The Palgrave Macmillan Dictionary of Finance, Investment and Banking

The Palgrave Macmillan Dictionary of Finance, Investment and Banking

Erik Banks

First published 2010 by
PALGRAVE MACMILLAN

Palgrave Macmillan in the UK is an imprint of Macmillan Publishers Limited, registered in England, company number 785998, of Houndmills, Basingstoke, Hampshire RG21 6XS.

Palgrave Macmillan in the US is a division of St Martin's Press LLC, 175 Fifth Avenue, New York, NY 10010.

Palgrave Macmillan is the global academic imprint of the above companies and has companies and representatives throughout the world.

Palgrave® and Macmillan® are registered trademarks in the United States, the United Kingdom, Europe and other countries

ISBN 978–0–230–23829–9

This book is printed on paper suitable for recycling and made from fully managed and sustained forest sources. Logging, pulping and manufacturing processes are expected to conform to the environmental regulations of the country of origin.

A catalogue record for this book is available from the British Library.

A catalog record for this book is available from the Library of Congress.

10 9 8 7 6 5 4
19 18 17 16 15 14 13 12 11

Printed and bound in the United States of America

Contents

Acknowledgments

I would like to extend my thanks and appreciation to Lisa von Fircks at Palgrave Macmillan for support in moving forward with a new version of this project. Thanks are also due to the editing, production, and marketing teams at Palgrave for their work in producing the book.

My deepest thanks, as always, go to Milena.

EB
Maine, 2009

The Author

Erik Banks is responsible for risk management of the Corporate and Investment Banking division at the European universal bank UniCredit. Over the past 23 years he has held senior risk positions at Citibank, Merrill Lynch, and in the hedge fund sector in New York, Tokyo, Hong Kong, London, and Munich. He is the author of more than 20 books on risk, derivatives, emerging markets, and governance.

Introduction

The Palgrave Macmillan Dictionary of Finance, Investment and Banking is a revised and comprehensive reference book that explains the formal and informal terminology of finance. We have structured the book much like any other dictionary so that it can be used as an easy (and hopefully frequent) guide and reference. Perhaps the hardest part in a project of this type is limiting the scope of content. Accordingly, as we set out to prepare this text we operated under two fundamental rules:

Rule 1: Include the most commonly encountered terms in a particular field.

Rule 2: Limit the fields to the essentials of the following:

- accounting
- business economics
- business law
- commercial banking
- corporate finance
- credit and equity analysis
- insurance/reinsurance
- investment banking
- risk management
- securities and investment
- trading/derivatives

In addition to formal terms, we decided to include some of the colloquialisms that have crept into the business vernacular over the years. We believe this is important because much of what happens in the banking, securities, asset management, and insurance industries is based to a degree on the informal language of the trade. So, when the reader hears of the "hung deal" in a securities underwriting, "stripping the yield curve" in a trading environment, or "spinning" in financial regulations, he or she is encountering the real language of finance; these terms convey concisely, efficiently, and sometimes colorfully what might otherwise take whole sentences to express. We have tried to take some care with colloquialisms by including terms that seem to have survived for a period of time. Obviously, new phases of market development can lead to the creation of new words, and these may ultimately fall out of use when the market phase subsides or changes. We have tried to be cognizant of this by focusing on the enduring terms of the marketplace.

There are, of course, instances where a particular concept or definition is known by different terms, even in the same marketplace. Rather than repeating definitions, we refer the reader to the single source for the definition, using some judgment about which of the two, and sometimes three, words serves as the "anchor" term.

How to use this dictionary

The dictionary contains clear, concise, easy-to-read financial definitions and descriptions, arranged in alphabetical order. Each definition ranges from two to ten sentences in length (depending on topic and complexity).

Cross-references to other terms in the dictionary are indicated in CAPITALS.

Foreign and colloquial terms are distinguished as follows:

- Arabic: ARB
- Colloquial: COL
- French: FR
- German: GER
- Italian: ITL
- Japanese: JPN
- Korean: KOR
- Latin: LAT
- Spanish: SPN

Where relevant "Also known as" references for terms that are known by multiple names are included.

Cross-references to additional terms within the dictionary are included where we believe these can add supplementary information or points of view.

References to external sources of information are included where we believe these may be of use to the reader.

Examples, charts, and figures are incorporated where additional clarity and information can be communicated. Where appropriate, we have also used very simple formulas and equations to convey certain terms, but these are non-technical and suitable for general business readers.

Summary of Colloquialisms, Foreign Language Terms, and Acronyms

Colloquialisms

ABOVE THE LINE
ACCELERATOR
ACTIVE BET
ACTIVE BOX
ACTUALS
AFTER THE BELL
ALGO
ALGO TRADING
ALL-IN
ALLIGATOR SPREAD
ALPHABET STOCK
ALT-A
ANGEL
ANKLE BITER
ARB
ARM'S LENGTH
ASIAN TAIL
ASSET STRIPPER
AUNT MILLIE
AXE
BABY BOND
BACK BOOK
BACK DOOR
BACK DOOR LISTING
BACK OFFICE
BACK UP THE TRUCK
BAD BANK
BANKMAIL
BAY STREET
BAZAAR
BEAR
BEAR CLOSING
BEAR HUG
BEAR RAID
BEAR SLIDE

BEAR SPREAD
BEAR SQUEEZE
BEAR TRAP
BEATING THE GUN
BEAUTY CONTEST
BED AND BREAKFASTING
BEIGE BOOK
BELLS AND WHISTLES
BELLWEATHER
BELLY OF THE CURVE
BELLYUP
BELOW THE LINE
BENCHMARK
BID WHACKER
BIG BANG
BIG BOARD
BIG DOG
BIG FIGURE
BIG UGLIES
BLACK BOX
BLACK KNIGHT
BLACK MONDAY
BLACK MONEY
BLACK SWAN
BLANK CHECK PREFERRED
BLIND BID
BLOWOUT
BLUE CHIP
BOARD LOT
BOBL
BOGEY
BOILER ROOM
BOILERPLATE
BOND CROWD
BOND VIGILANTES
BOOK
BOOKRUNNER
BOOTSTRAP
BOOTSTRAPPING
BOTTOM LINE
BOTTOM FISHING
BOUGHT DEAL
BOUTIQUE
BRADY BOND
BREAKING SYNDICATE

CLUB DEAL
COAT-TAILING
COLD CALLING
COMPS
CONCERT PARTY
CONSOL
CONTAGION
CONTRARIAN
COOKIE JAR ACCOUNTING
COOKING THE BOOKS
COOLING OFF PERIOD
CORNERING
CRACK SPREAD
CREEPING TAKEOVER
CREEPING TENDER
CROWDED TRADE
CROWN JEWEL DEFENSE
CROWN JEWELS
CRUSH SPREAD
CYLINDER
DAISY CHAIN
DARK POOL
DAWN RAID
DEAD CAT BOUNCE
DEAD HAND CLAUSE
DEAD HAND POISON PILL
DEAD MONEY
DEATH SPIRAL
DEEP MARKET
DIRTY FLOAT
DIRTY MONEY
DIRTY PRICE
DIRTY STOCK
DK
DOG
DOG AND PONY SHOW
DOGS OF THE DOW
DOUBLE DIPPING
DOWN ROUND
DRAGON
DRY POWDER
DUMMY DIRECTOR
DWARF
E-MINI

EASY MONEY
ELBOW
ELEPHANT
ELEPHANT HUNTING
EMBEDDO
EPS BOOTSTRAPPING
FALLEN ANGEL
FALLING KNIFE
FALSE MARKET
FANNIE MAE
FARMER MAC
FAST MARKET
FAST TAPE
FAT TAIL
FENCE
FIGHTING THE TAPE
FILL OR KILL
FINANCIAL SLACK
FINE PRINT
FIRE SALE
FIXED-FIXED
FIXED-FLOATING
FLASH PRICE
FLIGHT TO QUALITY
FLIP IN PILL
FLIP OVER PILL
FLIPPER
FLOATING-FLOATING
FLOW
FOLLOWING THE FORTUNES
FOOTSIE
FORWARD BUNDLE
FREDDIE MAC
FREE RIDER
FREEZE-OUT
FRONT BOOK
FRONT DOOR
FRONT OFFICE
FRONT RUNNING
FROTHY
GAMING
GATE
GATHER IN THE STOPS
GHOSTING

GINNIE MAE
GNOME
GNOMES OF ZURICH
GOLD BUG
GOLDBRICKS
GOLDEN HANDCUFFS
GOLDEN HANDSHAKE
GOLDEN HELLO
GOLDEN PARACHUTE
GOOD MONEY
GRAINS
GRANNY BOND
GRAVEYARD MARKET
GRAY KNIGHT
GRAY MARKET
GREEKS
GREENBACK
GREENMAIL
GREENSHOE
GUN JUMPING
GUNSLINGER
HAIRCUT
HANDLE
HARD LANDING
HARVEST
HEAD AND SHOULDERS
HEAVY MARKET
HIGH STREET BANK
HIT THE BID
HOT MONEY
HUNG DEAL
ICEBERG
IN PLAY
INCUBATOR
INFLATION HAWK
JOBBER
JOBBING
JUNK BOND
KAFFIRS
KANGAROOS
KICKER
KILLER BEES
KIWI
LADDERING

LAUNDERING
LEG
LEGGING
LIAR LOAN
LIFEBOAT
LIFT THE OFFER
LIFTING A LEG
LINE
LINKER
LOBSTER TRAP
LOCAL
LOCKBOX
LOCKED MARKET
LONG AND WRONG
LONG BOND
LONG END
LOONIE
LOOPHOLES
LOT
MACARONI DEFENSE
MAIN STREET
MAKING A BOOK
MAKING A MARKET
MAPLE BOND
MARRIED PUT
MATILDA
MIDGET
MINI
MIXED LOT
MOMO
MONEYNESS
MORNING NOTES
NAMES
NATURAL
NEAR MONEY
NIFTY FIFTY
NINJA LOAN
NOMING THE PIPES
NON-DEAL ROADSHOW
OFF-THE-RUN SECURITIES
OLD LADY
OMNIPRESENT SPECTER
ON-THE-RUN SECURITIES
ONE-MAN PICTURE

OPM
OVER THE WALL
OVERLINED
PAC MAN DEFENSE
PAINTING THE TAPE
PAPER MARKET
PARENT
PARKING
PASSING THE BOOK
PASSPORTING
PENNY JUMPING
PENNY STOCK
PEOPLE PILL
PHANTOM STOCK
PIERCING THE CORPORATE VEIL
PIG
PIG ON PORK
PIGGY-BACKING
PINGING
PINK SHEETS
PINNING THE STRIKE
PIP
PIPELINE
PIPETTE
PIT
POINT
POISION PILL
POISON PUT
POOP AND SCOOP
PORCUPINE PROVISION
PORTFOLIO PUMPING
POT
PRE-PACK
PRICE TALK
PUFFERY
PUKE POINT
PUMP AND DUMP
PUNT
PUNTER
PUP COMPANY
PURE PLAY
QUAD WITCH
QUANGO
QUIET PERIOD

RAIDER
RAINMAKER
RAMPING
RED HERRING
RED-LINING
REVERSE
REVERSE REPO
REVERSE TYING
REVOLVER
RICH
RIDING THE CURVE
RIGHTSIZING
RIO TRADE
ROADSHOW
ROLLER COASTER
ROLLING DOWN THE CURVE
ROUND TRIP
RUNNING THE BOOKS
SAFE HARBOR RULE
SANDWICH SPREAD
SATURDAY NIGHT SPECIAL
SCALPER
SCORCHED EARTH DEFENSES
SEAT
SELL-SIDE
SELLING AWAY
SELLING THE WINGS
SHADOW STOCK
SHARK
SHARK REPELLENT
SHELL
SHOE
SHORT AGAINST THE BOX
SHORT END
SHORT SQUEEZE
SIN STOCK
SINKER
SIV LITE
SIZE
SMART MONEY
SMOOTHING
SMURFING
SNAKE
SNIFFER

SNOWBALLING
SOFT LANDING
SOFTS
SPARK SPREAD
SPECIAL
SPIDER
SPINNING
SPOO
SPRING LOADING
SQUARE
SQUEEZE
STACK AND ROLL
STAGE
STALKING HORSE
STAPLED STOCK
STICKY DEAL
STICKINESS
STOPPED OUT
STORY PAPER
STREET
STREET NAME
STRONG HANDS
STUB
STUCK DEAL
SUCKER'S RALLY
SUPER SENIOR
SUPERSINKER
SWEEPER
SWEETENER
SWISSIE
TAG ALONG RIGHTS
TAIL
TAILGATING
TAKE THE OFFER
TARGET
TEASER
TEENY
TEXAS HEDGE
THIN MARKET
THIRD MARKET
TOM NEXT
TOMBSTONE
TON
TOO BIG TO FAIL

TOP TICK
TOPPY
TORPEDO STOCK
TOXIC ASSET
TOXIC POOL
TRADED AWAY
TRIPLE WITCHING DAY
TUNNEL
TURKEY
TURN
TWISTING
TYING
UNBUNDLING
UNDERWATER
VANILLA
VULTURE BID
VULTURE FUND
WALL STREET
WALLPAPER
WAR CHEST
WATERFALL
WEAK HANDS
WET BARRELS
WET LEASE
WHIPSAW
WHISPER NUMBERS
WHISPER STOCK
WHISTLEBLOWER
WHITE KNIGHT
WHITE SQUIRE
WIDOWS AND ORPHANS
WINDING UP
WITHOUT
WRAP
YANKEE
YARD
YIELD BURNING
ZOMBIE

Foreign language terms

AD VALOREM
AKTIEBOLAG
AKTIENGESELLSCHAFT

AMAKUDARI
ARBITRAGEUR
AUFSICHTSRAT
BANCASSURANCE
BANQUE D'AFFAIRE
BANQUE DE FRANCE
BANQUE DU CANADA
BESLOTEN VENNOOTSCHAP
BOLSA
BORDEREAU
BORSA
BOURSE
BUND
BUNDESANSTALT FUR FINANZDIENSTLEISTUNGSAUFSICHT
BUNDESBANK
CAVEAT EMPTOR
CEDULAS HIPOTECARIAS
CHAEBOL
COMMISSIONE NAZIONALE PER LA SOCIETA E LA BORSA
CONSEIL D'ADMINISTRATION
CONSEIL DU SURVEILLANCE
CORPUS
DAIMYO
DEUTSCHE AKTIENINDEX
DEUTSCHE BORSE
DEUTSCHE BUNDESBANK
ENTREPÔT
ENTREPRENEUR
EX-GRATIA
FILZ
FORCE MAJEURE
GEISHA
GENSAKI
GESELLSCHAFT MIT BESCHRÄNKTER HAFTUNG
GHARAR
GYOSEI SHIDO
HALAL
HARAAM
HAUSBANK
HYPOTHEKEN PFANDBRIEFE
IJARA
ITAYOSE
KABUSHIKI KAISHI
KEIDANREN

KEIRETSU
LAISSEZ-FAIRE
LETTRES DE GAGE
MOCHIAI
MUDARABA
MURABAHA
MUSHARAKA
NAAMLOZE VENNOOTSCHAP
NIPPON KEIDANREN
NOSTRO
NOYAU DUR
OBLIGATIONS FONCIERES
OFFENTLICHE PFANDBRIEFE
PARI PASSU
PER PRO
PFANDBRIEFE
PRIMA FACIE
PRO RATA
RENTES
RIBA
SALAM
SAMURAI
SCHATZ
SCHATZWECHSEL
SCHULDSCHEIN
SHIBOSAI
SHIKKO YAKUIN
SHOGUN
SHOKEN
SOCIEDAD ANONIMA
SOCIETA A RESPONSABILITA LIMITATA
SOCIETA PER AZIONI
SOCIETE ANONYME
SUKUK
TOKKIN
TRANCHE
UBERRIMAE FIDEI
ULTRA VIRES
VIS MAJOR
VORSTAND
VOSTRO
ZAIBATSU
ZAITECH

Abbreviations

AAU	ASSIGNED AMOUNT UNIT
AB	AKTIEBOLAG
ABA	AMERICAN BANKERS ASSOCIATION
ABCP	ASSET-BACKED COMMERCIAL PAPER
ABS	ASSET-BACKED SECURITY
ACCA	ASSOCIATION OF CHARTERED CERTIFIED ACCOUNTANTS
ACH	AUTOMATIC CLEARINGHOUSE
ADR	AMERICAN DEPOSITORY RECEIPT
ADS	AMERICAN DEPOSITORY SHARE
AFS	AVAILABLE FOR SALE
AG	AKTIENGESELLESCHAFT
AGM	ANNUAL GENERAL MEETING
AIM	ALTERNATIVE INVESTMENT MARKET
ALCO	ASSET LIABILITY COMMITTEE
ALM	ASSET-LIABILITY MANAGEMENT
AMEX	AMERICAN STOCK EXCHANGE
APACS	ASSOCIATION FOR PAYMENT CLEARING SERVICES
APR	ANNUAL PERCENTAGE RATE
APT	ARBITRAGE PRICING THEORY
ARCH	AUTOREGRESSIVE CONDITIONAL HETEROSCEDASTICITY
ARM	ADJUSTABLE RATE MORTGAGE
ASB	ACCOUNTING STANDARDS BOARD
ASEAN	ASSOCIATION OF SOUTH EAST ASIAN NATIONS
ATM	AUTOMATED TELLER MACHINE
ATS	ALTERNATIVE TRADING SYSTEM
B2B	EXCHANGE BUSINESS-TO-BUSINESS EXCHANGE
B2C	EXCHANGE BUSINESS-TO-CONSUMER EXCHANGE
BA	BANKER'S ACCEPTANCE
BACS	BANKERS AUTOMATED CLEARING SYSTEM
BAFIN	BUNDESANSTALT FUR FINANZDIENSTLEISTUNGSAUFSICHT
BBA	BRITISH BANKERS ASSOCIATION
BBA	RATE BRITISH BANKERS ASSOCIATION RATE
BOJ	BANK OF JAPAN
BTF	BLOCK TRADING FACILITY
BV	BESLOTEN VENNOOTSCHAP
CA	CHARTERED ACCOUNTANT
CAD III	CAPITAL ADEQUACY DIRECTIVE III
CATS	CERTIFICATE OF ACCURAL ON TREASURY SECURITIES
CBO	COLLATERALIZED BOND OBLIGATION

CCA	CHARTERED CERTIFIED ACCOUNTANT
CD	CERTIFICATE OF DEPOSIT
CDO	COLLATERALIZED DEBT OBLIGATION
CDS	CREDIT DEFAULT SWAP
CEO	CHIEF EXECUTIVE OFFICER
CESR	COMMITTEE OF EUROPEAN SECURITIES REGULATORS
CFA	CHARTERED FINANCIAL ANALYST
CFD	CONTRACT FOR DIFFERENCES
CFO	CHIEF FINANCIAL OFFICER
CFTC	COMMODITY FUTURES TRADING COMMISSION
CGS	COST OF GOODS SOLD
CHAPS	CLEARINGHOUSE AUTOMATED PAYMENT SYSTEM
CHIPS	CLEARINGHOUSE INTERBANK PAYMENT SYSTEM
CIF	COST, INSURANCE, FREIGHT
CIN	CUSIP INTERNATIONAL NUMBER
CLO	COLLATERALIZED LOAN OBLIGATION
CMBS	COMMERCIAL MORTGAGE BACKED SECURITY
CME	CHICAGO MERCANTILE EXCHANGE
CMO	COLLATERALIZED MORTGAGE OBLIGATION
CMS	CONSTANT MATURITY SWAP
CMT	CONSTANT MATURITY TREASURY
COD	CASH ON DELIVERY
CONSOB	COMMISSIONE NAZIONALE PER LA SOCIETA E LA BORSA
CP	COMMERCIAL PAPER
CPA	CERTIFIED PUBLIC ACCOUNTANT
CPI	CONSUMER PRICE INDEX
CPDO	CONSTANT PROPORTION DEBT OBLIGATION
CPPI	CONSTANT PROPORTION PORTFOLIO INSURANCE
CPR	CONDITIONAL PREPAYMENT RATE
CSA	CREDIT SUPPORT ANNEX
CTA	COMMODITY TRADING ADVISOR
CTD	CHEAPEST-TO-DELIVER
CUSIP	COMMITTEE ON UNIFORM SECURITIES IDENTIFICATION PROCEDURES
D&O COVER	DIRECTORS' AND OFFICERS' INSURANCE COVER
DAC/RAP	DELIVER AGAINST CASH/RECEIVE AGAINST PAYMENT
DAX	DEUTSCHE AKTIENINDEX
DCF	DISCOUNTED CASH FLOW
DIE	DESIGNATED INVESTMENT EXCHANGE
DIP FINANCING	DEBTOR-IN-POSSESSION FINANCING
DJIA	DOW JONES INDUSTRIAL AVERAGE
DMA	DIRECT MARKET ACCESS
DOT	DESIGNATED ORDER TURNAROUND

DPC	DERIVATIVE PRODUCT COMPANY
DPO	DIRECT PUBLIC OFFERING
DTCC	DEPOSITORY TRUST AND CLEARING CORPORATION
DVP	DELIVERY VERSUS PAYMENT
EAD	EXPOSURE AT DEFAULT
EAR	EFFECTIVE ANNUAL RATE
EBIT	EARNINGS BEFORE INTEREST AND TAXES
EBITDA	EARNINGS BEFORE INTEREST, TAXES, DEPRECIATION AND AMORTIZATION
EBRD	EUROPEAN BANK FOR RECONSTRUCTION AND DEVELOPMENT
ECB	EUROPEAN CENTRAL BANK
ECD	EURO CERTIFICATE OF DEPOSIT
ECN	ELECTRONIC COMMUNICATIONS NETWORK
ECP	EURO COMMERCIAL PAPER
ECU	EUROPEAN CURRENCY UNIT
EDF	EUROPEAN DEVELOPMENT FUND
EDI	ELECTRONIC DATA INTERCHANGE
EDS	EQUITY DEFAULT SWAP
EEA	EUROPEAN ECONOMIC AREA
EEC	EUROPEAN ECONOMIC COMMUNITY
EFP	EXCHANGE FOR PHYSICAL
EFT	ELECTRONIC FUNDS TRANSFER
EFTA	EUROPEAN FREE TRADE ASSOCIATION
EIB	EUROPEAN INVESTMENT BANK
ELOB	ELECTRONIC LIMIT ORDER BOOK
EMS	EUROPEAN MONETARY SYSTEM
EMTN	EURO MEDIUM TERM NOTE
EMU	EUROPEAN MONETARY UNION
EONIA	EURO OVERNIGHT INDEX AVERAGE
EPS	EARNINGS PER SHARE
ESOP	EMPLOYEE STOCK OWNERSHIP PLAN
ESOT	EMPLOYEE SHARE OWNERSHIP TRUST
ETF	EXCHANGE-TRADED FUND
EU	EUROPEAN UNION
EURIBOR	EURO INTERBANK OFFERED RATE
EURONIA	EURO OVERNIGHT INDEX AVERAGE
EVA	ECONOMIC VALUE ADDED
EVT	EXTREME VALUE THEORY
EXIMBANK	EXPORT IMPORT BANK
FASB	FINANCIAL ACCOUNTING STANDARDS BOARD
FCFE	FREE CASH FLOW TO EQUITY
FCFF	FREE CASH FLOW TO FIRM

FCM	FUTURES COMMISSION MERCHANT
FDIC	FEDERAL DEPOSIT INSURANCE CORPORATION
FHLB	FEDERAL HOME LOAN BANKS
FHLMC	FEDERAL HOME LOAN MORTGAGE CORPORATION
FIFO	FIRST IN FIRST OUT
FNMA	FEDERAL NATIONAL MORTGAGE ASSOCIATION
FOB	FREE ON BOARD
FOF	FUND OF FUND
FOMC	FEDERAL OPEN MARKETS COMMITTEE
FRA	FORWARD RATE AGREEMENT
FRCD	FLOATING RATE CERTIFICATE OF DEPOSIT
FRN	FLOATING RATE NOTE
FSA	FINANCIAL SERVICES AUTHORITY
FTC	FEDERAL TRADE COMMISSION
FX	FOREIGN EXCHANGE
G3	GROUP OF 3
G7	GROUP OF 7
G8	GROUP OF 8
G10	GROUP OF 10
GAAP	GENERALLY ACCEPTED ACCOUNTING PRINCIPLES
GAO	GOVERNMENT ACCOUNTABILITY OFFICE
GATT	GENERAL AGREEMENT ON TARIFFS AND TRADE
GC	GENERAL COLLATERAL
GDP	GROSS DOMESTIC PRODUCT
GDR	GLOBAL DEPOSITORY RECEIPT
GDS	GLOBAL DEPOSITORY SHARE
GEMM	GILT-EDGED MARKET MAKER
GIB	GUARANTEED INCOME BOND
GMBH	GESELLSCHAFT MIT BESCHRÄNKTER HAFTUNG
GMRA	GLOBAL MASTER REPURCHASE AGREEMENT
GNMA	GOVERNMENT NATIONAL MORTGAGE ASSOCIATION
GNP	GROSS NATIONAL PRODUCT
GO BOND	GENERAL OBLIGATION BOND
GP	GENERAL PARTNERSHIP
GPM	GRADUATED PAYMENT MORTGAGE
GSE	GOVERNMENT-SPONSORED ENTERPRISE
HICP	HARMONIZED INDEX OF CONSUMER PRICES
HKSE	HONG KONG STOCK EXCHANGE
HLT LOAN	HIGHLY LEVERAGED TRANSACTION LOAN
HSI	HANG SENG INDEX
IAS	INTERNATIONAL ACCOUNTING STANDARDS
IASB	INTERNATIONAL ACCOUNTING STANDARDS BOARD
IBF	INTERNATIONAL BANKING FACILITY

IBNR	INCURRED BUT NOT REPORTED
IBRD	INTERNATIONAL BANK FOR RECONSTRUCTION AND DEVELOPMENT
ICAAP	INTERNAL CAPITAL ADEQUACY ASSESSMENT PROCESS
ICE	INTERCONTINENTAL EXCHANGE
IDB	INTER-DEALER BROKER
IDR	INTERNATIONAL DEPOSITORY RECEIPT
IFC	INTERNATIONAL FINANCE CORPORATION
IFRS	INTERNATIONAL FINANCIAL REPORTING STANDARDS
ILS	INSURANCE-LINKED SECURITY
IMF	INTERNATIONAL MONETARY FUND
INC	INCORPORATED
IO	INTEREST-ONLY STRIP
IOI	INDICATION OF INTEREST
IOSCO	INTERNATIONAL ORGANIZATION OF SECURITIES COMMISSIONS
IPO	INITIAL PUBLIC OFFERING
IRA	INDIVIDUAL RETIREMENT ACCOUNT
IRB APPROACH	INTERNAL RATINGS-BASED APPROACH
IRR	INTERNAL RATE OF RETURN
IRS	INTERNAL REVENUE SERVICE
ISA	INDIVIDUAL SAVINGS ACCOUNT
ISDA	INTERNATIONAL SWAPS AND DERIVATIVES ASSOCIATION
ISIN	INTERNATIONAL SECURITIES IDENTIFICATION NUMBER
ISMA	INTERNATIONAL SECURITIES MARKETS ASSOCIATION
JGB	JAPANESE GOVERNMENT BOND
JV	JOINT VENTURE
KK	KABUSHIKI KAISHI
LBO	LEVERAGED BUYOUT
LDC	LESSER DEVELOPED COUNTRY
LEAPS	LONG-TERM EQUITY APPRECIATION SECURITY
LEPO	LOW EXERCISE PRICE OPTION
LGD	LOSS GIVEN DEFAULT
LIBID	LONDON INTERBANK BID
LIBOR	LONDON INTERBANK OFFERED RATE
LIFO	LAST IN FIRST OUT
LIMEAN	LONDON INTERBANK MEAN
LLC	LIMITED LIABILITY COMPANY
LLP	LIMITED LIABILITY PARTNERSHIP
LP	LIMITED PARTNERSHIP
LSE	LONDON STOCK EXCHANGE
LTD	LIMITED
LTPR	LONG-TERM PRIME RATE

LTV	LOAN-TO-VALUE
M&A	MERGERS and ACQUISITIONS
MAC	MATERIAL ADVERSE CHANGE CLAUSE
MAS	MONETARY AUTHORITY OF SINGAPORE
MBO	MANAGEMENT BUYOUT
MBS	MORTGAGE-BACKED SECURITY
METI	MINISTRY OF ECONOMY, TRADE, AND INDUSTRY
MFN	MOST FAVORED NATION
MIFID	MARKETS IN FINANCIAL INSTRUMENTS DIRECTIVE
MLP	MASTER LIMITED PARTNERSHIP
MNC	MULTINATIONAL CORPORATION
MOB SPREAD	MUNICIPALS OVER BONDS SPREAD
MOF	MULTIPLE OPTION FACILITY
MOS	MUTUAL OFFSET SYSTEM
MPC	MONETARY POLICY COMMITTEE
MPT	MODERN PORTFOLIO THEORY
MTN	MEDIUM-TERM NOTE
N.A.	NATIONAL ASSOCIATION
NAFTA	NORTH AMERICAN FREE TRADE AGREEMENT
NASD	NATIONAL ASSOCIATION OF SECURITIES DEALERS
NASDAQ	NATIONAL ASSOCIATION OF SECURITIES DEALERS AUTOMATED QUOTATIONS
NAV	NET ASSET VALUE
NBBO	NATIONAL BEST BID OFFER
NCD	NEGOTIABLE CERTIFICATE OF DEPOSIT
NGO	NONGOVERNMENTAL ORGANIZATION
NIC	NEWLY INDUSTRIALIZED COUNTRY
NIF	NOTE ISSUANCE FACILITY
NMS	NATIONAL MARKET SYSTEM
NNP	NET NATIONAL PRODUCT
NOPAT	NET OPERATING PROFIT AFTER TAX
NPV	NET PRESENT VALUE
NV	NAAMLOZE VENNOTSCHAP
NYSE	NEW YORK STOCK EXCHANGE
OAS	OPTION-ADJUSTED SPREAD
OECD	ORGANIZATION FOR ECONOMIC COOPERATION AND DEVELOPMENT
OID	ORIGINAL ISSUE DISCOUNT
OIS	OVERNIGHT INDEX SWAP
OPEC	ORGANIZATION OF PETROLEUM EXPORTING COUNTRIES
OPIC	OVERSEAS PRIVATE INVESTMENT CORPORATION
OSE	OSAKA STOCK EXCHANGE
OTC	OVER-THE-COUNTER
P/E	PRICE/EARNINGS

PAC BOND	PLANNED AMORTIZATION CLASS BOND
PAYE	PAY AS YOU EARN
PBOC	PEOPLE'S BANK OF CHINA
PD	PROBABILITY OF DEFAULT
PIPE	PRIVATE INVESTMENT IN PUBLIC EQUITY
PLC	PUBLIC LIMITED COMPANY
PPI	PRODUCER PRICE INDEX
QFII	QUALIFIED FOREIGN INSTITUTIONAL INVESTOR
QIB	QUALIFIED INSTITUTIONAL BUYER
QT	QUESTIONED TRADE
RAROC	RISK-ADJUSTED RETURN ON CAPITAL
RBA	RESERVE BANK OF AUSTRALIA
REIT	REAL ESTATE INVESTMENT TRUST
REMIC	REAL ESTATE MORTGAGE INVESTMENT CONDUIT
RFP	REQUEST FOR PROPOSAL
ROA	RETURN ON ASSETS
ROE	RETURN ON EQUITY
ROI	RETURN ON INVESTMENT
RPI	RETAIL PRICE INDEX
RUF	REVOLVING UNDERWRITING FACILITY
RWA	RISK WEIGHTED ASSETS
S&L	SAVINGS AND LOAN
S&P 500	STANDARD AND POOR'S 500
SA	SOCIETE ANONYME, SOCIEDAD ANONIMA
SDR	SPECIAL DRAWING RIGHTS
SEAQ	STOCK EXCHANGE AUOMATED QUOTATIONS
SEATS	STOCK EXCHANGE ALTERNATIVE TRADING SERVICE
SEC	SECURITIES AND EXCHANGE COMMISSION
SEDOL	STOCK EXCHANGE DAILY OFFICIAL LIST
SETS	STOCK EXCHANGE TRADING SYSTEM
SIFMA	SECURITIES INDUSTRY AND FINANCIAL MARKETS ASSOCIATION
SIPC	SECURITIES INVESTOR PROTECTION CORPORATION
SIV	STRUCTURED INVESTMENT VEHICLE
SNIF	STANDBY NOTE ISSUANCE FACILITY
SOES	SMALL ORDER EXECUTION SYSTEM
SONIA	STERLING OVERNIGHT INDEX AVERAGE
SOR	SMART ORDER ROUTER
SpA	SOCIETA PER AZIONI
SPE	SPECIAL-PURPOSE ENTITY
SPV	SPECIAL-PURPOSE VEHICLE
SrL	SOCIETA A RESPONSABILITA LIMITATA
SRO	SELF-REGULATORY ORGANIZATION
SSE	SHANGHAI STOCK EXCHANGE

STAGS	STERLING TRANSFER ACCURING GOVERNMENT SECURITY
STRIPS	SEPARATE TRADING OF REGISTERED INTERST AND PRINCIPAL SECURITIES
SWF	SOVEREIGN WEALTH FUND
TAC BOND	TARGETED AMORTIZATION CLASS BOND
TBA	TO BE ANNOUNCED
TERP	THEORETICAL EX-RIGHTS PRICE
TIBOR	TOKYO INTERBANK OFFERED RATE
TIGR	TREAUSRY INVESTORS GROWTH RECEIPT
TIPS	TREASURY INFLATION-PROTECTED SECURITY
TOPIX	TOKYO STOCK PRICE INDEX
TRIN	TRADING INDEX
TSE	TOKYO STOCK EXCHANGE
TWAP	TIME WEIGHTED AVERAGE PRICE
VAR	VALUE-AT-RISK
VAT	VALUE ADDED TAX
VIE	VARIABLE INTEREST ENTITY
VIX	VOLATILITY INDEX
VRCD	VARIABLE RATE CERTIFICATE OF DEPOSIT
VRN	VARIABLE RATE NOTE
VWAP	VOLUME WEIGHTED AVERAGE PRICE
WAC	WEIGHTED AVERAGE COUPON
WACC	WEIGHTED AVERAGE COST OF CAPITAL
WI	WHEN-ISSUED
WIT	WHEN-ISSUED TREASURY
WMBA	WHOLESALE MARKETS BROKERS ASSOCIATION
WTO	WORLD TRADE ORGANIZATION
XD	EX-DIVIDEND
XOL	AGREEMENT EXCESS OF LOSS AGREEMENT
XR	EX-RIGHTS
XW	EX-WARRANT

Numeric

1 AND 10 [COL] The fees typically charged by a FUND OF FUNDS, which include 1% annually for assets under management and 10% of any positive performance achieved during the year. Such fees are payable in addition to the 2 AND 20 paid on each underlying HEDGE FUND.

2 AND 20 [COL] The fees typically charged by a HEDGE FUND, which include 2% annually for assets under management and 20% of any positive performance achieved during the year. The performance fee is subject to restrictions imposed by any defined HIGH WATER MARK. See also 1 AND 10.

8-K In the United States, a report filed by a company with the SECURITIES AND EXCHANGE COMMISSION containing details on an event that may impact the company's FINANCIAL STATEMENTS or MARKET VALUE; the 8-K must be filed within 30 days of the event.

10-K In the United States, an audited ANNUAL REPORT filed by a company with the SECURITIES AND EXCHANGE COMMISSION. All ISSUERS of REGISTERED SECURITIES, all companies listed on an EXCHANGE, and companies with more than 500 shareholders must file a 10-K. See also 10-Q.

10-Q In the United States, a release of FINANCIAL STATEMENTS by a PUBLIC COMPANY, as required by the SECURITIES AND EXCHANGE COMMISSION. Though not as extensive as the ANNUAL REPORT, the quarterly report includes unaudited information on the BALANCE SHEET, INCOME STATEMENT and STATEMENT OF CASH FLOWS, and statement of retained earnings. All ISSUERS of REGISTERED SECURITIES, all companies listed on an EXCHANGE, and companies with more than 500 shareholders must file a 10-Q. Also known as QUARTERLY REPORT. See also 10-K.

12b-1 MUTUAL FUND A MUTUAL FUND that charges INVESTORS for its annual marketing and promotion expenses (which can range from under 25 BASIS POINTS to a maximum of 8.5%). 12b-1 funds are generally sold through

BROKERS or financial planners, who require the additional compensation in order to distribute fund SHARES.

13-D   In the United States, a document filed with the SECURITIES AND EXCHANGE COMMISSION by any SHAREHOLDER acquiring more than 5% of a PUBLIC COMPANY.

A-1 PAPER   See FIRST CLASS PAPER.

A-NOTE   A TRANCHE of SENIOR DEBT created out of a FIRST LIEN COMMERCIAL MORTGAGE. See also B-NOTE.

A-SHARE   (1) In the United Kingdom, a share of COMMON STOCK featuring RENT RIGHTS but no CONTROL RIGHTS. The lack of control rights generally causes A-shares to trade at a DISCOUNT to conventional shares. (2) On various STOCK EXCHANGES, the SHARES of the largest and most LIQUID listed companies. (3) Yuan-denominated STOCKS listed and traded on the SHANGHAI STOCK EXCHANGE and the Shenzhen Stock Exchange, and available to domestic INVESTORS and, on a limited basis, to foreign investors (under the QUALIFIED FOREIGN INSTITUTIONAL INVESTOR program). (2,3) See also B-SHARES.

AAU   See ASSIGNED AMOUNT UNIT.

AB   See AKTIEBOLAG.

ABA   See AMERICAN BANKERS ASSOCIATION.

ABA TRANSIT NUMBER   In the United States, a unique identifier assigned by the AMERICAN BANKERS ASSOCIATION to a BANK, which is used in routing of CHECKS and WIRE TRANSFERS.

ABANDON   The act of not exercising or selling an OPTION, occurring when the contract ends OUT-OF-THE-MONEY.

ABANDONED OPTION   An OPTION that has not been EXERCISED when IN-THE-MONEY. See also ABANDONMENT.

ABANDONMENT   (1) The voluntary surrender of right of title to real or financial property. (2) Within the INSURANCE sector, the transfer of rights to damaged or lost property from the INSURED to the INSURER. (2) See also ABANDONMENT CLAUSE.

ABANDONMENT CLAUSE   A clause in an INSURANCE POLICY that gives the INSURED the right to abandon property and make a CLAIM for a full SETTLEMENT from the INSURER; the same clause also gives the insurer rights to the abandoned property. See also ABANDONMENT.

ABANDONMENT OPTION   In REAL OPTION VALUATION, the OPTION a company has to abandon or exit an existing CAPITAL INVESTMENT before the end of the project's useful life. This option can be thought of as a form of PUT OPTION. See also DEFERRAL OPTION, EXPANSION OPTION.

ABATEMENT   A reduction in a payment due from an individual or company with insufficient funds or ASSETS to meet the full amount. An abatement may lead to cancellation of payments or some other form of RESTRUCTURING.

ABBREVIATED ACCOUNTS   In the United Kingdom, a short form set of FINANCIAL STATEMENTS that can be filed by qualified small or medium-sized enterprises.

ABCP   See ASSET-BACKED COMMERCIAL PAPER.

ABILITY TO PAY   See ABILITY TO PERFORM.

ABILITY TO PERFORM   A COUNTERPARTY's financial capacity to perform on its contractual obligations. Strong counterparties, with high CREDIT RATINGS, have a greater ability to perform than weak, or poorly rated, ones. Ability to perform is the essence of financial CREDIT ANALYSIS and is distinguished from WILLINGNESS TO PERFORM. Also known as ABILITY TO PAY.

ABOVE PAR   A trading price or valuation on a SECURITY, LOAN, or other ASSET that is greater than the original PAR VALUE (which is often set at 100). See also BELOW PAR.

ABOVE THE LINE   [COL] All INCOME STATEMENT entries that appear above the NET INCOME entry, i.e., prior to the distribution of residual profits. EXTRAORDINARY ITEMS and EXCEPTIONAL ITEMS appear above the line. See also BELOW THE LINE.

ABS   See ASSET-BACKED SECURITY.

ABSOLUTE LIABILITY   LIABILITY that occurs without fault, or an action deemed to be contrary to the public good that is neither negligent nor willful. A company found to be in breach of absolute liability may be required to provide restitution to injured parties.

ABSOLUTE PRICING MODEL   See EQUILIBRIUM PRICING MODEL.

ABSOLUTE PRIORITY RULE   A legal concept indicating that if a public company DEFAULTS, SHAREHOLDERS are only entitled to recover their INVESTMENTS after CREDITORS have been fully repaid. In most BANKRUPTCY cases shareholders receive little, if any, restitution since they are subordinate to all other claimholders. Absolute priority also extends to the broad category of creditors, where secured creditors receive payment before senior unsecured creditors, who receive payment before junior and subordinated creditors. See also SUBORDINATION.

ABSOLUTE RATE SWAP   An INTEREST RATE SWAP where the fixed leg is expressed as an outright FIXED RATE, rather than as an initial SPREAD to a BENCHMARK GOVERNMENT BOND.

ACCA   See ASSOCIATION OF CHARTERED CERTIFIED ACCOUNTANTS.

ACCELERATED DEPRECIATION   A DEPRECIATION mechanism that permits faster recovery of costs than conventional STRAIGHT-LINE DEPRECIATION methods, and generates greater TAX SHIELDS. Accelerated depreciation is applied to qualifying FIXED ASSETS, including those that are expected to become obsolete before the end of their economically useful lives. In the United States, the Accelerated Cost Recovery System became mandatory in the 1980s.

ACCELERATION   A clause in a CREDIT agreement, INDENTURE, or MASTER AGREEMENT that requires a COUNTERPARTY's outstanding sums to become due and payable when it triggers an EVENT OF DEFAULT or breaches a COVENANT. In some instances accelerated payments, except those related to DERIVATIVES and REPURCHASE AGREEMENTS, may be halted through an AUTOMATIC STAY, which is generally invoked in the event of a BANKRUPTCY filing.

ACCELERATOR   [COL] A firm that provides start-up ventures with initial, or seed, CAPITAL, administrative services, and business plan support. Accelerators often focus on start-ups that have been rejected by INCUBATORS or VENTURE CAPITAL groups because of insufficient development work. Accelerators may be compensated through fees or pre-INITIAL PUBLIC OFFERING EQUITY stakes.

ACCEPTANCE   (1) In INSURANCE, an agreement to an offer of coverage that creates a binding CONTRACT; this is generally accomplished when an INSURER issues a policy and an INSURED pays a PREMIUM. (2) In banking, a BANKER'S ACCEPTANCE or BILL OF EXCHANGE.

ACCEPTANCE CREDIT   (1) In international TRADE, a common means of FINANCING the sale of goods, where a COMMERCIAL BANK, MERCHANT BANK, or ACCEPTING HOUSE grants a CREDIT line to a foreign importer; an exporter in that foreign country can then draw against this line, creating a BILL OF EXCHANGE in the process. The bank accepts the bill, which can then be DISCOUNTED or held to MATURITY. (2) A form of LETTER OF CREDIT between buyer and seller that is paid via a time draft after a certain date. The letter of credit may be accepted by a bank, meaning the bank GUARANTEES payment if all terms are in compliance, or it may be unaccepted, meaning the seller assumes the risk of payment directly from the buyer. See also TRADE CREDIT.

ACCEPTING HOUSE   In the United Kingdom, a financial firm (i.e., BANK, MERCHANT BANK) that GUARANTEES that a BILL OF EXCHANGE or BANKER'S ACCEPTANCE created by a DRAWER will be paid to the BENEFICIARY or BEARER on the due date. The accepting house charges a fee in the form of a DISCOUNT on the amount of the bill for assuming the drawer's CREDIT RISK.

ACCEPTOR   A party that becomes liable for a BILL OF EXCHANGE that has been drawn by an original DRAWER. By signing acceptance, liability shifts to the acceptor.

ACCOMMODATION BILL   A BILL OF EXCHANGE signed by a party, who then becomes the guarantor of payment. If the ACCEPTOR fails to pay the bill when it comes due, the accommodation party assumes full liability.

ACCOMMODATION DIRECTOR   See DUMMY DIRECTOR.

ACCOMMODATION LINE   An agreement by an INSURER to UNDERWRITE a certain amount of business submitted by an INSURANCE BROKER, regardless of quality. The intent is for the insurer to develop a strong relationship with the broker, to the point where high-quality business (i.e., profitable and/or low RISK) can be regularly concluded.

ACCOMMODATION PAPER A NEGOTIABLE INSTRUMENT endorsed by a party that does not receive any value in return. Accommodation paper is generally used to help another party secure financing.

ACCOUNT (1) A portion of a ledger that is used to record financial transactions. Transactions based on the DOUBLE ENTRY ACCOUNTING system result in DEBITS and CREDITS into the relevant portion of the ledger. (2) An invoice reflecting charges and payments between two parties. (3) A separately held and managed balance of cash or ASSETS within a BANK or other financial institution.

ACCOUNT PAYEE The recipient of a CHECK from a third party, typically the original DRAWER; the check may feature parallel lines on the face that prohibits the payee from endorsing it to another party.

ACCOUNTING An area of practice concerned with the recording of transactions that impact the financial position of an individual or company, and the preparation of statements that reflect all such activity. Accounting is based on a series of principles and rules that ensures proper comparison over time and with peers, and provides stakeholders with a modicum of transparency regarding financial stability. See also ACCOUNTING CYCLE, ACCOUNTING ENTITY, ACCOUNTING PERIOD, DEFERRAL, FINANCIAL STATEMENTS.

ACCOUNTING CONCEPTS In certain ACCOUNTING regimes, 4 central tenets that are to be used in the preparation of a company's FINANCIAL STATEMENTS; these include the CONSISTENCY CONCEPT, the GOING CONCERN CONCEPT, the MATCHING CONCEPT, and the PRUDENCE CONCEPT.

ACCOUNTING CYCLE The process by which a company prepares and presents its FINANCIAL STATEMENTS. The process begins with recording of individual transactions via JOURNAL ENTRIES, often in a DOUBLE ENTRY ACCOUNTING framework, which are then posted to ledger accounts. Ledger accounts are then aggregated to create a TRIAL BALANCE. Thereafter adjusting entries are incorporated to reflect ACCRUALS and DEFERRALS, which leads to the creation of an adjusted trial balance. In the final stage, closing entries are completed, an AUDIT is performed and the final audited financial statements are published.

ACCOUNTING ENTITY Any unit, SUBSIDIARY, PARTNERSHIP, or company for which financial records are maintained and FINANCIAL STATEMENTS are prepared. The records and statements reflect the financial performance and standing of the entity, rather than the owners of the entity.

ACCOUNTING EQUATION The fundamental relationship reflected in the BALANCE SHEET of a company that indicates ASSETS must equal LIABILITIES plus CAPITAL.

ACCOUNTING PERIOD   A discrete time period for which an ACCOUNTING ENTITY records and prepares its financial records and FINANCIAL STATEMENTS. Internal accounts may have an accounting period of 1 month or 1 quarter, while external accounts (released to the public) may reflect an accounting period of 1 quarter, 6 months, or 1 year.

ACCOUNTING PROFIT   The difference between REVENUES and costs (including INTEREST, TAXES, and DEPRECIATION), prepared in accordance with applicable ACCOUNTING principles. Implicit costs, such as OPPORTUNITY COSTS, are excluded from the computation. See also ECONOMIC PROFIT, ECONOMIC VALUE ADDED.

ACCOUNTING RATIOS   See FINANCIAL RATIOS.

ACCOUNTING STANDARDS BOARD (ASB)   In the United Kingdom, the body responsible for establishing ACCOUNTING standards. PUBLIC COMPANIES (except small and medium-sized companies) must indicate whether their FINANCIAL STATEMENTS are prepared in accordance with ASB standards and explain any deviations. See also FINANCIAL ACCOUNTING STANDARDS BOARD, INTERNATIONAL ACCOUNTING STANDARDS BOARD.

ACCOUNTING VALUE   An approach to FINANCIAL ANALYSIS that values a company's COMMON STOCK as a function of EARNINGS PER SHARE and the PRICE/EARNINGS multiple. The higher either variable, the more valuable the stock, and thus the company. See also ENTERPRISE VALUE.

ACCOUNTS   In the United Kingdom, term for FINANCIAL STATEMENTS.

ACCOUNTS PAYABLE   Trade CREDIT created by a supplier when it permits a client to pay in the future for goods or services that have already been delivered by the supplier. Payables are a common source of short-term FINANCING for many industrial and service companies. A client company is generally required to arrange payment within 7 to 180 days, though in some cases terms may extend even further. In exchange for granting the payment extension, the supplier explicitly or implicitly charges a financing cost. Also known as TRADE CREDITORS. See also ACCOUNTS RECEIVABLE.

ACCOUNTS PAYABLE TURNOVER   An estimate of the time that it takes a company to pay on its ACCOUNTS PAYABLE. The resulting figure, number of days of purchases, fluctuates according to seasonal changes, and increasing or decreasing financing needs. The result, which is used in the CASH BUDGETING process, is computed as:

$$APT = \frac{CP}{AP}$$

where CP is purchases on CREDIT (per defined period), AP is accounts payable. The higher the ratio, the longer a company takes to pay on credit purchases. See also ACCOUNTS RECEIVABLE TURNOVER.

ACCOUNTS RECEIVABLE   Trade CREDIT created by a company when it permits a client to pay in the future for goods or services that have already been delivered by the company. A client company is generally required to arrange payment within 7 to 180 days, though in some cases terms may extend even further. In exchange for granting the payment extension, the company implicitly or explicitly charges its customers a financing cost. Receivables granted in the normal course of business are routinely sold to third parties on a NONRECOURSE basis (FACTORING) or used as COLLATERAL to secure funding (ACCOUNTS RECEIVABLE FINANCING); in some cases they are repackaged and sold through a SECURITIZATION. Also known as TRADE DEBTORS. See also ACCOUNTS PAYABLE.

ACCOUNTS RECEIVABLE FINANCING   Short-term FINANCING obtained by a company through a RECOURSE sale of ACCOUNTS RECEIVABLE to a third party. See also FACTORING, FORFAITING.

ACCOUNTS RECEIVABLE TURNOVER   An estimate of the time that it takes a company to collect on its ACCOUNTS RECEIVABLE. The resulting figure, number of days of CREDIT, fluctuates according to seasonal changes, and increasing or decreasing bad debts. The result, which can be used in the CASH BUDGETING process, is computed as:

$$ART = \frac{CS}{AR}$$

where CS is sales on credit (per defined period, net of returns), AR is accounts receivable. The higher the ratio, the longer it takes to convert credit sales into cash. See also ACCOUNTS PAYABLE TURNOVER.

ACCREDITED INVESTOR   Under the US SECURITIES AND EXCHANGE COMMISSION Regulation D, a wealthy INVESTOR with a minimum NET WORTH of $1 million or annual income of more than $200,000 that is permitted to invest in high-RISK investments that are normally intended only for INSTITUTIONAL INVESTORS that can withstand large economic losses.

ACCRETING CAP   A form of INTEREST RATE CAP based on an increasing NOTIONAL PRINCIPAL amount. See also ACCRETING SWAP.

ACCRETING SWAP   An OVER-THE-COUNTER SWAP featuring a NOTIONAL PRINCIPAL balance that increases on a preset schedule or through the triggering of a market event (generally a breach of a defined INTEREST RATE level). Accreting swaps typically have a LOCKOUT PERIOD during which increases are prohibited. See also ACCRETING CAP, AMORTIZING SWAP, INDEX PRINCIPAL SWAP, REVERSE INDEX PRINCIPAL SWAP, VARIABLE PRINCIPAL SWAP.

ACCRETION   A periodic increase in the value of an ASSET or LIABILITY originally issued, granted, or sold at a DISCOUNT to FACE VALUE. In general, the asset or liability will increase on a straight-line basis toward face value as maturity of the transaction approaches. See also ACCRETION OF DISCOUNT, AMORTIZATION, ORIGINAL ISSUE DISCOUNT.

ACCRETION OF DISCOUNT   The process of adjusting the BOOK VALUE of a BOND purchased at a DISCOUNT to reflect the effects of a noncash payment of INTEREST as MATURITY approaches. See also ACCRETION, AMORTIZATION, ORIGINAL ISSUE DISCOUNT.

ACCRUAL   A charge or EXPENSE incurred during an ACCOUNTING period but not paid or settled until the end of the period. See also ACCRUAL ACCOUNTING, DEFERRAL.

ACCRUAL ACCOUNTING   A general ACCOUNTING method that reports INCOME when it is earned and EXPENSES when they are incurred. Also known as ACCRUAL BASIS. See also CASH ACCOUNTING.

ACCRUAL BASIS   See ACCRUAL ACCOUNTING.

ACCRUAL BOND   (1) A TRANCHE of a COLLATERALIZED MORTGAGE OBLIGATION that pays no INTEREST or PRINCIPAL until all other tranches have been redeemed; this protects INVESTORS holding other tranches from PREPAYMENTS. The accrual bond is similar to a ZERO COUPON BOND but carries an explicit coupon rate and may ultimately pay both principal and coupons prior to final maturity. (2) A ZERO COUPON BOND. (1) Also known as Z-BOND.

ACCRUAL NOTE   See RANGE FLOATING RATE NOTE.

ACCRUED BENEFIT   Financial benefits that are due to BENEFICIARIES under a DEFINED BENEFIT PLAN. The accrual is computed in relation to current or expected EARNINGS and become due and payable upon the retirement of the employee.

ACCRUED INTEREST   The INTEREST on a BOND or LOAN that has been earned but not yet paid. Interest payable/receivable accumulates between COUPON payment periods; once a periodic interest payment is made, accrued interest reverts to zero and begins building on a daily basis until the next payment. Accrued interest of a FIXED INCOME instrument can be computed via:

$$AI = \frac{C(AD)}{2(n)}$$

where C is the coupon, AD is the actual number of days that have elapsed since the last coupon, and n is number of days in the coupon period. See also CLEAN PRICE, DIRTY PRICE.

ACCUMULATED DIVIDEND   A DIVIDEND that has been declared, but not yet paid, to INVESTORS holding CUMULATIVE PREFERRED STOCK. No dividends can be paid to holders of COMMON STOCK until accumulated dividends

have been paid. Since accumulated dividends are contractually owed to investors, they are reflected as a LIABILITY on the ISSUER's BALANCE SHEET until
they are fully paid.

ACCUMULATING SHARES   See STOCK DIVIDEND.

ACCUMULATION AREA   A TECHNICAL ANALYSIS charting figure reflecting a price range where buyers gradually build positions in a SECURITY, keeping the price above a minimum floor level. The steady buying interest is often
interpreted as a BULL signal, and may indicate a possible BREAKOUT to the
upside.

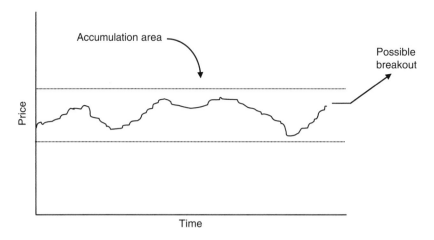

ACCUMULATION MAINTENANCE TRUST   A TAX-optimized TRUST that
transfers ASSETS to a named BENEFICIARY while still allowing the original
owner a modicum of control.

ACCUMULATION PERIOD   The period of time during which the purchaser
of an ANNUITY makes PREMIUM payments to an INSURER; once the accumulation period has ended, the annuity program provides the ANNUITANT
(i.e., the original purchaser or a designated BENEFICIARY) with contractual
payouts.

ACCUMULATION UNIT   A unit in a UNIT TRUST or investment trust where
after-TAX DIVIDENDS are reinvested in the same trust.

ACH   See AUTOMATIC CLEARINGHOUSE.

ACID TEST   See QUICK RATIO.

ACQUIRER   A company that seeks to purchase a TARGET company via a
HOSTILE TAKEOVER or a FRIENDLY TAKEOVER.

ACQUISITION   The purchase of one company by another in order to fulfill
particular strategic goals related to REVENUES, market share, product/service
offerings, or competition. An acquisition may be structured as a STOCK acquisition, where the acquiring company offers INVESTORS in the target company

a specific price for their COMMON STOCK, or an ASSET acquisition, where the acquiring company offers to buy a portion or majority of the target company's assets. Stock acquisitions based on full integration require tendering of all MINORITY INTEREST shares. See also CONSOLIDATION, MERGER, TAKEOVER.

ACQUISITION ACCOUNTING   The ACCOUNTING policies used when one company is acquired by another company. Under this process the purchase price of the company being acquired is divided between TANGIBLE ASSETS and INTANGIBLE ASSETS based on fair market value, and any resulting difference is reflected as an acquisition adjustment to the GOODWILL account. Also known as PURCHASE ACQUISITION ACCOUNTING. See also MERGER ACCOUNTING.

ACQUISITION COST   The cost associated with marketing and writing new INSURANCE business, generally comprised of AGENT COMMISSIONS, UNDERWRITING expenses, fees, and marketing support costs. A portion of these costs may be charged back to INSUREDS through EXPENSE LOADING.

ACQUISITION LINE   A form of SYNDICATED LOAN that is drawn by the BORROWER to fund an ACQUISITION. Once drawn, the loan typically becomes payable over the medium term, and may be structured with either regular AMORTIZATION of PRINCIPAL and INTEREST, or with a BULLET repayment.

ACT OF GOD   An event that is not predictable or preventable, and which can lead to significant physical, human, and/or financial damage. Such acts are often referenced as specific EXCLUSIONS in INSURANCE POLICIES, meaning they cannot be transferred from INSURED to INSURER. See also CATASTROPHIC HAZARD, CATASTROPHIC LOSS.

ACTIVE BET   [COL] The difference between an INVESTMENT MANAGER'S PORTFOLIO and the BENCHMARK portfolio, reflecting individual investments or strategies that specifically deviate from those contained in the benchmark. See also ACTIVE RETURN, ACTIVE RISK, TRACKING RISK.

ACTIVE BOX   [COL] See CAGE.

ACTIVE FUND   A FUND that seeks to outperform the market through the selection of ASSETS based on a defined INVESTMENT strategy. Active funds tend to feature higher costs than PASSIVE FUNDS. See also ACTIVE BET, ACTIVE RISK.

ACTIVE INVESTMENT STRATEGY   A process of dynamically managing a PORTFOLIO of SECURITIES by analyzing the RISK factors that influence each ASSET class (such as INTEREST RATES, interest rate VOLATILITY, CREDIT SPREADS, FOREIGN EXCHANGE RATES, and corporate earnings) and allocating CAPITAL to those where risk and RETURN appear attractive. An active strategy may require frequent rebalancing. See also INDEXING, PASSIVE INVESTMENT STRATEGY.

ACTIVE PARTNERSHIP   Any type of PARTNERSHIP where one or more of the PARTNERS provides CAPITAL and participates in the management of the operation. See also GENERAL PARTNERSHIP, LIMITED PARTNERSHIP, SILENT PARTNERSHIP.

ACTIVE RETURN   The results generated by an INVESTMENT MANAGER'S ACTIVE BETS, which can be computed as the realized outperformance or under-performance on an ex-post basis. See also ACTIVE RISK, TRACKING RISK.

ACTIVE RISK   The RISK that the ACTIVE BETS in an INVESTMENT MAN-AGER'S PORTFOLIO will lead to underperformance versus the BENCHMARK portfolio. Active risk is most often estimated through TRACKING RISK.

ACTIVE UNDERWRITER   An INSURANCE AGENT at LLOYD'S that under-writes on behalf of a SYNDICATE.

ACTUAL AUTHORITY   Powers granted by a PRINCIPAL to an AGENT to deal on its behalf. Actual authority may be explicit or implicit, and actions taken by the agent are generally binding on the principal. Also known as EXPRESS AUTHORITY.

ACTUAL CASH VALUE   The cost of replacing damaged or destroyed prop-erty, generally on the basis of new cost less DEPRECIATION. Actual cash value determination is the most common method of financial SETTLEMENT in INSURANCE unless an alternative method, such as full value (new cost), is specified.

ACTUAL EXPOSURE   The amount of CREDIT RISK exposure in a DERIVATIVE or financial transaction, typically reflected as a MARK-TO-MARKET valuation. If DEFAULT occurs when actual exposure is positive to the nondefaulting party, a credit loss arises; if negative, no credit loss occurs. Actual exposure is one of two components, along with FRACTIONAL EXPOSURE, in the deter-mination of total credit exposure. Also known as ACTUAL MARKET RISK, REPLACEMENT COST. See also POTENTIAL EXPOSURE.

ACTUAL MARKET RISK   See ACTUAL EXPOSURE.

ACTUALS   [COL] Physical COMMODITIES, such as GRAINS, SOFTS, metals, and energy, which are traded and delivered under COMMODITY DERIVATIVE contracts.

ACTUARIAL ADJUSTMENT   In INSURANCE, the process of modifying the PREMIUM rate and RESERVES to reflect actual loss experience.

ACTUARIAL EQUIVALENT   In INSURANCE, a statistical measure based on the expectation that a loss will occur, and the benefits that will become payable as a result. By computing this measure, the INSURER can vary the PREMIUM it charges INSUREDS. See also ACTUARIAL PRICING.

ACTUARIAL PRICING   In INSURANCE, the pricing of RISK based on prob-abilities of loss occurrence constructed from statistical distributions. Actuarial pricing is used to develop PREMIUMS that are intended to cover losses from underwritten risks and provide future benefits payable to BENEFICIARIES. See also ACTUARIAL EQUIVALENT.

AD VALOREM   [LAT] Literally, "according to the value." In general, a TAX applied to the value of goods and services, such as An AD VALOREM DUTY or VALUE-ADDED TAX.

AD VALOREM DUTY   A TAX that is levied as a percentage of the value of an ASSET, for example a STAMP DUTY.

ADD-ON   A NEW ISSUE of COMMON STOCK for a company that has already completed an INITIAL PUBLIC OFFERING. The add-on increases the ISSUER's PAID-IN CAPITAL account, generating additional funds for operations; however, since the transaction results in the creation of new shares it is considered dilutive. The UNDERWRITING SYNDICATE allocates add-on shares to new institutional and/or retail clients; if it is only offered to existing shareholders, the transaction takes the form of a RIGHTS ISSUE. See also PRIMARY OFFERING, SECONDARY OFFERING.

ADDITIONAL BONDS TEST   A COVENANT in an INDENTURE that limits the amount of new BONDS that an ISSUER can FLOAT. The test, which is intended to keep the issuer's total LEVERAGE in check, is often measured by a TIMES INTEREST EARNED ratio or a FIXED CHARGE COVERAGE ratio.

ADJUSTABLE PEG   See CRAWLING PEG.

ADJUSTABLE RATE MORTGAGE (ARM)   A MORTGAGE with a floating INTEREST RATE that resets every 1, 3, 6, or 12 months, and a final maturity of 5 to 30 years. In the United States, common floating ARM indexes include LIBOR, PRIME RATE, Cost of Funds Index, and the constant maturity TREASURY BOND rate. In order to protect the borrower and lender against extreme rate movements, ARMs generally feature periodic and lifetime CAPS, and lifetime FLOORS. In the United Kingdom, these are known as CAPPED MORTGAGES and CAP AND COLLAR MORTGAGES. Also known as VARIABLE RATE MORTGAGE.

ADJUSTABLE RATE MORTGAGE (ARM) SECURITY   A MORTGAGE-BACKED SECURITY created through the SECURITIZATION of a pool of ADJUSTABLE RATE MORTGAGES rather than conventional FIXED RATE mortgages. As a result of the FLOATING RATE component, ARM securities are generally more complex to value and HEDGE than standard fixed rate issues.

ADJUSTABLE RATE PREFERRED STOCK   PREFERRED STOCK that pays INVESTORS a floating DIVIDEND that resets periodically (generally every quarter or every 49 days); the floating dividend is typically pegged to TREASURY BILL rates or some other recognized MONEY MARKET rate. Also known as MONEY MARKET PREFERRED STOCK, VARIABLE RATE PREFERRED STOCK. See also DUTCH AUCTION PREFERRED STOCK.

ADJUSTED BASIS   The base price used to determine CAPITAL GAINS or CAPITAL LOSSES on an INVESTMENT, generally including a deduction for

COMMISSIONS at the time of purchase or sale, along with adjustments for any STOCK SPLITS that may have occurred.

ADJUSTED BREAKEVEN   A measure of the number of years it takes for an INVESTOR to recover the initial CONVERSION PREMIUM paid when purchasing a CONVERTIBLE BOND, after accounting for the fact that the investor may purchase more COMMON STOCK than represented by the CONVERSION RATIO. Adjusted breakeven is typically computed as:

$$ABE = \frac{Conv_{prem}}{C - \left(\frac{P_{CB}}{S}(DPS)\right)}$$

where $Conv_{prem}$ is the conversion premium, C is the COUPON, P_{CB} is the price of the convertible bond, S is the price of the common stock, and DPS is DIVIDENDS per share. See also EQUIVALENT BREAKEVEN, SIMPLE BREAKEVEN.

ADJUSTED PRESENT VALUE   An adaption of the NET PRESENT VALUE calculation that distinguishes the value of the underlying CAPITAL INVESTMENT project and the value of the LEVERAGE inherent in the project. The difference between an all-EQUITY financed project and a partially DEBT-financed project comes from the TAX SHIELDS generated by debt, as well as expected costs associated with FINANCIAL DISTRESS coming from greater use of leverage. See also ALL-EQUITY NET PRESENT VALUE.

ADJUSTED STRIKE PRICE   A STRIKE PRICE on an OPTION (or option-linked instrument, such as a CONVERTIBLE BOND) that is changed to reflect new or unexpected events, including STOCK SPLITS or STOCK DIVIDENDS.

ADJUSTMENT BOND   A BOND issued as a RECAPITALIZATION instrument by a company in FINANCIAL DISTRESS, often as an INCOME BOND that only pays INVESTORS COUPON interest as earnings permit.

ADMINISTRATION ORDER   In the United Kingdom, an order of the court in respect of a company in FINANCIAL DISTRESS that requires the business affairs of the company to be placed under the management of an ADMINISTRATOR and which prohibits CREDITORS from taking actions that would lead to liquidation of the company.

ADMINISTRATOR   See RECEIVER.

ADMITTED INSURANCE   An INSURANCE contract written by an ADMITTED INSURER that is authorized to do business in the state or jurisdiction where the policy is issued. See also NONADMITTED INSURANCE.

ADMITTED INSURER   An INSURER that is authorized to write INSURANCE business in a particular state or jurisdiction; the contracts it offers are classified as ADMITTED INSURANCE. Also known as AUTHORIZED INSURER, LICENSED CARRIER. See also NONADMITTED INSURER.

ADR   See AMERICAN DEPOSITORY RECEIPT.

ADS   See AMERICAN DEPOSITORY SHARE.

ADVANCE   See LOAN.

ADVANCE-DECLINE   A TECHNICAL ANALYSIS tool that measures the number of COMMON STOCKS that advance against the number that decline over a given period of time. A rising advance-decline is a generally regarded as a BULLISH signal, a falling advance-decline as a BEARISH signal.

ADVANCE OPTION   A short-term LINE OF CREDIT granted by an UNDERWRITER to an ISSUER of SECURITIES that can be drawn if the underwriter cannot successfully place the securities. The advance option thus guarantees the issuer access to short-term funds regardless of the relative success of the NEW ISSUE.

ADVANCE PREMIUM   In INSURANCE, a PREMIUM payment by the INSURED to the INSURER prior to the due date.

ADVANCE REFUNDING   An exchange of outstanding GOVERNMENT BONDS for a NEW ISSUE of SECURITIES prior to final maturity of the original issue, typically arranged to take advantage of a lower INTEREST RATE environment.

ADVANCE SETTLEMENT   In INSURANCE, payment of a CLAIM by the INSURER to the INSURED prior to the settlement date.

ADVANCED METHODOLOGY   A credit-based CAPITAL ALLOCATION process promulgated by the BANK FOR INTERNATIONAL SETTLEMENTS under the INTERNAL RATINGS-BASED (IRB) APPROACH. BANKS use internal models to determine EXPECTED CREDIT LOSSES and UNEXPECTED CREDIT LOSSES by estimating a COUNTERPARTY'S DEFAULT RISK, RISK EQUIVALENT EXPOSURE, and LOSS-GIVEN DEFAULT (as well as the impact of RISK mitigants and the relationship of COUNTERPARTY exposures to other exposures in the PORTFOLIO). CAPITAL is then allocated to cover the resulting exposure. See also FOUNDATION METHODOLOGY.

ADVERSE DEVELOPMENT COVER   A FINITE INSURANCE CONTRACT where the INSURED shifts the timing of losses that have already occurred, as well as those that have been INCURRED BUT NOT REPORTED, to the INSURER. In exchange for a PREMIUM the insurer assumes losses in excess of the insured's RESERVE, providing LOSS FINANCING up to a maximum amount dictated by the POLICY CAP. See also LOSS PORTFOLIO TRANSFER, RETROSPECTIVE FINITE POLICY.

ADVERSE OPINION   An AUDIT OPINION by an EXTERNAL AUDITOR indicating that a company's FINANCIAL STATEMENTS do not accurately reflect its financial position and cannot be relied on as a result of omissions, errors, lack of information, or lack of conformity to accepted ACCOUNTING PRINCIPLES. See also QUALIFIED OPINION, UNQUALIFIED OPINION.

ADVERSE SELECTION   Mispricing of RISK as a result of information asymmetries. This occurs when an INSURER cannot clearly distinguish between different classes of risks, and leads to a dearth or excess of risk coverage at a given price, i.e., charging a standard or low PREMIUM rate for a significant or UNINSURABLE RISK, or a high premium for a small or inconsequential risk. See also MORAL HAZARD.

ADVISED LINE   A BANK LINE that a BANK or other financial institution approves and maintains for a customer. The size of the line is specifically conveyed to the customer, though availability depends on the terms of the credit agreement and/or the payment of a COMMITMENT FEE. Also known as CONFIRMED LINE. See also GUIDANCE LINE.

ADVISING BANK   A BANK in an exporter's country that advises the exporter that a LETTER OF CREDIT has been opened with an international bank.

AFFILIATE   A company that is partly owned by a second company, and where the latter is able to direct or influence the operations of the former. See also JOINT VENTURE, SUBSIDIARY.

AFFIRMATIVE OBLIGATION   One or more duties that a SPECIALIST or MARKET MAKER must undertake, including taking one side of a purchase or sale ORDER through a proprietary account when the other side cannot be immediately matched, quoting TWO-WAY MARKETS at all times, and reporting all executed trades within a predefined time frame. Also known as POSITIVE OBLIGATION. See also INTERPOSITIONING, NEGATIVE OBLIGATION.

AFRICAN DEVELOPMENT BANK   A MULTILATERAL DEVELOPMENT BANK created in 1964 by African nations to support economic and social progress and to supply long-term development finance to member countries, modeled after the INTERNATIONAL BANK FOR RECONSTRUCTION AND DEVELOPMENT.

AFS ACCOUNTING   See AVAILABLE FOR SALE ACCOUNTING.

AFTER HOURS TRADING   TRADING in SECURITIES that occurs after the formal close of an EXCHANGE, through telephonic networks or ELECTRONIC COMMUNICATIONS NETWORKS supported by BROKER/DEALERS. In practice only BENCHMARK securities with a broad INVESTOR following trade after hours.

AFTER SIGHT   A term included on a BILL OF EXCHANGE indicating that the period of the bill starts from the date on which the DRAWEE has been presented with it. See also AT SIGHT.

AFTER THE BELL   [COL] The time period after the official close of an EXCHANGE. Market-moving information is often released after an exchange has closed.

AFTERMARKET   See SECONDARY MARKET.

AG   See AKTIENGESELLSCHAFT.

AGED ASSETS   ASSETS held for resale by a BANK or SECURITIES FIRM that have been owned for a long period of time (i.e., many months). Aged assets may indicate misvaluation.

AGED FAIL A FAIL TO RECEIVE or FAIL TO DELIVER between two parties that is not settled within 30 days. In most instances the party expecting to receive SECURITIES must remove the entry from the ASSET accounts on the balance sheet until the error is resolved. Aged fails may signal increased OPERATIONAL RISK.

AGENCY BILL See INLAND BILL.

AGENCY CAPTIVE A CAPTIVE, owned by one or more INSURANCE AGENTS, which is used to write INSURANCE cover for a large number of third party clients. See also GROUP CAPTIVE, PROTECTED CELL COMPANY, PURE CAPTIVE, RENT-A-CAPTIVE, SISTER CAPTIVE.

AGENCY COSTS Direct and indirect costs arising from the separation of ownership (i.e., COMMON STOCK shareholders) and control (i.e., DIRECTORS and managers) that ultimately lead to a reduction in ENTERPRISE VALUE. Agency costs can include the EXPENSES associated with implementing processes for monitoring, reporting, and auditing.

AGENCY PROBLEM A conflict based on the fundamental "mistrust" that arises between COMMON STOCK SHAREHOLDERS, DIRECTORS, and management. The agency problem centers on whether DIRECTORS and managers always act in good faith and seek to advance the interests of shareholders.

Additional reference: Berle and Means (1991).

AGENCY SECURITY In the United States, NOTES or BONDS issued by government-sponsored or government-guaranteed institutions (e.g., FEDERAL NATIONAL MORTGAGE ASSOCIATION, GOVERNMENT NATIONAL MORTGAGE ASSOCIATION, FEDERAL HOME LOAN MORTGAGE CORPORATION). The SECURITIES carry explicit or implicit government support related to PRINCIPAL and INTEREST payments, and thus carry the strongest CREDIT RATINGS. Agency securities, which are issued with short- to long-term maturities and fixed or floating COUPONS, are exempt from REGISTRATION requirements established by the SECURITIES AND EXCHANGE COMMISSION.

AGENT A party that acts as a representative of a PRINCIPAL, carrying express or implied authority to deal on behalf of the principal. In financial services a BROKER is an agent of the employing BANK or SECURITIES FIRM and is paid COMMISSIONS for client business. A bank may act as an agent for other banks in fulfilling certain duties related to arranging LOANS and NEW ISSUES. In INSURANCE, the independent agent represents at least two INSURERS and attempts to find the best possible deal for INSUREDS in exchange for a percentage of PREMIUMS charged. See also ACTUAL AUTHORITY, AGENT BANK, APPARENT AGENCY.

AGENT BANK A BANK forming part of a SYNDICATE arranging a LOAN for a BORROWER that is responsible for protecting the interests of all other syndicate banks. The lead bank arranging the loan is often selected as the agent bank. See also AGENT.

AGGREGATE DEMAND   The total amount spent on final goods and services. In an open economy this is generally considered to be the sum of consumption, INVESTMENT, government spending, and net EXPORTS. See also AGGREGATE SUPPLY, DEMAND, SUPPLY.

AGGREGATE EXCESS OF LOSS REINSURANCE   A REINSURANCE agreement where the REINSURER provides the CEDING INSURER with coverage on a large number of small losses arising from multiple policies, once an agreed ATTACHMENT point has been reached.

AGGREGATE INDEMNITY   The total INSURANCE coverage an INSURED has against a specific RISK, generally a combination of a primary policy and one or more secondary policies.

AGGREGATE LIMIT   See POLICY CAP.

AGGREGATE STOP LOSS INSURANCE   An INSURANCE contract that becomes effective once a company's SELF-INSURANCE threshold has exceeded a predefined value. Once in effect, the coverage assumes the form of a standard insurance contract with defined terms and conditions.

AGGREGATE SUPPLY   The total amount of goods and services enterprises are willing to provide consumers. See also AGGREGATE DEMAND, DEMAND, SUPPLY.

AGM   See ANNUAL GENERAL MEETING.

AGREED VALUE POLICY   An INSURANCE policy where the sum to be paid out in the event an insurable event occurs is specifically stated in the policy, e.g., life insurance.

AGREEMENT VALUE   The value that is settled between two COUNTER-PARTIES in the event a SWAP is subject to early termination.

AGRICULTURAL BANK   See LAND BANK.

AIM   See ALTERNATIVE INVESTMENT MARKET.

AJUSTABONOS   [SPN] Medium-term INFLATION-LINKED SECURITIES, issued by the Mexican government, which pay a regular fixed COUPON and adjust the PRINCIPAL every quarter based on the movement of the Mexican CONSUMER PRICE INDEX. The adjusted principal accumulates over the life of the bond and is paid to INVESTORS at maturity.

AKTIEBOLAG (AB)   [SWE] In Sweden, a JOINT STOCK COMPANY that may be either publicly traded or privately held; the term is also used in Finland to reflect a private company. In both countries minimum CAPITAL requirements must be met in order to qualify.

AKTIENGESELLSCHAFT (AG)   [GER]   In   Germany,   Switzerland,   and Austria, a STOCK CORPORATION which features both a VORSTAND and an AUFSICHTSRAT. In all countries minimum CAPITAL requirements must be met in order to qualify.

ALCO   See ASSET-LIABILITY COMMITTEE.

ALEATORY CONTRACT   A CONTRACT that can result in an unequal exchange of value between the contracting parties. INSURANCE is an aleatory contract, as the PREMIUM paid by the INSURED is generally larger or smaller than any SETTLEMENT received from the INSURER in the event of a loss and CLAIM.

ALGO   [COL] See ALGORITHM

ALGO TRADING   [COL] See ALGORITHMIC TRADING

ALGORITHM   A decision rule applied to trading strategies and incorporated into ALGORITHMIC TRADING platforms. Algorithms are employed for short-term trading and execution, and can be designed to perform a variety of functions, including searching for NONDISPLAYED LIQUIDITY, parceling trades into small orders to reduce MARKET IMPACT COST, executing trades at specific levels (such as VOLUME WEIGHTED AVERAGE PRICE or TIME WEIGHTED AVERAGE PRICE), and so forth. Also known as ALGO.

ALGORITHMIC TRADING   The use of computer-driven ALGORITHMS to EXECUTE financial transactions in the marketplace. The process is designed to be highly automated, with minimal need for manual intervention. Algorithmic trading is popularly used in the EQUITY markets, but is also found in the FOREIGN EXCHANGE and COMMODITIES markets. Also known as RULES BASED TRADING.

ALIEN INSURER   In the United States, an INSURER formed on the basis of the legal requirements of a country other than the United States. In order to qualify to write INSURANCE in the United States, the alien insurer must adhere to relevant state insurance regulations.

ALL-EQUITY NET PRESENT VALUE   A NET PRESENT VALUE calculation that is used when a CAPITAL INVESTMENT project is funded solely by EQUITY. The computation uses the cost of equity as the relevant DISCOUNT RATE and ignores any adjustments normally used for DEBT financing, e.g., TAX SHIELDS. See also ADJUSTED PRESENT VALUE.

ALL-IN   [COL] Abbreviated form of "all-included," referring to the total costs attributable to a firm's NEW ISSUE of SECURITIES or a BANK's issue of DEPOSITS. The all-in generally includes the core COST OF CAPITAL plus the UNDERWRITING SPREAD and COMMISSIONS; for bank funding instruments it may also include a PREMIUM for deposit INSURANCE. See also FLOTATION COST.

ALL LINES INSURANCE   See MULTIPLE PERIL POLICY.

ALL-OR-ANY PORTION ORDER   An ORDER to purchase or sell any, or all, of a specified quantity of SECURITIES, generally at the BROKER's discretion. See also ALL-OR-NONE ORDER.

ALL-OR-NONE ORDER   An ORDER to purchase or sell SECURITIES that must be filled at the limit price or better in its entirety or else cancelled. All-or-none orders are often marked FILL OR KILL. See also ALL-OR-ANY PORTION ORDER.

ALL-OR-NONE UNDERWRITING   A NEW ISSUE UNDERWRITING where the ISSUER has the right to cancel the entire transaction if the SYNDICATE is unable to successfully place the entire issue. See also BEST EFFORTS UNDERWRITING, BOUGHT DEAL.

ALL-OR-NOTHING OPTION   See BINARY OPTION.

ALL RISKS COVER   See ALL RISKS POLICY.

ALL RISKS POLICY   A broad INSURANCE policy that covers losses from all PERILS except those that are specifically excluded. Also known as ALL RISKS COVER. See also NAMED PERIL POLICY.

ALLIED LINES   A PROPERTY AND CASUALTY INSURANCE policy that provides coverage for fire and associated PERILS, including water damage, demolition, and contamination.

ALLIGATOR SPREAD   [COL] An OPTION SPREAD that is unprofitable even in favorable market conditions, as a result of large BROKER COMMISSIONS or fees. An alligator spread often comprises of many discrete transactions, which generate excessive costs and detract from any profits.

ALLOTMENT   The share of a NEW ISSUE of SECURITIES granted by the LEAD MANAGER to SYNDICATE members (and ultimately INVESTORS). Allotment may be determined by existing relationships between the lead manager and each syndicate member, or by the perceived or proven ability of a given member to place the securities with a particular base of investors.

ALM   See ASSET-LIABILITY MANAGEMENT.

ALPHA   (1) A measure of RISK-adjusted performance that focuses on the contributions of specific INVESTMENTS over and above the performance of the market at large, or the average difference between the RETURNS of a PORTFOLIO and a BENCHMARK INDEX. An investment strategy that has a high alpha effectively performs better than would be suggested by its BETA. Alpha is often used as a proxy of the skills and abilities of FUND managers that are involved in ACTIVE BETS. (2) The intercept of the line defining the expected RETURN of an ASSET and the BETA-adjusted return of the market portfolio. (1) See also PORTABLE ALPHA. (2) See also ARBITRAGE PRICING THEORY, CAPITAL ASSET PRICING MODEL.

ALPHA STOCKS   The most actively traded STOCKS on the United Kingdom's STOCK EXCHANGE AUTOMATED QUOTATIONS SYSTEM. See also NORMAL MARKET SIZE.

ALPHABET STOCK   [COL] Separate classes of COMMON STOCK issued by a company, where each class (often denoted by a letter of the alphabet) represents a different SUBSIDIARY. INVESTORS in an alphabet stock receive the RENT RIGHTS and CONTROL RIGHTS associated with that stock, but not those of the overarching parent company. See also CLASSIFIED STOCK.

ALT-A   [COL] A residential MORTGAGE that is granted to a BORROWER on the basis of a reduced amount of documentation or limited/no income verification. The credit quality of the borrowers ranks above that associated with SUBPRIME MORTGAGES but generally below that of PRIME MORTGAGES. Also known as ALTERNATIVE A MORTGAGE.

ALTERNATE DIRECTOR   A person who is authorized to act temporarily on behalf of a permanent DIRECTOR on a company's BOARD OF DIRECTORS.

ALTERNATIVE A MORTGAGE   See ALT-A.

ALTERNATIVE DELIVERY PROCEDURE Delivery terms under an EX-CHANGE TRADED DERIVATIVE that deviate from standard procedures.

ALTERNATIVE FINANCE ARRANGEMENTS   See ISLAMIC FINANCE.

ALTERNATIVE INVESTMENT   The broad category of INVESTMENTS that excludes the traditional classes of EQUITIES, FIXED INCOME, and cash. Alternative investments can include HEDGE FUNDS, COMMODITIES, real estate, PRIVATE EQUITY, managed FUTURES, and INSURANCE-LINKED SECURITIES. Alternatives are often selected by investors as they can be uncorrelated with traditional asset classes, helping improve PORTFOLIO DIVERSIFICATION.

ALTERNATIVE INVESTMENT MARKET (AIM) A market within the LONDON STOCK EXCHANGE that supports listing and TRADING of SMALL CAP STOCKS; AIM replaced the Unlisted Securities Market in 1995, which had performed a similar function.

ALTERNATIVE RISK TRANSFER (ART)   A product, channel, or solution that transfers RISK exposures between the INSURANCE and REINSURANCE sectors and the CAPITAL MARKETS in order to achieve specific RISK MANAGEMENT goals. As a result of regulatory rules and DIVERSIFICATION benefits, it is often desirable to shift INSURABLE RISKS to the financial sector and FINANCIAL RISKS to the insurance sector; ART mechanisms, such as CAPTIVES, DERIVATIVES, INSURANCE-LINKED SECURITIES, CONTINGENT CAPITAL, and ENTERPRISE RISK MANAGEMENT, make this possible. See also CONVERGENCE.

ALTERNATIVE TRADING SYSTEM (ATS)   An electronic venue that serves as an alternative to a traditional EXCHANGE, providing TRADING services by matching buyers and sellers directly, without the use of a BROKER or DEALER. See also ELECTRONIC COMMUNICATIONS NETWORK.

AMAKUDARI   [JPN] Literally, "descent from heaven"; a Japanese practice of appointing a senior financial REGULATOR to a senior executive position within a BANK or SECURITIES FIRM.

AMALGAMATION   The combination of two, or more, companies, through a series of MERGERS or ACQUISITIONS.

AMERICAN BANKERS ASSOCIATION (ABA)   A trade organization founded in 1875 that represents the interests of BANKS in the United States. The ABA is also responsible for assigning 9 digit ABA TRANSIT NUMBERS which uniquely identify every bank in the country, and which are used for WIRE TRANSFERS and CHECK routing.

AMERICAN BINARY OPTION   See BINARY-BARRIER OPTION.

AMERICAN DEPOSITORY RECEIPT (ADR)   A negotiable certificate issued by a US BANK representing a foreign company's COMMON STOCK (shares of which are held in CUSTODY by the bank). ADRs, denominated in US dollars, are registered with the SECURITIES AND EXCHANGE COMMISSION and are traded on an EXCHANGE or OVER-THE-COUNTER. ADRs may be sponsored (approved/backed by the company) or unsponsored (not backed/approved by the company). See also AMERICAN DEPOSITORY SHARE, GLOBAL DEPOSITORY RECEIPT, GLOBAL DEPOSITORY SHARE.

AMERICAN DEPOSITORY SHARE (ADS)   COMMON STOCK issued by a foreign company in the US marketplace. ADSs, denominated in US dollars, are registered with the SECURITIES AND EXCHANGE COMMISSION and are traded on an EXCHANGE or OVER-THE-COUNTER. See also AMERICAN DEPOSITORY RECEIPT, GLOBAL DEPOSITORY RECEIPT, GLOBAL DEPOSITORY SHARE.

AMERICAN OPTION   An OPTION that can be exercised at any time prior to, and including, maturity. See also BERMUDAN OPTION, EUROPEAN OPTION.

AMERICAN STOCK EXCHANGE (AMEX)   A secondary STOCK EXCHANGE in the United States that supports listing of individual STOCKS, EXCHANGE-TRADED FUNDS, and certain DERIVATIVES; the Exchange is now part of NEW YORK STOCK EXCHANGE.

AMERICAN TERMS   A commonly used quotation mechanism in the FOREIGN EXCHANGE markets that indicates how many US dollars can be exchanged for a unit of foreign CURRENCY. See also EUROPEAN TERMS, RECIPROCAL RATE.

AMEX   See AMERICAN STOCK EXCHANGE.

AMORTIZATION   A periodic reduction in the value of a LIABILITY or ASSET, as in a decrease in the PRINCIPAL balance of an AMORTIZING LOAN through repayments to the lender (or payments into a SINKING FUND), or a decrease in the value of a FIXED ASSET through periodic deductions for DEPRECIATION. Amortization may be based on constant, increasing, or decreasing payments, as defined in the AMORTIZATION SCHEDULE. See also ACCRETION, ACCRETION OF DISCOUNT.

AMORTIZATION SCHEDULE   A listing of the dates and amounts related to the repayment of an AMORTIZING LOAN or other FINANCING CONTRACT. See also AMORTIZATION.

AMORTIZING LOAN   A LOAN that requires the BORROWER to repay the BANK a certain amount of PRINCIPAL, along with contractual INTEREST, in accordance with an established AMORTIZATION SCHEDULE. See also BALLOON LOAN, BULLET LOAN.

AMORTIZING SWAP   An OVER-THE-COUNTER SWAP featuring a NOTIONAL PRINCIPAL balance that amortizes, or declines, on a preset schedule or through the triggering of a market event (commonly the breaching of an INTEREST RATE level). Amortizing swaps typically have a LOCKOUT PERIOD during which amortization is prohibited. See also ACCRETING SWAP, INDEX PRINCIPAL SWAP, REVERSE INDEX PRINCIPAL SWAP, VARIABLE PRINCIPAL SWAP.

AMOUNT AT RISK   (1)   In INSURANCE, the lesser of a POLICY CAP on a contract and the MAXIMUM PROBABLE LOSS to the INSURED. INSURERS use amount at risk to estimate potential losses within their PORTFOLIOS. (2) The difference between the PRINCIPAL outstanding on a LOAN and the value of any COLLATERAL securing the loan if it is liquidated forcibly.

ANALYSIS OF ACCOUNTS METHOD   A mechanism used by a company to create the PRO-FORMA BALANCE SHEET and PRO-FORMA INCOME STATEMENT. The process allocates to the start of period ASSET, LIABILITY, REVENUE and EXPENSE accounts the relevant DEBITS and CREDITS developed through CASH BUDGETING; the resulting end of period estimate is taken as the pro-forma estimate. See also PERCENTAGE OF SALES METHOD.

ANGEL   An INVESTOR or VENTURE CAPITAL partner that funds a private start-up company in exchange for a pre-INITIAL PUBLIC OFFERING EQUITY stake. The angel's participation in tactical and strategic decisions may be active or passive.

ANKLE BITER   [COL] A SMALL CAP STOCK, i.e., one with MARKET CAPITALIZATION of less than $1 billion.

ANNUAL ACCOUNTS   In the United Kingdom, the term for ANNUAL REPORT.

ANNUAL AGGREGATE LIMIT   The maximum amount that an INSURANCE contract will pay in SETTLEMENTS to an INSURED over a 12-month period, regardless of the number of CLAIMS submitted.

ANNUAL COMPOUNDING   See COMPOUNDING.

ANNUAL DEPRECIATION ALLOWANCE   The decrease in BOOK VALUE assigned to an ASSET as a result of DEPRECIATION, typically as a certain percentage per year.

ANNUAL EQUIVALENT RATE   See EFFECTIVE ANNUAL RATE.

ANNUAL GENERAL MEETING (AGM)   A meeting of a PUBLIC COMPANY's DIRECTORS, executives, and SHAREHOLDERS to review the year's financial performance and vote on specific agenda items (e.g., selection of directors, EXTERNAL AUDITOR, and so forth).

ANNUAL INFLATION SWAP   An OVER-THE-COUNTER SWAP involving the exchange of floating (actual) and fixed INFLATION at the end of each annual evaluation period. Annual inflation swaps, which generally reference an inflation INDEX of consumer prices, are often structured as long-term transactions, with maturities extending beyond 10 years. See also INFLATION SWAP, ZERO COUPON INFLATION SWAP.

ANNUAL PERCENTAGE RATE (APR)   The effective annual INTEREST RATE that is charged on a LOAN facility, CREDIT CARD facility or other debt FINANCING, or which is paid on an INVESTMENT, that expresses interest rate and fees as an annual rate. See also EFFECTIVE ANNUAL RATE.

ANNUAL REPORT   The yearly, AUDITED, FINANCIAL STATEMENTS published by a company. The annual report typically includes the BALANCE SHEET, INCOME STATEMENT, STATEMENT OF CASH FLOWS, along with accompanying FOOTNOTES and the AUDIT REPORT. See also ANNUAL ACCOUNTS.

ANNUITANT   A person or entity entitled to receive regular ANNUITY benefits based on capital that has been contributed into an annuity program during the ACCUMULATION PERIOD.

ANNUITY   An INVESTMENT CONTRACT, generally purchased from an INSURER through single or multiple tax-deferred CAPITAL contributions, that guarantees fixed or variable payments to an ANNUITANT starting at some future date, and lasting for a stated period of time. See also CERTAIN ANNUITY, PERPETUITY, PRESENT VALUE, FUTURE VALUE, LIFE ANNUITY.

ANTICIPATORY HEDGE   An ex-ante HEDGE that is created to reduce the variability associated with a future ASSET, LIABILITY, or cash inflow; the hedge may be created with DERIVATIVES or a LONG POSITION or SHORT POSITION in the UNDERLYING reference.

ANTIDILUTION PROVISION   See PREEMPTIVE RIGHT.

ANTITAKEOVER DEFENSE   A legal or structural tactic adopted by a company in order to protect it from being acquired by another company. Defenses may be used in conjunction with, or as a substitute for, ANTITAKEOVER LAWS. Also known as PORCUPINE PROVISION, SHARK REPELLENT. See also BLANK CHECK PREFERRED, POISON PILL, SCORCHED EARTH DEFENSES, STAGGERED BOARD.

ANTITAKEOVER LAWS   Laws enacted in certain national systems that prohibit, or severely limit, a company from acquiring another company, primarily in instances involving HOSTILE TAKEOVERS. See also ANTITAKEOVER DEFENSE.

ANTITRUST   Policies and REGULATIONS that restrict the formation of OLIGOPOLY or MONOPOLY power in order to promote free market competition.

ANY-AND-ALL BID   A TAKEOVER mechanism where a company seeking to acquire a TARGET firm agrees to pay the same price for any SHARES that are tendered. The any-and-all bid stands in contrast to the TWO-TIER BID (where INVESTORS receive an inducement PREMIUM for tendering their shares by an initial cutoff date.)

APACS   See ASSOCIATION FOR PAYMENT CLEARING SERVICES.

APPARENT AGENCY   Conduct by an AGENT that causes another party to believe the agent is authorized to conduct business on behalf of a PRINCIPAL, whether or not that is the case. A PRINCIPAL may be legally bound by apparent agency. See also ACTUAL AUTHORITY.

APPORTIONMENT   The practice of dividing an INSURED's CLAIMS covered under multiple INSURANCE contracts, typically in proportion to total insurance coverage. Apportionment is generally written into a contract through a separate clause. See also DIVIDED COVER, OVERLAPPING INSURANCE, PRIMACY, PRO-RATA.

APPRECIATION   An increase in the worth of a financial INVESTMENT or ASSET as a result of MARKET RISK factors. See also DEPRECIATION, DEVALUATION.

APPROPRIATION   The allocation of a company's NET INCOME to distinct accounts, such as DIVIDENDS, RETAINED EARNINGS, RESERVES, and so forth.

APR   See ANNUAL PERCENTAGE RATE.

APT   See ARBITRAGE PRICING THEORY.

ARB   [COL] Abbreviation for ARBITRAGEUR.

ARBITRAGE   An investment strategy involving the simultaneous purchase and sale of two ASSETS in order to capitalize on small price or rate discrepancies. The intent of the strategy is to generate a profit with a minimum amount of RISK; true arbitrage is RISK-free. Common arbitrage strategies include FIXED INCOME ARBITRAGE, CONVERTIBLE BOND ARBITRAGE, RISK ARBITRAGE, DUAL LISTED COMPANY ARBITRAGE, STATISTICAL ARBITRAGE, RELATIVE VALUE ARBITRAGE, VOLATILITY ARBITRAGE, as well as arbitrage related to MUNICIPAL BONDS and GLOBAL DEPOSITORY RECEIPTS. See also HEDGE, LONG ARBITRAGE, PURE ARBITRAGE, QUASI ARBITRAGE, SHORT ARBITRAGE, SPECULATION, YIELD ENHANCEMENT.

ARBITRAGE COLLATERALIZED DEBT OBLIGATION   A COLLATERALIZED DEBT OBLIGATION (CDO) arranged by a BANK or SECURITIES FIRM to take advantage of perceived profit opportunities created by assembling and managing a PORTFOLIO of credit-RISKY SECURITIES or CREDIT DERIVATIVES and issuing TRANCHES to fund the portfolio. See also BALANCE SHEET COLLATERALIZED DEBT OBLIGATION, CASH COLLATERALIZED DEBT OBLIGATION, SYNTHETIC COLLATERALIZED DEBT OBLIGATION.

ARBITRAGE-FREE CONDITION   See NO ARBITRAGE CONDITION.

ARBITRAGE-FREE MODEL   A model that values financial contracts in such a way that no ARBITRAGE opportunities can arise. Arbitrage-free models are often used in the TRADING of DERIVATIVES and may be specifically calibrated to actual market values. See also LAW OF ONE PRICE.

ARBITRAGE PRICING THEORY (APT)   A financial theory posited as a testable, and more flexible, alternative to the CAPITAL ASSET PRICING MODEL (CAPM), based on the concept that multiple linear RISK factors influence the return of a SECURITY, and the factors can be estimated through principal components/factor analysis. By understanding the risk and RETURN contribution of each factor, an optimal PORTFOLIO can be created. APT, like CAPM, makes use of BETA as a measure of risk. The single-factor APT return is given by:

$$E(r_j) = E(r_f) + \lambda_1 \beta_{1,j}$$

where $E(r_j)$ is the expected return of security j, $E(r_f)$ is the expected RISK-FREE RATE, λ_1 is the slope of risk factor 1, and $\beta_{1,j}$ is the beta related to risk factor 1 and security j. The equation can be expanded to multifactor form, with z risk factors:

$$E(r_j) = E(r_f) + \sum_{j=1}^{z} \lambda_1 \beta_{1,j}$$

Additional references: Roll (1977); Roll and Ross (1980); Ross (1976).

ARBITRAGEUR   [FR] An individual or institution engaged in ARBITRAGE transactions. See also ARB.

ARBITRATION   A formal mechanism to resolve disputes between parties out of court, widely used in the SECURITIES industry when conflicts appear between BROKERS and clients, and in the INSURANCE industry when disputes arise between INSUREDS and INSURERS. Parties submitting to arbitration may agree to a binding decision by the ARBITRATOR, or simply follow an indicative one.

ARBITRATION CLAUSE   A clause in an INSURANCE contract stating that the INSURED and INSURER agree to ARBITRATION in the event of disagreement on a CLAIM. Similar disclosure is common in INVESTMENT account agreements.

ARBITRATOR   A professional and independent party appointed to conduct ARBITRATION between two disputing parties.

ARCH   See AUTOREGRESSIVE CONDITIONAL HETEROSKEDASTICITY.

ARITHMETIC MEAN   See MEAN.

ARM   See ADJUSTABLE RATE MORTGAGE.

ARMS INDEX   See TRADING INDEX.

ARM'S LENGTH   [COL] A process of carrying out a transaction on purely market-driven commercial terms, regardless of the relationship between the two parties involved; no preferential pricing or treatment is granted to either party, even if they are related through common ownership.

ARRANGER   A BANK that is responsible for structuring a SYNDICATED LOAN facility for a BORROWER, and assembling a SYNDICATE to distribute portions of the loan to a broader group of INVESTORS.

ARREARS SWAP   An INTEREST RATE SWAP with a FLOATING RATE that is set in arrears rather than in advance; thus, the rate may be set two days before payment date, rather than six months plus two days before payment date (as on a standard semiannual swap). Also known as IN-ARREARS SWAP, LIBOR IN-ARREARS SWAP.

ARTICLES OF ASSOCIATION   In the United Kingdom, a document defining responsibilities and rights of key STAKEHOLDERS, including INVESTORS, DIRECTORS, and executive management. The articles can be used in the constitution of either a PRIVATE COMPANY or PUBLIC COMPANY. Changes may be made by special resolution at the ANNUAL GENERAL MEETING (public companies) or by written resolution (private companies). Articles of Association are submitted, along with the MEMORANDUM OF ASSOCIATION, as part of the COMPANY FORMATION process. See also ARTICLES OF INCORPORATION.

ARTICLES OF INCORPORATION   A legal document filed by the founders of a company that results in the issuance of a certificate of incorporation from an authorizing government or legal entity. The articles contain details on the company's business, founders, DIRECTORS, and authorized CAPITAL. Articles of incorporation, together with the CORPORATE CHARTER, give a company its legal form and existence.

ARTICLES OF PARTNERSHIP   A legally binding agreement between the PARTNERS involved in the formation and operation of a PARTNERSHIP. The form of agreement can vary, but generally defines the roles and responsibilities of the LIMITED PARTNER(S) and the GENERAL PARTNER(S), the sharing of profits, the payment of salaries, mechanisms of dissolution, mechanisms of ARBITRATION or dispute resolution, and so forth. Also known as PARTNERSHIP AGREEMENT.

ASB   See ACCOUNTING STANDARDS BOARD.

ASCENDING TOP   A TECHNICAL ANALYSIS formation that reveals repeatedly higher peaks in the price/level of a SECURITY or INDEX, reflecting a BULLISH trend. See also DESCENDING BOTTOM, FALLING TOP, RISING BOTTOM.

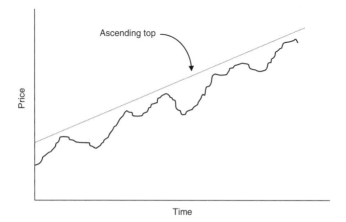

ASEAN   See ASSOCIATION OF SOUTH EAST ASIAN NATIONS.

ASIAN DEVELOPMENT BANK   A MULTILATERAL DEVELOPMENT BANK created in 1966 by Asian nations to support economic and social progress and to supply long-term development finance to member countries, modeled after the INTERNATIONAL BANK FOR RECONSTRUCTION AND DEVELOPMENT.

ASIAN OPTION   A COMPLEX OPTION that grants the buyer a payoff based on the geometric or arithmetic MEAN price of the UNDERLYING reference over a predetermined averaging period (i.e., ASIAN TAIL). The payoff can be determined by applying the average path to the price of the underlying (AVERAGE PRICE OPTION) or the STRIKE PRICE (AVERAGE STRIKE OPTION). Also known as AVERAGE OPTION.

ASIAN TAIL   [COL] The length of the averaging period in an ASIAN OPTION.

ASK   See OFFER.

ASSAY   The quantitative evaluation of the quality and purity of the chemical elements in a precious metal or industrial metal, often used in the specifications of a metals-based DERIVATIVE CONTRACT.

ASSENTED STOCK   A SHARE of STOCK held by an INVESTOR who has agreed to the terms of a TAKEOVER bid.

ASSET   A financial CONTRACT or physical object with value that is owned by an individual, company, or sovereign entity, which can be used to generate additional value/earnings or provide LIQUIDITY. Assets may include CASH, INVESTMENTS, ACCOUNTS RECEIVABLE, LOANS granted, INVENTORY, real estate, plant and equipment, and INTANGIBLES. Assets are characterized by varying degrees of LIQUIDITY, and may be funded through DEBT or EQUITY. See also LIABILITY.

ASSET ALLOCATION   The process of investing CAPITAL across, or within, a specific set of ASSET classes in order to achieve a desired RISK/RETURN profile. See also DISCRETIONARY TACTICAL ASSET ALLOCATION, STRATEGIC ASSET ALLOCATION, SYSTEMATIC TACTICAL ASSET ALLOCATION, TACTICAL ASSET ALLOCATION.

ASSET-AT-EXPIRY OPTION   A BINARY-BARRIER OPTION that grants the buyer a payoff at expiry equal to a fixed ASSET amount if the price of the UNDERLYING market reference breaches the BARRIER at any time during the transaction. See also ASSET-AT-HIT OPTION, BINARY OPTION.

ASSET-AT-HIT OPTION   A BINARY-BARRIER OPTION that grants the buyer an immediate payoff equal to a fixed ASSET amount if the price of the UNDERLYING market reference exceeds the BARRIER. See also ASSET-AT-EXPIRY OPTION, BINARY OPTION.

ASSET-BACKED COMMERCIAL PAPER (ABCP)   A form of COMMERCIAL PAPER issued by large FINANCIAL INSTITUTIONS or companies through a SPECIAL PURPOSE ENTITY or a CONDUIT, which is secured by pools of ASSETS, such as short-term LOANS, RECEIVABLES, or SECURITIES.

ASSET-BACKED SECURITY (ABS)   A NOTE or BOND collateralized by a POOL of ASSETS. Assets in the pool are transferred to a SPECIAL PURPOSE ENTITY established as a TRUST, which issues the securities to INVESTORS; investors hold an undivided interest in the asset pool and receive INTEREST and PRINCIPAL based on the CASH FLOWS generated by the assets. ABS can be arranged for a number of underlying asset pools, including credit card receivables, auto LOANS, student loans, small business loans, aircraft LEASES, and equipment leases, and so forth. While the CASH FLOW dynamics of each asset class can vary, all follow the same basic structural techniques.

ASSET-BASED LOAN   A RECOURSE or NONRECOURSE LOAN granted by a BANK or other financial institution to a customer for use in acquiring INVENTORY, machinery, equipment, or other FIXED ASSETS (apart from real estate). The underlying asset is often used to secure the loan. Also known as ASSET FINANCING.

ASSET CARD   See DEBIT CARD.

ASSET CONVERSION LOAN   See SELF-LIQUIDATING LOAN.

ASSET COVERAGE   The ability for a company to use its ASSETS to cover a particular financial CLAIM or LIABILITY, such as a class of DEBT or PREFERRED STOCK. Asset coverage can be computed via:

$$AC = \frac{TA - IN - Cl - Cl_{SR}}{Cl}$$

where TA equals total assets (expressed in terms of BOOK VALUE or LIQUIDATING VALUE), IN is INTANGIBLES, Cl is the claim being covered, Cl_{SR} is any claim ranking senior to Cl. The greater the asset coverage, the stronger the financial position and flexibility of the company.

ASSET FINANCING   See ASSET-BASED LOAN.

ASSET-FUNDING LIQUIDITY RISK   The RISK of loss arising from an inability to obtain unsecured funding at a reasonable economic cost, causing a forced pledge or sale of ASSETS at a loss. A subcategory of LIQUIDITY RISK. See also ASSET LIQUIDITY RISK, ENDOGENOUS LIQUIDITY, EXOGENOUS LIQUIDITY, FUNDING LIQUIDITY RISK.

ASSET IMPAIRMENT   A decline in the value of an ASSET as a result of damage, obsolescence, or DEFAULT. The value of an impaired asset can be reduced or written off in the FINANCIAL STATEMENTS of the organization, generally by an amount obtained from an impairment test.

ASSET-LIABILITY COMMITTEE (ALCO)   A management body within a BANK or financial institution that is responsible for establishing RISK MANAGEMENT and funding policies as related to ASSET-LIABILITY MANAGEMENT.

ASSET-LIABILITY MANAGEMENT (ALM)   A business and RISK MANA-
GEMENT practice where a BANK or financial institution manages the
CASH FLOWS generated by ASSETS (e.g., LOANS, REVERSE REPURCHASE
AGREEMENTS, INVESTMENTS), LIABILITIES (e.g., DEPOSITS, REPURCHASE
AGREEMENTS), and OFF-BALANCE SHEET ACTIVITIES (e.g., DERIVATIVES,
REVOLVING CREDIT AGREEMENTS, GUARANTEES). Depending on a bank's
view of INTEREST RATES, its willingness to assume RISK, and its REVENUE
goals, the ALM process may support a MISMATCH in the DURATION of assets
and liabilities in order to try to generate a profit. See also GAP, GAPPING, RATE-
SENSITIVE ASSETS, RATE-SENSITIVE LIABILITIES.

ASSET LIQUIDITY RISK   The RISK of loss arising from an inability to sell or
pledge ASSETS at, or near, their carrying value when needed. A subcategory of
LIQUIDITY RISK. See also ASSET-FUNDING LIQUIDITY RISK, ENDOGENOUS
LIQUIDITY, EXOGENOUS LIQUIDITY, FUNDING LIQUIDITY RISK.

ASSET MANAGEMENT   (1) The process of managing the INVESTMENT
CAPITAL of clients, with the aim of achieving specific goals which may
include preservation of capital, maximization of current income, optimization
of tax position, and so forth. The asset management function may be discretionary or nondiscretionary, and is typically performed by a financial institution, such as a BANK, BROKER/DEALER, HEDGE FUND, MUTUAL FUND,
or INSURER, for a fee. (2) The process of managing the ASSETS of a company
in order to achieve the best possible operating efficiencies. (1) Also known as
INVESTMENT MANAGEMENT.

ASSET MANAGER   See PORTFOLIO MANAGER.

ASSET-OR-NOTHING OPTION   A BINARY-BARRIER OPTION that grants the
buyer a payoff equal to a fixed ASSET value if the price of the UNDERLYING
market reference exceeds the STRIKE PRICE at EXPIRY. See also BINARY
OPTION, CASH-OR-NOTHING OPTION.

ASSET SECURITIZATION   See SECURITIZATION.

ASSET SENSITIVE   See POSITIVE GAP.

ASSET STRIPPER   [COL] A company or individual that engages in ASSET
STRIPPING. See also RAIDER.

ASSET STRIPPING   The process of selling corporate ASSETS acquired in a
TAKEOVER or ACQUISITION. Such disposals may occur when the value of
selling assets and using the proceeds to repay DEBT or invest in alternative
ventures is estimated to be greater than the value of preserving them on the
BALANCE SHEET. See also BREAKUP VALUE, LIQUIDATION VALUE.

ASSET SWAP   An OVER-THE-COUNTER INTEREST RATE SWAP that
exchanges BOND COUPONS from FIXED RATES into FLOATING RATES, or
vice versa, creating a synthetic investment that meets an INVESTOR's specifications. An asset swap can thus be viewed as a package of an interest rate
swap and a risky bond, where the bondholder pays the fixed coupon from
the risky bond and receives the floating coupon, itself a combination of the

ASSET SWAP SPREAD and the FLOATING RATE benchmark (e.g., LIBOR). See also LIABILITY SWAP.

ASSET SWAP SPREAD   The floating COUPON paid above a FLOATING RATE BENCHMARK in an ASSET SWAP, representing the CREDIT RISK of a risky BOND above the INTERBANK MARKET rate. See also BOND SWAP SPREAD, SWAP SPREAD.

ASSET SWAPTION   See SYNTHETIC LENDING FACILITY.

ASSET TURNOVER   A measure of a company's efficiency in utilizing its ASSETS, generally calculated as the number of times during the year the value of the company's assets is generated in REVENUES. It is computed as:

$$AT = \frac{Rev}{TA}$$

where Rev is the company's revenues, and TA is the company's total assets. The higher the ratio, the more effective is the company in utilizing its assets to generate value. Also known as CAPITAL TURNOVER.

ASSET VALUATION   The process of assigning an economic worth to a company's ASSETS. The valuation process depends on the specific nature of the asset: SECURITIES and other financial assets may be valued at a current market price, while FIXED ASSETS and INTANGIBLE ASSETS may require estimates provided by external assessors or experts. The process must generally be confirmed by AUDITORS for the purposes of publishing periodic FINANCIAL STATEMENTS.

ASSET VALUE   The value of a company's ASSETS less its LIABILITIES, providing a theoretical measure of its worth in the event of a breakup. The figure can be transformed to a per share value by dividing by the total number of SHARES outstanding.

ASSIGNED AMOUNT UNIT (AAU)   A tradable unit of a CARBON DIOXIDE EQUIVALENT.

ASSIGNEE   The party to whom an ASSIGNOR transfers TITLE, CLAIM, or property, as in a SECURED DEBT transaction.

ASSIGNMENT   (1) The sale or transfer of a financial CONTRACT, such as an OVER-THE-COUNTER DERIVATIVE or LOAN, from the original COUNTERPARTY to a third party; an assignment is often arranged in order to reduce CREDIT RISK exposure and typically requires permission from the original party to the contract. (2) The receipt of a notice of EXERCISE by an OPTION seller which obliges the sale (for a CALL) or purchase (for a PUT) of the UNDERLYING.

ASSIGNOR   The party assigning title, CLAIM, or property to the ASSIGNEE, as in a SECURED DEBT transaction.

ASSOCIATION FOR PAYMENT CLEARING SERVICES (APACS)   In the United Kingdom, an association that manages payment CLEARING and transfers.

APACS comprises of individual companies that focus on specific segments of the sector, including interbank clearing payments and settlements, direct DEBIT and CREDIT payments, interbank check clearing, and ELECTRONIC FUNDS TRANSFERS. See also CLEARINGHOUSE AUTOMATED PAYMENT SYSTEM.

ASSOCIATION OF CHARTERED CERTIFIED ACCOUNTANTS (ACCA)   In the United Kingdom, an association that represents the interests of CHARTERED CERTIFIED ACCOUNTANTS.

ASSOCIATION OF SOUTH EAST ASIAN NATIONS (ASEAN)   A group, formed in 1967 and including 10 Southeast Asian nations, which consults on economic and political matters, with an overarching goal of promoting regional economic progress. The membership includes Brunei, Cambodia, Indonesia, Laos, Malaysia, Myanmar, Philippines, Singapore, Thailand, and Vietnam.

ASSUMABLE MORTGAGE   A MORTGAGE that can be transferred from the original BORROWER to a new purchaser of the underlying property. The assumability feature eliminates the need for the original LOAN to be repaid and a new loan to be arranged, which reduces time and expense.

ASSUMED BOND   A BOND issued by one company that is the legal LIABILITY of another company, such as might be found between a PARENT and SUBSIDIARY or two JOINT VENTURE partners.

ASSUMED LOSS RATIO   See COMBINED RATIO.

ASSUMPTION OF RISK   See RETENTION.

ASSUMPTION REINSURANCE   A REINSURANCE mechanism where a REINSURER assumes the CEDING INSURER's obligations through a wholesale transfer of hundreds, or thousands, of individual INSURANCE policies.

ASSURANCE   In the United Kingdom, any form of INSURANCE against an event that will eventually occur, such as death.

ASSURED   In the United Kingdom, INSURED.

ASSURER   In the United Kingdom, INSURER.

ASYMMETRIC INFORMATION   Any instance where one party has more information than another party about a particular current or future event. This can be used to the advantage of the party with additional information – only, however, if it does not violate INSIDER TRADING laws or other rules.

ASYMMETRIC PAYOFF   A PAYOFF PROFILE on a DERIVATIVE contract where the gain or loss differs depending on the direction and magnitude of market price changes. An OPTION contract is characterized by an asymmetric profile, gaining or losing for a range of market prices in one direction, but capping gains or losses in the opposite direction. See also LINEAR PAYOFF, NONLINEAR PAYOFF, SYMMETRIC PAYOFF.

AT BEST   See AT BEST ORDER.

AT BEST ORDER   An ORDER to buy or sell SECURITIES at the best price available at the time the order is placed. An at best order is a form of MARKET ORDER. Also known as AT BEST.

AT CALL   Secured funds that have been lent by a BANK or DISCOUNT HOUSE on a short-term basis (often overnight) and which must be repaid immediately by the BORROWER upon demand.

AT-EXPIRY OPTION   A BINARY OPTION that grants the buyer a payoff at EXPIRY equal to a fixed ASSET or cash value if the price of the UNDERLYING market reference breaches the BARRIER at any time during the transaction. See also ASSET-AT-EXPIRY OPTION, AT-HIT OPTION, BINARY-BARRIER OPTION, CASH-AT-EXPIRY OPTION.

AT-HIT OPTION   A BINARY OPTION that grants the buyer an immediate payoff equal to a fixed ASSET or cash value if the price of the UNDERLYING market reference breaches the BARRIER at any time during the transaction. See also ASSET-AT-HIT OPTION, AT-EXPIRY OPTION, BINARY-BARRIER OPTION, CASH-AT-HIT OPTION.

AT LIMIT   See LIMIT ORDER.

AT SIGHT   A term included on a BILL OF EXCHANGE indicating that payment is due when the bill is presented for collection. See also AFTER SIGHT.

AT THE CLOSE ORDER   An ORDER to buy or sell SECURITIES at the market closing price; if the order cannot be fully executed, it is cancelled. See also AT THE OPEN ORDER.

AT THE FIGURE ORDER   See AT THE FULL ORDER.

AT THE FULL ORDER   An ORDER to buy or sell SECURITIES at the integer closest to the BID (for a purchase) or OFFER (for a sale). Also known as AT THE FIGURE ORDER.

AT-THE-MONEY   A condition where the STRIKE PRICE of an OPTION is precisely equal to the current price of the UNDERLYING reference ASSET. An at-the-money option has no INTRINSIC VALUE but features maximum TIME VALUE. See also IN-THE-MONEY, MONEYNESS, OUT-OF-THE-MONEY.

AT THE OPEN ORDER   An ORDER to buy or sell SECURITIES at the market open price; if the order cannot be fully executed, it is cancelled. See also AT THE CLOSE ORDER.

ATM   See AUTOMATED TELLER MACHINE.

ATS   See ALTERNATIVE TRADING SYSTEM.

ATTACHMENT   (1) The economic level at which INSURANCE or REINSURANCE coverage becomes effective, i.e., the first dollar above the INSURED's DEDUCTIBLE. An INSURER's total potential LIABILITY extends from the point of attachment to the POLICY CAP. (2) An addition or amendment to an insurance CONTRACT providing explanations or additional coverage or EXCLUSIONS; the attachment is often permanently replaced by an ENDORSEMENT or RIDER. (3) A procedure that legally permits a CREDITOR to obtain a payment from a DEBTOR's ASSETS or income.

ATTACHMENT METHOD   A process of combining several existing MONOLINE POLICIES i.e., separate INSURANCE covers for PROPERTY AND

CASUALTY, general LIABILITY, and others, under a single master agreement, without redrafting, in order to consolidate the individual components. See also SINGLE TEXT METHOD.

ATTORNEY-IN-FACT   A party holding POWER OF ATTORNEY, and who is therefore authorized to deal on behalf of the executor of the power of attorney.

AUCTION   A general market system where SECURITIES or other ASSETS are purchased and sold through competitive BIDS and OFFERS, through DEALERS or BROKERS acting as AGENTS for clients. Also known as AUCTION MARKET, ORDER-DRIVEN MARKET. See also DEALER MARKET, DUTCH AUCTION, ENGLISH AUCTION, REVERSE DUTCH AUCTION, QUOTE-DRIVEN MARKET, UNIFORM PRICE AUCTION.

AUCTION RATE PREFERRED STOCK   See DUTCH AUCTION PREFERRED STOCK.

AUDIT   The process of independently inspecting and analyzing the FINANCIAL STATEMENTS of a SOLE PROPRIETORSHIP, PARTNERSHIP, CORPORATION, or other economic entity, generally by performing a series of tests that ensure compliance with standards of financial control and reporting. The audit process may be carried out on a regular basis by an internal AUDITOR (in the form of an INTERNAL AUDIT) and supplemented for statutory requirements and the release of public financial statements by an external auditor, who is responsible for publishing an AUDIT OPINION at the conclusion of the EXTERNAL AUDIT.

AUDIT FEE   The amount paid by a company or economic entity for the services provided by an external AUDITOR.

AUDIT OPINION   An independent opinion rendered by a company's external AUDITOR after a review of FINANCIAL STATEMENTS and operations via an EXTERNAL AUDIT. The opinion generally takes one of three forms: UNQUALIFIED OPINION, meaning the financial statements are a fair and accurate representation of the company's financial position and conform to accepted ACCOUNTING PRINCIPLES; QUALIFIED OPINION, meaning the financial statements may contain some deviations or problems; and ADVERSE OPINION, meaning the financial statements do not accurately reflect the company's financial position.

AUDIT REPORT   The report prepared by internal and/or external AUDITORS that provides evidence of the findings and results obtained during the INTERNAL AUDIT and/or EXTERNAL AUDIT of a company's financial controls and reporting.

AUDIT TRAIL   The total of all documentation and records that evidence the financial recording and reporting used by a company in the preparation of its FINANCIAL STATEMENTS. AUDITORS frequently rely on the audit trail to perform their INTERNAL AUDIT and EXTERNAL AUDIT functions.

AUDITOR   An authorized ACCOUNTANT or financial expert that analyzes and verifies the nature and accuracy of a company's FINANCIAL STATEMENTS and the strengths of its control processes. The auditor may be part of the company (internal auditor) or a member of an external ACCOUNTING firm (external auditor).

AUFSICHTSRAT [GER] The SUPERVISORY BOARD of a German CORPORATION. See also VORSTAND.

AUNT MILLIE [COL] An unsophisticated INVESTOR. See also WIDOWS AND ORPHANS.

AUTARKY   An economic system without any external TRADE, or one where trade is reduced or eliminated through barriers and QUOTAS.

AUTHORIZATION RISK   The RISK of loss that occurs when an employee or AGENT of a company commits the firm to a legally binding, but unauthorized, transaction; in most instances the firm will be required to perform as contracted. A subcategory of OPERATIONAL RISK.

AUTHORIZED CAPITAL   The maximum number of SHARES of COMMON STOCK a company is permitted to issue, per the terms of its ARTICLES OF INCORPORATION. Issuance in excess of authorized capital requires an amendment to the articles. Also known as AUTHORIZED SHARE CAPITAL, NOMINAL CAPITAL, REGISTERED CAPITAL.

AUTHORIZED FINANCIAL ADVISOR   In the United Kingdom, an investment and finance advisor that has received authorization to provide professional services under the Financial Services Act of 1986. See also INVESTMENT ADVISOR.

AUTHORIZED INSURER   See ADMITTED INSURER.

AUTHORIZED INVESTMENTS INVESTMENTS that a TRUSTEE or INVESTMENT ADVISOR is legally permitted to execute on behalf of a TRUST fund.

AUTHORIZED SHARE CAPITAL   See AUTHORIZED CAPITAL.

AUTOCORRELATION   A statistical measure that indicates the degree of CORRELATION of a random variable with itself; specifically, it measures the relationship between a value in a time series and those that occur before and after. Positive autocorrelation indicates that deviations from the equilibrium exist across periods, while negative autocorrelation means that deviations tend to be reversed. See also CORRELATION.

AUTOMATED SCREEN TRADING   A trading mechanism that relies entirely on electronic communications, display, and EXECUTION to support incoming BIDS and OFFERS. Automated screen trading, which is a feature of many EXCHANGES and forms the central architecture of ELECTRONIC COMMUNICATIONS NETWORKS, removes the physical element of SECURITIES and COMMODITIES trading.

AUTOMATED TELLER MACHINE (ATM)   An electronic machine operated by a BANK, SAVINGS AND LOAN (BUILDING SOCIETY), or other financial institution that is able to dispense cash, accept DEPOSITS, and arrange transfers between a customer's accounts.

AUTOMATIC CLEARINGHOUSE (ACH)   In the United States, a national ELECTRONIC FUNDS TRANSFER network that clears and settles recurring payments between FINANCIAL INSTITUTIONS, as well as DEBITS and CREDITS generated through business-to-business commerce and trade transactions.

AUTOMATIC COVERAGE An INSURANCE CONTRACT that automatically comes into effect when an INSURED acquires new property or revalues existing property. Automatic coverage eliminates the possibility of UNDERINSURANCE.

AUTOMATIC NONPROPORTIONAL REINSURANCE   Automatic REINSURANCE coverage for an INSURER that becomes effective once a defined loss limit is exceeded, often implemented through a STOP LOSS AGREEMENT or a CATASTROPHE PER OCCURRENCE EXCESS OF LOSS CONTRACT. See also AUTOMATIC PROPORTIONAL REINSURANCE.

AUTOMATIC PROPORTIONAL REINSURANCE   Automatic REINSURANCE coverage for an INSURER that becomes effective once a defined loss limit is exceeded, generally implemented through a sharing agreement such as a SURPLUS SHARE or QUOTA SHARE. See also AUTOMATIC NONPROPORTIONAL REINSURANCE.

AUTOMATIC REINSTATEMENT CLAUSE A clause in an INSURANCE CONTRACT indicating that after the INSURER has paid the INSURED on a CLAIM, the original contract limits are automatically renewed.

AUTOMATIC STAY   A legal provision afforded to a DEBTOR in BANKRUPTCY that prohibits filing of lawsuits against the company and limits the ability of CREDITORS to dispose of COLLATERAL held as security or to take any other actions that would interfere with operations. While creditors in general cannot sell any of the debtor's collateral, those holding security against DERIVATIVES or REVERSE REPURCHASE AGREEMENTS are permitted to do so under exemption clauses or SAFE HARBOR RULES. The delay created by the automatic stay is necessary as the bankruptcy RECEIVER must complete a thorough analysis of the value of the company's ASSETS and LIABILITIES, as well as the nature of any payments made during PREFERENCE PERIODS.

AUTOREGRESSIVE CONDITIONAL HETEROSKEDASTICITY (ARCH)   An econometric model that uses multiple time-series factors as a way of estimating VOLATILITY. ARCH models are used in DERIVATIVES trading, particularly for contracts such as VOLATILITY SWAPS.

AVAILABILITY   The time at which point funds placed by a depositor in a BANK become usable. Availability can range from immediate (for WIRE TRANSFERS) to several days (for CHECKS written on banks in different locales). See also FINALITY.

AVAILABLE FOR SALE (AFS) ACCOUNTING An ACCOUNTING process used by a BANK where certain ASSETS, such as SECURITIES and DERIVATIVES that are held for TRADING purposes, follow a MARK-TO-MARKET approach to profit and loss recognition, with changes in fair value booked to the "other comprehensive income" account, which flows through the EQUITY account of the BALANCE SHEET.

AVAILABLE RESERVES The difference between a BANK's excess RESERVE balance with the CENTRAL BANK and net funds borrowed through the central banking system or via a DISCOUNT WINDOW.

AVAL A third party GUARANTEE on a BILL OF EXCHANGE, BANKER'S ACCEPTANCE, or PROMISSORY NOTE that is intended to reinforce the CREDITWORTHINESS of the obligation.

AVERAGE DOWN A strategy of buying additional SECURITIES at a lower price in order to reduce the average cost of the entire position. See also AVERAGE UP, AVERAGING.

AVERAGE EXPECTED RISK EXPOSURE POTENTIAL EXPOSURE of an OVER-THE-COUNTER DERIVATIVE that is based on the average maturity of the transaction and the expected movement of the underlying market reference. See also AVERAGE WORST-CASE RISK EXPOSURE, TERMINAL EXPECTED RISK EXPOSURE, TERMINAL WORST-CASE RISK EXPOSURE.

AVERAGE EXPOSURE The POTENTIAL EXPOSURE of an OVER-THE-COUNTER DERIVATIVE based on the average MATURITY of the transaction. See also TERMINAL EXPOSURE.

AVERAGE INVENTORY An INVENTORY management and ACCOUNTING approach where inventory is transferred at the average cost of all the goods held in stock. Also known as AVERAGE STOCK.

AVERAGE OPTION See ASIAN OPTION.

AVERAGE PRICE OPTION A COMPLEX OPTION that grants the buyer a payoff equal to the difference between an average price on an UNDERLYING market reference and a predefined STRIKE PRICE. See also ASIAN OPTION, AVERAGE STRIKE OPTION.

AVERAGE STOCK See AVERAGE INVENTORY.

AVERAGE STRIKE OPTION A COMPLEX OPTION that grants the buyer a payoff equal to the difference between an average STRIKE PRICE and the terminal value of the UNDERLYING market reference. See also ASIAN OPTION, AVERAGE PRICE OPTION.

AVERAGE TAX RATE The average TAX levied on a particular tax base, computed as the tax liability (due or paid) divided by the taxable income. See also EFFECTIVE TAX RATE, MARGINAL TAX RATE, STATUTORY TAX RATE.

AVERAGE UP A strategy of buying additional SECURITIES at increasing prices, thereby raising the average cost of the entire position. See also AVERAGE DOWN, AVERAGING.

AVERAGE WORST-CASE RISK EXPOSURE   POTENTIAL EXPOSURE of an OVER-THE-COUNTER DERIVATIVE that is based on the average MATURITY of the transaction and the worst-case movement of the UNDERLYING market reference. See also AVERAGE EXPECTED RISK EXPOSURE, TERMINAL EXPECTED RISK EXPOSURE, TERMINAL WORST-CASE RISK EXPOSURE.

AVERAGING   The process of buying or selling additional amounts of an INVESTMENT as the price falls or rises. Also known as DOLLAR COST AVERAGING. See also AVERAGE DOWN, AVERAGE UP.

AWAY FROM THE MARKET   A BID on a LIMIT ORDER that is lower than the current price, or an ASK that is higher than the current price. The order is held for later EXECUTION unless it is specifically identified as an ALL-OR-NONE ORDER.

AXE   [COL] A significant RISK position held on the books of a FINANCIAL INSTITUTION that it wishes to sell or reduce as a matter of priority. Axed positions generally feature attractive pricing or sales credits in order to incent salespeople to aggressively sell them to clients.

B

B-NOTE   A TRANCHE of SUBORDINATED DEBT created out of a FIRST LIEN COMMERCIAL MORTGAGE.

B-SHARES   (1) On various STOCK EXCHANGES, the SHARES of small companies or those with limited VOTING RIGHTS. (2) Dollar-denominated STOCKS listed and traded on the SHANGHAI STOCK EXCHANGE and the Shenzhen Stock Exchange, available to both domestic and foreign INVESTORS. (1,2) See also A-SHARE.

B2B EXCHANGE   See BUSINESS-TO-BUSINESS EXCHANGE.

B2C EXCHANGE   See BUSINESS-TO-CONSUMER EXCHANGE.

B&C LOAN   See SUBPRIME LOAN.

BA   See BANKER'S ACCEPTANCE.

BABY BOND   [COL] (1) A BOND with a small FACE VALUE denomination (e.g., $1000) that is targeted specifically at RETAIL INVESTORS. (2) In the United Kingdom, TAX-exempt bonds offered by FRIENDLY SOCIETIES that yield a specific sum over a return horizon of not less than 10 years.

BACK BOOK   [COL] A DEALER's proprietary trading BOOK, in which speculative positions can be held. See also FRONT BOOK.

BACK DOOR   [COL] In the United Kingdom, a process where the BANK OF ENGLAND attempts to influence MONEY SUPPLY indirectly by dealing in TREASURY BILLS through its own account, at market rates. See also FRONT DOOR.

BACK DOOR LISTING   [COL] A process where an unlisted or PRIVATE COMPANY gains a STOCK EXCHANGE listing through a MERGER or ACQUISITION with a company that is already listed.

BACK LOAD   A mechanism in which COMMISSIONS on a MUTUAL FUND or INVESTMENT TRUST are charged to INVESTORS at the time of sale or exit. See also FRONT LOAD.

BACK MONTH   See FURTHEST MONTH.

BACK OFFICE   [COL] The general operational and administrative infrastructure and functions of a BANK or financial institution that are used to support the activities of those generating revenues. The back office is responsible for SETTLEMENTS, CLEARING, financial controls, ACCOUNTING, reporting, and technology. See also FRONT OFFICE.

BACK-TO-BACK LOAN   (1) A pair of local CURRENCY LOANS between two companies, documented under a single agreement providing for the right of OFFSET, which allows the companies to on-lend the local currency funds to their own SUBSIDIARIES and eliminates the need for the subsidiaries to source their own local financing. (2) A loan commitment from a BANK to a real estate developer that includes a construction loan for initial building and a permanent MORTGAGE loan for ongoing financing once the project has been developed. (1) See also PARALLEL LOAN.

BACK-TO-BACK SWAP   A SWAP that acts as a mirror image of an existing swap on the books of an institution, serving to neutralize the MARKET RISKS. Such a swap does not, however, eliminate COUNTERPARTY CONTINGENT CREDIT RISK. See also UNWIND.

BACK UP THE TRUCK   [COL] The purchase of a large block of SECURITIES by an INVESTOR who is BULLISH and expects upward price movement.

BACKING AWAY   A situation where a MARKET MAKER refuses to perform on a quoted BID, generally in contravention of formal or informal market-making rules conveyed through AFFIRMATIVE OBLIGATIONS.

BACKSPREAD   An OPTION strategy designed to take advantage of VOLATILITY. A LONG backspread is created through the sale of a smaller quantity of closer-to-the-money PUT OPTIONS or CALL OPTIONS and the purchase of a larger quantity of farther-from-the-money puts or calls. See also RATIO VERTICAL SPREAD.

BACKTESTING   The process of determining the validity of a VALUE-AT-RISK model by comparing actual profit and loss experience with results predicted by the model. The process is also applicable in INVESTMENT management, where an investment strategy is applied to prior periods to create a hypothetical performance history. See also PROFIT AND LOSS EXPLAIN.

BACKUP CREDIT   See SWINGLINE.

BACKUP LINE   See SWINGLINE.

BACKWARDATION   See NORMAL BACKWARDATION.

BACS   See BANKERS' AUTOMATED CLEARING SYSTEM.

BAD BANK   [COL] A special BANK created and chartered to hold a sponsoring bank's NONPERFORMING LOANS. The sponsoring bank transfers the loans to the bad bank, thus improving its asset quality and becoming a "good bank." The bad bank, which is generally established as a self-liquidating TRUST, attempts to manage and liquidate the PORTFOLIO of loans in the most efficient manner possible.

BAD DEBT   Any extension of CREDIT that is no longer current with regard to PRINCIPAL and/or INTEREST payments and which is deemed unlikely to be repaid by the DEBTOR. When a debt is classified as bad it must be written off against income or against a previously established LOAN LOSS RESERVE or other reserve for bad debt. Also known as BAD LOAN.

BAD DEBT PROVISION   A noncash PROVISION reflected through a company's INCOME STATEMENT that is used to cover CREDIT extended to one or more DEBTORS that is not expected to be repaid in the current ACCOUNTING period. See also BAD DEBT RESERVE.

BAD DEBT RESERVE   Funds set aside by a company to cover the potential DEFAULT or impairment of an outstanding LOAN or DEBT granted to a third party. The reserve is created by a DEBIT to the bad debt expense account and a CREDIT to the BAD DEBT PROVISION account (establishing a CONTRA-ACCOUNT). See also LOAN LOSS RESERVE.

BAD LOAN   See BAD DEBT.

BAFIN   See BUNDESANSTALT FUR FINANZDIENSTLEISTUNGSAUFSICHT.

BALANCE CONCENTRATION   See POOLING.

BALANCE OF PAYMENTS   An economic account reflecting a country's transactions and dealings with other nations through its CURRENT ACCOUNT, CAPITAL ACCOUNT, and FOREIGN EXCHANGE RESERVES.

BALANCE OF TRADE   The difference between a country's VISIBLE and INVISIBLE EXPORTS and IMPORTS, and a primary component of the BALANCE OF PAYMENTS CURRENT ACCOUNT. A surplus balance of trade means exports are greater than imports, a deficit means imports are greater than exports.

BALANCE SHEET   A key FINANCIAL STATEMENT produced by a company that reflects its ASSETS, LIABILITIES, and CAPITAL (or EQUITY, NET WORTH) as of a specific date. Assets and liabilities are typically listed in order of their realizability into cash or their contractual maturity. In order to be "in balance" assets must equal liabilities plus capital. Presentation of the balance sheet can vary by country, accounting regime, and/or industry sector.

In the United States the balance sheet takes the following general form:

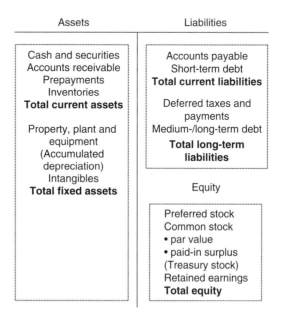

In the United Kingdom it assumes the following general form:

Property, plant and
equipment
(accumulated depreciation)
Intangibles
Long-term investments
Total fixed assets

Cash and securities
Accounts receivable
Prepayments
Inventories
Total current assets

Accounts payable
Short-term debt
Total current liabilities

Medium-and long-term debt

= *Net assets*

Preferred stock
Common stock
(Treasury stock)
Retained earnings

= *Net capital*

BALANCE SHEET COLLATERALIZED DEBT OBLIGATION A COLLAT-
ERALIZED DEBT OBLIGATION (CDO) arranged by a BANK or SECURITIES
FIRM in order to transfer the DEFAULT risk in its CREDIT PORTFOLIO to
INVESTORS. See also ARBITRAGE COLLATERALIZED DEBT OBLIGATION,
CASH COLLATERALIZED DEBT OBLIGATION, SYNTHETIC COLLATERALIZED
DEBT OBLIGATION.

BALANCE SHEET HEDGE A HEDGE transaction that is created to protect
against TRANSLATION RISK.

BALANCED BUDGET MULTIPLIER Under the KEYNESIAN FORMULA,
the result on AGGREGATE DEMAND (i.e., GROSS DOMESTIC PRODUCT) of
a change in government expenditures once these have been neutralized by an
equal change in TAXES.

BALANCING CHARGE A TAX charge that may be incurred by a company
when it sells ASSETS for more than their carrying value.

BALLOON See BALLOON LOAN.

BALLOON LOAN A LOAN structured with periodic INTEREST payments
and PRINCIPAL repayments throughout the transaction and a large principal repayment at MATURITY. The balloon structure can be applied equally to

COMMERCIAL LOANS and MORTGAGE LOANS. Also known as BALLOON. See also BULLET LOAN.

BALTIC EXCHANGE   A London-based membership organization that quotes INDEX prices for the BALTIC EXCHANGE DRY INDEX and the BALTIC EXCHANGE INTERNATIONAL TANKER ROUTE INDEX, which are used as references in a variety of DERIVATIVE contracts. The Baltic Exchange's indexes are often used as a general proxy of economic activity, with high or rising index levels representing high or rising demand and prices for shipping capacity related to commodities, and thus strong or strengthening economic activity; a low or declining index represents the reverse. The indexes are also directly and indirectly influenced by fleet supply, bunker fuel prices, port congestion and choke points, and so forth.

BALTIC EXCHANGE DRY INDEX   A weighted composite INDEX of the daily shipping rates compiled by the BALTIC EXCHANGE for four classes of ships carrying dry raw materials on various main shipping routes. The index tabulates subindex prices for moving dry bulk commodities of specific size and route on Capesize (100,000 dead weight tons), Panamax (60,000–80,000 tons), Supramax (45,000–59,000 tons), and Handysize (15,000–35,000 tons) ships. See also BALTIC EXCHANGE INTERNATIONAL TANKER ROUTE INDEX.

BALTIC EXCHANGE INTERNATIONAL TANKER ROUTE INDEX   A composite INDEX of the daily shipping rates compiled by the BALTIC EXCHANGE for oil tankers traveling on 19 shipping routes. The index tabulates subindex prices for dirty tankers and clean tankers. See also BALTIC EXCHANGE DRY INDEX.

BANCASSURANCE   [FR] In Europe, a financial conglomerate that engages in a broad range of financial services, including LOANS, DEPOSITS, INSURANCE, SECURITIES UNDERWRITING, INVESTMENT MANAGEMENT, and TRADING. Bancassurance groups often deal through separately incorporated and regulated entities but face no particular restriction on the scope of services they can offer. See also UNIVERSAL BANK.

BAND   A trading range for a SECURITY or CURRENCY that is bounded by upper and lower limits. A band may exist informally as a technical indicator, or formally to guide currency rates or trading activity.

BANK   A financial institution that is permitted, through its CORPORATE CHARTER, to accept DEPOSITS and extend commercial and retail LOANS, and perform various INTERMEDIATION and FIDUCIARY functions. COMMERCIAL BANKS specialize primarily in traditional forms of commercial lending and deposit taking, while INVESTMENT BANKS and SECURITIES FIRMS are active in CORPORATE FINANCE, SECURITIES UNDERWRITING, and TRADING. UNIVERSAL BANKS and BANCASSURANCE groups engage in a broader range of activities, including traditional banking, securities underwriting, INVESTMENT MANAGEMENT, INSURANCE, and trading. REGULATORS monitor the activities of banks to ensure that clients, particularly small depositors, are properly protected.

BANK ACCOUNT   An ACCOUNT opened by a customer with a BANK or other financial institution that can be used for effecting payments (e.g., through a CHECKING ACCOUNT or CURRENT ACCOUNT, via CHECKS or DIRECT DEBITS) or accumulating savings (e.g., via a SAVINGS ACCOUNT).

BANK ADVANCE   See LOAN.

BANK ADVISORY COMMITTEE   A form of CREDITOR COMMITTEE that deals with RESCHEDULING or RESTRUCTURING of a country's outstanding DEBTS, generally comprised of key BANKS and other lenders.

BANK CHARGE   Any fee levied by a BANK on its customers for the provision of specific services, such as transactions on AUTOMATED TELLER MACHINES, WIRE TRANSFERS, RETURNED CHECKS, and so forth.

BANK DEPOSIT   See DEPOSIT.

BANK DISCOUNT RATE   See BANKER'S ACCEPTANCE RATE.

BANK DRAFT   A CHECK that a BANK draws on itself, used when the PAYEE does not wish to accept the credit of the customer as DRAWER. The customer purchases the bank draft with good funds, which gives the payee confidence that the check will be honored. Also known as BANKER'S CHECK.

BANK FOR INTERNATIONAL SETTLEMENTS (BIS)   A supranational organization, often termed the "bank of the CENTRAL BANKS," that was created in 1930 to coordinate First World War reparation payments and provide basic international banking services (most of which were assumed by the INTERNATIONAL MONETARY FUND after the Second World War); the BANK also acted as TRUSTEE and CLEARING AGENT for various supranational organizations in the postwar period. Over the past few decades the BIS has focused primarily on promulgating RISK-BASED CAPITAL standards, and sponsoring a series of rules and directives related to capital adequacy standards for CREDIT RISK, MARKET RISK, and OPERATIONAL RISK (i.e., the BASLE ACCORD and BASLE II).

BANK GIRO   A mechanism where a payer can effect an electronic payment or transfer of funds from a BANK ACCOUNT to a payee's account, even if the accounts are with different BANKS. Also known as BANK TRANSFER. See also GIRO.

BANK GUARANTEE   A GUARANTEE issued by a BANK in support of the undertakings of a client or project. By providing the guarantee, the creditworthiness of the underlying client or project is substituted by that of the bank.

BANK HOLDING COMPANY   A CORPORATION that owns, or has control of, one or more individual BANKS and/or other financial SUBSIDIARIES.

BANK LINE   A REVOLVING CREDIT FACILITY established as an ADVISED LINE (i.e., the client is made aware of the size and terms of the facility) or a

GUIDANCE LINE (i.e., the client is not advised of the specific size of the line). See also COMMITTED FUNDING.

BANK LOAN   See LOAN.

BANK OF CANADA   The CENTRAL BANK of Canada, established in 1934 as a private CORPORATION before converting to a government-owned Crown Corporation in 1938. The Bank of Canada is responsible for issuing and enforcing REGULATIONS impacting its domestic financial markets and institutions, conducting MONETARY POLICY, issuing BANKNOTES, and managing RESERVES on behalf of the Canadian government. Also known as BANQUE DU CANADA.

BANK OF ENGLAND   The CENTRAL BANK of the United Kingdom, originally established as a private banking organization in 1694 to manage the country's national DEBT. It became the country's central bank through the passage of the Bank Charter Act of 1844, and was nationalized in 1946. The bank became independent once again in 1997, and is now responsible for managing the United Kingdom's debt and FOREIGN EXCHANGE RESERVES, issuing BANKNOTES, conducting MONETARY POLICY, supervising certain aspects the financial system, and acting as LENDER OF LAST RESORT. See also FINANCIAL SERVICES AUTHORITY.

BANK OF JAPAN (BOJ)   The Japanese CENTRAL BANK, founded in 1882 and reorganized in 1942, responsible for ensuring overall stability within the domestic financial system, managing MONETARY POLICY, issuing BANKNOTES, and operating interbank SETTLEMENT systems.

BANK RATE   See BASE RATE.

BANK REFERENCE   A general statement provided by a BANK to potential employers, CREDIT RATING AGENCIES, and TRADE CREDITORS regarding the credit standing of one of its customers. Bank references do not include specific details on balances or payment records in order not to prejudice the customer.

BANK RELEASE   An authorization that permits an importer to take possession of goods purchased through TRADE CREDIT.

BANK RUN   A crisis situation where a DEPOSIT-taking institution, such as a BANK, faces cash withdrawals from DEPOSITORS in excess of its access to ready cash. This lack of liquidity to meet deposit cash calls, which may be compounded by lack of access to a banking system that acts as a temporary lender or LENDER OF LAST RESORT, can lead to further withdrawals, in a self-fulfilling spiral that may lead ultimately to failure of the institution. Also known as RUN.

BANK STATEMENT   A periodic (generally monthly) statement issued by a BANK or financial institution to customers that reflects activity and balances in all relevant BANK ACCOUNTS.

BANK TRANSFER   See BANK GIRO.

BANKER   A professional involved in arranging LOANS or other FINANCING arrangements, structuring CORPORATE FINANCE deals, or managing client

INVESTMENT PORTFOLIOS. See also FINANCIER, INVESTMENT BANKER, PRIVATE BANKER.

BANKER'S ACCEPTANCE (BA)   A short-term LIABILITY or time DRAFT representing an order to pay a specified amount of funds to the holder at a defined time, generally 30 to 180 days after contract date. The BA is a DISCOUNT instrument drawn by a company on a BANK; once the bank accepts the draft it is obligated to pay the holder funds at maturity, and effectively substitutes the company's credit with its own. BAs are used for domestic and foreign TRADE transactions (including shipping, financing, and storage), and are generally backed by invoices or BILLS OF LADING. Also known as TIME DRAFT. See also BANKER'S ACCEPTANCE (BA) RATE.

BANKER'S ACCEPTANCE (BA) RATE   The INTEREST RATE representing the DISCOUNT between the FACE VALUE of a BANKER'S ACCEPTANCE and the amount a BANK is willing to pay for the draft, generally a function of the DRAWER's creditworthiness. Also known as BANK DISCOUNT RATE.

BANKERS' AUTOMATED CLEARING SYSTEM (BACS)   In the United Kingdom, a company which operates a computerized payment CLEARING service that is responsible for electronic processing of financial transactions. See also CLEARINGHOUSE AUTOMATED PAYMENT SYSTEM (CHAPS).

BANKER'S CHECK   See BANK DRAFT.

BANKERS' BLANKET BOND   An INSURANCE contract that protects a BANK from losses caused by employee FRAUD.

BANKING   The area of FINANCE related to taking of DEPOSITS, granting of LOANS, and provision of other financial services, which may include INVESTMENT, TRADING, and advisory.

BANKING ACT OF 1933   See GLASS-STEAGALL ACT.

BANKING BOOK ACCOUNTING   An ACCOUNTING process used by a BANK where certain ASSETS, such as LOANS and hold-to-maturity INVESTMENTS, follow an ACCRUAL approach to profit recognition and where impairments are taken on a periodic basis. See also AVAILABLE FOR SALE ACCOUNTING, TRADING BOOK ACCOUNTING.

BANKING CRISIS   See CREDIT CRISIS.

BANKING DIRECTIVE   In the EUROPEAN UNION, a series of requirements to which BANKS must adhere, including those related to CAPITAL ADEQUACY and solvency, MONEY LAUNDERING, CONCENTRATION RISKS, and cross-border licensing and marketing/distribution of INVESTMENTS. See also BASLE ACCORD, BASLE II, MARKETS IN FINANCIAL INSTRUMENTS DIRECTIVE.

BANKMAIL   [COL] An agreement between a BANK and a company attempting to acquire a TARGET company through a HOSTILE TAKEOVER that bars the bank from financing another company's competing bid, in exchange for a fee.

BANKNOTE   Paper CURRENCY of a country that serves as legal tender, typically issued by a CENTRAL BANK or other authorized monetary authority. Banknotes, which are effectively a form of FIAT MONEY since they are not backed by GOLD are a convenient MEDIUM OF EXCHANGE. Also known as NOTE.

BANKRUPTCY   A state where a company (or individual) is unable to meet its obligations and seeks the protection of the courts. The procedure may be based on VOLUNTARY BANKRUPTCY or INVOLUNTARY BANKRUPTCY and typically involves the filing of a bankruptcy petition. An AUTOMATIC STAY is invoked once the petition is filed, prohibiting lawsuits from being filed and CREDITORS from liquidating COLLATERAL or attempting to recover sums owed; the stay remains in place until the debt is discharged or a repayment plan is accepted. See also BANKRUPTCY ORDER, BANKRUPTCY PETITION, DEBTOR-IN-POSSESSION, RECEIVER, TRUSTEE.

BANKRUPTCY ORDER   In the United Kingdom, an order from the court making the DEBTOR referenced in a BANKRUPTCY PETITION an undischarged bankrupt who is no longer deemed owner of any property and who must assist the RECEIVER in its proper identification and collection.

BANKRUPTCY PETITION   In the United Kingdom, a document presented by CREDITORS (or the DEBTOR) to the courts that DEBTS have not been paid. Once the court accepts the petition the debtor is not permitted to dispose of any property and a RECEIVER may be appointed.

BANQUE D'AFFAIRE   [FR] In France, a MERCHANT BANK that invests its own CAPITAL in support of CORPORATE FINANCE transactions and engages in SECURITIES UNDERWRITING and TRADING.

BANQUE DE FRANCE   [FR] The French CENTRAL BANK, founded in 1800, nationalized in 1946, and granted independence in 1993. It is responsible for ensuring monetary stability within France and coordinating, as a member of the EUROPEAN MONETARY UNION (EMU), broader EMU MONETARY POLICY. The bank is a member of the European System of Central Banks.

BANQUE DU CANADA   [FR] See BANK OF CANADA.

BARBELL PORTFOLIO   An INVESTMENT PORTFOLIO comprised of NOTES and BONDS with short- and long-term MATURITIES but few, or no, SECURITIES with medium-term maturities. A barbell may be constructed to take advantage of a particular view of the YIELD CURVE or to meet specific CASH FLOW requirements. See also LADDERED PORTFOLIO.

BARGAIN   In the United Kingdom, any transaction that is executed on the LONDON STOCK EXCHANGE.

BARRIER   A price, YIELD, or INDEX level where a BARRIER OPTION becomes effective, causing an underlying EUROPEAN OPTION to be created or extinguished.

BARRIER CAP   A CAP with an embedded BARRIER OPTION.

BARRIER FLOOR   A FLOOR with an embedded BARRIER OPTION.

BARRIER OPTION   A COMPLEX DERIVATIVE that creates or extinguishes an underlying EUROPEAN OPTION as the price of the market reference moves through a specified BARRIER. Four versions of the barrier option are commonly used, including the DOWN AND IN OPTION, DOWN AND OUT OPTION, UP AND IN OPTION, and UP AND OUT OPTION. The fact that the underlying option may be extinguished, or may never be created, means that a barrier option is typically less expensive than an otherwise equivalent European option. Also known as KNOCK-IN OPTION, KNOCK-OUT OPTION. See also REVERSE BARRIER OPTION.

BARRIER SWAPTION   A PAYER SWAPTION or RECEIVER SWAPTION with an embedded BARRIER OPTION.

BASE CURRENCY   The currency against which others in the FOREIGN EXCHANGE market are quoted, generally selected as a result of one country's dominance in economic and TRADE matters. Since the mid-twentieth century the US dollar has assumed the role of base currency, succeeding the British pound sterling (which had been used as a base since the latter half of the nineteenth century). At various other times the French franc and Dutch florin (guilder) have also served as base currencies. See also RESERVE CURRENCY.

BASE RATE   (1) A BENCHMARK INTEREST RATE set by a CENTRAL BANK or monetary authority that is used as a reference for other commercial LOAN and DEPOSIT rates. (2) The rate at which a country's central bank or monetary authority will lend to other BANKS in the national system. (3) In the United Kingdom, the rate at which large banks are willing to lend to their best corporate customers. (1) Also known as BANK RATE. (3) See also PRIME RATE.

BASE WEIGHTED INDEX   A method of computing a weighted INDEX that uses base period quantities, computed as:

$$I_{bw} = \left(\frac{\sum p_c q_0}{\sum p_0 q_0} \right) \times 100$$

where p_c is the current period price, q_0 is the base period quantity, and p_0 is the base period price. Also known as LASPEYRES' INDEX. See also CURRENT WEIGHTED INDEX.

BASIS   The price differential between an underlying ASSET reference and a DERIVATIVE contract used as a HEDGE. The basis arises as a result of differences in SUPPLY/DEMAND, reference INDEXES, or FRICTION COSTS (including COST OF CARRY, storage, INSURANCE, transportation). See also BASIS RISK, NEGATIVE BASIS, POSITIVE BASIS.

BASIS POINT   1/100th of 1%, commonly used in the measurement of INTEREST RATES.

BASIS PRICE   The price used to calculate any capital gains or losses on an INVESTMENT, typically computed as the difference between the purchase and sale prices, plus COMMISSIONS paid.

BASIS RISK   A RISK that is generated by two ASSETS or INDEXES that track, but do not precisely replicate, one another. Basis risk is often assumed as a result of minimizing DIRECTIONAL RISK or VOLATILITY RISK, and can arise from HEDGING an asset with a DERIVATIVE contract on the same (or similar) asset, or hedging an asset with a second asset. Also known as RESIDUAL RISK. See also BASIS, CROSS-ASSET HEDGE.

BASIS SWAP   An INTEREST RATE SWAP involving the exchange of two FLOATING RATES for periods ranging from 1 to 10 years; common reference INDEXES include LIBOR, EURIBOR, COMMERCIAL PAPER rates, BANKER'S ACCEPTANCE RATES, and GOVERNMENT BILL rates. A basis swap may also be constructed by using floating rate indexes in two different CURRENCIES.

BASIS TRADING   An ARBITRAGE or TRADING strategy using a cash instrument and a related FUTURES contract to take advantage of perceived opportunities in the BASIS. See also BASIS RISK.

BASKET   A small PORTFOLIO of ASSETS that can be bought or sold or used as a reference in a DERIVATIVE. Baskets can be created from SECURITIES or other ASSETS from similar or different sectors/countries, depending on the specific HEDGE or INVESTMENT goals being sought. See also BASKET CREDIT SWAP, BASKET OPTION.

BASKET AGGREGATE   A total loss limit under an INSURANCE POLICY that covers multiple lines of coverage for different PERILS. See also BASKET DEDUCTIBLE.

BASKET CREDIT SWAP   A CREDIT DERIVATIVE that involves the exchange of a fixed or floating PREMIUM for a compensatory payment if one or more reference CREDITS in a predefined BASKET DEFAULTS. The swap provides the receiver of premium with a credit PORTFOLIO investment and the payer of premium with a credit HEDGE. See also FIRST-TO-DEFAULT SWAP.

BASKET DEDUCTIBLE   A single DEDUCTIBLE on an INSURANCE POLICY that covers multiple lines of coverage for different PERILS. See also BASKET AGGREGATE.

BASKET OPTION   An OVER-THE-COUNTER COMPLEX OPTION that grants the buyer a payoff based on the difference between the price of a BASKET of ASSETS and a predefined STRIKE PRICE. The basket can be comprised of assets from similar or different sectors/markets. See also MULTI-INDEX OPTION.

BASLE II   A new regulatory accord, introduced in 2004, which replaces the original BASLE ACCORD for participating BANKS. Basle II is formed atop PILLAR I, PILLAR II, and PILLAR III, which address computation of CREDIT RISK and OPERATIONAL RISK, the control of nonstandard risks, and the disclosure of RISK MANAGEMENT methods and risk parameters.

BASLE ACCORD   The original 1988 agreement between participating industrialized countries to adopt RISK-based CAPITAL methods developed by the BANK FOR INTERNATIONAL SETTLEMENTS. See also BASLE II, BASLE MARKET RISK AMENDMENT.

BASLE MARKET RISK AMENDMENT   A 1996 addendum to the original BASLE ACCORD that permits BANKS to use internally developed VALUE-AT-RISK models in computing required risk CAPITAL. See also BASLE II.

BAY STREET   [COL] The financial sector of Canada, so named for the location of various BANKS on Bay Street, Toronto.

BAZAAR   [COL] An unregulated market where participants cannot be assured of fairness or transparency.

BBA   See BRITISH BANKERS ASSOCIATION.

BBA RATE   See BRITISH BANKERS ASSOCIATION RATE.

BEAR   [COL] One who has a negative view on a market or ASSET. See also BEAR MARKET, BULL.

BEAR CLOSING   [COL] See SHORT COVERING.

BEAR HUG   [COL] A TAKEOVER BID received by a TARGET company that DIRECTORS urge SHAREHOLDERS to accept due to its attractive price. Though directors might prefer to reject the bid, the price makes it nearly impossible for them to do so; failure to recommend approval could constitute a breach of DUTY OF LOYALTY and result in legal action being taken.

BEAR MARKET   A market state that is characterized by declining prices and low volumes over an extended period of time, often resulting from weakened economic conditions (i.e., slow growth or contraction, poor corporate EARNINGS). A bear market is generally believed to be in effect when broad INDEX levels are at least 20% lower than the previous peak. See also BEARISH, BULL MARKET, CORRECTION.

BEAR NOTE   A STRUCTURED NOTE that is intended to provide an INVESTOR with CAPITAL GAINS and/or enhanced COUPONS through the declining value of an ASSET or market. The note can be designed to reference any type of financial asset or COMMODITY. See also BULL NOTE.

BEAR RAID   [COL] An attempt by a group of INVESTORS to drive down the price of a company's COMMON STOCK in a coordinated fashion in order to generate a profit. Bear raids conducted through circulation of negative news or unfounded rumors are illegal. UPTICK and ZERO PLUS TICK rules, which only allow SHORT SALES to be initiated on an upward move, are intended to help protect against this type of activity.

BEAR SLIDE   [COL] A rapidly declining market or ASSET price that is the result of a successfully executed BEAR RAID.

BEAR SPREAD   [COL] An OPTION strategy that attempts to take advantage of a BEARISH trend or BEAR MARKET; spreads can be structured as bearish

CALL SPREADS (purchase of a CALL OPTION and sale of a second call, where the short call is struck closer-to-the-money) or bearish PUT SPREADS (purchase of a PUT OPTION and sale of a second put, where the long put is struck closer-to-the-money). Also known as MONEY SPREAD, PRICE SPREAD, VERTICAL SPREAD. See also BULL SPREAD.

BEAR SQUEEZE   [COL] A rally in a market or ASSET price as a result of buying pressures that are intended to drive BEARS into SHORT COVERING.

BEAR TRAP   [COL] A situation where a SHORT SELLER, anticipating further declines in the price of a SECURITY, fails to COVER a position in a rapidly rallying market, sustaining losses. See also SHORT SQUEEZE.

BEARER   (1) One who presents a CHECK or BILL OF EXCHANGE for payment. This is only possible when the bill is made payable to "bearer" rather than a named BENEFICIARY. (2) One holding a BEARER SECURITY.

BEARER SECURITY   A SECURITY that can be transferred or redeemed by the holder, who may or may not be the BENEFICIAL OWNER, and for which no proof of ownership is required. Many securities are issued in bearer form, which eliminates the time and expense associated with re-registration. See also REGISTERED SECURITY.

BEARISH   A tendency for markets or ASSETS to assume a negative price trend. See also BEAR MARKET, BULLISH.

BEATING THE GUN   [COL] Any instance where an INVESTOR has an opportunity to purchase or sell a SECURITY before its price has been positively or negatively impacted by market-moving news or information.

BEAUTY CONTEST   [COL] A process where UNDERWRITERS competing for an ISSUER's DEBT or EQUITY NEW ISSUE MANDATE submit proposals and are evaluated on the basis of structure, timing, pricing, distribution, and other relevant factors. The winner of the beauty contest becomes the LEAD MANAGER of the issue.

BED AND BREAKFASTING   [COL] In the United Kingdom, the practice of selling COMMON STOCK of a company on one day and repurchasing it the following day in order to establish a gain or loss for TAX purposes; bed and breakfasting was outlawed starting in 1997. See also WASH SALE.

BEHAVIORAL FINANCE   An area of FINANCE that considers the behaviors and psychology of INVESTORS outside traditional economic and financial theory (which often call for "rational" actions, efficient markets, and optimal decision making). Behavioral finance attempts to incorporate cognitive biases and emotions in actions that drive individual and group investment and RISK decisions. Behavioral finance focuses on topics such as response to positive or negative news, reluctance to sell investments and incur losses, group feedback and panic selling, and so forth.

BEIGE BOOK   [COL] In the United States, a widely followed report on economic conditions issued by the FEDERAL RESERVE BOARD eight times per year.

BELLS AND WHISTLES Additional features added to a STRUCTURED NOTE or OVER-THE-COUNTER DERIVATIVE that more precisely match the PAYOFF PROFILE or RISK and RETURN characteristics to the needs of a client. Such additional features may imply a greater COMMISSION or fee charged by the arranging BANK.

BELLWETHER [COL] See BENCHMARK.

BELLY OF THE CURVE [COL] The intermediate maturities of the YIELD CURVE, generally considered to include the 3 to 7-year sector. See also LONG END, SHORT END.

BELLY-UP [COL] A failed venture, or a company that has filed for VOLUNTARY BANKRUPTCY or INVOLUNTARY BANKRUPTCY.

BELOW PAR Any SECURITY or ASSET that is valued at less than its initial PAR VALUE (often 100). See also ABOVE PAR.

BELOW THE LINE [COL] All INCOME STATEMENT entries that appear below the NET INCOME entry, focusing on the distribution of any residual profits to RETAINED EARNINGS or DIVIDENDS. See also ABOVE THE LINE.

BENCHMARK [COL] (1) A market-leading COMMON STOCK, BOND, COMMODITY, or INDEX that acts as a proxy for broader sentiment and movement in the market. Tradable benchmarks, which generally feature significant LIQUIDITY and narrow BID-OFFER SPREADS, are often used as an indexing, pricing, or HEDGING reference for other SECURITIES or DERIVATIVES. (2) An index that is used to gauge the relative performance of other ASSETS, securities, or PORTFOLIOS. (1) Also known as BELLWETHER.

BENEFICIAL INTEREST The right to use a particular ASSET or INVESTMENT, regardless of who retains legal interest. See also BENEFICIAL OWNER, LEGAL OWNER.

BENEFICIAL OWNER The actual owner of SECURITIES and the rightful recipient of the benefits accorded; the beneficial owner is often different from the title holder (generally a financial institution holding the securities on behalf of clients). A beneficial owner need not necessarily be the LEGAL OWNER.

BENEFICIARY The designated recipient of a contractual CASH FLOW or benefit from an INSURANCE contract, GUARANTEE, LETTER OF CREDIT, ANNUITY, TRUST, will, or other transaction. The beneficiary may be listed as primary (first recipient) or secondary (second recipient), and the selection may be revocable (changeable at any time) or irrevocable (changeable only with the express consent of the current beneficiary).

BENEFITS IN KIND Noncash compensation payable to employees or DIRECTORS and which may be subject to TAXES.

BERMUDA TRANSFORMER   A Class 3 Bermuda-registered INSURER that is authorized to write and purchase INSURANCE and REINSURANCE and deal in DERIVATIVES. In order to comply with regulatory restrictions, certain BANKS use transformers to convert derivatives into insurance or reinsurance and vice versa.

BERMUDAN OPTION   An OPTION that can only be EXERCISED on specific dates prior to maturity (e.g., once every month, quarter, or year). Also known as a MID-ATLANTIC OPTION. See also AMERICAN OPTION, EUROPEAN OPTION.

BESLOTEN VENNOOTSCHAP (BV)   [DUT] In the Netherlands, Netherlands Antilles, and Belgium, a LIMITED LIABILITY COMPANY. This form of business organization is frequently used in the establishment of offshore SPECIAL PURPOSE ENTITIES domiciled in the Antilles.

BEST EFFORTS UNDERWRITING   An agented NEW ISSUE of BONDS, COMMON STOCK, or PREFERRED STOCK, where the SYNDICATE attempts to place with INVESTORS as much of the issue as possible, but is not contractually obligated to fund any shortfall arising from SECURITIES that cannot be placed. See also ALL-OR-NONE UNDERWRITING, BOUGHT DEAL.

BETA   A statistical measure of an ASSET's VOLATILITY in relation to the average volatility of a market PORTFOLIO or reference INDEX, and a central component of ARBITRAGE PRICING THEORY and the CAPITAL ASSET PRICING MODEL. Beta is the slope of the line between the expected RETURN on an asset and the return on the market portfolio; the intercept of the line, termed ALPHA, is simply the difference between the return on the asset and the beta-adjusted return on the market portfolio. The computation of beta is given as:

$$\beta_j = \frac{Cov\left(E(r_j), E(r_m)\right)}{\sigma^2_{r_m}}$$

where $E(r_j)$ is the expected return on asset j, $E(r_m)$ is the expected return on the market portfolio, $Cov(E(r_j), E(r_m))$ is the COVARIANCE between asset j and the market portfolio, and $\sigma^2_{r_m}$ is the VARIANCE of the market portfolio.

The intercept, alpha, is simply:

$$\alpha = E(r_j) - \left(\left(\beta_j\left(E(r_m)\right)\right)\right)$$

A beta greater than 1.0 indicates that the asset is riskier than the market portfolio, but also has the possibility of generating higher returns; a beta less than 1.0 means that it is less risky than the portfolio. INVESTORS and FUND MANAGERS often use beta to determine overall risk levels within their investment portfolios. See also CAPITAL MARKET LINE, SECURITY MARKET LINE.

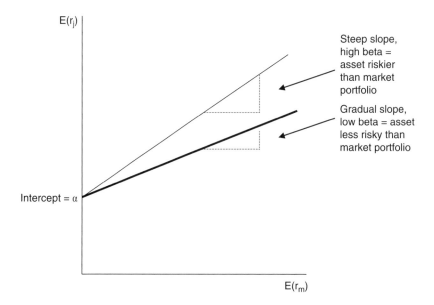

BIAS   The FEDERAL RESERVE BOARD's view on future INTEREST RATE movements and possible policy direction at future FEDERAL OPEN MARKETS COMMITTEE meetings; the board may express a bias toward tightening or easing of rates, or maintaining a neutral stance.

BID   A quoted purchase price for an ASSET from a DEALER or MARKET MAKER. See also OFFER.

BID-OFFER SPREAD   The difference between the buying (BID) and selling (OFFER) prices of any ASSET or SECURITY. The spread represents the profit to a DEALER or MARKET MAKER.

BID-TO-COVER   In the United States, the number of BIDS received in an AUCTION of TREASURY BILLS, NOTES, or BONDS versus the number actually accepted. The higher the bid-to-cover ratio the greater the demand by INVESTORS, and the more successful the auction. A low bid-to-cover ratio reflects a weak auction, and may be characterized by a long TAIL (i.e., a wide differential between the average and high yields).

BID WHACKER   [COL] Any INVESTOR that continuously sells SHARES at, or just below, the BID, rather than between the bid and OFFER, in hopes of temporarily forcing more selling pressure.

BIG BANG   [COL] Deregulation efforts occurring on the LONDON STOCK EXCHANGE and the TOKYO STOCK EXCHANGE during the 1980s that led to the elimination of fixed COMMISSIONS charged by BROKERS to their clients and allowed greater participation by foreign FINANCIAL INSTITUTIONS in the local institutions. In London it also removed a previous separation of duties between JOBBERS and brokers.

BIG BOARD   [COL] Informal name given to the NEW YORK STOCK EXCHANGE.

BIG DOG   [COL] A large and influential trader whose activities are closely followed by market watchers.

BIG FIGURE   [COL] A reference to the main digit(s) in a FOREIGN EXCHANGE quotation that are generally understood, and thus ignored, by traders. Quotes typically center on the last two digits of the CURRENCY rate. See also HANDLE.

BIG UGLIES   [COL] COMMON STOCK issued by companies in industrial sectors that are not considered to be "leading edge" or "glamorous" and are thus often shunned by investors, such as steel, chemicals, heavy equipment, and coal.

BILATERAL COLLATERAL   A COLLATERAL agreement between two COUNTERPARTIES that requires either party to post security, depending on the value of the PORTFOLIO of financial CONTRACTS (e.g., DERIVATIVES) and the level of unsecured CREDIT limits that have been established. This type of arrangement is often implemented when two counterparties have approximately equal CREDIT RATINGS. See also UNILATERAL COLLATERAL.

BILATERAL FACILITY   A CREDIT facility granted by one BANK to a company, allowing for the development of a more exclusive relationship. See also SYNDICATED LOAN.

BILATERAL NETTING   A form of NETTING between two COUNTERPARTIES, generally negotiated on a private basis between the involved parties, rather than through a CLEARINGHOUSE or EXCHANGE. Bilateral netting may be documented under a standard MASTER AGREEMENT or under a customized document. See also MULTILATERAL NETTING.

BILL   (1) An invoice requiring payment of a specified sum. (2) A short-term DEBT INSTRUMENT, typically issued by a government-related entity. (3) See BILL OF EXCHANGE. (2) See also TREASURY BILL.

BILL FUTURE   An INTEREST RATE FUTURES contract, bought or sold via an EXCHANGE, which references a short-term GOVERNMENT BILL rate. See also BOND FUTURE, DEPOSIT FUTURE.

BILL OF EXCHANGE   A payment order written by one party (the DRAWER) instructing another party (DRAWEE) to pay a third party (BENEFICIARY) at some future date. The beneficiary may endorse the bill of exchange, creating a NEGOTIABLE INSTRUMENT. The bill is transferable, meaning enforceable rights of payment travel from one party to another party. A financial institution accepting a bill creates a BANK BILL or BANKER'S ACCEPTANCE. Also known as COMMERCIAL BILL, DRAFT.

BILL OF LADING   A document used in the transportation of goods that evidences the receipt of goods by the shipper from the exporter. The bill must be presented under a BILL OF EXCHANGE, BANKER'S ACCEPTANCE, or DOCUMENTARY CREDIT, or if a CLAIM is being made under an INSURANCE POLICY. See also CLEAN BILL, DIRTY BILL OF LADING.

BILL RATE   See DISCOUNT RATE.

BILLS PAYABLE   BILLS OF EXCHANGE held by a company or financial institution that must be paid as they come due, classified on the BALANCE SHEET as a CURRENT LIABILITY. See also BILLS RECEIVABLE.

BILLS RECEIVABLE   BILLS OF EXCHANGE held by a company or financial institution that are due to be repaid, classified on the BALANCE SHEET as a CURRENT ASSET. See also BILLS PAYABLE.

BINARY-BARRIER OPTION   A hybrid of the BARRIER OPTION and BINARY OPTION that grants the buyer a payoff equal to a fixed cash or ASSET amount if the price of the UNDERLYING market reference breaches the BARRIER. Payoff may be immediate or at expiry of the CONTRACT. Also known as an AMERICAN BINARY OPTION, ONE TOUCH OPTION. See also ASSET-AT-EXPIRY OPTION, ASSET-AT-HIT OPTION, AT-EXPIRY OPTION, AT-HIT OPTION, CASH-AT-HIT OPTION, CASH-AT-EXPIRY OPTION.

BINARY CREDIT OPTION   See CREDIT DEFAULT OPTION.

BINARY OPTION   A COMPLEX OPTION that grants the buyer a payoff equal to a fixed cash or ASSET amount if the price of the UNDERLYING market reference breaches the STRIKE PRICE. Unlike a conventional OPTION, the INTRINSIC VALUE of the binary contract does not depend on the degree of MONEYNESS. A binary may be structured as an AMERICAN OPTION or EUROPEAN OPTION. Also known as ALL-OR-NOTHING OPTION, DIGITAL OPTION. See also ASSET-OR-NOTHING OPTION, AT-EXPIRY OPTION, AT-HIT OPTION, BINARY-BARRIER OPTION, CASH-OR-NOTHING OPTION.

BINDER   Temporary INSURANCE that provides an INSURED with coverage until the INSURER issues a permanent policy. Though insurers generally retain binding powers, certain AGENTS may have authority to bind.

BINOMIAL MODEL   An OPTION pricing model developed by Cox, Ross, and Rubinstein that traces price movements of an ASSET over discrete time intervals from trade date until EXPIRY DATE, making it possible to value AMERICAN OPTIONS. Under the parameters of the model the underlying asset can only move up or down by a specified amount in each period, meaning the process follows a binomial distribution. The general form of an American CALL OPTION under the binomial model is given as:

$$Call = S\Phi(a;n,p') - Xe^{-r_f t}\Phi(a;n,p)$$

where S is the stock price, X is the STRIKE PRICE, r_f is the RISK-FREE RATE, t is the time to expiry, n is the number of discrete periods until expiry, e is the exponential constant, p is equal to $(r' - d)/(u - d)$ (where r' is the risk-free rate for a single period, u is the possible upward move in S, and d is the possible downward move), a is the smallest nonnegative integer greater than $ln(X/Sd^n)/ln\,(u/d)$, and Φ is the binomial function. Also known as COX, ROSS, and RUBINSTEIN MODEL. See also BLACK-SCHOLES MODEL, LATTICE MODEL.

Additional references: Cox, Ross, and Rubinstein (1979); Cox and Rubinstein (1985); Rendleman and Bartter (1979).

BIS   See BANK FOR INTERNATIONAL SETTLEMENTS.

BLACK BOX   [COL] A quantitative, sometimes highly complex, proprietary mathematical model that may be used in certain forms of ARBITRAGE and TRADING. So named as the model lacks transparency to those interested in understanding its functioning.

BLACK KNIGHT   [COL] The party bidding for control of another company in a HOSTILE TAKEOVER. See also GRAY KNIGHT, WHITE KNIGHT, WHITE SQUIRE.

BLACK MONDAY   [COL] A reference to the two Mondays in STOCK market history during which major crashes occurred: Monday, October 28, 1929 and Monday, October 19, 1987.

BLACK MONEY   See DIRTY MONEY.

BLACK-SCHOLES MODEL   A closed-form OPTION pricing model developed by Black and Scholes to value EUROPEAN OPTIONS on non-DIVIDEND paying COMMON STOCKS. The Black-Scholes framework generates option prices based on a series of assumptions including continuous movement of the UNDERLYING (i.e., a STOCHASTIC PROCESS), unlimited borrowing at a RISK-FREE RATE, and absence of FRICTION COSTS. The equations for CALL OPTIONS and PUT OPTIONS are given as:

$$Call = SN(d_1) - Xe^{-r_f t} N(d_2)$$

and

$$Put = Xe^{-r_f t} N(-d_2) - SN(-d_1)$$

where S is the stock price, X is the STRIKE PRICE, t is the time to maturity, r_f is the risk-free rate,

$$d_1 = \frac{\ln\left(\frac{S}{X}\right) + \left(r_f + \frac{\sigma^2}{2}\right)t}{\sigma\sqrt{t}}$$

$$d_2 = d_1 - \sigma\sqrt{t}$$

σ^2 is the VARIANCE, and where the N values of $N(d_1)$ and $N(d_2)$ can be obtained from standard tables of probability functions. See also BINOMIAL MODEL.

Additional reference: Black and Scholes (1973).

BLACK SWAN   [COL] An extreme event that is difficult to predict and which is not well modeled by standard quantitative processes based on the NORMAL DISTRIBUTION.

BLANK BILL   A BILL OF EXCHANGE where the name of the PAYEE is blank.

BLANK CHECK   A CHECK where the name of the PAYEE is blank.

BLANK CHECK PREFERRED   [COL] PREFERRED STOCK that can be issued at the sole discretion of a company's BOARD OF DIRECTORS in order to resist a HOSTILE TAKEOVER. The issuance of preferred stock dilutes EARNINGS through payment of DIVIDENDS and provides additional cash to mount defensive measures, both of which may be sufficient to deter or combat a hostile action.

BLANKET LIMIT   The maximum amount of INSURANCE an INSURER is willing or able to UNDERWRITE in a specific geographic location. See also BLOCK LIMIT.

BLANKET POLICY   An INSURANCE policy that covers various named PERILS under a single limit, without specifying maximum coverage for any of the individual perils.

BLENDED FINITE RISK   An INSURANCE or REINSURANCE agreement with multiple lines of coverage, of which one or more is transferred through a FINITE RISK structure. See also BLENDED RISK.

BLENDED RISK   A FINITE RISK program that also includes a small amount of RISK TRANSFER. See also BLENDED FINITE RISK.

BLIND BID   [COL] The purchase of a POOL of STOCKS without specific knowledge of which companies are included in the pool. The seller typically provides basic MARKET CAPITALIZATION and volume data so that one or more bidders can submit a bid price reflecting a theoretical DISCOUNT to the assumed current market.

BLIND BROKERING   Brokered financial transactions where the BROKER does not give up the name of the underlying customer, even after the trade has been arranged and executed. Though the broker technically acts as AGENT, it de facto assumes the role of PRINCIPAL or DEALER. See also GIVE-UP.

BLIND TRUST   A form of DISCRETIONARY TRUST that is designed to manage the INVESTMENTS and financial affairs of an individual, without informing the individual as to the nature of the activity. A blind trust is used in any situation where an individual might otherwise have a conflict of interest.

BLOCK CROSSING   A CROSSED TRADE in an institutional block of SHARES, either on an EXCHANGE or through a DARK POOL.

BLOCK HOLDER   A significant SHAREHOLDER of a company's COMMON STOCK that has effective veto power over major company management decisions.

BLOCK LIMIT   The maximum amount of INSURANCE an INSURER is willing or able to UNDERWRITE in a given metropolitan city block. Block limits are often used in areas that are considered susceptible to CATASTROPHIC HAZARDS such as earthquakes or hurricanes. See also BLANKET LIMIT.

BLOCK ORDER EXPOSURE SYSTEM   In the United Kingdom, an electronic mechanism that provides QUOTES for BLOCK ORDERS of STOCK.

BLOCK TRADE   (1) A large trade in SECURITIES that is arranged through, and executed by, a BANK or other financial institution with sufficient CAPITAL to support the RISK exposure; the bank purchases the securities with its own resources at a DISCOUNT to the prevailing market price, and then attempts to distribute the block to INVESTORS. (2) A large trade, typically in excess of 1,000 or 10,000 SHARES (depending on marketplace).

BLOCK TRADING FACILITY (BTF)   A facility offered by certain FUTURES EXCHANGES where two parties agree to CROSS a large transaction away from the exchange in order not to skew prices. Once a transaction is concluded through the facility it is registered with the exchange and its CLEARINGHOUSE.

BLOCK VOLUME   The sum total of all BLOCK TRADES executed through an EXCHANGE or DARK POOL during a given trading day.

BLOCKED ACCOUNT   A BANK ACCOUNT or SECURITIES account that cannot be accessed by the holder, generally for legal reasons.

BLOCKED CURRENCY   A CURRENCY that cannot be withdrawn from a country as a result of the imposition of EXCHANGE CONTROLS.

BLOWOUT   [COL] The rapid sale of a NEW ISSUE of SECURITIES, leaving the UNDERWRITERS with no residual RISK position after BREAKING SYNDICATE.

BLUE CHIP   [COL] The COMMON STOCK of a high quality company, generally one with a large MARKET CAPITALIZATION, established reputation and market share, and a strong record of growth and EARNINGS.

BLUE SKY LAWS   In the United States, state SECURITIES laws intended to protect INVESTORS against FRAUD by BANKS, BROKER/DEALERS, SECURITIES FIRMS, INVESTMENT ADVISORS, or other FIDUCIARIES.

BOARD LOT   [COL] A minimum ORDER size established by an EXCHANGE, i.e., one board lot may be set equal to a given number of shares. See also LOT, ODD LOT, ROUND LOT.

BOARD OF DIRECTORS   The governing body of a public CORPORATION that acts as AGENT of the COMMON STOCK SHAREHOLDERS. In many companies the board of directors is responsible for developing strategy, overseeing management, and representing the interests of shareholders through DUTY OF CARE and DUTY OF LOYALTY. The structure of the board depends on whether the national system adheres to the SINGLE BOARD SYSTEM or the DUAL BOARD SYSTEM.

BOBL   [COL] Abbreviated form of Bundesobligationen, a subcategory of German federal GOVERNMENT BONDS (BUNDS), issued in the 5-year sector with fixed COUPONS.

BOGEY   [COL] A price target on a SECURITY, INDEX, or market that PORTFOLIO MANAGERS and other professional INVESTORS use to gauge performance. See also BENCHMARK.

BOILER ROOM   [COL] A suspicious BROKER/DEALER operation, established with a minimum of CAPITAL, that employs high-pressure sales tactics to sell dubious or risky INVESTMENTS to unsophisticated INVESTORS; some boiler room operations attempt to defraud investors by using illegal sales practices, CHURNING accounts, or embezzling funds. Also known as BUCKET SHOP.

BOILERPLATE   [COL] Standard legal language that is contained in financial documents such as RED HERRINGS, PROSPECTUSES, INDENTURES, GUARANTEES, and CREDIT AGREEMENTS. Boilerplate may include standard terminology related to REPRESENTATIONS, WARRANTIES, terminations, and EVENTS OF DEFAULT.

BOJ   See BANK OF JAPAN.

BOLLINGER BANDS   A TECHNICAL ANALYSIS tool that plots upper and lower boundaries above a MOVING AVERAGE level (typically 21 days). The bands are designed to capture two STANDARD DEVIATIONS (e.g., approximately 95%) of price movements over the moving average period.

BOLSA   [SPN] STOCK EXCHANGE.

BOND   (1) In INSURANCE, a form of SURETY to cover or reimburse a third party in the event of loss. (2) In the CAPITAL MARKETS, a financial obligation representing the ISSUER'S LIABILITY to repay DEBT CAPITAL provided by INVESTORS. Bonds are defined by the form of INTEREST RATE (e.g., FIXED RATE, FLOATING RATE, structured), COUPON frequency, MATURITY, COLLATERAL, price, REDEMPTION, AMORTIZATION, transfer, and market of issue. Though local market conventions differ among countries, bonds are generally characterized by long-term maturities, ranging from 10 to 30 years. Bonds may be issued onshore or offshore, as REGISTERED SECURITIES or BEARER SECURITIES, in any one of several CURRENCIES; securities are often listed on an EXCHANGE, although most TRADING occurs OVER-THE-COUNTER. The most common bonds are those paying a periodic coupon during the life of issue, together with PAR VALUE redemption at maturity; the price of such bonds is given as:

$$P = \sum_{n=1}^{t} \frac{C}{(1+r)^n} + \frac{M}{(1+r)^t}$$

where C is the coupon, r is the DISCOUNT RATE, n is the number of periods, t is the time to maturity, and M is the redemption value of the bond at maturity (generally par). (1) See also SURETY BOND, (2) see also BOND WITH WARRANT, CONVERTIBLE BOND, EUROBOND, FIXED-RATE BOND, FLOATING RATE NOTE, GLOBAL BOND, STRUCTURED NOTE, ZERO COUPON BOND.

BOND ANTICIPATION NOTE   A short-term DEBT obligation of a municipality that provides interim funds for a capital improvement project; the NOTE is typically redeemed and replaced with long-term funding once the project is underway.

BOND COVENANT   See COVENANT.

BOND CROWD   [COL] A group of SPECIALISTS that trade in BONDS on the floor of the NEW YORK STOCK EXCHANGE.

BOND DEALER   A DEALER who specializes in TRADING BONDS, acting as PRINCIPAL by taking positions and filling ORDERS through the commitment of RISK CAPITAL. Bond dealers may specialize in GOVERNMENT BONDS or other types of bonds, such as corporate BONDS, ASSET-BACKED SECURITIES, and so forth.

BOND EQUIVALENT YIELD   A measure that converts the YIELD of a FIXED INCOME discount instrument into terms of a standard COUPON instrument, permitting proper comparison of INVESTMENT alternatives. It is generally computed via:

$$BEY = \frac{(Face - P)}{P}\left(\frac{n_I}{n_{MAT}}\right)$$

where *Face* is FACE VALUE, P is purchase price, n_I is the number of days in the year following issuance, and n_{MAT} is the number of days until MATURITY. Also known as EQUIVALENT BOND YIELD. See also DISCOUNT YIELD, SIMPLE YIELD, TAXABLE EQUIVALENT YIELD, YIELD TO CALL, YIELD TO MATURITY.

BOND FLOOR   See BOND VALUE.

BOND FUTURE   An INTEREST RATE FUTURES CONTRACT, bought or sold via an EXCHANGE, which references a medium-term or long-term GOVERNMENT BOND rate. See also DEPOSIT FUTURE.

BOND MARKET   The general marketplace for issuing, buying and selling of BONDS, including GOVERNMENT BONDS, MUNICIPAL BONDS, corporate BONDS, and CONVERTIBLE BONDS. The bond market is a key element of the global CAPITAL MARKET, ensuring ISSUERS have the ability to raise DEBT capital and INVESTORS have access to trading LIQUIDITY. Each segment of each individual national bond market has its own characteristics, procedures, and conventions, though most trading occurs on an OVER-THE-COUNTER basis and most valuation and pricing follows standard formulae. See also COMMODITY MARKET, FOREIGN EXCHANGE MARKET, STOCK MARKET.

BOND ORDINANCE   See BOND RESOLUTION.

BOND PREMIUM   See INVESTMENT PREMIUM.

BOND RESOLUTION   In the United States, a law that authorizes the issuance of BONDS or other FIXED INCOME SECURITIES, typically applicable to municipal or other governmental ISSUERS. Also known as BOND ORDINANCE.

BOND SWAP   The sale of a BOND prior to its final MATURITY or REDEMPTION, and the purchase of another bond using the sale proceeds. A bond swap may involve an exchange of MATURITIES, COUPONS, taxable status, price, or REFERENCE CREDITS, and is a common PORTFOLIO management technique.

BOND SWAP SPREAD   The incremental BASIS POINT PREMIUM a company pays over the interbank SWAP SPREAD. The spread can be imputed by subtracting the basis point YIELD on one of its outstanding BONDS from the interbank swap rate of the same maturity.

BOND VALUE   The lowest TRADING value of a CONVERTIBLE BOND, which occurs when the embedded EQUITY OPTION is well OUT-OF-THE-MONEY and the bond is paying its normal COUPON. When a convertible is trading at bond value, its price is generally identical (or very similar) to a standard bond with the same coupon and maturity. Also known as BOND FLOOR.

BOND VIGILANTES   [COL] INSTITUTIONAL INVESTORS that actively sell holdings of GOVERNMENT BONDS when the specter of INFLATION begins to rise or when FISCAL POLICY and MONETARY POLICY indicate an over-reliance on deficit spending. Their actions can cause YIELDS on medium- and long-term bonds to rise sharply and rapidly.

BOND WITH WARRANT   A standard BOND that is issued with attached WARRANTS, which can often be detached and traded separately. By selling the package, the ISSUER lowers its effective COST OF CAPITAL. The bond, which can be denominated in one of various CURRENCIES and carry a MATURITY ranging from 1 to 10 years, is typically issued at PAR VALUE, but its ongoing value – with warrants retained – depends on the INTRINSIC VALUE and TIME VALUE of the warrants. While attached warrants can be issued on a range of references, they are often linked to the price of the issuer's COMMON STOCK or a broad equity INDEX. See also COVERED WARRANT, EQUITY WARRANT.

BONUS ISSUE   See STOCK DIVIDEND.

BONUS SHARE   See STOCK DIVIDEND.

BOOK   [COL] (1) To record the details of a financial transaction in the company's ledgers. (2) The total positions held by a DEALER in a particular ASSET class.

BOOK-BUILDING   [COL] The process of gathering firm ORDERS or INDICATIONS OF INTEREST for a NEW ISSUE of SECURITIES. UNDERWRITERS involved in the new issue carry out book-building, and the results are used to determine final deal pricing and order allocations.

BOOK ENTRY SECURITY   A DEBT or EQUITY SECURITY that is issued, traded, and transferred solely through electronic means, without SCRIP or physical certificates. Securities are increasingly issued in dematerialized form. See also DEFINITIVE SECURITY.

BOOK VALUE   (1) The original purchase price of an ASSET. (2) The current ACCOUNTING value of an asset, typically computed as MARKET VALUE or original purchase price less accumulated DEPRECIATION. (3) An estimate of a company's value, computed as total ASSETS less INTANGIBLES less LIABILITIES. (2) See also NET BOOK VALUE.

BOOKRUNNER   [COL] See LEAD MANAGER.

BOOTSTRAP   [COL] In ACQUISITIONS, a cash offer made for a controlling interest in a company.

BOOTSTRAPPING   [COL] See STRIPPING THE YIELD CURVE.

BORDEREAU   [FR] A report illustrating a history of losses and PREMIUMS on a specific RISK. The CEDING INSURER provides the report to the REINSURER so that an appropriate premium rate can be determined.

BORROWED RESERVES   In the United States, borrowing by BANKS from the FEDERAL RESERVE BANK on a short-term basis to bolster their RESERVES.

BORROWER   An individual or institution that obtains funds from a LENDER, either informally or formally, and with or without COLLATERAL. In exchange for use of funds, the borrower must typically pay recompense in the form of periodic INTEREST payments. See also DEBTOR.

BORSA   [ITL] STOCK EXCHANGE.

BOSTON OPTION   (1) Any OVER-THE-COUNTER OPTION where PREMIUM is paid at MATURITY rather than trade date. (2) See BREAK FORWARD.

BOTTOM FISHING   [COL] An INVESTMENT strategy based on purchasing SECURITIES that are perceived to be undervalued, out of favor, or CHEAP compared to other alternatives. CONTRARIAN INVESTORS are often bottom fishers.

BOTTOM LINE   [COL] NET INCOME earned by a company that can be distributed as DIVIDENDS and/or added to RETAINED EARNINGS.

BOUGHT DEAL   [COL] A NEW ISSUE of DEBT or EQUITY SECURITIES where the LEAD MANAGER and participating UNDERWRITERS commit to purchasing the entire block and then distributing to INVESTORS. The issuer is guaranteed a set amount of funds, regardless of the UNDERWRITERS' success in ultimately placing the securities with other investors. Also known as COMMITTED UNDERWRITING, FIRM UNDERWRITING. See also ALL-OR-NONE UNDERWRITING, BEST EFFORTS UNDERWRITING.

BOUNDED RATIONALITY   A theory of BEHAVIORAL FINANCE indicating that, in the absence of perfect information and in an environment where decisions must be taken quickly, an individual or company will attempt to achieve a satisfactory result rather than an optimal one.

BOURSE   [FR] A STOCK EXCHANGE, used generically for European exchanges.

BOUTIQUE   [COL] An INVESTMENT BANK that specializes in a particular area of business, such as CORPORATE FINANCE, LEVERAGED BUYOUTS, or MERGERS and ACQUISITIONS. Boutiques do not offer the full range of investment banking services (e.g., TRADING, ASSET MANAGEMENT, NEW ISSUE UNDERWRITING), but may cooperate with full-service firms in order to offer clients appropriate access.

BOX SPREAD   An OPTION strategy where the UNDERLYING is purchased synthetically at one price (i.e., LONG CALL, SHORT PUT) and sold at a different price (i.e., short call, long put) to generate an ARBITRAGE profit. A box spread that is created with EUROPEAN OPTIONS is equivalent to a ZERO COUPON BOND.

BRADY BOND   [COL] An EMERGING MARKET BOND resulting from an exchange of sovereign DEBT that has been rescheduled, named after former US Treasury Secretary Brady. Brady bonds, which were developed for a number of LESSER DEVELOPED COUNTRIES in the late 1980s and early 1990s, liquefied NONPERFORMING LOANS held by large BANKS, and became actively traded in the SECONDARY MARKETS. Securities were structured with 30-year ZERO COUPON TREASURY BONDS as COLLATERAL (guaranteeing PRINCIPAL repayment) and a rolling GUARANTEE from the INTERNATIONAL MONETARY FUND (covering interest COUPONS). Most Brady bonds have been retired in recent years by DEBTOR countries. See also DISCOUNT BOND, PAR BOND.

BREAK   A sharp and sudden decline in the price of an ASSET or market.

BREAK FORWARD   A FORWARD CONTRACT with a feature giving one party the ability to cancel the transaction at a future time in order to complete the underlying deal in the SPOT MARKET; if the party chooses to break the contract it pays the other party a cancellation fee. Also known as BOSTON OPTION.

BREAK ISSUE   An INITIAL PUBLIC OFFERING that trades below its issue price in the months following launch, as a result of poor demand, initial mispricing, or financial weakness of the issuing company.

BREAKING SYNDICATE   [COL] The process of disbanding the group of UNDERWRITERS involved in pricing, marketing, and distributing a NEW ISSUE of SECURITIES. Once the SYNDICATE is broken the underwriters are free to trade securities in the SECONDARY MARKET without restriction. A typical syndicate is broken 30 days after initial launch, though it can be broken earlier by mutual agreement of the underwriters.

BREAKING THE BUCK   [COL] A situation where the NET ASSET VALUE of a MONEY MARKET FUND falls below $1 per share. This occurs when INTEREST RATES fall to very low levels and the PORTFOLIO does not generate sufficient INTEREST INCOME to cover expenses. It may also occur when a fund uses LEVERAGE and suffers capital losses on its portfolio ASSETS.

BREAKOUT   A TECHNICAL ANALYSIS chart pattern reflecting movement in a security or index above a RESISTANCE LEVEL or below a SUPPORT LEVEL, which may portend future moves in the direction of the breakout.

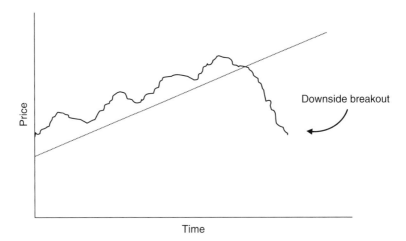

BREAKPOINT   An incremental ORDER size for MUTUAL FUND shares that causes sales COMMISSIONS to decline; the more breakpoints in an order, the lower the marginal rate of commissions.

BREAKUP FEE   A fee paid by an acquiring company to a TARGET company if the ACQUISITION fails to be consummated. See also TERMINATION FEE.

BREAKUP VALUE   The value of a company if operations are halted and the firm is decomposed and sold as a series of separate units. In most instances breakup value is less than "going-concern" value, meaning a breakup strategy is not advisable; in some cases, however, breakup opportunities exist, particularly if ASSETS have been underutilized. Estimating breakup value can be complex owing to the ILLIQUID nature of certain types of assets and the resulting uncertainty in cash values. Breakup value is distinct from LIQUIDATION VALUE, and ignores GOODWILL. Also known as TAKEOVER VALUE. See also ASSET STRIPPING.

BRETTON WOODS CONFERENCE   A forum held in 1944, which established the framework of fixed FOREIGN EXCHANGE RATES under the BRETTON WOODS SYSTEM and led to the creation of the INTERNATIONAL MONETARY FUND and the INTERNATIONAL BANK FOR RECONSTRUCTION AND DEVELOPMENT.

BRETTON WOODS SYSTEM   The system of fixed FOREIGN EXCHANGE RATES that existed until 1971, which required participating nations to intervene when necessary in order to preserve the value of their CURRENCIES within particular bands. Following the collapse of the system in 1971, the financial markets turned toward a free market process of floating exchange rates.

BRIC   [COL] The acronym given to 4 powerful emerging nations, Brazil, Russia, India, and China.

BRICKS AND MORTAR   [COL] The physical branches and infrastructure of a BANK or SECURITIES FIRM, distinct from the electronic banking platforms many institutions also operate.

BRIDGE EQUITY   A form of EQUITY (or deeply subordinated DEBT) supplied by BANKS or other INVESTORS to a LEVERAGED BUYOUT (LBO) FUND or PRIVATE EQUITY fund to support the FINANCING of an LBO. Bridge equity is intended to expedite the closing of an LBO transaction as it eliminates the need to find equity investors before the deal is funded. Bridge equity is intended as a temporary form of capital funding, to be replaced by other equity investors during the initial months of the LBO. Also known as EQUITY BRIDGE.

BRIDGE LOAN   A temporary LOAN granted by a BANK to a corporate or sovereign borrower, generally intended to be replaced by longer-term or permanent financing from the CAPITAL MARKETS. Bridge loans may be secured or unsecured and generally have maturities of less than one year. Also known as SWING LOAN.

BRIDGING LOAN   A short-term BRIDGE LOAN that is used to provide funds for the purchase of an ASSET and before the sale of a second asset.

BRITISH BANKERS ASSOCIATION (BBA)   A trade organization founded in 1919 to represent the interest of member BANKS in the United Kingdom. The BBA is also responsible for publishing the BBA RATE and LONDON INTERBANK OFFERED RATE (LIBOR).

BRITISH BANKERS ASSOCIATION (BBA) RATE   The official INTEREST RATES quoted for FORWARD RATE AGREEMENTS traded in the London market. BBA rates are quoted for various forward starting periods in the world's major interest rates.

BROAD EVIDENCE RULE   A rule allowing a wide scope of information to be used in determining the ACTUAL CASH VALUE of property that has been damaged or destroyed and which is subject to a CLAIM under an INSURANCE contract. Any evidence that is regarded as a relevant reflection of value is admissible.

BROAD MONEY   The broad definition of MONEY SUPPLY, often measured through M3. See also NARROW MONEY.

BROKEN DATE   [COL] An off-the-run COUPON payment date on a FIXED INCOME SECURITY, e.g., 28 or 58 days, rather than the conventional 30 or 60 days. The same concept can apply in the DERIVATIVE markets, where the broken date is taken to be any date that does not conform to standard quoting periods, which generally involve complete months.

BROKER   (1) An AGENT that matches buyers and sellers, earning a COMMISSION in the process. (2) In SECURITIES and INVESTMENT, a professional that brings together two parties and may also provide investment recommendations and EXECUTION services to an investing client. (3) In INSURANCE, a professional that represents an INSURED purchasing coverage from an INSURER, serving as agent of the client. (1) Also known as COMMISSION BROKER. See also COMMODITY BROKER, FOREIGN EXCHANGE BROKER, INTER-DEALER BROKER.

BROKER CALL LOAN   See BROKER LOAN.

BROKER/DEALER   A SECURITIES FIRM involved in INVESTMENT advice, BROKERAGE, and EXECUTION activities on behalf of clients, and TRADING activities for its own account. Some broker/dealers may also act as MARKET MAKERS or PRIMARY DEALERS.

BROKER LOAN   A short-term secured demand LOAN granted by a BANK to a SECURITIES FIRM or BROKER/DEALER that is used to fund client SECURITIES positions. The loan is backed by the underlying securities and is usually callable by the lender with 24 hours' notice. Also know as BROKER CALL LOAN. See also BROKER LOAN RATE, MONEY AT CALL.

BROKER LOAN RATE   The INTEREST RATE charged by a BANK on a short-term BROKER LOAN.

BROKERAGE   (1) An institution within the financial sector that specializes in providing BROKER services to its clients. (2) See COMMISSION.

BROKERED CERTIFICATE OF DEPOSIT (CD)   A large-denomination CERTIFICATE OF DEPOSIT issued by a BANK to a BROKER/DEALER, which splits the certificate into smaller denominations suitable for distribution to RETAIL INVESTORS. In some instances the bank may issue the certificate when the broker/dealer collects individual investments, amalgamates the funds, and deposits them with the bank as a lump sum. Also known as BROKERED DEPOSIT.

BROKERED DEPOSIT   See BROKERED CERTIFICATE OF DEPOSIT.

BROWNIAN MOTION   A continuous, normally distributed STOCHASTIC (random) PROCESS with MEAN zero and time increments that are serially independent, originally developed by Brown (1827) to describe the random nature of particle movement in gas or liquid. The original biological applications were extended in a mathematical framework by Wiener (1918) and have since been used as a way of characterizing the random movement of ASSET prices. Also known as GEOMETRIC BROWNIAN MOTION.

BTF   See BLOCK TRADING FACILITY.

BUBA   [COL] See BUNDESBANK.

BUBBLE   [COL] The speculative phase of a market cycle in which ASSET prices are BID up to unsustainably high levels through large amounts of LEVERAGED and unleveraged purchases by INVESTORS. The bubble may be burst through regulatory intervention (e.g., a tightening of INTEREST RATES) or general investor discomfort leading to withdrawal. See also FINANCIAL CRISIS.

BUCK   [COL] Common reference for million. See also TON, YARD.

BUCKET SHOP   [COL] See BOILER ROOM.

BUDGET   A financial statement or report regarding the REVENUES, EXPENSES, and CASH FLOWS expected to occur during a future fiscal period, often used as a performance measurement tool through analysis of deviations.

The budget may contain varying degrees of detail, focusing on INVENTORIES, CASH FLOWS, CAPITAL EXPENDITURES, and financings.

BUDGET DEFICIT   A state within a BUDGET where EXPENSES exceed REVENUES. Reducing or eliminating the deficit may require reduction in expenses and/or an increase in revenues, along with an increase in financing. See also BUDGET SURPLUS, DEFICIT FINANCING.

BUDGET SURPLUS   A state within a BUDGET where REVENUES exceed EXPENSES. The surplus may be used to offset future deficits. See also BUDGET DEFICIT.

BUFFER LAYER   A layer of INSURANCE coverage that exists between the PRIMARY LAYER and the ATTACHMENT point of the EXCESS LAYER.

BUILDING SOCIETY   In the United Kingdom, a DEPOSITORY institution that is primarily involved in accepting retail DEPOSITS and granting residential MORTGAGES; deregulation during the 1980s broadened the scope of permissible activities to include commercial banking business and DERIVATIVES dealing, but many continue to focus on the core mortgage credit sector. While most building societies were originally formed as mutual organizations, many have gone through DEMUTUALIZATION and converted to public CORPORATIONS. See also SAVINGS AND LOAN ASSOCIATION.

BULGE BRACKET   [COL] The small group of SECURITIES FIRMS, INVESTMENT BANKS, and BANKS that control the largest share of global CORPORATE FINANCE and securities UNDERWRITING business. Bulge bracket firms are often sought out by institutional clients as a result of their ability to arrange sophisticated transactions and distribute SECURITIES.

BULK RISK   Large concentrations of CREDIT RISK held by a BANK or other financial institution, typically subject to LEGAL LENDING LIMITS in order to minimize the likelihood of a lender encountering difficulties should a large borrower DEFAULT. Also known as LARGE EXPOSURES.

BULL   [COL] One who has a positive view on a market or ASSET. See also BEAR, BULL MARKET, BULLISH.

BULL MARKET   A general market phase characterized by low INFLATION and INTEREST RATES, strong consumer confidence, growing corporate EARNINGS, and rising COMMON STOCK prices and market INDEXES. See also BEAR MARKET.

BULL NOTE   A STRUCTURED NOTE that is intended to provide an INVESTOR with CAPITAL GAINS and/or enhanced COUPONS through the increasing value of an ASSET or market. The note can be designed to reference any type of financial asset or COMMODITY. See also BEAR NOTE.

BULL SPREAD   [COL] An OPTION strategy that attempts to take advantage of BULL MARKETS. The SPREAD can be structured as a BULLISH CALL SPREAD (purchase of a CALL and sale of a second call, where the long call is struck closer-to-the-money) or a bullish PUT SPREAD (purchase of a PUT and sale of a second put, where the short put is struck closer-to-the-money). Also known as MONEY SPREAD, PRICE SPREAD, VERTICAL SPREAD. See also BEAR SPREAD.

BULLET   See BULLET LOAN.

BULLET GUARANTEED INVESTMENT CONTRACT (GIC)   A GUARANTEED INVESTMENT CONTRACT where the INVESTOR funds the entire GIC with a single payment rather than periodic payments that are characteristic of standard GICs. All other features of the bullet GIC are similar to the conventional GIC. See also NONPARTICIPATING GUARANTEED INVESTMENT CONTRACT, PARTICIPATING GUARANTEED INVESTMENT CONTRACT, SYNTHETIC GUARANTEED INVESTMENT CONTRACT.

BULLET LOAN   A LOAN with a PRINCIPAL balance that is repaid by the BORROWER in a single installment at MATURITY, rather than standard AMORTIZATION of payments over the life. Also known as BULLET. See also BALLOON LOAN.

BULLISH   A tendency for markets or ASSETS to assume a positive price trend. See also BEARISH, BULL MARKET.

BUNCHING   [COL] The process of grouping together many small retail trade ORDERS (i.e., ODD LOTS) and combining them into a single large order. Bunching often permits better EXECUTION levels and reduces the administrative expenses associated with processing each small trade individually. BROKERS can only bunch orders if all INVESTORS agree.

BUND   [GER] Abbreviated form of Bundesanleihen, the broad category of German federal GOVERNMENT BONDS. Bunds, denominated in EUROS, feature maturities of 4 to 30 years (with 10-year securities constituting the BENCHMARK) and pay INTEREST COUPONS on an annual basis. They are issued through the federal bond SYNDICATE, via traditional UNDERWRITING, and through DUTCH AUCTION.

BUNDESANSTALT FUR FINANZDIENSTLEISTUNGSAUFSICHT (BAFIN) [GER] The German financial REGULATOR, responsible for supervising BANKS, INSURANCE COMPANIES, PENSION FUNDS, and other financial services institutions operating in the country. BAFIN ensures that institutions under its purview have a sufficiency of resources and controls to operate prudently, and enforces its role through market supervision and investor protection.

BUNDESBANK   [GER] The German CENTRAL BANK, founded in 1957, responsible for ensuring monetary stability within Germany and coordinating, as a member of the EUROPEAN MONETARY UNION (EMU), broader EMU MONETARY POLICY. Additional functions include supervising domestic BANKS and operating cashless payment systems and cash operations. The bank is a member of the European System of Central Banks. Also known as BUBA, DEUTSCHE BUNDESBANK.

BUNDLE   [COL] A strip of consecutive, quarterly EURODOLLAR FUTURES that can be traded as a package in blocks of 1, 2, or more years. See also FORWARD BUNDLE.

BUNNY BOND   [COL] A BOND with an embedded OPTION giving the INVESTOR the right to receive COUPONS or additional bonds (i.e., as a PAYMENT-IN-KIND SECURITY).

BURN RATE   The speed at which a company, especially a new venture, utilizes its available cash to fund ongoing operations and expansion plans. The burn rate is an important measure for suppliers of VENTURE CAPITAL, as it indicates when (if) further rounds of financing will be required to expand the operation.

BURNING COST RATIO   In INSURANCE, a measure indicating the degree to which losses exceed the PREMIUMS being charged; the burning cost ratio is generally computed as:

$$BC = \frac{Loss_{exc}}{Pr}$$

where $Loss_{exc}$ is excess loss and Pr is premium.

In general, the larger the ratio, the greater the shortfall between premiums and losses.

BURNING LAYER   See PRIMARY LAYER.

BUSINESS CYCLE   The series of phases that characterize an ECONOMY, including growth, downturn, RECESSION, and recovery. The business cycle impacts, and is impacted by, INTEREST RATES, INFLATION RATES, and employment, and may be of varying length and magnitude.

BUSINESS INTERRUPTION INSURANCE   INSURANCE coverage designed to protect against financial losses arising from a disruption in normal business or commercial activities. Such coverage effectively compensates for CONSEQUENTIAL LOSSES that come from damage or destruction to production processes, and is generally arranged as a supplement to direct coverage obtained through PROPERTY AND CASUALTY INSURANCE.

BUSINESS JUDGMENT RULE   A legal rule that permits DIRECTORS and executives of a company to make all relevant corporate business decisions, as long as they are made on an informed basis (i.e., with a DUTY OF CARE). The intent is to prevent the courts from adjudicating on whether or not a business decision is correct; they are limiting to judging only whether it has been made on the basis of appropriate facts and information.

BUSINESS LIABILITY INSURANCE   INSURANCE coverage for LIABILITIES arising from normal commercial activities, including direct and indirect liability, and medical payments.

BUSINESS RECOVERY RISK   The RISK of loss arising from a temporary disruption in business activities due to lack of accessibility to physical infrastructure. Business recovery risk is typically firm-, business- or product-specific and generally not as damaging as DISASTER RECOVERY RISK. Business recovery losses can be protected through specific BUSINESS INTERRUPTION INSURANCE. A subcategory of OPERATIONAL RISK.

BUSINESS-TO-BUSINESS (B2B) EXCHANGE An electronic commerce EXCHANGE where networks are used to connect institutional buyers and sellers of ASSETS, goods, or services. See also ALTERNATIVE TRADING SYSTEM, BUSINESS-TO-CONSUMER (B2C) EXCHANGE, ELECTRONIC COMMUNICATIONS NETWORK.

BUSINESS-TO-CONSUMER (B2C) EXCHANGE An electronic commerce EXCHANGE where networks are used to connect consumers and retail buyers of ASSETS, goods, or services with providers, manufacturers, or distributors. See also BUSINESS-TO-BUSINESS (B2B) EXCHANGE.

BUST-UP TAKEOVER A TAKEOVER or LEVERAGED BUYOUT where some of the TARGET company's ASSETS are sold to third parties in order to repay a certain portion of the DEBT assumed in acquiring the company.

BUSTED CONVERTIBLE [COL] A CONVERTIBLE BOND that stands little or no chance of being converted into the ISSUER's COMMON STOCK because the STOCK price is well below the bond's CONVERSION PRICE. A busted convertible trades on BOND VALUE alone and remains a FIXED INCOME security until it is redeemed.

BUTTERFLY SPREAD A COMPOUND OPTION STRATEGY designed to take advantage of VOLATILITY within a market range. Butterflies are always created with the same ratio of PUT OPTIONS or CALL OPTIONS (i.e., one with a low STRIKE PRICE, two with middle strikes, one with a high strike) that expire at the same time. SHORT butterflies, which are similar to LONG STRADDLES without the extreme upside, consist of short low and high strike options and long middle strike options; long butterflies, which are similar to short straddles without the extreme downside, consist of long low and high strike options and short middle strike options.

Payoff profile of long butterfly

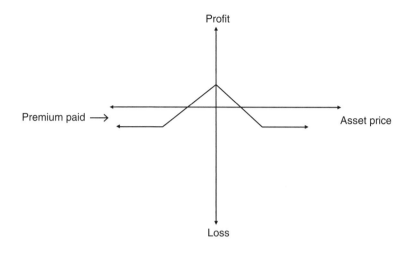

Payoff profile of short butterfly

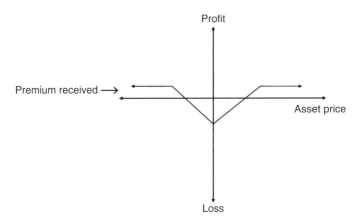

See also CONDOR SPREAD.

BUY AND HOLD   An INVESTMENT strategy, often based on FUNDAMENTAL ANALYSIS, where an INVESTOR commits CAPITAL to an investment with a view toward holding it for the long term.

BUY-BACK   (1) A process where a company repurchases some portion of outstanding SHARES from INVESTORS under a repurchase program. (2) A process where a government repurchases outstanding BONDS from the marketplace in order to retire them.

BUY-BACK DEDUCTIBLE   A DEDUCTIBLE on an INSURANCE POLICY that is eliminated through payment of an incremental PREMIUM, thus providing the INSURED with FIRST DOLLAR COVERAGE in the event of a loss.

BUY IN   (1) Covering of a SHORT POSITION by purchasing the UNDERLYING ASSET or taking delivery of SECURITIES. A SECURITIES FIRM expecting securities from another party that are not delivered buys them from another source and charges the original contracting firm any resulting price differential. (2) Purchase of securities from the open market to cover a FAIL TO DELIVER. The original contracting firm failing to deliver is invoiced for any differential between the contracted price and the actual price achieved. (3) See MANAGEMENT BUY-IN.

BUY MINUS   [COL] An ORDER to purchase a block of SECURITIES at a price that is lower than the current market price.

BUY/SELLBACK   A term sale and REPURCHASE AGREEMENT that is similar to the repurchase agreement but which is structured as a sale and simultaneous purchase of SECURITIES, where the purchase is agreed for a defined future date (i.e., no open-ended date), the BORROWER receives legal title and beneficial ownership of the securities and retains ACCRUED INTEREST. VARIATION MARGIN is generally not posted and COLLATERAL substitution is not possible.

BUY-SIDE   [COL] INVESTMENT firms, such as a HEDGE FUNDS, MUTUAL FUNDS, or PENSION FUNDS, that act as clients of the FINANCIAL INSTITUTION sector, paying fees and COMMISSIONS (i.e., "buying") in exchange for a range of services that can include investment advice, NEW ISSUES and other product offerings, and TRADE EXECUTION. See also SELL-SIDE.

BUY THE BOOK   [COL] An ORDER given by a client to a BROKER to purchase all of a SPECIALIST's or MARKET MAKER's inventory of a SECURITY, as well as the inventory of other BROKER/DEALERS, at the current market price.

BUY-WRITE   See COVERED OPTION.

BUYERS' CREDIT   A LOAN that is granted by a BANK or other financial institution to a buyer of exported goods.

BUYERS' MARKET   A market condition where SUPPLY exceeds DEMAND, causing prices to fall and giving potential buyers a greater opportunity to achieve a favorable BID price. See also SELLERS' MARKET.

BUYING FORWARD   The process of entering into a FORWARD contract or a FUTURES contract to achieve a future delivery of an ASSET or cash and/or to lock in a particular forward price.

BUYING THE DIPS   [COL] Purchasing STOCKS, BONDS, COMMODITIES, or other financial ASSETS after prices have fallen.

BV   See BESLOTEN VENNOOTSCHAP.

C

CA See CHARTERED ACCOUNTANT.

CABLE [COL] The sterling/US dollar FOREIGN EXCHANGE RATE.

CAD III See CAPITAL ADEQUACY DIRECTIVE III.

CAFETERIA PLAN [COL] A plan offered by companies to their employees that allows them to select from a variety of INSURANCE and retirement plans as a form of noncash benefit.

CAGE [COL] A physically secure location in a FINANCIAL INSTITUTION where physical-form SECURITIES are held in safekeeping. Also known as ACTIVE BOX.

CALAMITY CALL A provision in a COLLATERALIZED MORTGAGE OBLIGATION requiring a portion of the issue to be retired if PREPAYMENTS rise to a level where insufficient CASH FLOW exists to meet payments of PRINCIPAL and COUPON INTEREST.

CALENDAR See PIPELINE.

CALENDAR SPREAD See TIME SPREAD.

CALL See CALL OPTION.

CALL MONEY Funds placed in an INTEREST-bearing DEPOSIT account that can be withdrawn by the DEPOSITOR with one day's notice. In most instances call money refers to deposits placed by INSTITUTIONAL INVESTORS, which tend to be withdrawn more rapidly than those placed by retail customers. See also HOT MONEY.

CALL ON A CALL A COMPOUND OPTION that grants the buyer the right to purchase an underlying CALL OPTION from the seller of the compound. The option is generally purchased when the need for the underlying option is still uncertain. See also CALL ON A PUT, PUT ON A CALL, PUT ON A PUT.

CALL ON A PUT A COMPOUND OPTION that grants the buyer the right to purchase an underlying PUT OPTION from the seller of the compound. The option is generally purchased when the need for the underlying option is still uncertain. See also CALL ON A CALL, PUT ON A CALL, PUT ON A PUT.

CALL ON THE BEST OF N-ASSETS An OVER-THE-COUNTER COMPLEX OPTION that grants the buyer a payoff based on the difference between a pre-defined STRIKE PRICE and the best performing ASSET in a PORTFOLIO. See also CALL ON THE WORST OF N-ASSETS, MULTI-INDEX OPTION, OPTION ON THE BEST/WORST OF N-ASSETS, PUT ON THE BEST OF N-ASSETS, PUT ON THE WORST OF N-ASSETS.

CALL ON THE MAXIMUM   An OVER-THE-COUNTER COMPLEX OPTION that grants the buyer a payoff based on the difference between a predefined STRIKE PRICE and the highest price achieved by the UNDERLYING reference ASSET over the life of the transaction. See also LOOKBACK OPTION, OPTION ON THE MAXIMUM/MINIMUM, PUT ON THE MINIMUM.

C

CALL ON THE WORST OF N-ASSETS   An OVER-THE-COUNTER COMPLEX OPTION that grants the buyer a payoff based on the difference between a pre-defined STRIKE PRICE and the worst performing ASSET in a PORTFOLIO. See also CALL ON THE BEST OF N-ASSETS, MULTI-INDEX OPTION, OPTION ON THE BEST/WORST OF N-ASSETS, PUT ON THE BEST OF N-ASSETS, PUT ON THE WORST OF N-ASSETS.

CALL OPTION   A DERIVATIVE contract that gives the buyer the right, but not the obligation, to buy an UNDERLYING ASSET from the seller at a set STRIKE PRICE at, or before, EXPIRY. In exchange, the buyer pays the seller a PREMIUM. The payoff to the buyer is given as:

max(0, asset price – strike price)

Calls, which can be written on a broad range of financial and COMMODITY references, are available as EXCHANGE-traded and OVER-THE-COUNTER contracts, and can be structured as AMERICAN OPTIONS, BERMUDAN OPTIONS, or EUROPEAN OPTIONS.

Long call payoff profile

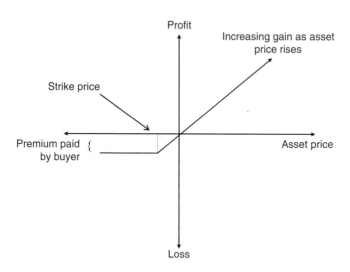

Short call payoff profile

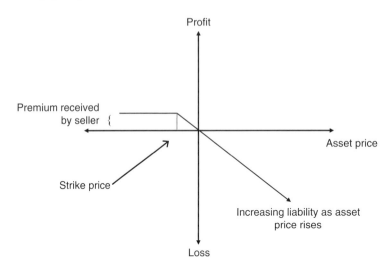

See also PUT OPTION.

CALL PREMIUM   (1) The differential between the redemption price and the PAR VALUE of a CALLABLE BOND. (2) The PREMIUM paid for a CALL OPTION.

CALL PRICE   The price paid to INVESTORS in a CALLABLE BOND if the OPTION to redeem is EXERCISED by the ISSUER. Also known as REDEMPTION PRICE.

CALL PROTECTION   A provision in a BOND INDENTURE that prevents the ISSUER from redeeming a BOND for a specific period of time (HARD CALL PROTECTION) or until certain price levels have been reached (SOFT CALL PROTECTION). See also CALL RISK, CALLABLE BOND, NONCALLABLE BOND.

CALL PROVISION   A clause contained in the INDENTURE of a BOND that specifies the terms under which the ISSUER may CALL the outstanding SECURITIES. The provision indicates the CALL PRICE and any relevant LOCKOUT PERIOD. See also PUT PROVISION.

CALL RISK   The RISK that the ISSUER will EXERCISE an embedded CALL and redeem a CALLABLE BOND when INTEREST RATES decline, exposing INVESTORS to reinvestment of CAPITAL at a lower rate.

CALL SPREAD   An OPTION position created by buying and selling CALL OPTIONS with the same EXPIRY DATE but different STRIKE PRICES (i.e., the purchaser of a call spread buys a closer-to-the-money call option and sells a farther out-of-the-money call option (a BULLISH strategy) the seller of a call spread does the reverse (a BEARISH strategy)). The spread limits the gain or LIABILITY to an area defined by the two strikes. See also BULL SPREAD, BEAR SPREAD, PUT SPREAD.

CALL SWAPTION See RECEIVER SWAPTION.

CALLABLE ASSET SWAP A structured DERIVATIVE comprised of a CALLABLE SWAP and an underlying BOND. The seller of the structure retains a CALL OPTION on the bond, allowing it to repurchase the asset at a given STRIKE CREDIT SPREAD at some future time. If the spread on the ASSET tightens during the life of the transaction (e.g., the price of the asset rises as a result of specific or general market/credit conditions), the seller calls the bond/swap package away from the INVESTOR; the investor receives proceeds equal to the strike spread plus invested PRINCIPAL from the seller. Also known as REMARKETABLE ASSET SWAP. See also PUTABLE ASSET SWAP.

CALLABLE BOND A BOND with embedded CALL OPTIONS that allows the ISSUER to redeem the SECURITY, generally at a PREMIUM to PAR VALUE. An issuer may call a bond if it can refinance at a lower INTEREST RATE (e.g., the PRESENT VALUE of the future CASH FLOWS from the bond is greater than the CALL PRICE) or no longer requires the CAPITAL proceeds; it is unlikely to call if prevailing rates are greater than the existing COUPON. From the INVESTORS' perspective, a callable bond can be considered the equivalent of a NONCALLABLE BOND and a SHORT POSITION in a call option(s) struck at the call price. In some cases investors are protected through CALL PROTECTION measures that limit an issuer's ability to redeem outstanding securities. See also CALL PREMIUM, CALL RISK, HYBRID BOND, PUTABLE BOND.

CALLABLE COMMON STOCK A form of COMMON STOCK where the SUBSIDIARY of a PARENT company issues SHARES that are subject to a stock purchase CALL OPTION agreement, giving the parent the right to repurchase the stock at a future time and STRIKE price. The strike price generally steps up over time, but effectively caps the CAPITAL GAINS that can accrue to the investor. See also PUTABLE COMMON STOCK.

CALLABLE SWAP An OVER-THE-COUNTER SWAP structure that gives the institution paying FIXED RATES the OPTION to cancel the transaction at a future date. See also CANCELLABLE SWAP, PUTABLE SWAP.

CALLOVER See RING TRADING.

CALLOVER PRICE The price of an ASSET that is established during a RING TRADING session, which becomes an officially reported figure.

CAMEL(S) [COL] Regulatory BANK ratings used in the US and UK financial systems based on a review of CAPITAL, ASSETS, management, MARKET RISK, EARNINGS, and LIABILITIES/LIQUIDITY. CAMEL ratings are used to reflect the overall strength of a bank; those awarded the highest ratings (e.g., 5 on a 1–5 scale) need little, if any, improvement, while those receiving lower ratings are expected to implement recommendations set forth by the REGULATORS.

CANCELLABLE SWAP   An OVER-THE-COUNTER SWAP structure that gives either party involved in the swap the OPTION to terminate the transaction at a future date. See also CALLABLE SWAP, PUTABLE SWAP.

CANCELLATION PRICE   In the United Kingdom, the price at which a UNIT TRUST will redeem individual units held by INVESTORS.

CANCELLATION PROVISION CLAUSE   A provision in a PROPERTY AND CASUALTY INSURANCE POLICY that gives the INSURED the right to cancel the CONTRACT prior to the stated expiration date, as long as adequate written notice is provided.

CANDLESTICK   [COL] A charting technique used in TECHNICAL ANALYSIS that divides TRADING periods (hours, days, weeks) into individual components of a histogram, with each period reflecting the open, close, high, and low.

CAP   (1) See POLICY CAP. (2) An OVER-THE-COUNTER INTEREST RATE OPTION that provides the buyer with a payoff when an underlying interest rate reference exceeds a predefined STRIKE PRICE. A cap can be viewed as a strip of options, where each individual option is known as a CAPLET and provides for a periodic payoff. More specifically, a cap is the equivalent of a strip of CALL OPTIONS on interest rates, or a strip of PUT OPTIONS on an underlying FIXED INCOME instrument (as a result of the inverse relationship between price and yield). This creates the following value relationships for rising and falling rates:

	Rising rates	Falling rates
Long cap	Value increases	Value decreases
Short cap	Value decreases	Value increases

The payoff to the purchaser of a cap on each settlement date is given as:

$$N * \left(r_{ref} - c\right) * \left(\frac{n}{d}\right)$$

where N is the NOTIONAL, r_{ref} is the value of the reference rate at the settlement date, c is the cap strike, n is the number of days in the settlement period, d is the number days in the year.

The cap provides no payoff to the purchaser if the reference rate is lower than the cap strike for any individual settlement period. (2) See also CAPLET, CAPTION, FLOOR, FLOORLET, FLOORTION.

CAP AND COLLAR MORTGAGE   See ADJUSTABLE RATE MORTGAGE.

CAP AND TRADE   A mechanism where emissions, such as carbon dioxide, sulfur dioxide, nitrous oxide and other pollutants, are capped and then traded between companies. The process depends on the creation of a maximum limit, or cap, by an international body on the amount of emissions that can be released. Individual companies are then issued emission permits and must hold a specific amount of credits (representing the right to emit a given amount). Companies that emit more must purchase more credits from those that emit less, in a TRADE. See also EMISSIONS TRADING.

CAPACITY The maximum amount an INSURER is willing or able to UNDERWRITE in a specific LINE of RISK, generally a function of the level of its RETAINED EARNINGS and CAPITAL. Capacity can be increased through the use of REINSURANCE CONTRACTS, which allow the insurer to release UNEARNED PREMIUM RESERVES and increase the size of the retained earnings account.

CAPITAL (1) The financial resources available to support a company's operations and absorb any unexpected losses. In a PUBLIC COMPANY capital typically comprises of COMMON STOCK, PAID-IN CAPITAL, CAPITAL SURPLUS, and RETAINED EARNINGS, though in some instances forms of SUBORDINATED PERPETUAL DEBT may also be included. (2) The MARKET VALUE of a company's EQUITY and long-term DEBT. (1) Also known as EQUITY. (1) See also ECONOMIC CAPITAL, NET WORTH, REGULATORY CAPITAL.

CAPITAL ACCOUNT (1) The national economic balance related to net direct INVESTMENT (inflows less outflows), purchases/sales of foreign SECURITIES by residents and domestic securities by nonresidents, and FOREIGN EXCHANGE RESERVES. (2) An account that reflects the individual elements of capital issued or generated by a company (e.g., PREFERRED STOCK, PAID-IN CAPITAL, RETAINED EARNINGS). (3) An account that reflects the capital contributions and GOODWILL attributable to individual partners in a PARTNERSHIP. (4) An account that reflects CAPITAL INVESTMENTS undertaken by a company. (1) See also BALANCE OF PAYMENTS, CURRENT ACCOUNT.

CAPITAL ADEQUACY In banking, a sufficiency of CAPITAL to support LENDING and TRADING activities and ensure proper protection of depositors and other CREDITORS. Minimum standards of capital adequacy, defined as qualifying capital in support of RISK-WEIGHTED ASSETS, are typically imposed by national regulators. See also BASLE ACCORD, BASLE II, CAPITAL ADEQUACY RATIO, INTERNAL CAPITAL ADEQUACY ASSESSMENT PROCESS.

CAPITAL ADEQUACY DIRECTIVE III (CAD III) A directive in Europe requiring BANKS to adopt the requirements prescribed under BASLE II.

CAPITAL ADEQUACY RATIO The measure of a BANK's CAPITAL ADEQUACY, measured as the ratio of qualifying CAPITAL to its total ASSETS. Under BASLE II, the minimum standard is set at 8%, but may be increased further at the discretion of national regulators. See also BASLE ACCORD, RISK-WEIGHTED ASSETS.

CAPITAL ALLOCATION CAPITAL used to cover the RISKS inherent in a transaction or line of business; funds allocated act as a buffer against unexpected losses and help ensure SOLVENCY is maintained. Capital can be allocated through both internally developed and regulatory mechanisms. See also ECONOMIC CAPITAL, REGULATORY CAPITAL, RESERVES, RISK-ADJUSTED CAPITAL, RISK-ADJUSTED RETURN ON CAPITAL.

CAPITAL ALLOWANCE   In the United Kingdom, an allowance granted to a party that has made CAPITAL INVESTMENTS in property, plant, or equipment used in the productive process.

CAPITAL ASSET   See FIXED ASSET.

CAPITAL ASSET PRICING MODEL (CAPM)   A financial theory indicating that RISK is a combination of DIVERSIFIABLE RISK and NONDIVERSIFIABLE RISK. Diversifiable risk can be reduced or eliminated through DIVERSIFICATION, meaning it is possible to create an optimal PORTFOLIO that maximizes return for a given level of risk. The nondiversifiable risk of an ASSET is fully measured by its sensitivity to the RISK PREMIUM of the market portfolio; in an efficient capital market the expected risk premium on an asset is proportional to BETA, a measure that indicates the riskiness, on a linear weighted basis, of the individual securities comprising the portfolio. Optimal portfolios are centered on the boundary of the EFFICIENT FRONTIER. Use of LEVERAGE (i.e., borrowing/lending at the RISK-FREE RATE) allows additional portfolios to be created, and is reflected in the CAPITAL MARKET LINE. CAPM assumes INVESTORS are risk averse and seek to maximize expected utility, asset return expectations are homogenous, assets are fixed, marketable, and divisible, a risk-free asset can be borrowed or lent without constraint, no friction costs exist, and all investors face the same investment horizon. Under CAPM the expected return of security j is given as:

$$E(r_j) = r_f + \beta\,[E(r_m) - r_f]$$

where r_f is the risk-free rate, β is beta, and $E(r_m)$ is the expected return on the market portfolio. See also ALPHA, ARBITRAGE PRICING THEORY.

Additional references: Jensen (1972); Merton (1973); Roll (1977); Ross (1976); Sharpe (1964, 1971).

CAPITAL AT RISK   (1) For an INVESTOR, the amount of invested CAPITAL that is exposed to one or more RISK types. (2) For a BANK, the amount of capital that is exposed to unexpected losses, typically derived from a CREDIT MODEL (for CREDIT RISK) and a VALUE-AT-RISK MODEL (for MARKET RISK).

CAPITAL BOND   In the United Kingdom a government savings BOND with a 5-year MATURITY offering a guaranteed rate of RETURN.

CAPITAL BUDGETING   A process carried out by a company based on estimating the future CASH FLOWS of potential medium- and long-term CAPITAL INVESTMENTS (including those related to nonfinancial ASSETS), determining the risk of the investments and their associated COST OF CAPITAL, and then deciding whether the investments will add value. Capital budgeting that involves cross-border investments must also take account of FOREIGN EXCHANGE risk, SOVEREIGN RISK and potential restrictions on capital repatriation.

CAPITAL COMMITMENT   (1) A CAPITAL financing transaction, such as a NEW ISSUE or LOAN, where the arranging/lending institution uses its own resources to fund the transaction, with a view toward subsequent distribution/SYNDICATION to other INVESTORS or lenders. (2) A plan developed by a company as part of its CAPITAL BUDGET process to enter into a specified amount and type of CAPITAL INVESTMENT during the fiscal year. (1) See also BOUGHT DEAL.

CAPITAL COST   See CAPITAL INVESTMENT.

CAPITAL EXPENDITURE   See CAPITAL INVESTMENT.

CAPITAL EXPENSE   See CAPITAL INVESTMENT.

CAPITAL FLIGHT   A sudden, and sometimes large, withdrawal of CAPITAL from a country, often as a result of SOVEREIGN RISK/COUNTRY RISK concerns or general political instability. A capital flight may involve nonresident (offshore) and resident INVESTORS; if the specter of loss appears real, investors will not be deterred by the potentially large transaction costs associated with shifting capital to a safe haven. See also FLIGHT TO QUALITY.

CAPITAL GAIN   A profit generated through the sale of an ASSET, computed as the difference between the sale price and the original purchase price. Capital gains may be generated over the short term (generally defined as less than one year) or long term, and may be taxable at varying rates (with lower rates applied to long-term capital gains in order to encourage the formation of long-term capital INVESTMENT). Also known as CAPITAL PROFIT. See also CAPITAL LOSS.

CAPITAL GEARING   See LEVERAGE.

CAPITAL GOOD   A FIXED ASSET that is used as a factor of production, e.g., plant, property, and equipment. See also DURABLE GOOD.

CAPITAL GROWTH   An increase in the value of CAPITAL that has been invested in a particular type of ASSET, such as STOCKS or BONDS. Capital growth may be driven by idiosyncratic or systemic factors such as profitability, market growth, and economic growth.

CAPITAL INFLOW   A change in a country's CAPITAL ACCOUNT that reflects an increase in the foreign ASSETS held within the country, or a decrease in the assets it holds in another country. See also CAPITAL OUTFLOW.

CAPITAL INVESTMENT   The allocation of CAPITAL by a company to ASSETS used in the creation of goods and services, such as property, plant and equipment, patents, copyrights, and so forth. Capital investments may be categorized according to their end use, and may include replacement projects, expansion projects, mandatory projects, and/or new markets projects. The evaluation of a capital investment may be undertaken during the CAPITAL BUDGETING process through a NET PRESENT VALUE calculation. Also known as CAPITAL COST, CAPITAL EXPENDITURE, CAPITAL EXPENSE.

CAPITAL LEASE   A long-term LEASE CONTRACT, structured in conventional or LEVERAGED form, where the LESSEE accepts most/all of the RISKS and benefits of the leased property. Since the risks and economics are transferable, ACCOUNTING rules generally require capital leases to be reflected on the corporate BALANCE SHEET. A capital lease is typically not cancellable, unless the lessee pays the LESSOR for any resulting losses. Also known as FINANCIAL LEASE. See also LEVERAGED LEASE, OPERATING LEASE.

CAPITAL LOSS   A loss generated through the sale of an ASSET, computed as the difference between the sale price and the original purchase price. Capital losses may be partly deductible against CAPITAL GAINS, with remaining TAX benefits carried over to future years.

CAPITAL MARKET   The general financial marketplace for primary and secondary transactions in COMMON STOCK, PREFERRED STOCK, medium to long-term BONDS, SECURITIZATIONS, and DERIVATIVES. See also MONEY MARKET.

CAPITAL MARKET LINE   A relationship within the CAPITAL ASSET PRICING MODEL (CAPM) that relates the expected RETURN of a PORTFOLIO to its expected RISK (as measured through STANDARD DEVIATION). Under CAPM, all INVESTORS will choose a position on the capital market line by borrowing or lending at the RISK-FREE RATE, since this maximizes return for a given level of risk. The capital market line, based on market portfolio M, can be estimated via:

$$ r_f + \left[\frac{E(r_M) - r_f}{\sigma(r_M)} \right] \sigma(r_p) $$

where r_f is the risk-free rate, $E(r_M)$ is the expected return of the market portfolio, $\sigma(r_M)$ is the standard deviation of the return of the market portfolio, $\sigma(r_p)$ is the standard deviation of the return of the target portfolio. See also SECURITY MARKET LINE.

CAPITAL MARKETS SUBSIDIARY   A dedicated SUBSIDIARY owned by an INSURER, REINSURER, or COMMERCIAL BANK that is authorized to deal directly in a range of CAPITAL MARKET financing transactions and/or DERIVATIVES, including businesses normally associated with SECURITIES FIRMS and INVESTMENT BANKS.

CAPITAL MOVEMENT The ability for CAPITAL to move between INVESTMENT alternatives and across national borders, without excessive FRICTION COSTS or controls. When costs and controls are minimized, capital is mobile, seeking the best possible RETURN over a particular time horizon.

CAPITAL NOTE   A NOTE (or BOND) issued by a BANK or bank HOLDING COMPANY that can qualify as TIER 2 CAPITAL. To be included in the Tier 2 computation, the SECURITY must be structured as a NONCALLABLE BOND with an original MATURITY of at least 7 years, or a MANDATORY CONVERTIBLE BOND that results in conversion into the bank's COMMON STOCK at maturity.

CAPITAL OUTFLOW   A change in a country's CAPITAL ACCOUNT that reflects a decrease in the foreign ASSETS held within the country, or an increase in the assets it holds in another country. See also CAPITAL INFLOW.

CAPITAL PROFIT See CAPITAL GAIN.

CAPITAL STRUCTURE The composition of LIABILITIES and EQUITY on a company's BALANCE SHEET, which in total are used to fund its productive ASSETS. Capital structure, which varies by firm and across industries, is typically a mix of different forms of DEBT (with varying degrees of SENIORITY) and one or more classes of STOCK (e.g., PREFERRED STOCK, COMMON STOCK).

CAPITAL SURPLUS A form of CAPITAL that can be created from issuance of COMMON STOCK at a PREMIUM over PAR VALUE, proceeds of stock repurchased and then resold (i.e., resale of TREASURY STOCK), a reduction in par value of common stock, or the purchase of another company with a surplus. The capital surplus does not include PAID-IN CAPITAL or RETAINED EARNINGS, which are treated separately for ACCOUNTING purposes. See also SHARE PREMIUM.

CAPITAL TURNOVER See ASSET TURNOVER.

CAPITALIZATION (1) The structure and amount of CAPITAL a company has on its BALANCE SHEET. (2) An ACCOUNTING practice where a cost is recorded as a CAPITAL INVESTMENT and depreciated over several periods instead of being recorded as an expense and charged off against EARNINGS in a single period. (3) See MARKET CAPITALIZATION.

CAPITALIZED VALUE The value of a FIXED ASSET on a company's BALANCE SHEET before any deduction for DEPRECIATION.

CAPITULATION [COL] A condition where the STOCK MARKET has declined dramatically on high volume as INVESTORS liquidate position en masse, in a form of panic selling. A capitulation may signal a bottoming phase in the market, luring in BOTTOM FISHERS and other investors seeking value.

CAPLET One of a series of INTEREST RATE CAPS comprising a CAP.

CAPM See CAPITAL ASSET PRICING MODEL.

CAPPED FLOATING RATE NOTE A FLOATING RATE NOTE (FRN) that features a COUPON that is capped at an upper STRIKE level. The INVESTOR therefore faces a maximum return on invested CAPITAL once rates move above the strike. See also FLOORED FLOATING RATE NOTE.

CAPPED MORTGAGE See ADJUSTABLE RATE MORTGAGE.

CAPTION An OVER-THE-COUNTER OPTION on a CAP, granting the buyer the right to purchase a cap at a predetermined STRIKE PRICE. See also FLOOR, FLOORTION.

CAPTIVE A vehicle established as an authorized INSURER or REINSURER that is used to facilitate a company's SELF-INSURANCE, RISK FINANCING, or RISK TRANSFER strategies. A captive, which can be controlled by a single owner or multiple owners (or sponsor(s)), can write INSURANCE/REINSURANCE business on behalf of one company/sponsor or many unrelated companies. Captives are often located in jurisdictions that have favorable insurance and tax laws, such as Bermuda, the Isle of Man, Guernsey, and Vermont. See also AGENCY CAPTIVE, GROUP CAPTIVE, PROTECTED CELL COMPANY, PURE CAPTIVE, RENT-A-CAPTIVE, SISTER CAPTIVE.

CAPTIVE AGENT   An AGENT that represents a single INSURER and is required to submit business only to that insurer. In exchange for acting in an exclusive capacity, the insurer generally helps the captive agent defray marketing costs and provides additional financial benefits.

CAPTIVE FINANCE COMPANY   See FINANCE COMPANY.

CARBON DIOXIDE EQUIVALENT   A standard metric used in EMISSIONS TRADING, where the warming potential of greenhouses gases is converted into the base carbon dioxide reference. Those with a higher warming potential (such as methane, nitrous oxide, hydrofluorocarbons, and sulfur hexafluoride) feature higher carbon dioxide equivalents.

CARBON TRADING   See EMISSIONS TRADING.

CARRIER   An INSURER that is authorized to UNDERWRITE and ISSUE an INSURANCE POLICY.

CARROT EQUITY   [COL] In the United Kingdom, a COMMON STOCK issue with a KICKER, or extra incentive, which allows INVESTORS to buy more stock if certain performance goals are met.

CARRY   [COL] The differential obtained after deducting INTEREST or funding charges from the RETURNS produced by an ASSET. Carry is positive if returns exceed funding, and negative if funding exceeds returns. See also CASH-AND-CARRY ARBITRAGE, CARRY TRADE, COST OF CARRY, LONG CARRY, NEGATIVE CARRY, POSITIVE CARRY, SHORT CARRY.

CARRY TRADE   Any transaction or TRADE that is designed to produce CARRY. A carry trade can be created using a variety of ASSETS, including FIXED INCOME instruments, EQUITIES, COMMODITIES, and CURRENCIES. See also NEGATIVE CARRY, POSITIVE CARRY.

CARRYBACK LOSS   See TAX CARRYBACK.

CARRYFORWARD LOSS   See TAX CARRYFORWARD.

CARRYING AMOUNT   See CARRYING VALUE.

CARRYING MARKET   Any COMMODITY market based on nonperishable commodities, where INVENTORY can be carried from period to period without risk of loss or damage, e.g., metals, energy.

CARRYING VALUE   The value of an ASSET or LIABILITY as reflected on a company's BALANCE SHEET. Also known as CARRYING AMOUNT.

CARTEL   A formal or informal agreement between firms in an industry or market to restrict competition by setting minimum price levels or maximum output QUOTAS, and/or by segregating products or markets. Although establishment of a cartel can lead to profit growth in the short run, members may find it difficult to monitor each other's actions over the long term, leading in some instances to the gradual erosion of the arrangement.

CARVE-OUT   See DEMERGER.

CASH ACCOUNTING   A general ACCOUNTING method that reports INCOME when it is received and EXPENSES when they are paid. Also known as CASH BASIS. See also ACCRUAL ACCOUNTING.

CASH AGAINST DOCUMENTS   In international TRADE, a process where shipping documents are sent to a BANK in the country to which the goods are being shipped, after which the buyer obtains the documents by paying the bank in cash. See also DOCUMENTS AGAINST ACCEPTANCE

CASH-AND-CARRY ARBITRAGE   A combination of ARBITRAGE and a CARRY TRADE used in the COMMODITY markets where an ARBITRAGEUR buys the commodity in the SPOT MARKET, sells it FORWARD, pays for the financing and storage costs, and is still able to generate a profit. See also REVERSE CASH-AND-CARRY ARBITRAGE.

CASH-AT-EXPIRY OPTION   A BINARY OPTION that grants the buyer a payoff at EXPIRY equal to a fixed cash amount if the price of the UNDERLYING market reference exceeds the STRIKE PRICE or BARRIER at any time during the transaction. See also BINARY-BARRIER OPTION.

CASH-AT-HIT OPTION   A BINARY OPTION that grants the buyer an immediate payoff equal to a fixed cash amount once the price of the UNDERLYING market reference breaches the STRIKE PRICE or BARRIER. See also BINARY-BARRIER OPTION.

CASH BASIS   See CASH ACCOUNTING.

CASH BUDGETING   A process carried out by a company that leads to development of estimated cash inflows and outflows during particular future periods. Cash budgeting provides a picture of how cash is generated, how it is used, and whether additional interim financing may be required. It also provides objective metrics by which to measure sales performance, INVESTMENT performance, and efficacy of ACCOUNTS RECEIVABLE and ACCOUNTS PAYABLE processes. See also OPERATING CASH FLOW.

CASH-CDS BASIS   For a given MATURITY, the differential between a REFERENCE ENTITY's CREDIT DEFAULT SWAP (CDS) spread and its BOND (e.g., the CASH MARKET). When the CDS–BOND spread is greater than 0, the basis is considered to be positive, and when it is less than 0 it is negative.

CASH COLLATERALIZED DEBT OBLIGATION   (CDO) A COLLATERALIZED DEBT OBLIGATION that is created on a funded basis through the use of actual DEBT SECURITIES rather than CREDIT DERIVATIVE CONTRACTS. A cash CDO may be structured as a BALANCE SHEET CDO or an ARBITRAGE CDO, and may be managed statically or dynamically. See also SYNTHETIC COLLATERALIZED DEBT OBLIGATION.

CASH CONVERSION CYCLE   The number of days it takes for a company to convert its INVENTORY and ACCOUNTS RECEIVABLE into cash, after taking into account its use of CREDIT via ACCOUNTS PAYABLE. It can be computed as:

$$CCC = DSI + DSO - DPO$$

where DSI is DAYS SALES INVENTORY, DSO is DAYS SALES OUTSTANDING, DPO is DAYS PAYABLES OUTSTANDING.

The larger the result, the longer it takes a company to create cash. See also CASH FLOW CYCLE, OPERATING CYCLE.

CASH COW   [COL] A company, SUBSIDIARY, or product that is able to generate significant, and dependable, REVENUES, OPERATING INCOME, and/or OPERATING CASH FLOW with little incremental invested CAPITAL.

CASH DELIVERY   Arrangement for immediate delivery of goods for cash, or vice-versa, as per the terms of any CONTRACT negotiated for cash or SPOT settlement. See also FORWARD DELIVERY.

CASH DISCOUNT   The DISCOUNT associated with the payment of an invoice within a particular period. A buyer of goods or services paying the invoice within the period specified receives a cash discount from the seller. From an ACCOUNTING perspective discounts received are considered a form of REVENUE while those which are granted are a form of EXPENSE.

CASH DIVIDEND   A DIVIDEND paid by a company in the form of cash. Cash dividends are the most common form of dividend payments in most national systems. See also STOCK DIVIDEND.

CASH FLOW   (1) A measure of a company's sources and uses of cash and the overall state of its LIQUIDITY. Cash flow is divided into OPERATING CASH FLOW, INVESTING CASH FLOW, and FINANCING CASH FLOW. (2) Any cash inflow or outflow associated with an INVESTMENT or FINANCING transaction.

CASH FLOW CYCLE   The time between the outflow of cash in support of raw material acquisition and the inflow of cash from sales of goods. Cash outflows may be delayed through the use of supplier CREDIT, while cash inflows may be delayed by granting customers sales credit. See also CASH CONVERSION CYCLE, OPERATING CYCLE.

CASH FLOW STATEMENT   See STATEMENT OF CASH FLOWS.

CASH FLOW TO CAPITAL INVESTMENT   A measure of the flexibility a company has to invest in new capital projects, which is particularly important for those in capital-intensive industries (e.g., utilities, transportation, manufacturing). It is computed as:

$$CFC = \frac{CF}{Capex}$$

where CF is the company's cash flow, Capex is the company's estimated capital expenditures

The greater the ratio, the greater the financial flexibility afforded the company. See also CASH FLOW TO DEBT.

CASH FLOW TO DEBT A measure of a company's ability to meet its DEBT obligations through its total CASH FLOW resources. It is computed as:

$$CFD = \frac{CF}{Debt}$$

where CF is the company's cash flow, Debt is the company's debt, either in total, or with reference to a specific maturity.

The greater the ratio, the greater the company's ability to meet its obligations. See also CASH FLOW TO CAPITAL INVESTMENT.

CASH FLOW UNDERWRITING In INSURANCE, a pricing strategy where the PREMIUM charged is less than the EXPECTED LOSS LEVEL. The intent is to generate a large amount of premiums through the underpricing and use proceeds from reinvested premiums to cover expected losses and generate a PROFIT MARGIN.

CASH FLOW WATERFALL See WATERFALL.

CASH MARKET See SPOT MARKET.

CASH ON DELIVERY (COD) See DELIVERY VERSUS PAYMENT.

CASH ON DELIVERY OPTION See CONTINGENT PREMIUM OPTION.

CASH-OR-NOTHING OPTION A BINARY OPTION that grants the buyer a payoff equal to a fixed cash amount if the price of the UNDERLYING market reference breaches the STRIKE PRICE at EXPIRY. See also BINARY OPTION.

CASH PRICE See SPOT PRICE.

CASH RATE See SPOT RATE.

CASH RATIO For a BANK, the amount of cash held as a percentage of total ASSETS to meet the claims of those withdrawing DEPOSITS.

CASH SETTLEMENT A SETTLEMENT process where two parties to a TRADE or DERIVATIVE CONTRACT exchange cash for the cash equivalent of a physical ASSET (such as a COMMODITY) on a net basis. This obviates the need for arranging or accepting delivery of the physical asset. Also known as FINANCIAL SETTLEMENT. See also PHYSICAL SETTLEMENT.

CASH SURRENDER VALUE See SURRENDER VALUE.

CASUALTY LIABILITY or loss arising from an accident, negligence, or omissions, which can be covered through different forms of INSURANCE (such as PROPERTY AND CASUALTY INSURANCE, COMMERCIAL GENERAL LIABILITY INSURANCE, or MULTIPLE PERIL INSURANCE).

CAT BOND   See CATASTROPHE BOND.

CATASTROPHE BOND   A SECURITIZATION of a CATASTROPHIC HAZARD, such as an earthquake, hurricane, or windstorm. Repayment of PRINCIPAL and/or COUPONS is contingent on the occurrence of a defined loss-making catastrophe; if a specified loss occurs, the ISSUER of the BOND (often an INSURER) may delay or cease making payments to INVESTORS, effectively transferring the RISK exposure to INVESTORS. The determination of whether payments are to be suspended under a catastrophe bond is based on one of three types of triggers: the INDEMNITY TRIGGER, INDEX TRIGGER, and PARAMETRIC TRIGGER. Also known as CAT BOND. See also INSURANCE-LINKED SECURITY, LIFE ACQUISITION COST SECURITIZATION, MORTGAGE DEFAULT SECURITIZATION, RESIDUAL VALUE SECURITIZATION, WEATHER BOND.

CATASTROPHE PER OCCURRENCE EXCESS OF LOSS   A REINSURANCE agreement providing the INSURER with cover for adverse loss experience from an accumulation of catastrophic events; such agreements often have an incremental DEDUCTIBLE and COINSURANCE.

CATASTROPHE REINSURANCE SWAP   A synthetic financial SWAP that provides one of the contracting parties with a cash inflow in the event of loss from a defined catastrophic event. In exchange for the contingent CASH FLOW, the second party receives an upfront fee. Although the swap assumes the function of standard INSURANCE or REINSURANCE, the underlying documentation is often simpler and quicker to negotiate. See also PURE CATASTROPHE SWAP.

CATASTROPHIC HAZARD   A RISK event that is characterized by high severity and low frequency, leading to a large difference between expected and actual aggregate losses. Common catastrophic hazards include natural and human-made events such as earthquakes, hurricanes, windstorms, and terrorism. Although many catastrophic hazards can be protected via INSURANCE, REINSURANCE, or INSURANCE-LINKED SECURITIES some cannot, as the risk of loss may be too large or the required PREMIUM too high. See also CATASTROPHIC LOSS, CLASH LOSS, SHOCK LOSS.

CATASTROPHIC LOSS   A high-severity, low-frequency loss event arising from a CATASTROPHIC HAZARD. A company often seeks to protect against catastrophic loss through INSURANCE, REINSURANCE, or CATASTROPHE BONDS. Catastrophic losses are often challenging to quantify since they are relatively rare and may, in some instances, be UNINSURABLE. See also CLASH LOSS, SHOCK LOSS.

CATCH A FALLING KNIFE   [COL] Any instance where an INVESTOR purchases the SHARES of a company that have fallen rapidly and dramatically in price. The investor is betting that OVERSOLD conditions exist and that the likelihood of a price rebound outweighs the risk of further price declines.

CATS   See CERTIFICATE OF ACCRUAL ON TREASURY SECURITIES.

CAVEAT EMPTOR   [LAT] Literally "buyer beware." The term is often given as a warning to RETAIL INVESTORS participating in risky or unproven INVESTMENTS.

CBO   See COLLATERALIZED BOND OBLIGATION.

CCA   See CHARTERED CERTIFIED ACCOUNTANT.

CD   See CERTIFICATE OF DEPOSIT.

CDO   See COLLATERALIZED DEBT OBLIGATION.

CDS   See CREDIT DEFAULT SWAP.

CEDANT   See INSURED.

CEDE   The process of transferring RISK from one party (the INSURED or CEDING INSURER) to another party (the INSURER or REINSURER) through an INSURANCE or REINSURANCE CONTRACT. See also RETROCEDE.

CEDED PREMIUMS   PREMIUMS that are paid by an INSURER or CAPTIVE to a REINSURER, which assumes coverage of the RISK being ceded.

CEDING COMPANY   A company that transfers, or CEDES, RISK to an INSURER. See also INSURED.

CEDING INSURER   An INSURER that transfers, or CEDES, RISK to a REINSURER.

CEDULAS HIPOTECARIAS   [SPN] In Spain, a form of COVERED BOND backed by a BANK's MORTGAGES. See also HYPOTHEKENPFANDBRIEFE, IRISH ASSET COVERED SECURITIES, JUMBO PFANDBRIEFE, LETTRES DE GAGE, OBLIGATIONS FONCIERES, OFFENTLICHE PFANDBRIEFE.

CELL CAPTIVE   See RENT-A-CAPTIVE.

CENTRAL BANK   A government-owned or controlled BANK or monetary authority that may be responsible for issuing local BANKNOTES, holding the country's own RESERVES, managing the value of the CURRENCY, regulating MONEY SUPPLY, setting RESERVE REQUIREMENTS, holding DEPOSITS of local banks, lending to the banking system, managing the local SECURITIES market, and/or acting as a LENDER OF LAST RESORT. See also BANK OF CANADA, BANK OF ENGLAND, BANK OF JAPAN, BANQUE DE FRANCE, BUNDESBANK, EUROPEAN CENTRAL BANK, FEDERAL RESERVE SYSTEM, MONETARY AUTHORITY OF SINGAPORE, PEOPLE'S BANK OF CHINA, RESERVE BANK OF AUSTRALIA.

CENTRAL LIMIT THEOREM   See LAW OF LARGE NUMBERS.

CENTRAL MOMENT   See MOMENT.

CEO   See CHIEF EXECUTIVE OFFICER.

CERTAIN ANNUITY   A form of ANNUITY that pays the ANNUITANT a fixed amount for a defined period of time, once the annuitant has reached a particular age.

CERTIFICATE OF ACCRUAL ON TREASURY SECURITIES (CATS)   In the United States, a ZERO COUPON BOND issued by the Treasury Department.

CERTIFICATE OF DEPOSIT (CD)   A time DEPOSIT issued by a BANK to a depositor that pays a fixed or variable INTEREST RATE; in most instances the deposit represents a senior, unsecured LIABILITY of the issuing bank. A CD may be issued onshore or offshore in any one of several CURRENCIES, with a final maturity ranging from 1 week to 10 years. Certain CDs (i.e., NEGOTIABLE CDs) can be actively traded in the SECONDARY MARKET. See also FLOATING RATE CERTIFICATE OF DEPOSIT, LOCKUP CERTIFICATE OF DEPOSIT.

CERTIFICATE OF INCORPORATION   A certificate issued by an authorized body (e.g., Registrar of Incorporations, Registrar of Associations) that confirms the legal creation and existence of a CORPORATION, typically based on the ARTICLES OF INCORPORATION that have been filed by the founders.

CERTIFIED PUBLIC ACCOUNTANT (CPA)   In the United States, an account-ant that receives a state license through the passage of relevant examinations and the accumulation of industry experience and is qualified to AUDIT a company's ACCOUNTS. See also CHARTERED ACCOUNTANT, CHARTERED CERTIFIED ACCOUNTANT.

CESR   See COMMITTEE OF EUROPEAN SECURITIES REGULATORS.

CESSION   A quantify of RISK transferred from one party to a second party via an INSURANCE CONTRACT; the second party becomes responsible for provid-ing coverage in exchange for CEDED PREMIUM.

CFA   See CHARTERED FINANCIAL ANALYST.

CFD   See CONTRACT FOR DIFFERENCES.

CFO   See CHIEF FINANCIAL OFFICER.

CFTC   See COMMODITY FUTURES TRADING COMMISSION.

CGS   See COST OF GOODS SOLD.

CHAEBOL   [KOR] The Korean form of conglomerate, generally comprised of a series of companies with cross-SHAREHOLDINGS and business relationships, but no central core company.

CHAPS   See CLEARINGHOUSE AUTOMATED PAYMENT SYSTEM.

CHAPTER 7   In the United States, the statute of the Bankruptcy Reform Act that relates to the LIQUIDATION proceedings of individuals, SOLE PROPRIETORSHIPS, PARTNERSHIPS, and CORPORATIONS that have entered FINANCIAL DISTRESS. The courts typically appoint a TRUSTEE to operate the business while liquidation negotiations are underway in order to preserve as much ASSET value as possible. See also CHAPTER 9, CHAPTER 11, CHAPTER 13, PREPACKAGED BANKRUPTCY.

CHAPTER 9   In the United States, the statute of the Bankruptcy Reform Act that relates to the REORGANIZATION proceedings of municipalities. Though this clause is not commonly used, in most instances a municipal DEBTOR continues to conduct municipal operations while concluding DEBT RESTRUCTURING negotiations with CREDITORS. See also CHAPTER 7, CHAPTER 11, CHAPTER 13, PREPACKAGED BANKRUPTCY.

CHAPTER 11   In the United States, the statute of the Bankruptcy Reform Act that relates to the REORGANIZATION proceedings of PARTNERSHIPS and CORPORATIONS. In most cases a Chapter 11 DEBTOR is allowed to remain in control of its business while concluding DEBT RESTRUCTURING negotiations with CREDITORS. See also CHAPTER 7, CHAPTER 9, CHAPTER 13, PREPACKAGED BANKRUPTCY.

CHAPTER 13   In the United States, the statute of the Bankruptcy Reform Act that relates to the RESTRUCTURING proceedings of individuals in FINANCIAL DISTRESS (as an alternative to CHAPTER 7). In most cases a personal DEBTOR is permitted to keep certain types of property and establish a DEBT repayment schedule covering 3 to 5 years. Also known as WAGE EARNER'S PLAN. See also CHAPTER 9, CHAPTER 11, PREPACKAGED BANKRUPTCY.

CHARGE   An interest in personal or corporate property that secures the payment of funds in favor of the chargee (often a BANK lender). See also FIXED CHARGE, FLOATING CHARGE.

CHARGE CARD   A card issued by a BANK or financial institution that conveys a short-term CREDIT line to the holder allowing the purchase of goods or services, with the agreement that any resulting balance becomes due and payable at the end of every month and cannot be carried forward. See also CREDIT CARD, DEBIT CARD.

CHARTERED ACCOUNTANT (CA)   In the United Kingdom, an accountant that is a member of the Institute of Charted Accountants, admitted through the passage of relevant examinations and the accumulation of industry experience, and qualified to AUDIT a company's ACCOUNTS. CAs may also engage in TAX and financial advisory duties. See also CERTIFIED PUBLIC ACCOUNTANT, CHARTERED CERTIFIED ACCOUNTANT.

CHARTERED BANK   In the United States and Canada, a BANK that is permitted to operate on a state/provincial or national level through the granting of a charter from the relevant regulatory authority.

CHARTERED CERTIFIED ACCOUNTANT (CCA)   In the United Kingdom, an accountant that is a member of the ASSOCIATION OF CHARTERED CERTIFIED ACCOUNTANTS, admitted through the passage of relevant examinations and the accumulation of industry experience, and qualified to AUDIT a company's ACCOUNTS. See also CERTIFIED PUBLIC ACCOUNTANT, CHARTERED ACCOUNTANT.

CHARTERED FINANCIAL ANALYST (CFA)   A professional designation awarded to those who have completed the examination requirements of the CFA program, which focuses on INVESTMENT MANAGEMENT, ECONOMICS, SECURITIES ANALYSIS, and ACCOUNTING.

CHASING THE MARKET   [COL] Any instance where an INVESTOR enters or exits a SECURITY or market after a significant upside or downside trend has already been established. Participating after such a lag may expose the investor to losses once a CORRECTION takes place.

CHASTITY BOND   A BOND that can be redeemed by the issuing company at PAR VALUE in the event that it becomes the target of a TAKEOVER offer from another company.

CHEAP   [COL] An ASSET that is perceived by market participants to be inexpensive compared to alternatives or proxies (i.e., the SPREAD is too wide in the case of a BOND or the price too low in the case of a COMMON STOCK, CURRENCY, or COMMODITY). Those believing the asset is cheap will seek to profit by purchasing it, directly, synthetically, or through an ARBITRAGE TRADE. See also RICH.

CHEAPEST-TO-DELIVER (CTD)   The cheapest of a series of ASSETS that are eligible for DELIVERY under an EXCHANGE-TRADED DERIVATIVE; the seller selects from the list of deliverables to determine the asset that will yield the greatest RETURN (i.e., lowest cost, narrowest BASIS, or smallest loss). See also CONVERSION FACTOR.

CHECK   A form that authorizes a BANK or other FINANCIAL INSTITUTION to pay a specified sum to the named PAYEE from the DRAWER's account. A check may carry an ENDORSEMENT which permits different degrees of transfer among third parties. Also known as CHEQUE.

CHECK KITING   [COL] An illegal practice involving the writing of CHECKS on two or more nonlocal BANKS, creating an unauthorized, INTEREST-free LOAN or displaying a larger account balance until the checks are cleared. Also known as KITING.

CHECKING ACCOUNT   A BANK ACCOUNT on which a CHECK can be drawn by the DRAWER in favor of a named PAYEE.

CHEQUE   In the United Kingdom, a CHECK.

CHERRY PICK   [COL] (1) A process where a RECEIVER or administrator in a BANKRUPTCY case attempts to have the court honor DERIVATIVE CONTRACTS (and/or REPURCHASE AGREEMENTS) that benefit the COUNTERPARTY in DEFAULT, while disallowing those that harm it. When a MASTER AGREEMENT is used to document the transactions and the legal jurisdiction recognizes the concept of NETTING, cherry picking cannot occur. (2) The process where a RAIDER engaged in ASSET STRIPPING selects only the best ASSETS for control or disposal, leaving behind less attractive or profitable ones.

CHEWABLE PILL   [COL] A POISON PILL defense clause that gives COMMON STOCK SHAREHOLDERS the right to revoke the pill in the face of a bona fide TAKEOVER offer, or which automatically nullifies the pill if the offer meets certain predefined criteria.

CHICAGO MERCANTILE EXCHANGE (CME)   A physical and electronic EXCHANGE, established in 1919, dealing in a wide variety of EXCHANGE-TRADED DERIVATIVES, including those referencing INTEREST RATES, CURRENCIES, EQUITY INDEXES, MACROECONOMIC indicators, real estate, weather, COMMODITIES, and energy. The CME was originally created as a mutual organization, but converted to public ownership in 2002. In recent years it has acquired other major exchanges, including the Chicago Board of Trade and the New York Mercantile Exchange.

CHIEF EXECUTIVE OFFICER (CEO)   The executive leader of a company, responsible for guiding the management team and defining and fulfilling tactical and strategic imperatives. The CEO is often appointed by the BOARD OF DIRECTORS and is accountable to them.

CHIEF FINANCIAL OFFICER (CFO)   A professional that is responsible for all aspects of financial affairs within a company, including ACCOUNTING, AUDITING, and TREASURY. In many jurisdictions the CFO is a signatory to the FINANCIAL STATEMENTS.

CHIEF INVESTMENT OFFICER   An individual working within a HEDGE FUND, MUTUAL FUND, or other investment management vehicle that is responsible for leading the management of one or more INVESTMENT PORT-FOLIOS. The chief investment officer may have strategic and tactical responsibilities, and may be in charge of the PORTFOLIO CONSTRUCTION process.

CHILD ORDER   A portion or slice of a PARENT ORDER that is executed independently, but according to price and/or time considerations embedded in the logic of an ALGORITHM.

CHINESE WALL   [COL] A process/structure within a BANK, INVESTMENT BANK, or SECURITIES FIRM that separates groups that call on clients and arrange deals (i.e., BANKERS) from those that are privy to NONPUBLIC INFORMATION related to those clients (i.e., INVESTMENT ANALYSTS). The intent is to minimize the exchange of sensitive information that might be used for competitive or personal gain. See also OVER THE WALL.

CHIPS   See CLEARINGHOUSE INTERBANK PAYMENT SYSTEM.

CHOICE PRICE   Identical BIDS and OFFERS provided by a MARKET MAKER or DEALER, meaning that a party can execute either side of the TRADE at the same price. See also LOCKED MARKET.

CHOOSER OPTION   An OVER-THE-COUNTER COMPLEX OPTION that permits the buyer to choose between an underlying CALL OPTION and PUT OPTION with identical STRIKE PRICES and MATURITIES from trade date until a defined "choice" date. Also known as a PREFERENCE OPTION, REGULAR CHOOSER OPTION. See also COMPLEX CHOOSER OPTION.

CHURNING   [COL] (1) An illegal practice where a BROKER urges clients to trade more actively than necessary in their INVESTMENT accounts in order to generate more COMMISSIONS. Accounts that reflect turnover of more than three to five times per year may indicate churning. (2) In the United Kingdom, a practice where a BANK or BUILDING SOCIETY encourages a holder of an ENDOWMENT MORTGAGE to surrender the current contract and take out a new, larger one, thereby generating additional COMMISSIONS. Also known as OVERTRADING, TWISTING.

CIF   See COST, INSURANCE, FREIGHT.

CIN   See CUSIP INTERNATIONAL NUMBER

CIRCLE   [COL] See INDICATION OF INTEREST.

CIRCUIT BREAKER   [COL] Measures taken to halt TRADING on an EXCHANGE in the event predefined price levels are reached. Circuit breakers are intended to allow market participants to rebalance their positions in an orderly manner without contributing to further price pressures. Common breakers include temporary trading halts, curbs, or bans on automated trading programs, and/or hourly/daily price limits.

CIRCULATING ASSET   See CURRENT ASSETS.

CITY   [COL] Short for City of London, a reference to London's financial district.

CITY CODE   [COL] Abbreviated form of the City Code on Takeovers and Mergers, a UK code of conduct established in 1968 under the direction of the BANK OF ENGLAND to ensure fair treatment for all parties involved in CORPORATE FINANCE transactions. The City Code defines the roles and responsibilities of BANKS (as advisors), acquiring companies, and TARGET companies involved in a MERGER or ACQUISITION.

CLAIM   (1) A request for loss INDEMNIFICATION made by an INSURED to an INSURER for a PERIL covered under an INSURANCE CONTRACT; the party submitting the claim is known as a claimant. In order for the claim to result in a SETTLEMENT, terms of the underlying contract must be met and proof of loss must generally be presented. (2) A general right to an ASSET or CASH FLOW.

CLAIMS MADE BASIS   Determination of whether a CLAIM is covered by an INSURANCE CONTRACT. If the contract is written on a claims made basis and if a claim is made when the policy is in effect, the INSURER must pay the INSURED up to the stated amount. See also CLAIMS OCCURRENCE BASIS.

CLAIMS OCCURRENCE BASIS   Determination of whether a CLAIM is covered by an INSURANCE CONTRACT. If the contract is written on a claims occurrence basis and a claim arises from an event when the policy is in force, the INSURER must pay the INSURED up to the stated amount, regardless of when the claim is actually filed (i.e., filing may occur after the policy has expired). See also CLAIMS MADE BASIS, OCCURRENCE LIMIT.

CLAIMS RESERVE Funds set aside by an INSURER for CLAIMS incurred or for claims outstanding that have not been settled. The claims reserve does not include ACCOUNTING for losses INCURRED BUT NOT REPORTED.

CLASH COVER A form of REINSURANCE that provides for additional coverage of RISK when the CEDANT's coverage results in two or more loss CLAIMS under the same occurrence.

CLASH LOSS A disaster scenario where various LINES of INSURANCE are simultaneously impacted by losses. The resulting CLAIMS may be particularly large and can negatively impact the financial condition of INSURERS and REINSURERS. See also CATASTROPHIC HAZARD, SHOCK LOSS.

CLASH REINSURANCE An EXCESS OF LOSS REINSURANCE CONTRACT where the INSURER is covered against property or casualty losses when a single CASUALTY event causes losses for at least two CEDING INSURERS.

CLASS ACTION A form of legal action where an individual brings suit as a representative of a broad class of plaintiffs who have a similar grievance or claim.

CLASSICAL ECONOMICS A field of ECONOMICS focused on markets, competition and self-interest, indicating that competitive, free market forces can regulate themselves, and that LAISSEZ-FAIRE/minimal government intervention in economic processes is desirable. The study was pioneered and popularized in the eighteenth and nineteenth centuries by Adam Smith, David Ricardo, David Hume, and John Stuart Mill, and carried through into the twentieth century by Alfred Marshall. See also KEYNESIAN ECONOMICS.

CLASSIFIED BOARD See STAGGERED BOARD.

CLASSIFIED STOCK Separate classes of COMMON STOCK issued by a company, with each class granting INVESTORS a distinct set of RENT RIGHTS and/or CONTROL RIGHTS. Classified stock is often used to increase or decrease the voting power of specific groups of SHAREHOLDERS. See also A-SHARE, ALPHABET STOCK, B-SHARES.

CLAWBACK [COL] (1) The repayment, to RECEIVERS of a company in BANKRUPTCY, of any PREFERENCE payments, or monies deemed to have benefited one party at the expense of others during the period of FINANCIAL DISTRESS. (2) An agreement, which may be used in PROJECT FINANCE, that requires the BORROWER or sponsor to pay future cash shortfalls with profits generated in previous periods. (1) See also PREFERENCE PERIOD.

CLEAN [COL] Matched buy and sell ORDERS on a BLOCK TRADE that leave the MARKET MAKER, DEALER, or INTERMEDIARY without a RISK position. Also known as NATURAL.

CLEAN BILL A BILL OF LADING reflecting the fact that goods being shipped are in good order. See also DIRTY BILL OF LADING.

CLEAN FLOAT   [COL] The practice of a CENTRAL BANK or monetary authority not to intervene in the FOREIGN EXCHANGE markets to influence the value of its CURRENCY. See also DIRTY FLOAT, STERILIZATION.

CLEAN OPINION   See UNQUALIFIED OPINION.

CLEAN PRICE   [COL] The price of a BOND quoted without ACCRUED INTEREST. See also DIRTY PRICE.

CLEAN RISK   See SETTLEMENT RISK.

CLEANUP REQUIREMENT   A requirement that a BORROWER regularly repay all funds drawn under a REVOLVING CREDIT FACILITY as a way of demonstrating its ability to generate FINANCING from other sources. Inability to meet the clean-up requirement may lead to a cancellation of the facility.

CLEARED BALANCE   The balance in a BANK ACCOUNT that reflects only items that have already been cleared and excluding those that are not yet classed as having cleared value.

CLEARING   (1) All services performed after the EXECUTION of a SECURITIES TRADE, except SETTLEMENT. (2) A process where all EXCHANGE-TRADED DERIVATIVES executed during a TRADING session are registered and reassigned to the CLEARINGHOUSE. Once reassigned, the clearinghouse becomes the official trade COUNTERPARTY on every transaction (which, along with a client's posting of MARGIN, helps to mitigate the effects of counterparty CREDIT RISK). (3) The exchange between BANKS and other FINANCIAL INSTITUTIONS of any CHECKS, DRAFTS, and NOTES, with a net sum paid or received. (2) See also CLEARING MARGIN, CLEARING MEMBER, HORIZONTAL CLEARING SERVICES.

CLEARING BANK   In the United Kingdom, a large retail or wholesale COMMERCIAL BANK. See also HIGH STREET BANK.

CLEARING CYCLE   The phases that comprise the transfer of cash or value from the PAYER to the PAYEE, typically spanning several days.

CLEARING MARGIN   MARGIN posted by a CLEARING MEMBER with an EXCHANGE on behalf of clients or proprietary accounts. See also INITIAL MARGIN, VARIATION MARGIN.

CLEARING MEMBER   An EXCHANGE member that is permitted to clear trades directly with the CLEARINGHOUSE, and which can accept trades for other clearing members and NONCLEARING MEMBERS.

CLEARINGHOUSE   (1) In the DERIVATIVES market, a SUBSIDIARY or division of an EXCHANGE or an independently owned entity that is responsible for CLEARING listed FUTURES and OPTIONS TRADES, computing and collecting daily MARGIN, and arranging for SETTLEMENT of financial or physical ASSETS related to trades. The CREDIT RISK normally associated with derivatives is neutralized as participants face the CLEARINGHOUSE, rather than each other, as their COUNTERPARTY. (2) In BANKING, a group of institutions that exchanges CHECKS, DRAFTS, and payment orders on a net basis, resulting in the creation of clearinghouse funds that are accessible within one to three business days. (2) See also CLEARINGHOUSE AUTOMATED PAYMENT SYSTEM, CLEARINGHOUSE INTERBANK PAYMENT SYSTEM.

CLEARINGHOUSE AUTOMATED PAYMENT SYSTEM (CHAPS) An automated CLEARINGHOUSE system in the United Kingdom that is used for large-value, same-day sterling transfers related to DRAFTS and payments. See also BANKERS' AUTOMATED CLEARING SYSTEM (BACS).

CLEARINGHOUSE INTERBANK PAYMENT SYSTEM (CHIPS) A private sector, fully automated CLEARINGHOUSE system in the United States that is used for dollar-based CHECKS and fund transfers, as well as payments associated with SECURITIES transactions and FOREIGN EXCHANGE TRADES.

CLEARSTREAM A European organization responsible for SETTLEMENT and CLEARING of EUROBONDS, created from the merger of Cedel and Deutsche Borse in 2000. See also EUROCLEAR.

CLIQUET OPTION An OVER-THE-COUNTER COMPLEX OPTION that allows the buyer to lock in gains at prespecified evaluation intervals if the option is IN-THE-MONEY at such points; gains are not relinquished if the market subsequently retraces. If the option is OUT-OF-THE-MONEY on an evaluation date the STRIKE PRICE resets AT-THE-MONEY based on the new market level. Also known as a RATCHET OPTION. See also LADDER OPTION, SHOUT OPTION.

CLO See COLLATERALIZED LOAN OBLIGATION.

CLO EQUITY The RESIDUAL TRANCHE of COLLATERALIZED LOAN OBLIGATION (CLO). The equity tranche stands as the FIRST LOSS PIECE in the SECURITIZATION, and is entitled to a portion of CASH FLOWS once the senior and subordinated tranches have received their payouts.

CLONE FUND [COL] A MUTUAL FUND or UNIT TRUST that attempts to replicate an existing fund through the use of DERIVATIVES rather than actual SECURITIES.

CLOSE COMPANY A company that is under the control of a small number of DIRECTORS or participants or where the participants would receive more than 50% of ASSETS in the event of LIQUIDATION. Close companies may be subject to different TAX rules. See also CLOSELY HELD COMPANY, PRIVATE COMPANY.

CLOSE-OUT The process of establishing an equal and opposite DERIVATIVE or ASSET position in order to neutralize or offset the RISK of an existing position. Although the close-out cancels the effects of risk, it grosses up the NOTIONAL amount of the contracts, which remain outstanding until final MATURITY.

CLOSE-OUT NETTING A contractual agreement where an institution and a COUNTERPARTY in DEFAULT agree to ACCELERATION, termination, and NETTING of all financial transactions. See also PAYMENT NETTING, SET-OFF.

CLOSED ECONOMY   An economy that is isolated and self-contained, engaging in no TRADE or commercial dealings with other economies.

CLOSED-END FUND   An INVESTMENT COMPANY that raises CAPITAL by issuing a limited number of SHARES on an EXCHANGE, and invests proceeds in a range of ASSETS on behalf of INVESTORS. Once the initial PORTFOLIO of assets is assembled no new securities are added and few, if any, are sold prior to final MATURITY. The fund generally provides investors with a fixed RETURN and typically allows no REDEMPTIONS prior to the stated maturity. Closed-end funds often invest in BONDS or other assets that are ILLIQUID or difficult to price. See also MUTUAL FUND. Also known as INVESTMENT TRUST, UNIT INVESTMENT TRUST.

CLOSELY HELD COMPANY   A company where no more than five individuals hold the controlling SHARES in the company; the SHAREHOLDERS may also be the primary managers. All closely held companies are PRIVATE COMPANIES, though not all private companies need be closely held.

CLOSING BALANCE   The final balance held on a ledger account after taking account of all DEBITS and CREDITS occurring during the reporting period; the balance is carried forward to the next reporting period.

CLOSING BELL   [COL] A signal marking the official close of the trading day on an EXCHANGE, typically announced via the ringing of an electronic bell. While the closing bell marks the end of official trading on an exchange, activity can still continue through AFTER HOURS TRADING.

CLOSING PRICE   The final price posted for a traded ASSET (e.g., STOCK, BOND, COMMODITY) at the end of trading day.

CLUB DEAL   [COL] A form of SYNDICATED LOAN that is jointly entered into by a small group of BANKS as a way of sharing the RISKS, CAPITAL INVESTMENT, and REVENUES; the club deal, which is managed by the ARRANGER, is generally used for smaller loan deals. Club deals can also apply to financings of LEVERAGED BUYOUTS, where PRIVATE EQUITY firms may join with banks in supplying funds.

CMBS   See COMMERCIAL MORTGAGE-BACKED SECURITY.

CME   See CHICAGO MERCANTILE EXCHANGE.

CMO   See COLLATERALIZED MORTGAGE OBLIGATION.

CMS   See CONSTANT MATURITY SWAP.

CMT   See CONSTANT MATURITY TREASURY.

COAT-TAILING   [COL] The practice of replicating the INVESTMENT strategies of INSTITUTIONAL INVESTORS who are known, or believed, to have exhibited good performance. Also known as PIGGYBACKING. See also TAILGATING.

COD (CASH ON DELIVERY)   See DELIVERY VERSUS PAYMENT.

COEFFICIENT OF DETERMINATION   A statistical measure that indicates the proportion of variability in a set of data observations that are accounted for by a given model, or the degree to which an observation varies from its BENCHMARK. The coefficient is measured on a scale of 0.0 to 1.0, with a result migrating toward 1.0 indicating a greater level of explanation. Also known as R-SQUARED.

COINSURANCE   A feature of an INSURANCE CONTRACT that results in a sharing of losses between the INSURED and INSURER on a predetermined basis once any DEDUCTIBLE has been met. The insurer's total obligation under an insurance contract with a coinsurance feature is generally computed via:

$$Coins_{pmt} = L\left(\frac{Ins}{V(Co)}\right)$$

where L is the amount of the loss, Ins is the amount of insurance carried, V is the value of the insured property, and Co is the coinsurance clause percentage.

Indemnification can never exceed the amount dictated by the coinsurance relationship, the POLICY CAP, or the amount of the actual loss.

COLD CALLING   [COL] A practice, used by BROKERS, of making unsolicited sales or marketing calls to gain new INVESTOR clients. Such calls are made without specific leads or targets, and may involve sourcing names from electronic directories.

COLLAR   A SPREAD consisting of a LONG CALL OPTION and a SHORT PUT OPTION, or long put and short call, with the same EXPIRY DATE. The LONG POSITION (which requires payment of PREMIUM) is intended to provide RISK protection or speculative opportunity, while the SHORT POSITION (which results in receipt of premium) helps defray, and in some cases eliminate, the cost of the long option.

Payoff profile of long collar

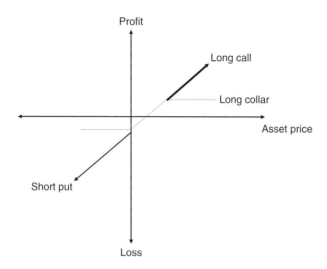

Also known as FENCE, RANGE FORWARD. See also ZERO COST COLLAR.

COLLATERAL   ASSETS, such as cash, SECURITIES, ACCOUNTS RECEIVABLE, INVENTORY, LETTERS OF CREDIT, or physical property, taken to secure a CREDIT RISK exposure. By taking collateral, the CREDITOR has an additional source of repayment should its COUNTERPARTY be unable to perform on its obligations. See also SECURITY.

COLLATERAL POOL   The ASSET PORTFOLIO that underlies a SECURITIZATION transaction. The pool is used to both secure the ASSET-BACKED SECURITIES (ABS) issued to INVESTORS and to generate CASH FLOWS which provide PRINCIPAL and INTEREST on the ABS. The pool generally comprises of a single form of asset (e.g., MORTGAGES, ACCOUNTS RECEIVABLE, automobile LOANS, and so forth), and is typically well diversified across obligors, regions, and sectors (though certain WHOLE LOAN securitizations are backed by a single large asset). The pool may be static (unchanging over the expected life of the securitization) or it may be dynamic (with substitution permitted).

COLLATERAL RISK   The RISK of loss arising from errors in the nature, quantity, pricing, or characteristics of COLLATERAL securing a transaction with CREDIT RISK. Institutions that actively accept and deliver collateral and are unable to manage the process accurately are susceptible to loss. A subcategory of OPERATIONAL RISK.

COLLATERAL TRUST BOND   A BOND secured by a PORTFOLIO of ASSETS owned by the ISSUER. Unlike a PASS-THROUGH SECURITY, the issuer retains sole ownership interest in the assets, which remain on the corporate BALANCE SHEET. See also MORTGAGE-BACKED BOND.

COLLATERALIZED BOND OBLIGATION (CBO)   A SECURITIZATION structure that repackages CREDIT-risky BONDS into TRANCHES with unique RISK and RETURN profiles. See also COLLATERALIZED DEBT OBLIGATION.

COLLATERALIZED DEBT OBLIGATION (CDO)   A SECURITIZATION structure that repackages CREDIT-risky instruments (such as LOANS, BONDS, or CREDIT DERIVATIVES) into TRANCHES with unique RISK and RETURN profiles. A CDO can be created by a sponsoring BANK or SECURITIES FIRM to transfer the DEFAULT risk in its credit PORTFOLIO to INVESTORS (BALANCE SHEET CDO) or to take advantage of profit opportunities in repackaging SECURITIES (ARBITRAGE CDO). A CDO can be structured as a COLLATERALIZED LOAN OBLIGATION (e.g., pools of loans) or COLLATERALIZED BOND OBLIGATION (e.g., pools of bonds) and can be created using physical instruments (CASH CDO) or credit derivatives (SYNTHETIC CDO). Portfolios may be managed statically (i.e., the portfolio is acquired and held until maturity) or dynamically (i.e., the portfolio changes during the life of the transaction, within certain parameters).

COLLATERALIZED LOAN OBLIGATION (CLO)   A SECURITIZATION structure that repackages CREDIT-risky LOANS into TRANCHES with unique RISK and RETURN profiles. See also COLLATERALIZED DEBT OBLIGATION.

COLLATERALIZED MORTGAGE OBLIGATION (CMO)   A SECURITIZATION structure that repackages pools of MORTGAGE-BACKED SECURITIES, WHOLE LOANS, or mortgage-backed STRIPS into TRANCHES with specific RISK and return (YIELD) profiles. CMO structures are available in many different forms, some of them esoteric, risky, and ILLIQUID. However, the largest portion of the market is centered on standard instruments with manageable RISK and LIQUIDITY parameters. The most common version of the CMO is based on sequential pay tranching, with COUPON payments, and then PRINCIPAL payments, allocated to INVESTORS in order of priority. Once all the tranches have been retired in sequence, the remaining ACCRUAL BOND (Z-BOND) is paid; since the accrual bond receives no CASH FLOWS until all others have been paid, it protects the cash flow payment stream for the entire structure. See also COMPANION BOND, INTEREST-ONLY STRIP, PLANNED AMORTIZATION CLASS BOND, PRINCIPAL-ONLY STRIP, TARGETED AMORTIZATION CLASS BOND.

COLLECTING BANK   (1) A BANK which is presented with an order for payment (e.g., a CHECK). (2) In TRADE CREDIT, a bank collecting payment from a buyer in exchange for a BILL OF LADING; the bank then forwards the payment to the seller's bank. (1) Also known as REMITTING BANK. (1,2) See also PAYOR BANK.

COLLECTION POLICY   The procedures established by a company that offers TRADE CREDIT to its customers, delineating the specific actions to be taken if a customer account has become delinquent. Such actions tend to increase in terms of escalation, often culminating in the transfer of delinquent ACCOUNTS RECEIVABLE to a collection agency.

COLLUSION   A practice where parties act in concert, but without any formal agreement, to set or fix prices on a good, service, or ASSET. Collusion is considered illegal in many national systems, as it reflects anticompetitive behavior. See also CARTEL.

COMBINED RATIO   A measure of an INSURER's profitability that compares earned PREMIUMS to losses from expenses and CLAIMS. The combined ratio is a summation of the LOSS RATIO and the EXPENSE RATIO, and is given as:

$$CR = \frac{L + LAE + IE}{Pr}$$

where L is the loss (from claims), LAE is LOSS ADJUSTMENT EXPENSE, IE is incurred expense (e.g., from UNDERWRITING activities), and Pr is premium.

If the ratio is greater than 100 the INSURANCE underwriting business is unprofitable, if it is less than 100 it is profitable.

COMFORT LETTER   A letter issued by a PARENT company to a BANK or other financial institution extending CREDIT indicating that it is aware of the fact that its SUBSIDIARY or AFFILIATE is seeking funds. The comfort letter does not serve as a legal GUARANTEE, suggesting that the bank has no RECOURSE to the parent should the subsidiary or affiliate DEFAULT. Also known as LETTER OF COMFORT.

COMMAND ECONOMY   An economic system where the government owns and operates the primary means of production and distribution, and controls the allocation of resources and the establishment of prices. The central planning and management characteristic of the command economy discourage competition. Also known as PLANNED ECONOMY. See also FREE MARKET ECONOMY.

COMMERCIAL BANK   A FINANCIAL INSTITUTION that is permitted through regulatory approval and CORPORATE CHARTER to accept retail and INTERBANK DEPOSITS, extend commercial and retail LOANS, and perform various INTERMEDIATION and FIDUCIARY duties. In some national systems commercial banks focus strictly on traditional banking services, while in others they have a broader scope, engaging in activities commonly associated with INVESTMENT BANKS or SECURITIES FIRMS, such as UNDERWRITING and TRADING of SECURITIES. See also BANCASSURANCE, BANK, UNIVERSAL BANK.

COMMERCIAL BILL   See BILL OF EXCHANGE.

COMMERCIAL GENERAL LIABILITY POLICY   An INSURANCE CONTRACT used by a firm seeking to cover RISK exposures to several LIABILITIES simultaneously, such as those arising from premises, products, contracts, contingencies, environmental damage, and FIDUCIARY breaches. See also COMMERCIAL UMBRELLA POLICY, MULTILINE POLICY, MULTIPLE PERIL POLICY.

COMMERCIAL LINES   The general category of INSURANCE coverage for business organizations (rather than individuals), including institutionally focused policies such as the COMMERCIAL GENERAL LIABILITY POLICY, COMMERCIAL UMBRELLA POLICY, and MULTILINE POLICY.

COMMERCIAL LOAN   A LOAN arranged and extended by a BANK or FINANCIAL INSTITUTION to a BORROWER. The loan may have a fixed or floating INTEREST RATE and PRINCIPAL repayment that amortizes according to a set schedule or which is in the form of a BALLOON LOAN or BULLET LOAN. The loan may be unsecured, or secured on a borrower's ASSETS.

COMMERCIAL MORTGAGE   A MORTGAGE that is granted to support the financing of a commercial property, such as an office building, industrial complex, retail center, hotel, or multifamily housing complex. A typical commercial mortgage is structured as a NONRECOURSE BALLOON LOAN with a 5 to 10 year MATURITY, though INTEREST-only options and longer maturities can also be arranged. PREPAYMENT of a commercial mortgage is unusual as a result of defined lockout periods as well as significant prepayment penalties.

COMMERCIAL MORTGAGE-BACKED SECURITY (CMBS) A form of MORTGAGE-BACKED SECURITY where the COLLATERAL pool underlying the security is comprised of COMMERCIAL MORTGAGES. In contrast to RESIDENTIAL MORTGAGE-BACKED SECURITIES, commercial mortgages do not feature unlimited ability to prepay, meaning PREPAYMENT RISK is relatively low and security cash flows are rather more predictable. A standard CMBS is structured as a PASS-THROUGH SECURITY, giving INVESTORS partial ownership in a pool of commercial mortgage assets and the attendant PRINCIPAL and INTEREST payments that occur over the life of the transaction. The commercial mortgage assets typically take one of five forms: traditional LOANS (pools where no single loan is greater than 10% of the total), large loans (pools where several loans may be greater than 10% of the total), fusion (pools where only a few loans may be greater than 10% of the total), LEASES (pools secured by property leases), and single assets (a pool with only a single loan/BORROWER). Since CMBS do not benefit from explicit GUARANTEES, numerous TRANCHES of various ratings are created through the SUBORDINATION mechanism.

COMMERCIAL PAPER (CP) Short-term, unsecured DISCOUNT DEBT SECURITIES issued by highly rated financial companies (as FINANCIAL PAPER) and industrial companies (as INDUSTRIAL PAPER) in a domestic market or in the EUROMARKETS (as EURO CP). Although most CP is unsecured, there is also a market for ASSET-BACKED CP and LETTER OF CREDIT-backed CP. CP programs are partially backed by SWINGLINES so that ISSUERS can access funds in the event they are unable to renew or roll over maturing notes. In the US market CP MATURITIES range from overnight to 270 days, while in the Euromarkets maximum maturity may extend to 360 days; the most common maturities in both markets are in the 14 to 30 day sector. Most CP is issued via DEALERS in the form of BEARER SECURITIES, although issues of REGISTERED SECURITIES are possible.

COMMERCIAL REAL ESTATE BOND A NONRECOURSE BOND that is secured by a specific commercial property or PORTFOLIO of properties. The bond may have a fixed or floating COUPON and a MATURITY that is medium- to long-term.

COMMERCIAL UMBRELLA POLICY An INSURANCE CONTRACT that provides protection for very large exposure amounts (well in excess of those that might be obtained through a standard PROPERTY AND CASUALTY INSURANCE POLICY, a COMMERCIAL GENERAL LIABILITY POLICY or a MULTILINE POLICY). The umbrella policy covers a broad range of INSURABLE RISKS, but serves as an EXCESS LAYER facility rather than a FIRST LOSS cover. See also MULTIPLE PERIL POLICY.

COMMISSION (1) A fee paid by a client to a BROKER for services rendered in arranging the EXECUTION of a TRADE. (2) A fee levied on the sale or purchase of real estate. (1) Also known as BROKERAGE.

COMMISSION BROKER See BROKER.

COMMISSIONE NAZIONALE PER LA SOCIETA E LA BORSA (CONSOB)   [ITA] The Italian Securities and Exchange Commission, established in 1974 to regulate, monitor, and control activities in the domestic financial markets. Its specific duties include regulating INVESTMENT services and intermediaries, authorizing controls and disclosures related to financial instruments, and monitoring TRADING activities.

COMMITMENT FEE   An upfront or annual fee a BANK charges a customer for providing COMMITTED FUNDING or a REVOLVING CREDIT FACILITY. Payment of the commitment fee ensures the facility will not be withdrawn prior to its stated MATURITY and the BORROWER will have access to the funds when needed, presuming no COVENANTS have been breached. Also known as FACILITY FEE.

COMMITTED FACILITY   See COMMITTED FUNDING.

COMMITTED FUNDING   A FINANCING facility provided by a BANK to a BORROWER, which the bank cannot withdraw unless the borrower breaches COVENANTS or other terms of the facility; this means the bank must provide funds when called on to do so, regardless of the market environment or borrower's financial condition. Funding facilities where the borrower has paid a COMMITMENT FEE and executed a CREDIT agreement without a MATERIAL ADVERSE CHANGE CLAUSE or CONTINGENT TRIGGER may be regarded as committed. Also known as COMMITTED FACILITY, COMMITTED LINE. See also BANK LINE, REVOLVING CREDIT FACILITY.

COMMITTED LINE   See COMMITTED FUNDING.

COMMITTED UNDERWRITING   See BOUGHT DEAL.

COMMITTEE OF EUROPEAN SECURITIES REGULATORS (CESR)   A body, formed in 2001, consisting of the SECURITIES REGULATORS of all EUROPEAN UNION nations, tasked with creating a uniform approach to REGULATION, advising the European Commission on relevant matters, and helping to implement practical rules and regulations on a timely basis.

COMMITTEE ON UNIFORM SECURITIES IDENTIFICATION PROCEDURES (CUSIP)   A 9-digit SECURITY identification code assigned by Standard and Poor's to US and Canadian BONDS and STOCKS. The first 6 digits identify the ISSUER, the next 2 digits identify the type of security issued, and the final digit serves as a check. See also CUSIP INTERNATIONAL NUMBER, INTERNATIONAL SECURITIES IDENTIFICATION NUMBER, STOCK EXCHANGE DAILY OFFICIAL LIST.

COMMODITY   A nonfinancial good representing an input or raw material for production or consumption. A commodity can be bought or sold in the COMMODITY MARKETS in cash or DERIVATIVE form, and can be divided into various sectors, including:

Precious Metals: Gold, Silver, Platinum, Palladium, Iridium, Osmium, Rhodium, Ruthenium

Industrial Metals: Aluminum, Chrome, Copper, Lead, Mercury, Nickel, Selenium, Tin, Titanium, Zinc

Energy: Crude oil, Gas oil, Heating oil, Unleaded gasoline, Natural gas, Coal

Livestock: Feeder cattle, Live cattle, Live hogs, Pork bellies

SOFTS: Coffee, Cocoa, Cotton, Orange Juice, Rubber, Sugar, Silk, Timber, Wool

GRAINS: Beans, Barley, Canola, Corn, Millet, Oats, Oilseed, Rice, Rye, Sorghum, Soybeans, Soybean meal, Wheat

COMMODITY BROKER   A BROKER that deals exclusively with clients in the COMMODITY markets, often specializing in a specific segment of the market (e.g., SOFTS, energy complex, metals complex). Commodity brokers are permitted to disclose their PRINCIPALS in certain markets, but not in all markets. See also FOREIGN EXCHANGE BROKER, INTER-DEALER BROKER.

COMMODITY DERIVATIVE   An EXCHANGE-TRADED DERIVATIVE or OVER-THE-COUNTER DERIVATIVE with an UNDERLYING reference based on nonfinancial COMMODITIES including chemicals, energy, base and precious metals, livestock, GRAINS, and SOFTS. A commodity derivative can be structured as a COMMODITY FUTURE, commodity FORWARD, commodity OPTION, or COMMODITY SWAP. See also CREDIT DERIVATIVE, CURRENCY DERIVATIVE, EQUITY DERIVATIVE, INTEREST RATE DERIVATIVE.

COMMODITY EXCHANGE-TRADED FUND   An EXCHANGE-TRADED FUND (ETF) that invests in physical COMMODITIES or in a recognized commodity INDEX. Commodity ETFs that gain exposure through DERIVATIVE contracts introduce a degree of LEVERAGE into their operation.

COMMODITY FUTURE   A FUTURES contract, bought or sold via an EXCHANGE, which references a nonfinancial physical commodity such as chemicals, energy, base and precious metals, livestock, GRAINS, and SOFTS. See also COMMODITY DERIVATIVE, CURRENCY FUTURE, INDEX FUTURE, INTEREST RATE FUTURE.

COMMODITY FUTURES TRADING COMMISSION (CFTC)   A US regulatory agency, established in 1974, that is responsible for overseeing the EXCHANGE-TRADED DERIVATIVE marketplace. It assigns certain daily regulatory monitoring duties to SELF-REGULATORY ORGANIZATIONS, including the National Futures Association and individual EXCHANGES.

COMMODITY MARKET   The general marketplace for buying and selling of COMMODITIES. The commodity market allows commodity producers to sell their INVENTORIES, and users (including consumers, HEDGERS, and SPECULATORS) to access the same commodities in physical, financial, or DERIVATIVE form. Each national commodity market has its own characteristics, procedures, and conventions, and TRADING may occur either via an EXCHANGE (electronic or physical) or OVER-THE-COUNTER. See also BOND MARKET, FOREIGN EXCHANGE MARKET, STOCK MARKET.

COMMODITY OPTION   An EXCHANGE-TRADED or OVER-THE-COUNTER OPTION involving a COMMODITY. VANILLA and COMPLEX OPTIONS can be bought and sold on a variety of commodities, and may be contracted for PHYSICAL SETTLEMENT or CASH SETTLEMENT. See also CURRENCY OPTION, EQUITY OPTION, INDEX OPTION, INTEREST RATE OPTION.

COMMODITY POOL   A pool of INVESTMENT CAPITAL, similar to a MUTUAL FUND or UNIT TRUST, that is invested by professional money managers solely in COMMODITY FUTURES and OPTIONS.

COMMODITY RISK   The RISK of loss due to an adverse move in the direction of COMMODITY prices. Commodity risk is a form of DIRECTIONAL RISK.

COMMODITY SWAP   An OVER-THE-COUNTER SWAP transaction involving the exchange of fixed and floating COMMODITY price references. Commodity swaps can be written on virtually any physical commodity (e.g., chemicals, energy, base and precious metals, livestock, GRAINS, and SOFTS) and can be structured to settle in cash or physical terms. See also COMMODITY DERIVATIVE.

COMMODITY TRADING ADVISOR (CTA)   An INVESTMENT ADVISOR that develops and executes INVESTMENT strategies for COMMODITY POOLS.

COMMON MARKET   See EUROPEAN ECONOMIC COMMUNITY.

COMMON SHARES   In the United Kingdom, COMMON STOCK.

COMMON STOCK   A CAPITAL instrument representing an ownership interest in a company. An INVESTOR in a company's common stock is granted RENT RIGHTS, including any DIVIDENDS that are declared and a share in any future capital appreciation, and CONTROL RIGHTS, including the ability to vote on specific issues at the ANNUAL GENERAL MEETING, file direct and derivative lawsuits, and receive regular financial information. Also known as EQUITY, ORDINARY SHARE, STOCK. See also PREFERRED STOCK.

COMPANION BOND   A TRANCHE of a COLLATERALIZED MORTGAGE OBLIGATION that accompanies PLANNED AMORTIZATION CLASS (PAC) BONDS and TARGETED AMORTIZATION CLASS (TAC) BONDS. The companion serves to absorb PREPAYMENT RISK, giving PACs and TACs greater CASH FLOW, and thus price stability. Also known as SUPPORT BOND.

COMPANY FORMATION   In the United Kingdom, the process of forming a company, which includes sending required information to the Registrar of Companies , indicating compliance with the provisions of the Companies Act, and providing the actual ARTICLES OF ASSOCIATION and MEMORANDUM OF ASSOCIATION.

COMPANY LIMITED BY GUARANTEE   In the United Kingdom, a company that does not issue SHARES and whose LIABILITIES are limited to the amounts noted in the MEMORANDUM OF ASSOCIATION. See also COMPANY LIMITED BY SHARES.

COMPANY LIMITED BY SHARES   In the United Kingdom, a company that issues SHARES and whose LIABILITIES are limited to the value of the shares, as noted in the MEMORANDUM OF ASSOCIATION. See also COMPANY LIMITED BY GUARANTEE.

COMPARABLES TRANSACTION ANALYSIS   See RELATIVE VALUATION.

COMPENSATING BALANCE   A non-interest-bearing DEMAND DEPOSIT placed by a customer with a BANK to compensate for LOANS or other services granted.

COMPETITION COMMISSION (CC)   In the United Kingdom, a body established in 1998 that ensures antiMONOPOLY and free competition rules are upheld, particularly as related to MERGERS and ACQUISITIONS. The work of the Commission is nonbinding and must be referred to the Office of Fair Trading for enforcement. The CC replaced the original Monopolies and Mergers Commission and Restrictive Practices Court.

COMPETITIVE BID   A BID submitted in an AUCTION MARKET process that is placed in direct competition with other bids, meaning it will only be filled if it ranks at, or near, the highest price/lowest YIELD. See also NONCOMPETITIVE BID.

COMPETITIVE BID UNDERWRITING   An UNDERWRITING of a NEW ISSUE of SECURITIES that is awarded by the issuing company to the UNDERWRITER that proposes the most favorable terms (generally a combination of lowest YIELD, lowest fees, broadest distribution, and strongest research and SECONDARY TRADING support). See also BEAUTY CONTEST, NEGOTIATED UNDERWRITING.

COMPETITIVE TENDER   A general process where a company acquires goods or services by extending to suppliers an invitation to tender a proposal. In general, the tender with the lowest price wins the order, although quality, shipping, timeliness, and efficiency may also be factors.

COMPLETION BOND   A GUARANTEE provided by an INSURER to a BANK, which is financing a project, that the bank will be repaid even if the project fails to be completed. See also PERFORMANCE BOND, SURETY BOND.

COMPLETION RISK   In PROJECT FINANCE, the RISK that a project will not be completed as scheduled, leading to difficulties in servicing contracted DEBT.

COMPLEX CHOOSER OPTION   An OVER-THE-COUNTER COMPLEX OPTION that permits the buyer to choose between an underlying CALL OPTION (with a certain STRIKE PRICE and MATURITY) and an underlying PUT OPTION (with a different strike and maturity) between trade date and choice date. See also CHOOSER OPTION.

COMPLEX OPTION   A conventional OPTION that is modified with respect to time, price, and/or payoff to produce unique RISK MANAGEMENT, INVESTMENT, or speculative results. Certain complex options have risky payoffs/LIABILITIES and demand considerable technical resources to ensure proper pricing and management. Also known as EXOTIC OPTION. See also COMPLEX STRUCTURED PRODUCT, COMPLEX SWAP, PATH-DEPENDENT OPTION, PATH-INDEPENDENT OPTION.

COMPLEX STRUCTURED PRODUCT   A CAPITAL MARKETS instrument, such as a BOND or NOTE, that contains embedded COMPLEX OPTIONS or COMPLEX SWAPS that alter RISK and RETURN characteristics in unique ways. Since complex structured products are highly customized they are often issued on a PRIVATE PLACEMENT basis and tend to feature very limited LIQUIDITY. See also STRUCTURED NOTE.

COMPLEX SWAP   An OVER-THE-COUNTER SWAP that is modified with respect to time, price, NOTIONAL PRINCIPAL, and/or payoff to produce unique RISK MANAGEMENT, INVESTMENT, or speculative results. Certain complex swaps have risky payoffs/LIABILITIES and demand considerable technical resources to ensure proper pricing and management. Also known as EXOTIC SWAP. See also COMPLEX OPTION, COMPLEX STRUCTURED PRODUCT.

COMPLIANCE   The processes used by BANKS and other FINANCIAL INSTI-TUTIONS to ensure adherence to the legal and regulatory rules governing their business.

COMPOSITE PEG   A MANAGED FOREIGN EXCHANGE RATE policy where a country's CENTRAL BANK or monetary authority pegs the value of its CUR-RENCY to a basket of several other currencies. See also SINGLE PEG.

COMPOUND OPTION   An OVER-THE-COUNTER COMPLEX OPTION that allows the buyer to EXERCISE into a second underlying option. Compound options are available in four forms, including a CALL ON A CALL (the right to buy an underlying CALL OPTION), a CALL ON A PUT (the right to buy an underlying PUT OPTION), a PUT ON A CALL (the right to sell an underlying call), and a PUT ON PUT (the right to sell an underlying put). Also known as NESTED OPTION.

COMPOUND OPTION STRATEGY   A package of OPTIONS created to pro-vide unique RISK MANAGEMENT, INVESTMENT, or speculative results that cannot be achieved through simple positions. Common compound strat-egies include COLLARS, CONDOR SPREADS, BUTTERFLY SPREADS, BULL SPREADS, BEAR SPREADS, STRADDLES, STRANGLES, and TIME SPREADS. See also DIRECTIONAL STRATEGY, SPREAD, VOLATILITY STRATEGY.

COMPOUNDING   The process of adding periodic INTEREST to an interest-bearing ASSET or LIABILITY, increasing the FUTURE VALUE to the INVESTOR or CREDITOR and LIABILITY to the BORROWER. Compounding can be com-puted in simple or complex form via the following:

Simple compounding:

$$FV = PV \, (1 + (t \, r))$$

Annual compounding:

$$FV = PV \, (1 + r)^t$$

Annual compounding, n times per year:

$$FV = PV \, (1 + (r/n))^{tn}$$

Continuous compounding:

$$FV = PV \, e^{rt}$$

where PV is the PRESENT VALUE of the sum invested or borrowed, r is the DISCOUNT RATE, t is the time to maturity, n is the number of compounding periods per year, and e is the exponential constant.

COMPREHENSIVE GENERAL LIABILITY A COMMERCIAL LINE of INSURANCE providing the INSURED with protection against all exposures except those specifically excluded, generally those arising from products, premises, and actions of independent contractors.

COMPS [COL] Abbreviation for "comparables": (1) A retailer's comparable same-store sales, allowing period-on–period comparison of expansion or contraction. (2) Proxy companies that can be used to provide additional pricing information for an INITIAL PUBLIC OFFERING of a new company's STOCK issue.

COMPTROLLER   See CONTROLLER.

COMPULSORY LIQUIDATION   In the United Kingdom, a process where the courts require the LIQUIDATION of a company, either through the official RECEIVER who acts in a temporary capacity, or through a court-appointed provisional LIQUIDATOR. See also CREDITORS' VOLUNTARY LIQUIDATION.

CONCENTRATION RISK   The RISK of loss arising from a large position in a single ASSET or market exposure. An excessive concentration can give rise to LIQUIDITY RISK or MARKET RISK losses.

CONCERT PARTY   [COL] A group of SPECULATORS who band together to quietly acquire COMMON STOCK in a company, either to deflect attention prior to a public TAKEOVER offer (legal) or to avoid disclosure rules (which may be illegal).

CONCURRENCY   The process of ensuring that the terms and conditions of multiple REINSURANCE CONTRACTS are synchronized so that no gaps or overlaps in RISK coverage exist.

CONDITIONAL PREPAYMENT RATE (CPR)   A PREPAYMENT rate used to value MORTGAGE-BACKED SECURITIES and COLLATERALIZED MORTGAGE OBLIGATIONS, generally computed as an annualized rate of monthly prepayments to outstanding pooled MORTGAGES.

CONDITIONAL PUT CONVERTIBLE BOND A CONVERTIBLE BOND with a PUT OPTION feature that allows INVESTORS to sell the SECURITY back to the ISSUER under certain market conditions (i.e., the underlying STOCK price reaches a particular level). See also PUTABLE CONVERTIBLE BOND.

CONDOR SPREAD   A COMPOUND OPTION STRATEGY designed to take advantage of VOLATILITY. Condors are created with the same ratio of PUT OPTIONS or CALL OPTIONS (i.e., one low STRIKE PRICE, one middle low strike, one middle high strike, one high strike) that expire at the same time. SHORT condors, similar to LONG STRANGLES without the extreme upside, consist of short low and high strike options and long middle low and high strike options. Long condors, similar to short strangles without the extreme downside, consist of long low and high strike options and short middle low and high strike options.

Payoff profile of long condor

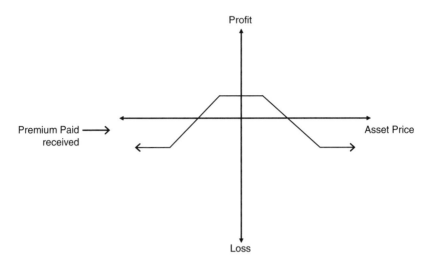

Payoff profile of short condor

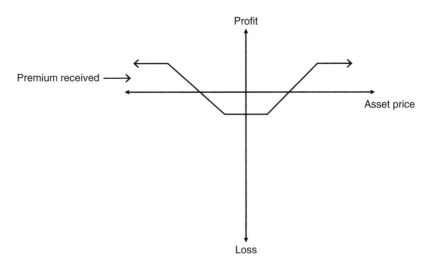

See also BUTTERFLY SPREAD.

CONDUIT   A SPECIAL PURPOSE ENTITY or TRUST that is used to acquire ASSETS forming part of a SECURITIZATION or ASSET-BACKED COMMERCIAL PAPER (ABCP) program. The conduit may be associated with (if not owned) by a private firm (e.g., a BANK or SECURITIES FIRM as sponsor), or it may be associated with a governmental or sovereign agency. The sponsor sells or conveys earmarked assets to the conduit, which accumulates them until the full asset PORTFOLIO is created. Once complete, the conduit issues NOTES or ABCP to INVESTORS under the terms of the securitization, or it sells the portfolio to a separate note-issuing vehicle. Conduits may accept assets from one seller or multiple sellers, and may be fully or partly supported by a third party GUARANTEE or LETTER OF CREDIT to minimize LIQUIDITY RISK and/ or CREDIT RISK.

CONFIDENCE LEVEL   A statistical interval that contains the actual parameter value of the population sampled to a stated PROBABILITY (e.g., 90%, 95%, 99%). The width of the confidence level is an increasing function of the probability required, and a decreasing function of sample size. Confidence levels are widely used in certain financial applications, including ACTUARIAL PRICING, CREDIT RISK models, and VALUE-AT-RISK models.

CONFIRMATION   A paper document or electronic slate that confirms all necessary details regarding a TRADE between two parties. The confirmation, which contains pertinent information related to trade size, price, reference ASSET/INDEX, CASH FLOWS, PREMIUM, fees, and SETTLEMENT, can be created in a manner that makes it legally binding on both parties.

CONFIRMED LETTER OF CREDIT   A transaction where a BANK *de facto* GUARANTEES ("confirms") an underlying LETTER OF CREDIT issued by another bank. If the original bank fails to perform under its contractual obligation, the confirming bank becomes liable to the BENEFICIARY. Confirmation often occurs when the original bank is small, less creditworthy, or located in a jurisdiction subject to a high degree of SOVEREIGN RISK. See also DIRECT PAY LETTER OF CREDIT, IRREVOCABLE LETTER OF CREDIT, STANDBY LETTER OF CREDIT, TRANSFERABLE LETTER OF CREDIT.

CONFIRMED LINE   See ADVISED LINE.

CONGLOMERATE MERGER   A MERGER between companies from unrelated sectors. Conglomerate mergers, which were popular during the 1960s and 1970s, have been relatively rare since many unsuccessful deals were dismantled in the 1980s. Academic and empirical evidence supports the idea that it is more efficient for an INVESTOR to hold a diversified PORTFOLIO of COMMON STOCKS, than for a company to merge with, or acquire, a diversified group of companies. See also HORIZONTAL MERGER, VERTICAL MERGER.

CONSEIL D'ADMINISTRATION   [FR] The EXECUTIVE BOARD of a French company that uses the DUAL BOARD SYSTEM. See also CONSEIL DU SURVEILLANCE.

CONSEIL DU SURVEILLANCE [FR] The SUPERVISORY BOARD of a French company that uses the DUAL BOARD SYSTEM. See also CONSEIL D'ADMINISTRATION.

CONSENSUS EARNINGS   An average of EARNINGS forecasts developed by financial analysts that follow the STOCK of a particular company. See also EARNINGS SURPRISE.

CONSEQUENTIAL LOSS   In INSURANCE, a loss arising from an inability to use property that has been damaged or destroyed by a covered PERIL. A consequential loss is generally not covered by a standard PROPERTY AND CASUALTY INSURANCE policy, and must therefore by insured separately through BUSINESS INTERRUPTION INSURANCE. Also known as INDIRECT LOSS. See also DIRECT LOSS.

CONSISTENCY CONCEPT   A central ACCOUNTING CONCEPT that indicates a company should apply the same ACCOUNTING policies and valuation methods from period to period when preparing its FINANCIAL STATEMENTS in order to permit comparative analysis. When a change in accounting policy is required, its effects should be clearly noted. See also GOING CONCERN CONCEPT, MATCHING CONCEPT, PRUDENCE CONCEPT.

CONSOB   See COMMISSIONE NAZIONALE PER LA SOCIETA E LA BORSA.

CONSOL   [COL] In the United Kingdom, abbreviated form of Consolidated Fund Annuities, representing PERPETUAL DEBT issued by the government as part of its GILT program. Consols, which form part of the government's TAX REVENUE account at the BANK OF ENGLAND, are redeemable at PAR VALUE at the government's discretion, but in practice are never redeemed. See also IRREDEEMABLE SECURITY.

CONSOLIDATED ACCOUNTS See CONSOLIDATED FINANCIAL STATEMENTS.

CONSOLIDATED DISPLAY   In ELECTRONIC TRADING, the minimum information that must be displayed according to REGULATION, including prices, quantities, and tickers of the NATIONAL BEST BID AND OFFER of a given SECURITY, along with consolidated information on last sales.

CONSOLIDATED FINANCIAL STATEMENTS   The FINANCIAL STATEMENTS of an entire group of companies, including the parent or HOLDING COMPANY and any associated SUBSIDIARIES, which are developed through the CONSOLIDATION process. Also known as CONSOLIDATED ACCOUNTS.

CONSOLIDATION   (1) A form of MERGER where two companies combine to form an entirely new company. (2) An ACCOUNTING process where the FINANCIAL STATEMENTS of group companies and SUBSIDIARIES are combined into a single set of ACCOUNTS that reflects the entire financial standing of the group. For any subsidiary that is not fully owned, the relevant percentage that is not owned must be adjusted as a MINORITY INTEREST. (1) See also ACQUISITION. (2) Also known as FULL CONSOLIDATION.

CONSORTIUM BANK   A form of MERCHANT BANK, popular in the EUROMARKETS during the 1970s and 1980s, jointly owned by several large international BANKS. Consortium banks were typically active in international LOAN origination and SYNDICATION, FOREIGN EXCHANGE and EUROBOND TRADING, and CORPORATE FINANCE transactions. With individual banks and INVESTMENT BANKS now operating similar businesses on their own, most consortium banks have scaled back their operations or ceased to exist.

CONSORTIUM UNDERWRITING   An UNDERWRITING process in the INSURANCE market where a group of LLOYD'S OF LONDON underwriting SYNDICATES write business on behalf of other syndicates.

CONSTANT MATURITY SWAP (CMS)   A form of INTEREST RATE SWAP where the FLOATING RATE reference used to compute the periodic interest exchange is based on a CONSTANT MATURITY TREASURY yield.

CONSTANT MATURITY TREASURY (CMT)   A rate computed and published by the FEDERAL RESERVE that reflects the YIELD of a TREASURY SECURITY of a given MATURITY as if it were issued on each business day. The CMT is used as a FLOATING RATE index in CONSTANT MATURITY SWAPS.

CONSTANT PROPORTION DEBT OBLIGATION (CPDO)   A form of LEVER-AGED CREDIT INVESTMENT where a SPECIAL PURPOSE ENTITY issues NOTES to INVESTORS, using the proceeds to purchase low RISK SECURITIES. The SPE simultaneously sells CREDIT DEFAULT SWAPS on a POOL of REFERENCE CREDITS on a leveraged basis (e.g., NOTIONAL in excess of the total of the notes outstanding). The transaction is adjusted on a periodic basis through a leverage rebalancing formula, and leads to increased leverage as SPREADS on the reference credits widen. See also CONSTANT PROPORTION PORTFOLIO INSURANCE.

CONSTANT PROPORTION PORTFOLIO INSURANCE (CPPI)   A form of LEVERAGED CREDIT INVESTMENT where a SPECIAL PURPOSE ENTITY issues NOTES to INVESTORS, using the proceeds to purchase low RISK SECURITIES. The SPE simultaneously sells CREDIT DEFAULT SWAPS on a POOL of REFER-ENCE CREDITS on a leveraged basis (e.g., NOTIONAL in excess of the total of the notes outstanding). The transaction is adjusted on a periodic basis through a leverage rebalancing formula, and deleverages as SPREADS on the reference credits widen. See also CONSTANT PROPORTION DEBT OBLIGATION.

CONSTRUCTIVE TOTAL LOSS   In INSURANCE, damage to property or ASSETS that is so significant that the cost of restoration is determined to be greater than the value of the restoration.

CONSUMER PRICE INDEX (CPI)   An INFLATION measure used in the United States, Mexico, and other countries, based on the retail prices of a weighted index basket of market goods and services, including transportation, housing, health, and food. CPI is used as a reference in certain INFLATION-LINKED SECURITIES and INFLATION SWAPS. See also HARMONIZED INDEX OF CONSUMER PRICES, PRODUCER PRICE INDEX, RETAIL PRICE INDEX.

CONTAGION [COL] The spreading of economic disruption or financial VOLATILITY from one financial system or country to another during a
FINANCIAL CRISIS. Contagion may occur or intensify as a result of excessive
speculative forces, global economic interdependencies, and mobile investment
CAPITAL. Government intervention is occasionally necessary when contagion spreads through the financial sector and threatens very broad systemic
dislocation.

CONTANGO   A market state where FUTURES prices are higher than expected
SPOT prices and decline as EXPIRY of the CONTRACT approaches. Also known
as FORWARDATION. See also NORMAL BACKWARDATION.

CONTESTED TRANSACTION   See HOSTILE TAKEOVER.

CONTINGENCY LOAN   A LINE OF CREDIT that a company arranges in
advance of a loss and invokes when one or more TRIGGER events occur; unlike
a traditional BANK line of CREDIT, the contingency loan can only be drawn to
cover losses arising from a defined event. See also CONTINGENT CAPITAL.

CONTINGENCY RESERVE   A RESERVE, established by INSURERS as a percentage of total retained surplus, which is used to cover unexpected losses and
any shortfall in a previously declared DIVIDEND.

CONTINGENT CAPITAL   A contractually agreed PRE-LOSS FINANCING
facility that a company accesses in the aftermath of a loss event. Funding may
take the form of CONTINGENT DEBT (i.e., COMMITTED CAPITAL FACILITIES,
CONTINGENCY LOANS, CONTINGENT SURPLUS NOTES), or CONTINGENT
EQUITY (e.g., PUT PROTECTED EQUITY, CATASTROPHE EQUITY PUT).

CONTINGENT CLAIM   (1) A financial CONTRACT or ASSET whose value is
dependent on other assets or INDEXES, e.g., a DERIVATIVE. (2) A claim in
BANKRUPTCY that may become a DEBT based on the occurrence of a future
event.

CONTINGENT CREDIT RISK   The RISK of loss arising from a potential
CREDIT RISK exposure that may appear in the future, such as draw down
on a REVOLVING CREDIT FACILITY or payment under a GUARANTEE or
LETTER OF CREDIT. A subcategory of CREDIT RISK. See also CONTINGENT
LIABILITY, CORRELATED CREDIT RISK, DIRECT CREDIT RISK, SETTLEMENT
RISK, SOVEREIGN RISK, TRADING CREDIT RISK.

CONTINGENT DEBT   A class of DEBT FINANCING that becomes effective
once a defined TRIGGER has been breached; the class includes COMMITTED
CAPITAL FACILITIES, CONTINGENT SURPLUS NOTES, CONTINGENCY
LOANS, and FINANCIAL GUARANTEES. See also CONTINGENT CAPITAL.

CONTINGENT EQUITY   A class of EQUITY FINANCING that becomes effective once a defined TRIGGER has been breached; the class includes LOSS EQUITY
PUTS and PUT PROTECTED EQUITY. See also CONTINGENT CAPITAL.

CONTINGENT LIABILITY   (1) The LIABILITY of an institution that
assumes the role of a GUARANTOR or endorser under a LETTER OF CREDIT,

GUARANTEE, or SURETY BOND. (2) ACCOUNTING and RISK classification of an undrawn REVOLVING CREDIT FACILITY granted by a BANK to a borrower. (1) See also CONTINGENT CREDIT RISK.

CONTINGENT PREMIUM OPTION An OVER-THE-COUNTER COMPLEX OPTION where the buyer is only obliged to pay the seller PREMIUM if the CONTRACT ends IN-THE-MONEY. If the option ends in-the-money but the INTRINSIC VALUE is less than the premium due to the seller, the purchaser is still obligated to exercise the option and pay the premium. Also known as PAY LATER OPTION, WHEN-IN-THE-MONEY OPTION.

CONTINGENT SURPLUS NOTES A form of PRE-LOSS FINANCING where an INSURER or REINSURER issues NOTES to INVESTORS via a TRUST if a pre-defined loss-making TRIGGER event occurs. The issuance provides funding to compensate for losses sustained. See also CONTINGENT CAPITAL.

CONTINGENT TRIGGER A COVENANT in a CREDIT agreement requiring a BORROWER to undertake certain actions (such as repaying DEBT, selling ASSETS, issuing COMMON STOCK) in the event a predefined TRIGGER event occurs. Common triggers include a CREDIT RATING downgrade or breach of a financial ratio, often those related to LIQUIDITY, LEVERAGE, or INTEREST COVERAGE.

CONTINGENTS TO ASSETS A measure of a company's off BALANCE SHEET financial LEVERAGE, or the degree to which contingent LIABILITIES feature in overall operations. It is computed as:

$$CTA = \frac{Con}{TA}$$

where Con is the company's contingent liabilities, TA is the company's total ASSETS.

The higher the ratio, the greater the company's financial leverage.

CONTINUOUS COMPOUNDING The process of COMPOUNDING the INTEREST on a DEPOSIT on an instantaneous, rather than periodic, basis. The general factor for continuous compounding for a 1-year period is derived from the base of the natural logarithm e, and is given as e^r where r is the ANNUAL PERCENTAGE RATE. See also CONTINUOUS DISCOUNTING, FUTURE VALUE.

CONTINUOUS DISCOUNTING The process of DISCOUNTING a CASH FLOW on an instantaneous, rather than periodic, basis. The general factor for continuous discounting for a 1-year period is derived from the base of the natural logarithm e, and is given as e^{-r} where r is the COST OF CAPITAL. See also CONTINUOUS COMPOUNDING, PRESENT VALUE.

CONTRA-ACCOUNT An account in a dual entry ACCOUNTING system that offsets or reverses the value of another account. Common contra-accounts include ACCUMULATED DEPRECATION as a contra-account to fixed, depreciable ASSETS, LOAN LOSS RESERVES as a contra-account to LOANS, and TREASURY STOCK as a contra-account to EQUITY.

CONTRA-LIQUIDITY   The opposing side of a TRADE, generally used in the context of BLOCK TRADES. ALGORITHMS and SMART ORDER ROUTERS handling an ORDER attempt to detect contra-liquidity in DARK POOLS and on EXCHANGES in order to try to get the best EXECUTION price and the quickest fill.

CONTRA-TRADING   The practice of buying and selling SHARES within the same SETTLEMENT period so that no payment need be made. Contra-trading is typically found in DAY TRADING, where a SPECULATOR purchases shares during the day and closes out the position before the close of business; since both transactions settle on the same day (e.g., T + 3), the speculator has no gross cash outflow.

CONTRACT   A legal agreement between two parties that specifies actions, duties, and payments. A contract is only enforceable if it is based on legal activities and involves the exchange of consideration (i.e., each party to the contract provides some value). See also MISREPRESENTATION.

CONTRACT FOR DIFFERENCES (CFD)   See TOTAL RETURN SWAP.

CONTRACT MONTH   The designated month(s) on which EXCHANGE-TRADED DERIVATIVES are offered for TRADING. Many derivative CONTRACTS are offered on a quarterly cycle, while those that are extremely popular and feature a high degree of LIQUIDITY may be offered on a sequential monthly basis. Although monthly and quarterly cycles are most common, some derivatives are deliberately designed with very short maturity periods (e.g., overnight or intraday) to allow for instantaneous HEDGING or RISK-taking.

CONTRARIAN   [COL] An INVESTOR with a view that runs contrary to popular market sentiment or belief. Contrarians may be willing to take RISK or provide LIQUIDITY when other parties cannot, or will not. See also BOTTOM FISHING.

CONTROL PREMIUM   The incremental value paid for a TARGET company in an ACQUISITION, reflecting the perceived benefits of being able to control management; in general this value is inversely proportional to the quality of management and its ability to maximize value.

CONTROL RIGHT   The legal entitlements granted to an INVESTOR holding a SHARE of COMMON STOCK, including the right to transfer shares, receive regular and accurate financial disclosure, vote on specific issues at the company's ANNUAL GENERAL MEETING, and file lawsuits (i.e., legal actions for abuses related to self-dealing, compensation, information disclosure, breaches of DUTY OF LOYALTY or DUTY OF CARE). See also RENT RIGHT.

CONTROL STOCK   (1) A special class of COMMON STOCK that carries enhanced voting rights, allowing its SHAREHOLDERS greater influence and control over operations. (2) A block of common stock held by a large shareholder, sufficient to permit influence and control over operations; the block need not necessarily be equal to 50% + 1 share, it may be some smaller amount. See also DUAL CLASS STOCK.

CONTROLLER   A professional within a company that is responsible for financial and ACCOUNTING matters. Also known as COMPTROLLER.

CONTROLLING INTEREST   An ownership stake in a company that provides the holder with the ability to effectively control management. Controlling interest generally requires 50% plus 1 SHARE, though in certain cases an effective controlling interest can be gained with a smaller percentage, particularly when votes on large amounts of the FREE FLOAT are not actively exercised. Also known as MAJORITY INTEREST. See also MINORITY INTEREST.

CONVENIENCE YIELD   The nonmonetary RETURN that is derived from holding an ASSET, such as not facing a shortfall in the event of excess DEMAND. The existence of a convenience yield creates an incremental RETURN that is included in FORWARD PRICE computations related to FUTURES or FORWARDS.

CONVERGENCE   (1) In the EXCHANGE-TRADED DERIVATIVE market, the gradual drawing together of SPOT PRICES and FUTURES PRICES as MATURITY approaches; the convergence means that the BASIS, or price difference, gradually narrows. (2) In the ALTERNATIVE RISK TRANSFER market a cross-sector fusion of business activities between INSURERS and BANKS; the two groups participate in each other's markets by creating mechanisms to assume and transfer various INSURABLE RISKS and FINANCIAL RISKS.

CONVERSION ARBITRAGE   An ARBITRAGE strategy that takes advantage of mispricing of OPTIONS in relation to PUT-CALL PARITY. The strategy may involve the purchase of "undervalued" OPTIONS and the sale of SYNTHETIC OPTIONS, or the sale of "overvalued" options and the purchase of synthetics. A RISK-free profit can be generated if the undervalued/overvalued options are truly mispriced.

Conversion arbitrage strategy

Undervalued put	Purchase put and sell synthetic put (synthetic = purchase underlying, sell call)
Overvalued put	Sell put and purchase synthetic put (synthetic = sell underlying, purchase call)
Undervalued call	Purchase call and sell synthetic call (synthetic = sell underlying, sell put)
Overvalued call	Sell call and purchase synthetic call (synthetic = purchase underlying, purchase put)

CONVERSION FACTOR   A multiplicative factor that is applied to a DELIVERABLE ASSET under an EXCHANGE-TRADED DERIVATIVE CONTRACT to determine the precise amount that needs to be delivered. Since different types and grades are often deliverable, the seller of the contract must use a conversion factor to make the appropriate adjustment. See also CHEAPEST-TO-DELIVER.

CONVERSION PARITY   The MARKET VALUE of the SHARES of COMMON STOCK into which a CONVERTIBLE BOND can be exchanged, generally computed as:

$$Conv_{pty} = Conv_{ratio} (S)$$

where Conv_{ratio} is the CONVERSION RATIO and S is the stock price. Also known as CONVERSION VALUE, PARITY. See also CONVERSION PREMIUM, CONVERSION PRICE, INVESTMENT VALUE.

CONVERSION PREMIUM The additional amount an INVESTOR in a CONVERTIBLE BOND pays above CONVERSION PARITY to acquire the bond, generally expressed as a percentage of parity:

$$Conv_{prem} = \left(\frac{P_{CB}}{Conv_{pty}} - 1 \right)(100\%)$$

where P_{CB} is the price of the convertible bond and Conv_{pty} is conversion parity. See also ADJUSTED BREAKEVEN, CONVERSION PRICE, CONVERSION RATIO, CONVERSION PARITY, EQUIVALENT BREAKEVEN, INVESTMENT PREMIUM, SIMPLE BREAKEVEN.

CONVERSION PRICE The price at which an INVESTOR holding a CONVERTIBLE BOND exchanges the bond for SHARES of COMMON STOCK, computed as:

$$Conv_{price} = \frac{Par_{CB}}{Conv_{ratio}}$$

where Par_{CB} is the PAR VALUE of the convertible bond and Conv_{ratio} is the CONVERSION RATIO. See also CONVERSION PARITY, CONVERSION PREMIUM.

CONVERSION RATIO The number of SHARES of STOCK an INVESTOR receives in converting the CONVERTIBLE BOND, computed via:

$$Conv_{ratio} = \frac{Par_{CB}}{Conv_{price}}$$

where Par_{CB} is the PAR VALUE of the convertible bond and Conv_{price} is the initial CONVERSION PRICE. See also CONVERSION PARITY, CONVERSION PREMIUM.

CONVERSION VALUE See CONVERSION PARITY.

CONVERTIBILITY The right to exchange one CURRENCY for another. Resident and nonresident holders can exchange a fully CONVERTIBLE CURRENCY at will, without seeking permission from government authorities; a NONCONVERTIBLE CURRENCY requires permission prior to exchange. Some currencies have restricted convertibility, where nonresidents may be able to exchange freely but residents may need to gain prior approval, or holders may be able to convert freely for CURRENT ACCOUNT purposes such as TRADE, but not for CAPITAL ACCOUNT purposes such as LOANS or ASSET acquisition. See also CONVERTIBILITY RISK, RESERVE CURRENCY.

CONVERTIBILITY RISK   The RISK of loss arising from an inability to convert local CURRENCY into a fully CONVERTIBLE CURRENCY and/or to repatriate convertible currency back to a home country as a result of EXCHANGE CONTROLS. A subcategory of SOVEREIGN RISK.

CONVERTIBLE BOND   A hybrid DEBT/EQUITY SECURITY that consists of a COUPON-bearing BOND and an embedded EQUITY OPTION that allows the INVESTOR to convert into a specified number of SHARES of COMMON STOCK once the CONVERSION PRICE is reached. Convertible bonds are generally issued at PAR with CONVERSION PREMIUMS of 15% to 25% and final MATURITIES of 10 to 15 years. See also CONDITIONAL PUT CONVERTIBLE BOND, LOW-PREMIUM CONVERTIBLE BOND, MANDATORY CONVERTIBLE BOND, PUTABLE CONVERTIBLE BOND, REVERSE CONVERTIBLE BOND, ZERO COUPON CONVERTIBLE BOND.

CONVERTIBLE BOND ARBITRAGE   A quantitative ARBITRAGE strategy where an INVESTOR or HEDGE FUND manager purchases a CONVERTIBLE BOND and simultaneously HEDGES or neutralizes the RISK on two of the three factors that influence the price of the convertible bond: STOCK PRICE, CREDIT SPREAD, and INTEREST RATE. The intent is to gain exposure to the remaining factor at a relatively inexpensive price.

CONVERTIBLE CURRENCY   A CURRENCY that can be freely exchanged into another currency for any purpose, without regulatory restrictions. Convertible currencies are generally associated with open and stable economies, and their prices are typically determined through SUPPLY and DEMAND forces in the FOREIGN EXCHANGE market. Also known as HARD CURRENCY. See also CONVERTIBILITY, EXOTIC CURRENCY, NONCONVERTIBLE CURRENCY, RESERVE CURRENCY.

CONVERTIBLE PREFERRED STOCK   A class of PREFERRED STOCK that allows the INVESTOR to convert into a specified number of shares of COMMON STOCK once a CONVERSION PRICE is reached. Convertible preferreds pay DIVIDENDS rather than INTEREST, often on a cumulative basis, and are generally perpetual. In certain cases issues are floated with mandatory conversion features, requiring conversion into new common stock by a specific date if a minimum price target is reached.

CONVEXITY   A mathematical measure that quantifies the sensitivity of an ASSET to large changes in price or YIELD. In OPTION contracts convexity (commonly termed GAMMA) measures the change in DELTA for a change in the price of the UNDERLYING; in FIXED INCOME products it measures the change in DURATION for a change in YIELD or INTEREST RATES. Mathematically, convexity is the first derivative of a change in value with respect to duration/delta, or the second derivative of a change in value with respect to yield/underlying.

The standard convexity calculation for a fixed income SECURITY with semiannual COUPONS is given by:

$$Cvx = \sum_{t=1}^{n} \frac{t(t+1)}{(1+y)^{t+2}} + \frac{n(n+1)M}{(1+y)^{n+2}}$$

where C is COUPON, t is the time to MATURITY, y is the semiannual yield, n is the number of semiannual periods, and M is the redemption value of the bond (generally PAR VALUE). Also known as OPTIONALITY. See also NEGATIVE CONVEXITY, NONLINEAR INSTRUMENT, POSITIVE CONVEXITY.

COOKIE JAR ACCOUNTING   [COL] The practice of liberally interpreting, or manipulating, ACCOUNTING rules in order to convey a stronger financial position. Smoothing income flows, reversing RESERVES, and capitalizing costs that should be expensed are forms of cookie jar accounting. Also known as COOKING THE BOOKS.

COOKING THE BOOKS   [COL] See COOKIE JAR ACCOUNTING.

COOLING OFF PERIOD   [COL] In the US markets, the period between the filing of a final PROSPECTUS and the offering of a NEW ISSUE of SECURITIES to INVESTORS in the public market. The cooling off period is typically 20 days.

CORE INFLATION   A measure of INFLATION at the consumer level, excluding certain items such as food and oil. See also CONSUMER PRICE INDEX, HARMONIZED INDEX OF CONSUMER PRICES, RETAIL PRICE INDEX.

CORNERING   [COL] An attempt to gain sufficient market share in an ASSET or SECURITY in order to manipulate the price for gain. Cornering attempts, which are generally illegal, are usually unsuccessful unless the asset is very thinly traded.

CORPORATE ACTIONS   Events undertaken by CORPORATIONS that impact SHAREHOLDERS, including STOCK SPLITS, STOCK BUYBACKS, SPIN-OFFS, MERGERS, or ACQUISITIONS.

CORPORATE CHARTER   An authorizing document issued by a government or legal authority that delineates the activities a CORPORATION is permitted to undertake. See also ARTICLES OF INCORPORATION.

CORPORATE CONTROL MARKET   The broad marketplace for transactions that are designed to change the ownership, structure, and/or control of a company. Common corporate control transactions include MERGERS, friendly or HOSTILE TAKEOVERS, LEVERAGED BUYOUTS, MANAGEMENT BUYOUTS, and RECAPITALIZATIONS. In some national systems the corporate control market also serves as a monitoring mechanism for GOVERNANCE purposes.

CORPORATE ETHICS   The broad area dealing with the way in which a company behaves toward, and conducts business with, its internal and external STAKEHOLDERS, including employees, INVESTORS, CREDITORS, customers, and REGULATORS. In certain national systems minimum standards are required or recommended in order to eliminate potential conflicts of interest or client/employee mistreatment.

CORPORATE FINANCE (1) The general class of financial transactions that a company may consider to alter its structure, operations, or business focus, including MERGER, ACQUISITION, DEMERGER, DIVESTITURE, RECAPITALIZATION, LEVERAGED BUYOUT, or MANAGEMENT BUYOUT. (2) General FINANCING activities carried out by a company through the CAPITAL MARKETS.

CORPORATE GOVERNANCE See GOVERNANCE.

CORPORATE SUSTAINABILITY The concept and action of ensuring that a corporate organization exists in perpetuity, providing returns and benefits for multiple generations of internal and external STAKEHOLDERS. Sustainability generally demands close ties and cooperation with a broad constituency of INVESTORS, customers, CREDITORS, employees, and REGULATORS, as well as the surrounding community.

CORPORATE VALUATION The process of estimating the value of a company based on its ability to generate future DIVIDENDS (DIVIDEND DISCOUNT MODEL), future earnings (EARNINGS-BASED MODEL) or future CASH FLOWS (DISCOUNTED CASH FLOW VALUATION MODELS). Corporate valuation is used in PORTFOLIO management, ACQUISITION analysis, and CORPORATE FINANCE considerations. Also known as EQUITY VALUATION, VALUATION.

CORPORATION Any company that issues COMMON STOCK to INVESTORS in order to raise CAPITAL; a corporation may be public or private, and is generally organized with LIMITED LIABILITY. See also JOINT STOCK COMPANY, LIMITED LIABILITY COMPANY, PUBLIC LIMITED COMPANY.

CORPUS [LAT] The PRINCIPAL component of a BOND. See also COUPON.

CORRECTION A temporary reversal of a SECURITY price or broader market sector lasting several days to several months; though the retracement is not as severe as it is in a BEAR MARKET, prices may ultimately fall by 20% from the previous peak. See also BEARISH, BULL MARKET.

CORRELATED CREDIT RISK The RISK of loss arising from CREDIT EXPOSURE that increases precisely as a COUNTERPARTY's ability to perform declines, or when COLLATERAL taken as SECURITY deteriorates in tandem with a counterparty's ability to pay. A subcategory of CREDIT RISK. See also CONTINGENT CREDIT RISK, DIRECT CREDIT RISK, SETTLEMENT RISK, SOVEREIGN RISK, TRADING CREDIT RISK.

CORRELATION A statistical measure that indicates the extent to which two or more variables (such as financial ASSET prices) move in the same direction, or different directions. Correlation is often used to price and manage certain COMPLEX DERIVATIVES (e.g., MULTI-INDEX OPTIONS), quantify

PORTFOLIO RISK exposures, and determine appropriate HEDGE RATIOS. See also CORRELATION COEFFICIENT, CORRELATION RISK.

CORRELATION COEFFICIENT A standard measure of CORRELATION, typically computed as:

$$\rho_{A,B} = \frac{Cov(A,B)}{\sigma_A, \sigma_B}$$

where Cov (A,B) is the COVARIANCE between ASSETS A and B, σ_A is the STANDARD DEVIATION of asset A and σ_B is the standard deviation of asset B.

A perfect positive correlation coefficient (+1) means a unit change in the price of one reference leads to the same unit change in the price of the second; a perfect negative correlation coefficient (-1) means they move in equal but opposite directions; a correlation of 0 indicates prices are uncorrelated, or independent. See also CORRELATED CREDIT RISK, CORRELATION RISK.

CORRELATION RISK The RISK of loss arising from a change in the historical relationships, or CORRELATIONS, between ASSETS. Correlation risk can be found in certain COMPLEX OPTIONS and COMPLEX SWAPS and may also impact HEDGE RATIOS, CREDIT PORTFOLIO MODELS, and VALUE-AT-RISK models. A subcategory of MARKET RISK.

CORRELATION TRADING An INVESTMENT strategy that involves going LONG of one STOCK and SHORT of a second stock in expectation of capturing the SPREAD movements between the two over some time horizon, based on deviations in the historical CORRELATIONS between the stock prices. Correlation trading is often done within a specific industry sector, e.g., one automobile stock versus a second one. See also PAIRS TRADING.

COST ACCOUNTING An element of MANAGEMENT ACCOUNTING focused on budgeted and actual costs within a company, including analysis of variances, in order to provide management with information on its ability to achieve specific targets. Cost accounting need not necessarily follow GENERALLY ACCEPTED ACCOUNTING PRINCIPLES as the results are used strictly for internal purposes. See also FINANCIAL ACCOUNTING.

COST INFLATION INFLATION that results from increased costs of production, including raw materials and labor. Higher production costs are priced into goods and services, leading labor to demand higher wages to meet the higher prices; the resulting rise in labor costs is also priced into the final goods and services, raising the overall rate of inflation. See also DEMAND INFLATION, MONETARY INFLATION.

COST, INSURANCE, FREIGHT (CIF) The declared value of imported goods, including the cost of purchase and associated INSURANCE and shipping charges from the point of EXPORT to the point of IMPORT. CIF does not include duties or the cost of freight within the country of import. See also FREE ON BOARD (FOB).

COST OF CAPITAL   The total costs a firm bears in funding its operations through CAPITAL, including DEBT and/or EQUITY, which is equal to the rate of RETURN needed to induce CAPITAL suppliers to invest or lend. The cost of capital is widely used for INVESTMENT, reinvestment, FINANCING, and capital budgeting decisions. Since most companies use a mix of debt and equity, the general cost of capital formula can also be considered as the WEIGHTED AVERAGE COST OF CAPITAL, computed as:

$$r_{coc} = \left[r_D (1-TR) \frac{D}{D+E} \right] + \left[r_E \frac{E}{D+E} \right]$$

where r_D is the average cost of debt, TR is the corporate tax rate (where $1 - TR$ provides benefits in the form of a TAX SHIELD), r_E is the average cost of equity (or expected return to COMMON STOCK shareholders), D is total amount of debt, and E is total amount of equity.

The formula can be further expanded to include a specific cost and amount of PREFERRED STOCK, if such capital features on the BALANCE SHEET.

COST OF CARRY   The FUTURE VALUE of costs and benefits associated with holding an ASSET, which typically includes the cost of FINANCING, INSURANCE, transportation and/or storage, less benefits derived from lending the asset and any CONVENIENCE YIELD. Cost of carry is used to determine theoretical FUTURES prices and ARBITRAGE opportunities.

COST OF GOODS SOLD (CGS)   The direct costs attributable to the production of goods, including the cost of raw materials and production inputs, as well as direct labor costs. CGS excludes administrative expenses, INTEREST, TAXES, and DEPRECIATION. See also REVENUE.

COST OF RISK   The implicit or explicit price a company must pay to manage its RISK exposures; typically it comprises of the expected costs and direct and indirect losses arising from RISK RETENTION, LOSS CONTROL, LOSS FINANCING, and RISK REDUCTION activities.

COUNTERPARTY   An institution that is a party to a financial transaction with CREDIT RISK, such as a LOAN, DERIVATIVE, or FINANCING.

COUNTERVAILING CREDIT   A mechanism of granting CREDIT in a commercial transaction without disclosing the name of one of the two parties. The FINANCIAL INSTITUTION standing between seller and buyer of goods on credit issues documentation to the buyer in its own name, so disguising the identity of the seller.

COUNTRY RISK   The RISK of loss due to adverse economic events or political instability within a country; country risk is often considered to be larger in scope than SOVEREIGN RISK as it includes actions that affect private sector, as well as governmental, obligations. A subcategory of CREDIT RISK.

COUPON   The periodic INTEREST CASH FLOW payable by an ISSUER or BORROWER to an INVESTOR or LENDER for the use of DEBT-based CAPITAL. Coupon payments may be based on FIXED or FLOATING RATES, and may be payable on a weekly, monthly, quarterly, semiannual, or annual basis, or accrued until final MATURITY of the LIABILITY. See also CORPUS, PRINCIPAL.

COUPON STRIPPING   See STRIPPING.

COVARIANCE   A statistical measure of the relationship between two variables (e.g., financial ASSET prices), often used to determine the magnitude of CORRELATION. The covariance between two assets can be computed via:

$$Cov(A,B) = \sum_{j=1}^{n} \frac{\left(x_{A,j} - \overline{x}_A\right)\left(x_{B,j} - \overline{x}_B\right)}{n-1}$$

where $x_{A,j}$ is an observation of asset A, $\overline{x}_A$ is the MEAN of asset A, $x_{B,j}$ is an observation of asset B, $\overline{x}_B$ is the mean of asset B, and n is the number of observations. See also CORRELATION COEFFICIENT, VARIANCE/COVARIANCE MATRIX.

COVENANT   A clause in a LOAN agreement or BOND INDENTURE that requires the BORROWER to adhere to certain conditions. The conditions may be affirmative, such as paying PRINCIPAL and COUPONS on a timely basis or preserving an adequate amount of INSURANCE coverage, or negative (restrictive), such as not disposing of certain ASSETS, not breaching financial ratios, or not taking actions that might impair the value of any assets pledged as COLLATERAL. Violation of a covenant can result in the loan or bond being terminated and becoming immediately due and payable. Common covenants relate to RESTRICTED RETAINED EARNINGS (limiting the payment of DIVIDENDS if the borrower sustains operating losses), net tangible assets (limiting investment, dividends, and new debt if net tangible assets fall below a particular level), WORKING CAPITAL (limiting CORPORATE FINANCE transactions, dividends, and new debt if working capital declines), and LEVERAGE (limiting new debt if total debt to equity becomes too large).

COVENANT LITE LOAN   A form of SYNDICATED LOAN where COVENANTS designed to protect the interests of lending BANKS are far less restrictive than those found in standard LOANS. Such covenants, which can appear similar to those found on BOND financings, grant the BORROWER greater flexibility with regard to its financial operations and management, particularly with regard to maximum LEVERAGE and minimum INTEREST COVERAGE. Covenant lite loans may be used in connection with LEVERAGED BUYOUTS. See also SECOND LIEN LOAN.

COVER   (1) The act of repurchasing or HEDGING a position previously SOLD SHORT or held naked. (2) Any form of INSURANCE or REINSURANCE.

COVERAGE TEST   A financial test that is performed in a COLLATERALIZED DEBT OBLIGATION to ensure that sufficient COLLATERAL and INTEREST COVERAGE exists. Successful passing of each coverage test allows CASH FLOW from the underlying reference POOL to flow to the TRANCHES with increasing levels of SUBORDINATION. See also INTEREST COVERAGE TEST, OVERCOLLATERALIZATION TEST, WATERFALL.

COVERED BOND   A BOND issued by FINANCIAL INSTITUTIONS that is collateralized by public sector LOANS or MORTGAGES. See also CEDULAS HIPOTECARIAS, HYPOTHEKENPFANDBRIEFE, IRISH ASSET COVERED SECURITIES, JUMBO PFANDBRIEFE, LETTRES DE GAGE, OBLIGATIONS FONCIERES, OFFENTLICHE PFANDBRIEFE.

COVERED CALL   An OPTION position where the seller of a CALL OPTION owns the UNDERLYING ASSET deliverable if the buyer EXERCISES the option. Selling covered calls is a relatively low RISK way of generating PREMIUM income since the cost of the underlying is already known. See also COVERED OPTION, COVERED PUT, NAKED CALL.

COVERED INTEREST ARBITRAGE   An ARBITRAGE transaction that takes advantage of any instance when the FORWARD PREMIUM or FORWARD DISCOUNT between two CURRENCIES does not equal the INTEREST RATE DIFFERENTIAL. When this occurs, ARBITRAGEURS can create an arbitrage position to generate profits until the relationships return to equilibrium. This may be done by buying one currency in the SPOT MARKET and simultaneously selling it in the FORWARD MARKET and using the spot proceeds to invest in an asset denominated in the spot currency; when the asset matures, the proceeds are used to fulfill the forward contract and the arbitrage transaction concludes with a risk-free profit. Also known as INTEREST ARBITRAGE.

COVERED OPTION   An OPTION position where the seller of the option already holds the UNDERLYING ASSET or cash deliverable if the buyer EXERCISES the option. Selling covered options is a relatively low RISK way of generating PREMIUM income since the cost of the underlying is already known or sufficient cash exists to cover the purchase. Also known as BUY-WRITE. See also COVERED CALL, COVERED PUT, COVERED WRITER, NAKED OPTION.

COVERED POSITION   An outright LONG POSITION or SHORT POSITION that is protected by an offsetting HEDGE. Depending on the nature of the hedge, a covered position may have only negligible MARKET RISK and CREDIT RISK exposures. See also NAKED POSITION.

COVERED PUT   An OPTION position where the seller of a PUT OPTION already has sufficient cash on hand to purchase the UNDERLYING ASSET if the buyer EXERCISES the option. Selling covered puts is a relatively low RISK way of generating PREMIUM income since the cash is available to cover the exercise. See also COVERED CALL, COVERED OPTION, NAKED PUT.

COVERED WARRANT   A long-dated EQUITY OPTION (i.e., 3 to 5 years) issued by a financial INTERMEDIARY on a company's COMMON STOCK, which can be EXERCISED by the holder into SHARES already outstanding in the market (making the transaction nondilutive). The covered warrant is not sponsored by the company and need not have the company's approval, since no new equity results. See also EQUITY WARRANT, WARRANT.

COVERED WRITER   The seller of a COVERED OPTION that either owns the UNDERLYING ASSET (deliverable under a CALL OPTION) or has sufficient cash on hand to acquire the asset (under a PUT OPTION) should EXERCISE occur. A covered writer seeks to earn PREMIUM income on a relatively low RISK basis. See also NAKED WRITER.

COX, ROSS, AND RUBINSTEIN MODEL   See BINOMIAL MODEL.

CP   See COMMERCIAL PAPER.

CPA   See CERTIFIED PUBLIC ACCOUNTANT.

CPDO   See CONSTANT PROPORTION DEBT OBLIGATION.

CPI   See CONSUMER PRICE INDEX.

CPPI   See CONSTANT PROPORTION PORTFOLIO INSURANCE.

CPR   See CONDITIONAL PREPAYMENT RATE.

CRACK SPREAD   [COL] A SPREAD in the energy market reflecting the price differential between crude oil and a refined product, generally gasoline or heating oil; the spread can be traded through a single FUTURE or OPTION on certain EXCHANGES. A HEDGER or SPECULATOR can buy the crack spread (e.g., purchase crude and sell heating oil or gas) to take advantage of positive margins in refining, and sell the spread (e.g., sell crude and purchase heating oil or gas) to profit from negative margins. See also CRUSH SPREAD, SPARK SPREAD.

CRAMDOWN   A process where CREDITORS with existing CREDIT RISK to a company that has filed a REORGANIZATION plan under BANKRUPTCY protection choose not to participate in the new plan and have their interests demoted or "crammed down." A bankruptcy court can approve cramdown if at least one creditor agrees to the repayment plan and the plan does not discriminate among participating creditor claims.

CRAWLING PEG   A FOREIGN EXCHANGE PEGGING process based on official CENTRAL BANK intervention activity that adjusts the value of the local CURRENCY through small preannounced changes or average target rates over a period of time. The crawling feature avoids sudden jumps or VOLATILITY characteristic of DEPRECIATION or DEVALUATION, but may still be difficult and expensive to maintain over the long term. Also known as ADJUSTABLE PEG. See also MANAGED FOREIGN EXCHANGE RATE.

CREDIT   (1) A LOAN, FINANCING, or other form of BORROWING. (2) Payment into an ACCOUNT. (3) An ACCOUNTING entry in a DOUBLE ENTRY ACCOUNTING system that reflects a decrease in ASSETS or an increase in LIABILITIES or CAPITAL. A credit balance also represents liabilities or revenues. (3) See also DEBIT.

CREDIT ANALYSIS   The process of analyzing a company's FINANCIAL STATEMENTS in order to establish its CREDITWORTHINESS, for the express purpose of determining its ability to repay its contractual obligations. BANKS and other financial institutions extending CREDIT rely on credit analysis in order to make credit decisions, while CREDIT RATING AGENCIES use it to assign a CREDIT RATING. See also FINANCIAL ANALYSIS.

CREDIT ANALYST   An analyst working for a BANK, CREDIT RATING AGENCY, or other FINANCIAL INSTITUTION that is responsible for analyzing the financial state and prospects of a company that is an ISSUER of DEBT or a borrower via CREDIT facilities. The output is used in accordance with the function of the credit analyst, which may be to establish an internal CREDIT RATING and recommend a credit decision, establish an external credit rating, or develop a recommendation on whether to buy, sell, or retain the company's debt. See also EQUITY ANALYST, INVESTMENT ANALYST.

CREDIT CARD   A card issued by a BANK or FINANCIAL INSTITUTION that conveys a CREDIT line to the holder and allows the purchase of goods or services on a credit basis. The resulting balance may be paid off by the holder immediately or over time, with INTEREST charges accruing on any unpaid balance. The credit line granted to the holder is, in most instances, unsecured. See also CHARGE CARD, DEBIT CARD.

CREDIT CONTROL   A government policy of controlling aggregate economic DEMAND by restricting access to CREDIT, generally by influencing INTEREST RATES, limiting the total amount of speculative LENDING, and setting minimum RESERVE requirements for BANKS.

CREDIT CRISIS   A severe form of FINANCIAL CRISIS, in which a national banking system ceases to function normally, making impossible the proper allocation of CREDIT. A credit crisis may be created through a consistent underpricing of RISK relative to RETURN during the growth phase of an economic cycle. Once a catalyst is triggered (e.g., a market crash, bursting of a speculative BUBBLE, rapid DELEVERAGING), FINANCIAL INSTITUTIONS sustain losses and may ration credit to corporate and individual clients. In extreme situations, the lack of credit leads to growing DEFAULTS, further losses in the banking sector, and so forth, in a self-fulfilling cycle. Also known as BANKING CRISIS. See also CURRENCY CRISIS, DEBT CRISIS.

CREDIT DEFAULT MODEL   An analytic model that is used to determine credit losses based on the PROBABILITY a COUNTERPARTY will DEFAULT at a future time. See also CREDIT DEFAULT RISK, CREDIT MARK-TO-MARKET MODEL, INTENSITY MODEL, STRUCTURAL MODEL.

CREDIT DEFAULT OPTION   An OVER-THE-COUNTER BINARY OPTION that grants the buyer a payoff if the REFERENCE CREDIT DEFAULTS on its DEBT; the STRIKE PRICE of the OPTION is typically set equal to the PAR VALUE of the REFERENCE OBLIGATION, and the contract only becomes EXERCISABLE in the event of a DEFAULT. Also known as BINARY CREDIT OPTION, DEFAULT OPTION. See also CREDIT DEFAULT SWAP, CREDIT DERIVATIVE, CREDIT SPREAD OPTION.

CREDIT DEFAULT RISK   The RISK of loss arising from a COUNTERPARTY's failure to perform on its contractual obligations, including DERIVATIVES, LOANS, BONDS, and other credit-sensitive instruments. Also known as DEFAULT RISK. See also CREDIT INVENTORY RISK, CREDIT RISK, CREDIT SPREAD RISK.

CREDIT DEFAULT SWAP   An OVER-THE-COUNTER SWAP involving the exchange of deferred PREMIUM (often in the form of a floating rate CASH FLOW) for a lump-sum payment if an UNDERLYING REFERENCE CREDIT DEFAULTS. The lump-sum payoff associated with the swap, which depends on the quoted price of the defaulted debt, is similar to that of a CREDIT DEFAULT OPTION. In addition to single references and broad CREDIT DEFAULT SWAP INDEXES, CDS can be bought and sold on a range of structured ASSETS, such as ASSET-BACKED SECURITIES, MORTGAGE-BACKED SECURITIES, and other STRUCTURED NOTES. Also known as DEFAULT SWAP. See also CREDIT DEFAULT OPTION, CREDIT DERIVATIVE.

CREDIT DEFAULT SWAP INDEX   A POOL of CREDITS that is used as a reference in a CREDIT DEFAULT SWAP transaction or an INDEX TRANCHE structure. ITRAXX INDEXES have emerged as the industry standard for liquid TRADING, though bespoke credit indexes also exist.

CREDIT DERIVATIVE   An OVER-THE-COUNTER DERIVATIVE with an UNDERLYING reference that is based on the credit performance of a REFERENCE CREDIT. Credit derivatives are available in various forms, including the BASKET SWAP, CREDIT DEFAULT OPTION, CREDIT DEFAULT SWAP, CREDIT FORWARD, CREDIT SPREAD OPTION, FIRST-TO-DEFAULT SWAP, Nth-TO-DEFAULT SWAP and TOTAL RETURN SWAP. See also COMMODITY DERIVATIVE, CURRENCY DERIVATIVE, EQUITY DERIVATIVE, INTEREST RATE DERIVATIVE, REFERENCE ENTITY, REFERENCE OBLIGATION, SYNTHETIC COLLATERALIZED DEBT OBLIGATION.

CREDIT EVENT   A trigger event used in the CREDIT DERIVATIVE market under INTERNATIONAL SWAPS AND DERIVATIVES ASSOCIATION (ISDA) documentation, which leads to the exchange of payments under any outstanding contracts related to the relevant REFERENCE ENTITY or REFERENCE OBLIGATION. The events include BANKRUPTCY, failure to pay, RESTRUCTURING, acceleration, and repudiation/MORATORIUM.

CREDIT EXPOSURE   See CREDIT RISK.

CREDIT FORWARD   A single period OVER-THE-COUNTER FORWARD CONTRACT that generates a payoff based on the difference between an agreed CREDIT SPREAD (or price) and the terminal credit spread (price) of a REFERENCE CREDIT. See also CREDIT DERIVATIVE.

CREDIT INVENTORY RISK   The RISK of loss arising from a borrower's financial deterioration (reflected in a widening of its CREDIT SPREAD) and/or its failure to perform on a LOAN or BOND obligation (reflected in DEFAULT). See also CREDIT DEFAULT RISK, CREDIT SPREAD RISK.

CREDIT MARK-TO-MARKET MODEL   An analytic model that is used to determine CREDIT losses based on the probability of a COUNTERPARTY's financial deterioration at various points in time. The MARK-TO-MARKET model considers losses due to both CREDIT SPREAD widening and DEFAULT (which is a single specific and unique state in the model). See also CREDIT DEFAULT MODEL, INTENSITY MODEL, STRUCTURAL MODEL.

CREDIT PORTFOLIO MODEL   A general model that estimates CREDIT losses arising from deterioration and DEFAULT in credit-risky PORTFOLIOS. Since the model examines portfolio losses, the analytics rely on default CORRELATION estimates between COUNTERPARTIES in the portfolio. A credit portfolio model can be used as a tool for RISK MANAGEMENT, business management, PORTFOLIO optimization, and CAPITAL ALLOCATION.

CREDIT RATING   A measure of an obligor's financial strength based on an assessment of financial standing, performance, and prospects. The rating analysis process focuses on the obligor's EARNINGS, LEVERAGE, LIQUIDITY, capitalization, ASSET quality, funding access, management experience, strategy, competition, and operating environment. A credit rating may be established internally by a firm's own credit department, or through external rating agencies such as Moody's, Standard and Poor's and Fitch IBCA.

CREDIT RESERVE   A CONTRA-ACCOUNT that is used to fund EXPECTED CREDIT LOSSES. Reserves are established by deducting required amounts from OPERATING REVENUES or current income, and are used when a COUNTERPARTY ceases to perform on a contractual obligation, such as a LOAN, BOND, payable, or DERIVATIVE. See also LOAN LOSS RESERVE.

CREDIT RISK   The RISK of loss arising from a COUNTERPARTY's failure to perform on a contractual obligation (CREDIT DEFAULT RISK) or from credit deterioration (CREDIT SPREAD RISK). Credit risk, which is a form of FINANCIAL RISK, can be subcategorized into CORRELATED CREDIT RISK, CONTINGENT CREDIT RISK, DIRECT CREDIT RISK, SETTLEMENT RISK, SOVEREIGN RISK (COUNTRY RISK), and TRADING CREDIT RISK.

CREDIT SCORE   A numeric score, assigned to an individual that has or is seeking CREDIT, representing a relative degree of creditworthiness. Credit scores are typically provided by one of several recognized credit bureaus, which specialize in gathering and analyzing credit-related data, including payment timeliness, income, past DEFAULTS, and so forth. See also CREDIT RATING.

CREDIT SPREAD   (1) A measure of the RISK PREMIUM a CREDIT-risky corporate or sovereign entity must pay to attract CAPITAL. The spread is generally quoted against a risk-free BENCHMARK, such as a GOVERNMENT BOND; the riskier the entity the wider the spread, and the worse the entity's financial condition/performance the larger the spread movements. Credit spreads are widely used in SECONDARY MARKET TRADING and as references for CREDIT DERIVATIVES. (2) Any OPTION SPREAD that results in a net inflow of PREMIUM. (1) See also CREDIT SPREAD RISK. (2) See also DEBIT SPREAD.

CREDIT SPREAD OPTION   An OVER-THE-COUNTER OPTION that generates a payoff based on the difference between a CREDIT SPREAD (or price) and a predefined STRIKE PRICE. In standard form credit options generate a continuum of payoffs based on credit appreciation or depreciation; a credit option structured in binary form (as a DEFAULT OPTION) generates a payoff based solely on DEFAULT by the REFERENCE CREDIT. See also CREDIT DERIVATIVE.

CREDIT SPREAD RISK   The RISK of loss arising from a deterioration in an entity's CREDITWORTHINESS, generally reflected by a widening in the CREDIT SPREAD. See also CREDIT DEFAULT RISK, CREDIT INVENTORY RISK, CREDIT RISK.

CREDIT SQUEEZE   [COL] A series of measures enacted by a CENTRAL BANK or monetary authority to control the MONEY SUPPLY of the country. Such policies may include raising INTEREST RATES, increasing RESERVE REQUIREMENTS, and/or imposing other restrictions on the creation of BANK-generated CREDIT.

CREDIT SUPPORT ANNEX (CSA)   An attachment to the MASTER AGREEMENT framework set forth by the INTERNATIONAL SWAPS AND DERIVATIVES ASSOCIATION that defines CREDIT terms between two COUNTERPARTIES, including credit thresholds, COLLATERAL requirements, and credit termination events.

CREDIT UNION   A form of BANK, generally structured as a cooperative organization, that accepts DEPOSITS from, and grants LOANS to, its members.

CREDITOR   A party that lends money. See also DEBTOR.

CREDITOR COMMITTEE   A group, formed by institutions that have a financial CLAIM on a company that has filed for BANKRUPTCY, which coordinates actions in order to maximize value in LIQUIDATION or REORGANIZATION.

CREDITORS' VOLUNTARY LIQUIDATION   In the United Kingdom, a common form of corporate LIQUIDATION, where a company in FINANCIAL DISTRESS is deemed INSOLVENT and a resolution is then passed regarding its liquidation; CREDITORS must be advised within 14 days of the passage of the resolution and a LIQUIDATOR is appointed to oversee the disposal of ASSETS. See also COMPULSORY LIQUIDATION.

CREDITWORTHINESS   A measure of the financial strength of an individual or company, and the resulting ABILITY TO PAY on any extension of CREDIT.

CREEPING TAKEOVER   [COL] See CREEPING TENDER.

CREEPING TENDER   [COL] A CORPORATE FINANCE transaction where an INVESTOR group or acquiring company gradually purchases the COMMON STOCK of a TARGET company. Once a specified block has been accumulated a formal TENDER OFFER is made for the balance of the company's SHARES. Also known as CREEPING TAKEOVER.

CREST   In the United Kingdom, an electronic platform used for the SETTLEMENT of SHARES that eliminates manual and paper-driven processes. The platform was original created by the BANK OF ENGLAND and is now owned and operated by EUROCLEAR.

CROSS   The process of executing a TRADE that has been MATCHED, often used in the context of off-EXCHANGE TRADING. See also CROSSING NETWORK, DARK POOL, MATCH.

CROSS-ASSET HEDGE   A proxy or substitute HEDGE that is used when an exact replicating hedge is not available, generally by identifying a reference (e.g., a DERIVATIVE) that has a high degree of CORRELATION with the underlying RISK exposure requiring protection. Although a highly correlated cross-asset hedge introduces elements of BASIS RISK, it reduces or eliminates first-order MARKET RISKS, including DIRECTIONAL RISK or VOLATILITY RISK. Also known as CROSS HEDGE.

CROSS COLLATERAL AGREEMENT   A single COLLATERAL agreement that covers multiple LOANS or CREDIT facilities. Also known as DRAGNET CLAUSE. See also POOLED PORTFOLIO COLLATERAL, TRANSACTION-SPECIFIC COLLATERAL.

CROSS CURRENCY REPURCHASE AGREEMENT   A REPURCHASE AGREEMENT where the cash lent and the SECURITIES taken as COLLATERAL are denominated in different CURRENCIES. The MARKED-TO-MARKET process may thus reflect changes in the value of the securities and the governing FOREIGN EXCHANGE RATE.

CROSS CURRENCY SWAP   See CURRENCY SWAP.

CROSS-DEFAULT CLAUSE   A clause in a LOAN, BOND, or DERIVATIVE agreement indicating that a technical DEFAULT on one obligation triggers a technical default in all other obligations. Cross-default clauses are commonly used in CREDIT agreements and MASTER AGREEMENTS.

CROSS GUARANTEE   A GUARANTEE provided by one company to another company that is often related, such as a SUBSIDIARY or JOINT VENTURE, and a reciprocal guarantee provided in the opposite direction. Cross guarantees have a high CORRELATION, meaning the financial performance of one GUARANTOR can improve or deteriorate at the same time as that of the second guarantor; this can magnify any associated CREDIT RISK exposures. Also known as PIG ON PORK. See also FINANCIAL GUARANTEE.

CROSS HEDGE   See CROSS-ASSET HEDGE.

CROSS-MARGIN AGREEMENT An agreement between two or more EXCHANGES that permits MARGIN requirements to be computed on a net, rather than gross, basis. Such an agreement avoids "double counting" of margins for LONG POSITIONS and SHORT POSITIONS, allowing clients to use their ASSETS more efficiently.

CROSS RATE A FOREIGN EXCHANGE RATE between two CURRENCIES that does not involve the US dollar.

CROSS SHAREHOLDING Minority stakes held by two companies in each other; this is often done to help strengthen long-term business relationships, and is particularly prevalent in RELATIONSHIP MODEL countries such as Germany and Japan.

CROSSED TRADE A practice where ORDERS to buy and sell listed SECURITIES are matched without being channeled through an EXCHANGE; once crossed, the details may be reported to the exchange. Crossed trades are not permitted in certain market jurisdictions as they are thought to reduce transparency and leave open the possibility for unfair pricing practices.

CROSSING (1) The process of executing buy and sale trades that have been MATCHED. (2) In the United Kingdom, a process where a BROKER or DEALER buys and then sells the same SECURITIES, without exposing them first to the market.(2) See also WASH SALE.

CROSSING NETWORK An electronic venue that matches STOCK orders, primarily large blocks from INSTITUTIONAL INVESTORS, on a continuous or predefined time schedule. The base price used to CROSS trades is generally the midpoint of the BID and OFFER on an EXCHANGE, meaning that the platform does not attempt to generate any PRICE DISCOVERY. A crossing network, which is a form of ALTERNATIVE TRADING SYSTEM, attempts to minimize costs and MARKET IMPACT while preserving client anonymity. See also DARK POOL.

CROSSOVER DISCOUNT RATE The DISCOUNT RATE which yields identical NET PRESENT VALUES for two different CAPITAL INVESTMENT projects.

CROSSOVER INVESTOR An INVESTOR that invests in a company before it goes public, and continues to do so during the INITIAL PUBLIC OFFERING stage and once it is a publicly listed company.

CROWDED TRADE [COL] An INVESTMENT or TRADE in a particular ASSET that has attracted a significant amount of interest and speculative CAPITAL, causing its price to move quickly and sharply. A crowded trade may be OVERBOUGHT and due for a CORRECTION.

CROWN JEWEL DEFENSE [COL] An ANTITAKEOVER DEFENSE used by a company seeking to avoid a future HOSTILE TAKEOVER by another company. In the event a hostile takeover is successful the crown jewel provision in the company's bylaws automatically triggers the sale of valuable corporate ASSETS, leaving the acquiring company with less value than anticipated. By publicizing in advance the existence of a crown jewel provision, a company hopes to deter any potential takeover attempts.

CROWN JEWELS   [COL] A company's most productive and/or profitable ASSETS/operations. See also CROWN JEWEL DEFENSE.

CRUSH SPREAD   [COL] A SPREAD in the GRAINS market reflecting the price differential between soybeans (as feedstock) and soybean oil or soybean meal (the two main by-products); the spread can be traded through a single FUTURE or OPTION on certain EXCHANGES. A HEDGER or SPECULATOR can buy the crush spread (e.g., purchase soybeans and sell oil or meal) to take advantage of positive margins, and sell the spread (e.g., sell soybeans and purchase oil or meal) to profit from negative margins. See also CRACK SPREAD, SPARK SPREAD.

CSA   See CREDIT SUPPORT ANNEX.

CTA   See COMMODITY TRADING ADVISOR.

CTD   See CHEAPEST-TO-DELIVER.

CUBIC SPLINE INTERPOLATION   A technique of INTERPOLATION that uses a polynomial function to reflect the shape of the YIELD CURVE. The process is done by fitting a series of linked lower order polynomials (known as cubic splines) to the curve using SPOT RATES or DISCOUNT RATES. The resulting interpolated values are generated without any "kinks" or discontinuities; each known point on the curve ("knot") is joined by a curved segment by making the slope and the rate of change of the slope equal at the knot. See also EXPONENTIAL INTERPOLATION, LINEAR INTERPOLATION.

CUMULATIVE PREFERRED STOCK   PREFERRED STOCK that includes a feature allowing any foregone or suspended DIVIDEND payments to automatically accumulate. When the company restarts its program, cumulative preferred stock INVESTORS are entitled to receive all accumulated dividends before dividends can be paid to COMMON STOCK or NONCUMULATIVE PREFERRED STOCK INVESTORS.

CUMULATIVE VOTING   A form of proportional representation that permits INVESTORS to allocate all of their votes in support of a single DIRECTOR or issue; this type of voting can favor MINORITY INTERESTS as it gives them greater ability to concentrate their otherwise limited voting influence.

CURE PERIOD   A time frame of 30 to 90 days during which a company that has gone into technical DEFAULT on a contractual payment is permitted to submit payment without further prejudice, and without being considered to have defaulted. See also GRACE PERIOD.

CURRENCY   (1) See MONEY, (2) See FOREIGN EXCHANGE.

CURRENCY BASKET   A group of CURRENCIES that may collectively be used as a reference value for another currency. Certain managed currencies in the emerging markets use currency baskets in this fashion.

CURRENCY CRISIS   A form of FINANCIAL CRISIS based on a fundamental and significant DEVALUATION in a country's national CURRENCY as a result of inconsistencies between its EXCHANGE RATE regime and its macroeconomic policies. The dislocation relates to a change in currency parity, dissolution of a peg, or migration from fixed to pure floating rates, leading to a very large devaluation that can destabilize other aspects of the national or regional economic system. See also CREDIT CRISIS, DEBT CRISIS.

CURRENCY DERIVATIVE   An EXCHANGE-TRADED DERIVATIVE or OVER-THE-COUNTER DERIVATIVE with an UNDERLYING reference based on FOREIGN EXCHANGE RATES. A currency derivative can be structured as a currency OPTION, currency forward, CURRENCY FUTURE, CURRENCY SWAP, or CURRENCY WARRANT. See also COMMODITY DERIVATIVE, CREDIT DERIVATIVE, EQUITY DERIVATIVE, INTEREST RATE DERIVATIVE.

CURRENCY FUTURE   A FUTURES contract, bought or sold via an EXCHANGE, which references a specific FOREIGN EXCHANGE RATE. Currency futures are available on both CONVERTIBLE CURRENCIES and select EXOTIC CURRENCIES. See also COMMODITY FUTURE, INDEX FUTURE, INTEREST RATE FUTURE.

CURRENCY OPTION An EXCHANGE-TRADED or OVER-THE-COUNTER OPTION involving two CURRENCIES. VANILLA and COMPLEX OPTIONS can be bought and sold on CONVERTIBLE CURRENCIES and EXOTIC CURRENCIES and may be traded concurrently with the DELTA-equivalent SPOT currency as a HEDGE. See also COMMODITY OPTION, EQUITY OPTION, INDEX OPTION, INTEREST RATE OPTION.

CURRENCY OVERLAY   An INVESTMENT technique related to the active management of CURRENCY exposures inherent in a PORTFOLIO of multicurrency ASSETS, where the currency RISKS of the portfolio are managed separately from the remaining MARKET RISKS of the portfolio. The currency overlay is implemented by creating a currency neutral position for the INVESTOR, and then permitting tactical flexibility that allows the portfolio manager to deviate from the base position in order to generate currency-based ALPHA. The overlay may be based on CARRY, momentum, and/or quantitative approaches.

CURRENCY SWAP   An OVER-THE-COUNTER SWAP involving the exchange of two CURRENCIES. A typical currency swap involves the exchange of a fixed payment in one currency for a floating payment in a second currency, although the exchange of two fixed or two floating payments can also be arranged. Currency swaps involve the initial and final exchange of principal, which results in a high degree of CREDIT RISK. Also known as CROSS CURRENCY SWAP. See also CURRENCY DERIVATIVE.

CURRENCY TRANSACTION RISK   See TRANSACTION RISK.

CURRENCY TRANSLATION RISK   See TRANSLATION RISK.

CURRENCY WARRANT   A long-dated CURRENCY OPTION (i.e., 3 to 5 years) that is typically attached to a BOND (as a BOND WITH WARRANTS). The warrant, which can be detached and traded separately, is generally denominated in a currency that is different from the currency of underlying bond issue and is included to give the ISSUER a lower overall cost of funding.

CURRENT ACCOUNT   (1) The sum of a country's activity in net TRADE (EXPORTS less IMPORTS), INVISIBLES, receipts/remittances from abroad, international payment transfers, and gifts. (2) In the United Kingdom, a CHECKING ACCOUNT. (1) See also BALANCE OF PAYMENTS, CAPITAL ACCOUNT.

CURRENT ASSETS   Any ASSET on the BALANCE SHEET with a final MATURITY of less than one year. Common current assets include cash, marketable SECURITIES (e.g., BONDS, COMMON STOCK, PREFERRED STOCK, and other INVESTMENTS), INVENTORY, and ACCOUNTS RECEIVABLE. Current assets generally exhibit a high degree of LIQUIDITY and can often be converted into cash very quickly, at a price near carrying value. Also known as CIRCULATING ASSET. See also CURRENT LIABILITIES, CURRENT RATIO.

CURRENT CAPITAL   See WORKING CAPITAL.

CURRENT EXPOSURE METHOD   A regulatory method of computing CREDIT RISK on a SWAP under the BANK FOR INTERNATIONAL SETTLEMENTS' original 1988 Capital Accord based on the sum of FRACTIONAL EXPOSURE (i.e., POTENTIAL EXPOSURE arising in the future) and ACTUAL EXPOSURE (i.e., the current or MARK-TO-MARKET value of the transaction). See also INTERNAL RATINGS-BASED APPROACH, ORIGINAL EXPOSURE METHOD.

CURRENT ISSUE   See ON-THE-RUN SECURITIES.

CURRENT LIABILITIES   Any LIABILITY CONTRACT on the corporate BALANCE SHEET with a final MATURITY of less than one year. Common current liabilities include COMMERCIAL PAPER, short-term NOTES, REPURCHASE AGREEMENTS, DEPOSITS, ACCOUNTS PAYABLE, and the current portion of MEDIUM- and LONG-TERM DEBT; certain deferred TAXES and charges may also be included as current liabilities. See also CURRENT ASSETS, CURRENT RATIO.

CURRENT RATIO   A measure of a company's LIQUIDITY and its ability to meet obligations that are coming due, typically computed as:

$$CR = \frac{CA}{CL}$$

where CA is CURRENT ASSETS and CL is CURRENT LIABILITIES.

A current ratio above 1.0 indicates that the company has sufficient CASH FLOW from maturing assets to meet its short-term obligations. A ratio below

1.0 suggests the possibility of greater LIQUIDITY RISK pressures. See also QUICK RATIO.

CURRENT WEIGHTED INDEX   A method of computing a weighted INDEX that uses current period quantities, computed as:

$$I_{cw} = \left(\frac{\sum p_c q_c}{\sum p_o q_c} \right) \times 100$$

where p_c is the current period price, q_c is the current period quantity, p_0 is the base period price. Also known as PAASCHE'S INDEX. See also BASE WEIGHTED INDEX.

CURRENT YIELD   A current measure of the return on a INTEREST-bearing FIXED INCOME SECURITY, generally computed as:

$$CY = \frac{C}{P}$$

where C is the COUPON, and P is the purchase price of the security. See also BOND EQUIVALENT YIELD, DISCOUNT YIELD, SIMPLE YIELD, TAXABLE EQUIVALENT YIELD, YIELD TO CALL, YIELD TO MATURITY.

CURVE RISK   The RISK of loss arising from a change in the shape of the YIELD CURVE (i.e., the TERM STRUCTURE of INTEREST RATES).

Curve positions	Short rates		Long rates	
	Rising	Falling	Rising	Falling
Long short end,	Loss	Profit		
Long long end			Loss	Profit
Long short end,	Loss	Profit		
Short long end			Profit	Loss
Short short end,	Profit	Loss		
Long long end			Loss	Profit
Short short end,	Profit	Loss		
Short long end			Profit	Loss

Although curve risk is generally associated with interest rates, it is also evident in other financial variables with a term structure, such as VOLATILITY of interest rates, FOREIGN EXCHANGE RATES, and EQUITIES. A subcategory of MARKET RISK.

CUSHION BOND   A CALLABLE BOND with a high COUPON that is selling for a PREMIUM. The cushion bond loses less value as rates rise and gains less value when rates fall when compared with a NONCALLABLE BOND.

CUSIP   See COMMITTEE ON UNIFORM SECURITIES IDENTIFICATION PROCEDURES.

CUSIP INTERNATIONAL NUMBER (CIN) The COMMITTEE ON UNIFORM SECURITIES IDENTIFICATION PROCEDURES' nine-digit identification code used for non-US and non-Canadian SECURITIES.

CUSTODIAN An AGENT that performs various duties on behalf of a client, including holding SECURITIES in safe CUSTODY, executing financial transactions under specific instructions, and collecting periodic CASH FLOWS from INVESTMENTS.

CUSTODY The act of holding SECURITIES or other ASSETS in safekeeping for another party. BANKS often provide custody services to their clients, reducing the inefficiency, inconvenience, and possible danger of conveying assets between locations/accounts. Also known as GLOBAL CUSTODY. See also CUSTODIAN.

CUSTOMER MARGIN MARGIN posted by a FUTURES COMMISSION MERCHANT or client with a CLEARING MEMBER to cover the requirements of TRADES that have been executed and temporarily covered by the member's own CLEARING MARGIN.

CUSTOMS UNION A confederation of two or more countries that agree to eliminate DUTIES on IMPORTS and EXPORTS on goods and services within the confederation.

CUTTING THE MELON [COL] The process of granting current SHAREHOLDERS of a company's COMMON STOCK a SPECIAL DIVIDEND (in SHARES or cash). The process is periodically used as a means of returning excess CAPITAL to INVESTORS.

CYCLICAL STOCK The STOCK of a company that tracks very closely the BUSINESS CYCLE, i.e., declining in price during an economic slowdown or RECESSION and rising during an economic expansion.

CYLINDER [COL] See ZERO COST COLLAR.

D

D&O COVER   See DIRECTOR AND OFFICER INSURANCE COVER.

DAC/RAP (DELIVER AGAINST CASH/RECEIVE AGAINST PAYMENT)   See DELIVERY VERSUS PAYMENT.

DAIMYO   [JPN, COL] A public BOND issued in Japanese yen by a non-Japanese company. Daimyos are generally listed on the Luxembourg Stock Exchange. See also GEISHA, SAMURAI, SHIBOSAI, SHOGUN.

DAISY CHAIN   [COL] An illegal TRADING scheme where a group of manipulators trade a company's COMMON STOCK among themselves in order to create the illusion of activity. Unsuspecting INVESTORS are lured into the scheme and bid prices up further, until a point where the manipulators sell their positions at a profit and leave remaining investors with losses as the market falls. Daisy chains are generally only possible in SECURITIES with relatively small FREE FLOAT and TRADING volume. Also known as PAINTING THE TAPE. See also PUMP AND DUMP.

DAMAGES   The financial compensation awarded by the courts to a plaintiff for losses, breach of CONTRACT, or infringement of protected RIGHTS. The compensation may equal the amount of financial loss sustained, or it may be set as some multiple of that amount. See also LIQUIDATED DAMAGES, STATUTORY DAMAGES, UNLIQUIDATED DAMAGES.

DARK ALGORITHM   An ALGORITHM that is specifically designed to detect, and interact with, a DARK POOL.

DARK LIQUIDITY   See NONDISPLAYED LIQUIDITY.

DARK POOL   [COL] An electronic venue or mechanism that accumulates NONDISPLAYED LIQUIDITY and provides MATCHES and CROSSES of BIDS and OFFERS generally based on a midpoint price obtained from an EXCHANGE (meaning that the platform does not attempt to generate any PRICE DISCOVERY). A dark pool can take the form of an ALTERNATIVE TRADING SYSTEM, INTERNALIZED order flow, or exchange HIDDEN ORDERS and RESERVE ORDERS, and is designed to minimize costs and MARKET IMPACT while preserving client anonymity. See also CROSSING NETWORK.

DATED SECURITY   Any SECURITY that has a defined MATURITY. See also PERPETUAL DEBT, UNDATED SECURITY.

DAWN RAID   [COL] A CORPORATE FINANCE tactic where a potential acquirer purchases a substantial block of a TARGET company's COMMON STOCK at the EXCHANGE open, but before the target's management is aware of what is occurring. If the initial raid is successful (i.e., enough SHARES are acquired at an appropriate price) a formal TAKEOVER is usually launched. See also PREMIUM RAID, SATURDAY NIGHT SPECIAL.

DAX   See DEUTSCHE AKTIENINDEX.

DAY COUNT CONVENTION   A mechanism for computing COUPON payments/receipts on a FIXED INCOME SECURITY. Day count conventions, which vary by instrument, market, and country, are based on the period between COUPON payments, the number of days in the month, and number of the days in the year. The most common conventions include:

- Actual/360, which computes the actual number of days between two coupon dates and assumes the year has 360 days.
- Actual/365, which computes the actual number of days between two coupon dates and assumes the year has 365 days.
- Actual/actual, which computes the actual number of days between two coupon dates and assumes the year has 365 days or 366 days (depending on leap year).
- 30/360, which assumes that each month has 30 days and the year has 360 days (a European version of this modifies the end-of-month computation).

DAY COUNT NOTE   See RANGE FLOATING RATE NOTE.

DAY ORDER   A LIMIT ORDER for the purchase or sale of SECURITIES that is automatically cancelled if it is not executed during the trading day. See also GOOD TILL CANCELLED ORDER.

DAY TRADING   The process of actively buying and selling SECURITIES throughout the day but holding little or no OPEN POSITION at market close; the practice was initially popularized by the advent of ELECTRONIC COMMUNICATIONS NETWORKS and Internet-based TRADING platforms. See also SWING TRADING.

DAYLIGHT EXPOSURE   See DAYLIGHT RISK.

DAYLIGHT OVERDRAFT   An intraday LOAN created when a BANK transfers funds in excess of its balance held in a RESERVE account with the CENTRAL BANK. OVERDRAFTS may also occur in the accounts of interbank payment members and in correspondent BANKS.

DAYLIGHT RISK   The RISK of loss arising from failure by a party to a CONTRACT to receive, within the same business day, cash or ASSETS after it has already delivered assets or cash to another party. Also known as DAYLIGHT EXPOSURE. See also SETTLEMENT RISK.

DAYS PAYABLES OUTSTANDING   A measure of a company's CASH FLOW CYCLE, reflecting the number of days it takes for a company to pay cash for its outstanding ACCOUNTS PAYABLE. It is computed as:

$$DPO = \frac{AP}{CP_{day}}$$

where AP is the company's accounts payable balance, CP_{day} is the company's average CREDIT purchases per day.

The higher the ratio, the longer the company takes to pay cash for its purchases.

DAYS SALES INVENTORY   A measure of a company's INVENTORY cycle, or the number of days of inventory it has on hand to meet sales demand. It is computed as:

$$DSI = \frac{Inv}{CGS_{day}}$$

where Inv is the company's inventory on hand, ready for sales (i.e., the FINISHED GOODS INVENTORY), CGS_{day} is the company's average day's COST OF GOODS SOLD.

The higher the ratio, the longer it takes to convert inventory into cash.

DAYS SALES OUTSTANDING   A measure of a company's CASH FLOW CYCLE, reflecting the number of days its takes for a CREDIT sale to be converted into cash. It is computed as:

$$DSO = \frac{AR}{CS_{day}}$$

where AR is the company's ACCOUNTS RECEIVABLE balance, CS_{day} is the company's average credit sales per day.

The higher the ratio, the longer it takes to convert sales into cash.

DCF   See DISCOUNTED CASH FLOW.

DEAD CAT BOUNCE   [COL] A temporary recovery in a market or SECURITY following a steady or sharp decline; the recovery is typically fleeting and the downward trajectory generally continues.

DEAD HAND CLAUSE   [COL] A provision contained within some POISON PILL defenses preventing the acquisition of the company by another firm even if a majority of SHAREHOLDERS approve of the offer. Only incumbent DIRECTORS can remove the provision. Also known as DEAD HAND POISON PILL.

DEAD HAND POISON PILL   See DEAD HAND CLAUSE.

DEAD MONEY   [COL] CAPITAL that has been invested in an ASSET or market which generates no RETURNS over a particular time horizon. See also DOG.

DEADWEIGHT DEBT   DEBT of a company that is used to fund operating losses or service other debt rather than support productive INVESTMENT or ACQUISITIONS, or create incremental ENTERPRISE VALUE. Although the debt is necessary to ensure survival, it can become burdensome unless the underlying ASSETS or operations being financed can be made productive or other BORROWINGS can be reduced.

DEALER   An institution acting as a PRINCIPAL, rather than as an AGENT of a customer, in a financial transaction. Dealers may be MARKET MAKERS (quoting TWO-WAY MARKETS), or simply RISK-takers on one side of a market. See also BROKER, DEALER MARKET, PRIMARY DEALER.

DEALER CREDIT   See TRADE CREDIT.

DEALER MARKET   A financial marketplace where activity is restricted to DEALERS acting as PRINCIPALS for their own accounts; BROKERS acting as AGENTS for their clients are not permitted to participate. See also AUCTION.

DEALER MARKET ELECTRONIC COMMUNICATIONS NETWORK (ECN)   An ELECTRONIC COMMUNICATIONS NETWORK where clients face a sponsor, rather than other clients, as price-maker and COUNTERPARTY. Dealer market ECNs can be regarded as an electronic mechanism of dealing with a single institution. See also HYBRID ELECTRONIC COMMUNICATIONS NETWORK, REGULATED ELECTRONIC COMMUNICATIONS NETWORK.

DEALING OVER TOMORROW   See TOM NEXT.

DEATH SPIRAL   [COL] A CONVERTIBLE BOND that allows INVESTORS to convert their bonds into the ISSUER'S COMMON STOCK at below market prices. Investors can therefore establish SHORT POSITIONS to drive the price of the stock down, obtaining more shares at the time of conversion and using converted proceeds to cover their shorts. A death spiral is typically issued by a company in FINANCIAL DISTRESS that is increasingly desperate for any source of CAPITAL. Also known as FLOORLESS CONVERTIBLE.

DEBENTURE   (1) In the United States, a medium- to long-term, unsecured BOND. (2) In the United Kingdom, a long-term bond that is generally secured by a FIXED CHARGE or FLOATING CHARGE on the issuing firm's ASSETS; the bond typically features fixed COUPONS that are payable before any DIVIDENDS. (2) See also NAKED DEBENTURE, PERPETUAL DEBENTURE.

DEBIT   An ACCOUNTING entry that leads to an increase in ASSETS or a decrease in LIABILITIES or CAPITAL. A debit balance also represents assets or expenses. See also CREDIT.

DEBIT CARD   A card issued by a BANK or FINANCIAL INSTITUTION that permits the holder to purchase goods or services through a direct DEBIT to funds in an account linked to the card. Since the ability to effect a transaction is based solely on a sufficiency of funds in the account, no CREDIT is extended to the card holder. Also known as ASSET CARD. See also CREDIT CARD.

DEBIT SPREAD   Any OPTION SPREAD that results in a net outflow of PREMIUM. See also CREDIT SPREAD.

DEBT   Money owed by one party to another party. Debt can take many forms, including ACCOUNTS PAYABLE, BILLS OF EXCHANGE, BONDS, DEPOSITS,

DRAFTS, LOANS, NOTES, and REPURCHASE AGREEMENTS, and is generally governed by a contractual agreement that reflects the borrowing party's LIABILITY and the specific obligations that must be met in order to discharge the liability.

DEBT CRISIS   A form of FINANCIAL CRISIS based on a country's inability to support its DEBT obligations. Failure to service PRINCIPAL and INTEREST associated with local and FOREIGN CURRENCY BONDS and LOANS may require a RESCHEDULING or RESTRUCTURING with CREDITORS, and may have a negative impact on the country's financial and ASSET markets. See also CREDIT CRISIS, CURRENCY CRISIS.

DEBT-EQUITY SWAP   An exchange of outstanding DEBT for EQUITY between a CREDITOR and a corporate or sovereign DEBTOR in order to ease the debtor's LEVERAGE burden and allow it to remain current on its remaining obligations; the swap is tantamount to a RESTRUCTURING of the debtor's LIABILITIES. In a sovereign debt-equity swap, the equity allocated to the creditor may be from an unrelated sovereign-owned or controlled entity.

DEBT FORGIVENESS   The process of cancelling a DEBTOR'S outstanding DEBTS, leading to a write-off on the accounts of CREDITORS. Debt forgiveness is most commonly associated with debt cancellation of distressed sovereign borrowers. See also OVERHANG, RESCHEDULING, RESTRUCTURING.

DEBT RESCHEDULING   See RESCHEDULING.

DEBT RESTRUCTURING   See RESTRUCTURING.

DEBT SERVICE   Contractually required CASH FLOWS that a BORROWER must pay on a LOAN, BOND, LEASE, or other form of DEBT, generally comprised of COUPON INTEREST, a fractional portion of PRINCIPAL (payable into a SINKING FUND), and/or a LEASE payment. See also DEBT SERVICE COVERAGE.

DEBT SERVICE COVERAGE   A company's ability to manage its DEBT SERVICE requirement. A company with strong coverage possesses financial strength and flexibility, while one with weak cover is susceptible to FINANCIAL DISTRESS. Debt service coverage may be computed through the FIXED CHARGE COVERAGE ratio. See also INTEREST COVERAGE.

DEBT TO ASSETS   A measure of a company's FINANCIAL LEVERAGE, or the degree to which DEBT features on the overall BALANCE SHEET. It is computed as:

$$DTA = \frac{D}{TA}$$

where D is the company's total debt, TA is the company's total ASSETS.

The higher the ratio, the great the company's financial leverage. See also CONTINGENTS TO ASSETS, DEBT TO EQUITY.

DEBT TO EQUITY   A measure of a company's FINANCIAL LEVERAGE, or the degree to which DEBT features in the capital structure. It is computed as:

$$DEq = \frac{D}{Eq}$$

where D is the company's total debt, Eq is the company's EQUITY.

The higher the ratio, the great the company's financial leverage. See also CONTINGENTS TO ASSETS, DEBT TO ASSETS.

DEBTOR   A party that borrows money. See also CREDITOR.

DEBTOR-IN-POSSESSION (DIP)   A firm filing for BANKRUPTCY protection and REORGANIZATION that is permitted to act as its own TRUSTEE. The DIP typically attempts to secure DIP FINANCING in order to continue its operations while preparing a reorganization plan for court approval.

DEBTOR-IN-POSSESSION (DIP) FINANCING   Funding arranged for a company in BANKRUPTCY that is filing a REORGANIZATION plan; the BANK group providing DIP financing generally assumes some level of control and/or COLLATERAL in order to protect its new FINANCING commitment.

DECLARATION OF DIVIDEND   An announcement by a company that it is recommending the payment of a DIVIDEND of a particular amount to SHAREHOLDERS of record as of a certain date.

DECLARATIONS   Statements the INSURED makes to the INSURER regarding salient facts needed to arrange an INSURANCE CONTRACT. Since the insurer relies on the declarations to UNDERWRITE the RISK of the policy, the information must be accurate in order for the policy to be accepted and remain valid and enforceable. See also MISREPRESENTATION, UBERRIMAE FIDEI.

DEDUCTIBLE   The initial amount paid by the INSURED in the event losses are sustained from PERILS covered via an INSURANCE CONTRACT. The deductible, which creates a FIRST LOSS position for the insured, can be regarded as SELF-INSURANCE or a RISK RETENTION. The INSURER is only obligated to pay its share of any losses once the deductible has been met. Also known as FIRST LOSS RETENTION, SELF-INSURANCE RETENTION.

DEED   A signed document that contains a legal transfer or CONTRACT.

DEEMED RISK   See FRACTIONAL EXPOSURE.

DEEP DISCOUNT BOND   Any BOND that is originally issued at a price well below PAR VALUE, such as a ZERO COUPON BOND. Distressed BONDS, which often trade at sharp discounts as a result of perceived or actual problems with the ISSUER's CREDITWORTHINESS are not typically considered deep discount bonds as they are usually issued at par. See also ORIGINAL ISSUE DISCOUNT.

DEEP MARKET   [COL] A financial market or specific SECURITY that is very LIQUID, featuring significant volume depth and narrow BID-OFFER SPREADS. See also THIN MARKET [COL].

DEFAULT   A state when an individual or a corporate, municipal, or sovereign entity fails to meet contractual obligations related to its outstanding LIABILITIES, such as nonpayment of PRINCIPAL and/or INTEREST, or triggers some other defined EVENT OF DEFAULT. Default may be partial, such as a delay in payments or nonpayment only on certain CONTRACTS, or total, such as a complete repudiation of all DEBT. Default can create CREDIT losses for those who have extended unsecured funds to the defaulting party; upon default, CREDITORS retain certain rights and may institute FORECLOSURE proceedings or ACCELERATION of contracts. See also CREDIT DEFAULT RISK.

DEFAULT CORRELATION   A measure of the strength of the DEFAULT relationship between two CREDIT-risky OBLIGORS, indicating the degree to which a default by one of the obligors influences the default of the second one.

DEFAULT LOSS RATE   The DEFAULT RATE applied to a company's LIABILITIES, adjusted for potential RECOVERIES. When combined with the MARKET VALUE of liabilities, it yields the EXPECTED LOSS. The general form of the computation is given as:

$$DLR = DR * (1 - RR)$$

where DR is the default rate, RR is the recovery rate. See also LOSS-GIVEN DEFAULT.

DEFAULT OPTION   See CREDIT DEFAULT OPTION.

DEFAULT RATE   The PROBABILITY that a company will enter into DEFAULT, generally expressed as a percentage per annum. INVESTMENT GRADE companies have lower default rates than HIGH YIELD companies. Also known as PROBABILITY OF DEFAULT. See also DEFAULT LOSS RATE, LOSS-GIVEN DEFAULT.

DEFAULT RISK   See CREDIT DEFAULT RISK.

DEFAULT SWAP   See CREDIT DEFAULT SWAP.

DEFEASANCE   A process where an ISSUER of a BOND makes periodic INTEREST payments into a TRUST and separately funds the trust with ASSETS (such as ZERO COUPON BONDS) that will yield sufficient proceeds to retire the bond at MATURITY. By defeasing the bond, the LIABILITY is carried off BALANCE SHEET.

DEFENDED TAKEOVER   A TAKEOVER that is opposed by the DIRECTORS of the TARGET company.

DEFENSIVE SECURITY   Any SECURITY that exhibits less VOLATILITY than the market as a whole (i.e., its BETA is less than 1.0), providing lower, but more stable, RETURNS. INVESTORS often acquire defensive securities during periods of financial turmoil or uncertainty.

DEFERRAL   See DEFERRED CREDIT, DEFERRED DEBIT.

DEFERRAL OPTION   In REAL OPTION VALUATION, the OPTION a company has to defer or adjust the timing of INVESTMENT until some future period, after which the CAPITAL INVESTMENT project may become positive. Also known as TIMING OPTION. See also ABANDONMENT OPTION, EXPANSION OPTION.

DEFERRED ANNUITY   An ANNUITY funded with single or multiple payments that entitles the ANNUITANT or BENEFICIARY to benefits at a future date.

DEFERRED ASSET   See DEFERRED DEBIT.

DEFERRED CREDIT   A payment received before it is earned (i.e., a prepayment), carried forward as a LIABILITY until the good or service is delivered. Also known as DEFERRED LIABILITY, DEFERRED REVENUE.

DEFERRED DEBIT   A prepaid, and often recurring, expense that is carried forward as an ASSET until the good or service is received.

DEFERRED EXPENSE   See DEFERRED DEBIT.

DEFERRED LIABILITY   See DEFERRED CREDIT.

DEFERRED ORDINARY SHARE   In the United Kingdom, DEFERRED STOCK.

DEFERRED PAYMENT AMERICAN OPTION   An OVER-THE-COUNTER AMERICAN OPTION that permits the seller to utilize option proceeds from the time the buyer EXERCISES the contract, until the original MATURITY of the option. In exchange for relinquishing use of proceeds until maturity, the buyer pays the seller a lower PREMIUM.

DEFERRED REVENUE   See DEFERRED CREDIT.

DEFERRED STOCK   A form of STOCK in which the SHAREHOLDERS are not entitled to any DIVIDEND payments for a fixed period of time, or until certain financial goals have been achieved. Deferred stock ranks SUBORDINATE to COMMON STOCK and PREFERRED STOCK.

DEFERRED STRIKE OPTION   An OVER-THE-COUNTER COMPLEX OPTION with a STRIKE PRICE that is set at a future time period, often as a specific function of the SPOT value of the UNDERLYING reference at that time. Once the strike is established, the CONTRACT assumes the form of a standard AMERICAN OPTION or EUROPEAN OPTION.

DEFERRED TAX   An amount reserved by a company for TAX payments that will become due and payable in a period other than the current one.

DEFICIENCY LETTER   In the United States, a letter from the SECURITIES AND EXCHANGE COMMISSION to a company planning a NEW ISSUE of securities, indicating that its RED HERRING requires further revisions before registration is considered complete and the issue can proceed.

DEFICIT FINANCING   The process of creating a BUDGET DEFICIT as a means of stimulating economic activity. Deficit financing may be funded through the issuance of BONDS.

DEFINED BENEFIT PLAN   A form of PENSION PLAN established by an employer on behalf of an employee that uses an established formula to determine the amount of an employee's financial benefit on retirement. See also DEFINED CONTRIBUTION PLAN.

DEFINED CONTRIBUTION PLAN   A form of PENSION plan where the employer and employee make joint contributions to the plan; the total, plus accrued INVESTMENT income, forms the employee's financial benefit on retirement. In the United States this is done via 401(K) and 403(b) accounts. See also DEFINED BENEFIT PLAN.

DEFINITIVE SECURITY   A DEBT or EQUITY SECURITY that is issued in the form of a physical certificate rather than as a dematerialized, electronic computer entry. See also BOOK ENTRY SECURITY, SCRIP.

DEFLATION   A phenomenon where prices of goods and services decline for an extended period of time as a result of limited DEMAND. Deflation is relatively uncommon, appearing only during certain severe RECESSIONS or DEPRESSIONS. See also DISINFLATION, INFLATION, STAGFLATION.

DELEVERAGING   See RECAPITALIZATION.

DELIVER AGAINST CASH (DAC)/RECEIVE AGAINST PAYMENT (RAP)   See DELIVERY VERSUS PAYMENT.

DELIVERABLE   See DELIVERABLE ASSET.

DELIVERABLE ASSET   The specific type and quality of a financial or physical ASSET that can be delivered under the terms of an EXCHANGE-TRADED DERIVATIVE. Many CONTRACTS provide the selling party with the ability to select from a range of deliverable assets. Also known as DELIVERABLE, DELIVERABLE GRADE. See also CHEAPEST-TO-DELIVER, CONVERSION FACTOR.

DELIVERABLE GRADE   See DELIVERABLE ASSET.

DELIVERY   The physical provision of an ASSET underlying a financial CONTRACT, generally associated with EXCHANGE-TRADED DERIVATIVES (though also applicable to certain OVER-THE-COUNTER DERIVATIVES, particularly those involving COMMODITIES). The selling party typically announces its intent to make delivery through a delivery note, which provides details regarding the asset and location.

DELIVERY DATE   The specific date(s) during which DELIVERY of a physical ASSET can be made under an EXCHANGE-TRADED DERIVATIVE . Each CONTRACT is governed by specific delivery dates and time periods, spanning from one day to more than a month.

DELIVERY FACTOR   An adjustment that is applied to the price of a BOND that is DELIVERABLE under a FUTURES CONTRACT. The factor adjustment is required since bond futures contracts typically allow for a number of different securities to be delivered.

DELIVERY OPTIONS   A series of selections that the seller of a FUTURES CONTRACT on a US GOVERNMENT BOND can make that can increase the value of the contract. The delivery options include the quality option (ability to select a specific bond for DELIVERY), the wildcard option (ability to delay announcement of intent to deliver for a period of up to several hours), the ACCRUED INTEREST option (ability to deliver a security with a particular amount of accrued interest), and the end-of-month option (ability to use closing futures prices 7 days before month end and deliver the bond at month end).

DELIVERY POINT   The specific location where a physical ASSET referenced through an EXCHANGE-TRADED DERIVATIVE can be accepted for DELIVERY or storage. Each contract is governed by specific dealing locations, including warehouse storage facility, port, or pipeline.

DELIVERY RISK   See SETTLEMENT RISK.

DELIVERY VERSUS PAYMENT (DVP)   A SETTLEMENT practice in the financial markets where payment, generally in cash, is due to the seller of SECURITIES once the buyer has received the securities in its account. If payment is to be made before securities are received, the buyer faces SETTLEMENT RISK. Also known as CASH ON DELIVERY, DELIVER AGAINST CASH (DAC)/ RECEIVE AGAINST PAYMENT (RAP).

DELTA   The change in the value of an OPTION for a change in the value of the UNDERLYING market reference, all other variables held constant. Thus, the value of a purchased CALL OPTION increases as the price of the underlying asset increases, by an amount estimated through delta. Similar determinations can be made for LONG POSITIONS and SHORT POSITIONS in PUTS and calls. The value of delta is often used as a measure of DIRECTIONAL RISK and can be used to create an appropriate DELTA HEDGE. The deltas of the call and put under the BLACK-SCHOLES MODEL are given by:

$$\Delta_c = \frac{\delta c}{\delta s} = N(d_1)$$

$$\Delta_P = \frac{\delta p}{\delta s} = N(-d_1)$$

where

$$d_1 = \frac{ln\left(\frac{S}{X}\right) + \left(r_f \frac{\sigma^2}{2}\right)t}{\sigma \sqrt{t}}$$

and S is the STOCK price, X is the STRIKE PRICE, t is the time to MATURITY, r_f is the RISK-FREE RATE, σ^2 is the VARIANCE, and where the N value of $N(d_1)$ can be obtained from a standard table of probability functions.

The deltas of LONG and SHORT puts and calls are given as:

	Long call	Long put	Short call	Short put
Option delta	+	−	−	+

See also DURATION, GAMMA, GREEKS, VEGA, THETA, RHO.

DELTA HEDGE   The process of reducing or neutralizing the exposure of an OPTION to the direction of the market. Delta HEDGING is accomplished by establishing a DELTA-equivalent LONG POSITION or SHORT POSITION in the UNDERLYING reference against a long or short position in the option. Long CALL OPTIONS have a positive delta, i.e., the value of the option increases as the market increases, and can thus be hedged with a delta-equivalent short position in the underlying; short calls have a negative delta and are thus neutralized with a delta-equivalent long position in the underlying. Similar hedges can be constructed for long and short PUT OPTIONS. Delta hedging also works in reverse, where an underlying position can be protected through delta-equivalent positions in options. To remain effective, a delta hedge must be rebalanced as the market moves, which may mean several times per day.

Option position	Option delta	Delta hedge
Long call	+	Delta-equivalent short underlying
Long put	−	Delta-equivalent long underlying
Short call	−	Delta-equivalent long underlying
Short put	+	Delta-equivalent short underlying

DELTA NEUTRAL   A PORTFOLIO of OPTIONS that is neutral with respect to its DELTA, meaning that it is HEDGED for small moves in the UNDERLYING. See also GAMMA NEUTRAL, VEGA NEUTRAL, THETA NEUTRAL.

DEMAND   The amount of a good or service that an individual or institution will be willing to purchase at a given price. In general, demand declines as price increases. See also ELASTICITY, SUPPLY.

DEMAND DEPOSIT   See SIGHT DEPOSIT.

DEMAND INFLATION   INFLATION that results from an excess of demand, which causes the prices of goods and services to be bid up; the greater the demand, the more aggressive the price increases, and the larger the resulting inflation. Also known as DEMAND PULL INFLATION. See also COST INFLATION, MONETARY INFLATION.

DEMAND PULL INFLATION   See DEMAND INFLATION.

DEMERGER   A CORPORATE FINANCE transaction where a company segregates a portion of its business, places it in a separate corporate entity, and sells it to a third party or floats it through an INITIAL PUBLIC OFFERING. A demerger may occur if the company seeks to permanently exit a business segment that is no longer deemed essential to strategic growth, or if it wishes to raise additional CAPITAL for other corporate operations. SHARES in the newly formed companies are allocated to SHAREHOLDERS in exchange for their shares in the parent company. Also known as CARVE-OUT, SPIN-OFF, SPLIT-OFF.

DEMUTUALIZATION   The process of converting a member-owned MUTUAL ORGANIZATION into a PUBLIC COMPANY through the flotation of COMMON STOCK. Once demutualization occurs, members/customers are separate and distinct from owners/INVESTORS.

DEPOSIT   Funds placed by an individual or institution with a BANK or authorized DEPOSITORY, which are then used to finance operations. Acceptance of the deposit creates a LIABILITY for the accepting bank and requires payment of periodic INTEREST and return of funds at MATURITY or on presentation. Deposits can be issued in a variety of forms, including CERTIFICATES OF DEPOSIT, LOCKUP CERTIFICATES OF DEPOSIT, INTERBANK DEPOSITS, NEGOTIABLE CERTIFICATES OF DEPOSIT, and TIME DEPOSITS, and can be floated in most major CURRENCIES with MATURITIES ranging from overnight to 10 years.

DEPOSIT FUTURE   An INTEREST RATE FUTURES contract, bought or sold via an EXCHANGE, that references a short-term INTERBANK DEPOSIT rate, such as LIBOR, EURIBOR, or TIBOR. See also BILL FUTURE, BOND FUTURE.

DEPOSIT INSURANCE   INSURANCE that protects funds placed by DEPOSITORS with BANKS, generally up to a maximum amount per account. The insurance is provided by a governmental agency (e.g., the Federal Deposit Insurance Corporation in the United States, the Deposit Protection Fund in the United Kingdom) and participating banks must pay a mandatory PREMIUM as a mechanism for financing the insurance fund.

DEPOSIT NOTE   A MEDIUM-TERM NOTE issued by a BANK in the US markets.

DEPOSIT-TAKING INSTITUTION   See DEPOSITORY.

DEPOSITARY   An AGENT authorized to place funds in a DEPOSITORY institution such as a BANK, SECURITIES FIRM, or SAVINGS AND LOAN.

DEPOSITORY   An institution, such as a BANK, SECURITIES FIRM, or SAVINGS AND LOAN, that is authorized to hold DEPOSITS or SECURITIES on behalf of third parties. Also known as DEPOSIT-TAKING INSTITUTION.

DEPOSITORY TRUST AND CLEARING CORPORATION (DTCC)   In the United States, a company created in 1972 that acts as a conduit in the SETTLEMENT of SECURITIES transactions and OPTIONS deliveries. DTCC holds ownership records in electronic form, allowing for electronic transfers among buyers and sellers, reducing settlement times and the RISK of operational errors.

DEPRECIATED VALUE   See NET BOOK VALUE.

DEPRECIATION (1) A decline in the value of a physical corporate ASSET as a result of use, normal "wear and tear," and/or obsolescence. From an ACCOUNTING perspective depreciation is generally treated as a noncash expense and the net value of an asset is typically reflected as BOOK VALUE less accumulated depreciation. Depreciation can be computed through one of several different methods depending on the asset, its use and estimated useful life, and the accounting rules of the jurisdiction. Common methods include STRAIGHT-LINE DEPRECIATION and ACCELERATED DEPRECIATION. (2) A decline in the worth of a financial INVESTMENT or ASSET as a result of MARKET RISK factors.

DEPRESSION A severe economic downturn, where the output of a national ECONOMY (as measured by GROSS DOMESTIC PRODUCT) drops sharply, for an extended period of time. A depression may feature falling INVESTMENT, falling prices, and very high UNEMPLOYMENT and may be triggered by a FINANCIAL CRISIS (e.g., market crash, CREDIT CRISIS).

DEREGULATION The process of removing or loosening rules, restrictions, and controls on companies, industries and/or markets, allowing for greater flexibilities and freedom in both tactical and strategic operations. Free market economies generally follow a policy of significant deregulation, with sufficient protections in place to guard consumers and other STAKEHOLDERS. See also REGULATION, REGULATOR.

DERIVATIVE A financial contract that derives its value from a specific market reference, such as a COMMON STOCK, index, INTEREST RATE, COMMODITY, or CURRENCY. Contracts are available as customized OVER-THE-COUNTER DERIVATIVES, including SWAPS, FORWARDS, OPTIONS, COMPLEX OPTIONS, COMPLEX SWAPS, and STRUCTURED NOTES with EMBEDDED OPTIONS, and standardized EXCHANGE-TRADED DERIVATIVES, including FUTURES, options, and FUTURES OPTIONS. Derivatives are commonly used to HEDGE, SPECULATE, and ARBITRAGE. See also COMMODITY DERIVATIVE, CREDIT DERIVATIVE, CURRENCY DERIVATIVE, EQUITY DERIVATIVE, INTEREST RATE DERIVATIVE.

DERIVATIVE LAWSUIT A legal action where one or more SHAREHOLDERS sue the CORPORATION to bring suit against the corporation's BOARD OF DIRECTORS or executives for breach of duties. See also DIRECT LAWSUIT.

DERIVATIVE PRODUCT COMPANY (DPC) A highly rated, BANKRUPTCY-remote SPECIAL PURPOSE ENTITY used by certain FINANCIAL INSTITU-TIONS to undertake DERIVATIVE transactions with COUNTERPARTIES demanding strong CREDIT RATINGS. Through design mechanics based on minimum CAPITAL, COLLATERAL, HEDGING, and DIVERSIFICATION, the DPC can often achieve AAA credit ratings, even if the sponsoring institu-tion's ratings are below that level. DPCs are capital-intensive and generally only suitable for institutions with sufficiently low INVESTMENT GRADE

CREDIT RATINGS that they cannot attract enough business without credit enhancement.

DESCENDING BOTTOM   A TECHNICAL ANALYSIS charting figure depicting a declining SECURITIES price or INDEX value over time, with ever-lower levels, generally considered to be a bearish signal. See also ASCENDING TOP, FALLING TOP, RISING BOTTOM.

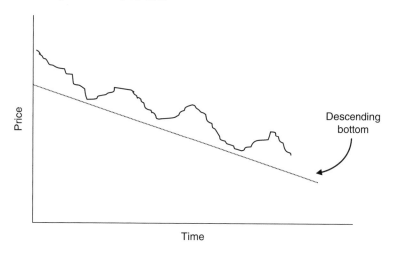

DESCENDING TOP   See FALLING TOP.

DESIGNATED INVESTMENT EXCHANGE (DIE)   In the United Kingdom, any EXCHANGE operating outside the country which is approved for dealing by the FINANCIAL SERVICES AUTHORITY.

DEUTSCHE AKTIENINDEX (DAX)   [GER] The BENCHMARK STOCK INDEX of the FRANKFURT STOCK EXCHANGE, comprised of 30 LARGE CAP STOCKS representing a broad range of industries.

DEUTSCHE BORSE   [GER] A financial EXCHANGE based in Germany established in 1992, which owns and operates the FRANKFURT STOCK EXCHANGE, the International Stock Exchange, and CLEARING and SETTLEMENT firm CLEARSTREAM, and co-owns DERIVATIVES exchange EUREX.

DEUTSCHE BUNDESBANK   [GER] See BUNDESBANK.

DEVALUATION   A sudden, and often large, decrease in the value of a national CURRENCY, arranged by a country's CENTRAL BANK or monetary authority in response to severe macroeconomic pressures, financial instability, speculative inflows/outflows, or capital imbalances. Once a currency has been devalued, its purchasing power in terms of other currencies declines, making EXPORTS cheaper abroad and IMPORTS more expensive domestically; this helps improve the country's BALANCE OF TRADE. Currency devaluation, a manifestation of SOVEREIGN RISK, is distinct from more gradual currency depreciation, which generally arises from the interaction of free market forces over a period of time.

DIE   See DESIGNATED INVESTMENT EXCHANGE.

DIFFERENCE IN CONDITIONS INSURANCE   INSURANCE coverage for physical structures, equipment, and INVENTORY against CATASTROPHIC HAZARD (although certain EXCLUSIONS for fire and vandalism are common). Also known as PARASOL POLICY.

DIFFERENCE OPTION   See SPREAD OPTION.

DIFFERENTIAL SWAP   An OVER-THE-COUNTER COMPLEX SWAP involving a single CURRENCY exchange of floating INTEREST RATE references denominated in two different currencies (e.g., dollar LIBOR versus EURIBOR, payable in dollars). The swap permits an institution to express a view on foreign interest rate movements without assuming currency RISK. Also known as a QUANTO SWAP.

DIFFUSION AND AMORTIZATION EFFECT   A concept indicating that the maximum CREDIT RISK of an INTEREST RATE SWAP occurs one-third to halfway through the life of a transaction. This occurs because simulated future INTEREST RATES used in the calculation of REPLACEMENT COST do not have a chance to move sufficiently in the early periods of a swap to pose the greatest economic loss (i.e., the "diffusion" effect), and insufficient payments remain to be made toward the end of the swap to pose the greatest economic loss (i.e., the "amortization" effect).

DIFFUSION PROCESS   A continuous, STOCHASTIC PROCESS where the market variable (e.g., a COMMON STOCK price or FOREIGN EXCHANGE RATE) exists in continuous time and its probability density function is continuous; the variable changes on a random and continuous basis, and as the time interval becomes larger, uncertainty in the returns increases in a predictable fashion. The diffusion process is widely used in modeling the value of certain financial contracts, such as DERIVATIVES.

DIGITAL OPTION   See BINARY OPTION.

DILUTION   The act of reducing the proportion of ownership held by current INVESTORS through issuance of new SHARES of COMMON STOCK (or through the EXERCISE of outstanding stock OPTIONS or the conversion of CONVERTIBLE BONDS). In order to protect investors against dilution from new issuance, a company may choose to float a RIGHTS ISSUE, giving existing SHAREHOLDERS the right of first refusal in taking up new shares. Also known as EQUITY DILUTION. See also FULLY DILUTED BASIS.

DIMINISHING MARGINAL RETURN   A MICROECONOMIC theory indicating that the marginal contribution obtained from increasing any variable factor of production declines once a particular point has been reached. The output declines as each incremental unit of input is added.

DIP FINANCING   See DEBTOR-IN-POSSESSION FINANCING.

DIRECT CREDIT RISK The RISK of loss due to DEFAULT by a COUNTERPARTY on a direct extension of CREDIT, such as a LOAN or DEPOSIT. Default on an unsecured direct credit risk transaction always results in a loss for the credit provider; this is in contrast to a situation involving TRADING CREDIT RISK, where the value of the CONTRACT may be in favor of the counterparty at the time of default. A subcategory of CREDIT RISK. See also CONTINGENT CREDIT RISK, CORRELATED CREDIT RISK, SETTLEMENT RISK, SOVEREIGN RISK.

DIRECT DEBIT A standing order granted by a PAYOR to a PAYEE to directly withdraw a fixed or variable sum of money from a BANK ACCOUNT.

DIRECT INVESTMENT See FOREIGN DIRECT INVESTMENT.

DIRECT LAWSUIT A legal action where one or more SHAREHOLDERS sue DIRECTORS or executives directly, rather than through the CORPORATION, for breach of duties. See also DERIVATIVE LAWSUIT.

DIRECT LOSS In INSURANCE, a loss where the covered PERIL is the PROXIMATE CAUSE of damage. PROPERTY AND CASUALTY INSURANCE policies often limit protection to direct loss rather than direct loss and CONSEQUENTIAL LOSS.

DIRECT MARKET ACCESS (DMA) A process where a BUY-SIDE client makes use of electronic trading systems to access a SECURITIES market directly, without any involvement or intervention by a SELL-SIDE firm or BROKER. This can result in faster EXECUTION at a lower cost, and provides a greater degree of anonymity.

DIRECT PAY LETTER OF CREDIT A LETTER OF CREDIT facility where a BANK automatically pays the BENEFICIARY an agreed amount and then seeks repayment from the underlying customer that has drawn the letter of credit; the beneficiary thus never faces the customer's CREDIT RISK. See also CONFIRMED LETTER OF CREDIT, IRREVOCABLE LETTER OF CREDIT, STANDBY LETTER OF CREDIT, TRANSFERABLE LETTER OF CREDIT.

DIRECT PLACEMENT The placement of a NEW ISSUE of SECURITIES by a company directly with an INSTITUTIONAL INVESTOR, without the use of a financial INTERMEDIARY. A direct placement, which can theoretically involve any type of security but in practice tends to involve DEBT issues, serves as an example of DISINTERMEDIATION. In general, only the largest companies directly place their securities, as the process requires name recognition and strong financial standing in order to attract a suitable base of INVESTORS. Also known as DIRECT PLACING. See also DIRECT PUBLIC OFFERING.

DIRECT PLACING See DIRECT PLACEMENT.

DIRECT PUBLIC OFFERING (DPO) A DIRECT PLACEMENT of COMMON STOCK that is offered by a company to INVESTORS, customers, and/or suppliers, without the use of an UNDERWRITER. Given the limited ability for companies to directly place their own SHARES and then encourage financial INTERMEDIARIES to produce EQUITY research and quote SECONDARY MARKETS, DPOs are relatively uncommon.

DIRECT STAKEHOLDERS   In GOVERNANCE, the parties most immediately and directly impacted by a company's activities, prospects, and actions, generally taken to include SHAREHOLDERS, CREDITORS, employees, customers, suppliers, professional service providers, and communities. See also INDIRECT STAKEHOLDERS.

DIRECT WRITE-OFF   The practice of charging off BAD LOANS directly to the INCOME STATEMENT rather than through LOAN LOSS RESERVES.

DIRECT WRITER   An INSURER that writes INSURANCE POLICIES through a direct selling process or an exclusive AGENCY arrangement, or a REINSURER that accepts ceded RISKS directly from other insurers rather than REINSURANCE BROKERS.

DIRECTED ORDER   An ORDER placed by a client with a BROKER or DEALER that instructs routing to a specific venue or EXCHANGE.

DIRECTIONAL RISK   The RISK of loss arising from exposure to the direction of a reference ASSET or market. An INVESTOR holding a LONG POSITION experiences a loss if market prices fall and a gain if they rise; one holding a SHORT POSITION generates a gain when market prices fall and a loss as they rise. A subcategory of MARKET RISK. See also DELTA, EQUITY RISK, FOREIGN EXCHANGE RISK, GAMMA, INTEREST RATE RISK.

DIRECTIONAL STRATEGY   An OPTION STRATEGY that seeks to take advantage of expected market direction rather than VOLATILITY to generate a profit. Common directional strategies include BULL SPREADS and BEAR SPREADS. See also VOLATILITY STRATEGY.

DIRECTOR   An individual acting as AGENT of the SHAREHOLDERS of a company. A director is responsible, along with other members of the BOARD OF DIRECTORS, for overseeing the activities of the EXECUTIVE MANAGEMENT team and exercising DUTY OF CARE and DUTY OF LOYALTY in protecting the interests of shareholders. See also EXECUTIVE DIRECTOR, INSIDE DIRECTOR, LEAD INDEPENDENT DIRECTOR, NONEXECUTIVE DIRECTOR, OUTSIDE DIRECTOR.

DIRECTOR AND OFFICER (D&O) INSURANCE COVER   INSURANCE coverage designed to protect the interests of DIRECTORS and executives from possible losses arising from lawsuits filed by SHAREHOLDERS (except those related to FRAUD).

DIRECTORS' INTERESTS   The SHARES, OPTIONS, and/or DEBENTURES held by a DIRECTOR in the company on whose board he or she serves. Such interests must be disclosed to STAKEHOLDERS.

DIRTY BILL OF LADING   A BILL OF LADING reflecting the fact that goods being shipped are in some way damaged. Also known as BILL.

DIRTY FLOAT [COL] A situation where a CENTRAL BANK or monetary authority does not adjust the nation's MONEY SUPPLY to offset any changes caused by active intervention in the FOREIGN EXCHANGE markets. The dirty float may ultimately result in rising INFLATION. See also STERILIZATION.

DIRTY MONEY [COL] MONEY that is earned illegally, and which may be placed through the MONEY LAUNDERING process in order to conceal its source. Also known as BLACK MONEY.

DIRTY PRICE [COL] The price of a BOND inclusive of ACCRUED INTEREST. Most SECONDARY MARKET bond transactions are quoted on dirty prices. See also CLEAN PRICE, INVOICE PRICE.

DIRTY STOCK [COL] Transferred COMMON STOCK that fails to convey good TITLE to the new buyer as a result of errors or omissions in form or authorization.

DISAPPEARING DEDUCTIBLE A DEDUCTIBLE on an INSURANCE CONTRACT that the INSURED is not obligated to cover if losses exceed a particular threshold. If the threshold is breached the INSURER pays the insured a CLAIM that includes the original amount of the deductible, causing it to "disappear." If the threshold is not breached the policy functions as any normal insurance contract with a deducible.

DISASTER RECOVERY RISK The RISK of loss arising from damage to physical infrastructure – which prohibits use of real estate, plant and equipment, technology, and communications – leading to a halt in operations; the disaster may be firm-specific, industry-based, regional, or system-wide. Disaster recovery risks can often be covered through specific BUSINESS INTERRUPTION INSURANCE. A subcategory of OPERATIONAL RISK. See also BUSINESS RECOVERY RISK.

DISBURSEMENT Granting of funds by a BANK to a client under a previously established CREDIT facility.

DISCHARGE The release of a party from a legally binding CONTRACT or other obligation as a result of satisfactory performance under the terms of the agreement, or as a result of a legal proceeding.

DISCOUNT (1) A reduction in the price of goods or the value of SECURITIES or other ASSETS as a result of SUPPLY and DEMAND or RISK factors. (2) The process of applying a DISCOUNT RATE to one or more future CASH FLOWS in order to obtain a PRESENT VALUE, NET PRESENT VALUE, or ENTERPRISE VALUE. DISCOUNT

DISCOUNT BOND (1) A BOND that trades at a DISCOUNT to its PAR VALUE. (2) A form of BRADY BOND with an initial discount to par value but a higher INTEREST COUPON than the PAR BOND alternative. (1) See also PREMIUM BOND.

DISCOUNT CURRENCY   A CURRENCY that trades at a lower value than another currency in the FORWARD market. See also PREMIUM CURRENCY.

DISCOUNT FACTOR   A factor that generates the PRESENT VALUE of a CASH FLOW when multiplied by a period's estimated CASH FLOW. It is computed as:

$$DF = \frac{1}{(1+r)^t}$$

where r is the relevant DISCOUNT RATE or COST OF CAPITAL, t is the time period. Also known as PRESENT VALUE FACTOR.

DISCOUNT HOUSE   In the United Kingdom, a FINANCIAL INSTITUTION that is active in MONEY MARKET dealing and which actively discounts BILLS OF EXCHANGE and deals in AT CALL funds.

DISCOUNT MARKET   In the United Kingdom, the sector of the MONEY MARKET that includes BANKS, DISCOUNT HOUSES, and BROKERS specializing in BILLS OF EXCHANGE. The discount market serves to generate short-term secured LIQUIDITY for these specialized institutions.

DISCOUNT RATE   (1) The COST OF CAPITAL that is applied to DISCOUNT FACTORS to obtain a DISCOUNTED CASH FLOW or PRESENT VALUE computation. (2) A company's cost of capital, often used to determine ENTERPRISE VALUE or the PRESENT VALUE or NET PRESENT VALUE of an INVESTMENT opportunity. It is generally computed as the sum of a RISK-FREE RATE and an appropriate RISK PREMIUM. (3) In the United States, the INTEREST RATE charged by FEDERAL RESERVE BANKS for LOANS taken by MEMBER BANKS through the DISCOUNT WINDOW; the rate need not be the same across all 12 Federal Reserve Banks. (4) The interest rate charged by ACCEPTANCE HOUSES or BANKS when accepting a BILL OF EXCHANGE or BANKER'S ACCEPTANCE. (5) The SPOT RATE of interest. (1,2) See also DISCOUNT.

DISCOUNT SWAP   An OVER-THE-COUNTER NONPAR SWAP where the receiver of FIXED RATES is granted an upfront payment by the FLOATING RATE payer in exchange for accepting a lower ongoing fixed rate inflow. See also PREMIUM SWAP.

DISCOUNT WINDOW   In the United States, a facility, made available by the FEDERAL RESERVE BANKS, that permits authorized MEMBER BANKS to borrow short-term funds on an emergency basis in order to balance cash outflows.

DISCOUNT YIELD   The effective YIELD of any FIXED INCOME instrument issued on a discount, rather than COUPON-bearing, basis, generally computed as:

$$DY = \frac{(Face - P)}{Face}\left(\frac{360}{n_{MAT}}\right)$$

where Face is FACE VALUE, P is purchase price, and n_{MAT} is the number of days until MATURITY. See also BOND EQUIVALENT YIELD, SIMPLE YIELD, TAXABLE EQUIVALENT YIELD, YIELD TO CALL, YIELD TO MATURITY.

DISCOUNTED CASH FLOW   A financial measurement technique used to evaluate the worth of capital INVESTMENTS, ACQUISITIONS, or other projects involving cash inflows and outflows over time. Net CASH FLOWS are DISCOUNTED at a company's COST OF CAPITAL in order to crystal-lize the economic impact in current terms. See also DISCOUNTED CASH FLOW VALUATION MODEL, INTERNAL RATE OF RETURN, NET PRESENT VALUE.

DISCOUNTED CASH FLOW VALUATION MODEL   A quantitative VALUATION measure used to estimate the fair value of a company's STOCK, or the entire firm, based on its ability to generate future CASH FLOWS. Similar methods can be applied using DIVIDENDS (DIVIDEND DISCOUNT MODEL) or earnings (EARNINGS-BASED MODEL) instead of cash flows. The basic form of this process assumes a constant growth rate in future cash flows and is given as:

$$S = \frac{CF}{(r-g)}$$

where CF is the estimated cash flow, r is the company's COST OF CAPITAL, g is the estimated, and constant, growth rate.

A more refined version assumes that cash flows vary from period to period, and is given as:

$$S = \sum_{t=1}^{\infty} \frac{CF_t}{(1+r)^t}$$

where CF_t is an estimated cash flow generated in time period t.

Since estimating cash flows into infinity is challenging a further refinement of the model uses a combination of discounted cash flow estimates over a spe-cific time horizon, along with an estimate of TERMINAL VALUE.

$$S = \sum_{t=1}^{N} \frac{CF_t}{(1+r)^t} + \frac{TV}{(1+r)^N}$$

where N is the number of periods over which a cash flow can be reasonably estimated, TV is the estimated terminal value of the company.

The model can also be adapted to value a company's stock based on FREE CASH FLOW TO EQUITY, under the following general formula:

$$S = \sum_{t=1}^{\infty} \frac{FCFE_t}{(1+r)^t}$$

where r is the company's cost of EQUITY.

Alternatively, it can be used to value the firm (rather than the stock) under the FREE CASH FLOW TO FIRM formula:

$$V = \sum_{t=1}^{\infty} \frac{FCFF_t}{(1+r)^t}$$

where *r* is the firm's WEIGHTED AVERAGE COST OF CAPITAL.

For both free cash flow methods, the terminal value estimate can also be used after a specific time horizon. See also DIVIDEND DISCOUNT MODEL, EARNINGS-BASED MODEL, FREE CASH FLOW TO EQUITY, FREE CASH FLOW TO FIRM.

DISCOUNTED PAYBACK PERIOD The time required to pay back the original INVESTMENTS in terms of DISCOUNTED future CASH FLOWS, generally expressed in terms of years. See also PAYBACK PERIOD.

DISCRETE BARRIER OPTION See PARTIAL BARRIER OPTION.

DISCRETIONARY ACCOUNT A customer BROKERAGE ACCOUNT where the client gives the BROKER authorization to act on his/her behalf in buying and selling SECURITIES. The client may limit the discretion through time and/ or price constraints.

DISCRETIONARY ORDER An ORDER for the purchase or sale of SECURITIES, COMMODITIES, or other financial ASSETS given by a client to a BROKER, where the broker has flexibility to execute a deal at the price and time deemed best.

DISCRETIONARY TACTICAL ASSET ALLOCATION A form of TACTICAL ASSET ALLOCATION where short-term adjustments to the PORTFOLIO are based on expert views of market forecasts and perceived market opportunities, making the process relatively subjective. See also SYSTEMATIC TACTICAL ASSET ALLOCATION.

DISCRETIONARY TRUST A TRUST or INVESTMENT trust where a TRUSTEE or other designated person has the ability to invest the BENEFICIARY'S ASSETS as deemed best, without specific constraints or within certain general parameters. See also BLIND TRUST.

DISCRIMINATING MONOPOLY A state where a company with MONOPOLY power charges different prices in different markets, according to the characteristics of each market. This presumes the monopolist can clearly identify the source of DEMAND in each market and can properly gauge PRICE ELASTICITY; if it can, it may be able to maximize its profitability.

DISECONOMIES OF SCALE   The relative cost increases that a company may experience once excessive expansion within a market segment has occurred. These may relate to duplicative efforts, slower response time, product cannibalization, regulatory challenges, and so forth. See also ECONOMIES OF SCALE.

DISENFRANCHISE   The process of removing VOTING RIGHTS from a class of COMMON STOCK so that INVESTORS in that class are only entitled to RENT RIGHTS. See also DISENFRANCHISING TRANSACTION.

DISENFRANCHISING TRANSACTION   A financial RESTRUCTURING transaction, such as a DUAL CLASS RECAPITALIZATION, that removes VOTING RIGHTS from certain COMMON STOCK INVESTORS.

DISHONOR   The act of refusing to accept or pay a BILL OF EXCHANGE or of failing to honor a CHECK or other financial CONTRACT.

DISINFLATION   A decline in the rate of INFLATION, indicating a decline in the rate at which prices of goods and services are rising. See also DEFLATION.

DISINTERMEDIATION   The process of removing FINANCIAL INSTITUTIONS, including BANKS, INVESTMENT BANKS, and SECURITIES FIRMS, from their traditional function in intermediating between suppliers and providers of CAPITAL and providing INVESTMENT and CORPORATE FINANCE advice. If BORROWERS and INVESTORS/LENDERS can properly identify each other and disintermediate traditional providers, borrowers may be able to realize a cheaper COST OF CAPITAL and investors a greater return, as neither party will be required to pay implicit or explicit intermediation fees. Equally, if companies can arrange their own MERGERS or ACQUISITIONS, INTERMEDIARIES can be excluded from the role and costs can be reduced. Disintermediation occurs in certain financing and corporate finance transactions, although the overall scope and volume are limited.

DISINVESTMENT   See DIVESTMENT.

DISPLAYED LIQUIDITY   TRADING VOLUME, particularly in STOCKS, that is visible to the market at large, and which reflects available MARKET DEPTH. Displayed liquidity excludes HIDDEN ORDERS, the hidden portion of RESERVE ORDERS, positions held back in the books of MARKET MAKERS, as well as those residing in DARK POOLS.

DISPOSABLE INCOME   The amount of discretionary income left for SAVINGS, INVESTMENT, or consumption once mandatory EXPENSES and TAXES have been paid. Disposable income can be measured at both the household level and the national level.

DISPOSAL VALUE   See RESIDUAL VALUE.

DISTRESSED ASSET   An ASSET, generally a SECURITY or real property, that features a sharply reduced value as a result of actual or potential losses created by an excess of CREDIT RISK, MARKET RISK, and/or LIQUIDITY RISK. Securities, LOANS, or MORTGAGES of obligors that are at high risk of DEFAULT and those that contain significant amounts of LEVERAGE or ILLIQUIDITY may trade at deep DISCOUNTS that are characteristic of distressed assets. VULTURE FUNDS and other sophisticated INSTITUTIONAL INVESTORS periodically invest in such assets. See also FIRE SALE.

DISTRESSED FUND   See VULTURE FUND.

DISTRIBUTABLE PROFITS   See DISTRIBUTABLE RESERVES.

DISTRIBUTABLE RESERVES   In the United Kingdom, the amount of money a company has available for distribution to INVESTORS in the form of DIVIDENDS. The maximum amount that is ultimately distributable by PUBLIC LIMITED COMPANIES is governed via the Companies Act, i.e., distributable reserves cannot exceed an amount that causes NET ASSETS to become less than SHARE CAPITAL plus UNDISTRIBUTABLE RESERVES. Also known as DISTRIBUTABLE PROFITS.

DIVERSIFIABLE RISK   A RISK that is unique to a company, ASSET, or market, meaning that it can be reduced or eliminated by holding a PORTFOLIO of assets that have little or no CORRELATION.

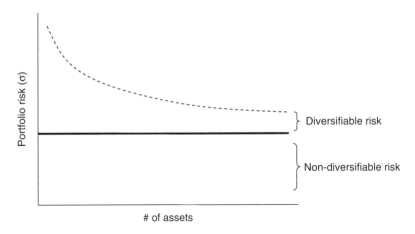

Also known as IDIOSYNCRATIC RISK, NONSYSTEMATIC RISK, UNSYSTEMATIC RISK, SPECIFIC RISK. See also DIVERSIFICATION, NONDIVERSIFIABLE RISK.

DIVERSIFICATION   A spreading or dispersion of RISK, achievable by combining ASSETS or exposures with little or no CORRELATION to one another; the process of diversification helps minimize concentrations of exposure and creates a more balanced set of risks. Ultimately, the risk of a diversified PORTFOLIO depends on the amount of risk that cannot be eliminated, i.e., NONDIVERSIFIABLE RISK, which is often measured by BETA, or the sensitivity of an INVESTMENT's RETURN compared to the market. The variability of returns for a given SECURITY can thus be divided into diversifiable and non-diversifiable components:

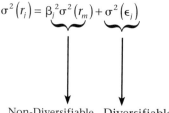

$$\sigma^2\left(r_j\right) = \beta_j^2 \sigma^2 \left(r_m\right) + \sigma^2 \left(\epsilon_j\right)$$

Non-Diversifiable   Diversifiable

where β_j^2 is the square of the beta of security j, $\sigma^2(r_m)$ is the VARIANCE of the market portfolio, and $\sigma^2(\epsilon_j)$ is the RESIDUAL VARIANCE of security j. See also DIVERSIFIABLE RISK, NONDIVERSIFIABLE RISK, PORTFOLIO DIVERSIFICATION.

Additional references: Markowitz (1952); Ross (1976); Sharpe (1971).

DIVERSITY SCORE   A scoring method used by CREDIT RATING agencies to evaluate the level of industry and ISSUER DIVERSIFICATION within a POOL of COLLATERAL underlying a COLLATERALIZED DEBT OBLIGATION. SECURITIES from different industry groups are assumed to have zero CORRELATION (providing maximum diversification), while those from the same industry group have some amount of positive correlation (reducing the diversification effects). Securities issued by the same ISSUER have a correlation of 1 (providing no diversification benefits).

DIVESTITURE   A CORPORATE FINANCE transaction where a company sells a SUBSIDIARY or a portion of its operations to a third party. A divestiture typically occurs when the company no longer views the ASSETS as essential to its business, prefers to refocus its operations more narrowly, or needs to raise CAPITAL for other purposes. See also DEMERGER.

DIVESTMENT   The process of removing invested CAPITAL from a project, INVESTMENT, or other ASSET as a result of a change in strategy or actual/perceived RISK in relation to RETURN. Also known as DISINVESTMENT.

DIVIDED COVER   INSURANCE CONTRACTS on the same property and PERIL purchased by the INSURED from two or more INSURERS. In the event of a CLAIM, the total SETTLEMENT will never exceed the amount of the loss, and will be divided on a PRO-RATA basis between insurers. See also APPORTIONMENT, OVERLAPPING INSURANCE, PRIMACY.

DIVIDEND   A periodic amount a company pays from its net EARNINGS to COMMON STOCK and/or PREFERRED STOCK INVESTORS; dividend payments are generally discretionary, meaning they can be suspended at will, though in certain instances they are made mandatory through terms of a SECURITIES issue. In most systems the BOARD OF DIRECTORS is responsible for setting dividend policy. Dividends are generally paid in cash (as CASH DIVIDENDS) though in some cases they may be paid in the form of additional SHARES (as STOCK DIVIDENDS). See also DIVIDEND YIELD, PAYOUT RATIO.

DIVIDEND COVER   See PAYOUT RATIO.

DIVIDEND DISCOUNT MODEL   A quantitative VALUATION measure, based on the DISCOUNTED CASH FLOW framework, that is used to estimate the fair value of a company's COMMON STOCK based on the discounted value of projected future DIVIDENDS. The price of a firm's stock can be estimated via:

$$S = \sum_{i=1}^{n} \frac{Div_i}{(1+r)^i}$$

where Div_i is the projected dividend payable in period i, r is the firm's DISCOUNT RATE, and n is the number of periods. Note that for stocks that do not currently pay out a dividend, the assumption is made that a dividend will be made starting in some future period.

Value can also be estimated through growth and dividend assumptions. No growth and constant dividend:

$$S = \frac{Div_i}{r}$$

Growth and constant dividend:

$$S = \frac{Div_i}{r - g}$$

where g is the dividend growth rate and all other terms are as defined above.

Additional levels of precision can be added by assuming that dividends will change in stages as the company progresses through its life cycle (e.g., two-stage growth, three-stage growth). See also DISCOUNTED CASH FLOW VALUATION MODEL, EARNINGS-BASED MODEL.

Additional references: Lintner (1956); Miller and Modigliani (1961).

DIVIDEND IN ARREARS   A DIVIDEND that has accumulated for one or more payment periods and is payable to the current holders of CUMULATIVE PREFERRED STOCK. Dividends cannot be paid to COMMON STOCK or NONCUMULATIVE PREFERRED STOCK INVESTORS until the arrears have been made current.

DIVIDEND PAYOUT RATIO   The amount of EARNINGS paid out in the form of DIVIDENDS by a company to its INVESTORS, computed as:

$$k = \frac{Div}{E}$$

where Div is the amount of dividends paid in the current period, E is the amount of earnings in the current period.

DIVIDEND WAIVER   A process where a significant INVESTOR in a company opts not to accept a DIVIDEND payment, allowing the company to retain the cash in its accounts.

DIVIDEND YIELD   The effective YIELD of a share of COMMON STOCK, typically calculated as:

$$y_{Div} = \frac{Div_i}{S_i}$$

where Div_i is the DIVIDEND paid in period i and S_i is the price of the stock in period i. See also PAYOUT RATIO.

DJIA   See DOW JONES INDUSTRIAL AVERAGE.

DK   [COL] Abbreviated form of "don't know," meaning one of the parties to a transaction disputes, refutes, or claims not to know, certain details of a trade. A trade that has been "DK'd" remains unreconciled until one of the parties concedes to a change in details or it is cancelled. Also known as OUT TRADE, QUESTIONED TRADE.

DMA   See DIRECT MARKET ACCESS.

DO NOT REDUCE ORDER   An ORDER with a price that is not to be adjusted in case of a STOCK SPLIT or DIVIDEND payout.

DOCUMENTARY CREDIT   A commercial LETTER OF CREDIT committing the BANK to pay a named BENEFICIARY, such as a seller of goods, once a confirming document has been delivered to the buyer; the documentary credit is widely used in international TRADE transactions, where BILLS OF LADING often serve as the evidencing document. Also known as DOCUMENTARY DRAFT.

DOCUMENTARY DRAFT   See DOCUMENTARY CREDIT.

DOCUMENTS AGAINST ACCEPTANCE   In international TRADE, a process where an exporter sends shipping documents with a relevant BILL OF EXCHANGE to a BANK, which releases the goods when the bill has been accepted. See also CASH AGAINST DOCUMENTS.

DOG   [COL] A STOCK that performs poorly compared to its peers or the broad market. See also DEAD MONEY.

DOG AND PONY SHOW   [COL] See ROADSHOW.

DOGS OF THE DOW   [COL] In the United States, an INVESTMENT strategy based on purchasing the 10 stocks in the DOW JONES INDUSTRIAL AVERAGE that provide the greatest DIVIDEND YIELD, and holding the stocks during the course of the year.

DOLLAR COST AVERAGING   See AVERAGING.

DOLLAR ROLL   A financial transaction involving the sale, and future repurchase, of MORTGAGE-BACKED SECURITIES for cash. Through the exchange the selling party effectively borrows funds from the purchasing party on a collateralized basis for a period that normally covers several days to several weeks. The dollar roll is essentially a form of mortgage-backed REPURCHASE AGREEMENT.

DOLLARIZATION   A process where a country adopts, either partially or wholly, the US dollar in place of its own CURRENCY.

DOUBLE AUCTION MARKET   An AUCTION MARKET featuring multiple sellers and buyers, who have full transparency into dealings. In the double auction process the first BID or OFFER is given priority, the high bid and low offer take precedence, and a new auction begins when all bids and offers at a given price are successfully matched. Certain STOCK EXCHANGES use a form of the double auction to match buyers and sellers.

DOUBLE BOTTOM   A TECHNICAL ANALYSIS charting formation that depicts two SUPPORT LEVELS followed by a BREAKOUT. The multiple rebounds are indicative of support and possible strength on the upside. Also known as a W FORMATION. See also DOUBLE TOP.

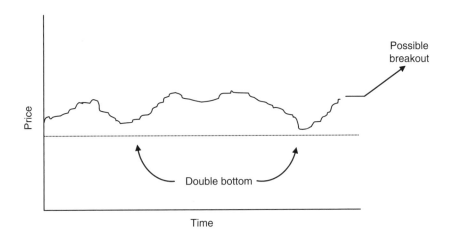

DOUBLE DIPPING   [COL] An unethical (and sometimes illegal) practice where a BROKER sells COMMISSION-based products through a client's fee-based account, earning REVENUES from two sources and effectively overcharging the client.

DOUBLE ENTRY ACCOUNTING   The standard ACCOUNTING framework used in many national jurisdictions that causes every transaction impacting the operations of a company to be reflected in the nominal ledgers via a DEBIT (left hand column) and a CREDIT (right hand column). The double entry system is used to accelerate the preparation of FINANCIAL STATEMENTS, improve their accuracy, and allow for simpler detection of errors or FRAUD, and is particularly important in a complex company with many transactions that daily affect its financial operations.

DOUBLE LEVERAGE   Borrowing at multiple levels within the corporate structure, such as the HOLDING COMPANY and a primary operating SUBSIDIARY. Double leverage is generally considered to be a more accurate reflection of a group's true indebtedness as it incorporates LIABILITIES from multiple entities. See also STRUCTURAL SUBORDINATION.

DOUBLE RECOVERY   An illegal attempt by an INSURED to file multiple CLAIMS on a single loss event with multiple INSURERS. Double recovery violates the principle of INDEMNITY, which states that an INSURANCE CONTRACT cannot result in a profit for the insured.

DOUBLE TAXATION   (1) A process where the income of an individual or company is taxed in multiple TAX jurisdictions. In order to avoid or reduce this burden, many countries have tax treaties that allow for an elimination or reduction. (2) The phenomenon where corporate earnings paid in the form of DIVIDENDS are taxed twice, once at the corporate level, and a second time at the INVESTOR level.

DOUBLE TOP   A TECHNICAL ANALYSIS charting formation that depicts two RESISTANCE LEVELS followed by a BREAKOUT. The multiple declines suggest resistance on the upside and possible weakness on the downside. Also known as a REVERSE W FORMATION. See also DOUBLE BOTTOM.

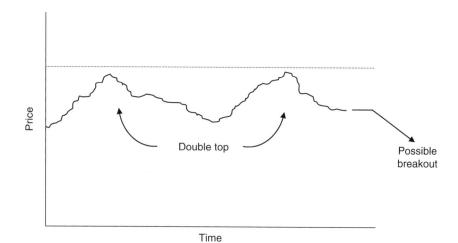

DOUBLING OPTION   A right granted by INVESTORS to an ISSUER of BONDS that allows the issuer to double the amount of the SINKING FUND provision in order to accelerate repayment and ultimate redemption.

DOW JONES INDUSTRIAL AVERAGE (DJIA)   A BENCHMARK price-weighted INDEX of the US STOCK market, comprised of 30 LARGE CAP STOCKS representing the industrial sector; the index is rebalanced periodically as industries and corporate leadership change. The DJIA, which is the oldest and most widely quoted US index, can be traded directly through EXCHANGE-TRADED FUNDS and DERIVATIVES.

DOW THEORY   The study of TECHNICAL ANALYSIS, efficient markets, and market cycles developed by Charles Dow in the early twentieth century. Under Dow theory, market cycles follow a primary trend (a long-term phase of approximately 4 years), which can be impacted by a secondary trend (short-term departures of STOCKS from trend lines) as well as a tertiary trend (short-term fluctuations in stock prices).

DOWN AND IN OPTION   A COMPLEX OPTION that creates a standard EUROPEAN OPTION if the price of the UNDERLYING market reference declines through a predefined BARRIER. See also BARRIER OPTION, DOWN AND OUT OPTION, KNOCK-IN OPTION, REVERSE KNOCK-IN OPTION, UP AND IN OPTION, UP AND OUT OPTION.

DOWN AND OUT OPTION   A COMPLEX OPTION that extinguishes a standard EUROPEAN OPTION if the price of the UNDERLYING market reference declines through a predefined BARRIER. If the barrier is not breached the European option remains in effect. See also BARRIER OPTION, DOWN AND IN OPTION, KNOCK-OUT OPTION, REVERSE KNOCK-OUT OPTION, UP AND IN OPTION, UP AND OUT OPTION.

DOWN ROUND   [COL] A second, third, or fourth round of VENTURE CAPITAL financing that is done at lower valuation levels than early rounds, suggesting the company may be worth less than initially predicted.

DOWNSIZING   A process where a company reduces its staffing and/or productive facilities as a means of managing costs more effectively and increasing its operating flexibility. Downsizing tends to occur when a company is becoming uncompetitive or during the contraction phase of the BUSINESS CYCLE. See also RIGHTSIZING.

DOWNSTREAM   (1) The process of channeling funds from a parent company or holding company to a SUBSIDIARY. This may occur when the parent or holding company can borrow on more favorable terms, or when the subsidiary is restricted in some way from raising funds directly. (2) The segment of the energy industry that is focused on refining, transportation, and marketing/retailing. See also UPSTREAM.

DOWNTICK   See MINUS TICK.

DPC   See DERIVATIVE PRODUCT COMPANY.

DPO   See DIRECT PUBLIC OFFERING.

DRAFT   (1) See BANK DRAFT. (2) See BILL OF EXCHANGE.

DRAG ALONG RIGHTS   Legal rights that allow majority SHAREHOLDERS of a company to force MINORITY INTERESTS to sell their SHARES in the event of a TAKEOVER bid; this is necessary in situations where the acquiring company requires 100% control. Drag along rights must be specifically negotiated in a CORPORATE FINANCE transaction. See also TAG ALONG RIGHTS.

DRAGNET CLAUSE   See CROSS COLLATERAL AGREEMENT.

DRAGON   [COL] A public BOND issued simultaneously in various Asian centers by a non-Asian company, denominated in a local Asian currency or US dollars. The dragon is effectively a regional form of the GLOBAL BOND.

DRAWDOWN   (1) A performance measure applied to HEDGE FUNDS, indicating the degree to which losses have reduced INVESTOR CAPITAL. (2) Reduction in capital within an investor's BROKER account as a result of losses. (3) The disbursement and use of funds by a BORROWER under a REVOLVING CREDIT FACILITY or other financing arrangement. (3) See also FLEXIBLE DRAWDOWN.

DRAWEE   A party that is instructed to pay under a BILL OF EXCHANGE or CHECK, as indicated by the DRAWER. In the case of a bill, the drawee may choose to have it accepted, or GUARANTEED, by an ACCEPTOR in exchange for a fee. See also DRAWER.

DRAWER   The person that issues a CHECK or executes a BILL OF EXCHANGE, requiring the DRAWEE to pay upon presentation and acceptance.

DROP LOCK   A mechanism where the INTEREST RATE on a FLOATING RATE NOTE or BOND is fixed once rates fall below a predefined level. The drop lock allows the ISSUER to lock in a lower rate of funding. See also DROP LOCK NOTE, SPREAD LOCK.

DROP LOCK NOTE   A FLOATING RATE NOTE or BOND that converts into a fixed COUPON obligation when a reference INTEREST RATE is breached on the downside. See also DROP LOCK.

DROPDOWN   A clause in a REINSURANCE CONTRACT that requires the REINSURER to provide coverage to an underlying INSURED if the INSURER cannot fulfill its obligations under the policy CEDED. A dropdown is most common in a FACULTATIVE REINSURANCE agreement where individual policies are analyzed and accepted.

DRY POWDER   [COL] (1) Excess cash reserves held by a company to meet future obligations or to capitalize on potential ACQUISITIONS or CAPITAL INVESTMENTS. (2) Cash held by INVESTORS that can be allocated to attractive INVESTMENT opportunities.

DTCC   See DEPOSITORY TRUST AND CLEARING CORPORATION.

DUAL BOARD SYSTEM   A corporate system where two separate BOARDS OF DIRECTORS are used to monitor and guide a company. Under a typical dual structure the SUPERVISORY BOARD is responsible for strategy and over-sight/supervision of EXECUTIVE MANAGEMENT, while the MANAGEMENT BOARD (or EXECUTIVE BOARD) is responsible for daily management and tactical issues. The supervisory board is often staffed with OUTSIDE DIRECTORS, while the management board comprises of senior executives of the company. See also SINGLE BOARD SYSTEM.

DUAL CLASS RECAPITALIZATION   A RESTRUCTURING of a company's existing COMMON STOCK into two classes with variable VOTING RIGHTS; creating a new class that conveys less than one vote per share is considered a DISENFRANCHISING TRANSACTION. A dual class recapitalization might be arranged to give a block of controlling SHAREHOLDERS even greater control over the firm.

DUAL CLASS STOCK   The COMMON STOCK of a CORPORATION that comes in two forms, one with enhanced VOTING RIGHTS and one with normal voting rights. The two classes may also carry different DIVIDEND rights. See also CONTROL STOCK, DUAL CLASS RECAPITALIZATION.

DUAL CURRENCY BOND   A BOND that pays INTEREST in one CURRENCY and PRINCIPAL redemption in a second currency. The FOREIGN EXCHANGE RATES associated with the COUPON and principal CASH FLOWS may be specified at the time of issuance, or they may be based on prevailing SPOT RATES at the time the coupons and principal are paid. A company may choose to issue a dual currency bond to HEDGE any FOREIGN EXCHANGE flows from its operations, or take a speculative view on currencies in order to obtain a lower COST OF CAPITAL. Also known as FOREIGN CURRENCY BOND.

DUAL LISTED COMPANY   Two PUBLIC COMPANIES that are constituted separately, retain separate identities, feature individual EXCHANGE listings but combine their business operations for purposes of creating goods and services. See also PUBLIC LIMITED COMPANY.

DUAL LISTED COMPANY ARBITRAGE   An ARBITRAGE strategy that seeks to exploit discrepancies between the SHARE prices of the constituent companies. An INVESTOR seeks to profit by purchasing the STOCK of the undervalued company and arranging a SHORT SALE of the overvalued company, with an expectation that the two will converge to a theoretical PARITY value over time.

DUAL PURPOSE FUND   A MUTUAL FUND or UNIT TRUST that issues two separate types of SECURITIES, including income shares, which are entitled only to the DIVIDEND flows from the underlying securities, and capital shares, which are entitled only to any resulting capital gains.

DUAL TRIGGER   An INSURANCE mechanism that provides the INSURED with a payout only if two separate TRIGGER events occur. One trigger is often related to a traditional insurable OPERATING RISK (e.g., damage or destruction in plant and equipment leading to business interruption), while the second may relate to a FINANCIAL RISK (e.g., a decline in OPERATING REVENUES to a particular amount, or a fall in the STOCK PRICE to a certain level). Since both events must occur in order for a SETTLEMENT to be paid, the PREMIUM is generally lower than on a conventional insurance CONTRACT. See also MULTIPLE TRIGGER PRODUCT, TRIPLE TRIGGER.

DUE DATE   The maturity date indicated on a BILL OF EXCHANGE.

DUE DILIGENCE   A process of detailed financial investigation into a company's operations and financial position, generally conducted by financial INTERMEDIARIES, lawyers, and accountants. Due diligence is commonly performed in advance of NEW ISSUE UNDERWRITINGS and CORPORATE FINANCE transactions, and to develop FAIRNESS OPINIONS; results are intended to inform and protect investors and corporate DIRECTORS by verifying the financial condition of the subject company.

DUMMY DIRECTOR   [COL] A DIRECTOR serving on the BOARD of a company who votes in favor of actions directed by a person who is not a director. Also known as ACCOMMODATION DIRECTOR.

DUOPOLY   A market that only features two sellers of goods or services, suggesting the sellers have a considerable degree of influence in setting prices. See also DUOPSONY, MONOPOLY, OLIGOPOLY.

DUOPSONY   A market that only features two buyers of goods or services, suggesting the buyers have an ability to influence the prices paid to suppliers. See also DUOPOLY, MONOPSONY, OLIGOPSONY.

DUPONT FORMULA   A financial performance which separates the traditional RETURN ON EQUITY (ROE) ratio into its constituent parts to provide further insight into performance and trends. Under this framework a company can isolate the effects of net profit margin, ASSET TURNOVER, and LEVERAGE. The Dupont formula is based on the fundamental ROE ratio:

$$ROE = \left(\frac{Inc}{Eq} \right)$$

$$\Rightarrow ROE = \left(\frac{Inc}{TA} \right)\left(\frac{TA}{Eq} \right)$$

$$\Rightarrow ROE = \left(\frac{Inc}{Sales} \right)\left(\frac{Sales}{TA} \right)\left(\frac{TA}{Eq} \right)$$

where Inc is net income, Sales is a measure of sales or turnover, TA is total assets, Eq is total equity.

DURABLE GOOD An ASSET that has a life span of at least three years, e.g., appliances, electronics, automobiles. Durable goods form part of the PERSONAL CONSUMPTION component of GROSS DOMESTIC PRODUCT (and GROSS NATIONAL PRODUCT). See also CAPITAL GOOD, NONDURABLE GOOD.

DURATION The average CASH FLOWS of an INTEREST RATE-sensitive ASSET or LIABILITY, takings account of YIELD, interest payments, MATURITY, and CALLABILITY. Duration quantifies the change in the price of a SECURITY for a small change in yield (e.g., the linear effects of market changes); the greater the duration, the more sensitive the price to changes in yield, the riskier the instrument. Securities with longer maturities or lower COUPONS have longer durations, which become even longer as yield declines. Duration is commonly used to estimate profit and loss on a bond, quantify INTEREST RATE RISK exposure, and create fixed income DELTA HEDGES. The standard dollar duration calculation for a semiannual pay security is given as:

$$Dur = -\frac{1}{(1+y)}\left[\frac{1C}{(1+y)^1} + \frac{2C}{(1+y)^2} + \ldots + \frac{nC}{(1+y)^n} + \frac{nM}{(1+y)^n}\right]$$

where C is semiannual coupon interest, y is the semiannual yield, n is the number of semiannual periods, and M is the maturity value of the bond (generally PAR VALUE).

Extensions of the duration formula include Macaulay's duration, computed as:

$$Dur\,(mac) = \frac{\sum_{i=1}^{n}\frac{iC}{(1+y)^i} + \frac{nM}{(1+y)^n}}{P}$$

and MODIFIED DURATION, calculated as:

$$Dur\,(mod) = \frac{Dur\,(mac)}{(1+y)}$$

See also DELTA, CONVEXITY.

DUTCH AUCTION An AUCTION MARKET technique used in certain marketplaces where the price of a SECURITY or ASSET being sold is lowered until a BID is obtained; the remaining orders are then filled at the same price. See also ENGLISH AUCTION.

DUTCH AUCTION PREFERRED STOCK ADJUSTABLE RATE PREFERRED STOCK with a floating DIVIDEND that is reset every 49 days through a DUTCH AUCTION process. Also known as AUCTION RATE PREFERRED STOCK.

DUTY   A TAX imposed by a government authority on a specific good or service. See also STAMP DUTY.

DUTY OF CARE   A legal requirement in certain systems where the BOARD OF DIRECTORS and EXECUTIVE MANAGEMENT must make informed decisions in discharging their FIDUCIARY responsibilities. An informed decision is generally based on gathering all relevant facts and material, giving such information due consideration, and then making a decision. A breach of duty of care can lead to legal action by SHAREHOLDERS. See also DUTY OF LOYALTY.

DUTY OF LOYALTY   A legal requirement in certain systems where the BOARD OF DIRECTORS and EXECUTIVE MANAGEMENT must ensure that any action taken is done in good faith and with the best interests of SHAREHOLDERS in mind. A breach of duty of loyalty can lead to legal action by shareholders. See also DUTY OF CARE.

DVP   See DELIVERY VERSUS PAYMENT.

DWARF   [COL] A 15-year MORTGAGE-BACKED SECURITY issued by the FEDERAL NATIONAL MORTGAGE ASSOCIATION. See also GNOME, MIDGET.

E

E-MINI [COL] An electronically traded EXCHANGE-TRADED DERIVATIVE contract with a denomination that is a fraction of a standard contract denomination, allowing retail or individual customers to participate. See also MINI.

E-TICKET See ELECTRONIC TICKET.

EAD See EXPOSURE AT DEFAULT.

EAR See EFFECTIVE ANNUAL RATE.

EARNED SURPLUS See RETAINED EARNINGS.

EARNINGS-BASED MODEL A quantitative VALUATION measure used to estimate the fair value of a company's STOCK based on its ability to generate future earnings.

The basic form of this process assumes a constant growth rate in earnings and is given as:

$$S = \frac{kE}{(r-g)}$$

where k is the DIVIDEND PAYOUT RATIO, r is the company's COST OF CAPITAL, g is the estimated, and constant, growth rate.

A changing growth coefficient requires estimates of the potential return on reinvested capital and its impact on dividend payouts from period to period. Since predicting earnings and dividends into infinity is challenging, a refinement of the model uses a combination of earnings and payout estimates over a specific time horizon, along with an estimate of TERMINAL VALUE.

$$S = \sum_{t=1}^{N} \frac{kE_t}{(1+r)^t} + \frac{TV}{(1+r)^N}$$

where N is the number of periods over which earnings can be reasonably estimated, TV is the estimated terminal value of the company. See also DISCOUNTED CASH FLOW VALUATION MODEL, DIVIDEND DISCOUNT MODEL.

EARNINGS BEFORE INTEREST AND TAXES (EBIT) A commonly used measure of a company's core operating profitability. By removing INTEREST and TAXES, the analysis focuses on a company's ability to generate REVENUES and manage production costs and noncash expenses associated with DEPRECIATION and AMORTIZATION. See also EARNINGS BEFORE INTEREST, TAXES, DEPRECIATION, AND AMORTIZATION.

EARNINGS BEFORE INTEREST, TAXES, DEPRECIATION, AND AMORTIZATION (EBITDA) A commonly used measure of a company's core operating profitability. By removing INTEREST, TAXES, DEPRECIATION, and AMORTIZATION, the analysis focuses on a company's ability to generate REVENUES and manage its production costs. See also EARNINGS BEFORE INTEREST AND TAXES.

EARNINGS PER SHARE (EPS) The amount of NET INCOME earned by a company, after PREFERRED STOCK DIVIDENDS have been distributed, which is attributable to each outstanding SHARE of COMMON STOCK. The EPS measure is used as a reflection of earnings power and corporate value; it is typically calculated on a FULLY DILUTED BASIS, which assumes that all outstanding stock OPTIONS are exercised, and any outstanding CONVERTIBLE BONDS are exchanged into new shares. The general computation is given as:

$$EPS = \frac{NI - Div_{pref}}{CS_{\frac{o}{s}}}$$

where NI is net income, Div_{pref} is preferred stock dividends, and $CS_{O/S}$ is the weighted average common stock shares outstanding (including those associated with options and convertible bonds for a fully diluted calculation).

EARNINGS RETAINED In the United Kingdom, RETAINED EARNINGS.

EARNINGS SURPRISE [COL] An unexpected difference between the EARNINGS announced by a company and the CONSENSUS EARNINGS estimated by financial analysts. Earnings surprises may be positive or negative.

EASY MONEY [COL] A policy stance taken by a CENTRAL BANK or other monetary authority that permits INTEREST RATES to remain low, in order to foster economic growth through cheap BORROWING.

EBIT See EARNINGS BEFORE INTEREST AND TAXES.

EBITDA See EARNINGS BEFORE INTEREST, TAXES, DEPRECIATION, AND AMORTIZATION.

EBRD See EUROPEAN BANK FOR RECONSTRUCTION AND DEVELOPMENT.

ECB See EUROPEAN CENTRAL BANK.

ECD See EURO CERTIFICATE OF DEPOSIT.

ECN See ELECTRONIC COMMUNICATIONS NETWORK.

ECONOMIC CAPITAL CAPITAL resources that a company allocates internally to conduct its operations and support its RISKS (including FINANCIAL RISK and OPERATING RISK). Economic capital, which is a key measure of SOLVENCY, serves to absorb unexpected losses and allows a firm to continue its operations. Also known as MANAGEMENT CAPITAL. See also CAPITAL

ALLOCATION, REGULATORY CAPITAL, RISK CAPITAL, TIER 1 CAPITAL, TIER 2 CAPITAL.

ECONOMIC COST   (1) OPPORTUNITY COST. (2) The total cost of a project, including financial costs and opportunity costs.

ECONOMIC INDICATORS Macroeconomic statistics released by government authorities that provide an indication of the relative strength or weakness of the economy and key markets (including labor, finance/banking, real estate/housing, construction, and so forth). Hundreds of statistics are released with varying frequencies and lags, and have different degrees of importance in shaping MONETARY POLICY and impacting financial markets. Those which are most closely watched by market participants include:

US

Average hourly earnings	Industrial production
Capacity utilization	International trade balance
Consumer confidence	Money supply
CPI	New home sales
PPI	Productivity
Durable goods orders	Nominal/Real GDP
Factory orders	Retail sales
Existing home sales	Unemployment
Housing starts	Federal reserve minutes

UK

GDP	Rics house price balance
GDP (NIESR estimate)	Nationwide consumer confidence
Current account balance	Retail sales volume
Trade balance	Bank of England minutes
Non-EU Trade balance UK	Employment/Unemployment rate
PPI (output and input)	CPI

Eurozone

GDP	Industrial production
Investment	Industrial new orders
External trade balance	Economic sentiment indicator
Current account balance	Retail trade turnover
HICP	Construction production
Unemployment/ employment rate	General gross government debt
Labor cost index	European Central Bank minutes
Industrial producer prices	

Japan

GDP	National CPI
Trade balance	Domestic corporate goods CPI
Merchandise trade balance	Bank of Japan minutes
Industrial production	Employment situation
Leading economic index	Tertiary industry index
Tankan Survey (Business Climate)	

Ex-Japan Asia, Rest of World

Real GDP	Foreign currency reserves
Nominal GDP	International debt
CPI	Direct foreign investment
Current account balance	Productivity index
Trade balance	Employment/
	unemployment rate

Also known as INDICATOR, MACROECONOMIC INDICATOR.

ECONOMIC PROFIT   The difference between REVENUES and costs (including INTEREST, TAXES, and DEPRECIATION, as well as implicit costs, such as OPPORTUNITY COSTS). See also ACCOUNTING PROFIT, ECONOMIC VALUE ADDED.

ECONOMIC VALUE   See ENTERPRISE VALUE.

ECONOMIC VALUE ADDED (EVA)   A measure of a company's value creation performance, computed as NET OPERATING PROFIT AFTER TAX (NOPAT) minus the COST OF CAPITAL. A company has positive EVA when its NOPAT exceeds the weighted average cost of the capital applied to its operations. See also ACCOUNTING PROFIT, ECONOMIC PROFIT, MARKET VALUE ADDED.

ECONOMICS   The area of study in social science concerned with scarce factors of production (including labor, land, CAPITAL) and the distribution and consumption of goods and services. Major subbranches focus on MICROECONOMICS and MACROECONOMICS.

ECONOMIES OF SCALE   The relative cost benefits that a company may obtain due to expansion within a market segment. This microeconomic theory centers on the decline in short- and long-term average costs that can be obtained by operating a larger operation more efficiently (e.g., through bulk discounts on raw material purchases, lower INTEREST costs from increased borrowing options, and so forth). Also known as SCALE EFFECT. See also DISECONOMIES OF SCALE.

ECONOMY   A system involving all activities related to the production and distribution of goods and services.

ECP   See EURO COMMERCIAL PAPER.

ECU   See EUROPEAN CURRENCY UNIT.

EDF   See EUROPEAN DEVELOPMENT FUND.

EDGE ACT BANK   A US BANK, owned by a state or nationally chartered BANK, with an international business scope. Edge Act banks are authorized to operate interstate branches, accept DEPOSITS from offshore sources, invest in foreign SECURITIES and projects, and grant foreign LOANS. See also INTERNATIONAL BANKING FACILITY.

EDI   See ELECTRONIC DATA INTERCHANGE.

EDS   See EQUITY DEFAULT SWAP.

EEA   See EUROPEAN ECONOMIC AREA.

EEC   See EUROPEAN ECONOMIC COMMUNITY.

EFFECTIVE ANNUAL RATE (EAR)   The INTEREST paid or received as a percentage of the PRINCIPAL, restated from its contracted compounding rate (e.g., continuous, monthly, quarterly) to an annual rate, allowing for comparison. EAR, which excludes any fees paid or received, can be computed as:

$$r = (1 + (i/n))^n - 1$$

where i is the nominal rate, n is the number of compounding periods per year. Also known as ANNUAL EQUIVALENT RATE, EFFECTIVE INTEREST RATE. See also ANNUAL PERCENTAGE RATE.

EFFECTIVE INTEREST RATE   See EFFECTIVE ANNUAL RATE.

EFFECTIVE RATE   The actual INTEREST RATE a BANK charges on a LOAN, after taking into account fees and COMPENSATING BALANCE requirements. See also YIELD TO MATURITY.

EFFECTIVE SPREAD   The actual difference between the BID and OFFER of a SECURITIES transaction, incorporating the direction of price movements. See also QUOTED SPREAD, REALIZED SPREAD.

EFFECTIVE TAX RATE   For an individual or a company, the actual income TAX paid divided by net taxable income before taxes. The effective tax rate may be different than the STATUTORY TAX RATE as a result of adjustments, gross-ups, and deductions. See also AVERAGE TAX RATE, MARGINAL TAX RATE.

EFFECTIVE YIELD   See YIELD TO MATURITY.

EFFICIENT FRONTIER   In the CAPITAL ASSET PRICING MODEL, a boundary defined by INVESTMENT PORTFOLIOS that provide INVESTORS with the maximum possible RETURN for a given level of RISK. See also CAPITAL MARKET LINE, SECURITY MARKET LINE.

EFFICIENT MARKET HYPOTHESIS   A theory stating that financial markets reflect all publicly available information, suggesting that all INVESTORS have an equal opportunity to earn a given minimum RETURN, and that it is not possible to predict whether one ASSET will generate a better RISK-adjusted return than another one. The "weak form" of the hypothesis indicates that market prices reflect all information contained in past prices, the "semi-strong form" indicates that market prices reflect all information contained in past prices and published information, and the "strong form" indicates that market prices reflect all information contained in past prices, published information, and all other nonpublic information. See also RANDOM WALK.

Additional reference: Fama (1970).

EFFICIENT PORTFOLIO A PORTFOLIO that gives an INVESTOR the highest EXPECTED PORTFOLIO RETURN amongst all FEASIBLE PORTFOLIOS with the same degree of RISK. See also EFFICIENT FRONTIER.

EFP See EXCHANGE FOR PHYSICAL.

EFT See ELECTRONIC FUNDS TRANSFER.

EFTA See EUROPEAN FREE TRADE ASSOCIATION.

EIB See EUROPEAN INVESTMENT BANK.

ELASTIC A state where a proportional change in one variable leads to the same or greater proportional change in another variable. Elastic DEMAND is a strong demand response to a change in price, i.e., a proportional decline in the purchase price results in a larger proportional increase in demand. Elastic SUPPLY is a strong supply response to a change in price, i.e., a proportional increase in the selling price results in a larger proportional increase in the amount supplied. See also ELASTICITY, INELASTIC.

ELASTICITY The degree to which a proportional change in one variable impacts the proportional change in another variable, commonly used in reference to prices, SUPPLY, and DEMAND. Price elasticity measures the proportional change in goods supplied or demanded for a proportional change in price; supply elasticity measures the proportional change in quantity supplied for a proportional change in price; and demand elasticity measures the proportional change in quantity demanded for a proportional change in price. See also ELASTIC, INELASTIC.

ELBOW [COL] An area of the YIELD CURVE that is deemed to be financially attractive (i.e., CHEAP) and where profits can be generated by simply ROLLING DOWN THE CURVE.

ELECTRICITY SWAP An OVER-THE-COUNTER SWAP involving the exchange of fixed and floating electricity prices based on the average level of a recognized electricity pool or pricing index; transactions are often settled monthly or quarterly (to coincide with billing cycles), on a physical or financial basis. Also known as POWER SWAP. See also POWER OPTION.

ELECTRONIC BANKING A computerized service offered by many BANKS and financial institutions that allows clients to conduct essential BANKING transactions (e.g., ACCOUNT balance inquiries, fund transfers, bill paying) via computer. See also ELECTRONIC TRADING.

ELECTRONIC COMMUNICATIONS NETWORK (ECN)   An electronic system that widely disseminates to third parties any ORDERS entered by a MARKET MAKER, and permits such orders to be executed. ECNs exclude any systems that CROSS multiple orders at one or more specified times at a single price set by the system (i.e., by ALGORITHM) and those that do not allow orders to be crossed or executed against directly by participants outside of such times, as well as any system operated by a market maker that executes customer orders primarily against the market maker's proprietary book. See also ALTERNATIVE TRADING SYSTEM, DEALER MARKET ELECTRONIC COMMUNICATIONS NETWORK, HYBRID ELECTRONIC COMMUNICATIONS NETWORK, REGULATED ELECTRONIC COMMUNICATIONS NETWORK.

ELECTRONIC DATA INTERCHANGE (EDI)   The exchange of information from computer system to computer system, in a standard form. EDI adheres to standard formatting of messages to ensure consistency and efficiency in communicating large blocks of data. The EDI framework is used for all manner of business communication, including purchasing, invoicing, payments transfers, and so forth.

ELECTRONIC FUNDS TRANSFER (EFT)   The transfer of cash through an electronic mechanism, such as an interbank wire system or a retail point-of-sale system, rather than a physical CHECK or DRAFT.

ELECTRONIC LIMIT ORDER BOOK (ELOB)   An electronic platform that operates as a form of electronic EXCHANGE, posting standard LIMIT ORDERS and, in some instances, also managing MARKET ORDERS HIDDEN ORDERS. An ELOB aggregates BIDS and OFFERS submitted buyers and sellers, posting varying degrees of price and volume information without attribution to the buyer or seller; as bids and offers are queued in the ELOB, price assumes priority, followed by time.

ELECTRONIC PORTAL   An integrated electronic interface where a sponsoring FINANCIAL INSTITUTION or EXCHANGE provides clients with access to a broad range of market information, research, quotes/pricing, analytics, and/ or EXECUTION.

ELECTRONIC TICKET   An electronically generated and communicated information "slate" used by certain EXCHANGES and ELECTRONIC COMMUNICATIONS NETWORKS to convey details of a TRADE. Relevant parties update the electronic ticket as new information becomes available during the TRADING and CLEARING processes. The resulting electronic ticket acts as a legally binding CONFIRMATION once accepted by both parties. Also known as E-TICKET.

ELECTRONIC TRADING   Any form of TRADING that is routed and executed through an electronic platform, such as an ALTERNATIVE TRADING SYSTEM or ELECTRONIC COMMUNICATIONS NETWORK, rather than through a physical

BROKER or MARKET MAKER on an EXCHANGE floor. Electronic trading exists in various ASSET classes, including STOCKS, BONDS, FOREIGN EXCHANGE, and COMMODITIES, and can be executed between platforms or through electronic capabilities on exchanges. See also ELECTRONIC BANKING.

ELEPHANT   [COL] A large institutional client, such as a PENSION FUND, MUTUAL FUND, HEDGE FUND, CORPORATION, or sovereign entity, that FINANCIAL INSTITUTIONS court in order to generate NEW ISSUE, CORPORATE FINANCE, or INVESTMENT MANAGEMENT business. See also ELEPHANT HUNTING.

ELEPHANT HUNTING   [COL] A process where FINANCIAL INSTITUTIONS attempt to win business or MANDATES from large institutional clients. Elephant hunting generally requires continuous communication with clients on deal-related ideas and a certain amount of pro-bono work in support of the ideas. See also ELEPHANT.

ELIGIBILITY   The characteristics that define ELIGIBLE PAPER.

ELIGIBLE LIABILITY   A BANK LIABILITY, such as an interbank or retail DEPOSIT, that attracts a regulatory RESERVE.

ELIGIBLE PAPER   Short-term financial instruments (such as GOVERNMENT BILLS, CERTIFICATES OF DEPOSIT, BANKER'S ACCEPTANCES, or BANK-endorsed corporate obligations) that can be used for collateralized borrowing in the REPURCHASE AGREEMENT market or through CENTRAL BANK mechanisms, such as the DISCOUNT WINDOW.

ELIGIBLE RESERVES   In the United States, cash held in a BANK plus funds held in the bank's name at the FEDERAL RESERVE.

ELIGIBLE SECURITIES   SECURITIES that BANKS are allowed to purchase, hold, and TRADE on a direct basis, including GOVERNMENT BONDS and AGENCY SECURITIES. Those ruled ineligible under regulations must often be traded through a separately incorporated and regulated subsidiary.

ELOB   See ELECTRONIC LIMIT ORDER BOOK.

EMBARGO   Prohibition on TRADE with another country either generally (all goods and services) or specifically (targeted goods and services). An embargo, which is one manifestation of SOVEREIGN RISK, may arise as a result of trade disputes, political constraints, REGULATIONS, or national security issues.

EMBEDDED OPTION   An OPTION that is incorporated into a STRUCTURED NOTE or OVER-THE-COUNTER SWAP to provide the INVESTOR or ISSUER with a lower funding cost, unique speculative payoff, or customized RISK MANAGEMENT solution. Also known as EMBEDDO.

EMBEDDO   [COL] See EMBEDDED OPTION.

EMBEZZLEMENT   The fraudulent appropriation of ASSETS that have been entrusted by the LEGAL OWNER, generally through secretive or deceptive measures. See also FRAUD.

EMERGING CURRENCY   See EXOTIC CURRENCY.

EMERGING MARKET   A market or economy that is in the initial stages of commercial progress, and which is subject to both development and profit opportunities and increased RISK levels.

EMISSIONS   Any gases emitted in the furtherance of productive processes, and which may be subject to control through a CAP AND TRADE system, allowing for EMISSIONS TRADING between countries and companies.

EMISSIONS TRADING   The TRADING of emissions allowances between companies, or ASSIGNED AMOUNT UNITS across borders, for those participating in a CAP AND TRADE mechanism.

EMPLOYEE BUYOUT   The ACQUISITION of a PUBLIC COMPANY by an employee-led group that leads to a controlling or majority stake in the outstanding EQUITY. The buyout may be financed through the collective resources of employees as well as external financing obtained from a BANK or other financial institution. See also MANAGEMENT BUYOUT.

EMPLOYEE RETIREMENT INCOME SECURITY ACT (ERISA)   In the United States, legislation passed in 1974 permitting the creation of private PENSION FUNDS and employee profit-sharing plans, and authorizing the creation of the Pension Benefit Guaranty Corporation to insure employee pensions.

EMPLOYEE SHARE OWNERSHIP TRUST (ESOT)   In the United Kingdom, a program where a TRUST acquires SHARES of a company's COMMON STOCK and distributes them to employees as a form of compensation. The ESOT builds employee ownership in the company and creates a TAX deduction for the company.

EMPLOYEE STOCK OWNERSHIP PLAN (ESOP)   In the United States, a program where a company provides SHARES of its COMMON STOCK to employees through a TRUST. The program builds employee ownership and aligns employee/INVESTOR interests, and creates a TAX deduction for the company.

EMS   See EUROPEAN MONETARY SYSTEM.

EMTN   See EURO MEDIUM-TERM NOTE.

EMU   See EUROPEAN MONETARY UNION.

ENCUMBRANCE   A real property CLAIM that passes with TITLE, often used in collateralized FINANCING; the BORROWER encumbers the property by granting the lending BANK a LIEN. The encumbrance does not impact ownership transfer, but it can reduce the MARKET VALUE and marketability of the property.

END OF DAY SWEEP   See SWEEP.

ENDOGENOUS LIQUIDITY   LIQUIDITY and LIQUIDITY RISK that are specific to a firm and the actions it takes in managing its ASSETS, LIABILITIES, and OFF-BALANCE SHEET ACTIVITIES. See also ASSET LIQUIDITY RISK, ASSET-FUNDING LIQUIDITY RISK, EXOGENOUS LIQUIDITY.

ENDORSEMENT   (1) A signature appearing on a NEGOTIABLE INSTRUMENT that transfers legal ownership from one party (the ENDORSER) to another party (the BENEFICIARY). While endorsements may be unqualified, allowing for the free transfer of ownership, they may also be qualified, conditional, or restrictive, limiting transferability and thus marketability. (2) An agreement attached to an INSURANCE CONTRACT that adds or removes particular coverages; the endorsement takes precedence over provisions incorporated in the original contract.

ENDORSER   The party signing a NEGOTIABLE INSTRUMENT; once the endorser signs the instrument, ownership is transferred to the BENEFICIARY. See also ENDORSEMENT.

ENDOWMENT ASSURANCE POLICY   In the United Kingdom, a form of INSURANCE that provides a lump sum payment to the BENEFICIARY, either on an agreed date or with the death of the INSURED. The policy, which has SAVINGS features that accumulate value, can also be used to secure a residential MORTGAGE (i.e., ENDOWMENT MORTGAGE).

ENDOWMENT MORTGAGE   In the United Kingdom, a form of residential MORTGAGE where the final PRINCIPAL balance is secured by an ENDOWMENT ASSURANCE POLICY.

ENGLISH AUCTION   An AUCTION MARKET technique applied in certain marketplaces where the price of a SECURITY being sold is publicly announced at each stage, allowing parties to submit higher BIDS. When no further bids are received, the orders are filled. See also DUTCH AUCTION.

ENTERPRISE RISK MANAGEMENT (ERM)   (1) A holistic RISK MANAGEMENT process that combines a company's current and anticipated RISKS into a single, multiyear risk management program using various products and markets. ERM in its broadest sense allows a firm to use ALTERNATIVE RISK TRANSFER techniques/products, including INSURANCE, REINSURANCE, DERIVATIVES, CAPTIVES, CONTINGENT CAPITAL, and/or INSURANCE-LINKED SECURITIES to manage exposures. (2) A consolidated approach to financial risk management used by certain BANKS and SECURITIES FIRMS that unites CREDIT RISK, MARKET RISK, and OPERATIONAL RISK under a single framework. (1,2) Also known as INTEGRATED RISK MANAGEMENT.

ENTERPRISE VALUE   A measure of the value of a firm, typically computed as the sum of expected future net CASH FLOWS, DISCOUNTED back to the present at a firm-specific DISCOUNT RATE. Enterprise value can be computed via:

$$EV = \sum_{t=1}^{n} \frac{NCF_t}{(1+r)^t}$$

where NCF_t is the expected net cash flow at time t, r is the discount rate, and n is the number of periods. Also known as ECONOMIC VALUE. See also ACCOUNTING VALUE.

ENTERPRISE ZONE   A special area designated by a government authority that accords TAX benefits and special exemptions to those establishing a business in the area. The enterprise zone is designed to use such incentives to increase employment and stimulate economic growth.

ENTREPÔT   [FR] A commercial TRADE center where goods are imported from several sources and then reexported to various destinations. Although the entrepôt produces no goods of its own it may be able to operate successfully as a result of ECONOMIES OF SCALE and efficiencies and comparative advantages related to transportation, warehousing, INSURANCE, FINANCING, and economic/political stability.

ENTREPRENEUR   [FR] A creative, RISK-taking, individual that develops a new business concept or product, or expands into new markets in order to generate profits.

ENVIRONMENTAL AUDIT   An AUDIT performed on a company by a qualified organization that focuses specifically on adherence to environmental standards or laws. The audit may be undertaken for legal, regulatory, or managerial purposes.

EONIA   See EURO OVERNIGHT INDEX AVERAGE.

EPS   See EARNINGS PER SHARE.

EPS BOOTSTRAPPING   [COL] A CORPORATE FINANCE practice where an acquirer buys a company with a low PRICE/EARNINGS RATIO through a STOCK SWAP in order to boost the post-acquisition EARNINGS PER SHARE (EPS) of the newly formed group and create a rise in the stock price.

EQUILIBRIUM PRICING MODEL   A theoretical mathematical model that attempts to establish market-clearing price levels (i.e., where SUPPLY and DEMAND for ASSETS meet and the market clears). Equilibrium models, such as the CAPITAL ASSET PRICING MODEL, are difficult to calibrate to actual markets and are therefore used primarily for theoretical purposes. Also known as ABSOLUTE PRICING MODEL.

EQUITABLE CONTROL   A theoretical concept in CORPORATE GOVERNANCE where managers obtain or receive power from diffuse SHAREHOLDERS and act in the best interests of the firm.

EQUITABLE INTEREST   An ownership interest in ASSETS that is conveyed via TITLE and which is considered fair and just by the courts but which may not represent a strict legal right, e.g., the interests of a BENEFICIARY in a TRUST are of an equitable nature. See also EQUITY.

EQUITAS   A vehicle established in 1996 to REINSURE, on a mandatory basis, the LIABILITIES of NAMES operating through LLOYD'S OF LONDON.

EQUITY   (1) In INSURANCE, the concept of pricing fairness across CONTRACTS. PREMIUMS must be set according to the loss expectations within RISK classifications; those with the same risk characteristics should face the same premium and should not be subject to any discriminatory pricing. (2) See CAPITAL, COMMON SHARES, COMMON STOCK, STOCK. (3) A beneficial interest in a specific ASSET. (4) A concept of RIGHTS , separate and apart from legal rights, which may be conveyed via an EQUITABLE INTEREST.

EQUITY ACCOUNTING A form of ACCOUNTING where a company records the relevant portion of the undistributed earnings and RESERVES of an AFFILIATE in which it holds an ownership interest, typically in relation to the percentage of its EQUITY ownership stake. This concept generally applies when the ownership stake is less than 50% but more than 20% (i.e., influence but not control).

EQUITY ANALYST An INVESTMENT ANALYST working for a BANK or other FINANCIAL INSTITUTION that is responsible for analyzing the financial state and prospects of a PUBLIC COMPANY and developing estimates of future EARNINGS PER SHARE and STOCK PRICE targets, with a view toward offering a recommendation on whether to buy, sell, or retain a position in the company's SHARES. See also CREDIT ANALYST.

EQUITY BRIDGE See BRIDGE EQUITY.

EQUITY CALL SWAP An OVER-THE-COUNTER SWAP involving the exchange of a floating INTEREST RATE for potential gains from the appreciation on an EQUITY INDEX (which may take the form of a single COMMON STOCK, a BASKET, or a broad market index). The equity call swap can be viewed as a long-dated CALL OPTION with a PREMIUM paid over time via the floating rate. See also EQUITY DERIVATIVE, EQUITY INDEX SWAP, EQUITY PUT SWAP.

EQUITY DEFAULT SWAP (EDS) A form of OVER-THE-COUNTER DERIVATIVE that provides the buyer with a compensatory payment if a reference company's COMMON STOCK declines by a large amount, in exchange for an upfront or periodic PREMIUM payment. The EDS is similar to a CREDIT DEFAULT SWAP (with the exception of the reference ASSET) or a deep OUT-OF-THE-MONEY digital American PUT OPTION.

EQUITY DERIVATIVE An EXCHANGE-TRADED DERIVATIVE or OVER-THE-COUNTER DERIVATIVE with an UNDERLYING reference based on COMMON STOCKS, BASKETS, and market indexes. An equity derivative can be structured as an equity OPTION, equity FUTURE, equity forward, EQUITY CALL SWAP, EQUITY INDEX SWAP, EQUITY PUT SWAP, or EQUITY WARRANT. See also COMMODITY DERIVATIVE, CREDIT DERIVATIVE, CURRENCY DERIVATIVE, INTEREST RATE DERIVATIVE.

EQUITY DILUTION See DILUTION.

EQUITY FINANCE The general class of STOCK LOANS and SHARE-based REPURCHASE AGREEMENT transactions.

EQUITY INDEX SWAP An OVER-THE-COUNTER SWAP involving the exchange of a floating INTEREST RATE for potential gains from the appreciation or depreciation of an EQUITY INDEX (which may be a COMMON

STOCK, a BASKET, or a broad market index). The equity index swap can be viewed as a long-dated OPTION with a PREMIUM paid over time via the floating rate. Also known as EQUITY SWAP. See also EQUITY CALL SWAP, EQUITY DERIVATIVE, EQUITY PUT SWAP.

EQUITY KICKER   See KICKER.

EQUITY-LINKED ENDOWMENT POLICY   See EQUITY-LINKED POLICY.

EQUITY-LINKED LIFE INSURANCE POLICY   See EQUITY-LINKED POLICY.

EQUITY-LINKED POLICY   A type of INSURANCE POLICY where the PREMIUMS paid by the INSURED are invested in EQUITIES. The SURRENDER VALUE of a standard equity-linked policy depends on the RETURNS achieved by the equity PORTFOLIO. Policies are also available with a minimum guaranteed ASSET value, to reduce the RISK to the insured. Also known as EQUITY-LINKED ENDOWMENT POLICY, EQUITY-LINKED LIFE INSURANCE POLICY.

EQUITY OPTION   An EXCHANGE-TRADED or OVER-THE-COUNTER OPTION involving a single STOCK. VANILLA and COMPLEX OPTIONS can be bought and sold on a broad range of stocks, and may be traded concurrently with the DELTA-equivalent amount of SHARES as a HEDGE. See also COMMODITY OPTION, CURRENCY OPTION, INDEX OPTION, INTEREST RATE OPTION.

EQUITY PUT SWAP   An OVER-THE-COUNTER SWAP involving the exchange of a floating INTEREST RATE for potential gains from the depreciation of an EQUITY INDEX (which may take the form of a single COMMON STOCK, a BASKET, or a broad market index). The equity put swap can be viewed as a long-dated PUT OPTION with a PREMIUM paid over time via the floating rate. See also EQUITY CALL SWAP, EQUITY DERIVATIVE, EQUITY INDEX SWAP.

EQUITY RISK   The RISK of loss due to an adverse move in the direction of EQUITY prices or INDEXES. Equity risk is a form of DIRECTIONAL RISK.

EQUITY SWAP   See EQUITY INDEX SWAP.

EQUITY TRANCHE   See RESIDUAL SECURITY.

EQUITY VALUATION   See CORPORATE VALUATION.

EQUITY VALUE   The pure EQUITY value of the firm, computed as FIRM VALUE less the MARKET VALUE of DEBT.

EQUITY WARRANT   A long-dated EQUITY OPTION (i.e., 3 to 5 years) issued by a financial INTERMEDIARY on a company's COMMON STOCK, which can be EXERCISED by the holder into new SHARES (making the transaction dilutive). Since new equity results in the event of EXERCISE, an equity warrant must be sponsored and approved by the issuing company. Also known as WARRANT. See also BOND WITH WARRANT, COVERED WARRANT.

EQUIVALENT BOND YIELD   See BOND EQUIVALENT YIELD.

EQUIVALENT BREAKEVEN   A measure of the number of years it takes for an INVESTOR to recover the initial CONVERSION PREMIUM paid in acquiring a CONVERTIBLE BOND, typically computed as:

$$EBE = \frac{Conv_{prem}}{C - (Conv_{ratio}DPS)}$$

where $Conv_{prem}$ is the conversion premium, C is the COUPON, $Conv_{ratio}$ is the CONVERSION RATIO, and DPS is DIVIDENDS per share. See also ADJUSTED BREAKEVEN, SIMPLE BREAKEVEN.

ERISA   See EMPLOYEE RETIREMENT INCOME SECURITY ACT.

ERM   See ENTERPRISE RISK MANAGEMENT.

ERRORS AND OMISSIONS   The general category of mistakes that arise in the ACCOUNTING or financial records of a company. Errors and omissions can be viewed as a form of PROCESS RISK and can be INSURED by an INSURER.

ESCROW ACCOUNT   A TRUST account that is used to collect from a DEBTOR periodic payments related to a MORTGAGE, an INSURANCE policy, or other contractual CASH FLOWS.

ESOP   See EMPLOYEE STOCK OWNERSHIP PLAN.

ESOT   See EMPLOYEE SHARE OWNERSHIP TRUST.

ESTOPPEL   A legal rule of evidence that prohibits a person from denying a statement or allegation that contradicts or reverses a previous statement, or which has otherwise already been legally established.

ETF   See EXCHANGE-TRADED FUND.

ETHICAL INVESTMENT   See SOCIALLY RESPONSIBLE INVESTMENT.

EU   See EUROPEAN UNION.

EUREX   An electronic EXCHANGE owned by DEUTSCHE BORSE and the Swiss Exchange that specializes in DERIVATIVES. Eurex was created in 1998 when the parent exchanges merged their derivative affiliates, Deutsche Terminborse and Swiss Options and Financial Futures Exchange.

EURIBOR   See EURO INTERBANK OFFERED RATE.

EURO   A unit of CURRENCY adopted in 1999 by countries comprising the EUROPEAN MONETARY UNION; early commercial exchange transactions were ultimately supplemented by circulation of SPECIE. The euro, which comprises of a fixed percentage of the domestic currencies of participating nations, is considered a RESERVE CURRENCY.

EURO CERTIFICATE OF DEPOSIT (ECD)   A EUROCURRENCY CERTIFICATE OF DEPOSIT issued by a BANK, often from a London-based branch or SUBSIDIARY. Like other CDs, ECDs can be issued with fixed or floating

COUPONS and in varying maturities and are often traded on a secondary basis between DEALERS.

EURO COMMERCIAL PAPER (ECP)   Short-term, unsecured discount DEBT SECURITIES with MATURITIES ranging from 1 to 360 days issued by companies in the EUROMARKETS. A SYNDICATE of DEALERS places ECP on a best efforts basis; unlike US COMMERCIAL PAPER, ECP issues may be unrated and need not be backed by SWINGLINES. See also EUROBOND, EURO MEDIUM-TERM NOTE, EURONOTE.

EURO DEPOSIT   A EUROCURRENCY time DEPOSIT issued by a BANK, often from a London-based branch of SUBSIDIARY. Unlike EURO CERTIFICATES OF DEPOSIT, Eurodeposits are generally not tradable on a secondary basis.

EURO INTERBANK OFFERED RATE (EURIBOR)   The OFFER side of the EURO-based interbank DEPOSIT market, or the rate at which prime BANKS are willing to lend funds. EURIBOR, which is set every business day at 11 am Brussels time by the European Banking Federation, is quoted for maturities of one week and monthly to 1 year, and serves as an important base reference for other financial instruments (e.g., DERIVATIVES, FLOATING RATE NOTES) with a floating rate component.

EURO MEDIUM-TERM NOTE (EMTN)   A FIXED INCOME SECURITY issued by a company or sovereign entity in the EUROMARKETS from a standing program arranged by an UNDERWRITER; once the program is registered issuance can take place at will. Financing via an EMTN program gives an ISSUER considerable flexibility in accessing funds in the form, and at a time, deemed most beneficial. EMTNs can be issued in a range of CURRENCIES and MATURITIES (up to 30 years), in FIXED RATE, FLOATING RATE, collateralized, amortizing, and CREDIT supported form. A single issue from an EMTN program can be likened to a EURONOTE or EUROBOND. See also EURO COMMERCIAL PAPER, MEDIUM-TERM NOTE.

EURO OVERNIGHT INDEX AVERAGE   EURO overnight INDEX average of INTEREST RATES on unsecured EURO DEPOSITS arranged by London-based BROKERS (quoted as EURONIA) or Continental markets (quoted as EONIA).

EUROBOND   A BOND issued by a company or sovereign entity in the EUROMARKETS. Eurobonds are typically sold as BEARER SECURITIES through a SYNDICATE or TENDER PANEL, or via EURO MEDIUM-TERM NOTE programs. Bonds may be issued in FIXED RATE or FLOATING RATE form, with MATURITIES ranging from 3 to 30+ years. Eurobonds are often listed on a national STOCK EXCHANGE, such as Luxembourg, Zurich, or London, although most SECONDARY TRADING occurs OVER-THE-COUNTER. See also EURONOTE, EURO COMMERCIAL PAPER.

EUROCLEAR   A European organization established in 1968 and responsible for SETTLEMENT and CLEARING of EUROBONDS, EQUITIES, and INVESTMENT FUNDS. See also CLEARSTREAM.

EUROCURRENCY   An ASSET or LIABILITY created outside the country of origin, e.g., a US dollar LOAN outside the United States is a EURODOLLAR loan, a yen DEPOSIT outside of Japan is a Euroyen deposit. Eurocurrency transactions are typically free of home market REGULATIONS and may attract favorable TAX and RESERVE treatment.

EURODOLLAR   A US dollar ASSET or LIABILITY located outside the United States, and the single largest element of the EUROCURRENCY market. Eurodollar LOANS are created when a BANK lends dollars through an offshore branch, an EDGE ACT BANK, or an INTERNATIONAL BANKING FACILITY (IBF). Eurodollar DEPOSITS arise through the acceptance of funds from offshore branches or IBFs.

EUROEQUITY ISSUE   (1) An issuance of SHARES by a company on an overseas EXCHANGE, denominated in the overseas CURRENCY rather than in the issuing company's home currency. (2) An issuance of shares by a company that occurs simultaneously, in several domestic markets, through an international SYNDICATE.

EUROMARKET   The international CAPITAL MARKETS, or the marketplace for offshore, or nondomestic, SECURITIES offerings and DERIVATIVE activity in support of such FINANCINGS. The Euromarket includes the PRIMARY MARKET and SECONDARY MARKET for INTERBANK DEPOSITS, EURO COMMERCIAL PAPER, EURONOTES, EURO MEDIUM-TERM NOTES, EUROBONDS, and GLOBAL BONDS, as well as related derivatives. Although issuance and TRADING can theoretically occur in any nondomestic currency, in practice it is limited to major RESERVE CURRENCIES. The Euromarkets are subject to a degree of regulatory oversight, although requirements related to REGISTRATION, DUE DILIGENCE, and market-making tend to be more flexible than in other domestic markets.

EURONIA   See EURO OVERNIGHT INDEX AVERAGE.

EURONOTE   A NOTE issued by a company or sovereign entity in the EUROMARKETS. Euronotes are typically sold as BEARER SECURITIES through a SYNDICATE or TENDER PANEL, or via EURO MEDIUM-TERM NOTE programs. Notes may be issued in FIXED RATE or FLOATING RATE form, in any one of several CURRENCIES, with MATURITIES ranging from 1 to 3 years. See also EURO COMMERCIAL PAPER, EURO MEDIUM-TERM NOTE, EUROBOND, NOTE ISSUANCE FACILITY, REVOLVING UNDERWRITING FACILITY.

EUROPE 1992   See SINGLE MARKET.

EUROPEAN BANK FOR RECONSTRUCTION AND DEVELOPMENT (EBRD)   A MULTILATERAL DEVELOPMENT BANK created in 1990 to assist in the economic development of Central and Eastern European nations via infrastructure and project LOANS to private and public sector BORROWERS.

EUROPEAN BARRIER OPTION   See POINT BARRIER OPTION.

EUROPEAN CENTRAL BANK (ECB) The CENTRAL BANK of the EUROPEAN MONETARY UNION (EMU), created in 1998 to manage MONETARY POLICY within the EMU (i.e., managing INTEREST RATES and the value of the EURO). The ECB features an EXECUTIVE BOARD consisting of representatives of member countries and a SUPERVISORY BOARD comprised of central bankers from member countries. Although the ECB operates independently, it works with the individual central banks of member countries, who are associated via the European System of Central Banks.

EUROPEAN COMMUNITY (EC) Three separate communities, including the EUROPEAN ECONOMIC COMMUNITY, European Atomic Energy Community, and European Coal and Steel Community, that joined together to promote FREE TRADE and economic cooperation. Charter members included Belgium, France, Italy, Luxembourg, the Netherlands, and Germany, and others joined at various points thereafter.

EUROPEAN CURRENCY UNIT (ECU) A unit of account, created by the EUROPEAN ECONOMIC COMMUNITY in 1979 as part of the European Monetary System, based on a weighted average of the CURRENCIES of the member countries. The ECU was superseded by the creation of the EUROPEAN MONETARY UNION and the introduction of the EURO in 1999.

EUROPEAN DEVELOPMENT FUND (EDF) A fund created via the TREATY OF ROME in 1957, operated by the EUROPEAN UNION, which provides grants and LOANS in Africa, the Caribbean, and the Pacific.

EUROPEAN ECONOMIC AREA (EEA) An organization that includes the EUROPEAN UNION plus Norway, Switzerland, and Liechtenstein.

EUROPEAN ECONOMIC COMMUNITY (EEC) A community of various European nations who originally joined in 1957 under the TREATY OF ROME to create a marketplace with lower TRADE BARRIERS and easier transfer of goods, services, and capital. The EEC has been superseded by the EUROPEAN UNION. Also known as COMMON MARKET. See also EUROPEAN COMMUNITY, EUROPEAN ECONOMIC AREA.

EUROPEAN FREE TRADE ASSOCIATION (EFTA) An association created in 1960 to promote FREE TRADE among a number of European countries (and whose membership has changed over the years with the creation of the EUROPEAN UNION (EU). EFTA was designed to reduce TRADE BARRIERS, and in 1984 succeeded in abolishing TARIFFS between EFTA nations and EU nations.

EUROPEAN INVESTMENT BANK (EIB) The EUROPEAN UNION's development and long-term CREDIT institution, established in 1957 under the TREATY OF ROME and active in providing LOANS to members states and to projects located in developing nations around the world.

EUROPEAN MONETARY SYSTEM (EMS) A framework of monetary cooperation and EXCHANGE RATE stabilization established in 1979 (and leading ultimately to a stronger union in 1989 via the EUROPEAN MONETARY

UNION). Under the EMS's Exchange Rate Mechanism, participating countries agreed to hold the value of their national currencies within pre-agreed bands referenced in terms of EUROPEAN CURRENCY UNITS and to take corrective actions as needed when drifting outside the band.

EUROPEAN MONETARY UNION (EMU)   The monetary system of member European nations that is based on coordinated management of INTEREST RATES, FOREIGN EXCHANGE rates, and INFLATION. The EMU created the EUROPEAN CENTRAL BANK to guide its policies, and developed and introduced the EURO as its core CURRENCY. The original 11 original participating countries – Austria, Belgium, Finland, France, Germany, Italy, Ireland, Luxembourg, Portugal, and Spain – were joined by various others in subsequent stages, including Greece, Slovenia, Slovakia, and Cyprus.

EUROPEAN OPTION   An OPTION contract that can only be EXERCISED by the buyer at MATURITY. See also AMERICAN OPTION, BERMUDAN OPTION.

EUROPEAN TERMS   A commonly used quotation mechanism in the FOREIGN EXCHANGE markets that indicates how many units of a foreign CURRENCY can be exchanged for a US dollar. See also AMERICAN TERMS, RECIPROCAL RATE.

EUROPEAN UNION (EU)   An economic and political union formed under the MAASTRICHT TREATY of 1993 which includes 27 participating nations (Austria, Belgium, Bulgaria, Cyprus, the Czech Republic, Denmark, Estonia, Finland, France, Germany, Greece, Hungary, Ireland, Italy, Latvia, Lithuania, Luxembourg, Malta, the Netherlands, Poland, Portugal, Romania, Slovakia, Slovenia, Spain, Sweden, and the United Kingdom). Membership is dependent on fulfilling specified human rights and economic standards. The EU ensures free transfer of people, CAPITAL, and resources across borders, helping to create a single, unified trading and economic marketplace. A subgroup of the EU has adopted the EURO as the national CURRENCY. See also EUROPEAN MONETARY UNION.

EUROSECURITY   A SECURITY (EQUITY, BOND, or other securitized and tradable ASSET) that is issued and traded in the EUROMARKETS.

EVA   See ECONOMIC VALUE ADDED.

EVENT DRIVEN   A common HEDGE FUND strategy where a manager may invest in DISTRESSED ASSETS and RISK ARBITRAGE positions, as well as other corporate restructuring events that may include CARVE-OUTS, STOCK BUYBACKS, BANKRUPTCIES, and REORGANIZATIONS.

EVENT OF DEFAULT   An instance of DEFAULT that is specific to a BORROWER or ISSUER of SECURITIES, caused by failure to make scheduled PRINCIPAL and/or INTEREST payments, failure to comply with obligations in an INDENTURE, TRUST DEED, or CREDIT agreement, triggering of a CROSS-DEFAULT CLAUSE, initiation of BANKRUPTCY proceedings by outside CREDITORS, or seizure of ASSETS by the courts.

EVENT RISK   The RISK of loss from an unexpected CREDIT or economic event/ action, such as a CREDIT RATING downgrade, DEFAULT, MORATORIUM, or EXCHANGE CONTROLS. The onset of event risk can be difficult to predict and the potential financial impact can be hard to estimate, as losses do not follow traditional STOCHASTIC PROCESSES.

EVERGREEN   [COL] (1) A REVOLVING CREDIT FACILITY without a specific MATURITY; the facility rolls over automatically every quarter or year until the BANK decides to convert it into a term LOAN with a defined maturity. (2) In the United Kingdom, a gradual infusion of CAPITAL into a new, or recapitalized, company.

EVT   See EXTREME VALUE THEORY.

EX-ALL   A share of COMMON STOCK that lacks DIVIDEND rights and VOTING RIGHTS and is only entitled to possible CAPITAL appreciation.

EX-ANTE PORTFOLIO RETURN   See EXPECTED PORTFOLIO RETURN.

EX-DIVIDEND   (1) A share of COMMON STOCK without any rights to the current period DIVIDEND. (2) The time period between the announcement and payment of dividends.

EX-GRATIA   [LAT] Literally, "from favor": a goodwill payment from an INSURER to an INSURED even though no SETTLEMENT is actually due or payable. Ex gratias are generally arranged to strengthen business relationships.

EX-RIGHTS (XR)   The purchase of a SHARE of STOCK for which the INVESTOR is not entitled to any associated RIGHTS.

EX-WARRANT (XW)   A SHARE of STOCK for which the INVESTOR is not entitled to any associated WARRANT.

EXCEPTIONAL ITEMS   Profit and loss items incurred in the normal course of a company's business which are of an unusually large magnitude. Exceptional items appear ABOVE THE LINE, as a separate disclosure item. See also EXTRAORDINARY ITEMS.

EXCESS   In the United Kingdom, a DEDUCTIBLE on an INSURANCE POLICY.

EXCESS INSURANCE   Any INSURANCE coverage that an INSURED arranges over and above the primary insurance CONTRACT, such as an UMBRELLA POLICY. Excess insurance is generally designed to protect against losses from LIABILITY or unexpected damage that are not adequately covered through the primary contract. Also known as EXCESS POLICY.

EXCESS KURTOSIS   An adjustment made to the computation of KURTOSIS so that the resulting kurtosis for a NORMAL DISTRIBUTION is zero. This indicates that any distribution with excess kurtosis > 0 has "fatter tails" than a comparable normal distribution. Excess kurtosis is obtained via:

$$\frac{1}{N\sigma^4}\sum_{i=1}^{N}(x_i - \mu)^4 - 3$$

where N is the number of observations, x_i is an observation, μ is the MEAN, σ is the STANDARD DEVIATION. See also SKEWNESS.

EXCESS LAYER   Any INSURANCE coverage that becomes effective once the INSURED's DEDUCTIBLE has been exhausted. The excess layer also applies to INSURERS or REINSURERS who choose to set their ATTACHMENT points at a particular distance above the EXPECTED LOSS level. See also HORIZONTAL LAYERING, VERTICAL LAYERING.

EXCESS OF LOSS (XOL) AGREEMENT   A REINSURANCE arrangement where a REINSURER assumes RISKS and RETURNS in specific horizontal or vertical layers; depending on the magnitude of losses and the sequence and level of ATTACHMENT, a reinsurer may or may not face some CESSION and allocation of losses on each loss event. See also PROPORTIONAL AGREEMENT, QUOTA SHARE, SURPLUS SHARE.

EXCESS POLICY   See EXCESS INSURANCE.

EXCESS RESERVES   RESERVES held by a BANK that are greater than the amount required by the regulatory authority. Excess reserves can be sold between banks.

EXCESS RETURN   The RETURN on an INVESTMENT over and above what the market expects or requires. Excess return can be generated through ACTIVE BETS, and is typically measured against a market BENCHMARK established through a framework such as the CAPITAL ASSET PRICING MODEL.

EXCESS SHARES   In a RIGHTS issue, the SHARES that are not taken up by existing SHAREHOLDERS; these may be taken up by the UNDERWRITING SYNDICATE.

EXCESS SPREAD   In a SECURITIZATION transaction, the difference between the CASH FLOW generated by the COLLATERAL POOL (after charge-offs and other EXPENSES) and the INTEREST payable to INVESTORS holding the ASSET-BACKED SECURITY. Excess spread may be held in ESCROW as an additional form of CREDIT enhancement until MATURITY of the transaction, at which time it may be paid to investors in the RESIDUAL TRANCHE.

EXCESS SURPLUS LINES INSURANCE   See SURPLUS LINES INSURANCE.

EXCHANGE   (1) A central physical or electronic marketplace, generally approved or authorized by a regulatory authority, which provides the facilities needed to bring together buyers and sellers of ASSETS (such as BONDS, COMMON STOCK, and DERIVATIVES), and allow for appropriate PRICE DISCOVERY. An exchange does not typically set prices or trade for its own account. (2) The process of swapping assets or cash between parties.

EXCHANGE CONTROLS   Restrictions imposed by national CENTRAL BANK or monetary authority on local CURRENCY flows that limit TRADING, prohibit exporters from drawing CREDIT from a BANK, or forbid residents from owning foreign BANK ACCOUNTS or local bank accounts with foreign currency. Such controls, which are a manifestation of SOVEREIGN RISK, are generally imposed to discourage speculative inflows or outflows. See also BLOCKED CURRENCY.

EXCHANGE FOR PHYSICAL (EFP)   A facility offered by certain EXCHANGES where two parties can agree to SWAP, off exchange, a FUTURES contract for a physical ASSET at the price quoted on the exchange. Before an EFP transaction can be concluded through the facility it must be registered with the CLEARINGHOUSE.

EXCHANGE OFFER   In a capital RESTRUCTURING, a proposal to existing INVESTORS in a company's DEBT and EQUITY to swap their current SECURITIES for new securities with different terms, which are typically less economically attractive. The exchange offer is used as a means of averting a filing for BANKRUPTCY.

EXCHANGE RATE   See FOREIGN EXCHANGE RATE.

EXCHANGE-TRADED DERIVATIVE   A DERIVATIVE, traded through an authorized EXCHANGE and cleared through a CLEARINGHOUSE, that is characterized by standard terms and conditions, and is subject to standard MARGIN requirements and clearing rules. Trading in exchange derivatives may occur in physical OPEN OUTCRY form, or in electronic form. The three main classes of exchange-traded derivatives are FUTURES, OPTIONS, and FUTURES OPTIONS. Contracts are available on a broad range of national and international ASSET references, including INTEREST RATES, FOREIGN EXCHANGE RATES, EQUITIES, COMMODITIES, CREDITS, and MACROECONOMIC INDICATORS. Also known as LISTED DERIVATIVE. See also OVER-THE-COUNTER DERIVATIVES.

EXCHANGE-TRADED FUND (ETF)   A MUTUAL FUND on a SECURITY, BASKET, or INDEX that trades on an EXCHANGE with continuously quoted and constantly changing prices, and which provides INVESTORS with the ability to engage in SHORT SALES and borrow against a position. Unlike CLOSED-END FUNDS, which often trade at a substantial PREMIUM or DISCOUNT to NET ASSET VALUE (NAV), ARBITRAGE activity in the creation and redemption process ensures that ETFs trade very close to NAV. Authorized participants deposit PORTFOLIOS of SECURITIES with the TRUSTEE to create ETF SHARES and withdraw them to redeem shares; accordingly, they are aware of the value of the underlying PORTFOLIOS versus the price of the ETF and can take advantage of any perceived arbitrage opportunities, which keeps the quoted price near the NAV. See also LEVERAGED EXCHANGE-TRADED FUND.

EXCHEQUER   (1) In the United Kingdom, an ACCOUNT held by the BANK OF ENGLAND that contains government funds, including REVENUES raised through TAXES. (2) A government department that is responsible for collecting taxes and other REVENUES (3) A treasury account.

EXCLUDED PERIL   See EXCLUSION.

EXCLUSION   Specific RISK exposures that are not covered through an INSURANCE CONTRACT. The more exclusions an insurance contract contains, the smaller the amount of risk transferred from INSURED to INSURER or INSURER to REINSURER. Common exclusions include losses from uninsurable CATASTROPHIC HAZARDS, losses from normal use/DEPRECIATION, and duplicative (though not excess) covers. Exclusions may be contained within the policy, or in an EXCLUSION RIDER or ENDORSEMENT.

Also know as EXCLUDED PERIL. See also RETENTION.

EXCLUSION RIDER An ENDORSEMENT attached to an INSURANCE CONTRACT eliminating coverage for previously included PERILS. The details of the rider supersede those contained in the original contract.

EXECUTION The process of agreeing and then consummating the terms of a SECURITIES trade. An execution results in the exchange of securities and cash between seller and buyer. See also EXECUTION RISK.

EXECUTION ONLY Services provided by a BROKER that are based strictly on EXECUTION and involve no INVESTMENT advice.

EXECUTION RATE The amount of trades that are CROSSED once MATCHED within a DARK POOL or on an EXCHANGE.

EXECUTION RISK (1) The RISK that a SECURITIES TRADE will not be executed under current market prices, or per the terms of an ORDER. (2) The RISK of lowering ENTERPRISE VALUE by not being able to successfully gain entry into a new market, introduce a new product or service, or absorb a new acquisition.

EXECUTIVE BOARD See MANAGEMENT BOARD.

EXECUTIVE DIRECTOR A board DIRECTOR that is also a member of the company's EXECUTIVE MANAGEMENT group. An executive director is not considered to be independent for GOVERNANCE and control purposes. See also LEAD INDEPENDENT DIRECTOR, NONEXECUTIVE DIRECTOR.

EXECUTIVE MANAGEMENT A team within a company that is responsible for managing the tactical and strategic operations of the firm. The head of the executive management team is the CHIEF EXECUTIVE OFFICER, who may be appointed by the BOARD OF DIRECTORS.

EXECUTOR An individual responsible for carrying out the terms of a will, including consolidating ASSETS, settling outstanding DEBTS, and distributing residual property to named BENEFICIARIES.

EXEMPT GILTS A form of GILT in which the TAX payable on INTEREST COUPONS is deducted by the government before distribution to INVESTORS.

EXEMPT SECURITY In the United States, a SECURITY that does not have to adhere to REGISTRATION requirements set forth by the SECURITIES AND EXCHANGE COMMISSION. Securities that are commonly exempted included TREASURY BILLS, TREASURY NOTES, TREASURY BONDS, AGENCY SECURITIES, MUNICIPAL BONDS, PRIVATE PLACEMENTS, and COMMERCIAL PAPER.

EXEMPT UNIT TRUST In the United Kingdom, a form of UNIT TRUST that is exempt from corporation TAX and CAPITAL GAINS tax and can only be purchased and sold by tax-exempt institutional INVESTORS, such as PENSION FUNDS.

EXERCISE The process of utilizing the rights granted an OPTION buyer under the terms of a CONTRACT; for a CALL OPTION this means purchasing the UNDERLYING at the STRIKE PRICE, and for a PUT OPTION it means selling the underlying at the strike price. Exercise may occur at MATURITY of the contract (EUROPEAN OPTION), at any time until maturity (AMERICAN OPTION), or on specified dates (BERMUDAN OPTION).

EXERCISE DATE The date on which an OPTION can be EXERCISED. For EUROPEAN OPTIONS and BERMUDAN OPTIONS this occurs on a date certain, for AMERICAN OPTIONS it may be any date.

EXERCISE NOTICE A written notice from the buyer to the seller of an OPTION that it intends to EXERCISE its rights under the CONTRACT, either buying or selling the UNDERLYING at the STRIKE PRICE.

EXERCISE PRICE See STRIKE PRICE.

EXHAUST The level at which the COLLATERAL securing a MARGIN LOAN or PURPOSE LOAN has been depleted, requiring the borrower to post additional collateral or forcing the BANK to liquidate the collateral on hand to repay the loan.

EXHAUSTION POINT See POLICY CAP.

EXIMBANK See EXPORT IMPORT BANK.

EXOGENOUS LIQUIDITY LIQUIDITY and LIQUIDITY RISK that relate to an entire industry or national system, and are not confined to, or significantly influenced by, a single firm and its actions. See also ASSET LIQUIDITY RISK, ASSET-FUNDING LIQUIDITY RISK, ENDOGENOUS LIQUIDITY, FUNDING LIQUIDITY RISK.

EXOTIC CURRENCY A CURRENCY that is not widely used in international TRADE and financial transactions and is thinly traded in the FOREIGN EXCHANGE markets; the general lack of LIQUIDITY can result in increased price VOLATILITY. Exotics, which are typically the currencies of LESSER DEVELOPED COUNTRIES or NEWLY INDUSTRIALIZED COUNTRIES, may be nonconvertible and subject to partial or complete EXCHANGE CONTROLS. See also NONCONVERTIBLE CURRENCY, RESERVE CURRENCY.

EXOTIC OPTION See COMPLEX OPTION.

EXOTIC SWAP See COMPLEX SWAP.

EXPANSION OPTION In REAL OPTION VALUATION, the OPTION a company has to expand the amount of capital allocated in CAPITAL INVESTMENT project, generally synchronized across discrete project phases (e.g., research and development, start-up, early growth, mid-cycle, and so forth). This option can be thought of as a form of CALL OPTION. See also ABANDONMENT OPTION, DEFERRAL OPTION.

EXPECTATIONS THEORY A theory of INTEREST RATES indicating that the expectations of INVESTORS influence the TERM STRUCTURE of rates. Thus, if investors expect future rates will be higher than current rates, the

YIELD CURVE will be upward sloping, and vice versa. Also known as MARKET EXPECTATIONS THEORY. See also LIQUIDITY PREFERENCE THEORY, MARKET SEGMENTATION THEORY.

Additional references: Lutz and Lutz (1951); Meiselman (1962).

EXPECTED CREDIT LOSS   An average, or mathematically expected, CREDIT loss, generally determined through a combination of expected CREDIT RISK exposure, PROBABILITY of DEFAULT, and anticipated RECOVERY in DEFAULT. FINANCIAL INSTITUTIONS allocate CREDIT RESERVES in support of expected credit losses. See also UNEXPECTED CREDIT LOSS, WORST-CASE CREDIT LOSS.

EXPECTED LOSS   The EXPECTED VALUE, or MEAN, of a statistical loss distribution function. The loss distribution function may be created to compute CREDIT losses, INSURANCE losses, or other financial losses.

EXPECTED LOSS RATIO   See LOSS RATIO.

EXPECTED PORTFOLIO RETURN   The INCOME expected to be generated by a group of ASSETS over a defined horizon. Income may be derived from DIVIDENDS, YIELD, and/or CAPITAL GAINS, depending on the characteristics of the SECURITIES. The expected return on any asset is derived from a probability distribution containing possible return outcomes. The value of a RANDOM VARIABLE drawn from the distribution is taken as the uncertain return of an asset and the resulting expected value of the return is simply the weighted average of possible outcomes. The total expected return of the portfolio is equal to the sum of the expected returns on each individual asset, and is given by:

$$E(R_p) = \sum^{z, x=1} w_x E(R_x)$$

where $E(R_p)$ is the expected return of the portfolio, $E(R_x)$ is the expected return of asset x in the portfolio, Wx is the weight of asset x in the portfolio, Z is the number of assets in the portfolio Also known as EX-ANTE PORTFOLIO RETURN. See also PORTFOLIO RETURN

EXPECTED RETURN   The estimated value of an ASSET or INVESTMENT, typically determined from a probability distribution of all possible return outcomes.

EXPECTED SHORTFALL   See EXPECTED TAIL LOSS.

EXPECTED TAIL LOSS   A form of VALUE-AT-RISK (VAR) that measures, for a given TAIL PROBABILITY, the average or EXPECTED LOSS conditional on the loss exceeding the corresponding VAR. Also known as EXPECTED SHORTFALL. See also EXTREME VALUE THEORY.

EXPECTED UTILITY   The weighted average utility value – or satisfaction from income or wealth – that is derived from a particular activity. Utility is generally used in an economic or theoretical RISK MANAGEMENT framework;

precise measurement of a company's utility is not generally considered feasible or practical.

EXPECTED VALUE   (1) The MEAN of a distribution of values that a random variable can take. (2) The value that is obtained given certain possible outcomes and PROBABILITIES of occurrence. In financial RISK MANAGEMENT terms this is often summarized as frequency (probability) times severity (outcome), or:

$$ExpV = (Prob\ (O_1)) + ((1 - Prob)\ (O_2))$$

where Prob is the probability of occurrence, O_1 is outcome 1 and O_2 is outcome 2.

EXPECTED VOLATILITY   An estimate of the VOLATILITY in a particular ASSET or market that is expected to occur in the future, used in the pricing of specific types of DERIVATIVES.

EXPENSE   A cost associated with the acquisition of goods or services or the production of goods intended for resale.

EXPENSE LOADING   A margin an INSURER adds in the PREMIUM LOADING process to cover expenses such as AGENT COMMISSIONS, PREMIUM TAXES, marketing support costs, and contingencies. See also FAIR PREMIUM, PURE PREMIUM.

EXPENSE RATIO   In INSURANCE, a measure of an INSURER's ability to cover its UNDERWRITING expenses with earned PREMIUM, computed as:

$$ER = \frac{IE}{Pr}$$

where IE is incurred expense and Pr is premium.

The lower the ratio, the more premium an insurer preserves as profit. See also COMBINED RATIO, LOSS RATIO.

EXPERIENCE ACCOUNT   (1) An account established for future DEBITS and CREDITS related to a FINITE INSURANCE CONTRACT. (2) The specific history of loss experience an INSURER has with a given INSURED, which is often used to help formulate future PREMIUM rates for a broader class of insureds. (2) See also EXPERIENCE RATING.

EXPERIENCE RATED POLICY   A LOSS-SENSITIVE INSURANCE CONTRACT where the INSURER charges a PREMIUM that is directly related to the INSURED's past loss experience: the greater the past losses, the higher the premium.

EXPERIENCE RATING   A procedure to calculate PREMIUM on an INSURANCE CONTRACT through modifications based on past loss experience. The INSURER examines actual CLAIMS and associated expenses for a group of INSUREDS in order to project possible future claims; based on its analysis it sets a premium that it believes will be sufficient to cover EXPECTED LOSS and PROFIT LOAD. See also EXPERIENCE ACCOUNT, SCHEDULE RATING.

EXPERIENCE REFUND   The amount of PREMIUM an INSURER returns to an INSURED if the loss record is better than the amount indicated by the PURE PREMIUM incorporated in the basic premium rate.

EXPIRATION CYCLE   The standard cycle of CONTRACT expiries related to EXCHANGE-TRADED DERIVATIVES. Certain contracts follow a quarterly expiration cycle, while others opt for a shorter cycle (daily, weekly, monthly).

EXPIRY   See EXPIRY DATE.

EXPIRY DATE   The date on which an OPTION contract comes due, after which it becomes invalid. Also known as EXPIRY.

EXPLODING OPTION   A BULL SPREAD or BEAR SPREAD that generates a payoff once the two STRIKE PRICES defining the SPREAD are breached, i.e., the spread "explodes," or terminates, resulting in an immediate payoff.

EXPONENTIAL INTERPOLATION   A technique of INTERPOLATION that uses DISCOUNT FACTORS to connect two points on a YIELD CURVE.

$$D_i = D_1 \frac{t_i}{t_1} \left[\frac{t_2 - t_i}{t_2 - t_1} \right] D_2 \frac{t_i}{t_2} \left[\frac{t_i - t_1}{t_2 - t_1} \right]$$

where t_i is the number of days required from known point t_1 to the target date, t_2 is the number of days at the end of the period, D_1 is the discount factor at the first known point, D_2 is the discount factor at the second known point. See also CUBIC SPLINE INTERPOLATION, LINEAR INTERPOLATION.

EXPONENTIAL SMOOTHING   A statistical mechanism where more recent data observations are given greater weight in computations than older observations. Such exponential smoothing is used in econometric modeling, and certain forms of VALUE-AT-RISK modeling. Also known as EXPONENTIAL WEIGHTING.

EXPONENTIAL WEIGHTING   See EXPONENTIAL SMOOTHING.

EXPORT IMPORT BANK   The US EXPORT CREDIT agency, created to encourage TRADE flows by providing export credit GUARANTEES and guaranteeing LOANS made by banks to US exporters. Also known as EXIMBANK.

EXPORTS   Goods and services produced domestically and sold to nonresidents, including VISIBLES (such as goods) and INVISIBLES (services). Some invisibles are sent abroad, while nonresident visitors use others domestically; capital exports can involve LOANS to nonresidents or the purchase of ASSETS or INVESTMENTS abroad. See also BALANCE OF TRADE, IMPORTS.

EXPOSED TO THE MARKET   [COL] A purchase or sale ORDER in the SECURITIES markets that must be shown to the market at large before it can be

INTERNALIZED or CROSSED on an alternative venue. See also SUNSHINE TRADE.

EXPOSURE AT DEFAULT (EAD)   A parameter used in the computation of CREDIT RISK under BASLE II's INTERNAL RATINGS-BASED APPROACH which reflects the degree of credit exposure inherent in a particular on-balance sheet or OFF-BALANCE SHEET item. For on-BALANCE SHEET items, such as LOANS, EAD is equal to the NOTIONAL VALUE. For off-balance sheet items, such as DERIVATIVES and REVOLVING CREDIT FACILITIES, a FRACTIONAL EXPOSURE method may be used.

EXPRESS AUTHORITY   See ACTUAL AUTHORITY.

EXPROPRIATION   The taking of private property by a government authority for public use, to enforce social equality, or to deny private ownership, generally outside the framework of laws. See also NATIONALIZATION, PRIVATIZATION.

EXTENDIBLE OPTION   An OVER-THE-COUNTER COMPLEX OPTION that allows the buyer to EXERCISE the CONTRACT on a particular reset date or reset the STRIKE PRICE to the current market level and extend the option for another reset period. The extendible option is a variation of the PARTIAL LOOKBACK OPTION.

EXTENDIBLE SWAP   A structured DERIVATIVE comprised of an INTEREST RATE SWAP and an OPTION that grants one party the right to require its COUNTERPARTY to continue a previously contracted swap under existing terms for an additional period of time. See also PAYER EXTENDIBLE SWAP, RECEIVER EXTENDIBLE SWAP.

EXTENSION RISK   The RISK that one party to a CONTRACT or financial transaction will choose to extend the terms of the contract, to the potential financial detriment of the second party.

EXTERNAL AUDIT   A form of AUDIT performed on a company or other organization by an independent AUDITOR. The issuance of an AUDIT OPINION requires the use of an external auditor. See also INTERNAL AUDIT.

EXTERNAL DEBT   DEBT raised by a country or company outside of its own national system, generally in a FOREIGN CURRENCY.

EXTRAORDINARY ITEMS   Profit and loss items incurred in a company's business which are not expected to recur in the future (and which may be excluded by analysts in order to perform an accurate period on period comparison). Extraordinary items appear ABOVE THE LINE, as a separate disclosure item. See also EXCEPTIONAL ITEMS.

EXTREME MORTALITY BOND   A form of INSURANCE-LINKED SECURITY that seeks to protect the sponsoring INSURER or REINSURER from an extreme, or catastrophic, rise in mortality rates within a defined target population that would trigger payout on life INSURANCE policies. Such bonds can be used by the sponsor to transfer the RISK associated with high mortality from a low PROBABILITY event, such as a terrorist attack or a pandemic.

EXTREME VALUE THEORY (EVT)   A statistical framework that attempts to model maximum excess losses of extreme events (e.g., CATASTROPHIC HAZARD, financial disasters) through estimation of the TAIL of a distribution. EVT is designed to estimate the maximum excess loss possible for a given confidence level, and liquidation period EVT is based on the external types theorem (i.e., "three types" theorem), stating that there are only three types of distributions needed to model the maximum or minimum of the collection of random observations from the same distribution. For N data sets generated from the same distribution a new data set is created that includes the maximum values from the N sets, and where the resulting data set can only be described by one of the three models – the Gumbel, Fréchet, and Weibull distributions. The primary difference between the distributions relates to the thickness of the tail, as defined by a shape parameter ε; for the Gumbel distribution, $\varepsilon = 0$, for Fréchet $\varepsilon > 0$, and for Weibull $\varepsilon < 0$.

F

FACE VALUE   The PRINCIPAL amount of a SECURITY; for standard securities transactions, face value and PAR VALUE are often equivalent. Face value is distinguished from MARKET VALUE, although they may converge to the same value at MATURITY.

FACILITY   A line of CREDIT granted by a BANK to a client. The availability of the facility depends on the nature of the CONTRACT and the fees paid by the client; the most reliable facilities, which are a form of COMMITTED FUNDING, command higher fees in relation to those that may be cancelled or withdrawn by the bank on short notice (e.g., ADVISED LINE).

FACILITY FEE   See COMMITMENT FEE.

FACTOR   A firm that specializes in FACTORING activities, generally a non-BANK FINANCIAL INSTITUTION with significant CREDIT RISK expertise.

FACTOR MODEL   See MULTIFACTOR RISK MODEL.

FACTOR OF PRODUCTION   The essential elements that are used in the production of goods, including land, labor, and CAPITAL (broadly defined to include all productive ASSETS, such as plant and equipment and raw material INVENTORIES).

FACTORING   The process of obtaining short-term FINANCING through the outright sale of ACCOUNTS RECEIVABLE to a third party FACTOR on a NONRECOURSE basis. See also ACCOUNTS RECEIVABLE FINANCING, FORFAITING.

FACULTATIVE   A process where a REINSURER can accept or reject coverage for individual RISKS presented for consideration by a CEDING INSURER. See also FACULTATIVE REINSURANCE.

FACULTATIVE OBLIGATORY TREATY   A hybrid of FACULTATIVE REINSU-RANCE and TREATY REINSURANCE where the CEDING INSURER can choose to assign certain RISKS to the REINSURER, who is then required to accept them.

FACULTATIVE REINSURANCE   A REINSURANCE agreement/process that involves a case-by-case submission of RISKS by a CEDING INSURER to a REINSURER, who can accept or reject them according to specific UNDERWRITING criteria. Unlike TREATY REINSURANCE, facultative reinsurance does not compel the ceding insurer to submit risks, nor does it require a reinsurer to accept them. The arrangement is often used for large or unique exposures that require special analysis. Risks that are ultimately CEDED/ accepted may be done via QUOTA SHARE or SURPLUS SHARE. See also FACULTATIVE OBLIGATORY TREATY.

FAIL TO DELIVER   A situation where a selling DEALER has not delivered SECURITIES to the buying dealer, and will thus not receive payment. Fails are commonly used as a measure of settlements-based OPERATIONAL RISK. See also FAIL TO RECEIVE, AGED FAIL.

FAIL TO RECEIVE   A situation where a buying DEALER has not received SECURITIES from the selling dealer, and will thus not make its payment. Fails are commonly used as a measure of settlements-based OPERATIONAL RISK. See also AGED FAIL, FAIL TO DELIVER.

FAIR PREMIUM   An INSURANCE pricing methodology where the PREMIUM charged an INSURED is intended to cover EXPECTED LOSSES and operating and administrative expenses, and provide an equitable RETURN to providers of CAPITAL. Fair premium comprises of PURE PREMIUM and PREMIUM LOADING (which also includes EXPENSE LOADING). Also known as GROSS RATE.

FAIR PRESENTATION   In the United States, a general ACCOUNTING concept indicating that the FINANCIAL STATEMENTS of a company should reflect the true financial position, and should not be misleading. See also TRUE AND FAIR VIEW.

FAIR PRICE PROVISION   A legal provision that protects a company from an ACQUISITION based on a TWO-TIER BID (i.e., a first tier comprised of an attractive front-loaded cash offer, and a second tier consisting of a lower price and/or lower percentage of cash). The provision requires that all of the TARGET's COMMON STOCK SHAREHOLDERS receive the same (or substantially similar) buyout price and terms.

FAIRNESS OPINION   An analysis and opinion prepared by a BANK or INVESTMENT BANK for a client company's MERGER, ACQUISITION, or LEVERAGED BUYOUT, to determine whether the price being paid or received is fair. The opinion is intended to convey the relative financial worth of the transaction and demonstrate that DIRECTORS have performed their DUTY OF CARE; the results can be used to protect against potential SHAREHOLDER lawsuits. The fairness opinion is typically developed from information generated via the DUE DILIGENCE process.

FALLEN ANGEL   [COL] A BOND with an INVESTMENT GRADE CREDIT RATING at the time of issuance that has been downgraded to SUBINVESTMENT GRADE status as a result of a deterioration in the ISSUER'S financial position. See also HIGH-YIELD BOND.

FALLING KNIFE   [COL] A SECURITY whose value has fallen sharply in a short period of time. A falling knife may represent an INVESTMENT opportunity for INVESTORS who believe the security is OVERSOLD. See also CATCH A FALLING KNIFE.

FALLING TOP   A TECHNICAL ANALYSIS charting figures depicting a declining SECURITIES price or INDEX value over time, with ever-lower resistance levels, generally considered to be a BEARISH signal. Also known as DESCENDING TOP. See also ASCENDING TOP, DESCENDING BOTTOM, RISING BOTTOM.

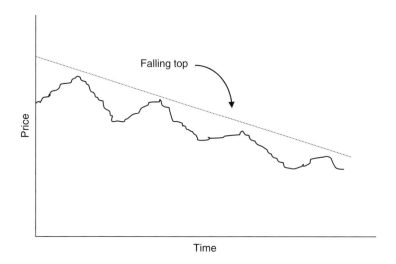

FALSE MARKET   [COL] A market where TRADING actions are influenced by erroneous information or misinformation, creating complications in the PRICE DISCOVERY process. A false market may develop in ILLIQUID SECURITIES or EMERGING MARKET securities, where standards of information transparency are not as rigorous.

FANNIE MAE   [COL] See FEDERAL NATIONAL MORTGAGE ASSOCIATION.

FARMER MAC   [COL] See FEDERAL AGRICULTURAL MORTGAGE CORPORATION.

FASB   See FINANCIAL ACCOUNTING STANDARDS BOARD.

FAST MARKET   [COL] A financial market that is characterized by heavy volume and high levels of market VOLATILITY, and which can generate ORDER IMBALANCES. See also LOCKED MARKET.

FAST TAPE   [COL] A market condition that occurs when TRADING in a particular SECURITY or contract is so rapid and heavy that the current price is unavailable.

FAT TAIL   [COL] See KURTOSIS.

FCFE   See FREE CASH FLOW TO EQUITY.

FCFF   See FREE CASH FLOW TO FIRM.

FCM   See FUTURES COMMISSION MERCHANT.

FDIC   See FEDERAL DEPOSIT INSURANCE CORPORATION.

FEASIBLE PORTFOLIO   Any PORTFOLIO an INVESTOR can construct from available ASSETS in the marketplace. A feasible portfolio represents any combination of investable assets, but need not necessarily provide the greatest RETURN for a given level of RISK. See also EFFICIENT PORTFOLIO.

FED FUNDS   See FEDERAL FUNDS.

FED WIRE   An electronic network connecting the FEDERAL RESERVE BOARD, the 12 FEDERAL RESERVE BANKS, the US Treasury and US agencies, which is used for immediate payments, FEDERAL FUNDS transfers, and TREASURY NOTE, TREASURY BOND, and AGENCY SECURITY transfers.

FEDERAL AGRICULTURAL MORTGAGE CORPORATION   In the United States, a federally chartered, publicly owned CORPORATION founded in 1988 that purchases agricultural MORTGAGES, issues standby commitments to purchase mortgages and swaps loans for MORTGAGE-BACKED SECURITIES in order to provide for a property SECONDARY MARKET in agricultural real estate and housing. Also known as FARMER MAC.

FEDERAL DEPOSIT INSURANCE CORPORATION (FDIC)   A US federal agency that is responsible for managing the INSURANCE funds for BANKS and SAVINGS AND LOANS, providing DEPOSITORS with protection of up to $100,000 per DEPOSIT account.

FEDERAL FUNDS   In the United States, unsecured LOANS available to MEMBER BANKS from excess balances held at one of the 12 FEDERAL RESERVE BANKS. The process of borrowing Federal Funds is represented as a purchase of funds, while lending is the sale of funds. The majority of Federal Funds transactions mature the business day after they are contacted, though term transactions for from 1 week to 6 months can be arranged. Federal Funds are available immediately (i.e., they are considered GOOD MONEY), an advantage over interbank CLEARINGHOUSE funds, which are generally only accessible 1 to 2 days after contracting. Also known as FED FUNDS. See also FEDERAL FUNDS RATE.

FEDERAL FUNDS RATE   The overnight INTEREST RATE charged on FEDERAL FUNDS, and a widely followed indicator of market rates.

FEDERAL HOME LOAN BANKS (FHLB)   In the United States, a network of 12 BANKS created in 1932 to ensure appropriate CREDIT availability for financial institutions granting residential MORTGAGES and loans to individuals. In recent years it has become focused on ensuring the smooth flow of credit into affordable housing and community development. FHLB also holds the outstanding SHARES in the FEDERAL HOME LOAN MORTGAGE CORPORATION, an organization involved in the SECONDARY MARKET for mortgages.

FEDERAL HOME LOAN MORTGAGE CORPORATION (FHLMC)   A US agency established in 1970 that purchases MORTGAGES from mortgage originators and pools them into MORTGAGE-BACKED SECURITIES known as PARTICIPATION CERTIFICATES; the certificates, which convert ILLIQUID mortgage ASSETS into MARKETABLE SECURITIES, carry the agency's GUARANTEE of repayment on both PRINCIPAL and INTEREST. Also known as FREDDIE MAC. See also FEDERAL NATIONAL MORTGAGE ASSOCIATION, GOVERNMENT NATIONAL MORTGAGE ASSOCIATION.

FEDERAL NATIONAL MORTGAGE ASSOCIATION (FNMA)   A US federally chartered, publicly owned CORPORATION founded in 1938 that purchases government GUARANTEED/INSURED residential MORTGAGES and pools them into MORTGAGE-BACKED SECURITIES (MBS); FNMA MBS, which essentially convert ILLIQUID mortgage ASSETS into MARKETABLE SECURITIES, carry the corporation's guarantee of repayment on both PRINCIPAL and INTEREST. Also known as FANNIE MAE. See also FEDERAL HOME LOAN MORTGAGE CORPORATION, GOVERNMENT NATIONAL MORTGAGE ASSOCIATION.

FEDERAL OPEN MARKETS COMMITTEE (FOMC) The US FEDERAL RESERVE SYSTEM's policy committee, responsible for developing and implementing MONETARY POLICY. The committee, which includes the 7 FEDERAL RESERVE BOARD governors and 5 of the 12 FEDERAL RESERVE BANK presidents, conducts monetary policy via OPEN MARKET OPERATIONS and adjustments to both the DISCOUNT RATE and RESERVE REQUIREMENTS.

FEDERAL RESERVE BANKS The 12 BANKS in the US FEDERAL RESERVE SYSTEM that are responsible for providing CENTRAL BANK services to MEMBER BANKS, LENDING via the DISCOUNT WINDOW, monitoring the activities of banks operating within their jurisdictions, and assisting in the formulation of MONETARY POLICY via the FEDERAL OPEN MARKETS COMMITTEE.

FEDERAL RESERVE BOARD The governing body of the US banking system, comprised of seven governors appointed by the US president. The board, which holds a voting majority on the FEDERAL OPEN MARKETS COMMITTEE, sets the DISCOUNT RATE and MARGIN requirements, establishes RESERVE REQUIREMENTS for national BANKS, and supervises the financial system at large through regulatory policies and declarations. See also FEDERAL RESERVE BANKS, FEDERAL RESERVE SYSTEM.

FEDERAL RESERVE SYSTEM The US CENTRAL BANK system, created in 1913 via the Federal Reserve Act, comprised of 12 FEDERAL RESERVE BANKS, the FEDERAL RESERVE BOARD, the FEDERAL OPEN MARKETS COMMITTEE, and MEMBER BANKS (which hold EQUITY in the 12 Federal Reserve banks). Operating responsibilities are divided between the board and the banks.

FEDERAL TRADE COMMISSION (FTC) A US federal agency responsible for promoting competitive behavior by preventing TRADE restraints, price discrimination, formation of MONOPOLY power, and illegal or predatory pricing policies. The FTC acts via voluntary enforcement and formal LITIGATION.

FEEDER FUND A FUND that invests CAPITAL gathered from INVESTORS solely or primarily in another fund (i.e., a MASTER FUND). The feeder fund structure is widely employed in the HEDGE FUND sector.

FENCE [COL] See COLLAR.

FHLB See FEDERAL HOME LOAN BANKS.

FHLMC See FEDERAL HOME LOAN MORTGAGE CORPORATION.

FIAT MONEY CURRENCY backed by an issuing nation's proclamation that it is legal tender rather than a specific RESERVE of GOLD or metal; fiat money is not specifically convertible into metal. Most currency in circulation through-out the world is fiat money.

FIDELITY BOND In INSURANCE, a BOND that GUARANTEES an INSURER will pay the INSURED for losses caused by dishonesty or FRAUD of employees.

FIDUCIARY   An individual or institution that is responsible for administer-ing duties for the express benefit of other parties. See also FIDUCIARY DUTY.

FIDUCIARY DEPOSIT   A DEPOSIT placed by a customer through an AGENT BANK with a second (recipient) bank; the recipient bank forwards INTEREST on the deposit to the agent bank for onward disbursement to the client. The recipient bank posts the funds on its BALANCE SHEET as an INTERBANK placement rather than a customer DEPOSIT.

FIDUCIARY DUTY   (1) The legal duty that DIRECTORS and executives have in representing SHAREHOLDER interests; this includes, but is not limited to, DUTY OF CARE and DUTY OF LOYALTY. (2) The legal duty that a FIDUCIARY has in administering assigned tasks or services.

FIFO   See FIRST IN FIRST OUT.

FIGHTING THE TAPE   [COL] The general practice of attempting to take a controlling position in a company's COMMON STOCK. Fighting the tape is generally unsuccessful in all but the most thinly traded stocks, and is illegal in certain jurisdictions unless accompanied by formal disclosure of holdings and/ or a full TENDER OFFER.

FILL OR KILL   [COL] A common form of designating an ALL-OR-NONE ORDER. Written trade tickets may be marked "FOK" as an abbreviation. See also GOOD TILL CANCELLED ORDER, MARKET ORDER, STOP LOSS ORDER.

FILZ   [GER] Literally "interwoven" material or fabric; the term is commonly used in Switzerland to describe the close, and sometimes conflicted, relation-ships that exist between board DIRECTORS, including instances of nepotism and INTERLOCKING DIRECTORSHIPS.

FINAL TRADING DAY   The last day during which TRADING can occur in an EXCHANGE-TRADED DERIVATIVE CONTRACT.

FINALITY   The time at which funds that have been placed by a depositor in a BANK become irrevocable and cannot be returned, unless consent is obtained from the PAYEE. Finality can range from immediate (for WIRE TRANSFERS) to several days (for CHECKS, which can be debited if rejected by the DRAWEE bank). See also AVAILABILITY.

FINANCE   The broad area of study and practice related to MONEY, BANKING, INVESTMENT, INSURANCE, and RISK MANAGEMENT.

FINANCE BILL   A form of BILL OF EXCHANGE used for short-term FINANCING purposes, and which cannot be sold or marketed to a third party.

FINANCE COMPANY   A non-BANK FINANCIAL INSTITUTION that provides CREDIT to customers that are either purchasing or LEASING a particular product, often a DURABLE GOOD or vehicle. The finance company generates REVENUES based on the differential between its own rate of borrowing and the rate at which it lends to customers. A finance company may be independent, or owned by a bank or an industrial company. Also known as CAPTIVE FINANCE COMPANY. See also FINANCE HOUSE.

FINANCE HOUSE   In the United Kingdom, a FINANCE COMPANY.

FINANCIAL ACCOUNTING   The recording and reporting of a company's financial transactions based on ACCOUNTING PRINCIPLES or other applicable standards, which is followed by an EXTERNAL AUDIT and interim/annual presentation to external STAKEHOLDERS. See also MANAGEMENT ACCOUNTING.

FINANCIAL ACCOUNTING STANDARDS BOARD (FASB)   A US self-regulatory advisory panel that is responsible for creating and promulgating ACCOUNTING STANDARDS for CERTIFIED PUBLIC ACCOUNTANTS via the Statements of FINANCIAL ACCOUNTING STANDARDS, the core of US GENERALLY ACCEPTED ACCOUNTING PRINCIPLES (GAAP). See also INTERNATIONAL ACCOUNTING STANDARDS BOARD.

FINANCIAL ANALYSIS   The process of analyzing a company's FINANCIAL STATEMENTS in order to determine its financial strength, its trends over time, and how it compares with peers in its industry. Financial analysis is used by BANKS extending loans to clients, INVESTMENT BANKS and SECURITIES FIRMS recommending specific INVESTMENT actions on STOCKS, and CREDIT RATING AGENCIES rating the LIABILITIES of ISSUERS. See also CREDIT ANALYSIS.

FINANCIAL CRISIS   A severe dislocation in the markets and/or institutions that support the effective flow of CREDIT and CAPITAL in the global economic system. A financial crisis may be created through the bursting of a SPECULATIVE BUBBLE, a rapid weakening of economic conditions, the accumulation of excessive amounts of LEVERAGE, the sudden loss of INVESTOR confidence in market mechanisms, and so forth, and may manifest itself in the form of a DEBT CRISIS, a CURRENCY CRISIS, or a CREDIT CRISIS.

FINANCIAL DISTRESS   A state of corporate financial weakness characterized by an increasing COST OF CAPITAL, deteriorating payment terms from CREDITORS and suppliers, lower LIQUIDITY, higher LEVERAGE, and steady departure of key personnel. Distress may be induced by poor operations, weak market conditions, and/or financial mismanagement. Companies unable to cope with the effects of financial distress may ultimately be forced to file for BANKRUPTCY.

FINANCIAL ENGINEERING   The area of FINANCE concerned with creating financing, INVESTMENT and RISK MANAGEMENT solutions through the development of new instruments or the repackaging of existing instruments, e.g., the development of new DERIVATIVES with unique payoff profiles or the creation of SYNTHETIC ASSETS and LIABILITIES formed from packages of derivatives and UNDERLYINGS. Financial engineering relies heavily on quantitative methods and modeling in order to generate solutions with very specific RISK and RETURN characteristics. See also STRUCTURED FINANCE.

FINANCIAL FUTURE   An EXCHANGE-TRADED FUTURES CONTRACT that references a financial ASSET or marketplace. Key contracts include INTEREST RATE FUTURES, CURRENCY FUTURES, EQUITY FUTURES, and INDEX FUTURES, and may be designed to settle on a PHYSICAL or CASH BASIS. See also COMMODITY FUTURE.

FINANCIAL GUARANTEE   (1) A CONTRACT that provides for timely payment of PRINCIPAL and INTEREST to providers of CAPITAL. (2) A RISK TRANSFER mechanism that functions as a form of CONTINGENT DEBT FINANCING by giving the BENEFICIARY access to funds from the GUARANTOR in the event a loss TRIGGER is breached.

FINANCIAL HOLDING COMPANY   In the United States, a HOLDING COMPANY authorized under the GRAMM-LEACH-BLILEY ACT to own entities involved in SECURITIES TRADING and UNDERWRITING, CORPORATE FINANCE, INSURANCE, INVESTMENT MANAGEMENT, and commercial banking.

FINANCIAL INFORMATION EXCHANGE (FIX) PROTOCOL   A communications protocol developed in 1992 to promote consistency in the transfer of front-office information within the financial services industry. FIX, which uses a specified data template that is available in the public domain, is used extensively in a variety of pre-TRADE messaging and EXECUTION functions between BUY-SIDE and SELL-SIDE firms.

FINANCIAL INSTITUTION   A regulated organization that provides a range of BANKING and INVESTMENT services. Such institutions can be constituted in different forms (e.g., COMMERCIAL BANK, INVESTMENT BANK, UNIVERSAL BANK, MERCHANT BANK, BOUTIQUE) and deal with disparate products and clients.

FINANCIAL INSURANCE   See FINITE INSURANCE.

FINANCIAL INTERMEDIARY   See INTERMEDIARY.

FINANCIAL LEASE   See CAPITAL LEASE.

FINANCIAL LEVERAGE   See LEVERAGE.

FINANCIAL PAPER   COMMERCIAL PAPER issued by a BANK or SECURITIES FIRM. See also INDUSTRIAL PAPER.

FINANCIAL RATIOS   Measures derived from information contained in the FINANCIAL STATEMENTS of a company that provide additional insight into financial strength and performance. Ratios, which vary by industry, can be computed for profitability, activity, LIQUIDITY, CASH FLOW, and

SOLVENCY/ LEVERAGE. Results can be compared on a historical basis to establish a trend, and against other peer companies.

Common profitability ratios: GROSS MARGIN, NET INTEREST MARGIN, NET PROFIT MARGIN, OPERATING MARGIN, RETURN ON ASSETS, RETURN ON EQUITY, RETURN ON INVESTMENT, DUPONT RATIO.

Common activity ratios: INVENTORY TURNOVER, ACCOUNTS PAYABLE TURNOVER, ACCOUNTS RECEIVABLE TURNOVER, ASSET TURNOVER.

Common liquidity ratios: CURRENT RATIO, QUICK RATIO, DAYS PAYABLES OUTSTANDING, DAYS SALES INVENTORY, DAYS SALES OUTSTANDING, DAYS COST OF GOODS SOLD.
Common cash flow ratios: CASH FLOW TO CAPITAL INVESTMENT, CASH FLOW TO DEBT.
Common solvency/leverage ratios: FIXED CHARGE COVERAGE, TIMES INTEREST EARNED, DEBT TO EQUITY, DEBT TO ASSETS, CONTINGENTS TO ASSETS. Also known as ACCOUNTING RATIOS.

FINANCIAL REINSURANCE   See FINITE REINSURANCE.

FINANCIAL REPORTING STANDARDS (FRS) In the United Kingdom, a series of standards and interpretations promulgated by the ACCOUNTING STANDARDS BOARD that address key ACCOUNTING issues. A number of revisions related to FRS are converging with the INTERNATIONAL FINANCIAL REPORTING STANDARDS promulgated by the INTERNATIONAL ACCOUNTING STANDARDS BOARD.

FINANCIAL RISK   The RISK of loss arising from the financial activities of a firm, broadly taken to include CREDIT RISK, MARKET RISK, and LIQUIDITY RISK. See also OPERATING RISK.

FINANCIAL SERVICE DIRECTIVE   A directive established by the EUROPEAN UNION in 1996 indicating that a BANK or other FINANCIAL INSTITUTION authorized to provide services in one member country can provide the same services in other member countries. See also MARKETS IN FINANCIAL INSTRUMENTS DIRECTIVE, PASSPORTING.

FINANCIAL SERVICES ACT 1986 In the United Kingdom, an Act of Parliament designed to increase regulatory and self-regulatory control over INVESTMENTS and provide INVESTORS with additional protections. It was amended through the FINANCIAL SERVICES AND MARKETS ACT 2000.

FINANCIAL SERVICES AND MARKETS ACT 2000 In the United Kingdom, an Act of Parliament updating the original FINANCIAL SERVICES ACT 1986 that led to the creation of the FINANCIAL SERVICES AUTHORITY as the central UK financial REGULATOR, responsible for oversight of BANKS, INSURERS, and other INVESTMENT vehicles and markets.

FINANCIAL SERVICES AUTHORITY (FSA) The United Kingdom's independent consolidated financial REGULATOR, formally created through the

FINANCIAL SERVICES AND MARKETS ACT 2000; though the FSA was formally created in 1997, it received its statutory powers in 2000. The FSA comprises bodies and functions that were previously divided among a number of separate regulatory entities, and is responsible for overseeing institutions and markets related to DEPOSIT-taking, INSURANCE, and INVESTMENTS. In addition to specific oversight of key financial sectors, the FSA is responsible for ensuring public confidence in the markets and to provide appropriate INVESTOR and consumer protections.

FINANCIAL SERVICES MODERNIZATION ACT OF 1999   See GRAMM-LEACH-BLILEY ACT.

FINANCIAL SETTLEMENT   See CASH SETTLEMENT.

FINANCIAL SLACK   [COL] The excess DEBT financing capacity available to a company, which can be applied to a future ACQUISITION or capital INVESTMENT.

FINANCIAL STATEMENTS   The key financial information conveyed by a company based on the use of standardized accounting standards. The main financial statements include the BALANCE SHEET, INCOME STATEMENT, and CASH FLOW STATEMENT, along with supplementary FOOTNOTES. Also known as ACCOUNTS, FINANCIALS.

FINANCIAL TIMES STOCK EXCHANGE (FTSE) 100   The BENCHMARK INDEX of the LONDON STOCK EXCHANGE, comprised of 100 LARGE CAP STOCKS that represent a broad range of industries. The FTSE 100 can be traded directly through EXCHANGE-TRADED FUNDS and DERIVATIVES. Also known as FOOTSIE.

FINANCIAL YEAR   See FISCAL YEAR.

FINANCIALS   See FINANCIAL STATEMENTS.

FINANCIER   A professional involved in originating and structuring business transactions and associated financing arrangements, employed by a BANK, MERCHANT BANK, or BOUTIQUE. See also BANKER, INVESTMENT BANKER, PRIVATE BANKER.

FINANCING CASH FLOW   The portion of the corporate STATEMENT OF CASH FLOWS depicting the cash inflows and cash outflows that impact a firm's LIABILITIES and CAPITAL, including issuance/repayment of short- and long-term DEBT, issuance of COMMON STOCK and PREFERRED STOCK, repurchase of TREASURY STOCK, and payment of DIVIDENDS. See also INVESTING CASH FLOW, OPERATING CASH FLOW.

FINE PAPER   See FIRST CLASS PAPER.

FINE PRINT   [COL] The detailed legal language often contained in CONTRACTS or other documentation that contains relevant conditions, REPRESENTATIONS, WARRANTIES, and other essential information. Also known as SMALL PRINT.

FINISHED GOODS INVENTORY   A class of INVENTORY held by a company that includes all goods that are finalized and ready for sale. See also RAW MATERIAL INVENTORY, WORK-IN-PROCESS INVENTORY.

FINITE INSURANCE   An INSURANCE CONTRACT that is used primarily to finance, rather than transfer, an INSURED's RISK exposures. Finite contracts may be structured in the form of RETROSPECTIVE FINITE POLICIES (encompassing LOSS PORTFOLIO TRANSFER, ADVERSE DEVELOPMENT COVER, and RETROSPECTIVE AGGREGATE LOSS COVER) and PROSPECTIVE FINITE POLICIES. Also known as FINANCIAL INSURANCE, FINITE RISK CONTRACT. See also FINITE REINSURANCE.

FINITE QUOTA SHARE   A FINITE REINSURANCE agreement where the REINSURER agrees to pay, on behalf of the CEDING INSURER, a fixed or variable proportion of CLAIMS and expenses as they occur; ceding COMMISSIONS and INVESTMENT income from RESERVES typically cover actual claims, but if they prove insufficient the reinsurer funds the shortfall and recovers the difference from the insurer over the life of the contract.

FINITE REINSURANCE   A REINSURANCE agreement used primarily to finance, rather than transfer, a CEDING INSURER's RISK exposures. The INSURER pays PREMIUMS into an EXPERIENCE ACCOUNT and the REINSURER covers losses under the policy once they exceed the funded amount (up to predefined maximum limits). Finite reinsurance can be written in a variety of forms, including SPREAD LOSS, FINITE QUOTA SHARE, LOSS PORTFOLIO TRANSFER, ADVERSE DEVELOPMENT COVER, FUNDED EXCESS OF LOSS, and AGGREGATE STOP LOSS. Also known as FINANCIAL REINSURANCE. See also FINITE INSURANCE.

FINITE RISK CONTRACT   See FINITE INSURANCE.

FIRE SALE   [COL] Liquidation of an ASSET at a distressed, or sharply DISCOUNTED, price. A fire sale may be required if an INVESTOR or company is in urgent need of cash resources. See also DISTRESSED ASSET, VULTURE BID.

FIRM COMMITMENT   (1) A contractual agreement by a BANK to a client to provide a maximum amount of financing under a FACILITY, generally in exchange for a commitment fee. (2) See BOUGHT DEAL. (1) Also known as COMMITTED FACILITY.

FIRM ORDER   An ORDER submitted by a client to a BROKER or DEALER that remains valid until it is cancelled by the client. If the specific parameters regarding price, quantity, and time can be executed the broker/dealer is not required to refer back to the client.

FIRM PRICE   See FIRM QUOTE.

FIRM QUOTE   A BID and/or OFFER supplied by a DEALER or MARKET MAKER to a BROKER or client that can be regarded as reliable and actionable. Also known as FIRM PRICE. See also INDICATIVE QUOTE, QUOTED SPREAD.

FIRM UNDERWRITING   See BOUGHT DEAL.

FIRM VALUE   The value of a firm, computed as EQUITY value plus the MARKET VALUE of DEBT.

FIRST CALL DATE   The first date on which an ISSUER can call back a CALLABLE BOND outstanding in the marketplace; a typical bond might have several sequential call opportunities appearing after the first date. The time period between the issuance of the security and the first call date is regarded as HARD CALL PROTECTION and protects the INVESTOR against REINVESTMENT RISK. See also YIELD TO CALL.

FIRST CLASS PAPER   BILLS OF EXCHANGE or other MONEY MARKET SECURITIES with the highest CREDIT RATING, typically backed by a top-rated BANK or DISCOUNT HOUSE. Also known as A-1 PAPER, FINE PAPER.

FIRST DOLLAR COVERAGE   An INSURANCE CONTRACT that is not subject to a DEDUCTIBLE or which is made equivalent to a "no deductible" policy through an EXCESS INSURANCE clause. Under first dollar coverage the INSURER, rather than the INSURED, occupies the FIRST LOSS position.

FIRST IN FIRST OUT (FIFO)   An INVENTORY management and ACCOUNTING methodology where the first raw materials or work-in-progress inventory acquired for production of final goods are used first. Costs and inventory valuation are thus based on the earliest, and then latest, items in inventory, regardless of whether this corresponds to the actual physical movement in the inventory. See also LAST IN FIRST OUT (LIFO).

FIRST LIEN COMMERCIAL MORTGAGE   A MORTGAGE LOAN granted on a NONRECOURSE basis to a BORROWER seeking to purchase or finance a commercial property. First lien loans are typically structured as 10-year BALLOON LOANS with 30-year AMORTIZATION schedules, though INTEREST-only structures are also possible. Most loans carry fixed rates and have little, or no, possibility of PREPAYMENT. In some instances the original first lien mortgage can be split into two separate TRANCHES, one as SENIOR DEBT (a so-called A-NOTE) and the other as SUBORDINATED DEBT (a B-NOTE), and traded or placed separately. See also MEZZANINE LOAN.

FIRST LOSS   In an INSURANCE or REINSURANCE arrangement, the position that absorbs the initial losses arising from damage or destruction. The first loss position can be created through a DEDUCTIBLE where the INSURED bears the losses up to the ATTACHMENT point. If no DEDUCTIBLE exists, the INSURER bears the first loss position up to the POLICY CAP, or the point at which REINSURANCE attaches. See also EXCESS LAYER.

FIRST LOSS PIECE   See RESIDUAL SECURITY.

FIRST LOSS POLICY   A form of INSURANCE POLICY that places a CAP on the total value being insured, even if this is less than the appraised value of the item or property being insured.

FIRST LOSS RETENTION   See DEDUCTIBLE.

FIRST MORTGAGE DEBENTURE In the United Kingdom, a DEBENTURE that is secured by a first priority FIXED CHARGE over a specific property.

FIRST NOTICE DAY In the EXCHANGE-TRADED DERIVATIVE market, the day on which the seller of a CONTRACT advises the buyer of its intent to deliver.

FIRST-TO-DEFAULT SWAP An OVER-THE-COUNTER DEFAULT SWAP comprised of a BASKET of REFERENCE ENTITIES that entitles the purchaser to a payout on the first one that DEFAULTS; once a default occurs, the transaction terminates. Since swap pricing generally takes account of reference credit CORRELATIONS, the DERIVATIVE is cheaper than the purchase of individual contracts on the same reference credits. See also CREDIT DERIVATIVE, Nth to DEFAULT SWAP.

FISCAL AGENT An AGENT in a BOND transaction that arranges for COUPONS to be paid to INVESTORS.

FISCAL POLICY TAX and spending activities undertaken by a government in order to influence growth in the ECONOMY. By altering national tax levels and the program of spending and INVESTMENT, authorities attempt to shape AGGREGATE DEMAND within the economy. Since fiscal actions may demand legislative change or lead-time in implementation, the effects often take longer to flow through the economy than those created through short-term MONETARY POLICY actions.

FISCAL YEAR A 12-month period that is used to compute income or REVENUES for TAX and other financial reporting purposes, and which may vary by country (e.g., in the United Kingdom, Canada, and Japan the fiscal year runs from April 1 to March 31, in the United States October 1 to September 30, and so forth). Also known as FINANCIAL YEAR, TAX YEAR.

FISHER EFFECT In MACROECONOMICS, a theory put forth by economist Irving Fisher indicating that the real INTEREST RATE is equal to the NOMINAL INTEREST RATE less expected INFLATION, implying that for a constant real rate, the nominal rate is a direct function of the expected inflation rate. Using CONTINUOUS COMPOUNDING, the relationship is given as:

$$r_r = r_n - inf^e$$

where r_n is the nominal interest rate, infl is the expected inflation rate, e is the exponential constant. Also known as FISHER PARITY.

FISHER PARITY See FISHER EFFECT.

FIX PROTOCOL See FINANCIAL INFORMATION EXCHANGE PROTOCOL

FIXED ANNUITY An ANNUITY where PREMIUMS received from the INVESTOR grow at a fixed rate (known as the credited rate) specified by the INSURER. The growing amount accrues and is added to the cash value of the annuity, which remains untaxed as long as it remains in its annuitized form. The most common types of fixed annuities include the flexible premium deferred annuity (with flexible timing and amount of contribution by the investor) and the single premium deferred annuity (with set timing and amounts). See also GUARANTEED INVESTMENT CONTRACT, VARIABLE ANNUITY.

FIXED ASSET   The tangible and/or INTANGIBLE ASSETS used by a company in the production of goods, generally having a medium- to long-term life. Tangible fixed assets include plant, property, and equipment, while intangibles may include patents, trademarks, or GOODWILL. Fixed assets must be written off over their useful life through DEPRECIATION (tangibles), or AMORTIZATION (intangibles). Also known as CAPITAL ASSET. See also FIXED CAPITAL.

FIXED CAPITAL   The CAPITAL of a company that is specifically used to support FIXED ASSETS.

FIXED CHARGE   A CHARGE on the specific ASSETS of a company in favor of the chargee (typically a lending BANK), which prohibits the company from disposing of the assets without prior consent. Fixed charge CREDITORS have a SENIOR, secured ranking in the event of BANKRUPTCY, and are repaid before outstanding PENSION and employee compensation obligations. See also FLOATING CHARGE.

FIXED CHARGE COVERAGE   A measure of a company's ability to repay its PRINCIPAL AMORTIZATION, INTEREST, LEASE payments, and other fixed charges with pretax EARNINGS. Fixed charge coverage is computed via:

$$FCC = \frac{E_{BFC} + Tax}{FC}$$

where E_{BFC} equals earnings before fixed charges, Tax is income tax paid, and FC is fixed charges.

The larger the ratio, the greater the company's ability to cover its obligations. See also DEBT SERVICE COVERAGE, INTEREST COVERAGE, TIMES INTEREST EARNED.

FIXED COST   An EXPENSE that does not change in proportion to a company's output, but which remains constant regardless of activity (e.g., rent, salaries). Fixed cost is one of two elements, along with VARIABLE COST, which comprise TOTAL COSTS.

FIXED EXCHANGE RATE   An EXCHANGE RATE that is set by a country's CENTRAL BANK or monetary authority based on its MACROECONOMIC policies and its intervention in the FOREIGN EXCHANGE markets. A fixed exchange rate is not freely determined by market forces.

FIXED-FIXED   [COL] A CURRENCY SWAP where each LEG of the swap carries a FIXED RATE. See also FIXED-FLOATING, FLOATING-FLOATING.

FIXED-FLOATING   [COL] A CURRENCY SWAP or INTEREST RATE SWAP where one LEG has a FIXED RATE and the second leg a FLOATING RATE. See also FIXED-FIXED, FLOATING-FLOATING.

FIXED INCOME   The general class of marketable DEBT, or any SECURITY that pays an implicit or explicit INTEREST RATE RETURN to INVESTORS on a DISCOUNT or COUPON-bearing basis, including BILLS, NOTES, and BONDS. Also known as FIXED INTEREST.

FIXED INCOME ARBITRAGE   An ARBITRAGE strategy where an INVESTOR or HEDGE FUND manager purchases one FIXED INCOME SECURITY while simultaneously selling a similar security, under the expectation that temporary mispricings will converge over some defined time horizon, generally MATURITY of the underlying ASSETS. By selling the security, the investor or manager neutralizes key MARKET RISK factors, so that the price discrepancy can be crystallized and turned into a profit. Since discrepancies may be small, LEVERAGE may be employed to magnify any potential RETURN. Fixed income arbitrage can be applied with GOVERNMENT BONDS, MORTGAGE-BACKED SECURITIES, MUNICIPAL BONDS, and so forth.

FIXED INTEREST   See FIXED INCOME.

FIXED INTEREST RATE   See FIXED RATE.

FIXED PERIOD ADJUSTABLE RATE MORTGAGE   See HYBRID ADJUSTABLE RATE MORTGAGE.

FIXED PREMIUM   PREMIUM payable by an INSURED for an INSURANCE CONTRACT that remains constant during the payment period. See also FLEXIBLE PREMIUM.

FIXED-PRICE REOFFER   An agreement among SYNDICATE members not to resell a NEW ISSUE of NOTES or BONDS at a price that is lower than the initial offer until issuance is complete and the syndicate has been broken.

FIXED-PRICE TENDER   A form of TENDER where a fixed price is set for an ASSET or SECURITY, allowing buyers and sellers to BID or OFFER any quantity they like.

FIXED RATE   An INTEREST RATE on a financial contract, ASSET, or LIABILITY that remains constant during the life of the contract. Also known as FIXED INTEREST RATE. See also FLOATING RATE.

FIXED-RATE BOND   A DEBT obligation, such as a domestic BOND, EUROBOND, or GLOBAL BOND, which pays a fixed COUPON on a monthly, quarterly, semiannual, or annual basis. Fixed-rate bonds, which carry MATURITIES ranging from 1 to 30 years, can be issued directly or from MEDIUM-TERM NOTE or EURO MEDIUM-TERM NOTE programs, and may be sold as publicly placed REGISTERED SECURITIES, BEARER SECURITIES, or PRIVATE PLACEMENTS. See also FLOATING RATE NOTE.

FIXED STRIKE LADDER OPTION   An OVER-THE-COUNTER COMPLEX OPTION that allows the buyer to lock in any accumulated gains prior to expiry as the price of the UNDERLYING exceeds prespecified market levels (or "rungs"); gains are not lost if the market subsequently retraces. This version of the option compares the terminal price and ladder rungs against a predefined STRIKE PRICE and allocates a gain to the larger of the two. See also CLIQUET OPTION, FLOATING STRIKE LADDER OPTION, LADDER OPTION, SHOUT OPTION.

FIXED STRIKE LOOKBACK OPTION   See OPTION ON THE MAXIMUM/ MINIMUM.

FIXED STRIKE SHOUT OPTION   An OVER-THE-COUNTER COMPLEX OPTION that allows the buyer to lock in any accumulated gains when a "shout" is declared (i.e., the buyer formally declares its intention to lock in); gains are not lost if the market subsequently retraces. This version of the option compares the terminal price and shout level against a predefined STRIKE PRICE and allocates a gain to the larger of the two. See also CLIQUET OPTION, FLOATING STRIKE SHOUT OPTION, LADDER OPTION, SHOUT OPTION.

FIXED TRIGGER   A TRIGGER in an INSURANCE CONTRACT that indicates whether or not an event has occurred; a fixed trigger does not typically impact the payoff value of the contract, it simply indicates whether a SETTLEMENT will occur.

FIXING   The process of setting or resetting a specific INTEREST RATE on a LOAN or DERIVATIVE. Fixing is done in relation to the specific mechanics of a transaction, and is defined by market, rate, time, and other particulars.

FLAG   A TECHNICAL ANALYSIS pattern where a SECURITY or INDEX price fluctuates in a narrow, and relatively stable, range (the body of the flag) preceded and/or followed by large upward or downward moves (the flagpole).

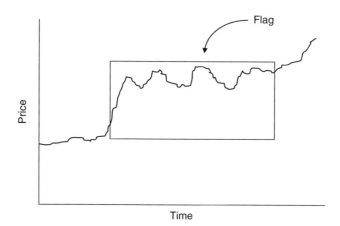

See also PENNANT.

FLASH   See FLASH PRICE.

FLASH PRICE   [COL] The current price of a SECURITY; during very heavy volume sessions on an EXCHANGE, quote tickers become delayed with "stale" price information, so flash prices periodically appear to signal the current value. Also known as FLASH.

FLAT BOND   A BOND that is bought or sold without ACCRUED INTEREST, either because the SETTLEMENT date is equal to the payment date, no COUPON is due, or the ISSUER is unable to pay a current coupon (e.g., the SECURITY is an INCOME BOND).

FLAT TAX   See PROPORTIONAL TAX.

FLAT YIELD   The current YIELD of a CONVERTIBLE BOND, typically computed via:

$$FY = \frac{C}{P_{CB}}$$

where C is the COUPON of the issue (in percentage terms) and P_{CB} is the current price of the convertible bond. Also known as RUNNING YIELD. See also EQUIVALENT BREAKEVEN, SIMPLE BREAKEVEN, YIELD ADVANTAGE.

FLAT YIELD CURVE   A TERM STRUCTURE where short-term INTEREST RATES are equal to long-term interest rates. See also KINKED YIELD CURVE, NEGATIVE YIELD CURVE, POSITIVE YIELD CURVE, YIELD CURVE.

FLATTENING   (1) The act of neutralizing a LONG POSITION or a SHORT POSITION, either by selling or covering, or by establishing an equal and opposite HEDGE. A position that has been flattened is no longer exposed to market movements. (2) A reshaping of the YIELD CURVE so that short-term and long-term INTEREST RATES appear approximately equal.

FLEX OPTION   See FLEXIBLE EXCHANGE OPTION.

FLEXIBLE DRAWDOWN   A DRAWDOWN under a REVOLVING CREDIT FACILITY or other financing arrangement that occurs in stages, often to correspond with specific CASH FLOW or INVESTMENT requirements of the BORROWER.

FLEXIBLE EXCHANGE (FLEX) OPTION   A standardized OPTION CONTRACT traded on an EXCHANGE that allows buyers and sellers to select key contract features such as STRIKE PRICE, EXERCISE style, and MATURITY. Though not as bespoke as an OVER-THE-COUNTER (OTC) OPTION, the flex structure provides a degree of customization that allows it to compete with certain OTC contracts.

FLEXIBLE PREMIUM   PREMIUM payable by an INSURED for an INSURANCE CONTRACT that may increase or decrease during the payment period. See also FIXED PREMIUM.

FLIGHT TO QUALITY   [COL] A market action or event where INVESTORS liquidate risky or speculative SECURITIES holdings and deposit proceeds with BANKS or purchase GOVERNMENT BONDS or other "safe haven" ASSETS. Flight to quality may occur when financial markets start becoming volatile and ILLIQUID, economic conditions deteriorate, and/or systemic threats grow. See also CAPITAL FLIGHT.

FLIP IN PILL   [COL] A POISON PILL that allows existing SHAREHOLDERS of a company that is the subject of a TAKEOVER to buy new SHARES at a DISCOUNT; the pill increases DILUTION, and is thus intended to dissuade a potential acquirer from bidding for the company. See also FLIP OVER PILL.

FLIP OVER PILL   [COL] A POISON PILL that allows existing SHAREHOLDERS of a company that is the subject of a TAKEOVER to buy the acquiring company's SHARES at a sharp DISCOUNT if the transaction is completed; the pill is intended to dissuade an acquirer from bidding for the company. See also FLIP IN PILL.

FLIPPER   [COL] An INVESTOR receiving an allocation in an INITIAL PUBLIC OFFERING, ADD-ON, or NEW ISSUE that sells the SECURITIES several hours or days after issuance to lock in a short-term capital gain. Also known as STAG.

FLOAT   (1) The value of all cash balances that result from delays in SETTLEMENT and processing of CHECKS, DRAFTS, and other payments; collection float represents lost INTEREST to DEPOSITORS while payment float represents a gain to payers. (2) Funds established by an INSURER to pay for incurred losses under INSURANCE contracts. (3) The act of issuing new SECURITIES in the PRIMARY MARKET.

FLOATER   (1) In INSURANCE, an ENDORSEMENT that allows cover age of moveable property to be transferred with the property between locations. (2) [COL] See FLOATING RATE NOTE.

FLOATING CHARGE   A charge on nonspecific ASSETS of company in favor of the chargee (typically a lending BANK), indicating that it floats across all assets and does not become fixed to any specific asset until an event of BANKRUPTCY. Floating charge CREDITORS are paid after outstanding PENSION and employee compensation obligations, but before unsecured creditors. Also known as FLOATING LIEN. See also FIXED CHARGE.

FLOATING-FLOATING   [COL] A CURRENCY SWAP or INTEREST RATE SWAP where each LEG references a different FLOATING RATE, i.e., a BASIS SWAP. See also FIXED-FIXED, FIXED-FLOATING.

FLOATING INSURANCE POLICY   See FLOATING POLICY.

FLOATING INTEREST RATE   See FLOATING RATE.

FLOATING LIEN   See FLOATING CHARGE.

FLOATING POLICY   (1) An INSURANCE POLICY that relates to movable personal property. (2) An insurance policy that is used to cover merchandise that is continuously changing, such as in maritime shipments of cargoes, or personal property which is substituted. Although the specific items being covered change over time, the policy remains in force until it is cancelled. Also known as FLOATING INSURANCE POLICY.

FLOATING RATE   An INTEREST RATE on a financial CONTRACT, ASSET, or LIABILITY that changes on a periodic basis, based on the specific rate benchmark that serves as a reference. Also known as FLOATING INTEREST RATE. See also FIXED RATE.

FLOATING RATE CERTIFICATE OF DEPOSIT (FRCD)   A CERTIFICATE OF DEPOSIT issued by a BANK that pays a monthly, quarterly, semiannual, or annual COUPON based on a floating INTEREST RATE, often LIBOR or EURIBOR. The most common FRCDs have a 6-month MATURITY and a 30-day roll (e.g., ACCRUED INTEREST is paid every 30 days and the new coupon is set) and a 12-month maturity with a 90-day roll. Also known as VARIABLE RATE CERTIFICATE OF DEPOSIT (VRCD). See also LOCKUP CERTIFICATE OF DEPOSIT, NEGOTIABLE CERTIFICATE OF DEPOSIT.

FLOATING RATE LOAN   A LOAN where the INTEREST paid by the BORROWER is based on a FLOATING RATE BENCHMARK, such as LIBOR or EURIBOR.

FLOATING RATE NOTE (FRN)   A DEBT obligation with a final MATURITY of 1 to 15 years that pays a monthly, quarterly, semiannual, or annual COUPON based on a floating INTEREST RATE reference, often LIBOR or EURIBOR. Floating rate notes can be issued directly or from MEDIUM-TERM NOTE or EURO MEDIUM-TERM NOTE programs, and may be sold as REGISTERED SECURITIES, BEARER SECURITIES, or PRIVATE PLACEMENTS in a range of CURRENCIES. FRNs are periodically issued as STRUCTURED NOTES such as RANGE FRNs, RANGE KNOCK-OUT FRNs, and INVERSE FRNs. Also known as FLOATER. See also FIXED-RATE BOND, PERPETUAL FLOATING RATE NOTE.

FLOATING RATE SECURITY   Any SECURITY with a COUPON that adjusts on a periodic basis with reference to a FLOATING RATE BENCHMARK. Common floating rate securities include FLOATING RATE CERTIFICATES OF DEPOSIT, FLOATING RATE NOTES, and VARIABLE RATE NOTES. Also known as VARIABLE RATE SECURITY.

FLOATING STRIKE LADDER OPTION   An OVER-THE-COUNTER COMPLEX OPTION that allows the buyer to lock in any accumulated gains prior to expiry as the price of the UNDERLYING exceeds prespecified market levels (or "rungs"); gains are not lost if the market subsequently retraces. This version of the option carries no preset STRIKE PRICE, it simply compares the terminal price and ladder rungs at maturity to determine the size of any gains. See also CLIQUET OPTION, FIXED STRIKE LADDER OPTION, LADDER OPTION, SHOUT OPTION.

FLOATING STRIKE LOOKBACK OPTION   An OVER-THE-COUNTER COMPLEX OPTION that provides the buyer with a maximum gain by "looking back" over the price path of the UNDERLYING and determining the point that creates the greatest economic profit. This version of the option carries no preset STRIKE PRICE, it simply compares the terminal price against the lowest buying price (for CALL OPTIONS) or highest selling price (for PUT OPTIONS). See also LOOKBACK OPTION.

FLOATING STRIKE SHOUT OPTION   An OVER-THE-COUNTER COMPLEX OPTION that allows the buyer to lock in any accumulated gains when a "shout" is declared (i.e., the buyer formally declares its intention to lock in); gains are not lost if the market subsequently retraces. This version of the option carries no predefined STRIKE PRICE, it simply compares the terminal price and shout level at maturity to determine any profit. See also CLIQUET OPTION, FIXED STRIKE SHOUT OPTION, LADDER OPTION, SHOUT OPTION.

FLOOR   (1) A location in an EXCHANGE for the TRADING of COMMODITIES, SECURITIES, or DERIVATIVES. (2) An OVER-THE-COUNTER INTEREST RATE OPTION that generates a payoff when an underlying INTEREST RATE reference falls below a STRIKE PRICE. A floor can be viewed as a strip of options, where each individual option is known as a FLOORLET and provides for a periodic payoff. More specifically, a floor is the equivalent of a strip of PUT OPTIONS on interest rates or a strip of CALL OPTIONS on an underlying FIXED INCOME instrument (as a result of the inverse relationship between price and yield). This creates the following value relationships for rising and falling rates:

	Rising Rates	**Falling Rates**
Long floor	Value decreases	Value increases
Short floor	Value increases	Value decreases

The payoff to the purchaser of a cap on each settlement date is given as:

$$N * (f - r_{ref}) * (n / d)$$

where N is the notional, r_{ref} is the value of the reference rate at the settlement date, f is the floor strike, n is the number of days in the settlement period, d is the number days in the year.

The floor provides no payoff to the purchaser if the reference rate is higher than the floor strike for any individual settlement period. (1) See also CAP, CAPTION, FLOORTION.

FLOOR BROKER   A BROKER that fulfills the BROKERAGE role on the FLOOR of an EXCHANGE. See also FLOOR TRADER.

FLOOR TRADER   A TRADER operating on the FLOOR of an EXCHANGE, EXECUTING relevant ORDERS for clients or for proprietary purposes. See also FLOOR BROKER.

FLOORED FLOATING RATE NOTE   A FLOATING RATE NOTE (FRN) that features a COUPON that is floored at a lower STRIKE level. The INVESTOR therefore faces a minimum return on invested capital once rates fall below the strike. See also CAPPED FLOATING RATE NOTE.

FLOORLESS CONVERTIBLE   See DEATH SPIRAL.

FLOORLET   One of a series of INTEREST RATE FLOORS comprising a FLOOR.

FLOORTION   An OVER-THE-COUNTER OPTION on a FLOOR, granting the buyer the right to purchase a floor at a predetermined STRIKE PRICE. See also CAP, CAPTION.

FLOTATION   The act of UNDERWRITING a NEW ISSUE of SECURITIES in the PRIMARY MARKET.

FLOTATION COST   The EXPENSE a company bears in issuing new SECURITIES, typically computed as the difference between the price received by the company on an issue and the amount charged to INVESTORS (the UNDERWRITING SPREAD) plus out of pocket expenses. See also ALL-IN.

FLOW   [COL] The total of customer ORDERS passing through a BROKER or DEALER.

FNMA   See FEDERAL NATIONAL MORTGAGE ASSOCIATION.

FOB   See FREE ON BOARD.

FOF   See FUND OF FUNDS.

FOLLOWING THE FORTUNES   [COL] A clause in a REINSURANCE CONTRACT indicating that the REINSURER will be subject to the same financial fate as the CEDING INSURER. The clause is designed to align the interests of the two parties.

FOMC   See FEDERAL OPEN MARKETS COMMITTEE.

FOOTNOTES   Additional, often detailed, explanation regarding the FINANCIAL STATEMENTS presented by a company. The explanatory material may related to the BALANCE SHEET, INCOME STATEMENT, and/or CASH FLOW STATEMENT, and may also include information on the operating environment, litigation, and other RISK FACTORS.

FOOTSIE   [COL] See FINANCIAL TIMES STOCK EXCHANGE (FTSE) 100.

FORBEARANCE   (1)   A decision by a BANK not to exercise its rights against a BORROWER in technical DEFAULT, in exchange for the borrower's promise to begin making regular payments of PRINCIPAL and/or INTEREST. (2) See REGULATORY FORBEARANCE.

FORCE MAJEURE   [FR] Literally "irresistible force"; in the corporate sector it is a financial event of such gravity (e.g., systemic dislocation, severe CREDIT RATING downgrade, BANKRUPTCY) that a relationship/transaction (such as a LOAN, NEW ISSUE, or CORPORATE FINANCE deal) may be cancelled or accelerated. See also MATERIAL ADVERSE CHANGE CLAUSE, VIS MAJOR.

FORCED CONVERSION   An act taken by an ISSUER to require the conversion of a CONVERTIBLE BOND into SHARES, taken when the structure of the SECURITY allows for such a step, e.g., as in a MANDATORY CONVERTIBLE BOND.

FORECLOSURE   A legal process where CREDITORS take possession of COLLATERAL securing a LOAN to a BORROWER in technical DEFAULT, generally through the filing of a foreclosure suit. In some systems the ability to seize ASSETS and foreclose may be limited or delayed by AUTOMATIC STAY provisions.

FOREIGN BILL   In the United Kingdom, a BILL OF EXCHANGE that is either drawn or payable outside the country.

FOREIGN CORRUPT PRACTICES ACT   In the United States, legislation designed to ban corruption and bribery in US companies operating in foreign jurisdictions.

FOREIGN CURRENCY BOND   (1) A BOND issued in a CURRENCY other than the ISSUER's home currency. (2) See DUAL CURRENCY BOND.

FOREIGN DIRECT INVESTMENT   A CAPITAL INVESTMENT by a company in one country in productive ASSETS located in another country, often through a controlled foreign affiliate. Also known as DIRECT INVESTMENT.

FOREIGN EXCHANGE (FX)   A transaction that involves the exchange of two CURRENCIES. TRADING in foreign exchange is extremely active, with institutions regularly using SPOT and DERIVATIVE contracts to HEDGE, ARBITRAGE, or SPECULATE. See also FOREIGN EXCHANGE (FX) RATE.

FOREIGN EXCHANGE (FX) BROKER   A BROKER that deals exclusively with clients in the FOREIGN EXCHANGE MARKET, generally across a broad range of currencies. Foreign exchange brokers are permitted to disclose their PRINCIPALS in certain markets, but not in all markets. See also COMMODITY BROKER, INTER-DEALER BROKER.

FOREIGN EXCHANGE (FX) DEALER   A DEALER who specializes in TRADING FOREIGN EXCHANGE, acting as PRINCIPAL by taking positions and filling ORDERS through the commitment of RISK CAPITAL.

FOREIGN EXCHANGE (FX) MARKET   The general marketplace for buying and selling of CURRENCIES. The FX market allows currency HEDGERS and SPECULATORS to establish prices and exchange both major and emerging market currencies. The market is global, operating 24 hours per day, and is conducted on an OVER-THE-COUNTER basis (though certain currency DERIVATIVES are traded on EXCHANGES). See also BOND MARKET, COMMODITY MARKET, STOCK MARKET.

FOREIGN EXCHANGE (FX) RATE   The price or value of a country's CURRENCY. Market forces may set a foreign exchange rate (i.e., a market exchange rate) or a country's CENTRAL BANK or monetary authority may control or influence the rate (i.e., a MANAGED FOREIGN EXCHANGE RATE, or a semifloating rate determined through PEGGING or CRAWLING PEGS). Fixed foreign exchange rates may or may not reflect the perceived market value of the currency; where significant discrepancies arise a black market, based purely on market SUPPLY and DEMAND forces, may develop. Also known as RATE OF EXCHANGE.

FOREIGN EXCHANGE (FX) RESERVES   ASSETS of a country, held with the CENTRAL BANK or monetary authority, which are used for currency management and intervention. RESERVES generally comprise of GOLD and major RESERVE CURRENCIES, along with SPECIAL DRAWING RIGHTS held with the INTERNATIONAL MONETARY FUND.

FOREIGN EXCHANGE (FX) RISK   The RISK of loss due to an adverse move in the direction of FOREIGN EXCHANGE RATES. Foreign exchange risk is a form of DIRECTIONAL RISK.

FOREIGN EXCHANGE (FX) SWAP   A transaction involving the simultaneous purchase and sale of one CURRENCY for a second one, each with a different VALUE DATE. In a conventional swap one of the value dates is for SPOT settlement and the other for future settlement, meaning the structure can be viewed as a package of a spot and a FORWARD; in some cases two forward dates may also be used. Note that this transaction is separate and distinct from a CURRENCY SWAP.

FORENSIC ACCOUNTING   A reconstruction of a company's past financial transactions and records in order to fulfill a court-order or legal investigation.

FORFAITING   A process where an exporter sells to a BANK or specialized financial institution a PORTFOLIO of discounted long-term ACCOUNTS RECEIVABLE or PROMISSORY NOTES (generally backed by GUARANTEES from the importer's own BANK). See also FACTORING.

FORM 3   In the United States, a document filed by a company with the SECURITIES AND EXCHANGE COMMISSION that details the amount of SHARES and OPTIONS held by the company's officers and its largest shareholders.

FORM F1   In the United States, a document filed by a company with the SECURITIES AND EXCHANGE COMMISSION indicating that a NEW ISSUE of SHARES is being sold to the public.

FORTUITOUS EVENT   An unforeseen, unexpected, or accidental occurrence; such an event is a general characteristic of an INSURABLE RISK and must be present in order for an INSURED to make a CLAIM under an INSURANCE CONTRACT.

FORWARD   A bilateral OVER-THE-COUNTER DERIVATIVE that permits the purchaser to buy, and the seller to sell, a reference ASSET at a predetermined future price and future date. Unlike a SWAP, a forward CONTRACT features no intervening cash FLOWS, simply a final cash exchange at the conclusion of the contract. Forwards are highly customizable; the two parties can negotiate terms regarding amount, SETTLEMENT, MATURITY, and UNDERLYING reference.

Long forward payoff profile

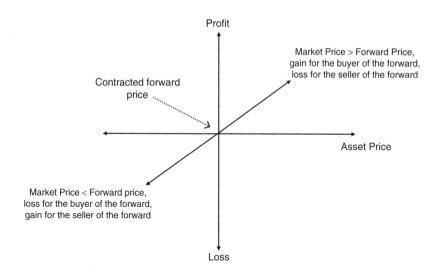

Short forward payoff profile

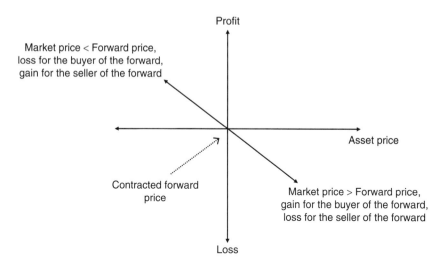

See also FORWARD DISCOUNT, FORWARD FORWARD, FORWARD PREMIUM, FORWARD PRICE, FORWARD RATE, FORWARD RATE AGREEMENT, NONDELIVERABLE FORWARD.

FORWARD BALANCE SHEET   A future depiction of a firm's BALANCE SHEET and OFF-BALANCE SHEET commitments and contingencies. Construction of a forward balance sheet is an important element in managing RISK, LIQUIDITY, and CAPITAL as it provides an estimate of how a firm's operations will change with the passage of time or the occurrence of contingent events.

FORWARD BUNDLE   [COL] A BUNDLE of EURODOLLAR FUTURES that does not begin with the FRONT MONTH contract, but with some future CONTRACT date.

FORWARD DELIVERY   Arrangement for the future delivery of goods for cash, or vice-versa, and an essential feature of a FUTURES contract and a FORWARD contract. See also CASH DELIVERY.

FORWARD DISCOUNT   A FORWARD PRICE (or rate) for future delivery of an ASSET that is lower than the SPOT PRICE (or rate) for immediate delivery. See also FORWARD PREMIUM.

FORWARD FOREIGN EXCHANGE (FX) CONVERSION   An ARBITRAGE strategy in the FOREIGN EXCHANGE market to take advantage of mispricing in CURRENCY FORWARDS. The conversion occurs when forwards appear CHEAP, and is created by buying a forward, selling a CALL OPTION, and buying a PUT OPTION (all with the same MATURITY); if the forward is mispriced, the strategy yields an arbitrage profit. See also FORWARD FOREIGN EXCHANGE REVERSAL.

FORWARD FOREIGN EXCHANGE (FX) REVERSAL   An ARBITRAGE strategy in the FOREIGN EXCHANGE market to take advantage of mispricing in CURRENCY FORWARDS. The conversion occurs when forwards appear RICH, and is created by selling a forward, buying a CALL OPTION, and selling a PUT OPTION (all with the same MATURITY); if the forward is mispriced, the strategy yields an arbitrage profit. See also FORWARD FOREIGN EXCHANGE CONVERSION.

FORWARD FORWARD   A FORWARD transaction that is contracted to start at a future date. See also FORWARD FORWARD RATE, FORWARD RATE AGREEMENT.

FORWARD FORWARD RATE   The FORWARD RATE used as a reference in a FORWARD RATE AGREEMENT or an INTEREST RATE FORWARD CONTRACT; it can be considered the interest rate for a certain period of time applicable to a certain future starting point.

FORWARD MARGIN   See FORWARD POINTS.

FORWARD MARKET   The general marketplace for ASSETS or financial CONTRACTS that are settled and delivered at a future time. See also FORWARD, SPOT MARKET.

FORWARD POINTS   The differential between a SPOT RATE and FORWARD RATE in the FOREIGN EXCHANGE markets. Forward points arise as a result of INTEREST RATE DIFFERENTIALS, market expectations related to CURRENCIES and INTEREST RATES, and/or currency SUPPLY and DEMAND. While forward points can be computed as the difference between spot and forward currency rates, they can also be estimated via:

$$FP = \frac{FX_s(r_{diff})(t)}{RB}$$

where FX_s is the spot currency rate, r_{diff} is the interest rate differential between the two currencies, t is the time to maturity (days), and RB is the rate basis (e.g., 360 or 365 days). Also known as FORWARD MARGIN.

FORWARD PREMIUM   A FORWARD PRICE (or rate) for future delivery of an ASSET that is higher than the SPOT PRICE (or rate) for immediate delivery. See also FORWARD DISCOUNT.

FORWARD PRICE   The price quoted for future delivery of an ASSET under a FORWARD or FUTURE, comprised of the SPOT PRICE and a positive or negative COST OF CARRY; a quoted price may reflect a FORWARD PREMIUM or FORWARD DISCOUNT. The equilibrium, no-ARBITRAGE forward prices for various assets are given as follows:

COMMON STOCK, no DIVIDENDS:

$$F = S\,e^{rt}$$

where S is the stock price, e is the exponential constant, r is a prevailing DISCOUNT RATE, and t is the time to MATURITY.

Stock, continuous dividends:

$$F = S\,e^{(r-\delta)t}$$

where δ is the DIVIDEND YIELD and all other terms are as defined above.

Currency:

$$F = Sp\,e^{(r_1-r_2)t}$$

where Sp is the spot price, r_1 is the discount rate for currency 1, r_2 is the discount rate for currency 2, and all other terms are as defined above.

Commodity with LEASE market:

$$F = Sp\,e^{(r-\varphi)t}$$

where φ is the lease payment rate and all other terms are as defined above.

Commodity with carry market:

$$F = Sp\,e^{(r+\lambda)t}$$

where λ is the cost of storage and INSURANCE, and all other terms are as defined above.

Commodity with carry market and CONVENIENCE YIELD:

$$F = Sp\,e^{(r+\lambda-cy)t}$$

where cy is the convenience yield, and all other terms are as defined above. See also FORWARD RATE.

FORWARD PRICE/EARNINGS RATIO   A PRICE/EARNINGS RATIO that is computed based on earnings forecasts of a company's results rather than its historical results. The earnings estimates may be based on consensus forecasts from EQUITY ANALYSTS. See also TRAILING PRICE/EARNINGS RATIO.

FORWARD RATE   (1) The rate quoted for future delivery of an ASSET, used in the calculation of FORWARDS and FUTURES. A quoted forward rate may reflect a FORWARD PREMIUM or FORWARD DISCOUNT. (2) See IMPLIED FORWARD RATE. (1) See also FORWARD PRICE.

FORWARD RATE AGREEMENT (FRA) An OVER-THE-COUNTER DERIVATIVE agreement to borrow or lend an amount of cash for a predefined period that does not exceed 1 year. In market terms, the buyer of an FRA is borrowing a specified amount, while the seller of an FRA is lending that amount. The FRA can be viewed as a single period FORWARD CONTRACT on INTEREST RATES that does not involve an exchange of PRINCIPAL; at MATURITY the parties exchange the differential prevailing between the interest rate and the rate agreed at the start of the transaction. The settlement amount at the end of the contract is defined by:

$$FRAset = \left(\frac{(r_{ref} - r_{FRA}) * N * (n/d)}{1 + (r_{ref} * n * (n/d))} \right)$$

where r_{ref} is the reference fixing rate, r_{FRA} is the FRA contract rate, N is the notional value of the contracts, n is the number of days in the contract period, d is the day count basis (360 or 365) Also known as INTEREST RATE FORWARD. See also FORWARD FORWARD RATE

FORWARD RATE MODEL   A form of mathematical model used in the pricing of INTEREST RATE DERIVATIVES which uses and evolves randomly the entire FORWARD curve of the short rate. See also SHORT RATE MODEL.

FORWARD START OPTION   An OVER-THE-COUNTER COMPLEX OPTION that is contracted on TRADE date t to commence on forward date t + 1, with the forward start date, STRIKE PRICE, and final MATURITY parameters established on trade date. Once the forward date is reached a conventional EUROPEAN OPTION comes into existence.

FORWARD SWAP   An OVER-THE-COUNTER SWAP that is contracted on TRADE date t and commences on forward date t + 1, with the INTEREST RATE and final MATURITY parameters established on trade date. Once the forward date is reached a conventional fixed/floating INTEREST RATE SWAP comes into existence.

FORWARDATION   See CONTANGO.

FOUNDATION METHODOLOGY   A credit-based CAPITAL ALLOCATION process promulgated by the BANK FOR INTERNATIONAL SETTLEMENTS (BIS) under the INTERNAL RATINGS-BASED (IRB) APPROACH. BANKS use internal models to determine a COUNTERPARTY'S DEFAULT RISK, but use BIS-supplied RISK factors to estimate RISK EQUIVALENT EXPOSURE and LOSS-GIVEN DEFAULT in order to obtain estimates of EXPECTED CREDIT LOSS and UNEXPECTED CREDIT LOSS. CAPITAL is then allocated to cover the resulting exposure. See also ADVANCED METHODOLOGY.

FRA   See FORWARD RATE AGREEMENT.

FRACTIONAL BANKING   See FRACTIONAL RESERVE BANKING.

FRACTIONAL EXPOSURE   The amount of future CREDIT RISK inherent in an OVER-THE-COUNTER DERIVATIVE transaction, typically combined with ACTUAL EXPOSURE to determine total credit exposure. The amount of fractional exposure in a derivative is dependent on market movements in the UNDERLYING reference: the greater the potential future market moves, the greater the fractional exposure. Fractional exposure, which can be estimated through statistical or simulation methods, is positive at the inception of a transaction and declines as MATURITY approaches, since the opportunity for further market moves that can affect value becomes limited. Also known as DEEMED RISK, POTENTIAL MARKET RISK, PRESETTLEMENT RISK, TIME-TO-DECAY RISK.

FRACTIONAL RESERVE BANKING   A banking framework where a BANK keeps a portion of its DEPOSITS in the form of cash reserves and uses the balance to grant LOANS. The responsible CENTRAL BANK or monetary authority can alter the RESERVE REQUIREMENTS in order to adjust the amount of new CREDIT flowing into the system (e.g., increasing the reserve requirement reduces the ability of a bank to create new loans, tightening the supply of credit in the system, and vice-versa).

FRANKFURT STOCK EXCHANGE   The primary STOCK EXCHANGE of Germany, founded in 1820 and now owned by DEUTSCHE BORSE, accounting for the majority of EQUITY TRADING in the country. The exchange sets prices on an AUCTION basis through BROKERS and, through separate divisions, deals in LARGE CAP, MID-CAP, and SMALL CAP STOCKS and GOVERNMENT BONDS.

FRAUD   An act of intentional deception or dishonesty perpetrated by one or more individuals, generally for financial gain. See also EMBEZZLEMENT, FRAUDULENT MISREPRESENTATION.

FRAUDULENT CONVEYANCE   The act of transferring ASSETS from one party (often an insolvent DEBTOR) to another party, with the express intent of keeping such assets away from CREDITORS or a BANKRUPTCY TRUSTEE or RECEIVER. Also known as FRAUDULENT TRANSFER. See also UNFAIR PREFERENCE.

FRAUDULENT MISREPRESENTATION   A false CLAIM made by one party in order to gain economic advantage from a second party. Proof of misrepresentation can result in termination of CONTRACTS. See also FRAUD.

FRAUDULENT TRANSFER   See FRAUDULENT CONVEYANCE.

FRCD   See FLOATING RATE CERTIFICATE OF DEPOSIT.

FREDDIE MAC [COL]   See FEDERAL HOME LOAN MORTGAGE CORPORATION.

FREE CAPITAL   In the United Kingdom, FREE FLOAT.

FREE CASH FLOW   A CASH FLOW measure that is computed as OPERATING CASH FLOW less capital expenditures, or as NET INCOME plus DEPRECIATION, less changes in WORKING CAPITAL, less changes in capital expenditures.

The resulting figure is generally considered to be an accurate reflection of a company's true cash position. See also FINANCING CASH FLOW, FREE CASH FLOW TO EQUITY, FREE CASH FLOW TO FIRM, INVESTING CASH FLOW.

FREE CASH FLOW TO EQUITY (FCFE)   Cash available to SHAREHOLDERS after all EXPENSES, INVESTMENTS, and INTEREST payments (after TAX) to DEBT holders have been made. It can be computed as OPERATING CASH FLOW less capital expenditures less debt payments. See also DISCOUNTED CASH FLOW VALUATION MODEL, FREE CASH FLOW TO FIRM.

FREE CASH FLOW TO FIRM (FCFF)   Cash available to BOND holders and SHAREHOLDERS after all EXPENSES and INVESTMENTS have been made. It can be computed as EARNINGS BEFORE INTEREST AND TAX times (1 – tax rate) plus DEPRECIATION less capital expenditures less changes in WORKING CAPITAL less changes in other ASSETS. See also DISCOUNTED CASH FLOW VALUATION MODEL, FREE CASH FLOW TO EQUITY.

FREE FLOAT   SHARES of a company that are held by the public at large rather than by controlling or major SHAREHOLDERS. See also FREE CAPITAL.

FREE MARKET ECONOMY   An economic system where the means of production and distribution are primarily owned by the private sector, and where government involvement is very limited. The economy encourages competition and resource allocation and pricing is driven primarily by market forces of SUPPLY and DEMAND. Also known as MARKET ECONOMY.

FREE ON BOARD (FOB)   The declared value of EXPORT goods, including the cost of production and transportation to the port of shipment. FOB does not include the cost of transportation from the port to the destination or the cost of INSURANCE, both of which are the responsibility of the importer. See also COST, INSURANCE, FREIGHT (CIF).

FREE RESERVES   Any cash RESERVES held by a regulated FINANCIAL INSTITUTION, such as a BANK, BUILDING SOCIETY, or SAVINGS AND LOAN, that exceed those required by the relevant REGULATOR.

FREE RIDER   [COL] An UNDERWRITER or SYNDICATE member that retains a portion of a PRIMARY MARKET offering in order to sell at what it hopes will be a higher SECONDARY MARKET price; the practice is illegal in many markets.

FREE TRADE   A process of exchanging goods, services, and resources without undue constraints, such as TARIFFS, surcharges, or QUOTAS.

FREEZE-OUT   [COL] The process of persuading MINORITY INTERESTS of a TARGET company to sell their SHARES after a TENDER OFFER has been made. The intent behind the freeze-out is for the acquiring company to accumulate all shares so that the transfer is complete. See also DRAG ALONG RIGHTS, TAG ALONG RIGHTS.

FRESH START ACCOUNTING   A revaluation of ASSETS and LIABILITIES that takes place when REORGANIZATION of a bankrupt company results in a general restatement of liabilities. The accounting is applied in the United States to any company operating under CHAPTER 11 that expects to complete a reorganization, as well as any company that is emerging from Chapter 11.

FRICTION COST   See TRANSACTION COST.

FRIENDLY SOCIETY   In the United Kingdom, a MUTUAL ORGANIZATION for savings and life INSURANCE that is owned and operated by its members; the organizational structure of the friendly society conveys certain TAX advantages to the mutual owners.

FRIENDLY TAKEOVER   An ACQUISITION that is agreed on amicable terms between the acquiring company and the TARGET. A friendly takeover may arise as a result of negotiations between the two companies, or it may be a WHITE KNIGHT response to a HOSTILE TAKEOVER offer from another party.

FRN   See FLOATING RATE NOTE.

FRONT BOOK   [COL] A trading BOOK managed by a DEALER in which customer ORDERS are handled. The front book is intended to feature regular turnover as the dealer places BIDS and OFFERS against customer orders. See also BACK BOOK.

FRONT DOOR   [COL] A process where the BANK OF ENGLAND attempts to influence UK MONEY SUPPLY by LENDING directly to DISCOUNT HOUSES and other financial institutions. See also BACK DOOR.

FRONT LOAD   A mechanism in which COMMISSIONS on a MUTUAL FUND or INVESTMENT TRUST are charged to INVESTORS at the time of purchase. See also BACK LOAD.

FRONT MONTH   See NEARBY CONTRACT.

FRONT OFFICE   [COL] The units and functions within a BANK or FINANCIAL INSTITUTION that are responsible for generating REVENUES through LENDING, TRADING, CORPORATE FINANCE, ASSET MANAGEMENT, and so forth. See also BACK OFFICE.

FRONT RUNNING   [COL] An illegal practice where a DEALER, MARKET MAKER, or SPECIALIST executes a transaction in advance of a customer trade in order to capture favorable price movements.

FRONTING COMPANY   See FRONTING INSURER.

FRONTING INSURER   An INSURER that is interposed between a CEDING INSURER or CAPTIVE, and a REINSURER. Use of a fronting insurer allows the insurer or captive to access the professional reinsurance market directly and obtain coverage at more favorable PREMIUM rates. Also known as FRONTING COMPANY.

FROTHY   [COL] A market condition reflecting excessive speculative buying or OVERBOUGHT conditions. Also known as TOPPY.

FSA   see FINANCIAL SERVICES AUTHORITY.

FTC   See FEDERAL TRADE COMMISSION.

FULL INSURANCE   An INSURANCE CONTRACT where the INSURER provides the INSURED with complete coverage of a RISK exposure in exchange for a larger PREMIUM. It can be considered a contract of maximum RISK TRANSFER, and is characterized by a small (or no) DEDUCTIBLE, large POLICY CAP, limited (or no) COINSURANCE, and limited (or no) EXCLUSIONS. Such a policy is most suitable for extremely risk averse companies or individuals. See also PARTIAL INSURANCE.

FULL RECOURSE LOAN   A LOAN with repayment that may come from the proceeds of the project/ASSET being financed or the sale of specific COLLATERAL, or from the resources of the borrower if project/collateral CASH FLOWS prove insufficient. See also RECOURSE, NONRECOURSE, NONRECOURSE LOAN, PARTIAL RECOURSE LOAN.

FULLY DILUTED BASIS   A method of computing a company's EARNINGS PER SHARE by taking account of any potential new SHARES of COMMON STOCK that may be created through a planned NEW ISSUE of EQUITY, exercise of outstanding stock OPTIONS, or conversion of any existing CONVERTIBLE BONDS. See also DILUTION.

FULLY PAID SHARES   The SHARES of a company that have been paid up to the full PAR VALUE at the time of initial issuance, and on which INVESTORS are not subject to a further call for CAPITAL. See also PARTLY PAID SHARES.

FUND   A vehicle that is established to gather and invest CAPITAL provided by INVESTORS. A fund can take various structural forms, such as a PENSION FUND, MUTUAL FUND, HEDGE FUND, CLOSED-END FUND, OPEN-END FUND, or UNIT INVESTMENT TRUST, and can be established to invest in specific ASSET classes.

FUND FAMILY   A group of diverse FUNDS offered by a single fund management company. INVESTORS allocating CAPITAL within a fund family can generally switch between available funds without incurring incremental charges. The largest fund families are able to offer investors a broad range of investment choices, which can include global STOCK and BOND funds, sector funds, and emerging market funds.

FUND MANAGER   See PORTFOLIO MANAGER.

FUND OF FUNDS (FOF)   A FUND that invests in other MUTUAL FUNDS or HEDGE FUNDS. In exchange for vetting individual funds and constructing, and tactically adjusting, PORTFOLIOS to achieve specific RETURNS, fund of fund managers charge their clients an annual fee and a performance fee. See also 1 AND 10.

FUNDAMENTAL ANALYSIS   An INVESTMENT ANALYSIS approach that focuses on a company's financial and ACCOUNTING value and its ability to generate core operating EARNINGS in order to increase the STOCK price. Fundamental analysts advocate the purchase of stocks selling below LIQUIDATION VALUE, which may be evidenced by a low PRICE/EARNINGS RATIO and CURRENT ASSETS that exceed CURRENT LIABILITIES and long-term DEBT. See also TECHNICAL ANALYSIS.

Additional reference: Graham and Dodd (1962).

FUNDAMENTAL FACTOR MODEL   A MULTIFACTOR RISK MODEL with inputs that include historical STOCK RETURNS and observable industry factors, such as PRICE/EARNINGS ratios, price/BOOK VALUE, economic growth, and so forth. The sensitivity of a stock price to each fundamental factor can be estimated through such a model, allowing the projection of EXPECTED RETURNS. See also MACROECONOMIC FACTOR MODEL, STATISTICAL FACTOR MODEL.

FUNDED DEBT   (1) Any DEBT obligation issued by a sovereign authority that need not be repaid, i.e., an instrument that exists in PERPETUITY, such as a CONSOL. (2) Any debt obligation of a company or sovereign authority that matures in more than one year.

FUNDED PENSION PLAN   A PENSION PLAN where all future LIABILITIES are fully covered by existing fund resources. See also UNFUNDED PENSION PLAN.

FUNDING   The general process of raising DEBT to finance operations.

FUNDING AGREEMENT   An unsecured FINANCING facility for an INSURER, often arranged as a PRIVATE PLACEMENT and placed directly with large INSTITUTIONAL INVESTORS (often MONEY MARKET FUNDS). Funding agreements generally have MATURITIES extending from several months to several years, but may contain investor PUT OPTIONS that allow redemption with 7, 30, 90, or 180 days' notice.

FUNDING LIQUIDITY RISK   The RISK of loss arising from an inability to roll over existing unsecured funding or obtain new unsecured funding without incurring a large cost. A subcategory of LIQUIDITY RISK. See also ASSET LIQUIDITY RISK, ASSET-FUNDING LIQUIDITY RISK, ENDOGENOUS LIQUIDITY, EXOGENOUS LIQUIDITY.

FUNGIBILITY   The ability to exchange or substitute one ASSET with another. Fungibility is important in COLLATERAL management for OVER-THE-COUNTER DERIVATIVES and REPURCHASE AGREEMENTS, and in delivery decisions for EXCHANGE-TRADED DERIVATIVES.

FUNGIBLE ISSUE   A SECURITY that can be exchanged for an identical or similar security of the same ISSUER.

FURTHEST MONTH   An EXCHANGE-TRADED DERIVATIVE CONTRACT with the longest MATURITY date featuring trading volume; contracts with even longer maturity dates that are inactive or dormant are not considered to be the furthest month contract. See also NEARBY CONTRACT, NEXT NEARBY CONTRACT.

FUTURE   An EXCHANGE-TRADED DERIVATIVE CONTRACT that permits the purchaser to buy, and the seller to sell, an ASSET at a predetermined future price and delivery date. Standardized futures contracts are available on assets/ SECURITIES from the FIXED INCOME, EQUITY, FOREIGN EXCHANGE, and COMMODITY markets, and can be settled in cash or physical (depending on contract specifications). Contracts are secured by INITIAL MARGIN and are MARKED-TO-MARKET on a daily basis by the CLEARINGHOUSE; VARIATION MARGINS are posted to cover daily market movement. Also known as FUTURES CONTRACT. See also FUTURES OPTION, FUTURES CALL, FUTURES PUT.

FUTURE VALUE   A financial computation where the value of a current CASH FLOW or lump sum is projected into the future through use of an appropriate RETURN or YIELD. The general form of the equation is given as:

$$FV = CF0 \ (1 + r)t$$

where CF_0 is the current cash flow, t is the time to MATURITY, and r is the DISCOUNT RATE or yield.

The future value of a cash flow that is subject to CONTINUOUS COMPOUNDING is given as:

$$FV = CFe^{rN}$$

where e is the exponential constant, N is the number of years over which the compounding occurs.

The base computation for multiple cash flows occurring over time expands to:

$$FV = \sum_{t=1}^{n} CF_t(1+r)^{n-t}$$

where n is the last period of the cash flows.

The future value of a stream of cash flows, such as those characterizing an ANNUITY, can be computed through an extension of the same equation:

$$FV_A = CF_P\left[\frac{(1+r)^t - 1}{r}\right]$$

where CF_P is the periodic future cash flow and other terms are as defined above. See also DISCOUNTED CASH FLOW, NET PRESENT VALUE, PRESENT VALUE.

FUTURES CALL   An EXCHANGE-TRADE OPTION CONTRACT granting the buyer the right, but not the obligation, to buy a FUTURES contract at a pre-specified STRIKE PRICE. See also FUTURES PUT.

FUTURES COMMISSION MERCHANT (FCM)   An intermediary that develops and executes FUTURES-based strategies and coordinates transactions with CLEARING MEMBERS on behalf of clients. FCMs are the only entities, apart from CLEARINGHOUSES, that can hold customer funds. In the United States, FCMs must meet certain minimum financial requirements and must be members of the National Futures Association, a SELF-REGULATORY ORGANIZATION; they may be structured as independent organizations or divisions of larger financial institutions.

FUTURES CONTRACT   See FUTURE.

FUTURES OPTION   An EXCHANGE-TRADE OPTION CONTRACT granting the buyer the right, but not the obligation, to buy or sell a FUTURES contract at a prespecified STRIKE PRICE. See also FUTURES CALL, FUTURES PUT.

FUTURES PUT   An EXCHANGE-TRADED OPTION CONTRACT granting the buyer the right, but not the obligation, to sell a FUTURES contract at a pre-specified STRIKE PRICE. See also FUTURES CALL.

FX   See FOREIGN EXCHANGE.

G

G3 See GROUP OF 3.

G7 See GROUP OF 7.

G8 See GROUP OF 8.

G10 See GROUP OF 10.

GAAP See GENERALLY ACCEPTED ACCOUNTING PRINCIPLES.

GAMING [COL] The act of taking advantage of information gained through PINGING to position an ORDER to capitalize on of a known large BID or OFFER residing in a DARK POOL. While not illegal, dark pool operators attempt to guard their pools from pinging and gaming, often by establishing minimum order size and tracking TRADING patterns of participants.

GAMING CONTRACT An agreement to enter into a game of chance for money. In certain jurisdictions DERIVATIVES may be defined as gaming contracts. Also known as WAGERING CONTRACT.

GAMMA The change in the value of an OPTION's DELTA for a change in the value of the UNDERLYING market reference, all other variables held constant. Gamma, as a measure of the CONVEXITY of option prices, is often used to gauge sensitivity to large and sudden market moves. The gammas of the CALL OPTION and PUT OPTION under the BLACK-SCHOLES MODEL are identical and given by:

$$\Gamma_c = \frac{\delta \Delta_c}{\delta S} = \frac{\delta^2 c}{\delta S^2} = \frac{1}{S\sigma\sqrt{t}} N'(d_1)$$

$$\Gamma_p = \frac{\delta \Delta_p}{\delta S} = \frac{\delta^2 p}{\delta S^2} = \frac{1}{S\sigma\sqrt{t}} N'(d_1)$$

where

$$N'(d_1) = \frac{1}{\sqrt{2\pi}} e^{\frac{-d_1^2}{2}}$$

and S is the stock price, t is the time to MATURITY, σ is the STANDARD DEVIATION, and where the value of N'(d1) can be obtained from a standard table of PROBABILITY functions.

The gammas of long and short puts and calls are shown as:

	Long call	Long put	Short call	Short put
Gamma	+	+	−	−

See also GAMMA HEDGE, NEGATIVE GAMMA, GREEKS, RHO, THETA, VEGA.

GAMMA HEDGE   A HEDGE technique used to establish a GAMMA NEUTRAL position, and used primarily to manage the effects of NEGATIVE GAMMA, which can create large losses if markets move sharply and quickly before DELTA HEDGES can be rebalanced. Creating a hedge for a negative gamma position generally requires the purchase or use of a position with POSITIVE GAMMA (e.g., an instrument with positive CONVEXITY, such as a LONG POSITION in a CALL OPTION or PUT OPTION).

GAMMA NEUTRAL   A PORTFOLIO of OPTIONS that is neutral with respect to its GAMMA, meaning that it is HEDGED for large moves in the UNDERLYING. See also DELTA NEUTRAL, GAMMA HEDGE, VEGA NEUTRAL, THETA NEUTRAL.

G

GAO   See GOVERNMENT ACCOUNTABILITY OFFICE.

GAP   (1) The differential between interest RATE-SENSITIVE ASSETS and INTEREST RATE-SENSITIVE LIABILITIES, often used as a measure of a BANK's exposure to LIQUIDITY RISK and MARKET RISK; the gap can be computed for individual MATURITY BUCKETS and in total. A gap computation based on the final contractual maturity of each rate-sensitive asset and liability fails to take account of interim CASH FLOWS, PREPAYMENTS, AMORTIZATION, or ACCRETION; accordingly, a preferred method calls for gaps computed through DURATION. A NEGATIVE GAP means the bank is BORROWING short-term and lending long-term and is thus exposed to rising short-term rates or an inversion of the YIELD CURVE. A POSITIVE GAP means the bank is borrowing long-term and lending short-term, and is therefore exposed to falling short-term rates or a steepening of the yield curve. (2) In TECHNICAL ANALYSIS an intraday or overnight upward or downward break in a SECURITY price or INDEX level. Gaps can be classified in different forms, including runaway gap (a gap in the same direction as recent large up/down moves), breakaway gap (a gap at the end of a consolidation period, signaling the beginning of a major market move), common gap (a one-day gap, often appearing in thinly traded markets), and exhaustion gap (a gap at the end of an extreme market move). (1) Also known as MATURITY GAP. (1) See also ASSET-LIABILITY MANAGEMENT, GAPPING.

GAPPING   The process of deliberately mismatching ASSETS and LIABILITIES in order to take advantage of an anticipated change in INTEREST RATES. Although gapping has the potential of generating greater RETURNS, it can also increase a firm's potential losses via DIRECTIONAL RISK, CURVE RISK, and/ or LIQUIDITY RISK. See also ASSET-LIABILITY MANAGEMENT, GAP, RATE-SENSITIVE ASSETS, RATE-SENSITIVE LIABILITIES.

GARMAN-KOHLHAGEN MODEL   A closed-form OPTION pricing model developed by Garman and Kohlhagen that is used to value EUROPEAN

OPTIONS on CURRENCIES. The model is an adaptation of the BLACK-SCHOLES MODEL. The equations are given as:

$$Call = Se^{-qt}(d_1) - Xe^{-rt}N(d_2)$$

and

$$Put = Xe^{-rt}N(-d_2) - Se^{-qt}N(-d_1)$$

where S is the current EXCHANGE RATE (domestic currency per unit of foreign currency), X is the STRIKE PRICE, t is the time to MATURITY, r is the CONTINUOUSLY COMPOUNDED domestic INTEREST RATE, q is the continuously compounded foreign interest rate,

$$d_1 = \frac{\ln\left(\frac{S}{X}\right) + \left(r - q + \frac{\sigma^2}{2}\right)t}{\sigma\sqrt{t}}$$

$$d_2 = d_1 - \sigma\sqrt{t}$$

σ^2 is the VARIANCE of the currency rate, and where the N values of $N(d_1)$ and $N(d_2)$ can be obtained from standard tables of probability functions.

GARN ST. GERMAIN ACT   In the United States, legislation passed in 1982 to deregulate aspects of the domestic banking sector. The Act allowed SAVINGS AND LOANS to expand their business scope by granting COMMERCIAL LOANS and using DERIVATIVES, and gave BANKS greater LEGAL LENDING LIMITS and allowed them to compete for customer DEPOSITS on the same terms as MONEY MARKET FUNDS.

GATE   [COL] A restriction imposed by a HEDGE FUND that limits the amount of REDEMPTIONS that can occur in a given period. A fund may be gated when the manager is attempting to preserve CAPITAL and avoid an acceleration of redemptions that would otherwise lead to forced disposal of ASSETS.

GATHER IN THE STOPS   [COL] Concentrated selling to drive a SECURITY price down to levels where STOP ORDERS are known to exist. This forces the stop orders to convert into buy or sell MARKET ORDERS, clearing the way for further upward or downward moves once executed. See also SNOWBALLING.

GATT   See GENERAL AGREEMENT ON TARIFFS AND TRADE.

GAUSSIAN DISTRIBUTION   See NORMAL DISTRIBUTION.

GC   See GENERAL COLLATERAL.

GDP   See GROSS DOMESTIC PRODUCT.

GDP DEFLATOR   A measure designed to express current GROSS DOMESTIC PRODUCT (GDP) in terms of GDP in a base year, effectively providing a gauge of INFLATION. It is computed as:

$$GDP_{defl} = \left(\frac{GDP_{nom}}{GDP_{real}} \right) \times 100$$

where GDP_{nom} is the current period GDP, GDP_{real} is the base year GDP. Also known as IMPLICIT PRICE DEFLATOR.

GDR   See GLOBAL DEPOSITORY RECEIPT.

GDS   See GLOBAL DEPOSITORY SHARE.

GEARING   See LEVERAGE.

GEISHA   [JPN, COL] A PRIVATE PLACEMENT, denominated in a CURRENCY other than Japanese yen, which is issued by a Japanese company. See also DAIMYO, SAMURAI, SHIBOSAI, SHOGUN.

GEMM   See GILT-EDGED MARKET MAKER.

GENERAL AGREEMENT ON TARIFFS AND TRADE (GATT)   An agency of the United Nations established in 1948 to promote international FREE TRADE. GATT was actively involved in coordinating issues related to multilateral quotas and tariffs, EXPORT restraints, and intellectual property rights until it was replaced by its successor, the WORLD TRADE ORGANIZATION, in 1994.

GENERAL AGREEMENTS TO BORROW   Agreements between GROUP OF 10 countries plus Switzerland to provide the INTERNATIONAL MONETARY FUND with LOANS on an emergency basis, which the IMF can then lend on to member countries in need of funds.

GENERAL COLLATERAL (GC)   COLLATERAL in the REPURCHASE AGREEMENT market that is in abundant SUPPLY and which does not therefore allow a repurchase agreement BORROWER to obtain a lower than normal BORROWING rate. See also SPECIAL.

GENERAL EQUILIBRIUM   A MICROECONOMIC framework that focuses on SUPPLY, DEMAND, and prices of individual markets, and how these interact simultaneously at a macroeconomic level. Multiple strands of study support this theory, including theories based on partial equilibrium, competitive equilibrium, and price transfer equilibrium.

GENERAL INSURANCE   In the United Kingdom, INSURANCE coverage for damage or loss to property. The UK market is broadly segmented into the three areas: large commercial RISK coverage (for large companies and unique risks, such as those UNDERWRITTEN through LLOYD'S OF LONDON), commercial lines (including small business properties), and personal lines (including home and automobile coverage for individuals). See also NONLIFE INSURANCE, PROPERTY AND CASUALTY INSURANCE.

GENERAL OBLIGATION (GO) BOND   In the United States, a MUNICIPAL BOND issued by a state or local authority that is typically used to finance nonrevenue-producing projects, such as schools and transportation systems. Bonds are generally repaid through the issuance of new DEBT or via TAX REVENUES. See also REVENUE BOND.

GENERAL PARTNER   A partner in a PARTNERSHIP that is generally responsible for managing tactical and strategic operations, and who bears UNLIMITED LIABILITY for DEBTS incurred.

GENERAL PARTNERSHIP (GP)   A form of unincorporated business organization that includes two or more general PARTNERS who manage the business operations and are ultimately liable for the organization's LIABILITIES. Since the PARTNERSHIP is constituted as an UNLIMITED LIABILITY structure, the personal assets of the general partners can be used to settle any claims. In addition, each general partner is liable for the actions and liabilities of all other general partners. General partnerships are typically established as separate tax-paying entities. See also LIMITED PARTNERSHIP, SILENT PARTNERSHIP.

GENERALLY ACCEPTED ACCOUNTING PRINCIPLES (GAAP)   ACCOUNTING rules adopted by public companies that are intended to provide uniform treatment of activities impacting the BALANCE SHEET, INCOME STATEMENT, and STATEMENT OF CASH FLOWS. Versions of GAAP are used in the United States, the United Kingdom, and various other counties. In the United States, the FINANCIAL ACCOUNTING STANDARDS BOARD establishes GAAP rules. See also INTERNATIONAL ACCOUNTING STANDARDS.

GENSAKI   [JPN] The broad Japanese MONEY MARKET, which includes trading in short-term GOVERNMENT BILLS, CERTIFICATES OF DEPOSIT, NOTES, REPURCHASE AGREEMENTS, and REVERSE REPURCHASE AGREEMENTS.

GEOMETRIC BROWNIAN MOTION   See BROWNIAN MOTION.

GEOMETRIC MEAN   See MEAN.

GESELLSCHAFT MIT BESCHRÄNKTER HAFTUNG (GMBH)   [GER] In Germany, Switzerland, and Austria, a company with LIMITED LIABILITY. In Germany the GMBH is incorporated but not publicly traded, and must adhere to a minimum number of PARTNERS and CAPITAL in order to qualify. In Austria at least two founding SHAREHOLDERS are required, and minimum capital hurdles apply. In Switzerland the entity cannot have any SHARES outstanding.

GHARAR   [ARB] A form of RISK or uncertainty, as defined under the rules of ISLAMIC FINANCE. A cost-benefit review of contracts may be conducted by a religious scholar, and those that are found to contain an excessive or unnecessary amount of risk may be prohibited. See also RIBA.

GHOSTING   [COL] A practice where two or more MARKET MAKERS attempt to jointly influence the price of a SECURITY; ghosting is illegal in many jurisdictions as market makers are meant to compete against each other.

GIB   See GUARANTEED INCOME BOND.

GILT   See GILT-EDGED STOCK.

GILT-EDGED MARKET MAKER (GEMM)   A PRIMARY DEALER in GILTS that commits to quoting TWO-WAY MARKETS and bidding competitively at primary AUCTIONS. While GEMMs were once required to be separately capitalized legal entities, they may now form part of larger financial groups.

GILT-EDGED STOCK   The broad category of UK GOVERNMENT BONDS used for general FINANCING and MONETARY POLICY purposes. Gilts, denominated in sterling, are issued as REDEEMABLE BONDS (or STRAIGHT BONDS) with BULLET repayment after 5 years (shorts), 5–15 years (mediums), or 15+ years (longs), CONVERTIBLE BONDS (exchangeable into gilts with a longer MATURITY), INDEX-LINKED GILTS (tied to the RETAIL PRICE INDEX INFLATION measure), and IRREDEEMABLE BONDS (CONSOLS, or PERPETUAL BONDS). Gilts, which may be callable (e.g., double-dated gilts), are issued by a number of government departments (e.g., Exchequer, Treasury, Funding, Conversion, Consolidated Fund Annuities). Securities are sold in the PRIMARY MARKET via GILT-EDGED MARKET MAKERS (GEMMs) or through special tap arrangements, and are traded in the SECONDARY MARKET by GEMMs, BANKS, and DISCOUNT HOUSES. Also known as GILT.

GILT STRIP   See STAGS.

GINI COEFFICIENT   A statistical measure developed by Italian statistician Corrado Gini that measures the INCOME DISTRIBUTION within an economic system. A Gini coefficient of 0.0 reflects perfect equality in INCOME distribution, while a coefficient of 1.0 indicates perfect inequality. Also known as INDEX OF CONCENTRATION.

GINNIE MAE [COL] See GOVERNMENT NATIONAL MORTGAGE ASSOCIATION (GNMA).

GIRO   A system of physical or electronic payment transfers for consumer purchases, used primarily in the United Kingdom, Europe, and Japan. The giro results in a direct transfer of cash from the consumer, PAYER, or DEBTOR to the seller or CREDITOR without the need for using a BANK ACCOUNT. Giro payments, which are often conducted via local post offices, fulfill the role of the CHECK in the US financial markets.

GIVE-UP   A brokered TRADE executed on behalf on another party; once executed, the name of the party to the trade is "given up" by the BROKER to the trader so that the proper party of record can be recorded. See also BLIND BROKERING.

GLASS-STEAGALL ACT   US Federal legislation enacted in 1933 to separate banking powers in the aftermath of the 1929 STOCK market crash. Glass-Steagall forced banking institutions to select between commercial banking (e.g., LENDING and DEPOSIT-taking) and investment banking (e.g., SECURITIES, UNDERWRITING, TRADING, and CORPORATE FINANCE). Restrictions under the act began eroding in 1987 when COMMERCIAL BANKS were permitted to underwrite and trade securities, and were largely eliminated in 1999 through passage of the GRAMM-LEACH-BLILEY ACT. Also known as BANKING ACT OF 1933.

GLOBAL BOND   A BOND that is issued simultaneously in a domestic market and the EUROMARKETS. Global bonds, which may be FIXED RATE or FLOATING RATE and carry MATURITIES ranging from 1 to 30 years, are generally issued by large, well-known CORPORATIONS or supranationals that have international operations and broad name recognition. See also DRAGON, EUROBOND.

GLOBAL CUSTODY   See CUSTODY.

GLOBAL DEPOSITORY RECEIPT (GDR)   A negotiable certificate issued by a local BANK representing a nonlocal company's COMMON STOCK (shares of which are held in CUSTODY by the bank). GDRs, denominated in local CURRENCY (and occasionally dollars) are generally registered with local REGULATORS and may be traded on an EXCHANGE or OVER-THE-COUNTER. GDRs may be sponsored (approved/backed by the company) or unsponsored (not backed/approved by the company). Also known as INTERNATIONAL DEPOSITORY RECEIPT. See also AMERICAN DEPOSITORY RECEIPT, AMERICAN DEPOSITORY SHARE, GLOBAL DEPOSITORY SHARE.

GLOBAL DEPOSITORY SHARE (GDS)   COMMON STOCK issued by a nonlocal company in a local marketplace. GDSs, generally denominated in the local CURRENCY (and occasionally in US dollars), are typically registered with local REGULATORS and may be traded on an EXCHANGE or OVER-THE-COUNTER. See also AMERICAN DEPOSITORY RECEIPT, AMERICAN DEPOSITORY SHARE, GLOBAL DEPOSITORY RECEIPT.

GLOBAL MACRO   A common HEDGE FUND strategy where a manager makes use of macroeconomic analysis to create an INVESTMENT strategy. Global macro strategies can invest broadly, on a cross-border basis, in FOREIGN EXCHANGE, INTEREST RATES, EQUITIES, CREDITS, and COMMODITIES.

GLOBAL MASTER REPURCHASE AGREEMENT (GMRA)   A form of standardized documentation used for REPURCHASE and REVERSE REPURCHASE AGREEMENTS and BUY/SELLBACKS. The documentation contains standard terms and conditions, as well as the rights of the transacting parties, and caters for different classes of underlying SECURITIES, including FIXED INCOME instruments and EQUITIES.

GLOBAL MEDIUM-TERM NOTE   A MEDIUM-TERM NOTE (MTN) that is issued simultaneously in a domestic market and the EUROMARKETS, typically through a registered filing that allows for issuance at will. As with a standard MTN, a global issue can be denominated in one of several CURRENCIES and carry fixed or floating COUPONS with MATURITIES extending from 1 to 30 years.

GLOBAL OFFERING Any NEW ISSUE of SECURITIES that involves selling, placing, and listing in more than one market, and which may involve more than one issuing CURRENCY.

GLOBEX An electronic TRADING platform, launched in 1992, allowing for 24-hour TRADING in specific EXCHANGE-TRADED DERIVATIVES. The initiative was developed and sponsored by the CHICAGO MERCANTILE EXCHANGE, which ultimately made use of the technology platform developed by the Paris Bourse (now part of NYSE EURONEXT).

GMBH See GESELLSCHAFT MIT BESCHRÄNKTER HAFTUNG.

GMRA See GLOBAL MASTER REPURCHASE AGREEMENT.

GNMA See GOVERNMENT NATIONAL MORTGAGE ASSOCIATION.

GNOME [COL] A 15-year PARTICIPATION CERTIFICATE issued by the FEDERAL HOME LOAN MORTGAGE CORPORATION. See also DWARF, MIDGET.

GNOMES OF ZURICH [COL] A reference to Swiss BANKERS, attributable primarily to their secrecy.

GNP See GROSS NATIONAL PRODUCT.

GO BOND See GENERAL OBLIGATION BOND.

GOING CONCERN CONCEPT A business concept that indicates that a firm should be viewed as a complete business that is intended to continue its operations and is not going to become INSOLVENT. Going concern value is generally greater than LIQUIDATION VALUE as it includes the worth of GOODWILL and other INTANGIBLE ASSETS that may be sacrificed in a liquidation scenario, particularly if ASSETS are sold on a piecemeal basis. See also CONSISTENCY CONCEPT, GOING CONCERN VALUE, MATCHING CONCEPT, PRUDENCE CONCEPT.

GOING CONCERN VALUE A fundamental ACCOUNTING principle based on the premise that a company intends to operate as a continuing business (going concern) and will not be liquidated, meaning that its ASSETS should be valued at historical cost rather than at liquidation value. See also GOING CONCERN CONCEPT.

GOING LONG The act of creating a LONG POSITION in an ASSET or a market. See also FLATTENING, GOING SHORT.

GOING PRIVATE The process of taking a PUBLIC COMPANY out of the public markets, typically through the acquisition of outstanding SHARES and delisting from a STOCK EXCHANGE. Going private may require the assumption of a significant amount of DEBT (to purchase outstanding shares), as in a LEVERAGED BUYOUT. See also GOING PUBLIC.

GOING PUBLIC The process of taking a PRIVATE COMPANY to the public markets, typically through an INITIAL PUBLIC OFFERING. By making the company public, those previously providing CAPITAL (e.g., original owners, VENTURE CAPITAL funds) convert their stakes into marketable SHARES, which they may retain or sell. See also GOING PRIVATE.

GOING SHORT   The act of creating a SHORT POSITION in an ASSET or a market. See also FLATTENING, GOING LONG.

GOLD   A precious metal that serves as a store of value and MEDIUM OF EXCHANGE. Gold is an actively traded COMMODITY, and can be bought and sold physically as bullion, coins, jewelry, or financially through cash-settled FUTURES, OPTIONS, and other DERIVATIVES.

GOLD BUG   [COL] An INVESTOR that holds a BULLISH view on the price of gold and invests in gold either through physical metal or via gold-related STOCKS or EXCHANGE-TRADED FUNDS.

GOLD FIXING   The process of establishing the price of GOLD in the London Bullion Market, which occurs at 10:30 a.m. and 3 p.m. every business day through the settling of buying and selling amongst authorized DEALERS.

GOLD RESERVES   The RESERVES of a country held in the form of GOLD, typically stored at a centralized repository. Such reserves can be used for specific purposes, such as INTERVENTION in the FOREIGN EXCHANGE markets; they can also be lent to other countries for defined periods of time.

GOLDBRICKS   [COL] COMMON STOCKS that appear to be financially sound on the surface, but which feature little substance when examined more closely.

GOLDEN HANDCUFFS   [COL] A compensation package intended to induce an executive to remain at a company; if the executive departs, some or all of the benefits conveyed through the golden handcuffs may have to be returned. See also GOLDEN HANDSHAKE, GOLDEN HELLO, GOLDEN PARACHUTE.

GOLDEN HANDSHAKE   [COL] A compensation clause that gives an executive a substantial guaranteed payout in the event of termination or dismissal (other than "for cause"). See also GOLDEN HANDCUFFS, GOLDEN HELLO, GOLDEN PARACHUTE.

GOLDEN HELLO   [COL] An upfront compensation package granted to an executive joining from another firm; depending on the structure of the package it may serve as a "buy out" of the package being left at the prior company, and thus limit the effectiveness of long-term, performance-driven financial rewards. See also GOLDEN HANDCUFFS, GOLDEN HANDSHAKE, GOLDEN PARACHUTE.

GOLDEN PARACHUTE   [COL] A compensation clause that gives top executives guaranteed payouts in the event they lose their jobs through a FRIENDLY TAKEOVER or HOSTILE TAKEOVER. See also GOLDEN HANDCUFFS, GOLDEN HANDSHAKE, GOLDEN HELLO.

GOLDEN SHARE   A SHARE or block of shares in a company conveying extraordinary VOTING RIGHTS, allowing for *de-facto* control. Golden shares are typically held for a period of time by a government in a company that is undergoing PRIVATIZATION.

GOOD DELIVERY   A SECURITY/certificate with all necessary details and ENDORSEMENTS that allows accurate and efficient transfer of TITLE from one party to another.

GOOD FOR MONTH ORDER   A LIMIT ORDER or STOP ORDER to buy or sell a SECURITY that remains in effect until the end of the current month.

GOOD MONEY   [COL] Any source of funds that is available for immediate use, such as FEDERAL FUNDS.

GOOD TILL CANCELLED ORDER   A LIMIT ORDER for the purchase or sale of a SECURITY at a specific price that remains in effect until the price target is met and the TRADE is executed, or is otherwise cancelled by the individual or institution placing the order. Also known as OPEN ORDER. See also DAY ORDER, MARKET ORDER, STOP ORDER.

GOODWILL   The primary INTANGIBLE ASSET of a company, generally comprised of reputation, contact networks, intellectual property, and branding. Although the ASSETS have value, they cannot be physically inspected and are extremely ILLIQUID. Goodwill may also include the PREMIUM a company pays in acquiring another company; although such additional value is generally reflected on the corporate BALANCE SHEET it must typically be amortized over a set period of time.

GOVERNANCE   A formal process/structure intended to ensure a company's executives and DIRECTORS perform their assigned duties and responsibilities diligently, so that STAKEHOLDERS generally, and SHAREHOLDERS specifically, are properly protected. Governance may be enforced internally, through a BOARD OF DIRECTORS with independent oversight of the executive team, financial controls, policies, and executive compensation which is aligned with shareholder interests. It may also be enforced externally through regulatory requirements, controlling shareholder oversight, and corporate control activities. Also known as CORPORATE GOVERNANCE.

GOVERNMENT ACCOUNTABILITY OFFICE (GAO)   In the United States, a nonpartisan investigative body of Congress that is responsible for verifying and auditing the receipt and use of public funds to ensure that the Federal government is using them properly.

GOVERNMENT BILL   A MONEY MARKET instrument issued by a governmental authority as a funding mechanism and a tool for conducting MONETARY POLICY. Bills are often issued on a DISCOUNT, rather than COUPON-bearing, basis, and typically have MATURITIES extending from 1 week to 1 year. Those issued by governments of industrialized nations are considered to be highly LIQUID and extremely creditworthy, with virtually no risk of DEFAULT. See also GOVERNMENT BOND.

GOVERNMENT BOND   A DEBT instrument issued by a governmental authority as a funding mechanism. Government bonds are generally issued on a FIXED RATE or FLOATING RATE, COUPON-bearing, basis, with MATURITIES extending from 1 to 30 years; those within the 1 to 10-year sector may be referred to as government notes. Some countries also feature INFLATION-LINKED SECURITIES within their government issuance programs. Government bonds issued by industrialized nations are generally quite LIQUID (and may be very liquid in the BENCHMARK) and extremely creditworthy, with virtually no risk of DEFAULT. See also GOVERNMENT BILL.

GOVERNMENT BOND DEALER   See BOND DEALER.

GOVERNMENT NATIONAL MORTGAGE ASSOCIATION (GNMA)   A US government-owned CORPORATION (and agency of the Department of Housing and Urban Development) that purchases residential MORTGAGES with a GUARANTEE from the Department of Veterans Affairs and the Federal Housing Administration and pools them into MORTGAGE-BACKED SECURITIES (MBS); GNMA MBS, which essentially convert ILLIQUID mortgage ASSETS into MARKETABLE SECURITIES, carry the agency's guarantee of repayment on both PRINCIPAL and INTEREST. Also known as GINNIE MAE. See also FEDERAL HOME LOAN MORTGAGE CORPORATION, FEDERAL NATIONAL MORTGAGE ASSOCIATION.

GOVERNMENT-SPONSORED ENTERPRISE (GSE)   In the United States, as authorized by the US Congress, a private CORPORATIONS that serve a significant public purpose, most related to vital sectors such as housing, agriculture, education, and energy. GSEs are responsible for ensuring the sufficient allocation of CREDIT into sectors deemed to serve the public interest. In other countries such tasks may be undertaken by state-owned enterprises, public sector undertakings, or QUASI AUTONOMOUS NONGOVERNMENTAL ORGANIZATIONS, and NONGOVERNMENTAL ORGANIZATIONS. See also FEDERAL AGRICULTURAL MORTGAGE CORPORATION, FEDERAL NATIONAL MORTGAGE ASSOCIATION, FEDERAL HOME LOAN MORTGAGE CORPORATION, GOVERNMENT NATIONAL MORTGAGE ASSOCIATION.

GOVERNMENT STOCK   In the United Kingdom, GILT-EDGED SECURITIES issued by the government. See also GOVERNMENT BOND.

GP   See GENERAL PARTNERSHIP.

GPM   See GRADUATED PAYMENT MORTGAGE.

GRACE PERIOD   (1) The additional days permitted for payment on a BILL OF EXCHANGE or certain types of CREDIT facilities once the due date has passed. (2) See CURE PERIOD.

GRADING   The standards applied in defining the quality of a COMMODITY in order to ensure consistency in pricing, trading, and delivery under both physical and DERIVATIVE CONTRACTS.

GRADUATED PAYMENT MORTGAGE (GPM) A MORTGAGE where the payments due and payable by the BORROWER increase over the life of the deal. A GPM is a form of NEGATIVE AMORTIZATION LOAN.

GRAINS [COL] The general group of COMMODITIES referencing wheat, corn, soybeans, maize, oats, oilseed, beans, rice, and sorghum. See also COMMODITY DERIVATIVE, SOFTS.

GRAMM-LEACH-BLILEY ACT US Federal legislation enacted in 1999 with various provisions related to financial DEREGULATION, including the repeal of significant portions of the GLASS-STEAGALL ACT which had previously separated the powers of COMMERCIAL BANKS and INVESTMENT BANKS and prohibited all BANKS from engaging in INSURANCE business. The legislation also eliminated bank restrictions on SECURITIES UNDERWRITING contained in the Bank Holding Company Act of 1956, and named the FEDERAL RESERVE BOARD as the primary regulator of financial HOLDING COMPANIES engaged in banking, securities, and insurance businesses. Also known as FINANCIAL SERVICES MODERNIZATION ACT OF 1999.

GRANNY BOND [COL] In the United Kingdom, an issue of GILTS with an enhanced COUPON or TAX benefits that is only available to INVESTORS that have reached a pensionable age.

GRANTOR TRUST In the United States, a TRUST in which the income generated by INVESTMENT activities is taxed at the level of the individual rather than the trust itself.

GRAVEYARD MARKET [COL] A phase appearing at the end of a prolonged BEAR MARKET where INVESTORS have sustained large losses and new investors are unwilling to commit CAPITAL; volumes are extremely light, and direction may be uncertain.

GRAY KNIGHT [COL] A second unsolicited bidder in a HOSTILE TAKEOVER transaction that attempts to take advantage of the TARGET company's reluctance to accept the BLACK KNIGHT's original BID by offering slightly more "attractive" terms. See also WHITE KNIGHT, WHITE SQUIRE.

GRAY MARKET [COL] The market for TRADING in new SECURITIES that have been priced but not yet allocated, or allocated but not yet settled. The gray market acts as an intersection between the PRIMARY MARKET and the SECONDARY MARKET, and TRADES are considered binding and enforceable (though members of a SYNDICATE involved in UNDERWRITING a NEW ISSUE may be expelled if they trade between pricing and allocation; any such trades would be considered null and void).

GREEKS [COL] RISK measures for DERIVATIVES that are used to determine the price sensitivity of CONTRACTS to changes in the UNDERLYING ASSET (DELTA, GAMMA), VOLATILITY (VEGA), passage of time (THETA), and INTEREST RATES (RHO). The greeks of individual contracts can be added to determine the sensitivities of an entire PORTFOLIO, allowing for efficient pricing and RISK MANAGEMENT. The general impact on the value of an option for a unit increase in the relevant variable is given as:

	Long call	Short call	Long put	Short put
Delta	+	−	−	+
Gamma	+	−	+	−
Vega	+	−	+	−
Theta	−	+	−	+
Rho	+	+	−	−

Also known as OPTION SENSITIVITIES.

GREENBACK [COL] The US dollar.

GREENMAIL [COL] A targeted repurchase by a company of a block of its own COMMON STOCK from a corporate RAIDER or hostile acquirer, generally at a PREMIUM to the current market price. Greenmail payments, which were prevalent during the TAKEOVER cycle of the 1980s, are not common in the marketplace of the millennium as certain legal/regulatory regimes have deemed such payments illegal.

GREENSHOE [COL] An OPTION granted by an issuing company to the SYNDICATE UNDERWRITING a NEW ISSUE of EQUITY, which permits the syndicate to sell additional shares as part of the PRIMARY MARKET offering in the face of excessive DEMAND, up to a maximum amount defined in advance. Also known as OVERALLOTMENT OPTION, SHOE.

GROSS DOMESTIC PRODUCT (GDP) A measure of the goods and services produced within a country's geographic boundaries. GDP is used as a primary indicator of a country's economic strength and progress; positive GDP indicates the country's economic base is expanding, while negative GDP reflects a contraction and possible RECESSION. GDP includes PERSONAL CONSUMPTION, government expenditures, investment spending (CAPITAL INVESTMENT, business INVENTORIES, residential housing), and net EXPORTS. See also GROSS NATIONAL PRODUCT.

GROSS INCOME (1) An individual's income, before deductions and exemptions. (2). A company's top level results, computed as pretax sales or REVENUE less COST OF GOODS SOLD. (2) Also known as GROSS PROFIT. (2) See also OPERATING INCOME

GROSS INTEREST INTEREST paid or received, excluding the impact of TAXES.

GROSS LEASE A form of LEASE in which the LESSEE is only responsible for paying the LESSOR lease rental payments, while the lessor pays general expenses, maintenance, and TAXES. OPERATING LEASES are typically created as gross leases, while CAPITAL LEASES are not. See also NET LEASE.

GROSS LINE   The total amount of INSURANCE cover an INSURER will UNDERWRITE on a particular RISK, including the amount to be CEDED via REINSURANCE.

GROSS MARGIN   A measure of a company's ability to translate REVENUES into GROSS PROFITS (i.e., revenues after removing the costs of producing the goods/services), typically calculated as:

$$GM = \frac{GP}{Rev}$$

where GP is gross profit, Rev is revenue.

The higher the gross margin, the greater the company's ability to convert its revenues into profits.

GROSS NATIONAL PRODUCT (GNP)   A measure of the goods and services produced by a country, regardless of location. Since this measure includes goods and services that are produced outside national borders, it is broader than the GROSS DOMESTIC PRODUCT measure.

GROSS PREMIUM   A measure of an INSURER's total profitability from INSURANCE UNDERWRITING activities (before EXPENSES), or the total of NET PREMIUMS plus load factors, computed as:

$$GP = Pr + OpE + AC$$

where Pr is premium (net), OpE is OPERATING EXPENSE, and AC is AGENT COMMISSIONS.

The greater the gross premium, the larger the amount of business being underwritten. Also known as GROSS PREMIUM WRITTEN, GROSS WRITTEN PREMIUM. See also FAIR PREMIUM.

GROSS PREMIUM WRITTEN   See GROSS PREMIUM.

GROSS PROFIT   See GROSS INCOME.

GROSS RATE   See FAIR PREMIUM.

GROSS REDEMPTION YIELD   In the United Kingdom, YIELD TO MATURITY.

GROSS REVENUE   See REVENUE.

GROSS SPREAD   See UNDERWRITING SPREAD.

GROSS WORKING CAPITAL   The sum of a company's CURRENT ASSETS and CURRENT LIABILITIES. See also NET WORKING CAPITAL, WORKING CAPITAL.

GROSS WRITTEN PREMIUM   See GROSS PREMIUM.

GROSS YIELD   The YIELD on a SECURITY or INVESTMENT before deducting TAXES and costs associated with acquiring the ASSET. See also NET YIELD.

GROUP CAPTIVE   A CAPTIVE formed as a licensed INSURER or REINSURER that is owned by a number of companies, and which writes INSURANCE cover for all of them. Since a group captive engages in a significant amount of third party business, it generally receives more favorable TAX treatment than a PURE CAPTIVE. Also known as an ASSOCIATION CAPTIVE or MULTIPARENT CAPTIVE. See also AGENCY CAPTIVE, CAPTIVE, PROTECTED CELL COMPANY, RENT-A-CAPTIVE, SISTER CAPTIVE.

GROUP LIFE ASSURANCE   In the United Kingdom, GROUP LIFE INSURANCE.

GROUP LIFE INSURANCE   A form of LIFE INSURANCE that is offered to an individual that forms part of a larger group, such as an employee of a company or an association. The insurance coverage may be conveyed through a single master policy, without specific or detailed health review of the individual members. Also known as GROUP LIFE ASSURANCE.

GROUP OF 3 (G3)   A grouping of the three large industrial economies, including the United States, Germany, and Japan.

GROUP OF 7 (G7)   International finance ministers from seven industrialized nations who attempt to influence economic and MONETARY POLICIES through coordinated actions. The original seven member nations were Japan, Germany, France, the United Kingdom, Italy, Canada, and the United States; Russia joined the group as a permanent member in 2002 to form the GROUP OF 8.

GROUP OF 8 (G8)   The GROUP OF 7 plus Russia, which joined the original seven members in 2002.

GROUP OF 10 (G10)   CENTRAL BANKS of 10 countries that attempt to coordinate supervision of financial markets and FINANCIAL INSTITUTIONS and also agree to make funds available to the INTERNATIONAL MONETARY FUND (IMF). The original 10 member nations were Japan, Germany, France, the United Kingdom, Italy, Canada, Belgium, Sweden, the Netherlands, and the United States; Switzerland, while not part of the IMF, is part of the GENERAL AGREEMENTS TO BORROW framework promulgated by the G10 and is thus included as a member, while Luxembourg participates as an associate member.

GROWTH FUND   A MUTUAL FUND or UNIT INVESTMENT TRUST that invests CAPITAL primarily or exclusively in GROWTH STOCKS.

GROWTH STOCK   The STOCK of a company that is expected to grow rapidly in the medium term, providing INVESTORS with CAPITAL GAINS. A growth stock may exhibit higher VOLATILITY and BETA than an INCOME STOCK. See also GROWTH FUND.

GSE   See GOVERNMENT-SPONSORED ENTERPRISE.

GUARANTEE   A contractual agreement where one party (the GUARANTOR) provides payment to a second party (the BENEFICIARY) should the original contracting party DEFAULT on its OBLIGATIONS. Through the provision of the guarantee, the obligations of the contracting party assume the CREDIT RATING of the guarantor, often a highly rated BANK or INSURER. See also CROSS GUARANTEE, FINANCIAL GUARANTEE.

GUARANTEED EXCHANGE RATE OPTION   See QUANTO.

GUARANTEED INCOME BOND (GIB)   In the United Kingdom, a BOND issued by an INSURER in which the INVESTOR receives a GUARANTEED monthly or annual income for a period ranging from 1 to 5 years. The bonds are considered to be stable and secure as they are issued by only the most creditworthy insurers.

GUARANTEED INVESTMENT CONTRACT (GIC)   A financial CONTRACT between an INSURER and an individual or PENSION PLAN (as BENEFICIARY) that provides the beneficiary with a specific RETURN on CAPITAL invested over the life of the contract. The insurer bears the INVESTMENT RISK associated with the SECURITIES in the GIC portfolio but is generally able to retain any excess it earns over the GUARANTEED return. See also NONPARTICIPATING GUARANTEED INVESTMENT CONTRACT, PARTICIPATING GUARANTEED INVESTMENT CONTRACT, SYNTHETIC GUARANTEED INVESTMENT CONTRACT.

GUARANTEED PRINCIPAL BOND   A STRUCTURED NOTE or BOND in which the PRINCIPAL amount of the INVESTOR's CAPITAL is GUARANTEED to redeem at PAR, and where intervening COUPONS are dependent on the performance of the UNDERLYING market or ASSET reference (which may be drawn from the COMMODITY, EQUITY, INTEREST RATE, CURRENCY, or CREDIT markets, and which may contain some degree of LEVERAGE). Also known as PRINCIPAL PROTECTED BOND.

GUARANTOR   A party that supplies a GUARANTEE to another party, becoming responsible for performance or payment in the event of nonperformance by a third party.

GUIDANCE LINE   A BANK LINE granted to a customer that is used by a BANK or other FINANCIAL INSTITUTION for internal management purposes and is not specifically communicated to the customer. Since the client pays no COMMITMENT FEE, the guidance line can be cancelled or withdrawn by the lender at any time. See also ADVISED LINE.

GUN JUMPING   [COL] (1) The public solicitation of orders for a PRIMARY OFFERING before REGISTRATION is complete. (2) TRADING of SECURITIES on the basis of nonpublic information (as a form of INSIDER TRADING). Gun jumping in either form is illegal in most national jurisdictions.

GUNSLINGER   [COL] A trader, INVESTOR, or INVESTMENT MANAGER that takes a considerable amount of speculative RISK in an attempt to generate high RETURNS.

GYOSEI SHIDO [JPN] The Japanese practice of bureaucratic control (or "administrative guidance") of CORPORATIONS, exercised through REGULATION, KEIRETSU group pressure, and access to BANK-supplied CREDIT.

H

HAIRCUT [COL] (1) The upfront DISCOUNT applied to the value of SECURITY taken as COLLATERAL on a LOAN, REVERSE REPURCHASE AGREEMENT, or DERIVATIVE in order to protect against price deterioration and the possibility of any CREDIT RISK exposure becoming unsecured. The same discounts are often applied to securities included in a firm's own LIQUIDITY WAREHOUSE to provide a more accurate reflection of LIQUIDATION value. In general, the greater the VOLATILITY of the reference security and the longer the time between valuation and MARGIN calls or LIQUIDATION, the larger the haircut. (2) In the United States, the formula used by BROKERS/DEALERS to compute NET CAPITAL requirements under rules established by the SECURITIES AND EXCHANGE COMMISSION.

HALAL [ARB] Any action or objective that is permissible under Islamic law, and a key factor in ISLAMIC FINANCE. See also HARAAM.

HAND SIGNAL A method of communicating BIDS and OFFERS between FLOOR TRADERS in an OPEN OUTCRY market.

HANDLE [COL] The whole number appearing to the left of the decimal in a SECURITIES or FOREIGN EXCHANGE price, often ignored by DEALERS and MARKET MAKERS quoting BIDS or OFFERS as they are implicitly understood. Also known as BIG FIGURE.

HANG SENG INDEX (HSI) The BENCHMARK INDEX of the HONG KONG STOCK EXCHANGE, originally developed in 1933 and computed on a MARKET CAPITALIZATION-weighted basis. The index comprises of 42 STOCKS (intended to increase to 50), and also features several key subindexes, including those related to BANKING, utilities, property, and commerce and industry.

HARAAM [ARB] Any action or objective that is forbidden under Islamic law, and which has led to the development of the ISLAMIC FINANCE sector. See also HALAL.

HARD CALL PROTECTION A CALL PROTECTION provision in a BOND INDENTURE that prevents the ISSUER from calling the SECURITY for a specific period of time. See also NONCALLABLE BOND, SOFT CALL PROTECTION.

HARD CURRENCY See CONVERTIBLE CURRENCY.

HARD DOLLARS Direct payments made by clients to FINANCIAL INSTITU-TIONS for services rendered. In commercial banking a client may pay a fee for a CREDIT facility; in SECURITIES a client may pay BROKERAGE COMMISSIONS for TRADE EXECUTION, or a fee for a financial plan. See also SOFT DOLLARS.

HARD LANDING [COL] A state where fiscal or monetary restraint intended to curb excess DEMAND and high INFLATION erodes confidence and activity, leading to economic slowdown and RECESSION. See also SOFT LANDING.

HARD MARKET   (1) Any market where DEMAND exceeds SUPPLY, causing prices to rise. (2) An INSURANCE market cycle where INSURERS reduce the amount of coverage they are willing to write, causing SUPPLY to contract and PREMIUMS to rise. A hard market can occur by the onset of very large and unexpected losses (i.e., CATASTROPHIC HAZARDS, CLASH LOSS, SHOCK LOSS) that causes a depletion of CAPITAL within the insurance and REINSURANCE sector; relative lack of CAPITAL creates a shortfall in RISK CAPACITY. A hard market may also arise from a gradual lowering of UNDERWRITING standards occurring during a SOFT MARKET cycle, leading to a greater loss experience over time.

HARMONIZED INDEX OF CONSUMER PRICES (HICP)   An INFLATION INDEX widely used throughout the EUROPEAN UNION that measures changes in consumer prices. Unlike various other CONSUMER PRICE INDEX measures, HICP excludes owner-occupied rental costs. See also PRODUCER PRICE INDEX, RETAIL PRICE INDEX.

HARVEST   [COL] In PRIVATE EQUITY and VENTURE CAPITAL, the process of crystallizing profits in a PORTFOLIO company through an INITIAL PUBLIC OFFERING or sale to a third party.

HAUSBANK   [GER] In Germany, a BANK acting as the primary relationship banker to a company, providing or arranging a variety of CREDIT-related services. Hausbanks often wield additional power by directly holding large shareholdings in client companies and by voting PROXIES on behalf of INVESTORS who leave their SHARES in bank CUSTODY.

HAZARD   An event that creates or increases PERIL. While hazards are not specifically covered in most INSURANCE contracts, the perils they create or magnify form the core of INSURABLE RISKS.

HEAD AND SHOULDERS   [COL] A TECHNICAL ANALYSIS charting figure of a SECURITY or INDEX that features a supporting price plateau, followed by a spike, then a reversal to a second supporting price plateau; the formation of a head and shoulders might then lead to a BREAKOUT on the upside or downside.

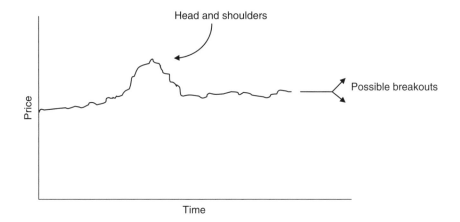

See also REVERSE HEAD AND SHOULDERS.

HEAVY MARKET [COL] A market or sector that suffers price declines through selling pressures generated by large ORDER IMBALANCES. See also FAST MARKET.

HEAVY SHARE A STOCK with a high price, and which may be a candidate for a STOCK SPLIT in order to lower its price and appeal to a broader number of INVESTORS, particularly those in the retail sector.

HEDGE A financial transaction that is intended to protect an underlying ASSET, LIABILITY, REVENUE, or EXPENSE from adverse movement in a particular reference; a correctly structured hedge transaction can offset losses by providing a gain when the UNDERLYING suffers a loss, and vice-versa. Hedges can be constructed using traditional financial instruments such as COMMON STOCKS, BONDS, FOREIGN EXCHANGE, and COMMODITIES, as well as OVER-THE-COUNTER DERIVATIVES and EXCHANGE-TRADED DERIVATIVES. The actual creation of a hedge may be quantified through a number of techniques, including HEDGE RATIOS. The process of hedging is often associated with RISKS that are uninsurable through a standard contractual INSURANCE framework and must therefore be transferred to a hedge COUNTERPARTY. See also ARBITRAGE, CROSS-ASSET HEDGE, HEDGER, HEDGING, SPECULATION.

HEDGE FUND A private PARTNERSHIP (for US INVESTORS) or INVESTMENT COMPANY (for non-US or TAX-exempt investors) that follows a specific strategy by establishing LONG POSITIONS or SHORT POSITIONS in a range of ASSETS, often using DERIVATIVES and LEVERAGE to enhance RETURNS. Funds may follow a specific strategy, including one based on market direction (i.e., MARKET NEUTRAL, LONG ONLY), ARBITRAGE (i.e., FIXED INCOME ARBITRAGE, CONVERTIBLE BOND ARBITRAGE, STATISTICAL ARBITRAGE, VOLATILITY ARBITRAGE, RELATIVE VALUE ARBITRAGE), RESTRUCTURING (i.e., DISTRESSED ASSETS, RISK ARBITRAGE, EVENT DRIVEN), or macro events (i.e., GLOBAL MACRO). Most funds have minimum LOCKUP periods and are considered to be quite ILLIQUID. Hedge fund managers charge investors an annual fee (typically 2%) and a performance fee (typically 20% of earnings generated). Since hedge funds are generally very risky, investors must be accredited (possessing minimum NET WORTH and able to sustain potential loss of CAPITAL).

HEDGE RATIO A measure that indicates the price relationship between a reference ASSET and a proxy HEDGE. The hedge ratio, which is generally based on a statistical process such as linear regression, reflects how much of an asset or DERIVATIVE is needed to protect or offset the RISK of the UNDERLYING reference. It can be computed via:

$$H = \frac{Cov(A, B)}{\sigma_B^2}$$

where Cov (A, B) is the COVARIANCE between asset A and hedge instrument B, and σ^2_B is the VARIANCE of B. Also known as MINIMUM VARIANCE HEDGE RATIO.

HEDGER   A party that employs HEDGING techniques in order to minimize, or neutralize, RISK. See also HEDGE, SPECULATOR.

HEDGING   The process of creating a HEDGE in order to minimize, or neutralize, RISK. Hedging requires the selection of the correct instrument(s) and quantities in order to be effective. See also DELTA HEDGE, HEDGE RATIO, HEDGER.

HERSTATT RISK   See SETTLEMENT RISK.

HICP   See HARMONIZED INDEX OF CONSUMER PRICES.

HIDDEN ORDER   A type of ORDER submitted to an EXCHANGE or ALTERNATIVE TRADING SYSTEM that remains completely obscured from public view. See also DARK POOL, RESERVE ORDER.

HIDDEN RESERVES   RESERVES, generally held by a BANK or other FINANCIAL INSTITUTION, that are not readily detectable through an examination of the BALANCE SHEET. Hidden reserves may be implicitly contained in an undervaluation of particular kinds of ASSETS, though such practice is often discouraged through ACCOUNTING rules as it fails to provide a fair estimate of financial condition.

HIGH-LOW OPTION   An OVER-THE-COUNTER COMPLEX OPTION that grants the buyer a payoff based on the difference between the high and low prices achieved by the UNDERLYING during the life of the transaction. See also CALL ON THE MAXIMUM, PUT ON THE MINIMUM.

HIGH STREET BANK   [COL] In the United Kingdom, a COMMERCIAL BANK that caters primarily to retail customers, accepting DEPOSITS and granting consumer, personal, and MORTGAGE LOANS. Although such banks also engage in other institutional banking business, their marketing and focus is weighted heavily toward individuals.

HIGH WATER MARK   The maximum value that has been attained by a HEDGE FUND or other INVESTMENT FUND. Performance fees are often synchronized to the high water mark, so that if RETURNS fall short of a previously established high water mark in a given year, the manager receives no performance fee.

HIGH-YIELD BOND   A BOND issued by a firm with a SUBINVESTMENT GRADE CREDIT RATING (i.e., below BBB– by Standard and Poor's, below Baa3 by Moody's Investors Services). The greater likelihood of DEFAULT compared with INVESTMENT GRADE bonds results in a greater COST OF CAPITAL for the ISSUER and a higher YIELD for INVESTORS. High-yield bonds were popularized during the corporate expansion and TAKEOVER phase of the mid- to late 1980s and have become an integral part of the CAPITAL MARKETS, particularly in the United States and Europe. Also known as JUNK BOND. See also FALLEN ANGEL.

HIGHLY LEVERAGED TRANSACTION (HLT) LOAN   A LOAN extended by a BANK to a company that already has a high degree of LEVERAGE. HLT loans may be secured or unsecured, and typically have stringent COVENANTS requiring the leveraged BORROWER to adhere to various financial operating ratios, including those related to minimum levels of LIQUIDITY and INTEREST COVERAGE.

HIRE PURCHASE   In the United Kingdom, INSTALLMENT CREDIT.

HISTORICAL COST ACCOUNTING   In ACCOUNTING, a method of valuation based on the original cost of an ASSET or LIABILITY. Though simple to implement, the historical cost method does not generally take account of current market values or DEPRECIATION, and may therefore not provide an accurate reflection of a company's true value. Note that INTERNATIONAL FINANCIAL REPORTING STANDARDS (IFRS) allow for a fair value assessment of plant and equipment, though this is strictly voluntary. In addition, IFRS and US GENERALLY ACCEPTED ACCOUNTING PRINCIPLES still require that DERIVATIVES be stated at fair value. See also INFLATION ACCOUNTING.

HISTORICAL METHOD   A CREDIT RISK exposure computation methodology for SWAPS using historical INTEREST RATES. Under the historical method past interest rate (or swap rate) data is used to create a statistical distribution of rates. Following an adjustment to a prespecified CONFIDENCE LEVEL, forward swap rates are determined, allowing the swap to be revalued at each forward point and discounted back to the present; the largest exposure obtained during the revaluation process becomes the swap's FRACTIONAL EXPOSURE. See also OPTION METHOD, SIMULATION METHOD.

HISTORICAL RATE ROLLOVER   A transaction in the FOREIGN EXCHANGE MARKET where a maturing FORWARD CONTRACT is extended for a subsequent period based on the originally contracted FORWARD RATE. This implies one of the two parties to the transaction is providing the other with a CREDIT line equal to the difference between the old forward rate and the new forward rate.

HISTORICAL VOLATILITY   A retrospective statistical measure of the price movement of an ASSET based on historical data, often conveyed in terms of VARIANCE or STANDARD DEVIATION. Historical volatility is applied to various financial and RISK valuation techniques, including FRACTIONAL EXPOSURE and VALUE-AT-RISK. See also IMPLIED VOLATILITY.

HIT THE BID   [COL] Any instance where one BROKER or DEALER is willing to sell at the BID price posted by another broker or dealer. See also TAKE THE OFFER.

HKSE   See HONG KONG STOCK EXCHANGE.

HLT LOAN   See HIGHLY LEVERAGED TRANSACTION LOAN.

HOLD HARMLESS AGREEMENT   An agreement by one party to assume the LIABILITY of a second party, holding it harmless or indemnifying against any potential financial loss; such an agreement may exist implicitly or explicitly between PRINCIPAL and AGENT.

HOLDING COMPANY A form of corporate organization that holds the ownership interest in a PARENT and/or a series of SUBSIDIARIES. A holding company may be constituted as a SHELL with no true operations and resources of its own (apart from ownership stakes in its subholdings) or it may be an operating company in its own right. See also BANK HOLDING COMPANY.

HOLDING PERIOD (1) The period of time that an INVESTMENT MANAGER holds an ASSET within a PORTFOLIO. (2) See LIQUIDATION PERIOD.

HOMOGENOUS EXPOSURE A group of RISKS that feature similar or identical characteristics, leading to the same EXPECTED LOSS levels. Homogenous exposures allow for more accurate and equitable ACTUARIAL PRICING of INSURANCE CONTRACTS and ultimately reduce the likelihood of ADVERSE SELECTION.

HONG KONG STOCK EXCHANGE (HKSE) The primary STOCK EXCHANGE of Hong Kong, established in 1891 and expanded through ACQUISITION of smaller regional exchanges in the 1960s and 1970s. HKSE converted from physical trading to ELECTRONIC TRADING in 1986. The HKSE acquired the Hong Kong FUTURES Exchange and the Hong Kong SECURITIES CLEARING Company in 2000, and now operates under a HOLDING COMPANY known as Hong Kong Exchanges and Clearing.

HORIZONTAL CLEARING SERVICES CLEARING services that are offered by the CLEARINGHOUSE of one EXCHANGE to other exchanges and ELECTRONIC COMMUNICATIONS NETWORKS as a means of generating additional REVENUES.

HORIZONTAL INTEGRATION See HORIZONTAL MERGER.

HORIZONTAL LAYERING A practice where different REINSURERS take percentage portions of the same loss layer under an EXCESS OF LOSS (XOL) REINSURANCE agreement. Each reinsurer becomes liable for its own fractional portion of coverage between the ATTACHMENT level and the POLICY CAP. Under this approach every reinsurer is exposed to losses and CLAIMS once the underlying DEDUCTIBLE is exceeded. See also EXCESS LAYER, VERTICAL LAYERING.

HORIZONTAL MERGER A MERGER between companies from the same industrial sector, sometimes direct competitors. A horizontal merger is often arranged in order to build market share or obtain better product or client coverage. Also known as HORIZONTAL INTEGRATION. See also CONGLOMERATE MERGER, VERTICAL MERGER.

HORIZONTAL SPREAD Any SPREAD where the OPTIONS being used have different EXPIRY DATES.

HOST SECURITY A SECURITY (typically a NOTE or BOND) to which a DERIVATIVE is attached (i.e., an OPTION or COMPLEX OPTION for a STRUCTURED NOTE, or a WARRANT for a BOND WITH WARRANT).

HOSTILE TAKEOVER An unsolicited ACQUISITION offer from a RAIDER or BLACK KNIGHT that the TARGET's DIRECTORS and executives do not favor and which they attempt to thwart through ANTITAKEOVER DEFENSES, ANTITAKEOVER LAWS, or SCORCHED EARTH DEFENSES, or by seeking a friendly partner in the form of a WHITE KNIGHT or WHITE SQUIRE. Also known as CONTESTED TRANSACTION.

HOT MONEY [COL] INTEREST RATE-SENSITIVE DEPOSITS, overnight REVERSE REPURCHASE AGREEMENTS, and interbank funds that can be withdrawn rapidly based on market events or CREDIT perceptions. BANKS funding their operations with a large amount of hot money, which is generally supplied by INSTITUTIONAL INVESTORS, may encounter a LIQUIDITY problem if they are unable to quickly replace funds that disappear within a span of hours or days. See also CALL MONEY.

HSI See HANG SENG INDEX.

HUNG DEAL [COL] A NEW ISSUE of SECURITIES that UNDERWRITERS fail to place at the primary launch SPREAD (or price). If the transaction is arranged as a BOUGHT DEAL the underwriters are obligated to take up the unsold securities and provide the ISSUER with funds as contracted; the group must then attempt to sell the securities on a secondary basis, often by widening the spread (lowering the price). Also known as STICKY DEAL, STUCK DEAL.

HURDLE RATE See COST OF CAPITAL.

HYBRID ADJUSTABLE RATE MORTGAGE An ADJUSTABLE RATE MORTGAGE (ARM) that features a longer period of FIXED RATES (i.e., up to 10 years) than a standard ARM, after which the rate resets to a specified MARGIN over a BENCHMARK FLOATING RATE. Also known as FIXED PERIOD ADJUSTABLE RATE MORTGAGE.

HYBRID BOND A FIXED INCOME SECURITY with EMBEDDED OPTIONS that alter RISK and RETURN characteristics. The general class of hybrids includes CALLABLE BONDS, PUTABLE BONDS, BONDS WITH WARRANTS, CONVERTIBLE BONDS, and STRUCTURED NOTES.

HYBRID CAPITAL SECURITY A SECURITY, generally issued by a BANK, with structural features that place it between DEBT and EQUITY in the CAPITAL structure. Such securities generally qualify as REGULATORY CAPITAL. Hybrids generally have a regular income stream via a COUPON or DIVIDEND, a fixed or perpetual MATURITY with OPTIONAL REDEMPTION, and rank above PREFERRED STOCK but below SUBORDINATED DEBT in terms of seniority in DEFAULT. Common forms of hybrids include TRUST

PREFERRED STOCK and JUNIOR SUBORDINATED DEBENTURES. See also PERPETUAL PREFERRED STOCK.

HYBRID ELECTRONIC COMMUNICATIONS NETWORK   An ELECTRONIC COMMUNICATIONS NETWORK (ECN) that incorporates the features of both DEALER MARKET ECNs and REGULATED ECNs.

HYBRID MODEL   A general corporate system that is characterized by ILLIQUID CAPITAL MARKETS, an inactive or nonexistent CORPORATE CONTROL MARKET, and nascent regulatory and legal frameworks; family interests often hold large ownership stakes in companies, related company conglomeration is common, and ownership ties between companies and BANKS can be significant. Emerging nations often use the hybrid model. See also MARKET MODEL, RELATIONSHIP MODEL.

HYPERINFLATION   A phenomenon of rapidly escalating prices for goods and services, leading to dramatic loss of purchasing power. Though metrics of hyperinflation are subjective, the INTERNATIONAL ACCOUNTING STANDARDS BOARD defines it to be three or more consecutive years of INFLATION reaching or exceeding 100% per annum. See also INFLATION ACCOUNTING.

HYPOTHECATION   A process where a BORROWER pledges ASSETS as COLLATERAL for a LOAN. No transfer of TITLE occurs through hypothecation, but the LENDER accepting hypothecated assets is granted the right to dispose of the assets if the borrower DEFAULTS. The same process applies when an INVESTOR pledges securities to a BROKER to secure a PURPOSE (or MARGIN) LOAN or SHORT SALE. See also REHYPOTHECATION.

HYPOTHEKENPFANDBRIEFE   [GER] A secured MORTGAGE-BACKED BOND forming part of the German PFANDBRIEFE sector, created when a MORTGAGE or mortgage POOL is converted into a negotiable SECURITY. Unlike standard SECURITIZATIONS, the ASSETS underlying the BONDS remain on the ISSUER's BALANCE SHEET, but are reserved (or RING-FENCED) for the benefit of INVESTORS, who receive a first priority claim in the event of DEFAULT. Also known as MORTGAGE PFANDBRIEFE. See also CEDULAS HIPOTECARIAS, IRISH ASSET COVERED SECURITIES, JUMBO PFANDBRIEFE, LETTRES DE GAGE, OBLIGATIONS FONCIERES, OFFENTLICHE PFANDBRIEFE.

I

IAS   See INTERNATIONAL ACCOUNTING STANDARDS.

IASB   See INTERNATIONAL ACCOUNTING STANDARDS BOARD.

IBF   See INTERNATIONAL BANKING FACILITY.

IBNR   See INCURRED BUT NOT REPORTED.

IBRD   See INTERNATIONAL BANK FOR RECONSTRUCTION AND DEVELOPMENT.

ICAAP   See INTERNAL CAPITAL ADEQUACY ASSESSMENT PROCESS.

ICE   See INTERCONTINENTAL EXCHANGE.

ICEBERG   [COL] See RESERVE ORDER.

IDB   See INTER-DEALER BROKER.

IDIOSYNCRATIC RISK   See DIVERSIFIABLE RISK.

IDLE BALANCE   Funds placed in a BANK by a DEPOSITOR that do not earn any INTEREST. Also known as TRANSACTION BALANCE.

IDR   See INTERNATIONAL DEPOSITORY RECEIPT.

IFC   See INTERNATIONAL FINANCE CORPORATION.

IFRS   See INTERNATIONAL FINANCIAL REPORTING STANDARDS.

IJARA   (ARB) A secured LEASE scheme used in ISLAMIC FINANCE, where a customer secures financing for a durable ASSET by leasing it from a BANK (which purchases the asset, and grants the customer the right to buy the asset at a defined value in the future).

ILLIQUID   (1) At a corporate level, the state of possessing insufficient cash to meet obligations. (2) At a market level, the state of having insufficient transaction volume to permit TRADING. See also LIQUID, LIQUID ASSETS, LIQUIDITY, ILLIQUIDITY.

ILLIQUIDITY   (1) At a corporate level, lack of cash, NEAR MONEY, unsecured funding access, or unencumbered LIQUID ASSETS to meet expected or unexpected payments. (2) The state of being ILLIQUID or lacking LIQUID ASSETS. (3) At a market level, lack of TRADING volume in a SECURITY or ASSET; an illiquid market is characterized by wide SPREADS, i.e., large differences between BIDS and OFFERS. See also ENDOGENOUS LIQUIDITY, EXOGENOUS LIQUIDITY, LIQUIDITY, LIQUIDITY RISK.

ILS   See INSURANCE-LINKED SECURITY.

IMF   See INTERNATIONAL MONETARY FUND.

IMMEDIATE ANNUITY   An ANNUITY contract that begins to make payments to the BENEFICIARY as soon as it is executed.

IMMEDIATE OR CANCEL ORDER   An ORDER to purchase or sell SECURITIES where the BROKER is instructed to fill as much of the order as possible as soon as it is entered and cancel any portion that is not immediately filled.

IMMUNIZATION   The process of protecting an INTEREST RATE-sensitive PORTFOLIO from future market movements so that a future LIABILITY or cash outflow can be met. To protect against any changes in rates the portfolio must be invested in FIXED INCOME SECURITIES that have a DURATION equal to the INVESTMENT horizon, and an initial PRESENT VALUE equal to the present value of a future liability. A portfolio is considered to be immunized when sufficient funds can be generated, or a target RETURN can be obtained, regardless of the movement of rates.

IMPACT DAY   The first day of official (rather than GRAY MARKET) TRADING in a NEW ISSUE of SECURITIES.

IMPLICIT PRICE DEFLATOR   See GDP DEFLATOR.

IMPLIED FINANCING RATE   See IMPLIED REPO RATE.

IMPLIED FORWARD CURVE   A YIELD CURVE representing the TERM STRUCTURE of DISCOUNT RATES, starting in any designated future period. The implied forward curve, which is constructed from IMPLIED FORWARD RATES derived from the ZERO COUPON YIELD CURVE (itself a product of the observable PAR YIELD CURVE), is used to price instruments, such as DERIVATIVES, that require a forward estimate of rates. The shape and slope of the implied curve depends on the shape and slope of the par and zero coupon curves, as well as INVESTOR expectations regarding future INTEREST RATES.

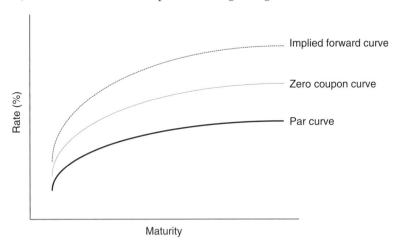

IMPLIED FORWARD RATE   The INTEREST RATE that can be earned for a defined period of time, starting at some future point. The implied forward rate is the rate necessary to make funds invested at a short rate and reinvested at a forward rate (i.e., multiple period) precisely equal to the return invested at a long rate (i.e., single period).

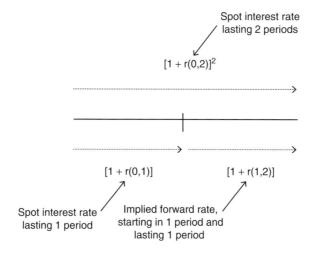

The t-year implied forward rate starting in n periods (semiannual) is given by:

$$f = \left[\frac{(1+r_{n+t})^{n+t}}{(1+r_n)^n} \right]^{\frac{1}{t}} - 1$$

where r is the prevailing semiannual SPOT RATE. Also known as FORWARD RATE. See also IMPLIED FORWARD CURVE, IMPLIED REPO RATE.

IMPLIED REPO RATE   The RETURN before FINANCING costs implied by a CASH-AND-CARRY ARBITRAGE involving BONDS. The implied repo rate can be computed via:

$$f = \left[\frac{\left(1+r_{0,b}\right)^b}{\left(1+r^*_{a,b}\right)^{b-a}} \right]^{\frac{1}{a}} - 1$$

where $r_{0,b}$ is the SPOT RATE to time period b and $r^*_{a,b}$ is the FUTURES rate covering periods a and b. Also known as IMPLIED FINANCING RATE. See also IMPLIED FORWARD RATE.

IMPLIED VOLATILITY   A prospective measure of the price movement of an ASSET imputed from the market prices of traded OPTIONS. VOLATILITY is one of the central inputs of option pricing models but is not directly observable in the market; accordingly, traders use observed option prices to derive volatility. See also HISTORICAL VOLATILITY.

IMPLIED YIELD   The YIELD on a SECURITY that is computed based on prevailing INTEREST RATES, as reflected in the current YIELD CURVE.

IMPORT DUTY   A TAX or TARIFF applied to goods that are being IMPORTED into a country, generally as a way of controlling the inflow of foreign goods and to generate additional tax-based REVENUES. An import duty may be levied via a fixed charge or on an AD VALOREM basis.

IMPORTS   Goods and services produced offshore, transported or brought into the country, and sold to residents of the nonproducing nation, including VISIBLES (goods) and INVISIBLES (services). See also BALANCE OF TRADE, EXPORTS.

IMPREST ACCOUNT   (1) An account established by a company as a SELF-INSURANCE mechanism to cover low-severity property losses. (2) A petty cash account that allows an individual to charge for small expenses.

IN-ARREARS SWAP   See ARREARS SWAP.

IN PLAY   [COL] The state of a company that is the subject of a TAKEOVER or which has put itself up for sale.

IN-THE-MONEY   A condition where the price of an UNDERLYING reference ASSET is higher than the STRIKE PRICE for a CALL OPTION or below the strike for a PUT OPTION, meaning the contract has immediate INTRINSIC VALUE if exercised. See also AT-THE-MONEY, MONEYNESS, OUT-OF-THE-MONEY.

INC   See INCORPORATED.

INCHOATE BILL OF EXCHANGE   A BILL OF EXCHANGE where one or more of the material terms are omitted, and which can be completed at the discretion of the possessor within a reasonable time frame. See also INCHOATE CONTRACT.

INCHOATE CONTRACT   A CONTRACT that has not been executed by all required parties, and which is therefore not considered enforceable. See also INCHOATE BILL OF EXCHANGE.

INCOME   A REVENUE stream that arises from INVESTMENT, sales, or labor, and which may be subject to some form of TAX.

INCOME BOND   A BOND that pays INTEREST only if the ISSUER's operations can support the payments without impairing core operations. Such a SECURITY is generally issued by a weak company, often in the context of a RESTRUCTURING effort. Income bonds are generally priced without ACCRUED INTEREST given the uncertainty over whether a COUPON will be paid in any given period; they may thus be considered as a form of FLAT BOND.

INCOME DISTRIBUTION   The allocation of national income across specific groups or classes, often computed for comparative purposes. The allocation can be measured via statistical measures, such as the GINI COEFFICIENT.

INCOME FUND   A MUTUAL FUND or UNIT INVESTMENT TRUST that invests CAPITAL primarily or exclusively in INCOME STOCKS.

INCOME STATEMENT   A key FINANCIAL STATEMENT that reflects a company's REVENUES and EXPENSES throughout the fiscal accounting period; the results it presents thus contain the cumulative effect of the reporting period. Presentation of the income statement can vary by country, accounting regime and/or industry sector. The summarized income statement takes the following general form:

```
        Gross revenues
      − Cost of goods sold
          = Gross profit
      − SG&A expenses
      − Interest expense
      + Interest income
      + Other income
      − Other expenses
      = Operating income
        − Income taxes
        = Net income
```

Also known as PROFIT AND LOSS ACCOUNT.

INCOME STOCK   The STOCK of a company that is expected to produce gradual, if stable, profits over the medium term, providing INVESTORS with DIVIDENDS rather than significant CAPITAL GAINS. An income stock may feature lower VOLATILITY and BETA than a GROWTH STOCK. See also INCOME FUND.

INCOME TAX   A TAX levied on INCOME by a government authority to fund the provision of government services and to enforce some degree of INCOME DISTRIBUTION. Income tax may be levied at a personal level (including individuals, households, SOLE PROPRIETORSHIPS, PARTNERSHIPS) and at a corporate level. Income tax is often designed as a PROGRESSIVE TAX.

INCOME WARRANT   A WARRANT that is structured to pay the holder INTEREST prior to being EXERCISED.

INCONVERTIBLE CURRENCY   See NONCONVERTIBLE CURRENCY.

INCORPORATED (INC)   In the United States, a CORPORATION that is publicly traded.

INCORPOREAL INTEREST   The right to an INSURABLE INTEREST in a designated ASSET, conveyed when the assets are pledged as COLLATERAL.

INCUBATOR   [COL] A firm that provides start-up ventures with seed CAPITAL, administrative services, and business plan support in exchange for a pre-INITIAL PUBLIC OFFERING EQUITY stake. Once the incubator has nurtured the start-up to a sufficient state of readiness the company is often referred to a VENTURE CAPITAL group for additional, and more formal, FINANCING and management. See also ACCELERATOR.

INCURRED BUT NOT REPORTED (IBNR)   A loss covered by an INSURANCE CONTRACT that has already occurred but has not been reported by the INSURED to the INSURER. Insurers generally establish a minimum level of RESERVES to cover the lag in CLAIMS arising from an anticipated amount of IBNR items.

INCURRED LOSS   In INSURANCE, a loss that has already occurred, whether or not the INSURER has paid a SETTLEMENT to the INSURED. See also INCURRED LOSS RATIO.

INCURRED LOSS RATIO   A measure of how much of an INSURER's PREMIUM is used to cover losses, computed as:

$$IL = \frac{Loss_{inc}}{Pr}$$

where $Loss_{inc}$ is the sum of INCURRED LOSSES and Pr is premium earned.

The larger the ratio, the greater the amount of premium that is used to cover losses.

INCURRED LOSS RETROSPECTIVE POLICY   A LOSS-SENSITIVE INSURANCE CONTRACT requiring the INSURED to pay an incremental PREMIUM during the year based on the INSURER's best estimate of losses (i.e., actual losses plus an estimate of future losses).

INDEMNIFICATION   The process of guaranteeing payment or recompense should a party suffer a specified loss.

INDEMNITY   A fundamental principle of INSURANCE indicating that an INSURED cannot profit from an insurance CONTRACT, which exists only to cover a loss and not generate a speculative gain. The maximum amount payable under a contract of indemnity is the amount required to return the insured to the financial position that existed prior to the loss. See also INDEMNITY CONTRACT, INSURABLE INTEREST, VALUED CONTRACT.

INDEMNITY COMPANY   An INSURER that specializes in UNDERWRITING a range of PROPERTY AND CASUALTY INSURANCE covers.

INDEMNITY CONTRACT   An INSURANCE CONTRACT that provides the INSURED with restitution for actual losses sustained. The indemnity contract, which includes PROPERTY AND CASUALTY INSURANCE and LIABILITY INSURANCE, is designed to return the insured to the financial state it occupied prior to the loss. See also INDEMNITY, VALUED CONTRACT.

INDEMNITY TRIGGER   A conditional event in an INSURANCE-LINKED SECURITY that causes suspension of INTEREST and/or PRINCIPAL when actual losses sustained by the ISSUER reach a predefined amount. See also INDEX TRIGGER, PARAMETRIC TRIGGER.

INDENTURE   (1) The written terms and conditions of a BOND or NOTE issue, which generally includes details regarding form of SECURITY, INTEREST,

CALL/PUT provisions, COVENANTS, EVENTS OF DEFAULT, and PRINCIPAL repayment. The indenture also defines the rights, privileges, and OBLIGATIONS of the ISSUER, INVESTOR, and TRUSTEE related to the initial provision of CAPITAL and the timely payment of interest and repayment of principal. (2) A DEED that relates to the transfer of a landed estate.

INDEPENDENT ADVISOR   A FINANCIAL ADVISOR that is licensed to provide financial advice to clients, is not affiliated with a specific BANK or financial institution, and is not required to sell products or services of any single institution. An independent advisor may act as a generalist, offering advice on a range of services/products, or a specialist, focusing on a dedicated discipline such as INVESTMENTS, INSURANCE, and so forth. Also known as INDEPENDENT FINANCIAL ADVISOR.

INDEPENDENT FINANCIAL ADVISOR   See INDEPENDENT ADVISOR.

INDEX   (1) A statistical measure that combines disparate data into a single reference, which becomes a BENCHMARK for some base year of computation. An index can be computed in various forms, either without a weighting (i.e., a pure price index equal to the price in the current period divided by the price in the base period), or with a weighting (i.e., as in the CURRENT WEIGHTED INDEX and the BASE WEIGHTED INDEX). (2) A basket of ASSETS that are combined into a single, often tradable, representation. (1) See also INDEXATION.

INDEX AMORTIZING RATE SWAP   See INDEX PRINCIPAL SWAP.

INDEX ARBITRAGE   An ARBITRAGE strategy that attempts to capitalize on price discrepancies between INDEX FUTURES and the individual COMMON STOCKS comprising the index. When index futures appear RICH to fair value, ARBITRAGEURS sell futures and purchase the underlying stocks; when they appear CHEAP, they buy futures and sell the stocks. The arbitrage can be preserved until the MATURITY of the underlying futures CONTRACTS, or rolled into the new contract cycle as trading becomes active. Also known as PROGRAM TRADING.

INDEX FUND   A MUTUAL FUND that GUARANTEES INVESTORS returns based on a defined market INDEX or subindex. Index funds generally feature lower costs than actively managed funds and are favored by investors who do not believe that a market index can be exceeded over the long term. Also known as TRACKER FUND. See also INDEXING, PASSIVE INVESTMENT STRATEGY.

INDEX FUTURE   A FUTURES CONTRACT, bought or sold via an EXCHANGE, which references a specific BENCHMARK EQUITY INDEX, index sector, or equity BASKET. See also COMMODITY FUTURE, CURRENCY FUTURE, INTEREST RATE FUTURE.

INDEX-LINKED ANNUITY   An ANNUITY with payments to the BENEFICIARY that are linked to a specified INDEX.

INDEX OF CONCENTRATION   See GINI COEFFICIENT.

INDEX OPTION An EXCHANGE-TRADED or OVER-THE-COUNTER OPTION involving a broad STOCK INDEX. VANILLA and COMPLEX OPTIONS can be bought and sold on a broad range of indexes, and are typically contracted for CASH SETTLEMENT. See also COMMODITY OPTION, CURRENCY OPTION, EQUITY OPTION, INTEREST RATE OPTION.

INDEX PRINCIPAL SWAP An OVER-THE-COUNTER SWAP with a NOTIONAL PRINCIPAL that amortizes as a FLOATING RATE reference declines through prespecified BARRIER levels. As the notional declines, fixed and floating rate payments associated with the swap become smaller. The swap is often used as a HEDGE against ASSETS or LIABILITIES with CASH FLOWS that amortize with rate movements. Also known as INDEX AMORTIZING RATE SWAP. See also ACCRETING SWAP, AMORTIZING SWAP, REVERSE INDEX PRINCIPAL SWAP, VARIABLE PRINCIPAL SWAP.

INDEX REBALANCING A periodic process where constituents of a traded or tradable INDEX are added or removed, to ensure that the index remains consistent with its definition of eligible constituents. Constituents may change as a result of MERGERS or ACQUISITIONS, increase or decrease in MARKET CAPITALIZATION beyond certain levels, and so forth. INVESTORS that BENCHMARK their PORTFOLIOS to particular indexes must go through similar readjustment exercises in order to minimize TRACKING ERROR.

INDEX TRANCHE A form of SINGLE TRANCHE COLLATERALIZED DEBT OBLIGATION that is based on standard quoted CREDIT DEFAULT SWAP INDEXES, including those related to ITRAXX INDEXES.

INDEX TRIGGER A conditional event in an INSURANCE-LINKED SECURITY that causes suspension of INTEREST and/or PRINCIPAL when the value of a recognized third-party index used to track RISK exposure or loss experience reaches a certain threshold. See also INDEMNITY TRIGGER, PARAMETRIC TRIGGER.

INDEXATION The process of linking a particular economic or financial action to a base reference INDEX. Indexation may be used to link payments and receipts to an INFLATION index in order to adjust for rising prices of goods and services.

INDEXING A PASSIVE INVESTMENT STRATEGY based on replicating the performance of a specific INDEX with a minimum of TRACKING ERROR. See also ACTIVE INVESTMENT STRATEGY, INDEX FUND.

INDICATED MARKET An estimated TRADING range for a SECURITY that has been halted on an EXCHANGE as a result of pending news or an ORDER IMBALANCE. The indicated market is a gauge of where the security may trade once it reopens, although SUPPLY and DEMAND forces ultimately determine the actual starting level.

INDICATION OF INTEREST (IOI) Preliminary indication by an INVESTOR of possible interest in purchasing a NEW ISSUE of SECURITIES. Since IOIs are gathered informally while securities are still in the REGISTRATION process, the interest is considered nonbinding; IOIs cannot be regarded as solicitation (by the UNDERWRITER) or commitment (by the investor). IOIs are an essential part of the BOOK-BUILDING process and provide UNDERWRITERS with valuable input on pricing and demand. Also known as CIRCLE.

INDICATIVE PRICE   See INDICATIVE QUOTE.

INDICATIVE QUOTE   A BID and/or OFFER supplied by a DEALER or MARKET MAKER to a BROKER or client that cannot be regarded as certain, but as a guide or estimate for informational purposes. Only when EXECUTION appears more likely to occur will the dealer provide an actionable FIRM QUOTE. Also known as INDICATIVE PRICE. See also QUOTED SPREAD.

INDICATORS   See ECONOMIC INDICATORS.

INDIRECT LOSS   See CONSEQUENTIAL LOSS.

INDIRECT SHAREHOLDER   See NOMINEE SHAREHOLDER.

INDIRECT STAKEHOLDERS   In GOVERNANCE, the parties impacted by a company's activities and actions in a less obvious, immediate, or direct manner than DIRECT STAKEHOLDERS; this group generally includes REGULATORS, taxpayers, and competitors.

INDIVIDUAL RETIREMENT ACCOUNT (IRA)   In the United States, a self-directed, TAX-deferred PENSION INVESTMENT account that can be invested in a broad range of ASSETS. Since the IRA is tax-deferred, DIVIDENDS or CAPITAL GAINS generated by the account's investments do not become taxable until withdrawal, which is typically at age 59 ½, at which point the BENEFICIAL OWNER is likely to be in a lower tax bracket. Individuals selecting an IRA forego the ability to participate in other company-sponsored pension plans.

INDIVIDUAL SAVINGS ACCOUNT (ISA)   In the United Kingdom, a TAX-free SAVINGS ACCOUNT that replaces other previously existing vehicles (including personal equity plans and tax-exempt special savings accounts), comprised of two elements: a cash component (i.e., tax-free DEPOSIT ACCOUNT), and a qualifying INVESTMENT component, which can be invested directly or via a BROKER, in a range of RISK investments, including STOCKS, GOVERNMENT BONDS, and corporate BONDS. INTEREST, DIVIDENDS, and CAPITAL GAINS generated by the ISA are tax-free and withdrawals may be taken at any time. The ISA is subject to maximum per annum contributions, though previous distinctions between Mini ISAs and Maxi ISAs have been abolished.

INDUSTRIAL DEVELOPMENT BOND   See INDUSTRIAL REVENUE BOND.

INDUSTRIAL PAPER   COMMERCIAL PAPER issued by a nonfinancial company. See also FINANCIAL PAPER.

INDUSTRIAL REVENUE BOND   In the United States, a form of MUNICIPAL BOND issued by a state or local government on behalf of a CORPORATION that is engaged in a development project on behalf of the municipality. The bond may be backed by real ASSETS, such as property or buildings. Also known as INDUSTRIAL DEVELOPMENT BOND.

INELASTIC A state where a proportional change in one variable leads to a smaller proportional change in a second variable. Inelastic DEMAND is a weak demand response to a change in price, i.e., a proportional decline in the purchase price results in a smaller proportional increase in demand. Inelastic SUPPLY is a weak supply response to a change in price, i.e., a proportional increase in the selling price results in a smaller proportional increase in the amount supplied. See also ELASTIC, ELASTICITY.

INELIGIBLE BILL A BILL OF EXCHANGE that cannot be DISCOUNTED by another BANK or CENTRAL BANK.

INFLATION The rate of increase in prices of goods and services. Inflation can be measured at the wholesale level through indexes such as the PRODUCER PRICE INDEX, or at the retail level through the CONSUMER PRICE INDEX, RETAIL PRICE INDEX, or HARMONIZED INDEX OF CONSUMER PRICES. See also COST INFLATION, DEFLATION, DEMAND INFLATION, NOMINAL INTEREST RATE, REAL INTEREST RATE.

INFLATION ACCOUNTING An ACCOUNTING approach that incorporates the fact that the value of MONEY changes over time as a result of INFLATION, which impacts the value of ASSETS and LIABILITIES carried on the BALANCE SHEET. Inflation accounting attempts to overcome deficiencies imposed by the simpler HISTORICAL COST ACCOUNTING approach by price-adjusting historical costs relative to a particular INDEX. Also known as PRICE LEVEL ACCOUNTING.

INFLATION FUTURE A FUTURES contract traded on an EXCHANGE that is based on a recognized INFLATION INDEX, such as CONSUMER PRICE INDEX or RETAIL PRICE INDEX.

INFLATION HAWK [COL] In the financial markets, one who has a negative view of INFLATION and its effects on the economy and generally prefers a tight MONETARY POLICY with stable to slightly increasing INTEREST RATES.

INFLATION-LINKED SECURITY A NOTE or BOND that pays a GUARAN-TEED RETURN based on realized INFLATION for INVESTORS holding the SECURITY until MATURITY. In most inflation securities the COUPON provides a fixed return while the PRINCIPAL is adjusted to take account of annual inflation recorded over the life of the security. Inflation-linked securities are issued by government authorities in the United States, the United Kingdom, the European Union, Mexico, and Canada. See also AJUSTABONOS, TREASURY INFLATION-PROTECTED SECURITY.

INFLATION OPTION An OVER-THE-COUNTER OPTION that references an INFLATION index such as the CONSUMER PRICE INDEX or RETAIL PRICE INDEX, or which is traded as a CAP or FLOOR on the individual COUPONS of ANNUAL INFLATION SWAPS.

INFLATION RISK   The risk of loss of value or RETURN on an ASSET due to INFLATION, which reduces purchasing power over the life of the ASSET. Also known as PURCHASING POWER RISK.

INFLATION SPIRAL   A phenomenon where the rising price of goods and services leads to hire wages, which in turn leads to higher prices.

INFLATION SWAP   An OVER-THE-COUNTER SWAP involving the exchange of fixed and actual INFLATION rates. Inflation swaps, which are generally structured as ANNUAL INFLATION SWAPS or ZERO COUPON INFLATION SWAPS, often have final MATURITIES of 10+ years. The market convention for inflation swap quotations is country-specific: United Kingdom (UK RPI, monthly with a 2-month lag), United States (US CPI, interpolated), France (French CPI, interpolated), Europe (European HICP, monthly with 3-month lag).

INFLATION TARGET   A policy used by certain CENTRAL BANKS or monetary authorities that establishes a medium-term range for acceptable INFLATION, and then calibrates MONETARY POLICY to attempt to achieve a result in the targeted range. See also INTEREST RATE POLICY.

INFORMATION RATIO   A measure of the success of an INVESTMENT manager computed as the ACTIVE RETURN of a PORTFOLIO divided by ACTIVE RISK. The ratio can be computed ex-ante through a forecast, or ex-post through realized performance.

INITIAL MARGIN   (1) SECURITY (generally cash, a LETTER OF CREDIT, or high-quality BONDS) posted by the buyer and seller of EXCHANGE-TRADED DERIVATIVE CONTRACTS at the inception of each transaction to protect the CLEARINGHOUSE against DEFAULT by a COUNTERPARTY. Initial margin is typically based on the price VOLATILITY of a contract's reference ASSET. (2) Security used to support PURPOSE LOANS or NONPURPOSE LOANS under the FEDERAL RESERVE BOARD's REGULATION T margin requirements. (1) Also known as ORIGINAL MARGIN. (1), (2) See also CLEARING MARGIN, MAINTENANCE MARGIN, VARIATION MARGIN.

INITIAL PUBLIC OFFERING (IPO)   An inaugural issue of a PRIVATE COMPANY's COMMON STOCK in the public EQUITY markets. A SYNDICATE of INVESTMENT BANKS or SECURITIES FIRMS typically UNDERWRITES an IPO, pricing the transaction within a range suggested by comparables (i.e., common stock of competing firms), SUPPLY/DEMAND forces, and INDICATIONS OF INTEREST. IPO shares are allocated by the syndicate to INSTITUTIONAL INVESTORS or RETAIL INVESTORS and are then traded through the SECONDARY MARKET. If demand is significant, the syndicate may exercise a GREENSHOE and float more shares. See also ADD-ON, RIGHTS ISSUE.

INITIAL YIELD   The YIELD on an ASSET computed at the time of acquisition as the annual INCOME (DIVIDENDS, INTEREST) divided by the initial cost of acquiring the asset. See also YIELD TO MATURITY.

INLAND BILL   In the United Kingdom, a BILL OF EXCHANGE that is purely domestic in nature, being drawn and payable inside the country. Also known as AGENCY BILL. See also FOREIGN BILL.

INLAND REVENUE   See REVENUE AND CUSTOMS, HM.

INSIDE DIRECTOR   A board DIRECTOR who is related to the company and/or its executives in some manner, such as through previous employment, business or consulting relationship, or personal relationships. Inside directors are generally not considered to be independent for GOVERNANCE purposes. See also OUTSIDE DIRECTOR.

INSIDE INFORMATION   Any item of information pertinent to a public company that is not in the public domain. Such information must be treated as confidential by those in possession, and in many legal jurisdictions cannot be used to create a profit. Also known as NONPUBLIC INFORMATION, PRICE-SENSITIVE INFORMATION. See also INSIDER TRADING.

INSIDE MARKET   BIDS and OFFERS between DEALERS expressly for dealer accounts, rather than those intended for BROKERS or their clients.

INSIDER DEALING   See INSIDER TRADING.

INSIDER SYSTEM   A corporate ownership system where controlling interests (e.g., family stakes, large corporate or BANK shareholdings) limit the ability of outside INVESTORS to influence the GOVERNANCE or management processes. Insiders systems are most commonly found in Continental Europe, Southeast Asia, and parts of Latin America. See also OUTSIDER SYSTEM.

INSIDER TRADING   Any instance where NONPUBLIC INFORMATION is used to purchase or sell SECURITIES in order to generate a profit. In some systems insider trading is a criminal activity and is monitored and regulated; violators may be punished through fines, disgorgement of profits, and/or incarceration. In other systems it is not considered a crime and/or rules against insider trading are widely ignored. Also known as INSIDER DEALING. See also GUN JUMPING.

INSOLVENCY   A state where a company's LIABILITIES exceed the MARKET VALUE of its ASSETS (giving rise to NEGATIVE EQUITY) or when it cannot pay DEBTS falling due in the normal course of business. Insolvency generally leads to filing of VOLUNTARY BANKRUPTCY or INVOLUNTARY BANKRUPTCY. See also DEFAULT, EVENT OF DEFAULT, SOLVENCY.

INSOLVENCY CLAUSE   A clause in a REINSURANCE CONTRACT indicating that the REINSURER is still liable for its share of any CLAIM submitted by an INSURED, even if the insured's primary INSURER (i.e., the CEDING INSURER) is in a state of INSOLVENCY.

INSOLVENCY RISK   The RISK that a company will be unable to perform on contractual obligations as a result of impending INSOLVENCY, resulting in a DEFAULT. See also CREDIT DEFAULT RISK.

INSTALLMENT CREDIT   A form of secured or unsecured CREDIT used by consumers for the purchase of DURABLE GOODS. The installment credit process allows the consumer to take possession of the goods being acquired immediately, in exchange for a down payment or deposit plus an agreement to pay INTEREST and remaining PRINCIPAL over time. See also HIRE PURCHASE.

INSTALLMENT OPTION   An OVER-THE-COUNTER COMPLEX OPTION allowing the buyer to pay the seller PREMIUM in installments, rather than upfront, and to cancel the CONTRACT at any time by suspending remaining payments. If the buyer completes all required payments, the seller grants a conventional EUROPEAN OPTION with contract details as specified on the trade date.

INSTITUTIONAL BROKER   A BROKER that deals strictly with INSTITUTIONAL INVESTORS in matching ORDERS.

INSTITUTIONAL INVESTOR   A large, professional INVESTOR, such as a PENSION FUND, INSURANCE FUND, MUTUAL FUND, UNIT INVESTMENT TRUST or HEDGE FUND, which often deals on behalf of a large number of small investors. The largest institutional investors manage significant amounts of CAPITAL and can have a decisive impact on market prices. See also RETAIL INVESTOR.

INSURABLE INTEREST   The possibility that an individual or institution will sustain a monetary loss from an event that can be covered by INSURANCE. An insurable interest can be created through direct ownership or indirect CLAIM (e.g., vendor/vendee, MORTGAGOR/MORTGAGEE). In order for an insurance CONTRACT to be valid, insurable interest must exist at the time a contract starts and when a loss occurs. See also INDEMNITY.

INSURABLE RISK   A RISK event that produces a loss that is definable, fortuitous, noncatastrophic, and homogenous, and that can be transferred through payment of a reasonably priced PREMIUM. Risk events that do not feature such characteristics may not always be insurable as the cost of RISK TRANSFER may be prohibitively expensive. See also UNINSURABLE RISK.

INSURANCE   A legally binding ALEATORY CONTRACT between two parties (the INSURER as protection provider and the INSURED as protection purchaser) that exchanges an ex-ante PREMIUM for an ex-post financial SETTLEMENT in the event of loss from a specified PERIL. In general, an insurance contract must represent INSURABLE RISKS, the insured must have an INSURABLE INTEREST and demonstrate an actual economic loss when making a CLAIM, and the risk of loss must be specifically transferred under a contract providing INDEMNITY. The insurance contract is one of UBERRIMAE FIDEI, executed in "utmost good faith" through the conveyance of material REPRESENTATIONS, and defines the insured's rights, the insurer's OBLIGATIONS, terms of coverage, rights of SUBROGATION, exceptions, EXCLUSIONS, limitations, conditions, and expiry. Common contracts include health insurance, life insurance, LIABILITY INSURANCE, PROPERTY AND CASUALTY INSURANCE, PROPERTY AND LIABILITY INSURANCE, and BUSINESS INTERRUPTION INSURANCE. Also known as ASSURANCE, INSURANCE POLICY. See also INDEMNITY CONTRACT, VALUED CONTRACT.

INSURANCE AGENT   An AGENT that specializes in providing clients with advice on, and access to, various types of INSURANCE products and insurance solutions from one or several INSURERS. An agent that acts only in the interest of one insurer may be considered a captive agent or tied agent.

INSURANCE BROKER   A BROKER that specializes in providing clients with advice on, and access to, various types of INSURANCE products and insurance solutions from a large number of INSURERS, earning a COMMISSION that is often set as a percentage of any PREMIUM earned by the ultimate provider.

INSURANCE COMPANY   See INSURER.

INSURANCE-LINKED SECURITY (ILS)   A NOTE or BOND that securitizes INSURABLE RISK by transferring exposures to the CAPITAL MARKETS; most ISSUERS are INSURERS seeking to reduce risk within their PORTFOLIOS. An ILS is created when an insurer issues securities through a special-purpose reinsurer (SPR), who places them with INVESTORS and channels proceeds to a TRUSTEE for further reinvestment in the BOND market. Simultaneously, the SPR grants the insurer a REINSURANCE contract covering the specified risk. Payment of INVESTOR PRINCIPAL and/or INTEREST is dependent on losses arising from defined INSURANCE events; if losses exceed a predetermined threshold, the insurer may suspend payments, which has the net effect of creating a HEDGE against the underlying insurable risks. Suspension of payments is generally based on breach of a threshold defined via an INDEX TRIGGER, INDEMNITY TRIGGER, or PARAMETRIC TRIGGER. Most ILSs are based on catastrophic PERILS such as hurricanes, earthquakes, and windstorms. See also CATASTROPHE BOND, EXTREME MORTALITY BOND, LIFE ACQUISITION COST SECURITIZATION, MORTALITY BOND, MORTGAGE DEFAULT SECURITIZATION, RESIDUAL VALUE SECURITIZATION, WEATHER BOND.

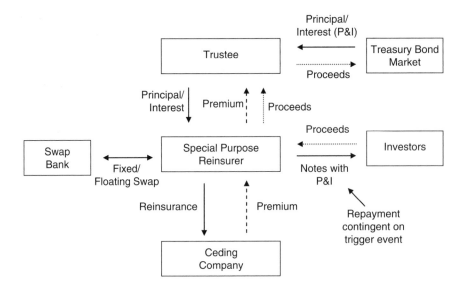

INSURANCE POLICY   See INSURANCE.

INSURED   A party in an INSURANCE CONTRACT that transfers, or CEDES, RISK to an INSURER by paying a PREMIUM. The amount of risk the insured cedes is typically a function of its own financial profile and its desire to retain or transfer specific types of risks. See also CEDING COMPANY. Also known as CEDANT (CEDENT).

INSURED PERIL   A PERIL that is specifically covered by an INSURANCE CONTRACT.

INSURER   A regulated institution that accepts the RISKS of INSUREDS or CEDANTS through the INSURANCE mechanism. In order to meet potential future LIABILITIES and cover EXPECTED LOSSES, an insurer manages the risk in its own operations through RISK POOLING, DIVERSIFICATION, and the purchase of REINSURANCE. To supplement EARNINGS from insurance UNDERWRITING activities, an insurer invests its ASSET PORTFOLIO in FIXED INCOME and EQUITY SECURITIES that generate INVESTMENT income and/ or CAPITAL GAINS. An insurer may be organized as a public company or a MUTUAL ORGANIZATION. Also known as ASSURER, INSURANCE COMPANY, PRIMARY INSURER. See also ADMITTED INSURER, NONADMITTED INSURER, REINSURER.

INTANGIBLE   See INTANGIBLE ASSET.

INTANGIBLE ASSET   An ASSET with value but without physical characteristics, such as GOODWILL, trademarks, copyrights, or intellectual property. Intangibles are generally heterogeneous across firms, and are typically very ILLIQUID. Also known as INTANGIBLE, INVISIBLE ASSET.

INTEGRATION   The third stage in the MONEY LAUNDERING process, in which the proceeds from layered transactions are used to enter into other seemingly common financial operations, such as redepositing layered proceeds into BANKS for further borrowing, lending to shell companies, and so forth. Once integrated, the ability of authorities to trace illicit funds becomes far more difficult.

INTELLECTUAL PROPERTY   A form of INTANGIBLE ASSET that typically includes patents, copyrights, brand names, trademarks, service marks, and images, which can be valued, licensed, or sold. In most countries a company's intellectual property is protected under the law, and any infringement can result in legal action and restitution.

INTENSITY MODEL   A form of CREDIT DEFAULT MODEL that estimates the time of a COUNTERPARTY'S failure with a particular intensity over an uncertain time horizon. Such models have no direct reference to a firm's value but derive the PROBABILITY of the event as an instantaneous likelihood of DEFAULT. See also STRUCTURAL MODEL, CREDIT MARK-TO-MARKET MODEL.

INTER-AMERICAN DEVELOPMENT BANK   A MULTILATERAL DEVELOPMENT BANK created in 1959 by Latin American nations to support economic and social progress and supply long-term development finance to member countries, modeled after the INTERNATIONAL BANK FOR RECONSTRUCTION AND DEVELOPMENT.

INTERBANK DEPOSIT   A DEPOSIT obligation issued by one BANK (the DEBTOR) to a second bank (the creditor). The deposit is generally short-term in nature, extending from overnight to several weeks, with a FLOATING RATE pegged to LIBOR, EONIA, EURIBOR, SONIA, TIBOR, or some other BENCHMARK rate. Funds from interbank deposits are generally held in a "due to" (VOSTRO/NOSTRO) account. Wholesale banks that lack a broad base of retail branches are often significant users of interbank deposits. See also HOT MONEY.

INTERBANK MARKET   The general marketplace for the pricing and TRADING of LIABILITIES of large BANKS.

INTERCONTINENTAL EXCHANGE (ICE)   A US-based electronic EXCHANGE created in 2000 to trade in energy-related DERIVATIVES, including standardized OVER-THE-COUNTER contracts and FUTURES. Through acquisition of the UK's International Petroleum Exchange and the New York Board of Trade the exchange has become a significant marketplace for trading in energy, SOFTS, and select financial UNDERLYINGS, including FOREIGN EXCHANGE and STOCK INDEXES.

INTER-DEALER BROKER (IDB)   A BROKER that deals exclusively with DEALERS and market professionals, rather than external clients. IDBs often execute their BROKERAGE business on a "blind" basis in order to preserve confidentiality about TRADES and positions in the competitive institutional marketplace.

INTEREST   (1) The amount paid or earned on DEBT CAPITAL that is borrowed or lent, based on a defined INTEREST RATE. (2) An ownership stake in a PARTNERSHIP or CORPORATION. See also COMPOUNDING, FUTURE VALUE, PRESENT VALUE, YIELD.

INTEREST ARBITRAGE   See COVERED INTEREST ARBITRAGE.

INTEREST COVERAGE   A financial indicator that measures a company's ability to manage its DEBT SERVICE, including payments of INTEREST, PRINCIPAL, and/or LEASE obligations. A company with good interest coverage demonstrates financial strength and flexibility, while one with weak cover may be susceptible to FINANCIAL DISTRESS. Interest cover is often computed through the TIMES INTEREST EARNED measure. See also DEBT SERVICE COVERAGE.

INTEREST COVERAGE TEST   An INTEREST-related financial test performed in a COLLATERALIZED DEBT OBLIGATION structure (or other SECURITAZATION) to determine whether the CASH FLOW WATERFALL can make payments to increasingly SUBORDINATED TRANCHES. The form of the test is given by:

(Interest due on COLLATERAL pool)/(Interest due on target TRANCHE + Interest due on all tranches ranking SENIOR to the target)

The test is considered successful if the interest coverage ratio is greater than or equal to the specified TRIGGER.

INTEREST EXPENSE   A COST that is incurred for borrowing money via LOANS, DEBT issuance, or certain other LIABILITIES. See also INTEREST INCOME.

INTEREST INCOME   INCOME that is generated by lending money or investing in FIXED INCOME SECURITIES. See also INTEREST EXPENSE.

INTEREST-ONLY MORTGAGE A type of MORTGAGE in which the BORROWER makes monthly payments which include INTEREST but no PRINCIPAL. The principal balance becomes due at MATURITY, implying that the mortgage is a form of BULLET LOAN.

INTEREST-ONLY (IO) STRIP   A component of a stripped MORTGAGE-BACKED SECURITY or COLLATERALIZED MORTGAGE OBLIGATION that is entitled only to INTEREST from the underlying SECURITIES; PRINCIPAL flows are redirected to the PRINCIPAL-ONLY (PO) STRIP. Unlike other FIXED INCOME securities, the price of an IO declines when INTEREST RATES decline since PREPAYMENTS increase and lead to a smaller amount of COUPON payments.

INTEREST RATE   The price of DEBT CAPITAL. For a BORROWER, it represents the cost of funds or the cost of borrowing; for INVESTORS or LENDERS it is the earning rate on capital invested or lent. Also known as RATE, RATE OF INTEREST.

INTEREST RATE CAP   See CAP.

INTEREST RATE DERIVATIVE An EXCHANGE-TRADED DERIVATIVE or OVER-THE-COUNTER DERIVATIVE with an UNDERLYING reference based on short-, medium- or long-term INTEREST RATES. An interest rate derivative may be structured as an INTEREST RATE FUTURE, interest rate OPTION, FORWARD RATE AGREEMENT, INTEREST RATE SWAP, or SWAPTION. See also CAP, CAPLET, CAPTION, COMMODITY DERIVATIVE, CREDIT DERIVATIVE, CURRENCY DERIVATIVE, FLOOR, FLOORLET, FLOORTION, PAYER SWAPTION, RECEIVER SWAPTION.

INTEREST RATE DIFFERENTIAL   The difference between the FORWARD RATES of two CURRENCIES. The interest rate differential can be determined via:

$$r_{diff} = \frac{FP(RB)(100)}{FX_s(t)}$$

where FP is the FORWARD POINTS, FX_s is the SPOT FOREIGN EXCHANGE rate, t is the time to maturity (days), and RB is the rate basis (e.g., 360, 365 days).

INTEREST RATE FLOOR   See FLOOR.

INTEREST RATE FORWARD   See FORWARD RATE AGREEMENT.

INTEREST RATE FUTURE   A FUTURES CONTRACT, bought or sold via an EXCHANGE, which references a short-term INTEREST RATE (such as a GOVERNMENT BILL rate or INTERBANK DEPOSIT rate) or a medium-term or long-term rate (generally a GOVERNMENT BOND rate). See also BILL FUTURE, BOND FUTURE, CURRENCY FUTURE, DEPOSIT FUTURE, INDEX FUTURE, INTEREST RATE FUTURE.

INTEREST RATE MARGIN   (1) The SPREAD charged by a BANK or other FINANCIAL INSTITUTION over and above its own cost of funding. (2) See NET INTEREST MARGIN.

INTEREST RATE OPTION An EXCHANGE-TRADED or OVER-THE-COUNTER OPTION involving an INTEREST RATE. VANILLA and COMPLEX OPTIONS can be bought and sold on various BENCHMARK rates, and may also form part of other structured DERIVATIVES, such as SWAPTIONS, CAPS, and FLOORS. See also COMMODITY OPTION, CURRENCY OPTION, EQUITY OPTION, INDEX OPTION.

INTEREST RATE PARITY A theory stating that the INTEREST RATE DIFFERENTIAL between two CURRENCIES approximates the difference between the FORWARD DISCOUNT or FORWARD PREMIUM implied in FOREIGN EXCHANGE RATES.

INTEREST RATE POLICY   A policy used by certain CENTRAL BANKS or monetary authorities that attempts to influence MONEY SUPPLY within a national system by setting the level of INTEREST RATES. This approach implies that properly calibrating rates and the money supply will lead to the proper balance of economic output and INFLATION. See also INFLATION TARGET.

INTEREST RATE RISK   The RISK of loss due to an adverse move in the direction of INTEREST RATES. Interest rate risk is a form of DIRECTIONAL RISK.

INTEREST RATE SWAP An OVER-THE-COUNTER SWAP involving the exchange of two INTEREST RATE references for periods ranging from less than 1 year to more than 10 years. An IRS is defined by specific terms that include the fixed swap rate, floating reference rate (e.g., LIBOR), payment frequency, term, and NOTIONAL amount. Under a standard IRS, the FIXED RATE payer receives the FLOATING RATE and pays the fixed rate, and so benefits from a rise in interest rates; the fixed rate receiver pays the floating rate and receives the fixed rate, and thus benefits from a decline in interest rates. A BASIS SWAP involves the exchange of two floating rates. Interest rate swaps do not involve the initial and final exchange of notional principal and thus feature less CREDIT RISK than CURRENCY SWAPS. Swaps are commonly used to HEDGE exposure to rates or take a specific view on the direction of rates and/or the shape of the YIELD CURVE.

INTERIM ACCOUNTS   See INTERIM FINANCIAL STATEMENTS.

INTERIM FINANCIAL STATEMENTS A set of FINANCIAL STATEMENTS produced by a company for a specific interim reporting period, which generally occurs quarterly or semiannually. Unlike a company's annual accounts, the interim statements may not be externally AUDITED. Also known as INTERIM ACCOUNTS.

INTERLOCKING DIRECTORATE See INTERLOCKING DIRECTORSHIP.

INTERLOCKING DIRECTORSHIP A practice where executives or DIRECTORS from one firm serve as DIRECTORS on another firm's board, and vice-versa. From a GOVERNANCE perspective this may create conflicts of interest and lack of independence. Also known as INTERLOCKING DIRECTORATE. See also FILZ.

INTERMARKET SPREAD A strategy that seeks to take advantage of price differences between two unique, though often related, markets or ASSETS; the SPREAD attempts to capitalize on movements in the spread, or BASIS, rather than the absolute direction or VOLATILITY, of the references.

INTERMARKET SWEEP ORDER In the United States, under REGULATION NMS, a LIMIT ORDER designated for automatic EXECUTION in a specified venue even when a better quote is available from another venue. In order to adhere to regulations, the order must be concurrently sent to the venues with better prices but is not subject to auto-routing.

INTERMARKET TRADING SYSTEM See NATIONAL MARKET SYSTEM.

INTERMEDIARY An institution that stands between two clients, or a client and a market, in the provision of financial services, including advice, EXECUTION, DEPOSIT-taking, and financing. Also known as FINANCIAL INTERMEDIARY.

INTERMEDIATION (1) A process or structure where a FINANCIAL INSTITUTION stands between the suppliers and users of CAPITAL (or other financial instruments, transactions, or ASSETS) helping arrange both sides in exchange for a fee. (2) A process where an originating BANK executes a financial transaction through another party rather than directly with the end-user; the INTERMEDIARY, rather than the bank, is thus exposed to the CREDIT RISK of the end-user. (1) See also DISINTERMEDIATION.

INTERNAL AUDIT A form of AUDIT performed within a company or other organization by its own AUDITORS. The purpose of such an audit is to verify the status of internal controls, rather than issue an AUDIT OPINION (which requires the use of an external auditor). See also EXTERNAL AUDIT.

INTERNAL CAPITAL ADEQUACY ASSESSMENT PROCESS (ICAAP) An element of PILLAR II of the BASLE II framework, in which a participating BANK creates appropriate GOVERNANCE and processes for reviewing all of its RISKS and its available CAPITAL resources, develops appropriate strategies, conducts STRESS TESTS, and documents its processes. These may be reviewed by the relevant national regulator through the SUPERVISORY REVIEW AND EVALUATION PROCESS.

INTERNAL CAPITAL GENERATION   The amount of CAPITAL a company generates through EARNINGS and allocates to its RETAINED EARNINGS account.

INTERNAL RATE OF RETURN (IRR)   The rate of INTEREST, compounded over each relevant period, which equates all net CASH FLOWS to the required outlay. IRR effectively measures the average YIELD or value of a project or financial INVESTMENT, and can be computed by setting the NET PRESENT VALUE to zero (breakeven) and solving for the rate that forces cash outflows and inflows to the breakeven NPV. It is also equivalent to the DISCOUNT RATE in a DISCOUNTED CASH FLOW computation, and YIELD TO MATURITY in a FIXED INCOME computation. IRR can be computed as the rate that solves the following equation:

$$\$0 = \sum_{t=1}^{N} \frac{CF_t}{(1+IRR)^t}$$

where CF_t is a cash flow in period t, N is the number of periods. See also PROFITABILITY INDEX.

INTERNAL RATINGS-BASED (IRB) APPROACH   A method of computing CREDIT RISK exposures under PILLAR I of BASLE II, which allows an institution to select between the: FOUNDATION METHODOLOGY (where it develops an internal model to compute PROBABILITY OF DEFAULT but accepts from its regulatory supervisor the LOSS-GIVEN DEFAULT, EXPOSURE AT DEFAULT, and MATURITY parameters) to determine the appropriate RISK weighting; and the ADVANCED METHODOLOGY (where it develops all of the required parameters internally). See also STANDARDIZED APPROACH.

INTERNAL REVENUE SERVICE (IRS)   In the United States, an agency of the Federal Government under the Department of Treasury that is responsible for TAX collection and application of the internal revenue laws. Created in 1862 and reorganized at various points, including 1998, the IRS now operates through 4 distinct divisions focused on large/medium businesses, small businesses/self-employed persons, wages and investment (individuals), and tax-exempt organizations.

INTERNATIONAL ACCOUNTING STANDARDS (IAS) A body of ACCOUNTING rules, adopted by PUBLIC COMPANIES in many countries, intended to create uniform treatment of activities impacting the BALANCE SHEET, INCOME STATEMENT, and STATEMENT OF CASH FLOWS. IAS has been subsumed by INTERNATIONAL FINANCIAL REPORTING STANDARDS. See also GENERALLY ACCEPTED ACCOUNTING PRINCIPLES.

INTERNATIONAL ACCOUNTING STANDARDS BOARD (IASB)   The international advisory panel that is responsible for creating and promulgating accounting standards and interpretations, in conjunction with the International ACCOUNTING Standards Committee Foundation, known collectively as INTERNATIONAL FINANCIAL REPORTING STANDARDS. The IASB also adopted all previously developed INTERNATIONAL ACCOUNTING STANDARDS developed by its predecessor organization, the International Accounting Standards Committee. See also FINANCIAL ACCOUNTING STANDARDS BOARD.

INTERNATIONAL BANK FOR RECONSTRUCTION AND DEVELOPMENT (IBRD) A MULTILATERAL DEVELOPMENT BANK established in 1946 to help reconstruct postwar economies and promote economic development and stability. The IBRD makes LOANS to public sector BORROWERS and state-GUARANTEED projects, and is funded by member countries through CURRENCIES, GOLD, and open call CAPITAL. Also known as WORLD BANK. See also INTERNATIONAL FINANCE CORPORATION (IFC).

INTERNATIONAL BANKING FACILITY (IBF) An international banking center within a US BANK that is permitted by the FEDERAL RESERVE BOARD to participate in EUROCURRENCY lending and accept RESERVE-free offshore DEPOSITS. The IBF is competitive with other offshore transactions as business is not subject to FEDERAL DEPOSIT INSURANCE CORPORATION PREMIUM payments and INTEREST on deposits payable to foreign depositors is exempt from withholding TAXES.

INTERNATIONAL DEPOSITORY RECEIPT (IDR) See GLOBAL DEPOSITORY RECEIPT.

INTERNATIONAL FINANCE CORPORATION (IFC) An international INVESTMENT BANK, created in 1956 as an affiliate of the INTERNATIONAL BANK FOR RECONSTRUCTION AND DEVELOPMENT (IBRD), which is responsible for making development LOANS to private sector BORROWERS, primarily in LESSER DEVELOPED COUNTRIES and NEWLY INDUSTRIALIZED COUNTRIES.

INTERNATIONAL FINANCIAL REPORTING STANDARDS (IFRS) A series of standards and interpretations promulgated by the INTERNATIONAL ACCOUNTING STANDARDS BOARD that address key ACCOUNTING issues, and which are increasingly adopted as a global standard. IFRS has adopted the standards previously set forth via the INTERNATIONAL ACCOUNTING STANDARDS.

INTERNATIONAL MONETARY FUND (IMF) A supranational organization created in 1946 to assist in maintaining financial stability and administer the fixed FOREIGN EXCHANGE RATE regime that existed until 1971. The IMF now focuses on granting LOANS, managing external DEBT programs (via the Supplemental Reserve Facility and Country Credit Line program), and creating stability plans for DEBTOR nations. The organization is financed via subscriptions from member countries.

INTERNATIONAL ORGANIZATION OF SECURITIES COMMISSIONS (IOSCO) An agency, formed in 1983, comprised of national SECURITIES REGULATORS, that addresses issues related to consistent REGULATION and surveillance of securities markets and enforcement of securities laws.

INTERNATIONAL SECURITIES IDENTIFICATION NUMBER (ISIN) A 12-digit SECURITY identification code developed by the International Standards Organization. The first 2 digits represent a country code, the next 9 characters represent a national securities identifier code (unique to each country) and the final digit serves as a check. See also COMMITTEE ON UNIFORM SECURITIES IDENTIFICATION PROCEDURES, CUSIP INTERNATIONAL NUMBER, STOCK EXCHANGE DAILY OFFICIAL LIST.

INTERNATIONAL SECURITIES MARKETS ASSOCIATION (ISMA) An industry trade group representing the SECONDARY TRADING marketplace for international BONDS. The ISMA is responsible for establishing and promulgating the bond-dealing practices and pricing and SETTLEMENT conventions, which are widely used in the international bond markets.

INTERNATIONAL SWAPS AND DERIVATIVES ASSOCIATION (ISDA) An industry trade group created in 1985 to represent the interests of the OVER-THE-COUNTER DERIVATIVES marketplace. ISDA has been instrumental in developing and advancing key product and RISK MANAGEMENT mechanisms, including NETTING and MASTER AGREEMENTS.

INTERPOLATION A mathematical method for computing missing or unobserved INTEREST RATES along the YIELD CURVE. A point can be interpolated using LINEAR INTERPOLATION, EXPONENTIAL INTERPOLATION, or CUBIC SPLINE INTERPOLATION. Also known as YIELD CURVE INTERPOLATION.

INTERPOSITIONING The act of placing a BROKER or SPECIALIST between two PRINCIPALS to facilitate a TRADE. Interpositioning is illegal when a broker intercedes simply to generate additional COMMISSIONS, or when a specialist intercedes to take one side of the TRADE for proprietary purposes. See also AFFIRMATIVE OBLIGATION, NEGATIVE OBLIGATION.

INTERVENTION The process used by CENTRAL BANKS or monetary authorities to purchase or sell a CURRENCY in the FOREIGN EXCHANGE markets in order to influence its value. Intervention is generally taken by a country to support the value of its currency (i.e., purchasing the national currency and selling a foreign currency from its RESERVE holdings, directly or via CURRENCY SWAPS), though the reverse may also occur when the home currency is considered to be overvalued and negatively impacting on EXPORT flows.

INTRADAY LIMIT (1) A price band on an ASSET traded on an EXCHANGE that cannot be exceeded. (2) A RISK limit granted by a BANK or other financial institution to a COUNTERPARTY or to its own proprietary TRADING operation that can be used during a single trading day. In most instances any resulting risk exposure must be reduced or flattened by the close of business.

INTRINSIC VALUE   (1) One of two components, along with TIME VALUE, comprising the value of an OPTION. Intrinsic value measures the current MONEYNESS of an option, or the difference between the STRIKE PRICE and the UNDERLYING reference price. A CONTRACT that is IN-THE-MONEY has intrinsic value and can be EXERCISED for an immediate gain; one that is OUT-OF-THE-MONEY or AT-THE-MONEY has no intrinsic value. (2) The inherent worth of a particular object.

INTRODUCING BROKER   An INTERMEDIARY standing between a client and a FUTURES COMMISSION MERCHANT (FCM) that develops and executes client strategies. Since the introducing broker cannot hold customer funds, it must deal through an FCM, which has proper authority.

INVENTORY   ASSETS on the corporate BALANCE SHEET that are ultimately used to meet customer DEMAND. In general, companies attempt to minimize their inventories so that they can deploy their ASSETS in other productive endeavors; however, they must balance this against the need to provide customers with finished goods as needed. The cost of holding inventory is a combination of the cost of FINANCING and storage, cost of obsolescence, and the OPPORTUNITY COSTS associated with CAPITAL deployment. Inventory is typically classified in one of three categories that reflect their degree of completion, including RAW MATERIAL INVENTORY, WORK-IN-PROCESS INVENTORY and FINISHED GOODS INVENTORY. See also INVENTORY FINANCING, INVENTORY TURNOVER.

INVENTORY FINANCING   A WORKING CAPITAL LOAN used to finance the purchase of INVENTORY that a company ultimately uses for production and sales to customers. The proceeds of the inventory sale are typically used to repay the loan, making the transaction self-liquidating. Inventory financing may be secured or unsecured; if secured, the loan may include a charge over specific inventory or a FLOATING LIEN applicable to inventories in general.

INVENTORY TURNOVER   A measure of a company's ability to sell INVENTORIES of finished goods, typically calculated as:

$$INV_{TO} = \frac{CGS}{INV_{AVG}}$$

where CGS is the COST OF GOODS SOLD, and INV_{AVG} is average inventory on hand during the period.

A high turnover ratio is generally an indication of efficiency in managing the inventory process.

INVERSE FLOATER SWAP An OVER-THE-COUNTER COMPLEX SWAP involving the exchange of a FIXED RATE and an inverse rate defined by the general form [x% – FLOATING RATE]. The payment flows add a degree of LEVERAGE, making the transaction far more sensitive to rate changes than a standard INTEREST RATE SWAP. Also known as REVERSE FLOATER SWAP. See also INVERSE FLOATING RATE NOTE.

INVERSE FLOATING RATE NOTE (FRN) A STRUCTURED NOTE that provides the INVESTOR with a COUPON based on an inverse INTEREST RATE, generally defined by the form [x% – FLOATING RATE]; rising rates create a lower interest coupon and falling rates a higher coupon. The inverse nature of the payment adds a degree of LEVERAGE to the structure, making it far more sensitive to changes in rates. Also known as REVERSE FLOATING RATE NOTE. See also CAPPED FLOATING RATE NOTE, INVERSE FLOATER SWAP, PERPETUAL FLOATING RATE NOTE, RANGE FLOATING RATE NOTE.

INVERTED YIELD CURVE See NEGATIVE YIELD CURVE.

INVESTING CASH FLOW The portion of the STATEMENT OF CASH FLOWS depicting the flows impacting a firm's ASSET and INVESTMENT accounts, including additions to, or disposals of, property, plant and equipment, MARKETABLE SECURITIES, and other corporate or SUBSIDIARY interests. See also FINANCING CASH FLOW, OPERATING CASH FLOW.

INVESTMENT An allocation of CAPITAL by an INVESTOR in real or financial ASSETS in expectation of a fair RETURN.

INVESTMENT ADVISOR A FIDUCIARY that acts as an AGENT for an investing client, ensuring all business is transacted in the best interests of that client. In most jurisdictions investment advisors must be registered with REGULATORS and disclose any conflicts of interest they may have in providing particular investment recommendations. See also BROKER.

INVESTMENT ANALYST An analyst working for a BANK or other FINANCIAL INSTITUTION that is responsible for analyzing the financial state and prospects of a company that is an ISSUER of EQUITY or DEBT, with a view toward developing a recommendation on whether to buy, sell, or retain a position in the issuer's SECURITIES. Investment analysts rely on FINANCIAL ANALYSIS, FUNDAMENTAL ANALYSIS, and/or TECHNICAL ANALYSIS to develop their recommendations. See also CREDIT ANALYST, EQUITY ANALYST.

INVESTMENT BANK In the United States, a BANK that provides clients with CORPORATE FINANCE, RISK MANAGEMENT, and investment management advice, and deals actively in securities UNDERWRITING and TRADING. Unlike a COMMERCIAL BANK, an investment bank does not typically accept DEPOSITS or grant LOANS as a main line of business (although certain investment banks hold commercial bank licenses and perform the functions as an additional business line). Pure investment banks are relatively few in number, as many of those that have traditionally occupied the sector have converted into BANK HOLDING COMPANIES. See also BOUTIQUE, MERCHANT BANK, UNIVERSAL BANK.

INVESTMENT BANKER   A BANKER working at an INVESTMENT BANK, MERCHANT BANK, or BOUTIQUE that is primarily involved in CORPORATE FINANCE, MERGERS and ACQUISITIONS, or CAPITAL MARKETS financings. See also BANKER, FINANCIER, PRIVATE BANKER.

INVESTMENT COMPANY   A registered company that raises CAPITAL from INVESTORS by selling SHARES or units, and invests in a range of ASSETS on a LEVERAGED of unleveraged basis. In the United States, MUTUAL FUNDS (OPEN-END FUNDS) and UNIT INVESTMENT TRUSTS (CLOSED-END FUNDS) are the most popular forms of investment companies; in the United Kingdom, UNIT TRUSTS and INVESTMENT TRUSTS perform a similar function.

INVESTMENT CREDIT PROGRAM   A tax-advantaged LOSS-SENSITIVE INSURANCE CONTRACT that contains elements of RISK FINANCING and RISK TRANSFER. Under the program the INSURED pays the INSURER an amount intended to cover EXPECTED LOSSES up to a desired DEDUCTIBLE. Funds are placed in a TRUST account and used to finance losses as they occur. If the trust account moves into deficit, the insured pays an additional PREMIUM, and if it builds to a surplus, it receives the excess. Since funds are held in trust (and cannot be withdrawn by the insured) INVESTMENT earnings are not taxed.

INVESTMENT GRADE   A CREDIT RATING designation applied to any ISSUER of SECURITIES that is rated between AAA and BBB– by Standard and Poor's, or Aaa and Baa3 by Moody's Investors Services. Investment grade companies have the strongest financial profiles and the lowest likelihood of encountering FINANCIAL DISTRESS leading to DEFAULT. See also SUBINVESTMENT GRADE.

INVESTMENT INCOME   Any form of INCOME generated from INVEST-MENT activities, which may include DIVIDENDS, INTEREST, and/or CAPITAL GAINS.

INVESTMENT LETTER   In the United States, a document between the buyer and seller of a PRIVATE PLACEMENT indicating that SECURITIES will not be offered for resale to the general public for a specific period of time; once the time period passes, they may be sold to a limited population under Rule 144A of the SECURITIES AND EXCHANGE COMMISSION.

INVESTMENT MANAGEMENT   See ASSET MANAGEMENT.

INVESTMENT MANAGER   See PORTFOLIO MANAGER.

INVESTMENT-ORIENTED INSURANCE   An INSURANCE policy that features a cash value even if a predefined INSURABLE RISK event does not occur, distinguishing it from a standard PURE RISK insurance policy. The main invest-ment-oriented insurance products include cash value life insurance (whole life, variable life, universal life), and ANNUITIES (variable, fixed, GUARANTEED INVESTMENT CONTRACT). In the case of whole life insurance, universal life insurance, guaranteed investment contracts, and fixed annuities, the INSURER bears the MARKET RISK of the cash value investment (providing the INSURED with a *de-facto* GUARANTEE), while with variable life insurance and variable annuities, the insured bears the risk.

INVESTMENT PORTFOLIO   See PORTFOLIO.

INVESTMENT PREMIUM   The additional amount an INVESTOR pays over the INVESTMENT VALUE of a CONVERTIBLE BOND to reflect the EQUITY OPTION features of the convertible; the premium is typically expressed as a percentage of investment value:

$$IPrem = \left(\frac{P_{CB}}{IV} - 1 \right)(100\%)$$

where P_{CB} is the price of the convertible bond and IV is investment value. Also known as BOND PREMIUM. See also CONVERSION PREMIUM.

INVESTMENT RATIO   In INSURANCE, a measure of the extent to which an INSURER's gains come from INVESTMENT, rather than UNDERWRITING, activities, typically computed as:

$$IR = \frac{Inv}{Pr}$$

where Inv is gain on PORTFOLIO investments and Pr is PREMIUM earned.

The higher the ratio, the greater the insurer's reliance on investment income rather than core insurance underwriting.

INVESTMENT TRUST   (1) In the United Kingdom, a PUBLIC LIMITED COMPANY traded on an EXCHANGE that raises CAPITAL through the placement of COMMON STOCK and DEBENTURES and invests the funds in a range of financial ASSETS. Since investment trusts are permitted to issue debentures they can invest on a LEVERAGED basis, magnifying potential gains and losses. (2) In the United States, see CLOSED-END FUND. (1,2) See also INVESTMENT COMPANY, MUTUAL FUND.

INVESTMENT VALUE   The value of a CONVERTIBLE BOND if no EQUITY conversion rights existed, i.e., the equivalent straight BOND with identical MATURITY and COUPON. Knowledge of investment value allows INVESTORS to determine the theoretical price of the equity OPTION embedded in the convertible bond. Also known as PURE BOND VALUE. See also CONVERSION PARITY, INVESTMENT PREMIUM.

INVESTOR   Any party that provides CAPITAL in expectation of a future RETURN. See also INSTITUTIONAL INVESTOR, INVESTMENT, RETAIL INVESTOR.

INVISIBLE ASSET   See INTANGIBLE ASSET.

INVISIBLE BALANCE   See INVISIBLES.

INVISIBLES   International TRADE involving services rather than goods; invisible EXPORTS include sales of services to nonresidents, while invisible IMPORTS are based on the purchase of services from nonresidents. Key items within the invisibles account include transportation, banking, INSURANCE, ACCOUNTING, legal services, medical practices, and hotel/leisure services. Invisibles are a key element of a country's BALANCE OF TRADE and BALANCE OF PAYMENTS accounts. Also known as INVISIBLE BALANCE. See also VISIBLE.

INVOICE PRICE   The total amount the buyer of a BOND pays the seller; in most markets this is the bond's current market value plus ACCRUED INTEREST (i.e., the DIRTY PRICE).

INVOLUNTARY BANKRUPTCY   A process where CREDITORS file a petition to force a DEBTOR into BANKRUPTCY after the debtor commits an "act of bankruptcy," generally a DEFAULT on a payment due. If the court accepts the petition the proceedings follow those established for LIQUIDATION or REORGANIZATION under VOLUNTARY BANKRUPTCY.

IO   See INTEREST-ONLY STRIP.

IOI   See INDICATION OF INTEREST.

IOSCO   See   INTERNATIONAL   ORGANIZATION   OF   SECURITIES COMMISSIONS.

IPO   See INITIAL PUBLIC OFFERING.

IRA   See INDIVIDUAL RETIREMENT ACCOUNT.

IRB APPROACH   See INTERNAL RATINGS-BASED APPROACH.

IRISH ASSET COVERED SECURITIES   In Ireland, a form of COVERED BOND backed by MORTGAGES and issued by designated CREDIT institutions.

IRR   See INTERNAL RATE OF RETURN.

IRRATIONAL OPTION   An OPTION embedded in a STRUCTURED NOTE, such as CONVERTIBLE BOND or MORTGAGE-BACKED SECURITY, that is not EXERCISED when it is IN-THE-MONEY, or which is exercised when it is OUT-OF-THE-MONEY. The reasons for irrational exercise may relate to over-arching macroeconomic or idiosyncratic factors that override pure economic rationale.

IRREDEEMABLE SECURITY   A SECURITY without a final MATURITY date, such as a PERPETUAL BOND, PERPETUAL DEBENTURE, or a CONSOL. This includes undated securities that are redeemable at the option of the BORROWER/ISSUER, but in practice are allowed to remain outstanding.

IRREVOCABLE LETTER OF CREDIT   A LETTER OF CREDIT that can only be cancelled by agreement of both parties (i.e., the DRAWER and the BANK).

The facility remains in place until mutual cancellation or final MATURITY. See also CONFIRMED LETTER OF CREDIT, DIRECT PAY LETTER OF CREDIT, STANDBY LETTER OF CREDIT, TRANSFERABLE LETTER OF CREDIT.

IRS   See INTERNAL REVENUE SERVICE.

ISA   See INDIVIDUAL SAVINGS ACCOUNT.

ISA MORTGAGE   In the United Kingdom, a form of INTEREST-ONLY MORTGAGE where the BORROWER makes monthly INTEREST payments but no PRINCIPAL payments. In lieu of a principal payment, the borrower makes a DEPOSIT into an INDIVIDUAL SAVINGS ACCOUNT (ISA), the balance of which is used to repay outstanding principal at MATURITY of the mortgage.

ISDA   See INTERNATIONAL SWAPS AND DERIVATIVES ASSOCIATION.

ISIN   See INTERNATIONAL SECURITIES IDENTIFICATION NUMBER.

ISLAMIC FINANCE   A general form of structured FINANCE followed in Islamic countries that adheres to religious interpretations and legal rulings related to permissible financing and INVESTMENT. Under Islamic finance all contracts, including those of a financial nature, are permissible unless they are characterized by one or both of RIBA (interest) and GHARAR (uncertainty), which renders them null and void. Islamic finance permits trading of goods or ASSETS today for a sum of money in the future (a *de-facto* credit sale) or the trading of money today for goods or assets in the future (a prepaid FORWARD) where the sale of an asset under one CONTRACT is matched by the purchase of the asset under a second contract for a value that is greater. It prohibits the trading of goods or assets in the future for money in the future (a *de-facto* FUTURE or FORWARD contract). Common structural techniques include the SALAM (prepaid forward), IJARA (secured LEASE), MURABAHA (TRUST sale), and SUKUK (rent certificate). Though interest cannot explicitly govern such transactions, it can be defined as a profit in a credit sale or rent in a LEASE, and may be benchmarked to a recognized market rate, such as LIBOR. Also known as ALTERNATIVE FINANCE ARRANGEMENTS. See also HALAL, HARAAM, MUDARABA, MUSHARAKA.

ISMA   See INTERNATIONAL SECURITIES MARKETS ASSOCIATION.

ISSUE DATE   The date on a SECURITY which is used in the computation of ACCRUED INTEREST.

ISSUE PRICE   The price at which a NEW ISSUE of SECURITIES is offered by a SYNDICATE or UNDERWRITING GROUP to the market. The price is generally established between the underwriters and the ISSUER based on analysis of INDICATIONS OF INTEREST, COMPARABLES, and general market conditions. Also known as OFFER PRICE.

ISSUED AND OUTSTANDING   See OUTSTANDING SHARES.

ISSUER   Any corporate or sovereign entity that floats SECURITIES in the CAPITAL MARKETS.

ITAYOSE   [JPN] In the Japanese financial markets, a method of establishing a market clearing price based on submitted ORDERS. This occurs when a provisional price on a COMMODITY or ASSET is submitted to floor members, who revert with BIDS and OFFERS, which are then taken into account in establishing the initial clearing price. This mechanism assigns full priority to price without regard to the time orders are placed.

ITRAXX INDEXES   Standard quoted CREDIT DEFAULT SWAP INDEXES, which include REFERENCE CREDIT POOLS divided by region or sector (index level) and industry/rating/country (subindex level). CREDIT DEFAULT SWAPS and INDEX TRANCHES referencing the Dow Jones iTraxx/CDX indexes represent a standardized way of gaining exposure to, or HEDGING against, diverse pools of CREDIT. A new reference index is created every 6 months; reference credits comprising the index, which are all equally weighted, are reviewed prior to the launch of each new 6-month series, and any credits that are seen to be deteriorating rapidly or are in a state of FINANCIAL DISTRESS are removed.

Index	Region	Main index	Subindexes
DJ CDX North America – Investment grade	North America	125 corporate credits	Consumer, energy, financials, industrials, technology, high volatility
DJ CDX North America – High yield	North America	100 corporate credits	BB, B, High Beta
DJ iTraxx Europe	Europe	125 corporate credits	Autos, consumers, consumer cyclicals, nonconsumer cyclicals, energy, senior financials, subordinate financials, industrials, technology, large corporates, lower-rated corporates, high volatility
DJ iTraxx Japan	Japan	50 corporate credits	Capital goods, financials, technology, high volatility
DJ iTraxx Asia ex-Japan	Asia ex-Japan	50 corporate and sovereign credits	China and Taiwan, Korea, rest of ex-Japan Asia
DJ iTraxx Australia	Australia	25 corporate credits	n/a
DJ CDX Emerging Markets	Emerging markets	15 sovereign credits	n/a
DJ CDX Emerging Markets Diversified	Emerging markets	40 sovereign and corporate credits	Asia, Eastern Europe, Latin America

J

J-CURVE (1) The theoretical REVENUE profile of a PRIVATE EQUITY or VENTURE CAPITAL INVESTMENT over time, which begins at zero, becomes negative as CAPITAL is invested, and then becomes positive as a venture solidifies its business structure and starts to generate revenues. (2) In foreign TRADE, the evolution of BALANCE OF PAYMENTS (BOP) over time, where an initial DEVALUATION results in a BOP deficit as IMPORTS continue to flow into the country, but which eventually reverses into a surplus as cheaper EXPORTS resulting from the devaluation take hold.

JANUARY EFFECT An observable condition in the STOCK market that appears to reflect rallies, particularly in SMALL CAP and MID-CAP STOCKS, at the beginning of each year; some of the buying support may come from a reversal of positions that are sold in December to crystallize any TAX losses to offset CAPITAL GAINS.

JAPANESE GOVERNMENT BOND (JGB) The general category of SECURITIES issued by the Japanese government for general financing and MONETARY POLICY purposes. JGBs, denominated in Japanese yen, are issued as DISCOUNT bills with MATURITIES of less than one year, and COUPON-bearing instruments with medium-term maturities (i.e., 5 and 10 years, the latter constituting the BENCHMARK) and long-term maturities (i.e., the 20-year "super-long" bond). Securities are issued through a SYNDICATE of DEALERS and through an AUCTION MARKET process; SECONDARY MARKET trading is heavily concentrated in the 10-year BENCHMARK and a small number of associated issues.

JENSEN INDEX A common measure of the RISK-adjusted performance of an INVESTMENT PORTFOLIO that compares the average RETURN on the portfolio with the risk of the portfolio, as measured through BETA. The Jensen index, which uses the SECURITY MARKET LINE as a BENCHMARK, can be computed via:

$$JI = E(r_p) - (E(r_f) + (E(r_m) - E(r_f)) \beta_p)$$

where $E(r_p)$ is an estimate of the expected return of the target portfolio, $E(r_f)$ is the RISK-FREE RATE, $E(r_m)$ is the expected average return of the market portfolio, and β_p is the beta of the target portfolio. See also TREYNOR INDEX, SHARPE INDEX.

Additional reference: Jensen (1969).

JGB See JAPANESE GOVERNMENT BOND.

JOBBER [COL] An individual or institution that takes positions in SECURITIES, generally on a very short-term basis, in expectation of generating profits. A jobber may or may not also be an authorized MARKET MAKER. See also JOBBING.

JOBBING [COL] The practice of continuously buying and selling SECURITIES or other ASSETS in an attempt to make small profits. See also JOBBER.

JOINT AND SEVERAL A legal condition where multiple GUARANTORS, BORROWERS, or obligors are liable for the entire amount of an agreed LIABILITY should the other party (or parties) fail to perform. Any party to a joint and several transaction can be sued for nonpayment. See also SEVERAL BUT NOT JOINT.

JOINT BOND A BOND where payment of INTEREST and/or PRINCIPAL is the legal responsibility of more than one party, such as an issuing SUBSIDIARY and its parent company.

JOINT STOCK COMPANY In the United Kingdom, a form of corporate organization where INVESTORS pool their CAPITAL and trade it jointly rather than individually. Such organizations were popular during the seventeenth century but are now relatively uncommon. See also CORPORATION, PUBLIC LIMITED COMPANY.

J

JOINT VENTURE (JV) A contractual arrangement between two or more CORPORATIONS or business organizations to participate in the development and production of specific goods, services, or intellectual property. The parties to the joint venture may agree to provide specific resources, expertise and/or CAPITAL, and share in revenues and expenses on an agreed basis. The JV may have a finite life, exist in perpetuity, or become cancellable at the option of one or both parties.

JOURNAL ENTRY The recording of financial data related to a particular transaction. In a DOUBLE ENTRY ACCOUNTING system the journal entry involves both a DEBIT and a CREDIT.

JUMBO PFANDBRIEFE Any PFANDBRIEFE issue that has a minimum size of EUR1 billion, designed to ensure there is enough volume to promote liquid SECONDARY TRADING.

JUMP PROCESS A mathematical process used to describe the movement of ASSET prices that are impacted by sudden, discontinuous moves, such as those generated by EVENT RISKS. Certain OPTION pricing models utilize a jump process, rather than a continuous STOCHASTIC PROCESS, to estimate values. See also JUMP-TO-DEFAULT.

JUMP-TO-DEFAULT A JUMP PROCESS that is used in the CREDIT markets to reflect the fact that a company may DEFAULT on its DEBT instantaneously, causing a sharp and rapid downward jump in the price of its LIABILITIES to default-based levels.

JUNIOR DEBT See SUBORDINATED DEBT.

JUNIOR SUBORDINATED DEBENTURE A type of HYBRID CAPITAL SECURITY where an ISSUER (often a BANK), places junior ranking SUBORDINATED DEBT with INVESTORS directly or via a TRUST, paying periodic COUPONS over the life of the security, which may range from 60 years to perpetuity. Most issues feature OPTIONAL REDEMPTION and qualify as REGULATORY CAPITAL. The securities have a ranking in DEFAULT that is senior to COMMON STOCK and PREFERRED STOCK and PARI PASSU to other junior subordinated debt. See also PERPETUAL PREFERRED STOCK, TRUST PREFERRED STOCK.

JUNIOR SUBORDINATED DEBT The lowest ranking form of JUNIOR DEBT. Junior subordinated claims receive payment after junior INVESTORS or CREDITORS, but before EQUITY investors.

JUNK BOND   [COL] See HIGH-YIELD BOND.

JV   See JOINT VENTURE.

K

KABUSHIKI KAISHI (KK) [JAP] In Japan, a PUBLIC COMPANY.

KAFFIRS [COL] The COMMON STOCK of South African gold mining companies listed and traded in the UK stock market on a direct basis, and in the US market via AMERICAN DEPOSITORY RECEIPTS and AMERICAN DEPOSITORY SHARES. See also KANGAROOS.

KANGAROOS [COL] The COMMON STOCK of Australian companies listed and traded on the LONDON STOCK EXCHANGE. See also KAFFIRS.

KAPPA See VEGA.

KEEPWELL AGREEMENT A CONTRACT or GUARANTEE between a PARENT company or HOLDING COMPANY and its AFFILIATE or SUBSIDIARY agreeing to maintain a certain level of ownership and/or financial SOLVENCY for a stated period of time.

KEIDANREN [JPN] The Japan Business Federation, created in 2002 from the merger of the Japan Federation of Economic Organizations and the Japan Federation of Employers' Associations, which acts as a representative for companies, industrial associations, and regional economic organizations on important business-related matters. Also known as NIPPON KEIDANREN.

KEIRETSU [JPN] A Japanese business conglomerate, generally comprised of a series of companies with cross-SHAREHOLDINGS and business relationships but no central core company. A main BANK generally serves as a provider of funding and *de-facto* corporate monitor. The keiretsu replaced the centralized ZAIBATSU conglomerate that existed until the mid-1940s. See also CHAEBOL.

KEOGH PLAN In the United States, a TAX-deferred PENSION account that can be established by self-employed individuals or small, unincorporated businesses. Funds in the account are taxable upon withdrawal, but generally occur when the BENEFICIAL OWNER is retired, and thus in a lower tax bracket. See also INDIVIDUAL RETIREMENT ACCOUNT.

KEY MAN RISK The RISK arising from the departure of a person or team that is critically responsible for a vital management or business function within a company. Excessive reliance on such an individual(s) can lead to loss of REVENUES and/or an increase in PROCESS RISK.

KEYNESIAN ECONOMICS A theory of MACROECONOMICS developed by economist John Keynes in the twentieth century that supports the notion of government intervention in economic progress (via FISCAL POLICY and MONETARY POLICY) in order to overcome any suboptimal decisions taken by the private sector. See also CLASSICAL ECONOMICS, KEYNESIAN FORMULA.

Additional reference: Keynes (1936).

KEYNESIAN FORMULA   A general MACROECONOMIC equation developed by economist John Keynes, which is given as:

$$Y = C + I + G + (X - M)$$

where Y is GROSS DOMESTIC PRODUCT (or AGGREGATE DEMAND), C is consumption (or personal income less TAXES less amount not saved), I is INVESTMENT, G is government spending, X is EXPORTS, M is IMPORTS.

KICK-IN OPTION   See REVERSE KNOCK-IN OPTION.

KICK-OUT OPTION   See REVERSE KNOCK-OUT OPTION.

KICKER   [COL] An EQUITY stake offered by a company to a BANK providing LOAN funding or an INVESTOR supplying CAPITAL through a NOTE or BOND. Although the compensation can take different forms, in practice it is often provided in the form of a WARRANT, generating gains if the company's STOCK price rises. Also known as EQUITY KICKER, SWEETENER. See also CARROT EQUITY.

KILLER BEES   [COL] Investment bankers hired by a company to help defend against a HOSTILE TAKEOVER.

KINKED YIELD CURVE   A TERM STRUCTURE where short-term INTEREST RATES and long-term interest rates are approximately equal, but medium-term rates are higher. See also FLAT YIELD CURVE, NEGATIVE YIELD CURVE, POSITIVE YIELD CURVE, YIELD CURVE.

KITING   See CHECK KITING.

KIWI   [COL] (1) A BOND, NOTE, or CERTIFICATE OF DEPOSIT issued in New Zealand dollars in the New Zealand markets by a foreign company or BANK. (2) The New Zealand dollar.

KK   See KABUSHIKI KAISHI.

KNOCK-IN OPTION   A COMPLEX OPTION that leads to the creation of a EUROPEAN OPTION if the price of the UNDERLYING market reference moves above or below a predefined BARRIER level. See also BARRIER OPTION, DOWN AND IN OPTION, UP AND IN OPTION.

KNOCK-OUT OPTION   A COMPLEX OPTION that extinguishes a EUROPEAN OPTION if the price of the UNDERLYING reference moves above/below a predefined BARRIER level. See also BARRIER OPTION, DOWN AND OUT OPTION, UP AND OUT OPTION.

KONDRATIEFF WAVE   An observation put forth by Russian economist Nikolai Kondratieff that BUSINESS CYCLES are of a long-term nature, spanning 50 years or more, during which time they alternate between periods of growth and contraction. Also known as SUPERCYCLE.

KRUGERRAND   A coin minted by the South African government which contains 1 troy ounce of GOLD, commonly purchased by INVESTORS seeking physical gold.

KURTOSIS   A measure of how much the VARIANCE of a distribution is affected by extreme values. A distribution characterized by "FAT TAILS" and a tighter peak has high kurtosis, while one with thinner tails and a round peak has low kurtosis. When a distribution has fat tails, the PROBABILITY of an extreme event occurring is greater than if the tails are thinner, and is often referred to as the fourth MOMENT about the MEAN. Kurtosis is given by:

$$\frac{1}{N\sigma^4}\sum_{i=1}^{N}(x_i - \mu)^4$$

where N is the number of observations, x_i is an observation, μ is the mean, σ is the STANDARD DEVIATION.

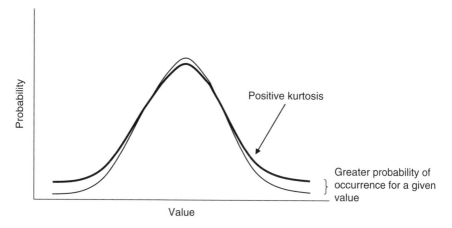

See also EXCESS KURTOSIS, LOGNORMAL DISTRIBUTION, NORMAL DISTRI-BUTION, SKEWNESS

L

L A broad measure of liquid money supply, generally defined as M3 plus GOVERNMENT BILLS, COMMERCIAL PAPER, BANKER'S ACCEPTANCES, and EUROCURRENCY DEPOSITS of residents.

LABOR CODETERMINATION A legal rule, found primarily in Continental European nations, requiring a certain number of labor representatives to be elected to a company's BOARD OF DIRECTORS in order to give employees proper input into corporate affairs.

LADDER OPTION An OVER-THE-COUNTER COMPLEX OPTION that allows the buyer to lock in any accumulated gains prior to EXPIRY as the price of the UNDERLYING market reference exceeds prespecified market levels (or "rungs"); gains are not surrendered if the market subsequently retraces. Also known as a RATCHET OPTION. See also CLIQUET OPTION, FIXED STRIKE LADDER OPTION, FLOATING STRIKE LADDER OPTION, SHOUT OPTION.

LADDERED PORTFOLIO An INVESTMENT PORTFOLIO comprised of NOTES and BONDS with short-, medium- and long-term MATURITIES, generally in approximately equal amounts. Such a portfolio provides the INVESTOR with exposure to the entire YIELD CURVE, generating INTEREST and PRINCIPAL redemptions on a steady basis over time. See also BARBELL PORTFOLIO.

LADDERING [COL] An illegal practice where the UNDERWRITER of a NEW ISSUE of COMMON STOCK allocates SHARES to an INVESTOR if the investor agrees to purchase additional shares in the SECONDARY MARKET (which will help support the price and generate additional COMMISSIONS). See also SPINNING.

LAG The time period between the occurrence of a loss, or filing of a CLAIM by the INSURED, and the receipt of a SETTLEMENT from the INSURER.

LAISSEZ-FAIRE [FR] An economic and business philosophy indicating that government intervention in commercial affairs should be limited so that market forces can play the leading role in resource allocation. Though free market economies adhere to basic tenets of laissez-faire, in practice some government involvement via REGULATION and monitoring is necessary in order to reduce inequalities and promote competition.

LAMBDA See VEGA.

LAND BANK A specialized banking institution dedicated to financing of agricultural development, often with a long-term horizon. Also known as AGRICULTURAL BANK.

LAPSE RATIO In INSURANCE, a measure indicating the degree to which new policies are written and existing policies are renewed, generally computed by comparing the percentage of policies in force at the start of the year versus those outstanding at the end of the year. A rising lapse ratio means policies are rolling off faster than new policies are being written and existing policies are being renewed.

LAPSED OPTION An IN-THE-MONEY OPTION that has expired and which has not been EXERCISED, resulting in an economic loss for the holder of the option.

LARGE CAP STOCK The COMMON STOCK of a company with a large MARKET CAPITALIZATION, generally in excess of $5 billion. See also MICROSTOCK, MID-CAP STOCK.

LARGE-DEDUCTIBLE POLICY A LOSS-SENSITIVE INSURANCE CONT-RACT that features a DEDUCTIBLE that is much larger than one found on a standard fixed PREMIUM, full INSURANCE contract. The INSURED retains a much larger amount of RISK and pays the INSURER a smaller PREMIUM.

LARGE LINE CAPACITY The ability for an INSURER or REINSURER to UNDERWRITE a large RISK exposure under a single policy. Insurers and rein-surers with strong financial standing and significant CAPITAL resources are generally able to offer a greater amount of large line capacity without seeking REINSURANCE and RETROCESSION.

LARGE LOSS PRINCIPLE In INSURANCE, the concept of transferring high severity/low frequency losses to an INSURER. Assuming fair PREMIUM pri-cing, the principle is often considered to be a prudent and cost-effective form of corporate RISK MANAGEMENT, as catastrophic loss events are very difficult to predict and quantify and can create significant FINANCIAL DISTRESS in the absence of proper LOSS FINANCING.

LASPEYRES' INDEX See BASE WEIGHTED INDEX.

LAST IN FIRST OUT (LIFO) An INVENTORY management and ACCOUN-TING approach where the last raw materials or work-in-progress inventory acquired for production of final goods are used first. Costs and inventory valuation are thus based on the latest, and then earliest, items in inventory, regardless of whether this corresponds to the actual physical movement in the inventory. See also FIRST IN FIRST OUT (FIFO).

LAST SALE See LAST TRADE.

LAST TRADE The latest TRADE in a particular ASSET or SECURITY, which yields the most current price at which identical positions can be valued. Also known as LAST SALE.

LAST TRADING DAY The final day on which TRADING in a specific EXCHANGE-TRADED DERIVATIVE CONTRACT can occur.

LATE TRADING An illegal practice where clients enter MUTUAL FUND pur-chase ORDERS after the official market close in order to take advantage of late market-moving events.

LATENT LIQUIDITY Blocks of STOCK held by INSTITUTIONAL INVESTORS in their PORTFOLIOS that may be available for sale, but which are not actively advertised or marketed. Latent liquidity may be brought to market through the efforts of BROKERS, who communicate with investors and ascertain their willingness to sell portions of their positions.

LATTICE MODEL A general class of OPTION pricing models (e.g., BINOMIAL MODEL) that is based on the construction of a framework of upward and downward movements with specific probabilities of occurrence. The model examines possible terminal values of the UNDERLYING ASSET and works backward through the lattice (via a process known as recombination) to generate a price of the option at each interval (or node). By valuing the option at each interval, the lattice model can be used to compute early EXERCISE of the contract, and is thus useful for pricing AMERICAN OPTIONS and BERMUDAN OPTIONS. Also known as RECOMBINING TREE. See also NONRECOMBINING TREE.

LAUNDERING [COL] See MONEY LAUNDERING.

LAW OF LARGE NUMBERS A statistical theorem indicating that the average outcome approaches the EXPECTED VALUE or MEAN of the distribution as the number of observations or random samples becomes very large. The Law of Large Numbers is commonly used by INSURERS in developing ACTUARIAL PRICING methodologies, and is also incorporated in certain DERIVATIVE pricing models. Also known as CENTRAL LIMIT THEOREM.

LAW OF ONE PRICE A financial theory indicating that ASSETS with CASH FLOWS that are equal but structured differently must still yield the same price, or else will give rise to an ARBITRAGE opportunity. Although the cash flows can be structured differently, they must have the same FRICTION COSTS and RISKS. INTEREST RATE PARITY and PUT-CALL PARITY are forms of this theorem. See also NO ARBITRAGE CONDITION.

LAYERING The second stage in the MONEY LAUNDERING process, in which cash deposited during the PLACEMENT phase is used in a series of complex financial transactions in order to separate illicit funds from their real source and obscure any AUDIT trail. Layering can include wiring cash to other institutions, purchasing BONDS, STOCKS, or other INVESTMENTS, or funding shell companies.

LBO See LEVERAGED BUYOUT.

LDC See LESSER DEVELOPED COUNTRY.

LEAD The first UNDERWRITER or SYNDICATE on an INSURANCE POLICY underwritten via LLOYD'S OF LONDON, and the party responsible for establishing the PREMIUM, issuing the policy, and collecting premiums.

LEAD INDEPENDENT DIRECTOR A DIRECTOR that serves as leader of the other independent members of the BOARD OF DIRECTORS. The role can be found in a SINGLE BOARD SYSTEM when the roles of the chairman and CHIEF

EXECUTIVE OFFICER are combined, and is intended to reinforce external scrutiny of management affairs. Also known as PRESIDING DIRECTOR. See also EXECUTIVE DIRECTOR, NONEXECUTIVE DIRECTOR.

LEAD MANAGER An institution leading a SYNDICATE in the UNDERWRITING of a NEW ISSUE of SECURITIES on behalf of a corporate or sovereign ISSUER. The lead manager is responsible for assembling the syndicate, filing for REGISTRATION, organizing DUE DILIGENCE and ROADSHOWS, acting as AGENT for other syndicate members, finalizing terms, conditions, and pricing, allocating securities, and stabilizing the price of securities upon launch. In exchange for performing these functions the lead manager receives a greater share of deal fees and receives LEAGUE TABLE credit for managing the process. Also known as BOOKRUNNER, SYNDICATE MANAGER.

LEAGUE TABLE   A tabulation of deals underwritten or advisories completed by financial intermediaries on behalf of companies and sovereigns.

LEAPS   See LONG-TERM EQUITY APPRECIATION SECURITY.

LEASE   A transaction that gives one party (the LESSEE) possession and use of an ASSET for a period of time in exchange for periodic payments to another party (the LESSOR). A lease, which may be carried on or off the corporate BALANCE SHEET and feature full TAX deductibility, generally has a MATURITY of several years, but can often be cancelled by the lessee. Although most lease transactions involve a single asset, master lease agreements covering multiple assets can also be arranged. See also CAPITAL LEASE, LEVERAGED LEASE, NET LEASE, OPERATING LEASE, WET LEASE.

LEASE PURCHASE AGREEMENT   A form of LEASE where payments made by the LESSEE are allocated to the eventual purchase of the ASSET.

LEASEBACK   See SALE AND LEASEBACK.

LEG   [COL] One component of a multicomponent financial transaction, often associated with structured DERIVATIVES, STRUCTURED NOTES, and other complex dealings.

LEGAL LENDING LIMIT   The maximum amount that a BANK can lend to a single BORROWER on a consolidated basis, generally set as a percentage of a bank's EQUITY and/or ASSETS. The limit exists in order to avoid concentrated CREDIT RISK exposures to a single borrower and possible FINANCIAL DISTRESS that might arise should that borrower DEFAULT, e.g., in the United States, the legal lending limit for national banks is 15% of equity on an unsecured basis and 25% on a secured basis. Also know as LENDING LIMIT.

LEGAL MECHANISM CONTROL   A structure or process where effective control of a company is obtained through legal or structural mechanisms (e.g., a pyramid holding company) rather than the purchase of a majority share of COMMON STOCK. See also MAJORITY CONTROL, MANAGEMENT CONTROL, MINORITY CONTROL, TOTAL CONTROL, VOTING TRUST CONTROL.

LEGAL OWNER A person or institution that holds legal TITLE to an ASSET or INVESTMENT and can arrange for its sale or transfer, but who may not be entitled to right of use (i.e., it may lack a BENEFICIAL INTEREST). See also BENEFICIAL OWNER.

LEGAL RESERVES (1) RESERVES held by BANKS in support of demand and time DEPOSIT balances, generally necessary in order to comply with RESERVE REQUIREMENTS imposed by a governing CENTRAL BANK or monetary authority. (2) Reserves established by a company to cover possible legal contingencies or lawsuits.

LEGAL RISK The RISK of loss arising from failures in the legal process, including unenforceability of CONTRACTS or lack of appropriate documentation related to business arrangements such as GUARANTEES, MASTER AGREEMENTS, or LOAN agreements.

LEGAL TENDER MONEY that must be accepted in the settlement of amounts due.

LEGGING [COL] (1) Establishing or unwinding one of two segments of a STRADDLE, or STRANGLE, or INDEX ARBITRAGE program, or other complex TRADE, thus creating an exposure to the direction of the SECURITY or market until the accompanying position is added or the second LEG is unwound. (2) The process of slowly accumulating a position in a security.

LENDER An individual or institution that provides funds to a BORROWER, either informally or formally, and with or without COLLATERAL. In exchange for providing funds, the lender generally expects recompense, which is levied via periodic INTEREST payments. See also CREDITOR.

LENDER OF LAST RESORT A government institution, generally a CENTRAL BANK or monetary authority, that supplies emergency CREDIT to BANKS or the broader banking system in order to avoid systemic dislocation arising from a bank DEFAULT or payment disruption. Existence of lender of last resort facilities is often implicit rather than explicit in order to avoid instances of MORAL HAZARD, and actual support is typically reserved for those institutions that are considered to be "TOO BIG TO FAIL."

LENDING The act of granting a LOAN to a customer. Lending is typically undertaken by BANKS and nonbank FINANCIAL INSTITUTIONS, and generates CREDIT RISK.

LENDING LIMIT See LEGAL LENDING LIMIT.

LEPO See LOW EXERCISE PRICE OPTION.

LESSEE A party in a LEASE transaction that contracts to lease an ASSET from another party, paying periodic payments in exchange for use of the asset during a stated period. See also LESSOR.

LESSER DEVELOPED COUNTRY (LDC) A country that features an economy that is gradually developing and strengthening, but lacks a sufficiently robust industrial production base to contribute in a meaningful way to national income and EXPORTS. LDCs may impose certain TRADE barriers and/or EXCHANGE CONTROLS in order to protect their economies from excessive IMPORTS or speculative inflows. As a result of nascent market conduits and often weak financial standing, LDCs are typically characterized by a high degree of SOVEREIGN RISK.

LESSOR   A party in a LEASE transaction that leases an ASSET to another party, receiving periodic payments in exchange for providing use of the asset during a stated period. See also LESSEE.

LETTER OF COMFORT   See COMFORT LETTER.

LETTER OF CREDIT   A CREDIT-based instrument issued by a BANK that GUARANTEES the payments of its customer (the DRAWER) to a third-party BENEFICIARY. The letter of credit, which effectively substitutes the customer's credit standing with the bank's, is widely used in banking and international TRADE transactions. See also CONFIRMED LETTER OF CREDIT, IRREVOCABLE LETTER OF CREDIT, STANDBY LETTER OF CREDIT, TRANSFERABLE LETTER OF CREDIT.

LETTRES DE GAGE   In Luxembourg, a form of COVERED BOND backed by a BANK's MORTGAGES. See also CEDULAS HIPOTECARIAS, HYPOTHEKENPFANDBRIEFE, IRISH ASSET COVERED SECURITIES, JUMBO PFANDBRIEFE, OBLIGATIONS FONCIERES, OFFENTLICHE PFANDBRIEFE.

LEVEL PREMIUM   In INSURANCE, a PREMIUM that remains unchanged over time, even if the amount of RISK the INSURER assumes from the INSURED increases.

LEVERAGE   The degree to which a company uses on- and OFF-BALANCE SHEET DEBT to fund its operations. Use of leverage magnifies the potential RETURNS and RISKS of an INVESTMENT or corporate strategy. In general, the greater the amount of leverage, the riskier the financial standing of the company and the greater the expectation of higher returns by suppliers of CAPITAL. Also known as FINANCIAL LEVERAGE, GEARING. See also DEBT SERVICE, INTEREST COVERAGE, LEVERAGE RATIOS, MODIGLIANI-MILLER THEORY, OPM, OPERATING LEVERAGE.
   Additional reference: Miller and Modigliani (1958).

LEVERAGE ARBITRAGE   An ARBITRAGE scheme intended to take advantage of a misperception that creates a gap between a company's CREDIT RATING and its actual financial activities/condition. This generally occurs when a highly rated company uses its strong rating to borrow a significant amount of DEBT at favorable rates and then invest in a range of speculative ASSETS.

LEVERAGE EFFECT   The degree to which the use of DEBT on a company's BALANCE SHEET impacts its EARNINGS PER SHARE and its DIVIDEND

PAYOUT. Greater use of leverage magnifies earnings and losses, and its effects can be estimated via:

$$LE = \frac{\left(\dfrac{\Delta EPS}{EPS}\right)}{\left(\dfrac{\Delta EBIT}{EBIT}\right)}$$

where EPS is EARNINGS PER SHARE, EBIT is EARNINGS BEFORE INTEREST AND TAXES, Δ is the change in the respective variable.

LEVERAGE RATIOS   Measures that reflect the degree to which a company uses DEBT in its operations. Common ratios include DEBT TO EQUITY, DEBT TO ASSETS, and CONTINGENTS TO ASSETS.

LEVERAGED BUYOUT (LBO)   The ACQUISITION of a PUBLIC COMPANY by a specialist or management group that results in retirement of the public EQUITY through the assumption of a large amount of DEBT (i.e., the company is taken private through LEVERAGE). The ultimate goal of the control group is to refocus operations, reduce EXPENSES, spin off unwanted operations, then refloat or sell the company over the medium term. The debt package used in a typical LBO generally comprises of senior loan TRANCHES with MATURITIES ranging from 1 to 7 years, subordinated loan tranches of 7+ years, and mezzanine tranches with BULLET repayments (and often with attached WARRANTS to provide equity-like RETURNS). See also MANAGEMENT BUYOUT, REVERSE LEVERAGED BUYOUT.

LEVERAGED EXCHANGE-TRADED FUND   Any EXCHANGE-TRADED FUND (ETF) that makes use of explicit or implicit LEVERAGE in order to increase the RISK, and thus RETURN, profile. Leveraged ETFs can be constructed by introducing an explicit leverage factor, or by using DERIVATIVE contracts that provide implicit leverage to an ASSET or INDEX.

LEVERAGED LEASE   A CAPITAL LEASE where the underlying ASSET is acquired with borrowed funds. The LESSOR establishes a TRUST and contributes 20% to 40% of the purchase price of the asset; the trust then borrows the balance from a BANK on a NONRECOURSE basis and buys the asset. The LOAN to the trust is secured by a first LIEN and an assignment of the lease and lease payments. Through the leveraged lease structure the lessor obtains the DEPRECIATION benefits from the asset and INTEREST deduction from the loan.

LEVERAGED NOTE   A STRUCTURED NOTE that provides an INVESTOR with the opportunity of earning an enhanced RETURN through a COUPON that is leveraged to a particular financial reference, such as EQUITIES, INTEREST RATES or FOREIGN EXCHANGE RATES. Since the leverage magnifies the movement of the underlying reference, the note can be very risky; in some instances, PRINCIPAL may be at RISK. See also INVERSE FLOATING RATE NOTE.

LEVERAGED OPTION   See POWER OPTION.

LEVERAGED RECAPITALIZATION (1) A defensive strategy where a company borrows a large amount of funds from a BANK to make a SPECIAL DIVIDEND payment to existing SHAREHOLDERS. Through this type of recapitalization the company effectively leverages its BALANCE SHEET, making it appear less attractive to a potential acquirer. (2) A CAPITAL restructuring technique that transfers value of a PUBLIC COMPANY to its INVESTORS through a STOCK REPURCHASE or CASH DIVIDEND.

LEVERAGED SWAP See POWER SWAP.

LEVERAGED UNIT TRUST A UNIT TRUST that is permitted to use LEVERAGE, either through the issuance of DEBT or the use of DERIVATIVES, in order to enhance INVESTOR RETURNS. The RISK profile of the leveraged unit trust is greater than a standard unit trust, with the potential of producing greater returns and greater losses. See also LEVERAGED EXCHANGE-TRADED FUND.

LGD See LOSS-GIVEN DEFAULT.

LIABILITY A legal OBLIGATION to make a payment or repay a DEBT; a liability is often used to fund the purchase of a productive ASSET. Common liabilities include ACCOUNTS PAYABLE, COMMERCIAL PAPER, DEPOSITS, LOANS, NOTES, BONDS, and certain deferred TAXES and charges and OFF-BALANCE SHEET items. An increase in liabilities results in a CREDIT, while a decrease leads to a DEBIT.

LIABILITY INSURANCE An INSURANCE CONTRACT providing an INSURED with coverage for losses sustained from payments it makes related to bodily injury or property damage. Coverage can be created for both personal and business exposures, including comprehensive personal liability, COMMERCIAL GENERAL LIABILITY, employers liability, and workers compensation.

LIABILITY MANAGEMENT The general practice of using a mix of funding instruments and markets, and INTEREST RATE and FOREIGN EXCHANGE HEDGES, in order to manage the LIQUIDITY RISK and MARKET RISK inherent in the corporate BALANCE SHEET.

LIABILITY SENSITIVE See NEGATIVE GAP.

LIABILITY SWAP An OVER-THE-COUNTER INTEREST RATE SWAP or CURRENCY SWAP that exchanges COUPONS or CURRENCIES from an underlying LIABILITY in order to create a synthetic liability that meets a company's preferred profile. See also ASSET SWAP.

LIAR LOAN [COL] A residential MORTGAGE that is granted by a BORROWER to a LENDER on the basis of little or no documentation proving INCOME and NET WORTH, and which is therefore subject to falsification. Liar loans have historically been part of the SUBPRIME MORTGAGE and ALT-A mortgage sector. See also NINJA LOAN.

LIBID See LONDON INTERBANK BID.

LIBOR See LONDON INTERBANK OFFERED RATE.

LIBOR IN ARREARS SWAP   See ARREARS SWAP.

LICENSED CARRIER   See ADMITTED INSURER.

LIEN   See SECURED INTEREST.

LIEN STATUS   The seniority of a LOAN backed by property (or other ASSETS) in the event of BORROWER DEFAULT and forced liquidation. The first lien holder has first claim on the RESIDUAL VALUE of the asset, and is followed by the second lien holder and other junior lien holders.

LIFE ACQUISITION COST SECURITIZATION An INSURANCE-LINKED SECURITY that transfers the upfront costs associated with writing LIFE INSURANCE policies to CAPITAL MARKETS INVESTORS. See also CATASTROPHE BOND, MORTGAGE DEFAULT SECURITIZATION, RESIDUAL VALUE SECURITIZATION, WEATHER BOND.

LIFE ANNUITY   An ANNUITY that stops payments to the ANNUITANT or BENEFICIARY once the person covered is deceased. See also CERTAIN ANNUITY.

LIFE ASSURANCE   In the United Kingdom, LIFE INSURANCE.

LIFE INSURANCE   An INSURANCE CONTRACT providing for a payment to a named BENEFICIARY in the event the INSURED dies; life insurance is available in many forms, including term life, whole life, ordinary life, and group life, each with different characteristics related to coverage, costs, and savings. See also LIFE ASSURANCE, LIFE REINSURANCE.

LIFE REINSURANCE   A REINSURANCE agreement where an INSURER cedes LIFE INSURANCE policies to a REINSURER individually (through FACULTATIVE REINSURANCE) or as a PORTFOLIO (TREATY REINSURANCE).

LIFEBOAT   [COL] A rescue fund established by a CENTRAL BANK or monetary authority to ensure BANKS have access to sufficient CAPITAL in the event of a FINANCIAL CRISIS.

LIFETIME FLOOR   An INTEREST RATE FLOOR embedded in a long-term CONTRACT that limits the lowest rate a BORROWER may pay on an ADJUSTABLE RATE MORTGAGE. The lifetime floor prevents the LENDER's mortgage rate from falling below some predefined level in a falling rate environment.

LIFO   See LAST IN FIRST OUT.

LIFT THE OFFER   See TAKE THE OFFER.

LIFTING A LEG   [COL] The process of LEGGING out of a transaction.

LIMEAN   See LONDON INTERBANK MEAN.

LIMIT   (1) Any MARKET RISK or CREDIT RISK limit established by a BANK or other FINANCIAL INSTITUTION in order to control RISK exposure to a particular market risk factor or COUNTERPARTY. (2) A price threshold established by an EXCHANGE on a traded ASSET or INDEX that dictates the maximum amount of upward or downward movement that can occur during a day or TRADING period. (2) See also CIRCUIT BREAKER.

LIMIT BUY ORDER   An ORDER to buy SECURITIES if a target level is reached, with no assurance the order can be filled at the limit price. See also LIMIT SELL ORDER.

LIMIT ON CLOSE ORDER   An ORDER to buy or sell SECURITIES at the market close, but only if the closing price is better than the limit specified.

LIMIT ORDER   An ORDER for the purchase or sale of a SECURITY at a specific price limit. If the price is not attained the order expires unfilled or it remains open until the client instructs otherwise. See also MARKET ORDER, STOP ORDER, TIME ORDER.

LIMIT PRICE   An EXECUTION price on an ORDER the reflects a specific BID or OFFER. See also MARKET PRICE.

LIMIT SELL ORDER   An order to sell SECURITIES if a target level is reached, with no assurance the order can be filled at the LIMIT PRICE. See also LIMIT BUY ORDER.

LIMITED (LTD)   In the United Kingdom and former colonies, as well as Japan and the United States, a LIMITED COMPANY that is INCORPORATED and thus has LIMITED LIABILITY.

LIMITED COMPANY   In the United Kingdom, a form of private LIMITED LIABILITY COMPANY where the LIABILITY of participants for the company's outstanding DEBTS is limited to their INVESTMENT in fully paid SHARES. See also LIMITED, PUBLIC LIMITED COMPANY.

LIMITED LIABILITY   A structural and legal concept where INVESTORS in a LIMITED LIABILITY COMPANY are financially responsible only up to the value of the CAPITAL they have invested in the company's COMMON STOCK; personal ASSETS are not at RISK in the event the company suffers losses that deplete capital. Limited liability is common in entities structured as public or private CORPORATIONS. See also PIERCING THE CORPORATE VEIL, UNLIMITED LIABILITY.

LIMITED LIABILITY COMPANY (LLC)   A form of business organization with one or more owners, each one with LIMITED LIABILITY. While similar to a CORPORATION, an LLC is cheaper to establish and operate as it has less requirements related to GOVERNANCE and SHAREHOLDER REGULATIONS. An LLC does not exist as a separate TAX-paying entity; all income is passed through to the tax returns of individual owners. See also JOINT STOCK COMPANY, PUBLIC COMPANY, PUBLIC LIMITED COMPANY.

LIMITED LIABILITY PARTNERSHIP (LLP)   A hybrid organization that draws on features of the LIMITED PARTNERSHIP and the LIMITED LIABILITY CORPORATION. The LLP features individual PARTNERS who have limited liability (which is in contrast to the standard limited partnership, where all members have UNLIMITED LIABILITY). In some jurisdictions the LLP must feature a GENERAL PARTNER who bears UNLIMITED LIABILITY.

LIMITED MARKET   Any marketplace that is either ILLIQUID or where the number of active buyers is very small.

LIMITED PARTNERSHIP (LP)   (1) A form of PARTNERSHIP that includes one or more GENERAL PARTNERS who manage the business operations and are ultimately responsible for the organization's LIABILITIES, and one or more limited partners who benefit from any PROFITS on a PRO-RATA or specified basis, and who face LIMITED LIABILITY. Limited partners are prohibited from actively managing the business operation, and any resulting income generated by the partnership is passed through to the TAX returns of the individual partners. (2) An unregistered private PARTNERSHIP open to a certain number of ACCREDITED INVESTORS, or a registered public partnership that is open to a larger population of investors, which invests in a broad range of ASSETS. Limited partnerships often acquire real estate, oil, and gas properties, or equipment LEASES and provide INVESTORS with any RETURNS generated. (1) See also GENERAL PARTNERSHIP, MASTER LIMITED PARTNERSHIP, SILENT PARTNERSHIP.

LIMITED PRICE INDEX SWAP   A form of INFLATION SWAP used in the United Kingdom that features a CAP and/or a FLOOR to limit the inflation-based payout to one or both parties.

LIMITED RECOURSE LOAN   See PARTIAL RECOURSE LOAN.

LINE   [COL] A general class of INSURANCE offered by INSURERS, typically grouped into one of five types: LIFE INSURANCE, health insurance, ANNUITY, PROPERTY AND CASUALTY INSURANCE, and LIABILITY INSURANCE. See also LINE LIMIT.

LINE LIMIT   The maximum LINE of INSURANCE an INSURER will UNDERWRITE without seeking excess protection via REINSURANCE. The size of the line limit depends on an insurer's financial resources and expertise, its ability to diversify and reinsure, and its willingness to assume RISK of a particular type and magnitude.

LINE OF CREDIT   See REVOLVING CREDIT FACILITY.

LINEAR INSTRUMENT   A financial ASSET or transaction, such as a COMMON STOCK, FORWARD, or FUTURE that provides a unit payoff for a unit move in the underlying asset. Linear instruments feature no CONVEXITY. See also NONLINEAR INSTRUMENT.

LINEAR INTERPOLATION   A technique of INTERPOLATION that uses a straight line to connect two points on a YIELD CURVE. The missing point can be computed by first determining the fractional number of days:

$$\lambda = \frac{t_i - t_1}{t_2 - t_1}$$

where t_i is the number of days required from known point t_1 to the target date, t_2 is the number of days at the end of the period.

And then determining the interpolated rate:

$$S_t = S_1(1 - \lambda) + s_2(\lambda)$$

where S_1 is the first known SPOT RATE, S_2 is the second known spot rate. Also known as STRAIGHT LINE INTERPOLATION. See also CUBIC SPLINE INTERPOLATION, EXPONENTIAL INTERPOLATION.

LINEAR PAYOFF   A linear and constant economic gain or loss that may be expected under a conventional DERIVATIVE (e.g., FUTURE or FORWARD) for a given range of market prices. For every unit move up or down in the market price, the gain or loss is a linear function of that unit move. See also ASYMMETRIC PAYOFF, NONLINEAR PAYOFF, SYMMETRIC PAYOFF.

LINKER   [COL] In the United Kingdom, an INFLATION-LINKED SECURITY.

LIQUID   (1) At a corporate level, the state of possessing sufficient cash to meet obligations. (2) At a market level, the state of having sufficient transaction volume to permit TRADING. See also ILLIQUID, LIQUID ASSETS, LIQUIDITY.

LIQUID ASSETS   ASSETS that can be converted into cash when needed at, or near, carrying value. Apart from cash, this generally includes very high-quality, short-dated SECURITIES, such as GOVERNMENT BILLS, highly rated MONEY MARKET instruments (i.e., COMMERCIAL PAPER, CERTIFICATES OF DEPOSIT, REPURCHASE AGREEMENTS, BANKER'S ACCEPTANCES); it may also include short-term, high-quality ACCOUNTS RECEIVABLE and certain classes of fungible INVENTORY. See also LIQUIDITY, NEAR MONEY.

LIQUID RATIO   See QUICK RATIO.

LIQUIDATED DAMAGES   DAMAGES awarded to a plaintiff that can be quantified very precisely, e.g., through ex-ante definition in a CONTRACT. See also STATUTORY DAMAGES, UNLIQUIDATED DAMAGES.

LIQUIDATING DIVIDEND   A DIVIDEND, payable by a company to SHAREHOLDERS, that represents a final return of CAPITAL. The dividend is paid when a company is halting its operations and no longer requires capital.

LIQUIDATION   (1) A state of corporate BANKRUPTCY that culminates in the disposal of ASSETS and payment of any RESIDUAL VALUE to CREDITORS; liquidation generally occurs when efforts at REORGANIZATION have failed. (2) The sale of assets by a company to cover an expected or unexpected payment, or the sale of COLLATERAL held by a creditor to cover funds due from the BORROWER/DEBTOR. (1) Also known as WINDING-UP. (1) See also CREDITORS' VOLUNTARY LIQUIDATION, VOLUNTARY LIQUIDATION.

LIQUIDATION PERIOD   (1) In a VALUE-AT-RISK model, the assumed horizon over which a PORTFOLIO of ASSETS can be sold in order to neutralize RISK and recognize gains or losses. In most models a single liquidation period is applied to all asset classes, regardless of the inherent level of risk or LIQUIDITY. (2) In the INSURANCE sector, the period during which a previously funded ANNUITY provides CASH FLOWS to the ANNUITANT. (1) Also known as HOLDING PERIOD.

LIQUIDATION VALUE   The value of an ASSET, business, or company that is to be sold to a third party. If the sale of an entire business or company occurs on a piecemeal basis the value obtained may be less than if it is sold as a going-concern, which reflects the financial worth of GOODWILL. If the sale must occur rapidly, the resulting liquidation value may also be lower as the seller will be recognized as a price taker. See also ASSET STRIPPING, BREAKUP VALUE.

LIQUIDATOR   An AGENT, typically appointed by a court, that is responsible for carrying out the LIQUIDATION of a company in BANKRUPTCY.

LIQUIDITY   (1) At a corporate level, access to cash, NEAR MONEY, unsecured funding and unencumbered ASSETS that can be used to cover expected or unexpected payments. (2) The state of being LIQUID or having LIQUID ASSETS. (3) Activity or turnover in a SECURITY or ASSET; a liquid market is characterized by small differences between BIDS and OFFERS, while an ILLIQUID market features potentially large differences. See also CURRENT RATIO, ILLIQUIDITY, LIQUIDITY RISK, QUICK RATIO.

LIQUIDITY FACILITY   A CREDIT line provided by a BANK to a customer that is used to cover short-term funding requirements arising from CASH FLOW gaps. Such facilities may be drawn on a revolving basis, and are generally repayable within 1 year.

LIQUIDITY PREFERENCE THEORY   A theory of INTEREST RATES indicating that INVESTORS will expect a higher return for ASSETS they prefer not to hold, leading to the creation of a LIQUIDITY PREMIUM (which is often expressed as the difference between FORWARD RATES and expected future SPOT RATES). The theory also allows for the fact that investor expectations help determine the shape of the YIELD CURVE, as set forth via the EXPECTATIONS THEORY. See also MARKET SEGMENTATION THEORY.

Additional references: Hicks (1946); Lutz and Lutz (1951); Meiselman (1962).

LIQUIDITY PREMIUM   The additional SPREAD that INVESTORS demand for holding ASSETS they prefer not to hold (including those that may be risky or ILLIQUID). Under the LIQUIDITY PREFERENCE THEORY the liquidity premium is also an increasing function of expectations regarding rising INTEREST RATES.

LIQUIDITY RISK   The RISK of being unable to raise funding or sell or pledge ASSETS when needed without incurring a significant cost. Liquidity risk, which is a form of FINANCIAL RISK, is commonly segregated into three components: ASSET LIQUIDITY RISK, FUNDING LIQUIDITY RISK, and ASSET-FUNDING LIQUIDITY RISK. See also ENDOGENOUS LIQUIDITY, EXOGENOUS LIQUIDITY, LIQUIDITY, LIQUIDITY SPIRAL.

LIQUIDITY SPIRAL   A self-fulfilling cycle where concerns about a company's LIQUIDITY cause CREDITORS to cancel CREDIT facilities, which leads to a repeated cycle of ASSET sales, CREDIT RATING downgrades, and further credit facility cancellations. The cycle continues until the company is able to secure sufficient funding or enters a stage of FINANCIAL DISTRESS. See also LIQUIDITY RISK.

LIQUIDITY TRAP   (1) A situation during a RECESSION or DEPRESSION where individuals hold an excessive amount of MONEY relative to actual needs and are insensitive to the RETURN offered via savings or INVESTMENT vehicles. In practice INTEREST RATES cannot be lowered without risking further damage to the economy. (2) A phenomenon where a ONE-WAY MARKET (i.e., offered-only) temporarily exhibits signs of two-way business, causing new buyers to enter and creating the illusion of strong LIQUIDITY. Once new buyers stop entering, liquidity quickly erodes and the market returns to its normal one-way state, "trapping" those that still hold positions.

LIQUIDITY WAREHOUSE   A PORTFOLIO of unencumbered INVESTMENT GRADE SECURITIES that a company maintains in order to manage LIQUIDITY requirements that cannot be adequately met via existing unsecured funding. When additional cash is required a company can pledge or sell the unencumbered ASSETS from the warehouse at, or near, carrying value. The liquidity warehouse generally comprises of short- and medium-term securities with stable prices and strong CREDIT RATINGS.

LISTED COMPANY   A company that is listed and traded on a STOCK EXCHANGE. See also PRIVATE COMPANY, PUBLIC COMPANY.

LISTED DERIVATIVE   See EXCHANGE-TRADED DERIVATIVE.

LISTING REQUIREMENTS   The specific rules that a company must fulfill in order to become a LISTED COMPANY with its SHARES traded on a STOCK EXCHANGE. Such requirements vary by national jurisdiction and exchange, but generally relate to the disclosure of full and complete FINANCIAL STATEMENTS on a regular basis, and the maintenance of a particular ASSET value.

LITIGATION   The process of taking legal action in a court of law, with a plaintiff bringing suit against a defendant.

LLC   See LIMITED LIABILITY COMPANY.

LLOYD'S BROKER   A BROKER that specializes in placing INSURANCE with LLOYD'S SYNDICATES operating in the LLOYD'S OF LONDON marketplace.

LLOYD'S OF LONDON   A London-based INSURANCE marketplace comprised of LLOYD's SYNDICATES (i.e., a group of NAMES) that UNDERWRITE a broad range of insurance, REINSURANCE, and RETROCESSION covers. Lloyd's itself does not write any insurance, though it maintains a backup RESERVE fund to cover any possible crisis situation. See also LLOYD'S BROKER.

LLOYD'S SYNDICATE   A group of NAMES within LLOYD'S OF LONDON that specializes in UNDERWRITING specific types of RISKS.

LLP   See LIMITED LIABILITY PARTNERSHIP.

LOAD   (1) In INVESTMENT MANAGEMENT, the sales COMMISSION charged to INVESTORS buying certain MUTUAL FUNDS. (2) In INSURANCE, see EXPENSE LOADING, PREMIUM LOADING. (1) See also LOAD FUND.

LOAD FUND   A MUTUAL FUND that levies an upfront sales charge on INVESTORS; sales COMMISSIONS are generally added to the NET ASSET VALUE to generate the total purchase price. Despite the sales charge, load funds are not always more expensive than NO-LOAD FUNDS, which may have higher management and/or exit fees.

LOAN   A DEBT financing extended by a BANK to a personal, corporate, or sovereign BORROWER. A loan may be granted with a FIXED RATE or FLOATING RATE and PRINCIPAL that amortizes on a regular basis (although certain loans, including BALLOON LOANS and BULLET LOANS, are structured with back-end principal repayments). A loan may have a fixed MATURITY (i.e., TERM LOAN) or it may be rolled over prior to each contractual maturity date (i.e., EVERGREEN); it may also allow for instant drawdown, or be available as needed (i.e., a BANK LINE or REVOLVING CREDIT FACILITY). A loan may be unsecured, or secured on physical ASSETS; unsecured loans may be ranked as SENIOR DEBT or SUBORDINATED DEBT. Loans are typically documented through formal credit agreements that specify precise terms and conditions, including interest and principal repayment schedule, COVENANTS, and EVENTS OF DEFAULT. Also known as ADVANCE, BANK ADVANCE, BANK LOAN. See also LOAN COMMITMENT.

LOAN COMMITMENT   A DEBT commitment extended by a BANK to a corporate or sovereign BORROWER. The commitment permits the borrower to draw on the facility at any time it chooses, up to a stated amount; if the borrower has not breached any COVENANTS, the bank is obligated to provide funds. In exchange for the commitment, the borrower pays the bank a fee (regardless of whether it ever uses the facility). See also LOAN, REVOLVING CREDIT FACILITY.

LOAN LOSS PROVISION   A noncash expense reflected through a BANK's INCOME STATEMENT that is used to increase the LOAN LOSS RESERVE established for NONPERFORMING LOANS.

LOAN LOSS RESERVE   A CREDIT RESERVE established by a BANK to cover the potential charge-off of NONPERFORMING LOANS (i.e., those that are classed as past-due or nonaccrual). The reserve is typically shown as a CONTRA ACCOUNT on the ASSET portion of the BALANCE SHEET, and is increased through LOAN LOSS PROVISIONS taken via the INCOME STATEMENT.

LOAN PARTICIPATION See PARTICIPATION LOAN.

LOAN SALE The process of selling a portion of a SYNDICATED LOAN between BANKS, or to INVESTORS. Although loans are not traded in a SECONDARY MARKET as actively as SECURITIES, the loan sale makes it possible to create a certain degree of LIQUIDITY.

LOAN SERVICING See SERVICING.

LOAN-TO-VALUE (LTV) The percentage amount a BANK is willing to lend a BORROWER against the appraised value of the ASSET being financed, often real estate or plant and equipment. The higher the LTV the greater the LEVERAGE granted to the borrower, and the lower the protection afforded the bank in the event the borrower DEFAULTS. LTVs in the residential and commercial real estate sector typically range from 70% to 100%; those in the plant and equipment sector can range from 50% to 100%.

LOANBACK In the United Kingdom, a transaction where an individual borrows against funds accumulated in a PENSION account, generally on a short-term basis.

LOBSTER TRAP [COL] An ANTITAKEOVER DEFENSE provision that prevents an INVESTOR (or RAIDER) holding more than 10% of a company's COMMON STOCK from exchanging any CONVERTIBLE BONDS into voting class stock. See also SCORCHED EARTH DEFENSES.

LOCAL [COL] An individual TRADING on an EXCHANGE using personal CAPITAL.

LOCAL AUTHORITY BILL In the United Kingdom, a BILL OF EXCHANGE that is drawn on a local government authority.

LOCAL AUTHORITY BOND In the United Kingdom, a BOND that is issued by a local government authority. Such bonds are typically issued with fixed COUPONS and medium-term MATURITIES.

LOCKBOX [COL] A service provided by a BANK to corporate customers where it receives payments by mail into a post box which it collects several times per day; the payments are deposited by the bank immediately so that the corporate customers can begin earning INTEREST immediately.

LOCKED MARKET [COL] A temporary market phenomenon where the BID and OFFER for an ASSET are precisely equal. A locked market, which generally lasts only for short periods of time, can appear when there is little news driving the market and participants lack strong directional views, or when extremely competitive forces on both sides of the market draw the bid and offer SPREAD in.

LOCK-IN PROVISION See RATE LOCK.

LOCKOUT PERIOD (1) A time period during which the NOTIONAL PRINCIPAL of an AMORTIZING SWAP or ACCRETING SWAP cannot be decreased or increased, regardless of the movement of reference INTEREST RATES. The lockout provision protects the party that has sold the embedded OPTIONS in the swap from a sudden movement in rates soon after the transaction commences. (2) The period during which the OPTION embedded in a CALLABLE BOND or a PUTABLE BOND cannot be exercised, generally the first few years of a multiyear bond transaction.

LOCKUP   A time period in a financial transaction that must pass before an action can occur or be taken such as REDEMPTION, LIQUIDATION or CONVERSION.

LOCKUP CERTIFICATE OF DEPOSIT (CD)   A CERTIFICATE OF DEPOSIT that functions as a TIME DEPOSIT. Although a lock-up CD is technically negotiable, it is held in CUSTODY by the issuing BANK on behalf of the DEPOSITOR and generally held until MATURITY. See also FLOATING RATE CERTIFICATE OF DEPOSIT, NEGOTIABLE CERTIFICATE OF DEPOSIT.

LOCKUP OPTION   An OPTION, granted to a friendly WHITE KNIGHT by a company that is a potential TAKEOVER TARGET, which allows the friendly party to purchase the company's most valuable ASSETS (i.e., the CROWN JEWELS) in the event of a HOSTILE TAKEOVER.

LOGNORMAL DISTRIBUTION   A single-tailed statistical distribution of a RANDOM VARIABLE where the logarithm is normally distributed, i.e., for any normally distributed variable x, y = exp(x) features a lognormal distribution. Financial ASSETS are often modeled using the lognormal distribution. The probability density function is given as:

$$f(x;\mu,\sigma) = \frac{1}{x\sigma\sqrt{2\pi}} e^{\frac{-(\ln(x)-\mu)^2}{2\sigma^2}}$$

where x is an observation, μ is the MEAN, σ is the STANDARD DEVIATION. See also KURTOSIS, NORMAL DISTRIBUTION, SKEWNESS.

LOMBARD RATE   (1)   A short-term INTEREST RATE used in the German market, generally applied to LOANS collateralized by SECURITIES. (2) The interest rate charged by BANKS in Europe against SECURITIES pledged as COLLATERAL.

LONDON BULLION MARKET   The official marketplace for the wholesale TRADING of GOLD and silver and the establishment of prices, conducted by DEALERS (e.g., major international BANKS and bullion specialists) under the general auspices of the BANK OF ENGLAND. See also GOLD FIXING.

LONDON INTERBANK BID (LIBID)   The BID side of the London INTERBANK DEPOSIT market, or the INTEREST RATE that a prime BANK must pay for interbank funds. See also LONDON INTERBANK MEAN, LONDON INTERBANK OFFERED RATE.

LONDON INTERBANK MEAN (LIMEAN)   The MEAN of the LONDON INTERBANK BID and LONDON INTERBANK OFFERED RATES, or the average

INTEREST RATE at which a BANK will DEPOSIT or accept interbank funds. See also LONDON INTERBANK BID, LONDON INTERBANK OFFERED RATE.

LONDON INTERBANK OFFERED RATE (LIBOR)   The OFFER side of the London INTERBANK DEPOSIT market, or the rate at which a prime BANK is willing to lend funds. LIBOR, which is set every business day at 11 am London time by the BRITISH BANKERS ASSOCIATION, is quoted for deposits in a range of MATURITIES and RESERVE CURRENCIES, and serves as an important base reference for other financial instruments with a FLOATING RATE component (e.g., DERIVATIVES, FLOATING RATE NOTES). See also LONDON INTERBANK BID, LONDON INTERBANK MEAN.

LONDON STOCK EXCHANGE (LSE)   The primary STOCK EXCHANGE of the United Kingdom, with origins dating back to the seventeenth century and formal constitution arriving in 1802; major structural changes followed in 1986 through DEREGULATION known as the BIG BANG. The LSE trades in domestic and international STOCKS, BONDS, COVERED WARRANTS, CONTRACTS FOR DIFFERENCES, EQUITY DERIVATIVES, and EXCHANGE-TRADED FUNDS through separate divisions, and in 2007 expanded its geographic scope by acquiring Borsa Italiana, the primary stock exchange of Italy.

LONG   See LONG POSITION.

LONG AND WRONG   [COL] A LONG POSITION (purchased or owned) that loses money as a result of sudden or steady price declines.

LONG ARBITRAGE   An ARBITRAGE strategy employed in the FUTURES market when the FORWARD RATE is lower than the futures rate, indicating that the cash market is overpriced when compared with the futures market; the strategy calls for selling the UNDERLYING ASSET and buying futures. See also SHORT ARBITRAGE.

LONG BOND   [COL] In the United States, the 30-year TREASURY BOND issued by the government.

LONG CARRY   The CARRY generated by a LONG position, defined for FIXED INCOME positions as daily COUPON income less daily financing costs; daily price AMORTIZATION/ACCRETION can also be included. See also SHORT CARRY.

LONG-DATED FORWARD   Any FORWARD transaction with a final MATURITY in excess of 1 year.

LONG END   [COL] The long MATURITIES of the YIELD CURVE, generally taken to mean those in excess of seven to ten years. See also BELLY OF THE CURVE, SHORT END.

LONG HEDGE   A LONG POSITION in a DERIVATIVE CONTRACT or financial instrument that is used to protect a natural SHORT POSITION. As rising prices cause a loss on the natural short position, the long hedge produces an offsetting gain; the reverse occurs with falling prices. See also SHORT HEDGE.

LONG ONLY A common HEDGE FUND or INVESTMENT strategy where a manager creates a PORTFOLIO of LONG positions in an EQUITY market. The strategy only permits the manager to express views on stocks that are believed to be undervalued. A long only portfolio generates SYSTEMATIC RISK and IDIOSYNCRATIC RISK. See also MARKET NEUTRAL.

LONG POSITION A purchased or owned position in a financial ASSET that benefits from price appreciation. In order to realize a gain generated by rising prices, the long position must be sold or offset. Also known as LONG. See also SHORT POSITION.

LONG-TERM DEBT Any form of DEBT with a MATURITY date of more than 10 years, depending on jurisdiction or ACCOUNTING rules. In some jurisdictions long-term debt is interpreted more narrowly as any debt maturity in the forthcoming fiscal period. See also MEDIUM-TERM DEBT, SHORT-TERM DEBT.

LONG-TERM EQUITY APPRECIATION SECURITY (LEAPS) Long-dated EQUITY CALL OPTIONS and PUT OPTIONS traded on various EXCHANGES and OVER-THE-COUNTER. LEAPS, which are available as EUROPEAN OPTIONS and AMERICAN OPTIONS, feature MATURITIES ranging from 2 to 5 years, and can be purchased or sold on a range of INDEXES and LARGE CAP STOCKS.

LONG-TERM PRIME RATE (LTPR) In Japan, a key long-term fixed INTEREST RATE, historically set as a fixed spread above the 5-year funding rate of select domestic BANKS.

LONG THE BASIS An ARBITRAGE or TRADING strategy where a LONG POSITION in a cash instrument is HEDGED by a SHORT POSITION in FUTURES or FORWARDS.

LONGEVITY BOND See MORTALITY BOND.

LOOKBACK OPTION An OVER-THE-COUNTER COMPLEX OPTION that grants the buyer a maximum gain by "looking back" over the price path of the ASSET and determining the point that creates the greatest economic profit. See also FLOATING STRIKE LOOKBACK OPTION, OPTION ON THE MAXIMUM/MINIMUM.

LOONIE [COL] The Canadian dollar.

LOOPHOLES [COL] Exceptions or exemptions in a TAX code that can be legally exploited in order to reduce tax LIABILITIES. See also TAX AVOIDANCE, TAX EVASION.

LOSS Any deficit remaining after all costs have been subtracted from the REVENUE or selling price of a good or service or any deficit arising from the disposal of an asset at a price that is unfavorable compared to its original contract price. See also PROFIT.

LOSS ADJUSTER A professional appointed by, but remaining independent of, an INSURER to negotiate settlement of a CLAIM under an INSURANCE POLICY. See also LOSS ASSESSOR.

LOSS ADJUSTMENT EXPENSE   The cost an INSURER must bear in adjusting a CLAIM under an INSURANCE contract; some portion of the expense is generally passed back to INSUREDS through LOAD charges. Insurers that are efficient in their claims procedures have greater ability to lower their loss adjustment expenses and either improve their margins or reduce their load charges.

LOSS ASSESSOR   A professional appointed by an INSURED to negotiate settlement of a CLAIM with an INSURER under the terms of an INSURANCE POLICY. See also LOSS ADJUSTER.

LOSS AVERSION   The degree to which an INVESTOR alters behavior in the face of a loss. While conventional financial theories assume behaviors for gains or losses are perfectly symmetric, theories of loss aversion suggest that investors may be reluctant to realize losses as quickly as they realize gains.

LOSS-BASED MODEL   See CREDIT DEFAULT MODEL.

LOSS CONTROL   A RISK MANAGEMENT TECHNIQUE where a firm employs safety precautions to reduce the likelihood that a particular RISK will impact its operations and create a loss. Loss controls may be physical, such as fire or security safety equipment, or intangible, such as training and education. Also known as LOSS PREVENTION. See also LOSS FINANCING, RISK REDUCTION.

LOSS EQUITY PUT   A CONTINGENT EQUITY structure that results in the issuance of new EQUITY in the event a predefined TRIGGER event, such as a large loss from a CATASTROPHIC HAZARD, is breached. Although COMMON STOCK and PREFERRED STOCK can be issued under the put, preferred stock is often used in order to prevent DILUTION. If the trigger event occurs and the put is EXERCISED the put seller, generally a BANK, provides the put purchaser with funds in exchange for SHARES. See also PUT PROTECTED EQUITY.

LOSS FINANCING   A broad class of RISK MANAGEMENT TECHNIQUES, including RISK TRANSFER, RISK RETENTION, and HEDGING, that is primarily concerned with ensuring the availability of funds in the event of a loss. Loss financing may be funded from internal sources (e.g., through self-retention RESERVES) or external sources (e.g., through compensatory payments from INSURANCE or DERIVATIVE CONTRACTS). See also LOSS CONTROL, POST-LOSS FINANCING, PRE-LOSS FINANCING, RISK REDUCTION.

LOSS FREQUENCY METHOD   In INSURANCE, a mechanism used to establish a core PREMIUM level by projecting the expected number of future losses in a given RISK class over a particular time frame. Also known as LOSS RATE. See also LOSS RATIO METHOD.

LOSS GIVEN DEFAULT   A value or percentage estimate of the amount, net of RECOVERY, which a BANK expects to lose if a COUNTERPARTY DEFAULTS (i.e., –1 RECOVERY RATE). Loss given default is an essential input into internal and regulatory CREDIT DEFAULT MODELS as it provides a financial estimate of the net amount that may ultimately be lost should a counterparty fail.

LOSS PORTFOLIO TRANSFER   A FINITE RISK CONTRACT where the INSURED transfers a PORTFOLIO of unclaimed losses from previous LIABILITIES. The insured pays the INSURER a fee, PREMIUM, and the PRESENT VALUE of net RESERVES needed to cover existing portfolio LIABILITIES, and the insurer assumes responsibility for the losses. Through this mechanism uncertain "lump sum" liabilities are transformed into certain liabilities, with a present value that is equal to the net present value of unrealized losses. See also RETROSPECTIVE AGGREGATE LOSS COVER, RETROSPECTIVE FINITE POLICY.

LOSS PREVENTION   See LOSS CONTROL.

LOSS RATE   See LOSS FREQUENCY METHOD.

LOSS RATIO   In INSURANCE, a measure of an INSURER's ability to cover losses and LOSS ADJUSTMENT EXPENSE with PREMIUMS, generally computed as:

$$LR = \frac{L + LAE}{Pr}$$

where L is loss (from CLAIMS), LAE is loss adjustment expense, and Pr is premium.

   The lower the ratio, the more premium the insurer preserves as profit. Also known as EXPECTED LOSS RATIO, PERMISSIBLE LOSS RATIO. See also COMBINED RATIO, EXPENSE RATIO.

LOSS RATIO METHOD   In INSURANCE, a mechanism used to modify a core PREMIUM level by uniform percentages for related types of RISKS in order to align actual and expected LOSS RATIOS. See also LOSS FREQUENCY METHOD.

LOSS RESERVES   A RESERVE account established by an INSURER or REINSURER that includes an estimate of CLAIMS reported and adjusted but not yet paid, claims reported and filed but not yet adjusted, and claims INCURRED BUT NOT REPORTED; the latter is often difficult to estimate on an *ex-ante* basis and actual results only appear over time.

LOSS-SENSITIVE INSURANCE CONTRACTS   The general class of partial INSURANCE contracts with PREMIUMS that depend on loss experience. Common loss-sensitive contracts include EXPERIENCE RATED POLICIES, INVESTMENT CREDIT PROGRAMS, LARGE-DEDUCTIBLE POLICIES, and RETROSPECTIVELY RATED POLICIES.

LOSSES INCURRED   In INSURANCE, a measure of the amount of PREMIUMS earned by the INSURER that must be allocated to cover losses; losses incurred can serve as a basis for establishing LOSS RESERVES. See also LOSSES OUTSTANDING.

LOSSES OUTSTANDING   In INSURANCE, the amount of losses representing CLAIMS received but not yet paid by the INSURER to INSUREDS. See also LOSSES INCURRED.

LOT   [COL] A minimum standard tradable quantity of a SECURITY, COMMODITY, or ASSET, typically set by an EXCHANGE or established through market convention. See also BOARD LOT, ODD LOT, ROUND LOT.

LOW EXERCISE PRICE OPTION (LEPO)   An EXCHANGE-TRADED or OVER-THE-COUNTER OPTION with a STRIKE PRICE that is set very close to zero. The creation of a low strike price allows the option's value to track closely the price of the UNDERLYING reference ASSET.

LOW-PREMIUM CONVERTIBLE BOND   A CONVERTIBLE BOND, generally issued with a 10- to 15-year final MATURITY, which has a CONVERSION PRICE set at a small (i.e., < 5%) PREMIUM to the market price of the ISSUER's COMMON STOCK; the PROBABILITY of rapid conversion into SHARES is thus very high. Since a low-premium convertible is essentially an EQUITY substitute, the coupon on the bond is usually only slightly higher than the existing DIVIDEND YIELD on the underlying common stock.

LP   See LIMITED PARTNERSHIP.

LSE   See LONDON STOCK EXCHANGE.

LTD   See LIMITED.

LTPR   See LONG-TERM PRIME RATE.

LTV   See LOAN-TO-VALUE.

M

M&A   Abbreviated form of MERGERS and ACQUISITIONS.

M0   CURRENCY in circulation plus BANK balances at the CENTRAL BANK.

M1   M0 plus COMMERCIAL BANK demand DEPOSITS and demand SAVINGS ACCOUNTS.

M2   M1 plus OVERNIGHT REPURCHASE AGREEMENTS, overnight EUROCURRENCY DEPOSITS, traditional SAVINGS ACCOUNTS, small time deposits, and MONEY MARKET MUTUAL FUND shares.

M3   M2 plus large time DEPOSITS and term REPURCHASE AGREEMENTS. See also L.

MAASTRICHT TREATY   A treaty, signed in 1992 in Maastricht, Netherlands, that led to the creation of the EUROPEAN UNION. The treaty defined the development and timeline for EUROPEAN MONETARY UNION and the creation of a single currency, the EURO.

MAC   See MATERIAL ADVERSE CHANGE CLAUSE.

MACARONI DEFENSE   [COL] An ANTITAKEOVER DEFENSE where a potential TARGET company issues BONDS with a REDEMPTION clause forcing the SECURITIES to be redeemed at a very substantial PREMIUM to PAR VALUE in the event of a TAKEOVER; the provision makes the company unattractive to any potential acquirer. See also SCORCHED EARTH DEFENSES.

MACAULAY DURATION   See DURATION.

MACROECONOMIC FACTOR MODEL   A MULTIFACTOR RISK MODEL with inputs that include historical STOCK RETURNS and observable macroeconomic indicators, such as INTEREST RATES, INFLATION, INVESTOR confidence, and business activity. The sensitivity of a stock price to each macroeconomic variable can be estimated through such a model, allowing the projection of EXPECTED RETURNS. See also FUNDAMENTAL FACTOR MODEL, STATISTICAL FACTOR MODEL.

MACROECONOMIC INDICATORS   See ECONOMIC INDICATORS.

MACROECONOMICS   The study, within the broad area of ECONOMICS, of the total economic activity of a system, with a focus on NATIONAL INCOME, industrial production, INFLATION/prices, UNEMPLOYMENT, MONEY SUPPLY, INTEREST RATES, and FOREIGN EXCHANGE RATES. See also MICROECONOMICS.

MACROHEDGE   A proxy HEDGE, put in place by a company or BANK, that is designed to protect REVENUES and earnings in the event of a deterioration in economic conditions (upto, and including, a RECESSION). Since there is no single instrument or financial CONTRACT that can replicate such conditions, a macrohedge is generally constructed from a variety of UNDERLYINGS that perform well in poor market conditions.

MAIN STREET   [COL] In the United States, the broad class of RETAIL INVESTORS.

MAINTENANCE MARGIN   (1) The minimum MARGIN each party to an EXCHANGE-TRADED DERIVATIVE transaction must preserve, generally an amount that is somewhat less than the INITIAL MARGIN. Once the maintenance margin level has been breached, VARIATION MARGIN must be posted to return the position to initial margin levels or the transaction will be closed out. (2) The minimum margin an INVESTOR must retain in a SECURITIES account in support of a collateralized PURPOSE LOAN or NONPURPOSE LOAN. If the maintenance level is not preserved, the BROKER is authorized to sell COLLATERAL in the account to repay the loan.

MAINTENANCE PERIOD   A specified period for computing BANK compliance with relevant RESERVE requirements.

MAJORITY CONTROL   A process or structure where effective corporate control is gained by taking a majority, though not absolute, stake in the company's COMMON STOCK. See also CONTROLLING INTEREST, LEGAL MECHANISM CONTROL, MANAGEMENT CONTROL, MINORITY CONTROL, TOTAL CONTROL, VOTING TRUST CONTROL.

MAJORITY INTEREST   See CONTROLLING INTEREST.

M

MAKING A BOOK   [COL] In the United Kingdom, taking a LONG POSITION or SHORT POSITION in SECURITIES, COMMODITIES, or other ASSETS for proprietary, rather than client-driven, purposes. Such activity is typical for the proprietary TRADING desks at BANKS and SECURITIES FIRMS, as well as HEDGE FUNDS. See also BACK BOOK.

MAKING A MARKET   [COL] See TWO-WAY PRICES.

MANAGED COLLATERALIZED DEBT OBLIGATION   A COLLATERALIZED DEBT OBLIGATION (CDO) that permits the manager to substitute REFERENCE CREDITS in the POOL. This form of CDO allows the substitution of deteriorating credits, but does not provide INVESTORS with transparency on the composition of the PORTFOLIO and carries higher fees than STATIC COLLATERALIZED DEBT OBLIGATIONS. See also SINGLE TRANCHE COLLATERALIZED DEBT OBLIGATION, SYNTHETIC COLLATERALIZED DEBT OBLIGATION.

MANAGED FLOATING   See MANAGED FOREIGN EXCHANGE RATE.

MANAGED FOREIGN EXCHANGE RATE   A FOREIGN EXCHANGE RATE whose value is set by a CENTRAL BANK or monetary authority via small/regular purchases and sales of CURRENCY and through macroeconomic policies. Managed rates are not strictly fixed or pegged by government authorities, nor are they freely determined through pure market SUPPLY and DEMAND forces. Also known as MANAGED FLOATING. See also CRAWLING PEG, PEGGING.

MANAGED FUND   Any form of INVESTMENT FUND (e.g., MUTUAL FUND, UNIT INVESTMENT TRUST) that features active management by the FUND MANAGER, who typically has significant discretion regarding the nature and timing of ASSETS that can be bought and sold within the fund (but must in all cases adhere to the terms of an approved investment policy).

MANAGEMENT ACCOUNTING   The measuring and analyzing of a company's financial information in order to provide management with insight on its progress in achieving specific financial targets and fulfilling strategic management, performance management, and RISK MANAGEMENT goals. Management accounting may include confidential information that is never disclosed to external STAKEHOLDERS, as well as forward-looking projections of operations. See also COST ACCOUNTING, FINANCIAL ACCOUNTING.

MANAGEMENT BOARD   The second BOARD OF DIRECTORS in a DUAL BOARD SYSTEM, approximately equivalent to the EXECUTIVE MANAGEMENT team in companies operating under the SINGLE BOARD SYSTEM. This board, which typically includes 5 to 15 senior executives appointed by the SUPERVISORY BOARD, is headed by a chairman and is responsible for daily management of individual businesses/divisions or control functions. Also known as EXECUTIVE BOARD.

MANAGEMENT BUY-IN   The ACQUISITION of a PRIVATE COMPANY or PUBLIC COMPANY by an external PRIVATE EQUITY or VENTURE CAPITAL group with a dedicated management team assembled expressly to manage the operations of the company. A buy-in generally occurs when the company is seen to have potential for growth and value-generation, but where the existing management is believed to have insufficient qualifications. Also known as BUY-IN. See also MANAGEMENT BUYOUT.

MANAGEMENT BUYOUT (MBO)   The ACQUISITION of a PUBLIC COMPANY by a management group that results in retirement of the public EQUITY through the assumption of a large amount of DEBT (i.e., the company is taken private through the use of LEVERAGE); such transactions have the advantage of placing in direct control those who are most familiar with the company and its operations. The ultimate goal of the management team is to refocus operations, reduce expenses, spin off unwanted operations, and then refloat or sell the company over the medium term. See also EMPLOYEE BUYOUT, LEVERAGED BUYOUT, REVERSE LEVERAGED BUYOUT, MANAGEMENT BUY-IN.

MANAGEMENT CAPITAL   See ECONOMIC CAPITAL.

MANAGEMENT COMPANY   The primary company of a MUTUAL FUND or other FUND MANAGEMENT organization, responsible for managing all aspects of the support, infrastructure, and policy surrounding an entire group of associated funds.

MANAGEMENT CONTROL   A process or structure where management gains effective corporate control by accumulating a sufficiently large block of a company's COMMON STOCK to direct activities; as with MINORITY CONTROL, this process only works when ownership is so diffuse that even an organized MINORITY INTEREST fails to dominate the company and its actions. See also LEGAL MECHANISM CONTROL, MAJORITY CONTROL, TOTAL CONTROL, VOTING TRUST CONTROL.

MANDATE   An authorization or approval to arrange a NEW ISSUE of SECURITIES or CORPORATE FINANCE transaction, awarded by a company or sovereign entity to a FINANCIAL INSTITUTION acting as an INTERMEDIARY. COMMERCIAL BANKS, INVESTMENT BANKS, and SECURITIES FIRMS that hope to generate fee income and gain LEAGUE TABLE credit compete aggressively for mandates.

MANDATORY BID   In the United Kingdom, a requirement under the CITY CODE stipulating that an acquiring company must submit a formal BID for a TAKEOVER target once it has amassed 30% of the target's SHARES in the market.

MANDATORY CONVERTIBLE BOND   A CONVERTIBLE BOND that must be EXERCISED into the ISSUER's COMMON STOCK prior to final MATURITY. The convertible can be issued as an EQUITY CONTRACT note, where the issuer exchanges the bond for common stock at maturity; if the INVESTOR chooses not to accept the stock, the issuer sells the newly issued securities in the market and delivers cash proceeds to the investor. It can also be structured as an equity commitment note, where the investor does not have to exchange notes for new common stock, but the issuer commits to floating new stock and using the proceeds to redeem the outstanding bonds. See also REVERSE CONVERTIBLE BOND.

MANUSCRIPT INSURANCE   A customized INSURANCE POLICY with terms that are tailored to an INSURED's specific requirements. A manuscript contract, which is used when coverage cannot be accommodated via a standard insurance form, reflects special needs, conditions, and PERIL coverages. Also know as MANUSCRIPT POLICY.

MANUSCRIPT POLICY   See MANUSCRIPT INSURANCE.

MAPLE BOND   [COL]] A BOND, NOTE, or CERTIFICATE OF DEPOSIT issued in Canadian dollars in the Canadian markets by a foreign company.

MARGIN   (1) SECURITY, such as cash, a LETTER OF CREDIT, or certain high-quality BONDS, posted by the buyer and seller of an EXCHANGE-TRADED DERIVATIVE at the start of the trade (in the form of INITIAL MARGIN) and periodically thereafter (as VARIATION MARGIN). Use of margin helps mitigate the effects of CREDIT RISK. (2) Security posted by an INVESTOR buying or selling STOCKS or BONDS on a LEVERAGED basis through a BROKER-DEALER. (3) See PREMIUM. (4) A profit component added to a LOAN or other financing transaction. (1), (2) See also MAINTENANCE MARGIN. (2) See also NONPURPOSE LOAN, PURPOSE LOAN.

MARGIN ACCOUNT   (1) An ACCOUNT at a BANK, BROKER, or other FINAN-CIAL INSTITUTIONS in which an INVESTOR can borrow against a speci-fied percentage of SECURITIES or COMMODITIES held within the account. The resulting LOAN is known as a MARGIN LOAN, and is subject to INITIAL MARGIN, MAINTENANCE MARGIN, VARIATION MARGIN, and MARGIN CALLS. (2) An account that is used by an INVESTOR to buy and sell EXCHANGE-TRADED DERIVATIVES, and which is subject to periodic evaluation of margin and posting of additional COLLATERAL in the event of a margin call.

MARGIN CALL   A CALL made by a BANK, BROKER, or other FINANCIAL INSTITUTION to an INVESTOR holding a MARGIN LOAN in a MARGIN ACCOUNT when the MAINTENANCE MARGIN has declined below a specified threshold. The investor must supply additional VARIATION MARGIN to return to the specified MAINTENANCE MARGIN or risk a closeout of its position.

MARGIN LOAN   See PURPOSE LOAN.

MARGIN TRADING   A form of LEVERAGED TRADING arising when an INVESTOR secures a MARGIN LOAN through a MARGIN ACCOUNT.

MARGINAL COST   The change in TOTAL COST that comes from producing an incremental unit of a good or service. Marginal cost can change at each new level of production, so the marginal cost at any point relates to the change in cost for that unit. It is computed as the first derivative of total cost with respect to quantity, or:

$$MC = \frac{\partial TC}{\partial Q}$$

where MC stands for marginal cost, TC for total cost and Q for quantity. See also MARGINAL REVENUE, VARIABLE COST.

MARGINAL REVENUE   The change in REVENUE that comes from selling an incremental unit of a good or service. Marginal revenue can change at each new level of sales, so the marginal revenue at any point relates to the change in revenue for that unit. It is computed as the first derivative of total revenue (TR) with respect to quantity (Q), or:

$$MR = \frac{\partial TR}{\partial Q}$$

Since revenue is itself a function of price times quantity, MR can also be expressed as the first derivative of price (P) with respect to quantity, or:

$$MR = (P + Q)\frac{\partial P}{\partial Q}$$

See also MARGINAL COST.

MARGINAL TAX RATE   The incremental TAX levied for an additional unit of INCOME (or earnings), computed as the change in tax liability (due or paid) divided by the change in taxable income (earnings). See also AVERAGE TAX RATE, EFFECTIVE TAX RATE, STATUTORY TAX RATE.

MARINE INSURANCE   A general form of PROPERTY AND CASUALTY INSURANCE used to cover goods in transit (i.e., via air, land, or waterway) and the vehicles used for transportation.

MARK-TO-MARKET   The process of revaluing a financial transaction based on closing market prices or rates. In the United States, FINANCIAL ACCOUNTING STANDARDS Rule 115 states that FINANCIAL INSTITUTIONS are required to mark-to-market their TRADING ASSETS every business day (although assets held in an INVESTMENT account until MATURITY need not be). Marking-to-market is used to estimate daily PROFITS and LOSSES and quantify actual CREDIT RISK and MARKET RISK exposures. It is also an essential process for transactions that are based on MARGIN or COLLATERAL, such as EXCHANGE-TRADED DERIVATIVES and MARGIN LOANS, since daily fluctuations in value can result in the call for, or return of, collateral. See also MARK-TO-MODEL, PROFIT AND LOSS EXPLAIN.

MARK-TO-MARKET VALUE   See ACTUAL EXPOSURE.

MARK-TO-MODEL   The process of valuing a financial transaction based on mathematical models rather than market prices. This type of valuation occurs when a transaction is very unique (e.g., long-dated or complex) or ILLIQUID, and transparent market prices are not available. Certain COMPLEX DERIVATIVES, esoteric STRUCTURED NOTES, and COLLATERALIZED MORTGAGE OBLIGATIONS are valued using models. Although marking-to-model provides an estimate of value where none would otherwise exist, it also introduces an element of MODEL RISK. See also MARK-TO-MARKET.

MARKER CRUDE   A BENCHMARK reference crude oil that is used in pricing and TRADING. Different qualities of oil from different regions may be pegged to particular marker crudes, such as Brent Blend, West Texas Intermediate, Dubai, and so forth.

MARKET CAPITALIZATION   A measure of a PUBLIC COMPANY's current value, computed as:

$$MC = S \times Shs$$

where S is the current price of the COMMON STOCK and Shs is the number of OUTSTANDING SHARES.

Since the stock price changes on a daily basis, the market capitalization of the firm changes in tandem. Also known as MARKET VALUE.

MARKET DEPTH The number of SHARES of STOCK in a given company that are BID and OFFERED, ranked by price. Market depth contributes to the DISPLAYED LIQUIDITY that all INVESTORS can see.

MARKET ECONOMY See FREE MARKET ECONOMY.

MARKET EXPECTATIONS THEORY See EXPECTATIONS THEORY.

MARKET FLEX Legal language contained in a LOAN transaction that allows the ARRANGER to change pricing based on INVESTOR demand, itself a function of market conditions. Market flex also allows the arranger to reallocate portions of the loan across various TRANCHES.

MARKET IF TOUCHED ORDER An ORDER to purchase or sell a SECURITY if a particular price is reached; once attained, the order converts into a MARKET ORDER and is filled at the best available market price.

MARKET IMPACT The effect of information transfer from an ORDER on the market price of a quoted SECURITY.

MARKET IMPACT COST The deviation of the price of a transaction from the market price that would have existed had the transaction not been executed. This approach disregards the BID-OFFER SPREAD, which is assumed to be an explicit cost. Market impact cost may be temporary (as related to the incremental LIQUIDITY required to execute a TRADE), or it may be permanent (as related to the new price demanded by the market once it becomes aware of the trade).

MARKET MAKER An institution that is obliged to quote BIDS and OFFERS at all times and fill either side of any ORDER received; for standard-sized transactions, the market maker must generally provide FIRM QUOTES rather than INDICATIVE QUOTES. In exchange for quoting a TWO-WAY MARKET and providing LIQUIDITY, the market maker is often given additional visibility into TRADING flows and pending orders.

MARKET MICROSTRUCTURE The study of the specific mechanics of financial marketplaces, focusing particularly on the way in which SUPPLY and DEMAND interact and the way in which PRICE DISCOVERY is achieved.

MARKET MODEL A general corporate system that is characterized by very diffuse SHAREHOLDINGS, deep and LIQUID CAPITAL MARKETS, dynamic CAPITAL reallocation, advanced legal and regulatory frameworks, and an active CORPORATE CONTROL MARKET. The United States, the United Kingdom, and Canada are representative examples of the market model. See also HYBRID MODEL, RELATIONSHIP MODEL.

MARKET NEUTRAL A common HEDGE FUND or INVESTMENT strategy where a manager creates a PORTFOLIO of LONG and SHORT positions in an EQUITY market. The construction of a market neutral portfolio allows the manager to simultaneously express views on stocks believed to be undervalued and those that are overvalued. A market neutral portfolio can result in the elimination of SYSTEMATIC RISK in favor of IDIOSYNCRATIC RISK arising from individual long and short positions. See also LONG ONLY.

MARKET ON CLOSE ORDER   An ORDER to purchase or sell a SECURITY at the price prevailing at market close. The market on close is effectively equivalent to a delayed MARKET ORDER.

MARKET ORDER   An ORDER for the purchase or sale of a SECURITY at the current market level; as long as sufficient LIQUIDITY is available, the order will be filled at the market price. See also LIMIT ORDER, MARKET IF TOUCHED ORDER, MARKET ON CLOSE ORDER, STOP ORDER, TIME ORDER.

MARKET OUT CLAUSE   See MATERIAL ADVERSE CHANGE CLAUSE.

MARKET OVERHANG   See OVERHANG.

MARKET POWER   A situation where a purchaser or supplier of raw materials or finished goods has such a significant presence that it can dictate, to a significant degree, favorable pricing terms. Such power is limited to a small number of companies that effectively operate as MONOPOLIES or OLIGOPOLIES.

MARKET PRICE   (1) The price for a good or service that is determined through the interaction of SUPPLY and DEMAND in a free market setting. (2) An EXECUTION price on an ORDER that reflects the current market BID or market OFFER. (2) See also LIMIT PRICE.

MARKET RISK   The RISK of loss due to an adverse move in the MARKET VALUE of an ASSET or market indicator, such as a COMMON STOCK, BOND, LOAN, FOREIGN EXCHANGE RATE, or COMMODITY. Market risk, which is a form of FINANCIAL RISK, can be subcategorized into BASIS RISK, CURVE RISK, DIRECTIONAL RISK, SPREAD RISK, and VOLATILITY RISK.

MARKET RISK AMENDMENT   An amendment to the BASLE ACCORD framework, agreed in 1996, permitting participating BANKS to use their internal models in the computation of VALUE-AT-RISK for CAPITAL ALLOCATION purposes. See also BASLE II.

MARKET SEGMENTATION THEORY   A theory of INTEREST RATES indicating that each MATURITY segment of the YIELD CURVE is separate and distinct; INVESTORS commit CAPITAL to the sector of their choice, impeding the free flow of capital to other segments. See also EXPECTATIONS THEORY, LIQUIDITY PREFERENCE THEORY.
   Additional references: Lutz and Lutz (1951); Meiselman (1962).

MARKET SWEEP   A second offer for the purchase of outstanding SHARES of COMMON STOCK, made by an acquiring company to INVESTORS in the TARGET company. The market sweep, which comes after an initial TENDER OFFER has been made, is intended to build the acquirer's position to a controlling stake and may be executed at a price that is higher than the initial tender.

MARKET TIMING An INVESTMENT strategy used by certain FUND MANAGERS and proprietary TRADING operations that attempts to select the proper points through which to establish a LONG POSITION or SHORT POSITION in a particular ASSET. In reality such a strategy is difficult to implement consistently.

MARKET VALUE   (1) The current value of an ASSET or LIABILITY based on quoted BIDS or OFFERS, reflecting a realizable economic value in the marketplace. (2) See MARKET CAPITALIZATION. (1) See also BOOK VALUE.

MARKET VALUE ADDED   A measure of a company's financial performance that compares its MARKET VALUE with CAPITAL invested. The greater the market value added, the greater the company's ability to use its capital resources effectively. See also ACCOUNTING PROFIT, ECONOMIC PROFIT, ECONOMIC VALUE ADDED.

MARKETABLE SECURITY   Any SECURITY that can be sold without limitation in a SECONDARY MARKET, thus featuring a high degree of LIQUIDITY. While many securities can be freely traded and are thus marketable some, such as PRIVATE PLACEMENTS, are designed primarily as "hold to maturity" ASSETS and are more accurately considered NONMARKETABLE SECURITIES. Certain ILLIQUID assets, such as MORTGAGES, LOANS, and ACCOUNTS RECEIVABLE, can be converted into marketable securities via the SECURITIZATION process.

MARKETS IN FINANCIAL INSTRUMENTS DIRECTIVE (MIFID)   A legislative directive enacted in 2007 within the EUROPEAN ECONOMIC AREA in order to protect INVESTORS, increase transparency for those dealing in financial markets, promote cost efficiencies, and ensure harmonization across member states. MIFID replaced the Investment Services Directive.

MARKOV PROCESS   A STOCHASTIC PROCESS where only the current price of an ASSET is relevant in determining what may happen in the future, i.e., previous prices and the number of periods preceding the current observation are irrelevant. The Markov process is used in numerous DERIVATIVE pricing models.

MARKOWITZ PORTFOLIO OPTIMIZATION   A single-period optimization process based on MEAN VARIANCE ANALYSIS that is designed to identify the best-performing PORTFOLIO for a given level of RISK. The inputs into the process include the EXPECTED RETURN of each ASSET in the portfolio, the VARIANCE of each asset, and the VARIANCE/COVARIANCE MATRIX between the assets. The resulting output is the EFFICIENT FRONTIER. See also MULTIPERIOD PORTFOLIO OPTIMIZATION.

MARRIED PUT   [COL] A PUT OPTION that is acquired by an INVESTOR as a HEDGE at the same time as the UNDERLYING reference ASSET is purchased. As the price of the underlying asset declines the value of married put increases, and vice versa.

MAS   See MONETARY AUTHORITY OF SINGAPORE.

MASTER AGREEMENT   A formal agreement between two COUNTERPARTIES that documents the legal and CREDIT aspects of DERIVATIVE transactions. A properly executed master agreement allows subsequent trades to be evidenced by short-form CONFIRMATIONS (rather than extensive long-form confirmations) and permits CREDIT RISK exposures to be managed on a net, rather than gross, basis. Common master agreements include the INTERNATIONAL SWAPS AND DERIVATIVES ASSOCIATION Master Agreement, the French Association Française Banque agreement and the German Rahmenverstrag agreement.

MASTER FUND   A FUND that invests CAPITAL gathered from INVESTORS through one or more FEEDER FUNDS. The master fund structure is widely employed in the HEDGE FUND sector.

MASTER LIMITED PARTNERSHIP (MLP)   A form of organization where the legal structure mirrors a conventional LIMITED PARTNERSHIP but where the business structure assumes that of a CORPORATION. An MLP may be publicly traded on an EXCHANGE.

MASTER NOTE   COMMERCIAL PAPER offered by a direct ISSUER to the INVESTMENT management or TRUST department of a BANK or an INSTITUTIONAL INVESTOR that has periodic amounts to invest in short-term FIXED INCOME instruments. The master note, which pays a particular SPREAD above a stated commercial paper rate, is a dependable source of funds for the issuer and eliminates the administrative burden that would otherwise arise through the issuance of smaller denomination notes.

MASTER TRUST   A vehicle often used to hold a POOL of ASSETS securing an ASSET-BACKED SECURITY.

MATCH   The process of matching a buyer and seller of an ASSET, typically STOCK. See also CROSS, CROSSING NETWORK, DARK POOL.

MATCHED BARGAIN   In the United Kingdom, the pairing of an ORDER to buy and an order to sell a specific STOCK.

MATCHED BOOK   A PORTFOLIO of ASSETS and LIABILITIES (such as the LOANS and DEPOSITS of a BANK, or the REPURCHASE AGREEMENTS and REVERSE REPURCHASE AGREEMENTS of a SECURITIES FIRM), with equal (or nearly equal) MATURITIES or DURATIONS. A matched book minimizes or eliminates an institution's exposure to MARKET RISK and/or LIQUIDITY RISK, but generates a smaller RETURN on CAPITAL. See also GAP, GAPPING, MISMATCH, OPEN BOOK, UNMATCHED BOOK.

MATCHING CONCEPT   A central ACCOUNTING CONCEPT that indicates a company should properly match its INCOME with its EXPENSES in any given accounting period (e.g., on an ACCRUAL BASIS). See also CONSISTENCY CONCEPT, GOING CONCERN CONCEPT, PRUDENCE CONCEPT.

MATERIAL ADVERSE CHANGE (MAC) CLAUSE   A COVENANT contained in certain LOAN agreements that permits a BANK to cancel undrawn CREDIT facilities and/or demand repayment of existing facilities if the BORROWER experiences a materially adverse change in its financial condition, or is subject to an adverse operating environment; triggering of a MAC can lead to the cancellation of facilities that otherwise appear to be available and committed. A material adverse change may be defined objectively (e.g., a CREDIT RATING downgrade or a rise in LEVERAGE) or subjectively. Also known as MARKET OUT CLAUSE. See also FORCE MAJEURE, VIS MAJOR.

MATERIALITY An assessment of information classified as material, and which must be considered in the ACCOUNTING process and in any relevant financial disclosure. Though the classification of materiality is at least partly subjective, a general guideline suggests that the exclusion of material information may have an adverse effect on STAKEHOLDERS.

MATILDA [COL] A BOND, NOTE, or CERTIFICATE OF DEPOSIT issued in Australian dollars in the Australian markets by a foreign company.

MATURITY See MATURITY DATE.

MATURITY BUCKET [COL] A framework of time bands used by BANKS and other FINANCIAL INSTITUTIONS to manage their ASSETS and LIABILITIES, <1 year, 1–3 years, 3–5 years, 5–7 years, and so forth. Assets and liabilities are assigned to their respective buckets and then used to compute a GAP.

MATURITY DATE The date on which a financial CONTRACT, ASSET, or LIABILITY matures or comes due. Also known as MATURITY. See also EXPIRY DATE, REDEMPTION DATE.

MATURITY GAP See GAP.

MAXIMUM FORESEEABLE LOSS A worst-case loss scenario applied by an INSURER or REINSURER to a potential CATASTROPHIC HAZARD. See also MAXIMUM PROBABLE LOSS.

MAXIMUM LOSS A loss measure indicating the amount a firm might lose across a PORTFOLIO of MARKET RISKS by ignoring any offsetting effects obtained from DIVERSIFICATION. Maximum loss can be regarded as an extreme form of the VALUE-AT-RISK computation. See also SCENARIO ANALYSIS.

MAXIMUM PROBABLE LOSS An EXPECTED LOSS computation applied by an INSURER or REINSURER to a catastrophic or noncatastrophic RISK event. See also AMOUNT AT RISK, MAXIMUM FORESEEABLE LOSS.

MBO See MANAGEMENT BUYOUT.

MBS See MORTGAGE-BACKED SECURITY.

MEAN The unweighted average of a set of observations, which can be computed in arithmetic or geometric form:

Arithmetic mean:

$$\mu = \frac{\sum_{i=1}^{N} x_i}{N}$$

Geometric mean:

$$\mu = (\Pi_i x_i)^{\frac{1}{N}}$$

where x_i is an observation and N is the number of observations. See also MEDIAN, MODE.

MEAN REVERSION The observable tendency for INTEREST RATES, EQUITIES, and certain other financial variables to return to a MEAN level over the long term. Mean reversion is incorporated into certain DERIVATIVE pricing models.

MEAN VARIANCE ANALYSIS The process of evaluating the riskiness of a PORTFOLIO based on the EXPECTED RETURN and RISK (or VARIANCE) of potential outcomes. A portfolio can be optimized for single or multiple frameworks through this process. Also known as MEAN VARIANCE OPTIMIZATION. See also MARKOWITZ PORTFOLIO OPTIMIZATION, MODERN PORTFOLIO THEORY, MULTIPERIOD PORTFOLIO OPTIMIZATION.

Additional reference: Markowitz (1952).

MEAN VARIANCE OPTIMIZATION See MEAN VARIANCE ANALYSIS.

MEDIAN A form of obtaining an average figure, typically obtained by ordering the values from largest to smallest and then selecting the center value (when the number of observations is odd) or the average of the two center values (when the number of observations is even). See also MEAN, MODE.

MEDIUM OF EXCHANGE A mechanism (often with little INTRINSIC VALUE) to store and transfer value, allowing for the efficient payment of goods and services. While all manner of COMMODITIES have historically been used as a medium of exchange, money is now the most common form. See also BANKNOTE, FIAT MONEY.

MEDIUM-TERM DEBT Any form of DEBT with a MATURITY DATE of 1 to 10 years, depending on jurisdiction or ACCOUNTING rules. See also LONG-TERM DEBT, SHORT-TERM DEBT.

MEDIUM-TERM NOTE (MTN) A FIXED INCOME SECURITY issued by a company or sovereign entity in the US markets from a standing program arranged by an UNDERWRITER; once the program is registered issuance can take place at will. Financing via an MTN program gives an ISSUER considerable flexibility in accessing funds in the form, and at a time, deemed most opportune. MTNs can be issued in FIXED RATE, FLOATING RATE, collateralized, amortizing, and CREDIT-supported form, with MATURITIES extending up to 30 years. Standard fixed-rate notes generally pay semiannual COUPONS; floating rate notes typically pay monthly or quarterly coupons referenced to LONDON INTERBANK OFFERED RATE, COMMERCIAL PAPER, TREASURY BILLS, or the PRIME RATE. See also EURO MEDIUM-TERM NOTE (EMTN).

MEMBER BANK   A BANK that is officially part of a country's CENTRAL BANK or monetary authority system, or part of a national CLEARING system.

MEMORANDUM OF ASSOCIATION   In the United Kingdom, a document that presents essential information on a new company that seeks to be recognized as a REGISTERED COMPANY. The memorandum is filed with the Registrar of Companies.

MERCHANDISE CREDIT   See TRADE CREDIT.

MERCHANT BANK   In the United Kingdom, a BANK that provides clients with CORPORATE FINANCE, RISK MANAGEMENT, and INVESTMENT management advice, and deals actively in SECURITIES UNDERWRITING and TRADING and PRIVATE EQUITY investments. A merchant bank does not actively accept DEPOSITS or grant LOANS as a main line of business. See also BOUTIQUE, INVESTMENT BANK.

MERGER   A CORPORATE FINANCE transaction where two companies combine their operations into a single venture, through a POOLING OF INTERESTS, an outright purchase, or a CONSOLIDATION. In a standard merger, SHAREHOLDERS of the two companies agree to the deal on a friendly basis and share in a specific percentage of SHARES in the new company. In a strict legal sense only transactions where one of the two original companies survives is classified as a merger; in practice, however, nontaxable poolings of interests and statutory consolidations are considered mergers. See also ACQUISITION, HORIZONTAL MERGER, TAKEOVER, VERTICAL MERGER.

MERGER ACCOUNTING   The ACCOUNTING policies used when two companies arrange a MERGER as equals. Under this process the BALANCE SHEET accounts of the two companies are simply added together, and no changes to GOODWILL are affected. Also known as POOLING OF INTERESTS ACCOUNTING. See also ACQUISITION ACCOUNTING.

MERGER ARBITRAGE   See RISK ARBITRAGE.

METI   See MINISTRY OF ECONOMY, TRADE, AND INDUSTRY.

MEZZANINE FINANCING   (1) A second or third round of financing in a VENTURE CAPITAL, LEVERAGED BUYOUT, or RESTRUCTURING transaction, which is generally SUBORDINATE to BANK LOANS but senior to early rounds of venture capital funding. Mezzanine financing is often considered to be pre-INITIAL PUBLIC OFFERING funding. (2) See SUBORDINATED DEBT.

MEZZANINE LOAN   A JUNIOR ranking NONRECOURSE LOAN, often used in the context of commercial real estate financing. Such loans, which may carry MATURITIES ranging from 1 to 10 years and feature AMORTIZATION or INTEREST-only payments, are not typically secured on the underlying property being financed, but on the creditworthiness of the entity that owns the property. See also FIRST LIEN COMMERCIAL MORTGAGE.

MFN   See MOST FAVORED NATION.

MICROCAP STOCK See MICROSTOCK.

MICROCREDIT A sector of development BANKING that is based on the granting of very small LOANS (e.g., $50–100) in order to promote small-scale, local business initiatives.

MICROECONOMICS The study, within the broad area of ECONOMICS, of how individuals and firms make decisions related to the allocation of scarce resources. Focus is placed on microstructures of SUPPLY and DEMAND, and how these interact to establish relative prices. See also MACROECONOMICS.

MICROSTOCK The COMMON STOCK of a very small company, typically one with a MARKET CAPITALIZATION in the tens, or hundreds, of thousands of dollars. Such stocks, which are generally speculative and unproven, TRADE infrequently in the informal OVER-THE-COUNTER bulletin board market. Also known as MICROCAP STOCK. See also LARGE CAP STOCK, MID-CAP STOCK, SMALL CAP STOCK.

MID-ATLANTIC OPTION See BERMUDAN OPTION.

MID-CAP STOCK The COMMON STOCK of a company with a medium-sized MARKET CAPITALIZATION, generally in the range of $1 billion to $5 billion. See also LARGE CAP STOCK, MICROSTOCK, SMALL CAP STOCK.

MID-MARKET The midpoint of a BID and OFFER on an ASSET. Also known as MID-PRICE.

MID-PRICE See MID-MARKET.

MIDDLE OFFICE A group of functions found in BANKS, SECURITIES FIRMS and INVESTMENT BANKS that center on verifying pricing of TRADES and providing technology and infrastructure support to TRADERS.

MIDGET [COL] A 15-year GOVERNMENT NATIONAL MORTGAGE ASSOCIATION PASS-THROUGH SECURITY. See also DWARF, GNOME.

MIFID See MARKETS IN FINANCIAL INSTRUMENTS DIRECTIVE.

MIGRATION See RATING MIGRATION.

MINI [COL] An EXCHANGE-TRADED DERIVATIVE CONTRACT designed primarily for use by RETAIL INVESTORS. Minis are structurally identical to other exchange FUTURES and OPTIONS but are offered in small denominations that make them suitable for those preferring smaller exposures. Given their size, minis are usually only traded through electronic mechanisms (even when an EXCHANGE features a physical TRADING floor). See also E-MINI.

MINIMUM FLUCTUATION The smallest price movement on a SECURITY or DERIVATIVE, typically set in relation to the specific characteristics of an ASSET or market. See also TICK VALUE.

MINIMUM FUNDING REQUIREMENT In the United Kingdom, a requirement that the ASSETS of a PENSION not be less than 90% of its LIABILITIES.

MINIMUM SUBSCRIPTION   The minimum size (in value terms) of a NEW ISSUE of STOCK or a RIGHTS OFFERING that must be raised in order for the transaction to proceed. If the minimum subscription amount is not met, the transaction is cancelled.

MINIMUM VARIANCE HEDGE RATIO   See HEDGE RATIO.

MINISTRY OF ECONOMY, TRADE, AND INDUSTRY (METI)   In Japan, a government ministry, formed in 2001 from the consolidation of the Ministry for International TRADE and Industry, the Economic Planning Agency, and various other governmental agencies, which is responsible for overseeing the country's industrial sector and its trade practices.

MINORITY CONTROL   A process or structure where a small group of INVESTORS cooperates to gain effective control of a company; this is generally accomplished by attracting enough PROXIES from diffuse owners and can only work if no other large block holder exists. See also LEGAL MECHANISM CONTROL, MAJORITY CONTROL, MANAGEMENT CONTROL, MINORITY INTEREST, TOTAL CONTROL, VOTING TRUST CONTROL.

MINORITY INTEREST   An ownership stake of less than 50% in a company, which leaves SHAREHOLDERS with no effective control of management. A minority interest arises when a CONTROLLING INTEREST is held by another party. Also known as MINORITY OWNERSHIP. See also MINORITY CONTROL.

MINORITY OWNERSHIP   See MINORITY INTEREST.

MINORITY PROTECTION   See MINORITY SHAREHOLDER RIGHTS.

MINORITY SHAREHOLDER RIGHTS   A set of rights accorded to the MINORITY SHAREHOLDERS to ensure that they are not treated unfairly by the MAJORITY INTERESTS. Specific rights vary by jurisdiction, but include access to FINANCIAL STATEMENTS, ability to take legal actions, and so forth. Also known as MINORITY PROTECTION.

MINUS TICK   Sale of a SECURITY at a price that is lower than the prior transaction, generally indicated through the display of a "-" next to the screen or tape price. In some jurisdictions a SHORT SALE cannot be initiated on a minus tick. Also known as DOWNTICK. See also PLUS TICK, ZERO PLUS TICK, ZERO MINUS TICK.

MISMATCH   A state where a BANK's RATE-SENSITIVE ASSETS and RATE-SENSITIVE LIABILITIES are not perfectly matched with regard to MATURITY or DURATION. A mismatch implies the existence of LIQUIDITY RISK, INTEREST RATE RISK, and/or CURVE RISK, but may generate a greater RETURN on invested CAPITAL. See also GAP, GAPPING, MATCHED BOOK, UNMATCHED BOOK.

MISMATCHED SWAP   See BASIS SWAP.

MISREPRESENTATION   An untrue statement of fact that is made by a party in entering into a CONTRACT, and which may result in losses or damages to the other party. The misrepresentation may be negligent (indicating that the party makes the statement without any reason to believe it is untrue) or fraudulent (indicating that the party makes the statement knowing that it is untrue). See also FRAUD, RESCISSION.

MIXED LOT   [COL] A total ORDER comprised of ROUND LOTS and ODD LOTS. See also BOARD LOT, LOT.

MIXED PERIL CONTRACT   See MULTILINE POLICY.

MLP   See MASTER LIMITED PARTNERSHIP.

MNC   See MULTINATIONAL CORPORATION.

MOB SPREAD   See MUNICIPALS OVER BONDS SPREAD.

MOCHIAI   [JPN] The network of cross-SHAREHOLDINGS held by KEIRETSU companies.

MODE   The value of a series of observations that occurs with greatest frequency. See also MEAN, MEDIAN.

MODEL   A mathematical framework used by a BANK, INSURER, INVESTMENT MANAGER, or other FINANCIAL INSTITUTION to perform specific financial computations, such as pricing DERIVATIVES or other instruments or determining a quantum of RISK. While often useful, such computations are prone to MODEL RISK.

MODEL RISK   The RISK of loss arising from flaws in the mathematical models/analytics used to value financial CONTRACTS such as DERIVATIVES. Sources of model risk include incorrect model specification, incorrect model application or usage, and incorrect implementation of a developed model. Endogenous factors may also play a role, including flaws in the technological or software platform or problems with data feeds used to supply the model with raw information. See also MARK-TO-MODEL.

MODERN PORTFOLIO THEORY (MPT)   A theory of INVESTMENT that considers how INVESTORS make use of DIVERSIFICATION to create an optimized PORTFOLIO that maximizes EXPECTED RETURNS for a given level of RISK (as specified through VARIANCE or STANDARD DEVIATION). MPT assumes an investor displays RISK AVERSION and must be compensated for incremental risk, and that risk preferences can be designated through a quadratic utility function, which requires only the definition of portfolio returns and variance (higher order moments, such as SKEWNESS and KURTOSIS are thus ignored). See also ALPHA, BETA, CAPITAL MARKET LINE, EFFICIENT FRONTIER, MARKOWITZ PORTFOLIO OPTIMIZATION, MULTIPERIOD PORTFOLIO OPTIMIZATION, MEAN VARIANCE ANALYSIS, SECURITY MARKET LINE.

MODIFIED DURATION   A common measure of DURATION, or the average CASH FLOWS of a FIXED INCOME instrument, which estimates the change in the value of the instrument for a small change in YIELD.

MODIFIED INTERNAL RATE OF RETURN (MIRR)   An adaptation of the INTERNAL RATE OF RETURN measure that generates a YIELD based on the use of a specific rate reinvested CASH FLOWS. Unlike the NET PRESENT VALUE computation, which reinvests at the project's COST OF CAPITAL, and standard internal rate of return computation, which reinvests at the internal rate of return, the MIRR uses specific rates for cash inflows.

MODIFIED LADDER OPTION   See FIXED STRIKE LADDER OPTION.

MODIFIED PASS-THROUGH SECURITY   A form of MORTGAGE-BACKED SECURITY that GUARANTEES to INVESTORS the timely payment of INTEREST and the payment of PRINCIPAL as it is collected, but not later than the final MATURITY DATE.

MODIFIED SHOUT OPTION   See FIXED STRIKE SHOUT OPTION.

MODIGLIANI-MILLER THEORY   A key financial theory indicating that in a perfect market a firm's COST OF CAPITAL is independent of the financing method chosen (i.e., DEBT, EQUITY, RETAINED EARNINGS) and that management should be indifferent to the actual mix of CAPITAL employed. In practice market imperfections and frictions such as TAXES and RISK mean that management generally focuses closely on LEVERAGE, DIVIDEND policy, and the proper mix of capital in order to minimize its overall cost of capital.

Additional reference: Miller and Modigliani (1958).

MOF   See MULTIPLE OPTION FACILITY.

MOMENT   In statistical theory, operators that describe the shape of a distribution. In general, the

First moment is 0

Second moment is the VARIANCE

Third moment is SKEWNESS

Fourth moment is KURTOSIS

Also known as CENTRAL MOMENT.

MOMENTUM INDICATOR   A TECHNICAL ANALYSIS measure used to gauge the speed of upward and downward movements in a SECURITY or market INDEX. Common momentum measures include relative strength indicators, MOVING AVERAGES, and convergence/divergence metrics.

MOMENTUM TRADING   A TRADING strategy that is based purely on the short-term movement and momentum of a SECURITY or INDEX rather than on FUNDAMENTAL ANALYSIS or TECHNICAL ANALYSIS. See also MOMO, NEGATIVE MOMENTUM TRADING, POSITION TRADING, SWING TRADING.

MOMO   [COL]   A TRADER or INVESTOR engaged in MOMENTUM TRADING.

MONETARISM   A theory of ECONOMICS popularized by economist Milton Friedman indicating that MONEY SUPPLY is the driving force in determining national output and INFLATION, and that policies should be geared toward ensuring an equilibrium in SUPPLY and DEMAND for MONEY.

Additional reference: Friedman and Schwartz (1963).

MONETARY AUTHORITY OF SINGAPORE (MAS)   The CENTRAL BANK of Singapore, which was established in 1970 and began operations in 1971, assuming many functions that had previously been managed in a decentralized manner by various government agencies. MAS is responsible for conducting MONETARY POLICY, issuing CURRENCY, overseeing the domestic payment systems, establishing REGULATIONS for the domestic financial sector, managing the country's RESERVES and developing the country as an international financial nexus.

MONETARY BASE   The core amount of MONEY circulating in a national system, precise measurement of which can vary by country and desired breadth. In a narrow sense it includes notes and coins and BANK RESERVES held with the CENTRAL BANK or monetary authority; a broader definition also includes customer DEPOSITS held by BANKS. See also M0, M1, M2, M3.

MONETARY INFLATION   An expansion in a country's MONEY SUPPLY which, under MONETARISM, leads to an increase in INFLATION.

MONETARY POLICY   An action taken by a country's CENTRAL BANK or monetary authority to influence the SUPPLY, DEMAND, and cost of CREDIT in order to promote economic growth and full employment, while keeping INFLATION pressures under control. Policy actions may be developed through a review of key data, e.g., ECONOMIC INDICATORS. Although specific approaches vary by national system, common techniques include buying/selling GOVERNMENT BILLS and GOVERNMENT BONDS through OPEN MARKET OPERATIONS, establishing RESERVE REQUIREMENTS for BANKS, and adjusting the official DISCOUNT RATE. See also FISCAL POLICY.

MONETARY POLICY COMMITTEE (MPC)   In the United Kingdom, a committee within the BANK OF ENGLAND that meets monthly to consider MONETARY POLICY and economic issues, culminating in a decision on setting of INTEREST RATES.

MONETIZATION   (1) A process, transaction, or strategy that allows financial value embedded in an ASSET to be converted into cash. Through monetization ILLIQUID, yet valuable, CONTRACTS and properties (such as ACCOUNTS RECEIVABLE, EMBEDDED OPTIONS, fixed plant and equipment) can be transformed into cash form so that proceeds can be used for other purposes. DERIVATIVES are often used to monetize value. (2) A process where a government prints MONEY in order to purchase outstanding GOVERNMENT BONDS from the market. (3) A process where a government sells government bonds to BANKS in order to finance a budgetary shortfall.

MONEY   (1) A MEDIUM OF EXCHANGE which is in circulation in the financial system. A narrow definition of MONEY includes paper and coins, while a broader definition includes measures such as M1, M2, and M3. (2) A medium of exchange used in a particular country. (1,2) Also known as CURRENCY. See also FIAT MONEY.

MONEY AT CALL   Secured funds lent by BANKS, BROKERS, DEALERS, and other FINANCIAL INSTITUTIONS to one another which must be repaid on demand. See also MONEY AT SHORT NOTICE.

MONEY AT SHORT NOTICE   Secured funds lent by BANKS, BROKERS, DEALERS, and other FINANCIAL INSTITUTIONS to one another which must typically be repaid within 1 to 2 weeks. See also MONEY AT CALL.

MONEY BROKER   In the United Kingdom, a BROKER that specializes in arranging short-term funding between BANKS, DISCOUNT HOUSES, and other FINANCIAL INSTITUTIONS that are active in the MONEY MARKET, in exchange for a COMMISSION.

MONEY CENTER BANK   A large BANK operating from one of the main money centers of the world.

MONEY LAUNDERING   The process of disguising illegally earned money so that it becomes part of the mainstream financial system. Money laundering generally comprises the three general stages of PLACEMENT, LAYERING, and INTEGRATION. Also known as LAUNDERING.

MONEY MARKET   The short-term financial marketplace for issuance and TRADING of ASSETS and LIABILITIES with MATURITIES extending from 1 day to 24 months. Instruments of the money market include GOVERNMENT BILLS, REPURCHASE AGREEMENTS, REVERSE REPURCHASE AGREEMENTS, BANKER'S ACCEPTANCES, CERTIFICATES OF DEPOSIT, COMMERCIAL PAPER, EURO COMMERCIAL PAPER, and short-term notes. Money market instruments are very LIQUID and generally feature only modest amounts of MARKET RISK and CREDIT RISK. See also CAPITAL MARKET.

MONEY MARKET BASIS   A day count convention applied to MONEY MARKET instruments, which is based on the actual number of days divided by 360 (for the United Kingdom) or 365 (for the United States and most other countries).

MONEY MARKET FUND   A MUTUAL FUND that invests exclusively in MONEY MARKET instruments, including COMMERCIAL PAPER, GOVERNMENT BILLS, BANKER'S ACCEPTANCES, and CERTIFICATES OF DEPOSIT. Money market funds are generally highly LIQUID and relatively low RISK, although returns are not GUARANTEED.

MONEY MARKET INSTRUMENT   Any financial instrument with a MATUR-ITY of less than 1 year, which can be traded and is often priced on a DISCOUNT basis. Common instruments include GOVERNMENT BILLS, CERTIFICATES OF DEPOSIT, COMMERCIAL PAPER, BILLS OF EXCHANGE, and BANKER'S ACCEPTANCES, among others.

MONEY MARKET PREFERRED STOCK   See ADJUSTABLE RATE PREFERRED STOCK.

MONEY SPREAD   See BEAR SPREAD, BULL SPREAD.

MONEY SUPPLY   The amount of MONEY circulating within a national ECONOMY, measured in various ways (i.e., M0, M1, M2, M3); though subtle differences exist in measuring money supply between M categories across countries, a general guide indicates that M0 is CENTRAL BANK money supply, and M1 – M3 is BANK money supply. The size and trend of money supply is directly and indirectly influenced by a country's MONETARY POLICY and FISCAL POLICY. See also MONETARY BASE.

MONEYNESS   [COL] The degree to which an OPTION possesses or lacks INTRINSIC VALUE. An option with moneyness is said to be IN-THE-MONEY and has intrinsic value; an option without moneyness is OUT-OF-THE-MONEY and has no intrinsic value.

MONOLINE INSURER   An INSURER that provides CREDIT enhancement (or WRAP) via GUARANTEES for MUNICIPAL BONDS and ASSET-BACKED SECURITIES (ABS), based on its ability to maintain a strong CREDIT RATING (e.g., AAA) of its own. If the bond or ABS being secured does not pay INVESTORS contractual INTEREST and PRINCIPAL, the monoline insurer is required to do so, and must therefore have a sufficiency of CAPITAL to meet obligations. Also known as MONOLINER.

MONOLINE POLICY   An INSURANCE CONTRACT that only covers one LINE or class of RISK. If a loss occurs in the referenced PERIL, the INSURED is covered to a net amount that reflects a DEDUCTIBLE and POLICY CAP. See also MULTILINE POLICY.

MONOLINER   See MONOLINE INSURER.

MONOPOLY   A market that features only one seller of goods or services, suggesting the seller has a significant degree of influence in setting prices. A monopoly can take the form of a natural monopoly, owing to the exclusive ownership of an input or process that would be prohibitively expensive to replicate, or a statutory monopoly, arising from approval given by a government or REGULATOR. In some national systems monopolies are prohibited or severely restricted, as they may be anticompetitive and create unfair pricing and price INFLATION pressures. See also DUOPOLY, MONOPSONY, OLIGOPOLY.

MONOPSONY   A market that features only one buyer of goods or services, suggesting the buyer has an ability to influence the prices paid to suppliers. See also DUOPSONY, MONOPOLY, OLIGOPSONY.

MONTE CARLO SIMULATION   A computer-intensive statistical process that generates ASSET paths based on user-defined inputs and drawings from a random number generator. Monte Carlo simulation is widely used for pricing DERIVATIVES, computing CREDIT RISK exposures and scenarios, and measuring PORTFOLIO RISKS. See also SIMULATION.

MORAL HAZARD   Altering behavior by becoming less conservative and more reckless, knowing that INSURANCE or RISK protection exists to compensate for damage or loss. INSURERS attempt to protect against moral hazard by remaining diligent in the UNDERWRITING procedures and requiring prospective INSUREDS to bear a portion of the economic exposure through DEDUCTIBLES, COINSURANCE, and/or POLICY CAPS. See also ADVERSE SELECTION.

MORAL SUASION   The process of attempting to convince institutions (e.g., BANKS) to follow a particular policy or set of actions, without specifically mandating such through laws, rules, or REGULATIONS. Moral suasion may be used by a CENTRAL BANK or monetary authority in the pursuit of a specific MONETARY POLICY.

MORATORIUM   A sovereign suspension of INTEREST and/or PRINCIPAL payments on DEBT, and a direct manifestation of SOVEREIGN RISK. Declaration of a moratorium, which may apply to all or selected classes of debt, is generally considered an EVENT OF DEFAULT under CREDIT agreements and may ultimately lead to a RESCHEDULING of payment terms and a write-off of the debt by the LENDERS/INVESTORS.

MORNING NOTES   [COL] Late-breaking research information conveyed to INVESTORS by research analysts of INVESTMENT BANKS and SECURITIES FIRMS during morning conference calls.

MORTALITY BOND   A form of INSURANCE-LINKED SECURITY that transfers longevity RISK, or the risk of unanticipated changes in longevity as related to ACTUARIAL or statistical estimates, from a sponsoring INSURER, REINSURER, or provider of ANNUITIES or defined benefits, to the CAPITAL MARKETS. Under the terms of a typical structure, INVESTORS receive a payment at MATURITY if a selected survivor INDEX (referencing a specific demographic) is either above or below a benchmark value. Since some sponsors are financially impacted by a rise in mortality rates (e.g., an insurer providing a payout on life insurance policies over and above its estimates) while others are affected by a decline in mortality rates (e.g., an annuities provider that must pay out additional sums as longevity extends), the market for such BONDS is two-sided. Also known as LONGEVITY BOND. See also EXTREME MORTALITY BOND.

MORTGAGE   A LOAN granted by a BANK for the purchase of residential or commercial property, generally secured by the property being acquired. The mortgage may carry a FIXED RATE or FLOATING RATE, and a MATURITY extending from 5 to 30 years, LOAN-TO-VALUE of 50%–100%, and PRINCIPAL repayment in conventional form (straight-line repayment), graduated form (increasing repayment), or BALLOON/BULLET form (larger or total back-end repayment).

MORTGAGE-BACKED BOND   A BOND that is collateralized by a MORTGAGE PLEDGE. Unlike MORTGAGE-BACKED SECURITIES, which convey an ownership interest in a POOL of mortgages to INVESTORS, the ISSUER retains the ownership interest of the mortgage; the transaction is thus considered DEBT FINANCING rather than a sale of ASSETS. Also known as MORTGAGE BOND. See also COLLATERAL TRUST BOND.

MORTGAGE-BACKED SECURITY (MBS)   A SECURITIZATION of a POOL of MORTGAGES that results in the creation of a PASS-THROUGH SECURITY; INVESTORS acquiring the SECURITIES acquire an ownership interest in the underlying pools. MBSs can be assembled with small-size (conforming) retail mortgages, jumbo (nonconforming) retail mortgages, and commercial real estate mortgages. Mortgage originators often sell their pools into a CONDUIT managed by a sponsoring financial institution, which then packages them into MBSs and issues them in the PRIMARY MARKET; once issued they are actively TRADED in the SECONDARY MARKET. MBSs have MATURITIES ranging from 1 to 30 years and are available in FIXED RATE and FLOATING RATE form. See also COLLATERALIZED MORTGAGE OBLIGATION, PARTICIPATION CERTIFICATE, FEDERAL NATIONAL MORTGAGE ASSOCIATION, FEDERAL HOME LOAN MORTGAGE CORPORATION, GOVERNMENT NATIONAL MORTGAGE ASSOCIATION.

MORTGAGE BOND   See MORTGAGE-BACKED BOND.

MORTGAGE DEBENTURE   A LOAN granted by a BANK or other FINANCIAL INSTITUTION that is secured on a specific real property of the BORROWER.

MORTGAGE DEFAULT SECURITIZATION An INSURANCE-LINKED SECURITY that permits purchasers of MORTGAGES to obtain protection against DEFAULT by the BORROWER. Repayment of PRINCIPAL and/or COUPONS is contingent on the repayment history of the underlying mortgages; if a specified loss occurs, the ISSUER of the BOND may delay or cease making payments to INVESTORS, meaning that it has HEDGED its RISK to instances of mortgage default. See also CATASTROPHE BOND, LIFE ACQUISITION COST SECURITIZATION, RESIDUAL VALUE SECURITIZATION, WEATHER BOND.

MORTGAGE SWAP (1) An OVER-THE-COUNTER AMORTIZING SWAP that replicates the CASH FLOW characteristics of a physical MORTGAGE-BACKED SECURITY, meaning it can be used as a synthetic MORTGAGE or HEDGE for a PORTFOLIO of MORTGAGES. (2) An exchange of mortgages for PARTICIPATION CERTIFICATES or PASS-THROUGH SECURITIES backed by the same mortgages. Mortgage originators in the US market commonly swap seasoned mortgages with the FEDERAL NATIONAL MORTGAGE ASSOCIATION, GOVERNMENT NATIONAL MORTGAGE ASSOCIATION, and FEDERAL HOME LOAN MORTGAGE CORPORATION for tradable SECURITIES or certificates, thereby adding LIQUIDITY to their BALANCE SHEETS.

MORTGAGEE   A LENDER of funds who takes as SECURITY a pledge of some underlying property. See also MORTGAGOR.

MORTGAGEE IN POSSESSION A LENDER that has completed FORE-CLOSURE on a MORTGAGE in DEFAULT and assumes control of the underlying property. As mortgagee in possession the lender is entitled to any INCOME produced by the property and to any proceeds generated upon its sale.

MORTGAGOR   A BORROWER of funds who pledges an underlying property as SECURITY. See also MORTGAGEE.

MOS   See MUTUAL OFFSET SYSTEM.

MOST FAVORED NATION (MFN)   Favorable TRADE status granted to certain nations, where IMPORTS from trading partner countries are treated no less favorably than imports from other countries, and no other foreign goods face a lower TARIFF than the partner country. Countries seek MFN status in order to bolster their trade activities and ultimately expand their own GROSS DOMESTIC PRODUCT.

MOVING AVERAGE   A TECHNICAL ANALYSIS charting technique that computes the average price of a SECURITY or INDEX over a particular time period, depicting general upward or downward trends. The averaging period rolls with each new observation period, which is generally set to daily, weekly, or monthly intervals.

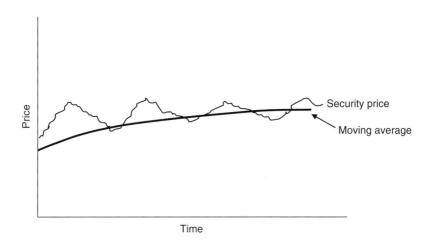

MPC   See MONETARY POLICY COMMITTEE.

MPT   See MODERN PORTFOLIO THEORY.

MTN   See MEDIUM-TERM NOTE.

MUDARABA   [ARB] A form of silent PARTNERSHIP used in ISLAMIC FINANCE. See also MUSHARAKA.

MULTICURRENCY NOTE FACILITY   A short- or medium-term EURONOTE facility that permits an ISSUER to float NOTES in any one of several CURRENCIES. Although the BORROWER can select the borrowing currency, the LENDER can demand repayment in another currency at MATURITY.

MULTIFACTOR MODEL   A type of mathematical model used in the pricing of INTEREST RATE DERIVATIVES in which all of the uncertainty related to the future movement of interest rates is captured by two or more factors. The factors vary by model and may include a short-term real interest rate and INFLATION, a short-term rate and a long-term rate, a short-term rate and a mean-reverting drift parameter, a short-term rate and a volatility parameter, and so forth. See also FORWARD RATE MODEL, SHORT RATE MODEL, SINGLE FACTOR MODEL.

MULTIFACTOR OPTION   See MULTI-INDEX OPTION.

MULTIFACTOR RISK MODEL   An ASSET pricing model used to estimate EXPECTED RETURNS on the basis of more than one RISK FACTOR. Common multifactor risk models include MACROECONOMIC FACTOR MODELS, STATISTICAL FACTOR MODELS, and FUNDAMENTAL FACTOR MODELS. The generic form of a linear factor model is given as:

$$r_i = \sum_{x=1}^{n} b_{ix} f_x e_i$$

where r_i is the asset return of the i-th asset, b_{ix} are the sensitivities to the common risk factors, e_i is the idiosyncratic return of the i-th asset. Also known as FACTOR MODEL. See also ARBITRAGE PRICING THEORY.

MULTI-INDEX NOTE   A STRUCTURED NOTE that pays INVESTORS an enhanced COUPON based on the performance of multiple INDEXES drawn from the same, or different, ASSET classes/markets. The most common multi-index notes are based on broad EQUITY indexes.

MULTI-INDEX OPTION   An OVER-THE-COUNTER COMPLEX OPTION that grants the buyer a PAYOFF based on the difference between two or more reference ASSETS and a predefined STRIKE PRICE; assets may be drawn from the same, or different, asset classes/markets. Also known as MULTIFACTOR OPTION, RAINBOW OPTION. See also BASKET OPTION, MULTIPLE STRIKE OPTION, OPTION ON THE BEST/WORST OF N-ASSETS, OPTION ON THE BEST/WORST OF N-ASSETS AND CASH, SPREAD OPTION.

MULTILATERAL DEVELOPMENT BANK   A supranational organization that is constituted to provide financing and financial and economic advice, primarily to developing nations. Such institutions are generally funded through contributions from the governments of industrialized nations. See also AFRICAN DEVELOPMENT BANK, ASIAN DEVELOPMENT BANK, EUROPEAN BANK FOR RECONSTRUCTION AND DEVELOPMENT, INTERNATIONAL BANK FOR RECONSTRUCTION AND DEVELOPMENT, INTER-AMERICAN DEVELOPMENT BANK.

MULTILATERAL NETTING   A form of NETTING between three or more COUNTERPARTIES. Since it involves more than two institutions, such netting is often carried out by an independent CLEARINGHOUSE or EXCHANGE. See also BILATERAL NETTING.

MULTILINE POLICY   An INSURANCE CONTRACT that covers multiple PERILS within the COMMERCIAL LINES areas. The standard multiline policy contains common policy declarations and conditions and details on specific coverages, each with their own declarations and coverage forms. If a loss occurs in any of the mentioned perils, the INSURED is covered to a net amount that reflects a DEDUCTIBLE and POLICY CAP. Also known as MIXED PERIL CONTRACT, PACKAGE POLICY. See also MONOLINE POLICY, MULTIPLE PERIL POLICY.

MULTINATIONAL CORPORATION (MNC)   A large CORPORATION that operates directly, or through SUBSIDIARIES and/or JOINT VENTURES, in various countries. An MNC may diversify its sourcing of RAW MATERIALS, production, marketing and/or distribution across national borders in an attempt to take advantage of the lowest cost factors of production, so that it is able to maximize PROFITS and ENTERPRISE VALUE.

MULTIPERIOD PORTFOLIO OPTIMIZATION   A multiple period optimization process based on MEAN VARIANCE ANALYSIS that is designed to identify the best-performing PORTFOLIO for a given level of RISK. Analytically more complex than the single-period approach, the inputs into the process include the arithmetic MEAN RETURN of each ASSET in the portfolio, the VARIANCE of each asset, and the VARIANCE/COVARIANCE MATRIX between the assets. The resulting output is the arithmetic mean EFFICIENT FRONTIER. Alternatively, the full historical market data set can be used as an input, and the resulting output will take the form of a geometric mean efficient frontier. See also MARKOWITZ PORTFOLIO OPTIMIZATION.

MULTIPLE   See PRICE/EARNINGS RATIO.

MULTIPLE BARRIER OPTION   An OVER-THE-COUNTER COMPLEX OPTION package that contains at least two BARRIER OPTIONS that create or extinguish an underlying EUROPEAN OPTION. Sine the multiple barrier option has two barriers the PROBABILITY of knock-in or knock-out increases. See also TWIN-IN BARRIER OPTION, TWIN-OUT BARRIER OPTION.

MULTIPLE OPTION FACILITY (MOF)   A medium-term EURONOTE facility that allows an ISSUER to access funds in a range of CURRENCIES, reference INTEREST RATES, and MATURITIES. The range of options available to the BORROWER are contained within the MOF agreement.

MULTIPLE PERIL POLICY   An INSURANCE POLICY that provides coverage for multiple classes of related or unrelated PERILS. Within the PROPERTY AND CASUALTY INSURANCE sector coverage generally extends to property, LIABILITY, crime, and boiler and machinery. Also known as ALL LINES INSURANCE. See also COMMERCIAL GENERAL LIABILITY POLICY, MULTILINE POLICY.

MULTIPLE STRIKE OPTION   An OVER-THE-COUNTER COMPLEX OPTION that grants the buyer a PAYOFF based on the best or worst performing of a series of ASSETS, each with a specific STRIKE PRICE. Option references may be drawn from the same, or different, asset classes/markets. See also MULTI-INDEX OPTION.

MULTIPLE TRIGGER PRODUCT An INSURANCE POLICY that provides the INSURED with a compensatory payment only if multiple events occur (i.e., two or more TRIGGERS are breached). Since the PROBABILITY of several events happening simultaneously is lower than the probability of single event occurrence, the protection provided through the multiple trigger product is generally cheaper than it is for a standard single trigger contract. Since multiple trigger products can be structured to protect against different dimensions of RISK, they are frequently applied in the management of VOLUMETRIC RISK, which is driven by both volume and price factors. See also DUAL TRIGGER, TRIPLE TRIGGER.

MULTIRISK PRODUCT An INSURANCE POLICY that combines multiple RISKS in a single structure, allowing the client to obtain a consolidated, and often cheaper and more efficient, RISK MANAGEMENT solution. See also MULTIPLE PERIL POLICY, MULTIPLE TRIGGER PRODUCT.

MULTITRADING FACILITY Any alternative or electronic EXCHANGE for TRADING of SECURITIES, permissible in Europe under the MARKETS IN FINANCIAL INSTRUMENTS DIRECTIVE.

MUNICIPAL BOND A BOND issued by a state or municipal authority or agency in order to fund general obligations or specific projects. Bonds can be issued with FIXED RATES or FLOATING RATES and MATURITIES ranging from 1 to 30 years, and can be backed by the specific CREDIT of the municipal issuer, the CASH FLOWS of a project (as a NONRECOURSE obligation), or through CREDIT enhancement provided by a MONOLINE INSURER. INTEREST earned on municipal bonds is generally exempt from federal TAX, although it is taxable at the state or municipal level. Notes are available in various forms, including tax, revenue, and bond anticipation notes, project notes, short COUPON notes, and 7-day demand notes. See also GENERAL OBLIGATION BOND, REVENUE BOND.

MUNICIPAL BOND INSURANCE An INSURANCE CONTRACT written by an INSURER (e.g., a MONOLINE INSURER) to cover an event of DEFAULT by the ISSUER of a MUNICIPAL BOND. The insurance, which may assume the form of a FINANCIAL GUARANTEE, is designed to protect INVESTORS from loss of PRINCIPAL and/or COUPON interest.

MUNICIPALS OVER BONDS (MOB) SPREAD The YIELD differential between TAX-free MUNICIPAL BONDS and TREASURY BONDS of the same MATURITY. The spread provides an indication of the relative CREDIT perception of a municipal ISSUER, with a widening reflecting deterioration, and a tightening indicating an improvement.

MURABAHA [ARB] A TRUST sale scheme used in ISLAMIC FINANCE, where a FINANCING is structured as a credit sales contract with a markup over a negotiated invoice price. See also IJARA, SALAM, SUKUK.

MUSHARAKA [ARB] A form of simple PARTNERSHIP used in ISLAMIC FINANCE. See also MUDARABA.

MUTUAL ASSENT   A condition that only permits a CONTRACT to become valid when both parties have agreed to the terms and conditions.

MUTUAL FUND   (1) In the United States, an INVESTMENT COMPANY that raises CAPITAL from INVESTORS and uses the proceeds to purchase ASSETS; owners of mutual fund SHARES own a proportional share in the pool of invested assets. Mutual funds can issue an unlimited number of shares, which are redeemable on demand at the quoted NET ASSET VALUE (or the net asset value less a back-end LOAD, or COMMISSION charge). Mutual funds are an extremely popular form of INVESTMENT, particularly among RETAIL INVESTORS who often lack the expertise, time, and/or resources, to create and manage a PORTFOLIO of SECURITIES. (2) See UNIT TRUST. (1) Also known as OPEN-END FUND, OPEN-END INVESTMENT COMPANY. (1) See also CLOSED-END FUND, LOAD FUND, NO-LOAD FUND, 12b-1 MUTUAL FUND.

MUTUAL OFFSET SYSTEM (MOS)   A formal arrangement between two EXCHANGES where EXCHANGE-TRADED DERIVATIVE CONTRACTS initiated on one exchange can be transferred to, or closed out on, another exchange. The MOS extends TRADING hours significantly, and can increase the LIQUIDITY of a given contract. In order for the MOS mechanism to work the contracts on the participating exchanges must be fungible.

MUTUAL ORGANIZATION   A corporate structure where members, rather than external INVESTORS, own the organization. Although the mutual has the advantage of limiting external influence on corporate affairs, it generally caps the amount of CAPITAL that is available for expansion.

N

N.A. See NATIONAL ASSOCIATION.

NAAMLOZE VENNOOTSCHAP (NV) [DUT] In the Netherlands and Belgium, a CORPORATION that is publicly traded. In the Netherlands Antilles, a SUBSIDIARY established as a TAX SHELTER.

NAFTA See NORTH AMERICAN FREE TRADE AGREEMENT.

NAKED CALL An OPTION position where the seller of a CALL OPTION does not own the UNDERLYING ASSET that must be delivered if the buyer EXERCISES the CONTRACT. Selling naked calls is generally a high RISK strategy since the seller must acquire the asset in the open market should exercise occur, at a prevailing price that will be higher than the STRIKE PRICE. See also COVERED CALL, NAKED OPTION, NAKED PUT.

NAKED DEBENTURE In the United Kingdom, a DEBENTURE that is not secured.

NAKED OPTION An OPTION position where the seller of the option does not own the UNDERLYING ASSET or cash that must be delivered if the buyer EXERCISES the CONTRACT. Selling naked options is generally a high RISK strategy since the seller must acquire the underlying asset in the open market or source cash should exercise occur. Also known as UNCOVERED OPTION. See also COVERED OPTION, NAKED CALL, NAKED PUT, NAKED WRITER.

NAKED POSITION An outright LONG POSITION or SHORT POSITION that is not protected by an offsetting HEDGE. A naked position may be exposed to elements of MARKET RISK, CREDIT RISK, and/or LIQUIDITY RISK. See also COVERED POSITION.

NAKED PUT An OPTION strategy where the seller of a PUT OPTION does not have cash on hand to purchase the UNDERLYING ASSET if the buyer EXERCISES the CONTRACT. Selling naked puts can be a high RISK strategy since the seller must be able to source enough cash to cover the higher STRIKE PRICE. Simply selling the asset will not generate enough proceeds, meaning the put seller must be able to borrow funds from alternative sources. See also COVERED PUT, NAKED CALL, NAKED OPTION.

NAKED SHORTING An illegal SHORT SALE of SECURITIES that are not certain to exist. In certain jurisdictions parties contemplating a short sale must first confirm that sufficient securities exist and can be borrowed to fulfill the short.

NAKED SWAP A SWAP transaction that creates a LONG POSITION or SHORT POSITION in a series of CASH FLOWS, without any offsetting position from other sources.

NAKED WRITER   The seller of a NAKED OPTION that does not have the UNDERLYING ASSET (deliverable under a CALL OPTION) or sufficient cash on hand to acquire the asset (under a PUT OPTION) should EXERCISE occur. A naked writer attempts to earn PREMIUM income through a relatively high RISK strategy. See also COVERED WRITER.

NAMED INSURED   The party in an INSURANCE POLICY that is designated as an INSURED.

NAMED PERIL COVER   See NAMED PERIL POLICY.

NAMED PERIL POLICY   An INSURANCE POLICY that provides coverage only for PERILS that are specifically enumerated in the policy; coverage is thus much narrower than it is under an ALL RISKS POLICY, although the corresponding PREMIUM payable by the INSURED to the INSURER is smaller. Also known as NAMED PERIL COVER.

NAMES [COL]   Individuals providing CAPITAL to SYNDICATES UNDERWRITING INSURANCE and REINSURANCE CONTRACTS through LLOYD'S OF LONDON. In the event CLAIMS exceed RESERVES, participating names must cover their share of the losses (as well as those that cannot be met by other participants, as most syndicates feature JOINT AND SEVERAL LIABILITY). Since names face UNLIMITED LIABILITY, their personal ASSETS are at RISK. Although individuals have historically been the primary providers of capital, Lloyd's allowed CORPORATIONS to act as names in the provision of underwriting CAPITAL starting in the mid-1990s.

NARROW MARKET   A market in a financial ASSET or COMMODITY that is not actively traded.

NARROW MONEY   The narrow definition of MONEY SUPPLY, often measured through M1. See also BROAD MONEY.

NASD   See NATIONAL ASSOCIATION OF SECURITIES DEALERS.

NASDAQ See NATIONAL ASSOCIATION OF SECURITIES DEALERS AUTOMATED QUOTATIONS.

NASDAQ 100   A BENCHMARK technology INDEX comprised of 100 LARGE CAP STOCKS in the technology sector. The index can be traded directly through EXCHANGE-TRADED FUNDS and DERIVATIVES.

NATIONAL ASSOCIATION (N.A.)   In the United States, a term appended to certain federally chartered BANKS, which are required by REGULATORS to include the term "national" in their names.

NATIONAL ASSOCIATION OF SECURITIES DEALERS (NASD)   A US SELF-REGULATORY ORGANIZATION, comprised of BROKER/DEALERS and SECURITIES FIRMS dealing in OVER-THE-COUNTER SECURITIES, which is responsible for enforcing INVESTOR protection rules promulgated by the SECURITIES AND EXCHANGE COMMISSION. The NASD also oversees TRADING of securities through the NATIONAL ASSOCIATION OF SECURITIES DEALERS AUTOMATED QUOTATIONS.

NATIONAL ASSOCIATION OF SECURITIES DEALERS AUTOMATED QUOTATIONS (NASDAQ) An electronic EXCHANGE that lists the COMMON STOCKS of over 5000 US companies through a system of MARKET MAKERS. The NATIONAL ASSOCIATION OF SECURITIES DEALERS oversees the exchange. It features two separate markets, the NASDAQ National Market, which supports LARGE CAP STOCKS, and the NASDAQ Capital Market, which supports emerging companies. The exchange also owns the Philadelphia Stock Exchange and the Nordic-based OMX group of exchanges.

NATIONAL BANK   In the United States, a BANK that holds a Federal charter and is a part of the FEDERAL RESERVE SYSTEM and the FEDERAL DEPOSIT INSURANCE CORPORATION.

NATIONAL BEST BID AND OFFER (NBBO)   In the United States, the best available BID and OFFER on a quoted STOCK, which must be made available to any buyer or seller under REGULATION NMS. A similar market concept exists in Europe and Canada under relevant local rules.

NATIONAL DEBT   The cumulative total of a country's borrowing, both domestically and offshore, which arises from annual deficit spending. Responsibility for managing the national debt is generally assigned to a country's CENTRAL BANK or monetary authority.

NATIONAL MARKET SYSTEM (NMS)   In the United States, an electronic system created in 1975 to link different STOCK EXCHANGES, giving INVESTORS access to consolidated information on the prices of individual STOCKS. NMS continues to provide, through its Intermarket Trading System, access to price and volume data.

NATIONALIZATION   A process where a government assumes control of a specific company or sector in order to achieve specific political or economic goals. See also EXPROPRIATION, PRIVATIZATION.

NATURAL   [COL] See CLEAN.

NAV   See NET ASSET VALUE.

NBBO   See NATIONAL BEST BID AND OFFER.

NCD   See NEGOTIABLE CERTIFICATE OF DEPOSIT.

NEAR MONEY   [COL] ASSETS that are nearly equivalent to cash, meaning they can be liquidated immediately at carrying value, but which still generate a small YIELD or RETURN. Common examples of near money include short-term GOVERNMENT BILLS, COMMERCIAL PAPER, BANKER'S ACCEPTANCES, and sight DEPOSITS. See also L, M0, M1, M2, M3.

NEARBY CONTRACT The current, or closest, EXCHANGE-TRADED DERIVATIVE on a reference ASSET, generally the most LIQUID until several days or weeks prior to EXPIRY, when participants often begin rolling positions into the NEXT NEARBY CONTRACT. Also known as FRONT MONTH, PROMPT MONTH.

NEGATIVE AMORTIZATION LOAN   A LOAN where the periodic payment made is less than the INTEREST being charged, and where the difference is added to the outstanding PRINCIPAL balance. Negative amortization loans are specifically agreed between BORROWER and LENDER, and are often associated with certain types of MORTGAGES, such as a GRADUATED PAYMENT MORTGAGE.

NEGATIVE BASIS   (1)   A market state where the price of the cash or SPOT MARKET SECURITY is below the price of the underlying FUTURES CONTRACT. (2) A market state where the CREDIT SPREAD on a CREDIT DEFAULT SWAP (CDS) is narrower than the spread on a REFERENCE OBLIGATION BOND of the same ISSUER (e.g., the bond is CHEAP to the CDS, or the CDS is RICH to the bond), typically as a result of greater LIQUIDITY in the CDS, large issuance of SYNTHETIC COLLATERALIZED DEBT OBLIGATIONS and/or large issuance of bonds by the issuer. (1) See also BASIS RISK, POSITIVE BASIS, (2) see also NEGATIVE BASIS TRADE.

NEGATIVE BASIS TRADE   An ARBITRAGE TRADE created when a NEGATIVE BASIS exists between a REFERENCE CREDIT's CREDIT DEFAULT SWAP (CDS) and its BOND. Under this strategy an INVESTOR can buy the bond and buy the CDS, earning a POSITIVE CARRY.

NEGATIVE CARRY   Any transaction or TRADE where the RETURNS generated by an ASSET are smaller than the costs of financing and storing the asset. See also CARRY, CARRY TRADE, POSITIVE CARRY.

NEGATIVE CONVEXITY   A characteristic of certain financial ASSETS where losses are greater, and gains are smaller, than those of linear CONTRACTS or those with POSITIVE CONVEXITY. SHORT OPTIONS and certain types of MORTGAGE-BACKED SECURITIES (e.g., INTEREST-ONLY STRIPS) feature negative convexity. See also NEGATIVE GAMMA, NONLINEAR INSTRUMENT.

NEGATIVE EQUITY   (1) A financial state when the value of an ASSET is worth less than the amount of financing used to acquire the asset, e.g., a property whose value is less than the MORTGAGE. (2) See NEGATIVE NET WORTH.

NEGATIVE GAMMA   MARKET RISK exposure to large price moves in the UNDERLYING generated through the sale of PUT OPTIONS or CALL OPTIONS. A seller of options can suffer a loss from negative gamma as it may not have an opportunity to properly rebalance a DELTA HEDGE. In common with other NEGATIVE CONVEXITY instruments, negative gamma positions feature losses that are greater and gains that are smaller than instruments with POSITIVE CONVEXITY. See also GAMMA, GAMMA HEDGE, POSITIVE GAMMA.

NEGATIVE GAP   A general measure of a company's exposure to INTEREST RATE REPRICING RISK. A negative gap arises when RATE SENSITIVE LIABILITIES reprice faster than its ASSETS (e.g., have shorter DURATION), and means the firm will experience a loss if rates rise and a gain if rates fall. Also known as LIABILITY SENSITIVE. See also GAP, GAPPING, POSITIVE GAP.

NEGATIVE MOMENTUM TRADING   A short-term, speculative TRADING strategy based on purchasing COMMON STOCKS that have fallen quickly and dramatically as a result of bad or unexpected news. Negative momentum traders believe market moves may be an overreaction, and attempt to profit by purchasing SHARES for the very short term, until the negative news has been absorbed and other INVESTORS reenter the market. See also MOMO, MOMENTUM TRADING.

NEGATIVE NET WORTH   A financial state where the value of an individual's or company's LIABILITIES exceed the value of ASSETS, indicating a state of INSOLVENCY. Also known as NEGATIVE EQUITY.

NEGATIVE OBLIGATION   The duty for a SPECIALIST or MARKET MAKER dealing in a COMMON STOCK not to take one side of an ORDER on a proprietary basis when it can be matched directly with another order. See also AFFIRMATIVE OBLIGATION, INTERPOSITIONING.

NEGATIVE PLEDGE   A COVENANT in a LOAN agreement or BOND INDENTURE that prohibits a BORROWER from pledging unencumbered ASSETS in support of new FINANCING unless existing debt holders remain equally secured and/or their seniority rankings remain unchanged. If a borrower violates the negative pledge, existing debt holders can generally demand repayment of their funds.

NEGATIVE WORKING CAPITAL   A financial state where a company's CURRENT LIABILITIES exceed its CURRENT ASSETS. Negative working capital generally indicates the presence of LIQUIDITY problems, since insufficient assets exist to cover obligations coming due. See also NET WORKING CAPITAL, POSITIVE WORKING CAPITAL.

NEGATIVE YIELD CURVE   A TERM STRUCTURE where short-term INTEREST RATES are higher than long-term interest rates. A negative curve may be caused by strong demand for short-term CREDIT, high INFLATION, and/or weak INVESTOR confidence. Also known as INVERTED YIELD CURVE. See also FLAT YIELD CURVE, KINKED YIELD CURVE, POSITIVE YIELD CURVE, YIELD CURVE.

NEGLIGENCE   A failure to use reasonable care or diligence in executing a particular action or duty, and which may lead to particular damages. See also DUTY OF CARE.

NEGOTIABLE CERTIFICATE OF DEPOSIT (NCD)   A large denomination marketable CERTIFICATE OF DEPOSIT (i.e., $100,000+) with a FIXED RATE or FLOATING RATE, issued by a BANK; the negotiability feature allows the NCD to be traded in the SECONDARY MARKET. NCDs have MATURITIES ranging from one week to over 10 years and can be floated in a broad range of CURRENCIES. See also FLOATING RATE CERTIFICATE OF DEPOSIT, LOCKUP CERTIFICATE OF DEPOSIT.

NEGOTIABLE INSTRUMENT   A written order, such as a BILL OF EXCHANGE, PROMISSORY NOTE, or CHECK, which is signed by the endorser as being payable to the holder/bearer without conditions. See also NONNEGOTIABLE INSTRUMENT.

NEGOTIATED SWAP A CORPORATE FINANCE transaction involving an exchange of ASSETS (e.g., a SUBSIDIARY, company, or block of SHARES) between two parties. Use of a negotiated swap is an efficient way for a firm to substitute assets that it no longer requires for others that may represent a better strategic fit.

NEGOTIATED UNDERWRITING A noncompetitive UNDERWRITING of a NEW ISSUE of SECURITIES where the ISSUER and UNDERWRITER agree in advance on an appropriate UNDERWRITING SPREAD, deal size, and distribution strategy. See also COMPETITIVE BID UNDERWRITING.

NESTED OPTION See COMPOUND OPTION.

NET ASSET VALUE (NAV) The per SHARE market price of a MUTUAL FUND or CLOSED-END FUND, generally based on the previous day's closing prices for the underlying ASSETS held in the fund. NAV can be computed via:

$$NAV = \frac{(Sec_{MV} + Cash + AI - Liab)}{OS}$$

where Sec_{MV} is the MARKET VALUE of quoted SECURITIES in the PORTFOLIO, Cash is cash on hand, AI is ACCRUED INTEREST, Liab is LIABILITIES, and OS is the number of outstanding SHARES in the fund.

NET ASSETS In the United Kingdom, total ASSETS less CURRENT LIABILITIES. In other jurisdictions the net assets computation also deducts from total assets all medium- and long-term liabilities.

NET BOOK VALUE The value of an ASSET on the corporate BALANCE SHEET, typically reflecting the original cost of purchase or the latest valuation, less accumulated DEPRECIATION. Also known as BOOK VALUE, DEPRECIATED VALUE.

NET BORROWED RESERVES In the United States, the amount a BANK has borrowed from the FEDERAL RESERVE SYSTEM minus the amount of RESERVES it holds above the required minimum. See also NONBORROWED RESERVES.

NET CAPITAL A company's NET WORTH less any additional deductions taken to reflect difficulty in selling ASSETS at their stated value. See also NET CAPITAL RATIO.

NET CAPITAL RATIO In the United States, a measure of LEVERAGE applied by the SECURITIES AND EXCHANGE COMMISSION to BROKER/DEALERS that limits to 15 times the ratio of indebtedness to LIQUID ASSETS. See also NET CAPITAL.

NET CURRENT ASSETS   See WORKING CAPITAL.

NET EARNINGS   See NET INCOME.

NET INCOME   The final result of a company's operations, prior to distribution of DIVIDENDS or allocation to RETAINED EARNINGS. Net income can be computed as OPERATING REVENUE less OPERATING EXPENSE less INTEREST and TAXES. Also known as NET EARNINGS, NET PROFIT.

NET INTEREST MARGIN   In banking, a measure of the INCOME differential between interest-generating ASSETS (e.g., LOANS, FIXED INCOME SECURITIES) and interest-bearing LIABILITIES required to fund the assets (e.g., DEPOSITS, REPURCHASE AGREEMENTS, BONDS), generally computed as:

$$NIM = II - IE$$

where II is INTEREST INCOME and IE is INTEREST EXPENSE.

The larger the *NIM*, the greater the profitability of core banking operations. Also known as INTEREST RATE MARGIN.

NET INVESTMENT   The total within an economic system of new CAPITAL INVESTMENTS less DEPRECIATION on existing investment.

NET LEASE   A form of LEASE in which the LESSEE is responsible for paying the LESSOR lease rental payments as well as general EXPENSES, maintenance, and TAXES. CAPITAL LEASES are typically created as net leases, while OPERATING LEASES are not. See also GROSS LEASE.

NET LINE LIMIT   The maximum amount of INSURANCE an INSURER will write on a given LINE of RISK; a limit is used to control the insurer's exposure and cap potential losses.

NET LOSS   In INSURANCE, the actual loss sustained by an INSURER in meeting an INSURED's CLAIMS, after taking account of REINSURANCE coverage and any amounts recovered via SUBROGATION or ABANDONMENT.

NET NATIONAL PRODUCT (NNP)   The total of a country's GROSS NATIONAL PRODUCT less DEPRECIATION on capital goods, where depreciation reflects the amount that must be invested on new capital goods to maintain the same level.

NET OPERATING PROFIT AFTER TAX (NOPAT)   A measure of a company's profitability, computed as EARNINGS BEFORE INTEREST AND TAXES minus TAXES.

NET POSITION   The difference between a LONG POSITION and a SHORT POSITION in the same ASSET or SECURITY.

NET PREMIUM   The total amount of an INSURER's PREMIUMS less premium ceded for any REINSURANCE cover. Also known as NET PREMIUM WRITTEN, NET WRITTEN PREMIUM. See also FAIR PREMIUM, GROSS PREMIUM.

NET PREMIUM WRITTEN   See NET PREMIUM.

NET PRESENT VALUE (NPV)   A measure of the net value of an INVESTMENT or CAPITAL project, measured by DISCOUNTING future CASH FLOWS to the present using an appropriate DISCOUNT RATE or COST OF CAPITAL (which is also equal to the INTERNAL RATE OF RETURN); the original cost of the investment made at the inception of the project is deducted in order to provide a net figure. The general form of the equation is given as:

$$NPV = \sum_{t=1}^{n} \frac{CF_t}{(1+r)^t} - I_0$$

where CF_t is the expected cash flow at time t, r is the discount rate, n is the number of periods, and I_0 is the original cost of the investment. Under NPV in general, if NPV > 0 the investment is expected to create shareholder value and should be accepted; if NPV < 0 the investment should be rejected, and if NPV = 0, then the company should be indifferent. See also PRESENT VALUE, FUTURE VALUE.

NET PROFIT   See NET INCOME.

NET PROFIT MARGIN   A measure of a company's ability to transform its REVENUES into NET INCOME, typically calculated as:

$$NP = \frac{EBITDA - Tax}{Rev}$$

where EBITDA is EARNINGS BEFORE INTEREST, TAXES, DEPRECIATION, AND AMORTIZATION, Tax is taxes paid, and Rev is revenues.

The greater the net profit margin, the stronger the operating efficiencies and cost control.

NET RESIDUAL VALUE   The RESIDUAL VALUE of an ASSET, less any costs associated with disposal.

NET RETAINED LINES   The net amount of INSURANCE held by an INSURER after taking account of any REINSURANCE coverage.

NET SINGLE PREMIUM   In INSURANCE, the core PREMIUM designed to cover the PRESENT VALUE of future CLAIMS, excluding any LOAD factor to account for costs or PROFIT margin.

NET UNDERWRITING PROFIT   In INSURANCE, a measure of profitability associated with core insurance UNDERWRITING business, generally computed as:

$$NUP = P_{C\&E} - Div$$

where $P_{C\&E}$ is profit after CLAIMS and EXPENSES, and Div is policy holder DIVIDENDS.

The greater the net underwriting profit, the stronger the INSURER's core business.

NET WORKING CAPITAL   A general measure of corporate LIQUIDITY, typically calculated as CURRENT ASSETS less CURRENT LIABILITIES. Positive net working capital indicates that a company is likely to have sufficient resources to meet payments or OBLIGATIONS coming due, while a negative figure is a signal of potential LIQUIDITY problems. See also CURRENT RATIO, GROSS WORKING CAPITAL, NEGATIVE WORKING CAPITAL, POSITIVE WORKING CAPITAL, QUICK RATIO, WORKING CAPITAL.

NET WORTH   The difference between an individual's or company's ASSETS and its LIABILITIES, and an indication of overall SOLVENCY. See also CAPITAL, NEGATIVE EQUITY.

NET WRITTEN PREMIUM   See NET PREMIUM.

NET YIELD   The YIELD on a SECURITY or INVESTMENT after deducting TAXES and costs associated with acquiring the ASSET. See also GROSS YIELD.

NETTING   An arrangement that condenses payments between two or more COUNTERPARTIES into a single CASH FLOW, allowing CREDIT RISK exposures to be offset. In order to be effective, netting must be legally documented through an appropriate MASTER AGREEMENT and recognized by the relevant legal system where dealing occurs; if these prerequisites are not fulfilled, a non-defaulting counterparty may be CHERRY PICKED in a BANKRUPTCY court by a defaulting counterparty's RECEIVERS. See also BILATERAL NETTING, MULTILATERAL NETTING, NOVATION, PAYMENT NETTING, SET-OFF.

NEW ISSUE   An offering of COMMON STOCK, BONDS, or PREFERRED STOCK in the PRIMARY MARKET. A new issue is generally UNDERWRITTEN by a SYNDICATE comprised of BANKS, INVESTMENT BANKS, and/or SECURITIES FIRMS, who may agree to place SECURITIES on an agented basis (i.e., a BEST EFFORTS UNDERWRITING) or as PRINCIPALS (i.e., a BOUGHT DEAL). An ISSUER's inaugural launch of securities is known as a PRIMARY OFFERING, and any subsequent new issue is considered to be a SECONDARY OFFERING.

NEW YORK STOCK EXCHANGE (NYSE)   The largest US stock EXCHANGE, founded in 1792, which trades over 3000 COMMON STOCKS (along with WARRANTS, OPTIONS, and RIGHTS ISSUES) through a network of DEALERS and SPECIALISTS. BOND trading is conducted on a separate floor through traders known as the BOND CROWD. The exchange continues to feature a physical trading floor where it conducts OPEN OUTCRY trades, although portions of the process are now managed electronically. The exchange converted into a public company in 2006 through the ACQUISITION of publicly listed ELECTRONIC COMMUNICATIONS NETWORK Archipelago, and proceeded to acquire pan-European exchange Euronext in 2007 and the American Stock Exchange in 2008. NYSE EURONEXT now serves as the NYSE's HOLDING COMPANY. Also known as BIG BOARD.

NEWLY INDUSTRIALIZED COUNTRY (NIC)   A country that features a strong, and rapidly growing, industrial production base that contributes substantially to both national INCOME and EXPORTS. NICs generally possess greater industrial development and exports than LESSER DEVELOPED COUNTRIES.

NEXT NEARBY CONTRACT   An EXCHANGE-TRADED DERIVATIVE on a reference ASSET with the second closest MATURITY. Though generally not as actively traded as the NEARBY CONTRACT, the next nearby is usually very LIQUID and becomes even more liquid as the nearby contract approaches MATURITY and participants start rolling their positions.

NGO   See NONGOVERNMENTAL ORGANIZATION.

NIC   See NEWLY INDUSTRIALIZED COUNTRY.

NIF   See NOTE ISSUANCE FACILITY.

NIFTY FIFTY   [COL] The top 50 COMMON STOCK holdings of large US INSTITUTIONAL INVESTORS; the list changes periodically but generally includes a core of BLUE CHIP stocks that INVESTORS hold for the long term.

NIKKEI 225   One of two BENCHMARK INDEXES of the Japanese STOCK market (along with the TOKYO STOCK PRICE INDEX), comprised of 225 LARGE CAP STOCKS listed on the TOKYO STOCK EXCHANGE. The Nikkei 225, which is a PRICE-WEIGHTED INDEX, can be traded directly through EXCHANGE-TRADED FUNDS and DERIVATIVES.

NINJA LOAN   [COL] A LOAN, often a residential MORTGAGE, granted to a BORROWER with "no income, no job, or assets," i.e., an applicant with potentially poor CREDITWORTHINESS. Ninja mortgage loans have historically been part of the SUBPRIME MORTGAGE sector.

NIPPON KEIDANREN   [JPN] See KEIDANREN.

NMS   See NATIONAL MARKET SYSTEM.

NNP   See NET NATIONAL PRODUCT.

NO ARBITRAGE CONDITION   A key theory of FINANCE that indicates that RISK-free EXCESS RETURNS cannot be obtained in the financial marketplace.

NO-LOAD FUND   A MUTUAL FUND that does not carry a sales COMMISSION charge (or LOAD). Despite the lack of a commission no-load funds are not always cheaper than LOAD FUNDS, as they may feature higher annual management fees or exit fees. See also NET ASSET VALUE.

NOMINAL   See NOTIONAL.

NOMINAL CAPITAL   See AUTHORIZED CAPITAL.

NOMINAL INTEREST RATE   A measure of the level of INTEREST RATES, computed as the REAL INTEREST RATE plus INFLATION.

NOMINAL PRICE   The price of a SECURITY at the time it is issued, generally equal to some defined PAR VALUE. In most cases the nominal price has little or no relationship to the MARKET VALUE of the security, particularly over time.

NOMINAL VALUE   See PAR VALUE.

NOMINEE   A party acting as registered owner of SECURITIES (i.e., the holder of record) on behalf of a client, either for ease of EXECUTION/transfer or for reasons related to client anonymity. BROKERS commonly act as nominees by holding client securities in STREET NAME.

NOMINEE SHAREHOLDER   A registered SHAREHOLDER who holds SHARES on behalf of a BENEFICIAL OWNER. Also known as INDIRECT SHAREHOLDER.

NOMING THE PIPES   [COL] Abbreviated form of "nominating the pipes," a scheduling process in natural gas TRADING where physical delivery of gas is allocated through the network of interconnecting gas pipelines based on SUPPLY, DEMAND, time, and price constraints.

NONACCRUAL LOAN   See NONPERFORMING LOAN.

NONADMITTED INSURANCE   An INSURANCE POLICY written by an INSURER that is not licensed in the state or jurisdiction where the INSURED'S RISK exists. Also known as UNAUTHORIZED INSURANCE. See also ADMITTED INSURANCE, SURPLUS LINES INSURANCE.

NONADMITTED INSURER   An INSURER that is not licensed to sell an INSURANCE POLICY in a given state or jurisdiction. Also known as UNAUTH-ORIZED INSURER. See also ADMITTED INSURER.

NONBORROWED RESERVES   In the United States, the amount of RESERVES a BANK has created through its core business operations, rather than through specific borrowings from the FEDERAL RESERVE SYSTEM. See also NET BORROWED RESERVES.

NONCALLABLE BOND   A BOND that cannot be called or redeemed by the ISSUER prior to final MATURITY under any circumstances. A noncallable bond provides the INVESTOR with protection against REINVESTMENT RISK until final maturity. Also known as STRAIGHT BOND. See also CALL RISK, CALLABLE BOND, HARD CALL PROTECTION, SOFT CALL PROTECTION.

NONCLEARING MEMBER   An EXCHANGE member that is not permitted to clear TRADES directly with the CLEARINGHOUSE, and must therefore direct all CLEARING activities through a CLEARING MEMBER.

NONCOMPETITIVE BID   In an AUCTION MARKET, a BID that is not placed in competition with other bids. Noncompetitive bids are generally filled at the average price of the COMPETITIVE BIDS.

NONCOMPETITIVE TRADING   An illegal practice where a DEALER or MARKET MAKER executes a client ORDER within a proprietary account, with-out first exposing it to the market. Noncompetitive trading reduces transpar-ency into order flows and allows dealers to profit at the expense of clients.

NONCONCURRENCY   A situation where an INSURED's multiple INSURANCE policies are not properly structured or synchronized, and fail to provide com-prehensive cover in the event of a loss.

NONCONFORMING LOAN   A residential MORTGAGE that exceeds standard specifications related to size and LOAN-TO-VALUE established for inclusion in a POOL of PASS-THROUGH SECURITIES (such as those created by FEDERAL NATIONAL MORTGAGE ASSOCIATION, GOVERNMENT NATIONAL MORTGAGE ASSOCIATION, or FEDERAL HOME LOAN MORTGAGE CORPORATION). If a mortgage originator wishes to securitize nonconforming loans, it must generally do so through a private label CONDUIT sponsored and managed by a financial institution.

NONCONTRIBUTORY PENSION   A PENSION scheme where the sponsoring company makes all contributions to the account and the employee makes none.

NONCONVERTIBLE CURRENCY   A CURRENCY that cannot be freely exchanged into another currency without prior regulatory approval. Some currencies are nonconvertible for all holders, and for any purpose. Others feature restricted convertibility: nonresidents may be able to exchange holdings but residents may require approval, or holders may be permitted to convert freely for CURRENT ACCOUNT purposes such as TRADE, but not for CAPITAL ACCOUNT purposes such as LOANS or ASSET purchases. Nonconvertible currencies are generally associated with COMMAND ECONOMIES, and their prices are often set or influenced by the local CENTRAL BANK or monetary authority. Also known as INCONVERTIBLE CURRENCY. See also CONVERTIBILITY, CONVERTIBLE CURRENCY, EXCHANGE CONTROLS.

NONCUMULATIVE PREFERRED STOCK   PREFERRED STOCK that pays DIVIDENDS to INVESTORS when, and if, they are declared and paid, and provides for no right to, or CLAIM on, dividends that have been suspended for one or more periods. Since the dividends do not accumulate, they are permanently sacrificed. See also CUMULATIVE PREFERRED STOCK.

NONDEAL ROADSHOW   [COL] A ROADSHOW that is conducted by a company (or other organization) with the aim of updating potential current and future INVESTORS on the state of financial and strategic topics, without being specifically associated with a definite and planned NEW ISSUE of SECURITIES.

NONDELIVERABLE FORWARD   A bilateral OVER-THE-COUNTER DERIVATIVE that permits the purchaser to buy, and the seller to sell, an ASSET at a predetermined future price and future date with SETTLEMENT in financial/cash terms, rather than via delivery of the UNDERLYING reference asset. Nondeliverable forwards are commonly used in transactions where sourcing and/or delivery of an asset is restricted, such as NONCONVERTIBLE CURRENCIES that are subject to EXCHANGE CONTROLS.

NONDISPLAYED LIQUIDITY   Trading volume, particularly in STOCKS, that is not displayed to the market, but which is available for EXECUTION. Nondisplayed liquidity, which in total comprises the DARK POOL sector, may be held within EXCHANGES in the form of RESERVE ORDERS and HIDDEN ORDERS or on the books of SPECIALISTS, or within dedicated venues, such as ELECTRONIC COMMUNICATIONS NETWORKS and CROSSING NETWORKS. Also known as DARK LIQUIDITY. See also DISPLAYED LIQUIDITY.

NONDIVERSIFIABLE RISK   A RISK that is common to all companies, ASSETS, or markets and cannot therefore be reduced or eliminated through DIVERSIFICATION. Also known as SYSTEMATIC RISK. See also DIVERSIFIABLE RISK

NONDURABLE GOOD   An ASSET that has a life span of less than three years and which tends to be consumed immediately, e.g., food, clothing. Nondurable goods form part of the PERSONAL CONSUMPTION component of GROSS DOMESTIC PRODUCT (and GROSS NATIONAL PRODUCT). See also CAPITAL GOOD, DURABLE GOOD.

NONEQUITY SHARE   A form of CAPITAL that contains features of both DEBT and EQUITY, but which is defined for ACCOUNTING purposes as a SHARE that is redeemable, where DIVIDEND rights exist for a finite time period, and where the participation in any proceeds generated through LIQUIDATION are limited.

NONEXECUTIVE DIRECTOR   In the United Kingdom and various other European countries, a DIRECTOR who is not a member of the EXECUTIVE MANAGEMENT team and, presuming no conflicts of interest, may be considered to be independent from a GOVERNANCE perspective. See also EXECUTIVE DIRECTOR, LEAD INDEPENDENT DIRECTOR.

NONGOVERNMENTAL ORGANIZATION (NGO)   A nonprofit, often volunteer-driven, organization on the local, state, or national level, that attempts to promote and address specific public sector issues, often related to humanitarian causes. See also GOVERNMENT-SPONSORED ENTERPRISE, QUASI AUTONOMOUS NONGOVERNMENTAL ORGANIZATION.

NONINSURANCE TRANSFER   A RISK TRANSFER technique that makes use of contractual relationships, such as HOLD HARMLESS AGREEMENTS or PRINCIPAL/AGENT relations, rather than traditional INSURANCE arrangements.

NONLIFE INSURANCE   In Europe, INSURANCE coverage for damage or loss to property, which includes both personal line coverage and commercial line coverage. See also GENERAL INSURANCE, PROPERTY AND CASUALTY INSURANCE.

NONLINEAR INSTRUMENT   A financial CONTRACT, such as an OPTION or WARRANT, with a payout that varies with changes in the movement of the UNDERLYING reference market or ASSET. A unit change in the value of the reference leads to a greater than unit change in the contract, which may be positive or negative depending on whether the instrument has POSITIVE

CONVEXITY or NEGATIVE CONVEXITY. See also CONVEXITY, GAMMA, LINEAR INSTRUMENT, NEGATIVE GAMMA, POSITIVE GAMMA.

NONLINEAR PAYOFF   A nonlinear economic gain or loss that may be expected under a DERIVATIVE (e.g., EXOTIC OPTION) for a given range of market prices. For every unit move up or down in the market price, the gain or loss is a nonlinear function of that unit move. See also ASYMMETRIC PAYOFF, LINEAR PAYOFF, SYMMETRIC PAYOFF.

NONNEGOTIABLE INSTRUMENT   Any financial instrument which cannot be assigned or transferred to another party, such as those with restrictive endorsements or defined PAYEES. See also NEGOTIABLE INSTRUMENT.

NONPAR SWAP   An OVER-THE-COUNTER SWAP, such as a PREMIUM SWAP or DISCOUNT SWAP, which is transacted at off-market INTEREST RATES. Also known as OFF-MARKET SWAP.

NONPARTICIPATING GUARANTEED INVESTMENT CONTRACT (GIC)   A GUARANTEED INVESTMENT CONTRACT with a fixed RETURN and a fixed term; the INVESTOR does not receive any excess benefit from surplus returns generated by the INSURER in managing the ASSET PORTFOLIO. See also PARTICIPATING GUARANTEED INVESTMENT CONTRACT, SYNTHETIC GUARANTEED INVESTMENT CONTRACT.

NONPERFORMING LOAN   A LOAN in which the BORROWER is no longer making regular payments of INTEREST and/or PRINCIPAL. A nonperforming loan is generally classified as a substandard ASSET and must be supported by appropriate LOAN LOSS RESERVES. If the loan is not made current by the borrower over a particular period it is generally written off against reserves; legal actions may then be taken against the borrower to recover amounts due. Also known as NONACCRUAL LOAN.

NONPRIME LOAN   See SUBPRIME LOAN.

NONPUBLIC INFORMATION   See INSIDE INFORMATION.

NONPURPOSE LOAN   A LOAN, collateralized by SECURITIES and subject to MARGIN rules, where the proceeds are not used to acquire additional securities. See also PURPOSE LOAN.

NONRECOMBINING TREE   A LATTICE MODEL used to price OPTIONS where the assumed upward and downward movements are not equal. This yields an uneven or skewed lattice, and causes option value to be weighted more heavily in the direction of the larger market moves. See also BINOMIAL MODEL.

NONRECOURSE   The lack of a CLAIM on a contracting party. A nonrecourse transaction is dependent solely on the ASSETS or CASH FLOWS associated with the transaction, indicating that the financial position/capabilities of the sponsor or contracting party are irrelevant and cannot be considered. See also NONRECOURSE LOAN, RECOURSE.

NONRECOURSE LOAN   A LOAN with repayment that depends solely on the proceeds from the project or ASSET being financed, or the sale of specific COLLATERAL supporting the transaction. The lending BANK has no ability to seek repayment from the BORROWER in the event of a shortfall. See also FULL RECOURSE LOAN, NONRECOURSE, PARTIAL RECOURSE LOAN, RECOURSE.

NONREFUNDABLE DEBT   A BOND or NOTE that cannot be redeemed and replaced by alternative DEBT. In some instances the INDENTURE of a nonrefundable bond will allow limited refunding, but only if INTEREST RATES decline to a particular level. See also CALL PROTECTION, NONCALLABLE BOND.

NONSYSTEMATIC RISK   See DIVERSIFIABLE RISK.

NONVOTING STOCK   COMMON STOCK that carries standard RENT RIGHTS, but only limited CONTROL RIGHTS – including the right to obtain financial disclosure and file lawsuits, but not to vote. See also DISENFRANCHISING TRANSACTION.

NOPAT   See NET OPERATING PROFIT AFTER TAX.

NORMAL BACKWARDATION   A market state where the SPOT PRICE on a FUTURE or FORWARD is higher than the FORWARD PRICE, often as a result of temporary ASSET shortages or an excess SUPPLY for future delivery. Also known as BACKWARDATION. See also CONTANGO.

NORMAL DISTRIBUTION   A continuous probability distribution function that focuses on data centered around the MEAN. The probability density function is given as:

$$p(x) = \frac{1}{\sigma\sqrt{2\pi}} \exp\left(-\frac{(x-\mu)^2}{2\sigma^2}\right)$$

where μ is the mean, and σ is the STANDARD DEVIATION.

Given a mean of 0 and standard deviation of 1, the equation simplifies to:

$$p(x) = \frac{1}{\sigma\sqrt{2\pi}} e^{\frac{-x^2}{2}}$$

Under the properties of the distribution, approximately 68% of observations lie within +/– one standard deviation of the mean, 95% within approximately +/– two standard deviations, and 99.7% within approximately +/– three standard deviations. The normal distribution is widely used in a variety of financial and ACTUARIAL PRICING techniques.

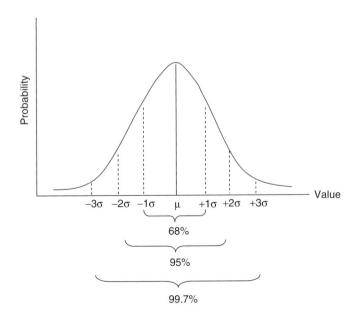

Also known as GAUSSIAN DISTRIBUTION. See also LAW OF LARGE NUMBERS, LOGNORMAL DISTRIBUTION.

NORMAL MARKET SIZE   A method of classifying the TRADING volume of STOCKS on the United Kingdom's LONDON STOCK EXCHANGE, based on 12 different categories. The classifications are used to impose certain requirements on MARKET MAKERS and to set requirements for publishing transaction data.

NORTH AMERICAN FREE TRADE AGREEMENT (NAFTA)   A law passed in 1993 to abolish TARIFFS, DUTIES, and fees on goods flowing between the United States, Canada, and Mexico, in order to promote FREE TRADE.

NOSTRO   [LAT] Literally "our account"; a local account a foreign BANK maintains with a local bank to accommodate local CURRENCY business, e.g., a US bank has a yen nostro with a Japanese bank to manage its yen inflows and outflows. See also VOSTRO.

NOTARY   An official that is legally authorized to witness signatures and certify the validity of a document. Also known as NOTARY PUBLIC.

NOTARY PUBLIC   See NOTARY.

NOTE   (1) In the CAPITAL MARKETS, a financial OBLIGATION representing the ISSUER's LIABILITY to repay CAPITAL provided by INVESTORS. Notes are defined by form of INTEREST RATE (e.g., FIXED RATE, FLOATING RATE, structured), COUPON frequency, CURRENCY, MATURITY, COLLATERAL, price, redemption, AMORTIZATION, transfer, and market of issue. Notes are generally floated with maturities ranging from 1 to 10 years. They may be issued onshore or offshore, as REGISTERED SECURITIES or BEARER SECURITIES, in any one of several currencies; securities are often listed on an EXCHANGE, although most TRADING occurs OVER-THE-COUNTER. (2) A PROMISSORY NOTE. (3) A BANKNOTE. (1) See also BOND, EURONOTE, MEDIUM-TERM NOTE, EURO MEDIUM-TERM NOTE, FLOATING RATE NOTE, GOVERNMENT BOND, LEVERAGED NOTE, NOTE ISSUANCE FACILITY, STRUCTURED NOTE.

NOTE ISSUANCE FACILITY (NIF)   A EURONOTE program where a BORROWER issues unsecured NOTES to INVESTORS via a TENDER PANEL. If the notes cannot be successfully placed, the underwriting BANKS agree to purchase them through the extension of medium-term LOANS, thus guaranteeing the borrower good funds. See also REVOLVING UNDERWRITING FACILITY.

NOTIONAL   A common method of denominating the size, though not necessarily the RISK, of a DERIVATIVE transaction (generally SWAPS and FORWARDS). In most instances notional is used only as a reference to compute amounts payable and/or receivable, although for CURRENCY SWAPS the full notional is typically exchanged on TRADE date and at final MATURITY. Also known as NOMINAL, NOTIONAL PRINCIPAL.

NOTIONAL POOLING   See POOLING.

NOTIONAL PRINCIPAL   See NOTIONAL.

NOVATION   A process where all contractual payments between two parties are amalgamated and settled during a particular interim period (monthly or quarterly). Remaining CONTRACTS are then rewritten at the current MARKET VALUE and the process is repeated during the next netting period. Novation creates greater efficiencies in the CASH FLOW settlement process. See also PAYMENT NETTING, RECOUPONING, SET-OFF.

NOYAU DUR   [FR] The French concept of SHAREHOLDER loyalty; stakes taken by certain institutional or corporate shareholders in other companies with which they have long-standing ties or business relationships are used to support EXECUTIVE MANAGEMENT and DIRECTORS in their attempt to direct the company.

NPV   See NET PRESENT VALUE.

NPV MODEL   See CREDIT MARK-TO-MARKET MODEL.

N-TH-TO-DEFAULT SWAP   A generalized version of an OVER-THE-COUNTER DEFAULT SWAP comprised of a BASKET of REFERENCE ENTITIES that entitles the purchaser to a payout on the n-th one to DEFAULT, where n is agreed between the two parties to the CONTRACT in advance; once the n-th reference entity occurs, the transaction terminates. See also FIRST-TO-DEFAULT SWAP.

NV   See NAAMLOZE VENNOOTSCHAP.

NYSE   See NEW YORK STOCK EXCHANGE.

NYSE EURONEXT   An international HOLDING COMPANY formed from the 2007 MERGER of the NEW YORK STOCK EXCHANGE and EURONEXT, itself the product of a merger of the STOCK exchanges of Amsterdam, Brussels, Paris, and Lisbon, and the DERIVATIVES exchange London International Financial Futures and Options Exchange. The NYSE Euronext group exchanges are active in TRADING, SETTLEMENT, and CLEARING of stocks, BONDS, and a range of derivatives.

O

OAS See OPTION-ADJUSTED SPREAD.

OBJECTIVE RISK A measure of the deviation between an INSURER's actual losses and its EXPECTED LOSSES (as predicted through ACTUARIAL PRICING techniques). The greater the objective risk, the larger the losses and the less accurate the pricing methodologies.

OBLIGATION The requirement of a BORROWER to repay a LENDER under the terms of a CONTRACT.

OBLIGATIONS FONCIERES In France, a form of COVERED BOND backed by MORTGAGES, issued exclusively by Sociétés de Crédit Foncier. See also CEDULAS HIPOTECARIAS, HYPOTHEKENPFANDBRIEFE, IRISH ASSET COVERED SECURITIES, JUMBO PFANDBRIEFE, LETTRES DE GAGE, OFFENTLICHE PFANDBRIEFE.

OCCURRENCE LIMIT The maximum amount an INSURER is required to pay the INSURED for a loss occurrence that leads to a CLAIM, even if the total loss is larger than the amount specified by the limit. See also CLAIMS OCCURRENCE BASIS.

ODD LOT An ORDER that is smaller than the standard institutional TRADING size in a particular SECURITY or market. Odd lots, which are most often associated with RETAIL INVESTORS, are generally subject to higher COMMISSIONS/fees than ROUND LOTS.

ODD LOT THEORY A theory indicating that as ORDERS executed on an ODD LOT basis rise, speculative forces may be at work in pushing individual SECURITIES or broader markets to new peaks, as individual INVESTORS often drive the final stages of a BUBBLE.

OECD See ORGANIZATION FOR ECONOMIC COOPERATION AND DEVELOPMENT.

OFF-BALANCE SHEET ACTIVITIES Contingent financial transactions that are not fully reflected through the corporate BALANCE SHEET. For FINANCIAL INSTITUTIONS this may include STANDBY LETTERS OF CREDIT, IRREVOCABLE LETTERS OF CREDIT, REVOLVING CREDIT FACILITIES, REVOLVING UNDERWRITING FACILITIES, NOTE ISSUANCE FACILITIES, written GUARANTEES, ASSET sales with RECOURSE, RISK participations in BANKER'S ACCEPTANCES, DERIVATIVES, and certain types of LEASES; for companies it may be limited to leases, SUBSIDIARY guarantees and/or derivatives. Institutions active in these businesses face varying degrees of contingent risk exposure and must generally set aside sufficient CAPITAL to cover potential risks.

OFF-MARKET A price or feature assigned to a SECURITY, DERIVATIVE, or other financial transaction that is different than the current market or accepted market standard. An off-market transaction may be created in order to shift profit and loss parameters, alter funding costs, or reduce RISK exposures. See also NONPAR SWAP.

OFF-MARKET SWAP   See NONPAR SWAP.

OFF-THE-RUN SECURITIES   [COL] A SECURITY that has been issued at some time in the past. Off-the-runs continue to trade until they mature or are redeemed, but often feature less LIQUIDITY and wider SPREADS than ON-THE-RUN SECURITIES.

OFFENTLICHE PFANDBRIEFE   [GER] A form of COVERED BOND in the German market that is fully collateralized by public sector LOANS. Also known as PUBLIC PFANDBRIEFE.

OFFER   A quoted selling price for an ASSET from a DEALER or MARKET MAKER. Also known as ASK. See also BID.

OFFER BY PROSPECTUS   The offering of a NEW ISSUE of SECURITIES directly by the ISSUER to INVESTORS by means of a PROSPECTUS. An offer by prospectus is a relatively uncommon method of placing new securities. See also OFFER BY SALE.

OFFER BY SALE   The offering of a NEW ISSUE of SECURITIES through one or more INTERMEDIARIES (e.g., a SYNDICATE of UNDERWRITERS), and the most common means of placing new securities with INVESTORS. See also OFFER BY PROSPECTUS.

OFFER DOCUMENT   A document submitted to SHAREHOLDERS of a company that is the subject of an ACQUISITION offer that contains relevant details of the proposed transaction.

OFFERING CIRCULAR   See PROSPECTUS.

OFFERING MEMORANDUM   A document used to describe relevant details of a PRIVATE PLACEMENT, including information related to the ISSUER and particulars of the transaction. See also PROSPECTUS.

OFFICIAL LIST   The list of all STOCKS traded on the main board of the LONDON STOCK EXCHANGE.

OFFICIAL RECEIVER   In the United Kingdom, a RECEIVER that is appointed to manage the BANKRUPTCY of a company. The official receiver may also serve as liquidator of ASSETS in the event of a LIQUIDATION.

OFFSET   (1) The right of a CREDITOR to take possession of financial ASSETS of a delinquent DEBTOR through a process known as garnishment. (2) The right of a firm with amounts payable to a COUNTERPARTY in DEFAULT to deduct any amounts receivable from the counterparty. (2) See also NETTING.

OFFSHORE COMPANY   (1) A company or SPECIAL PURPOSE ENTITY that is generally established in a TAX-friendly jurisdiction to help fulfill specific INVESTMENT or tax goals. (2) Any company or SUBSIDIARY operating outside the national borders of a PARENT or HOLDING COMPANY.

OID   See ORIGINAL ISSUE DISCOUNT.

OIS   See OVERNIGHT INDEX SWAP.

OLD LADY   [COL] A term for the BANK OF ENGLAND, abbreviated from the "Old Lady of Threadneedle Street" in reference to the location of the Bank's headquarters.

OLIGOPOLY   A marketplace with only a few sellers who can collectively influence selling prices. If each has enough of a market share, then the actions of other sellers must be considered when developing pricing and distribution strategies. See also DUOPOLY, MONOPOLY, OLIGOPSONY.

OLIGOPSONY   A marketplace with only a few buyers who can collectively influence overall purchase prices. If each has enough of a market share, then the actions of other buyers must be considered when developing pricing and acquisition strategies. See also DUOPSONY, MONOPSONY, OLIGOPOLY.

OMEGA   See THETA.

OMNIBUS ACCOUNT   An ACCOUNT held by one BROKER or FUTURES COMMISSION MERCHANT in the name of a second one, and which contains individual subaccounts for separate clients.

OMNIPRESENT SPECTER   [COL] A legal rule requiring a BOARD OF DIRECTORS to demonstrate that it is not acting in its own self-interest when rejecting a corporate control transaction such as a TAKEOVER, i.e., that rejection of the bid and the creation of any ANTITAKEOVER DEFENSES are required in order to protect SHAREHOLDERS.

ON-THE-RUN SECURITIES   [COL] The most recently AUCTIONED issue of GOVERNMENT BILLS or GOVERNMENT BONDS or the most recently issued BOND from a corporate or financial ISSUER from a standing program. On-the-run securities tend to become the most actively traded issues in the market, replacing previously issued securities, which become OFF-THE-RUN SECURITIES. The relatively more LIQUID characteristics lead to narrower SPREADS. Also known as CURRENT ISSUE.

ONE-FACTOR MODEL   See SINGLE FACTOR MODEL.

ONE-MAN PICTURE   [COL] A market situation where the only available BID and OFFER on a transaction come from the same source.

ONE-SIDED MARKET   A market in which only one price, either a BID or OFFER, is quoted. This tends to be characteristic of ILLIQUID markets or those that are undergoing a period of financial stress, when DEALERS and SPECULATORS are unwilling to put up RISK CAPITAL.

ONE-TOUCH OPTION   See BINARY-BARRIER OPTION.

ONE-WAY MARKET   A market situation in which interest or activity exists only on one side, typically the selling or OFFER side. A one-way market may arise during a period of FINANCIAL CRISIS, when RISK appetite is on the wane.

OPEC See ORGANIZATION OF PETROLEUM EXPORTING COUNTRIES.

OPEN BOOK A general financial strategy of BORROWING on a short-term basis and LENDING on a long-term basis. BANKS routinely run an open book in a normal POSITIVE YIELD CURVE environment in order to maximize NET INTEREST MARGIN. In doing so, however, they are subject to CURVE RISK, and possible losses should the curve begin to flatten or invert. SECURITIES FIRMS and BROKER/DEALERS may follow a similar strategy with their REPURCHASE AGREEMENT/REVERSE REPURCHASE AGREEMENT operations. See also MISMATCH.

OPEN CONTRACT A LONG POSITION or SHORT POSITION in a single unit of an EXCHANGE-TRADED DERIVATIVE. See also OPEN POSITION.

OPEN DISPLAY The electronic LIMIT ORDER book of BIDS and OFFERS in a given STOCK as supplied by an ELECTRONIC COMMUNICATIONS NETWORK. Open displays provide full visibility on all orders that are not held back as RESERVE ORDERS or HIDDEN ORDERS.

OPEN-END FUND See MUTUAL FUND.

OPEN-END INVESTMENT COMPANY See MUTUAL FUND.

OPEN INTEREST A measure of EXCHANGE-TRADED DERIVATIVE CONTRACT LIQUIDITY, generally computed as the number of outstanding FUTURES or OPTION contracts that are not offset by opposing transactions or accommodated by DELIVERY.

OPEN MARKET OPERATIONS A technique of MONETARY POLICY involving the purchase or sale of GOVERNMENT BILLS or GOVERNMENT BONDS by a CENTRAL BANK or monetary authority, with the express intent of influencing the level of INTEREST RATES and MONEY SUPPLY. A purchase of SECURITIES causes prices to rise, rates to fall, and money supply to expand; a sale causes prices to fall, rates to rise, and money supply to contract.

OPEN MARKET PURCHASE The purchase of a block of a company's COMMON STOCK in the open market by another firm, generally as a prelude to a formal TENDER OFFER.

OPEN ORDER See GOOD TILL CANCELLED ORDER.

OPEN OUTCRY A TRADING process/mechanism based on physical communication between FLOOR TRADERS working on an EXCHANGE. Floor traders agree on purchase and sale terms through verbal discussion and/or hand-signals.

OPEN POSITION A LONG POSITION or a SHORT POSITION in a financial ASSET, COMMODITY, or DERIVATIVE, which exposes the holder to one or more RISK FACTORS. The risk of an open position can only be offset through a HEDGE, closeout, or offsetting position. See also OPEN CONTRACT.

OPEN REPURCHASE AGREEMENT A REPURCHASE AGREEMENT with no specific MATURITY, cancellable on 24 hours' notice by either party to the transaction. This is akin to an OVERNIGHT REPURCHASE AGREEMENT that is automatically rolled over every day as a continuing FINANCING CONTRACT. The DEALER in an open repo retains the right to substitute COLLATERAL. The opposite side of the transaction is referred to as open REVERSE REPURCHASE AGREEMENT. See also OVERNIGHT REPURCHASE AGREEMENT, TERM REPURCHASE AGREEMENT.

OPENING BANK   A BANK that creates a LETTER OF CREDIT at the request of an importer so that payment for an exporter's goods can be arranged.

OPERATING CASH FLOW   The portion of the STATEMENT OF CASH FLOWS that reflects the cash activities of a firm's core operations, and can be computed as NET INCOME plus DEPRECIATION, benefits, and provisions, and DEBIT/CREDIT adjustments related to changes in ACCOUNTS RECEIVABLE, INVENTORIES, accrued LIABILITIES, and deferred income TAXES. It can also be computed as EARNINGS BEFORE INTEREST AND TAXES minus TAXES plus DEPRECIATION, or NET OPERATING PROFIT AFTER TAX plus DEPRECIATION. See also FINANCING CASH FLOW, INVESTING CASH FLOW.

OPERATING CYCLE   The time between the acquisition of raw materials or other resources needed to prepare goods and the sale of goods to customers. The difference between cash outflows in support of raw material acquisition and cash inflows from sales must be financed through internal (e.g., cash on hand) or external sources (e.g., LOANS). The operating cycle can be viewed as the sum (in days) of the INVENTORY cycle (as measured through e.g., DAYS SALES INVENTORY) and the CASH FLOW CYCLE (as measured through, e.g., DAYS SALES OUTSTANDING). See also CASH CONVERSION CYCLE, CASH FLOW CYCLE.

OPERATING EXPENSE   The cost associated with supporting the normal business operations of a company, typically including COST OF GOODS SOLD, DEPRECIATION, administrative costs (e.g., salaries, rent, research and development); some companies exclude cost of goods sold in the computation. Operating expenses always exclude INTEREST and TAX EXPENSES.

OPERATING INCOME   The results of a company's operations before taking account of INTEREST and TAX EXPENSES. It can be computed as REVENUE less OPERATING EXPENSES (if operating expenses includes COST OF GOODS SOLD) or GROSS INCOME less operating expenses (if operating expenses exclude cost of goods sold). Also known as OPERATING PROFIT.

OPERATING LEASE   A LEASE with a CONTRACT period that is shorter than the expected economic life of the underlying ASSET; the contract is generally cancellable at the option of the LESSEE. Operating leases, which are generally classified as OFF-BALANCE SHEET ACTIVITIES, are commonly written on equipment. See also CAPITAL LEASE.

OPERATING LEVERAGE   The degree to which a company's costs are fixed; the greater the percentage of a company's costs that are fixed, rather than variable, the greater the resources it has flowing to the NET INCOME account once the breakeven point has been reached. Also known as OPERATIONAL GEARING. See also LEVERAGE.

OPERATING MARGIN A measure of a company's ability to translate REVENUES into OPERATING INCOME, computed as:

$$OM = \frac{OI}{Rev}$$

where OI is operating income, Rev is revenue

The higher the margin, the more efficient a company is in managing the costs of its business.

OPERATING PROFIT See OPERATING INCOME.

OPERATING RISK The RISK of loss arising from temporary or permanent disruption in the daily physical operating and production activities of a firm and/or changes in nonfinancial inputs and outputs. See also FINANCIAL RISK.

OPERATIONAL ERROR RISK The RISK of loss due to problems or errors involving internal operations, such as late or misdirected payments or mishandling/misdirecting securities. A subcategory of PROCESS RISK.

OPERATIONAL GEARING See OPERATING LEVERAGE.

OPERATIONAL RISK The RISK of loss arising from control/process inadequacies or failures, including DISASTER RECOVERY RISK, BUSINESS RECOVERY RISK, COLLATERAL RISK, KEY MAN RISK, OPERATIONAL ERROR RISK, and REGULATORY COMPLIANCE RISK. Also known as PROCESS RISK.

OPIC See OVERSEAS PRIVATE INVESTMENT CORPORATION.

OPM [COL] Abbreviation for "other people's money," typically employed in describing a company's use of financial LEVERAGE in its operations or in the context of a potential ACQUISITION.

OPPORTUNITY COST The cost or value lost in opting not to pursue the next best alternative. Analysis of opportunity costs is integral for those involved in INVESTMENT and CAPITAL EXPENDITURES, for example. Also known as ECONOMIC COST.

OPTION A DERIVATIVE CONTRACT granting the buyer the right, but not the obligation, to buy or sell a reference ASSET at a predefined STRIKE PRICE; in exchange for the right, the buyer pays the seller a PREMIUM. Options are available on many UNDERLYING asset references from the FIXED INCOME, EQUITY, FOREIGN EXCHANGE, COMMODITY, and CREDIT markets, and can be bought or sold as OVER-THE-COUNTER DERIVATIVES or EXCHANGE-TRADED DERIVATIVES. See also CALL OPTION, PUT OPTION, COMPLEX OPTION.

OPTION-ADJUSTED ANALYSIS   Quantitative analysis that is performed on a SECURITY that has one or more EMBEDDED OPTIONS. The analysis may focus on determining the OPTION-ADJUSTED DURATION, OPTION-ADJUSTED CONVEXITY, and/or OPTION-ADJUSTED SPREAD.

OPTION-ADJUSTED CONVEXITY   The CONVEXITY of a CALLABLE BOND, PUTABLE BOND, or other FIXED INCOME SECURITY with OPTIONALITY, which reflects the actual convexity of the security after adjusting for the effects of the EMBEDDED OPTION(s). The option-adjusted convexity of a callable bond is given as:

$$Cvx_{OA} = \left[\frac{P_{noncall}}{P_{call}} \right] [Cvx(1 - \Delta)] - [P_{noncall}(\Gamma)(Dur)^2]$$

where $P_{noncall}$ is the price of the equivalent NONCALLABLE BOND, P_{call} is the price of the callable bond, Cvx is the convexity of a noncallable bond, Dur is the DURATION of a noncallable bond, and Γ is the GAMMA of the option.

Similar computations can be made for other option-embedded securities. See also OPTION-ADJUSTED DURATION, OPTION-ADJUSTED SPREAD, OPTION-ADJUSTED YIELD.

OPTION-ADJUSTED DURATION   The DURATION of a CALLABLE BOND, PUTABLE BOND, or other FIXED INCOME SECURITY with OPTIONALITY, which reflects the actual duration of the security after adjusting for the effects of the EMBEDDED OPTION(s). The option-adjusted duration of a callable bond is given as:

$$Dur_{OA} = \left[\frac{P_{noncall}}{P_{call}} \right] [Dur(1 - \Delta)]$$

where $P_{noncall}$ is the price of the equivalent NONCALLABLE BOND, P_{call} is the price of the callable bond, Dur is the duration of a noncallable bond, and Δ is the DELTA value of the option.

Similar computations can be made for other option-embedded securities. See also OPTION-ADJUSTED CONVEXITY, OPTION-ADJUSTED SPREAD, OPTION-ADJUSTED YIELD.

OPTION-ADJUSTED SPREAD (OAS)   A quantitative valuation technique applied to BONDS with EMBEDDED OPTIONS, such as MORTGAGE-BACKED SECURITIES, CALLABLE BONDS, PUTABLE BONDS, or STRUCTURED NOTES, where the OAS is equal to the SPREAD over the BENCHMARK RISK-FREE RATE after taking account of the fact that the option will cause the bond's CASH FLOWS to change as INTEREST RATES change. See also OPTION-ADJUSTED DURATION, OPTION-ADJUSTED YIELD, OPTION-ADJUSTED CONVEXITY.

OPTION-ADJUSTED YIELD   The YIELD of a CALLABLE BOND, PUTABLE BOND, or other FIXED INCOME SECURITY with OPTIONALITY that results if the security is held until maturity, i.e., the yield that makes the PRESENT VALUE of the CASH FLOWS from the bond (held to maturity) equal to the implied price of a BOND with no CALL OPTION or PUT OPTION features. See also OPTION-ADJUSTED CONVEXITY, OPTION-ADJUSTED DURATION, OPTION-ADJUSTED SPREAD.

OPTION METHOD   A methodology where the FRACTIONAL EXPOSURE of a SWAP is estimated through an OPTION pricing framework. The swap is viewed as a package of options giving the holder the right to buy a FIXED RATE BOND and sell a FLOATING RATE NOTE (or vice-versa); the options are exercised jointly in the event of DEFAULT by the COUNTERPARTY, but only if they are IN-THE-MONEY. See also HISTORICAL METHOD, SIMULATION METHOD.

OPTION MONEY   See PREMIUM.

OPTION ON THE BEST/WORST OF N-ASSETS   An OVER-THE-COUNTER COMPLEX OPTION that grants the buyer a PAYOFF based on the best or worst performing of a PORTFOLIO of ASSETS against a predefined STRIKE PRICE; assets in the portfolio may be from identical or different asset classes/markets. See also CALL ON THE BEST OF N-ASSETS, CALL ON THE WORST OF N-ASSETS, MULTI-INDEX OPTION, PUT ON THE BEST OF N-ASSETS, PUT ON THE WORST OF N-ASSETS.

OPTION ON THE BEST/WORST OF N-ASSETS AND CASH   An OVER-THE-COUNTER COMPLEX OPTION that grants the buyer a PAYOFF based on the best or worst performing of a PORTFOLIO of ASSETS and cash; assets may be from identical or different asset classes/markets. The option has no STRIKE PRICE and always produces a minimum payoff equal to the predefined cash amount. See also MULTI-INDEX OPTION.

OPTION ON THE MAXIMUM/MINIMUM   An OVER-THE-COUNTER COMPLEX OPTION that grants the buyer a maximum gain by "looking back" over the price path of the ASSET and determining the point that creates the greatest economic value. This version of the LOOKBACK OPTION carries a preset STRIKE PRICE and produces a gain based on the difference between the strike and the maximum price (for a CALL ON THE MAXIMUM) or minimum price (for a PUT ON THE MINIMUM) achieved by the asset. Also known as FIXED STRIKE LOOKBACK OPTION.

OPTION REPRICING   The practice of converting an OPTION that is OUT-OF-THE-MONEY into one with INTRINSIC VALUE by resetting the STRIKE so that the contract is IN-THE-MONEY. See also UNDERWATER.

OPTION SENSITIVITIES   See GREEKS.

OPTIONAL REDEMPTION   The right granted to the ISSUER of a SECURITY, particularly those with long or perpetual MATURITIES, to repurchase or redeem the outstanding securities at a predefined fixed price, or a price that steps up over time. Optional redemption may be incorporated into the terms of HYBRID CAPITAL SECURITIES.

OPTIONALITY   See CONVEXITY.

ORDER   Instructions from one party (e.g., BROKER or client) to a second party (e.g., DEALER or MARKET MAKER) to execute the purchase or sale of SECURITIES or other ASSETS. There are four broad classes of orders: MARKET ORDERS, LIMIT ORDERS, STOP ORDERS, and TIME ORDERS, each with their own variations related to time, price, and discretion.

ORDER-DRIVEN MARKET   A physical or electronic marketplace where SECURITIES ORDERS are grouped in the books of INTERMEDIARIES such as PRINCIPALS, SPECIALISTS, or AGENTS, and are then matched according to certain auction-based rules, often related to price-time priority; many public EQUITY markets are order-driven. See also AUCTION, QUOTE-DRIVEN MARKET.

ORDER GENERATION LOGIC   The mathematical instructions embedded in an ALGORITHM that dictate how a PARENT ORDER is to be parceled into separate CHILD ORDERS for individual execution over a specific time horizon. See also ORDER PLACEMENT LOGIC, ROUTER LOGIC.

ORDER IMBALANCE   An excess of purchase or sale ORDERS waiting to be filled via an EXCHANGE or OVER-THE-COUNTER that can disrupt LIQUIDITY and cause divergences between BIDS and OFFERS; in more extreme cases an imbalance can lead to temporary suspension of TRADING. An imbalance can arise from positive or negative news or rumors about a company or marketplace.

ORDER PLACEMENT LOGIC   The mathematical instructions embedded in an ALGORITHM that indicate how each individual CHILD ORDER in a PARENT ORDER should be executed, e.g., as a LIMIT ORDER, a MARKET ORDER, a limit order that converts to a market order after a period of time, and so forth. See also ORDER GENERATION LOGIC, ROUTER LOGIC.

ORDINARY SHARE   In the United Kingdom, COMMON STOCK.

ORGANIC GROWTH   The natural business expansion a company gains in products/markets through its own resources, improvements, or innovations, rather than through external ACQUISITIONS.

ORGANIZATION FOR ECONOMIC COOPERATION AND DEVELOPMENT (OECD)   An international economic organization, comprised primarily of industrialized countries (and a small number of NEWLY INDUSTRIALIZED COUNTRIES) created to assist members in developing policies to promote economic growth and general financial stability.

ORGANIZATION OF PETROLEUM EXPORTING COUNTRIES (OPEC)   An organization of countries that produce and export crude oil, established in 1973 to coordinate production levels and dealings with oil companies; OPEC essentially functions as an oil CARTEL and has some ability to influence global oil prices over the short term. Member countries have at various points included Algeria, Iran, Iraq, Kuwait, Libya, Nigeria, Saudi Arabia, the United Arab Emirates, and Venezuela.

ORIGINAL EXPOSURE METHOD   A regulatory method of computing SWAP CREDIT RISK, under the original 1988 BASLE ACCORD put forth by the BANK FOR INTERNATIONAL SETTLEMENTS, which focuses solely on future credit exposure (*de facto* ignoring ACTUAL EXPOSURE or MARK-TO-MARKET value). Since the methodology takes no account of ongoing mark-to-market value, it features higher future exposure risk factors. See also CURRENT EXPOSURE METHOD, INTERNAL RATINGS-BASED APPROACH.

ORIGINAL ISSUE DISCOUNT (OID)   The size of the price DISCOUNT to PAR VALUE at the time of a BOND's issuance. Accretion of the price from OID to par value is treated as INTEREST income for TAX purposes.

ORIGINAL MARGIN   See INITIAL MARGIN.

OSAKA STOCK EXCHANGE (OSE)   The second largest STOCK EXCHANGE of Japan, originally established in 1878, consolidated in 1943, and reformed in 1949. In addition to electronic TRADING of individual STOCKS, the OSE lists and trades FUTURES and OPTIONS on the BENCHMARK NIKKEI 225 INDEX, in both standard and MINI form. See also TOKYO STOCK EXCHANGE.

OSCILLATOR   In TECHNICAL ANALYSIS, a measure of market movements used to identify OVERBOUGHT or OVERSOLD conditions; different oscillators exist, including the relative strength of the market (average number of days ending up divided by number of days ending down).

OSE   See OSAKA STOCK EXCHANGE.

OTC   See OVER-THE-COUNTER.

OUT-OF-COURT WORKOUT   Private negotiations held outside a court between a company that is in some degree of FINANCIAL DISTRESS and its CREDITORS, centering on extending CREDIT facilities and establishing a payback schedule. A turnaround plan generally accompanies such negotiations and may reflect a more favorable end result for creditors than a pure LIQUIDATION or REORGANIZATION.

OUT-OF-THE-MONEY   A condition where the price of an UNDERLYING reference ASSET is lower than the STRIKE PRICE for a CALL OPTION, or higher than the strike for a PUT OPTION, meaning the CONTRACT has no immediate INTRINSIC VALUE if EXERCISED or sold. See also AT-THE-MONEY, IN-THE-MONEY, MONEYNESS.

OUT TRADE   See DK.

OUTPERFORMANCE OPTION   An OVER-THE-COUNTER COMPLEX OPTION that grants the buyer a PAYOFF based on the degree to which a market reference or SPREAD outperforms a predefined STRIKE PRICE. See also SPREAD OPTION, UNDERPERFORMANCE OPTION.

OUTSIDE BARRIER OPTION   An OVER-THE-COUNTER COMPLEX OPTION with a BARRIER that is triggered by a market reference that is distinct from the one defining the UNDERLYING option, leading to the creation of a multivariate structure. The likelihood of a payout to the buyer is dependent, in part, on the relative CORRELATIONS between the barrier reference and the underlying reference. See also BARRIER OPTION.

OUTSIDE DIRECTOR   In the United States, a board DIRECTOR that is not related to the company or its EXECUTIVE MANAGEMENT in any fashion, i.e., the director has no former employment ties, or any existing business, consulting, or personal relationships with executives. Outside directors are typically considered to be independent for GOVERNANCE purposes. See also INSIDE DIRECTOR.

OUTSIDER SYSTEM   A corporate ownership system where no significant controlling interests exist and SHAREHOLDER influence over the GOVERNANCE and management processes is theoretically strong. The outsider system is found in the United States, the United Kingdom, Canada, and Australia. See also INSIDER SYSTEM.

OUTSTANDING SHARES   The total amount of SHARES issued by a company and which are currently held by INVESTORS, including shares held by employees and executives but excluding shares that have been repurchased from the market under a TREASURY STOCK program. Also known as ISSUED AND OUTSTANDING, SHARES OUTSTANDING.

OVER-THE-COUNTER (OTC)   Any financial transaction that is arranged or traded away from a formal EXCHANGE. Dealing may be done in telephonic form or in electronic form (via ELECTRONIC COMMUNICATIONS NETWORKS, ALTERNATIVE TRADING SYSTEMS, and other network-based platforms), and may feature varying degrees of price transparency. Most trading in FIXED INCOME, FOREIGN EXCHANGE, and customized DERIVATIVES occurs over the counter rather than via exchange.

OVER-THE-COUNTER (OTC) DERIVATIVES   Customized DERIVATIVE CONTRACTS that are traded directly between two parties rather than via a formal EXCHANGE. The flexibility regarding transaction size, trade and settlement dates, MATURITIES, UNDERLYING market references, and PAYOFF profiles makes OTC derivatives extremely popular with institutional HEDGERS and SPECULATORS. However, the lack of standardized dealing terms means many OTC contracts are not as LIQUID as EXCHANGE-TRADED DERIVATIVE contracts; in addition, the lack of MARGINS or CLEARINGHOUSES means that many OTC contracts feature some amount of COUNTERPARTY CREDIT RISK. Broad classes of OTC derivatives include SWAPS, FORWARDS, OPTIONS, COMPLEX OPTIONS, and COMPLEX SWAPS. Contracts are regularly purchased and sold on references from the FIXED INCOME, EQUITY, FOREIGN EXCHANGE, COMMODITY, and CREDIT markets. See also COMMODITY DERIVATIVE,

CREDIT DERIVATIVE, CURRENCY DERIVATIVE, EQUITY DERIVATIVE, INTEREST RATE DERIVATIVE, WEATHER DERIVATIVE.

OVER THE WALL   [COL] A process where bankers inform a research analyst within the BANK about an impending CORPORATE FINANCE or NEW ISSUE transaction for a company; once "over the CHINESE WALL," the analyst cannot produce research information as it is apt to be influenced by, or contain details of, NONPUBLIC INFORMATION.

OVERALLOTMENT OPTION   See GREENSHOE.

OVERBOUGHT   A situation where a SECURITY or market has been the focus of aggressive buying over a short period of time, and which may be due for a correction due to a relative lack of new buyers. See also OVERSOLD.

OVERCAPITALIZATION   Any instance where a company has an excess of CAPITAL and is unable to justify its use in the pursuit of productive endeavors. In such instances the company may seek to return excess EQUITY capital to SHAREHOLDERS through a special cash DIVIDEND or through a SHARE repurchase program, while it may reduce excess DEBT capital by retiring outstanding MEDIUM-TERM DEBT or LONG-TERM DEBT.

OVERCOLLATERALIZATION   In a SECURITIZATION transaction, the excess of the PAR VALUE of the collateral ASSET pool over the par value of the ASSET-BACKED SECURITIES being issued to INVESTORS, or the advance rate against the pool. Overcollateralization serves as a form of internal credit enhancement for transactions using the SENIOR and SUBORDINATED TRANCHE structure. See also TIME TRANCHING.

OVERCOLLATERALIZATION TEST   A COLLATERAL-related financial test performed in a COLLATERALIZED DEBT OBLIGATION or SECURITIZATION structure to determine whether the CASH FLOW WATERFALL can make payments to increasingly SUBORDINATED TRANCHES. The form of the test is given by:

(PRINCIPAL value of the collateral pool)/(Principal of a target TRANCHE + Principal of all tranches ranking SENIOR to the target)

The test is considered successful if the interest coverage ratio is greater than or equal to the specified TRIGGER.

OVERHANG   (1) A sizeable amount of SECURITIES known to be held by INVESTORS or INTERMEDIARIES, which, if placed in the market, would cause significant price declines. An overhang can result from a large block of unsold NEW ISSUE securities. (2) A measure of COMMON STOCK and OPTIONS awarded or subject to conversion under executive compensation plans; a large overhang (10% + of outstanding shares) can depress a company's stock price since award and/or conversion results in DILUTION. (3) An excess of DEBT at the sovereign level, leaving it with insufficient resources to continue servicing its obligations. The overhang may lead to a RESTRUCTURING or RESCHEDULING action. (1) Also known as MARKET OVERHANG.

OVERHEAD The administrative costs associated with operating a business, such as costs for salaries, rents, insurance, utilities, and supplies.

OVERHEATING A stage in the expansion of an ECONOMY or the appreciation in a market or ASSET where speculative factors force growth/prices to move up rapidly, at what may ultimately be an unsustainable pace.

OVERHEDGING Excessive HEDGE protection that might not be required when broader PORTFOLIO exposures with "beneficial" CORRELATIONS that produce natural offsets are considered.

OVERINSURANCE Any instance where an INSURED carries too much INSURANCE coverage against a specific PERIL. Since an insured can never profit from a CLAIM (being entitled only to fair restitution related to the amount lost), overinsurance results in wasted PREMIUM payments. See also UNDERINSURANCE

OVERISSUE Issuance of COMMON STOCK by a company in excess of its authorized SHARE limit. The corporate registrar is typically responsible for ensuring that overissue does not occur.

OVERLAPPING INSURANCE A situation where an INSURED has two or more INSURANCE policies covering the same RISK. If a CLAIM is made, the insured will not be able to receive payment under all policies, since insurance cannot result in a net profit; the amount of the claim is generally divided on PRO-RATA basis between the policies. See also APPORTIONMENT, DIVIDED COVER, PRIMACY.

OVERLINED [COL] A temporary situation where a COMMERCIAL PAPER ISSUER has repaid all outstanding NOTES and has excess SWINGLINE availability.

OVERNIGHT INDEX SWAP (OIS) An INTEREST RATE SWAP which exchanges a FIXED RATE for a FLOATING RATE, where the floating rate INDEX is computed on an overnight basis as a geometric MEAN of a specific reference such as FEDERAL FUNDS, EONIA, SONIA, and so forth. No interim payments are made during the life of the transaction, but are settled at MATURITY, which is generally 1 week to 2 years from inception. The OIS essentially functions as a form of synthetic LENDING/BORROWING (e.g., the fixed rate receiver is *de facto* a lender, and vice-versa).

OVERNIGHT MONEY Funds borrowed on an overnight basis by a BANK or other financial institution. Such overnight funding is payable within one day, and can be accessed through direct interbank borrowings (unsecured) or OVERNIGHT REPURCHASE AGREEMENTS (secured).

OVERNIGHT RATE Any INTEREST RATE reference that is computed on, and reflective of, an overnight period, e.g., EONIA, SONIA.

OVERNIGHT REPURCHASE AGREEMENT A REPURCHASE AGREEMENT with a 24-hour MATURITY, which is generally renewed or rolled over on a daily basis. The opposite side of the transaction is referred to as an overnight

REVERSE REPURCHASE AGREEMENT. See also OPEN REPURCHASE AGREEMENT, TERM REPURCHASE AGREEMENT.

OVERSEAS PRIVATE INVESTMENT CORPORATION (OPIC)   A US government agency created in 1971 to help US companies INVEST in foreign countries and to provide FINANCING and POLITICAL RISK INSURANCE for those dealing in both developed and emerging markets.

OVERSOLD   A situation where a SECURITY or market has been the focus of aggressive selling over a short period of time, and which may be due for a price rebound due to a lack of additional sellers. See also OVERBOUGHT.

OVERSUBSCRIPTION   A situation where the number of ORDERS for a NEW ISSUE of SECURITIES is greater than the available SUPPLY, suggesting the price of the security will rise sharply at launch. If an EQUITY issue is oversubscribed, the UNDERWRITERS may exercise the GREENSHOE and float more shares; if a DEBT issue is oversubscribed, the issuer may authorize the underwriters to increase the size of the deal. See also UNDERSUBSCRIPTION.

OVERTRADING   See CHURNING.

P

P/E RATIO   See PRICE/EARNINGS RATIO.

PAASCHE'S INDEX   See CURRENT WEIGHTED INDEX.

PAC BOND   See PLANNED AMORTIZATION CLASS BOND.

PAC MAN DEFENSE   [COL] An ANTITAKEOVER DEFENSE where a TARGET company initiates a counterbid for the company that is attempting a HOSTILE TAKEOVER of its operations. The counterbid may involve the use of a considerable amount of LEVERAGE, making the defense strategy financially risky.

PACKAGE INSURANCE   See MULTILINE POLICY.

PAID-IN CAPITAL   CAPITAL received by a company from the flotation of COMMON STOCK through an INITIAL PUBLIC OFFERING, RIGHTS ISSUE, or ADD-ON. Also known as PAID-IN SURPLUS. See also RETAINED EARNINGS, CAPITAL SURPLUS.

PAID-IN SURPLUS   (1) A measure of an INSURER's SOLVENCY, computed as the excess of an insurer's admitted ASSETS over the total value of its LIABILITIES and minimum required CAPITAL. (2) See PAID-IN CAPITAL.

PAID LOSS RETROSPECTIVE POLICY   A LOSS-SENSITIVE INSURANCE CONTRACT where the INSURED's incremental PREMIUM is due when the INSURER makes actual SETTLEMENT payments; since the payment period can span several years, the insured gains the benefit of a multiyear financing.

PAID-UP POLICY   In the United Kingdom, an ENDOWMENT ASSURANCE policy where the INSURED ceases to make PREMIUM payments, and where the SURRENDER VALUE is then used to purchase some amount of cheaper life assurance coverage.

P

PAINTING THE TAPE   [COL] See DAISY CHAIN.

PAIRED SHARES   The COMMON STOCK of two companies, managed by the same EXECUTIVE MANAGEMENT team, that are traded together through a single certificate. Also known as STAPLED STOCK.

PAIRS TRADING   An INVESTMENT strategy that involves going LONG of one STOCK (perceived to be CHEAP) and SHORT of a second stock (RICH) in expectation of capturing the SPREAD movements between the two over some time horizon, typically based on some impending event (e.g., earnings announcements). Since the investor hopes to capture the spread, the strategy is MARKET NEUTRAL, meaning the absolute level of the market is not relevant to success. Pairs trading is often done within a specific industry sector, e.g., one automobile stock versus a second one, but is also characteristic of takeover and acquisition stocks in RISK ARBITRAGE.

PAPER LOSS   See UNREALIZED LOSS.

PAPER MARKET   [COL] See PAPER SWAP.

PAPER PROFIT   See UNREALIZED PROFIT.

PAPER SWAP   (1) An OVER-THE-COUNTER SWAP based on a physical COMMODITY (often an energy product) that is transacted strictly on paper, with no attempt or intent to make or take delivery of the underlying physical goods; paper swaps are always settled on a cash, or financial, basis, or are OFFSET prior to EXPIRY. (2) A COMMODITY DERIVATIVE involving the exchange of fixed and floating prices related to paper products, such as pulp, paperboard, and newsprint. The paper swap can serve as a HEDGE for firms exposed to the selling or buying price of paper products. (1) Also known as PAPER MARKET.

PAR   See PAR VALUE.

PAR BOND   (1) A BOND that trades at its PAR VALUE. (2) A form of BRADY BOND with no price discount but with a smaller INTEREST COUPON than the DISCOUNT BOND alternative. (1) See also PREMIUM BOND.

PAR VALUE   The stated value, or FACE VALUE, of a SECURITY established at the time of issuance, and generally also its REDEMPTION VALUE. For BONDS and NOTES it is the amount to be repaid to INVESTORS at MATURITY, for COMMON STOCK or PREFERRED STOCK it is simply an artificial value that has no bearing after the initial launch of SHARES. Also known as NOMINAL VALUE, PAR.

PAR YIELD CURVE   A YIELD CURVE representing observable INTEREST RATES across a spectrum of MATURITIES, obtained from FIXED INCOME SECURITIES traded in the marketplace. The par yield curve is used for pricing, investment, HEDGING, and RISK MANAGEMENT, and is the foundation for developing the IMPLIED FORWARD CURVE used to price DERIVATIVES and other financial CONTRACTS that rely on a forward estimate of rates. See also TERM STRUCTURE, ZERO COUPON YIELD CURVE.

PARALLEL LOAN   A pair of LOANS between two companies and their two offshore SUBSIDIARIES, which permits efficient funding of local CURRENCY requirements across borders; parallel loans are effectively BALANCE SHEET versions of CURRENCY SWAPS. One company lends the local subsidiary of a second company funds in the local currency, while the second company lends the subsidiary of the first company funds in its local currency. This arrangement eliminates the need for the two companies to convert proceeds before on-lending to their local operations. The loans are governed by separate agreements that do not normally include the right of OFFSET. See also BACK-TO-BACK LOAN.

PARALLEL MONEY MARKETS   A sector of the financing market that occurs between users and suppliers of short-term funds without the use of specialized INTERMEDIARIES, such as DISCOUNT HOUSES. The development of parallel money markets is a form of DISINTERMEDIATION.

PARALLEL SHIFT   The process of moving the YIELD CURVE up or down by an equal number of BASIS POINTS throughout every MATURITY point on the curve and recalculating the value of a FIXED INCOME transaction or PORTFOLIO. The parallel shift reveals the sensitivity of the fixed income position(s) to equal changes in the curve, and can be used to calculate hypothetical PROFITS and LOSSES and the effectiveness of possible HEDGES. See also TWIST.

PARAMETRIC TRIGGER   A conditional event in an INSURANCE-LINKED SECURITY that results in suspension of INTEREST and/or PRINCIPAL when a specific damage metric reaches a certain value. The metric is generally based on location and severity parameters. See also INDEMNITY TRIGGER, INDEX TRIGGER.

PARASOL POLICY   See DIFFERENCE IN CONDITIONS INSURANCE.

PARENT   [COL] The primary operating entity in a CORPORATION, and often the one with the most significant operations and financial resources. A parent company may be called on by potential CREDITORS to GUARANTEE the LIABILITIES of any SUBSIDIARIES. See also HOLDING COMPANY.

PARENT ORDER   An overarching ORDER to execute a particular transaction that can be divided up into smaller CHILD ORDERS. A parent order is commonly used as a fundamental starting point in ALGORITHMIC TRADING. See also ORDER GENERATION LOGIC, ORDER PLACEMENT LOGIC.

PARI PASSU   [LAT] Literally "on equal standing." In FINANCE it applies to granting a party the same rights/seniority that have been granted to others. A pari passu clause is often included in VENTURE CAPITAL, BOND, and LOAN agreements to ensure that seniority classes remain unaffected by future financial transactions. See also NEGATIVE PLEDGE, STRUCTURAL SUBORDINATION.

PARIS CLUB MEETING   A meeting between a sovereign DEBTOR and government CREDITORS and BANKS (generally those from GROUP OF 10 countries), to consider bilateral RESCHEDULINGS of the debtor country's DEBT in order to avoid MORATORIUM or DEFAULT. So named as the meetings are coordinated via the French finance ministry.

PARITY   See CONVERSION PARITY.

PARKING   [COL] The transfer of ASSETS, LIABILITIES, or CASH FLOWS to another party, without the transfer of associated RISKS, for the purpose of altering a FINANCIAL STATEMENT. Parking is illegal in many jurisdictions as it conveys a false profile of financial standing.

PARTIAL BARRIER OPTION   A BARRIER OPTION with a BARRIER that is only in effect during a portion of the option's life, often one week, month, or quarter of a multiquarter or multiyear deal. See also POINT BARRIER OPTION.

PARTIAL INSURANCE   An INSURANCE POLICY providing fractional RISK TRANSFER in exchange for a smaller PREMIUM. For INSUREDS with the proper RISK TOLERANCE, the lower cost of protection achieved via partial insurance may be preferable under a cost/benefit framework. Fractional coverage is generally achieved through DEDUCTIBLES, EXCLUSIONS, and/or POLICY CAPS. See also FULL INSURANCE.

PARTIAL LOOKBACK OPTION An OVER-THE-COUNTER COMPLEX OPTION that allows the purchaser to reset the STRIKE PRICE on a particular evaluation date if the option is OUT-OF-THE-MONEY. Also known as RESET OPTION. See also LOOKBACK OPTION.

PARTIAL PLAN TERMINATION A CORPORATE FINANCE scheme designed to take advantage of an overfunded PENSION PLAN to free up cash for use in other endeavors. Under the termination transaction, the pension plan is split into two distinct components and the overfunded portion is terminated, releasing cash into the general corporate account. Partial plan termination only works when the total plan is overfunded with respect to both retirees and current employees.

PARTIAL RECOURSE LOAN A LOAN where the lending BANK must initially rely on CASH FLOWS from the ASSET or project being financed for repayment but may then turn to the BORROWER for repayment. Also known as LIMITED RECOURSE LOAN. See also FULL RECOURSE LOAN, NONRECOURSE, NONRECOURSE LOAN, RECOURSE.

PARTICIPATING DIVIDEND An additional DIVIDEND paid to INVESTORS holding a company's participating PREFERRED STOCK. See also PARTICIPATING FORWARD.

PARTICIPATING FORWARD A FORWARD CONTRACT with a feature that allows the first party to share in any gains earned by the second party on a predetermined basis. In exchange, the second party receives a more favorable forward price.

PARTICIPATING GUARANTEED INVESTMENT CONTRACT (GIC) A form of a GUARANTEED INVESTMENT CONTRACT granting the INVESTOR a share of any INVESTMENT EARNINGS from the ASSET PORTFOLIO exceeding the guaranteed rate. See also NONPARTICIPATING GUARANTEED INVESTMENT CONTRACT, SYNTHETIC GUARANTEED INVESTMENT CONTRACT.

PARTICIPATING OPTION An OPTION CONTACT with a feature that allows the buyer to only benefit from a certain amount of any gains earned; the option seller retains a portion of the profits, in return for levying a smaller PREMIUM.

PARTICIPATING POLICY An INSURANCE CONTRACT where the INSURED receives periodic DIVIDENDS from the INSURER, thus sharing in the insurer's overall profitability. The participating policy essentially grants the insured an increasing PREMIUM rebate as the insurer's UNDERWRITING and INVESTMENT MANAGEMENT performance improves.

PARTICIPATING PREFERRED STOCK A form of PREFERRED STOCK that pays INVESTORS a standard preferred DIVIDEND and a portion of a COMMON

STOCK dividend if certain financial performance targets are met. Such issues are relatively rare.

PARTICIPATION CERTIFICATE   A SECURITY that represents an interest in an underlying POOL of ASSETS, generally MORTGAGES; the term is often used generically to refer to MORTGAGE-BACKED SECURITIES. See also PASS-THROUGH SECURITY.

PARTICIPATION FINANCING   See PARTICIPATION LOAN.

PARTICIPATION LOAN   A LOAN that is extended by several BANKS to a single BORROWER, and which is serviced by one of the participating banks on behalf of the group. The banks all enter into the agreement simultaneously and jointly (in contrast to a SYNDICATED LOAN, which is originated by the lead bank and syndicated to the participating group). A participation loan is arranged when the financing is so large that it exceeds any single bank's LEGAL LENDING LIMIT. Also known as LOAN PARTICIPATION, PARTICIPATION FINANCING.

PARTLY PAID SHARES   The SHARES of a company that have not been paid up to the full PAR VALUE at the time of initial issuance, and on which INVESTORS are subject to a further call for additional CAPITAL. The mechanism is relatively uncommon, used primarily in very large transactions or PRIVATIZATIONS. See also FULLY PAID SHARES.

PARTNER   A participant in a form of an unincorporated business organization. Depending on the structure of the organization, a partner may have unlimited personal responsibility with regard to incurred DEBTS. See also GENERAL PARTNERSHIP, LIMITED PARTNERSHIP, PARTNERSHIP, SILENT PARTNERSHIP.

PARTNERSHIP   A form of unincorporated business organization that features two or more PARTNERS contractually associated in the furtherance of a particular type of business. Depending on structure, the partners may have unlimited personal responsibility with regard to incurred LIABILITIES. The term can also be used to mean a GENERAL PARTNERSHIP. See also LIMITED PARTNERSHIP, SILENT PARTNERSHIP.

PASS-THROUGH SECURITY   A generic SECURITIZATION structure that provides INVESTORS with the CASH FLOWS generated by an underlying ASSET or PORTFOLIO. A pass-through can be issued in modified form (guaranteeing payment of PRINCIPAL and INTEREST, but only timely payment of interest) or fully modified form (guaranteeing timely payment of both principal and interest). Pass-through securities can be created from a range of assets, including MORTGAGES, ACCOUNTS RECEIVABLE, LOANS, and BONDS. Common examples include MORTGAGE-BACKED SECURITIES (MBS) issued by the GOVERNMENT NATIONAL MORTGAGE ASSOCIATION and FEDERAL NATIONAL MORTGAGE ASSOCIATION, PARTICIPATION CERTIFICATES issued by the FEDERAL HOME LOAN MORTGAGE CORPORATION, MBS and COLLATERALIZED MORTGAGE OBLIGATIONS issued by private-label CONDUITS, and COLLATERALIZED BOND OBLIGATIONS and COLLATERALIZED LOAN OBLIGATIONS issued by BANKS and SECURITIES FIRMS.

PASSING THE BOOK   [COL] The practice followed by large international BANKS and other FINANCIAL INSTITUTIONS of transferring OPEN POSITIONS in FOREIGN EXCHANGE and other ASSETS that trade on a 24-hour basis among TRADING centers as each one becomes the primary locus of trading activity during part of the business day.

PASSIVE FUND   A FUND that seeks to match a BENCHMARK market INDEX through a replication strategy, with no attempt to outperform the benchmark. Passive funds, such as INDEX FUNDS, feature lower costs than ACTIVE FUNDS.

PASSIVE INVESTMENT STRATEGY   A process of managing a PORTFOLIO of SECURITIES by relying on a minimum amount of ASSET reallocation; passive strategies are often implemented through INDEXING. See also ACTIVE INVESTMENT STRATEGY, INDEX FUND.

PASSIVE LOSS RULES   Rules that limit the amount of deductions or INCOME that can be sheltered from TAXES. Deductions on passive losses are generally limited to an amount equal to earnings from passive sources; in addition, losses and gains must generally come from similar businesses or INVESTMENTS.

PASSIVE RETENTION   A state where a company unknowingly retains RISK and is therefore not actively managing exposure through RESERVES or SELF-INSURANCE. Passive retentions can lead to unexpected losses. See also RETENTION, RISK RETENTION.

PASSPORTING   [COL] The ability for BANKS and other FINANCIAL INSTITUTIONS operating in the EUROPEAN UNION to provide services in all EU countries once they have been approved to provide such services in any one country.

PATENT   Exclusive rights that are granted by a government authority to the designer or inventor of an innovative product or service, generally for a specified period of time (e.g., the WORLD TRADE ORGANIZATION recommends a minimum of 20 years). A patent is typically classified on the BALANCE SHEET as an INTANGIBLE.

PATH-DEPENDENT OPTION   A VANILLA or COMPLEX OPTION whose PAYOFF at EXPIRY or EXERCISE is dependent on the price path of the UNDERLYING reference ASSET at previous points in time. Common path-dependent options include BARRIER OPTIONS, ASIAN OPTIONS, FLOATING STRIKE LOOKBACK OPTIONS, HIGH-LOW OPTIONS, LADDER OPTIONS, CLIQUET OPTIONS, SHOUT OPTIONS, and INSTALLMENT OPTIONS. See also PATH-INDEPENDENT OPTION.

PATH-INDEPENDENT OPTION   A VANILLA or COMPLEX OPTION whose PAYOFF at EXPIRY or EXERCISE is dependent solely on the price of the

UNDERLYING reference ASSET at expiry or exercise. Common path-independent options include BINARY OPTIONS, MULTI-INDEX OPTIONS, COMPOUND OPTIONS, CHOOSER OPTIONS, CONTINGENT PREMIUM OPTIONS, DEFERRED PAYMENT AMERICAN OPTIONS, EXPLODING OPTIONS, and FORWARD START OPTIONS. See also PATH-DEPENDENT OPTION.

PATHFINDER PROSPECTUS   In the United Kingdom, a RED HERRING.

PAY AS YOU EARN (PAYE)   In the United Kingdom, a scheme where employers deduct from the current salary of employees the amount of estimated TAX due and payable.

PAY LATER OPTION   See CONTINGENT PREMIUM OPTION.

PAYABLE   See ACCOUNTS PAYABLE.

PAYBACK PERIOD   Also know as PAYBACK RULE.

PAYBACK RULE   A measure of the amount of time it takes for a company or INVESTOR to recover an initial INVESTMENT. The rule is based strictly on CASH FLOWS occurring over a stated period of time, with no weight given to those generated after the stated cutoff period, which can skew the result. A refinement of the payback rule DISCOUNTS the cash flows by a relevant DISCOUNT RATE. The basic form of the computation is given as:

$$PB = \frac{CI}{CF_{p.a}}$$

where CI is the initial capital investment, $CF_{p.a.}$ is the annual cash flow from the investment. Also known as PAYBACK PERIOD. See also INTERNAL RATE OF RETURN, NET PRESENT VALUE.

PAYE   See PAY AS YOU EARN.

PAYEE   A party that is due a payment, as under a CHECK, DRAFT, BILL OF EXCHANGE, or other CONTRACT. See also PAYER.

PAYER   A party that is required to make a payment, as under a CHECK, DRAFT, BILL OF EXCHANGE, or other CONTRACT. See also PAYEE.

PAYER EXTENDIBLE SWAP   An EXTENDIBLE SWAP that is formed from a combination of a fixed payer SWAP and a PAYER SWAPTION.

PAYER SWAPTION   A SWAPTION granting the buyer the right to enter into an OVER-THE-COUNTER INTEREST RATE SWAP to pay FIXED RATES and receive FLOATING RATES. The buyer is likely to exercise the swaption as floating rates rise above a particular STRIKE PRICE. Also known as PUT SWAPTION. See also RECEIVER SWAPTION.

PAYING AGENT   A BANK of other FINANCIAL INSTITUTION that is responsible for disbursing INTEREST and PRINCIPAL on a particular DEBT facility or instrument.

PAYMENT DATE The date on which INTEREST and/or PRINCIPAL due on a SECURITY is paid to INVESTORS.

PAYMENT IN KIND Payment that is made in goods or services rather than cash.

PAYMENT IN KIND (PIK) SECURITY A SECURITY that pays COUPONS or DIVIDENDS in the form of additional securities rather than cash (e.g., PIK BONDS pay interest in the form of additional PIK bonds, PIK PREFERRED STOCK pays dividends with additional PIK preferreds). PIK securities are generally issued by companies that have difficulty raising cash or are attempting to preserve cash to fund corporate operations. See also RESET PAYMENT IN KIND BOND.

PAYMENT NETTING A NETTING arrangement where an institution and its COUNTERPARTY agree to net all payments in the normal course of business. See also NOVATION, SET-OFF.

PAYMENT TERMS The specific terms defined by a seller or supplier for buyers or DEBTORS, indicating the amount of DISCOUNT that will be granted if payments are made over particular time horizons.

PAYOFF The economic result generated by a DERIVATIVE CONTRACT based on the market price of the UNDERLYING at a point in time or at the MATURITY of the contract. See also PAYOFF PROFILE.

PAYOFF PROFILE The economic gain or loss that may be expected under a DERIVATIVE CONTRACT for a given range of market prices, providing a relative gauge of upside and downside RISK. Common payoff profiles include the ASYMMETRIC PAYOFF characteristic of OPTIONS and the SYMMETRIC PAYOFF characteristic of FUTURES and FORWARDS; contracts may further be characterized as having LINEAR PAYOFFS or NONLINEAR PAYOFFS.

PAYOR BANK A BANK that is the DRAWEE of a DRAFT or CHECK. See also COLLECTING BANK.

PAYOUT RATIO The amount of corporate earnings paid out to SHAREHOLDERS in the form of COMMON STOCK DIVIDENDS, calculated as:

$$Payout = \frac{DIV_n}{EPS_n}$$

where DIV_n is the dividend paid in period n and EPS_n is the EARNINGS PER SHARE achieved in period n. See also DIVIDEND YIELD, PLOWBACK RATIO.

PBOC See PEOPLE'S BANK OF CHINA.

PD See PROBABILITY OF DEFAULT.

PEGGING (1) In the FOREIGN EXCHANGE markets, the process of linking the value of a national CURRENCY to the value of a foreign currency (or a BASKET of currencies). This implies that the national currency is not free-floating, but

dependent on the MONETARY POLICY and TRADE activities of reference countries. (2) In the SECURITIES markets, an illegal practice where manipulators
attempt to keep the price of a listed security trading close to its PAR VALUE. (3)
In the NEW ISSUE market, the legal practice of stabilizing the price of a new
offering, generally through buying efforts coordinated by the LEAD MANAGER.
(1) See also CRAWLING PEG, MANAGED FOREIGN EXCHANGE RATE.

PENNANT   A TECHNICAL ANALYSIS charting figure of a SECURITY or market that resembles the FLAG, but features a narrowing of the tip as the peaks
and troughs draw closer together; once at the tip of the pennant, the price of
the security or market is expected to rise or fall sharply.

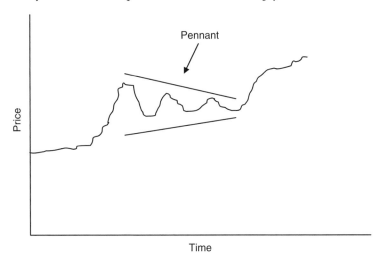

PENNY JUMPING   [COL] An illegal practice where a SPECIALIST or MARKET
MAKER in a COMMON STOCK does not match offsetting LIMIT ORDERS and
MARKET ORDERS, filling only one side and keeping the other for its proprietary book until it determines how the market moves. If the market moves
favorably, the specialist retains the position and profits; if it moves unfavor-
ably, it fills the order for the original client. Under this scenario the most the
specialist risks is a penny per share.

PENNY STOCK   [COL] The COMMON STOCK of a company that trades for
less than $1 per share, generally associated with a firm that has a short his-
tory of financial performance or one that has entered a phase of FINANCIAL
DISTRESS and has been delisted from a larger EXCHANGE. Penny stocks are
traded OVER-THE-COUNTER and are quoted on the PINK SHEETS.

PENSION FUND   See PENSION PLAN.

PENSION MORTGAGE   In the United Kingdom, a form of MORTGAGE where
the MORTGAGOR pays the lending BANK periodic INTEREST payments, and
makes additional contributions to a PENSION account, which is designed to
provide funds for repayment of PRINCIPAL when the mortgagor retires.

PENSION PLAN   A retirement program for the employees of a company, based on employer- and/or employee-funded contributions, that generates periodic, often monthly, payments for those that have retired. Funds are held in a TRUST and managed by TRUSTEES who may be nominated by the employer. In order to ensure sufficient funds to pay pension obligations, the plan may be invested in a range of FIXED INCOME and EQUITY SECURITIES. Plans may be fully funded (e.g., already actuarially solvent under a range of scenarios) or partially funded (e.g., the employer must cover any shortfall as it comes due). In some jurisdictions the pension plan can be one of defined contribution (e.g., a variable payment) or defined benefit (e.g., a fixed monthly payment). Also known as PENSION FUND.

PENSION SYSTEM   A national system for defining and administering PENSION PLANS, either at a public level or within the private sector. A system may be structured on the basis of UNFUNDED PENSIONS or FUNDED PENSIONS.

PEOPLE PILL   [COL] An ANTITAKEOVER DEFENSE where a well-regarded management team threatens to depart, en masse, in the event of a TAKEOVER. See also POISON PILL.

PEOPLE'S BANK OF CHINA (PBOC)   The CENTRAL BANK of the People's Republic of China, established in 1948 and granted central banking powers in 1983. PBOC is responsible for issuing and enforcing REGULATIONS impacting its domestic financial markets and institutions, developing and implementing MONETARY POLICY, issuing CURRENCY and managing FOREIGN EXCHANGE activities, managing official RESERVES and operating national payment SETTLEMENTS.

PER CAPITA INCOME   The average amount of INCOME earned by a defined group, system, or country, which is determined by dividing total income by the number of people in the group, system, or country. Per capita income can be used for comparative purposes across groups and over time.

PER PRO   [LAT] Abbreviated form of per procurationem, signifying an act by an AGENT who is authorized to deal on behalf of a PRINCIPAL.

PERCENTAGE OF LOSS DEDUCTIBLE   In INSURANCE, a CONTRACT with a percentage-based DEDUCTIBLE that increases as the INSURED's losses grow larger. Through this feature the insured preserves, or even increases, its RISK RETENTION.

PERCENTAGE OF SALES METHOD   A mechanism used by a company to create the PRO-FORMA BALANCE SHEET and PRO-FORMA INCOME STATEMENT. The process is based on adjusting ASSET, LIABILITY, REVENUE, and EXPENSE accounts based on a historical analysis of past sales activity (and the resulting percentage impact on individual accounts) along with incremental changes in sales forecasts derived from the CASH BUDGETING process. See also ANALYSIS OF ACCOUNTS METHOD.

PERFORMANCE BENCHMARKING   The process of analyzing the financial performance of an INVESTMENT PORTFOLIO against a predefined

BENCHMARK. Proper performance benchmarking requires selection of the correct benchmark INDEX and proper consideration of exogenous factors including COMMISSIONS and TAXES levied on the portfolio.

PERFORMANCE BOND   A FINANCIAL GUARANTEE providing payment to a third party BENEFICIARY if the purchaser of the guarantee fails to perform as contracted. Common performance bonds include SURETY BONDS and COMPLETION BONDS (purchased from INSURERS) and STANDBY LETTERS OF CREDIT (purchased from banks).

PERIL   A cause of loss, and an exposure that individuals and institutions often seek to protect against through INSURANCE. See also HAZARD.

PERIOD BILL   See TERM BILL.

PERIODIC CAP   An INTEREST RATE CAP embedded in a long-term CONTRACT that relates to a specific period of time. A new periodic cap may come into force once a previous one has expired, and this process may continue for the entire life of the contract. The periodic cap is a common feature of ADJUSTABLE RATE MORTGAGES, and prevents the BORROWER's mortgage cost from rising too rapidly from period to period in a rising rate environment. See also CAPLET, FLOORLET, LIFETIME FLOOR.

PERIODIC COLLATERAL   A process where a FINANCIAL INSTITUTION extending CREDIT to a COUNTERPARTY takes a smaller amount of initial COLLATERAL but revalues the credit exposure and collateral periodically and makes necessary adjustments (i.e., calling for additional collateral if in deficit, returning excess collateral if in surplus). See also UPFRONT COLLATERAL.

PERMISSIBLE LOSS RATIO   See LOSS RATIO.

PERPETUAL DEBENTURE   In the United Kingdom, a DEBENTURE that is issued as an UNDATED SECURITY. See also IRREDEEMABLE SECURITY.

PERPETUAL DEBT   A BOND that is issued without a stated final MATURITY. The DEBT acts as a PERPETUITY, paying INVESTORS regular COUPONS but never repaying the PRINCIPAL balance. See also CONSOL, IRREDEEMABLE SECURITY, PERPETUAL FLOATING RATE NOTE, UNDATED SECURITY.

PERPETUAL FLOATING RATE NOTE (FRN)   A hybrid SECURITY comprised of a FLOATING RATE NOTE and PERPETUAL DEBT that is issued without a stated final MATURITY. The perpetual FRN pays INVESTORS a regular FLOATING RATE COUPON, often based on LIBOR or EURIBOR, but does not repay PRINCIPAL. See also CAPPED FLOATING RATE NOTE, INVERSE FLOATING RATE NOTE, RANGE FLOATING RATE NOTE.

PERPETUAL PREFERRED STOCK   A form of CUMULATIVE PREFERRED STOCK with no fixed MATURITY date, OPTIONAL REDEMPTION that makes the securities callable at the ISSUER'S option, and a ranking in DEFAULT that is senior to COMMON STOCK and PARI PASSU with other PREFERRED STOCK. See also HYBRID CAPITAL SECURITY, TRUST PREFERRED STOCK.

PERPETUAL SUCCESSION   A concept in corporate law that allows for the permanent and continuing existence of a CORPORATION, regardless of the departure or demise of founders or executives, or the sale of SHARES by original or existing SHAREHOLDERS.

PERPETUITY   An ASSET or financial CONTRACT that pays INVESTORS a stated CASH FLOW on a continuous basis but does not provide for PRINCIPAL repayment. The PRESENT VALUE of constant and growing perpetuities is given as:

Constant:

$$PV_{cp} = \frac{CF}{r}$$

Growing:

$$PV_{gp} = \frac{CF}{r - g}$$

where CF is the stated cash flow, r is the DISCOUNT RATE, and g is the growth rate. See also ANNUITY.

PERSONAL CONSUMPTION   A component of GROSS DOMESTIC PRODUCT (and related GROSS NATIONAL PRODUCT) that includes DURABLE GOODS, NONDURABLE GOODS, and services.

PETRODOLLARS   Dollar CASH FLOWS paid for oil to oil-producing nations, which are often redeposited (or recycled) through the Western banking system.

PFANDBRIEFE   [GER] COVERED BONDS issued in the German market which are collateralized by public sector LOANS or MORTGAGES; the COLLATERAL remains on the BALANCE SHEET of the issuing BANK. The securities may carry MATURITIES ranging from 4 to 20 years, and can also be issued in global form (for placement in the United States) or structured form (with embedded DERIVATIVES). See also CEDULAS HIPOTECARIAS, HYPOTHEKENPFANDBRIEFE, IRISH ASSET COVERED SECURITIES, JUMBO PFANDBRIEFE, LETTRES DE GAGE, OBLIGATIONS FONCIERES, OFFENTLICHE PFANDBRIEFE.

PHANTOM STOCK   [COL] A corporate SECURITY that gives employees, executives, and DIRECTORS the RENT RIGHTS associated with the company's COMMON STOCK (e.g., any CAPITAL GAINS, DIVIDENDS) without granting physical SHARES or CONTROL RIGHTS (e.g., PROXY voting). Also known as SHADOW STOCK.

PHYSICAL DELIVERY   See PHYSICAL SETTLEMENT.

PHYSICAL SETTLEMENT A SETTLEMENT process where two parties to a TRADE or DERIVATIVE CONTRACT exchange cash for a physical ASSET (such as a COMMODITY or physical form SECURITY). Also known as PHYSICAL DELIVERY. See also CASH SETTLEMENT.

PHYSICALS A COMMODITY or physical good that can be bought and sold, and which can be settled through PHYSICAL DELIVERY.

PIERCING THE CORPORATE VEIL [COL] An exceptional legal circumstance where the tenet of LIMITED LIABILITY is suspended and SHAREHOLDERS become liable for paying for corporate losses from their personal ASSETS. Actual instances of such "piercing" are rare, occurring primarily when the PRINCIPALS of very closely held companies have violated their duties and generated losses. See also UNLIMITED LIABILITY.

PIG [COL] An INVESTOR that, having earned PROFITS on certain INVESTMENTS, has unrealistic expectations about further profits and continues to hold the positions.

PIG ON PORK [COL] See CROSS GUARANTEE.

PIGGYBACKING [COL] See COAT-TAILING.

PIK SECURITY See PAYMENT IN KIND SECURITY.

PILLAR I One of three "pillars" under the BASLE II framework, centered on the computation of minimum CAPITAL requirements for BANKS. Pillar I provides for greater precision in defining CREDIT RISK (under the INTERNAL RATINGS-BASED APPROACH, STANDARDIZED APPROACH) and OPERATIONAL RISK; MARKET RISK is covered under the BASLE MARKET RISK AMENDMENT. See also PILLAR II, PILLAR III.

PILLAR II One of three "pillars" under the BASLE II framework, centered on the capture of RISKS that may not be covered by PILLAR I or the BASLE MARKET RISK AMENDMENT. The intent of Pillar II is to ensure a participating BANK has adequate control processes in place to capture unusual or nonstandard risks that may appear over time. The INTERNAL CAPITAL ADEQUACY ASSESSMENT PROCESS and the SUPERVISORY REVIEW AND EXAMINATION PROCESS are used to verify adherence to Pillar II. See also PILLAR I, PILLAR III.

PILLAR III One of three "pillars" under the BASLE II framework, based on ensuring improved market discipline through detailed public disclosures. A participating BANK is required to provide additional qualitative comments on its RISK MANAGEMENT policies, processes and methodologies, and quantitative details on its key CREDIT RISK, MARKET RISK, and OPERATIONAL RISK exposures. See also PILLAR I, PILLAR II.

PIN RISK The RISK of loss that arises when a very large OPTION position (or many small ones) trades near the STRIKE PRICE as EXPIRY approaches. A small move above/below the strike price can dramatically change the HEDGE requirement and potentially induce large losses (or gains).

PINGING   [COL] The act of sending in small ORDERS into a DARK POOL as a way of discovering whether a large BID or OFFER exists in a particular STOCK. If the small orders are executed the pinging is said to be successful and can lead to GAMING of the pool.

PINK SHEETS   [COL] A mechanism used to quote OVER-THE-COUNTER SECURITIES, including PENNY STOCKS. Pink sheets were previously printed and distributed on pink paper, but are now accessible electronically.

PINNING THE STRIKE   [COL] A tendency for the price of a COMMON STOCK with heavily traded OPTIONS to close near the STRIKE PRICE of the most actively traded PUT OPTIONS or CALL OPTIONS.

PIP   [COL] The fifth decimal point in a FOREIGN EXCHANGE quotation, e.g., 0.00001. See also POINT.

PIPE   See PRIVATE INVESTMENT IN PUBLIC EQUITY.

PIPELINE   [COL] Future deal flow being arranged by BANKS, INVESTMENT BANKS, and SECURITIES FIRMS on behalf of clients. The pipeline includes future NEW ISSUES and CORPORATE FINANCE transactions, and serves as a measure of strength/weakness in the financial and corporate sectors. Also known as CALENDAR, VISIBLE SUPPLY. See also SHADOW CALENDAR.

PIPETTE   [COL] One tenth of a PIP.

PIT   [COL] See TRADING PIT.

PLACED BUSINESS   An INSURANCE POLICY that has been completed and delivered to the INSURED, and where the INSURER has received its PREMIUM.

PLACEMENT   (1) The distribution of new SHARES of COMMON STOCK, either via an INITIAL PUBLIC OFFERING or a RIGHTS ISSUE. (2) The first stage in the MONEY LAUNDERING process, in which cash derived from illegal sources is deposited in BANKS or other FINANCIAL INSTITUTIONS or money broking operations. Once deposited, the cash is used in the LAYERING and INTEGRATION stages.

PLAIN VANILLA   See VANILLA.

PLANNED AMORTIZATION CLASS (PAC) BOND   A TRANCHE of a COLLATERALIZED MORTGAGE OBLIGATION (CMO) that exhibits considerable price and RETURN stability by deflecting PREPAYMENT RISK to a COMPANION BOND. The companion bond shields the PAC from accelerating PREPAYMENTS, providing INVESTORS with a constant YIELD for a band of PREPAYMENT SPEEDS (rather than a specific speed, as is characteristic of the TARGETED AMORTIZATION CLASS BOND). Unlike other CMO tranches, the PAC bond has a SINKING FUND that remains in effect while prepayments remain within the specified prepayment speed bands. Also known as SIMULTANEOUS PAY BOND. See also SEQUENTIAL PAY BOND.

PLANNED ECONOMY   See COMMAND ECONOMY.

PLC   See PUBLIC LIMITED COMPANY.

PLEDGE   The act of assigning an ASSET to a LENDER to support a BORROW-ING. The BORROWER retains ownership, but not possession, of the asset unless a DEFAULT occurs, at which point the lender takes legal ownership and can liquidate the asset to repay the loan. See also HYPOTHECATION.

PLOWBACK RATIO   The amount of CAPITAL a firm reinvests in its operations, such as EARNINGS that are retained and reinvested rather than paid to SHAREHOLDERS in the form of DIVIDENDS. The formula is given as:

$$PBR = 1 - Payout$$

where Payout is the PAYOUT RATIO.

PLUS TICK   Sale of a SECURITY at a price that is higher than the prior transaction, generally indicated through the display of a "+" next to the screen or tape price. A SHORT SALE can be initiated on a plus tick. Also known as UPTICK See also MINUS TICK, ZERO PLUS TICK, ZERO MINUS TICK.

PO STRIP   See PRINCIPAL-ONLY STRIP.

POINT   [COL] The fourth decimal point in a FOREIGN EXCHANGE quotation, e.g., 0.0001. See also PIP.

POINT AND FIGURE CHART   A TECHNICAL ANALYSIS chart that depicts upward and downward moves in a SECURITY or market but ignores time dimensions. A typical chart is comprised of Xs to depict upward moves and Os for downward moves. Continuous up or down moves are reflected in the same column for each occurrence, but when the trend shifts (e.g., to a new down or up) a new column is started. The chart that results is intended to reveal directional momentum.

POINT BARRIER OPTION   A BARRIER OPTION with a BARRIER that is only in effect at a single point in time, often MATURITY, rather than the entire life of the transaction. Also known as EUROPEAN BARRIER OPTION. See also PARTIAL BARRIER OPTION.

POISON PILL   [COL] A general class of ANTITAKEOVER DEFENSES designed to make a TARGET's COMMON STOCK look less attractive to a potential acquirer planning a TAKEOVER, often through excessive DILUTION. See also CHEWABLE PILL, FLIP IN PILL, FLIP OVER PILL.

POISON PUT   [COL] An OPTION contained within a company's BOND INDENTURE that allows INVESTORS to present BONDS for redemption if certain defined events occur, such as a HOSTILE TAKEOVER, payment of excessively large DIVIDENDS to SHAREHOLDERS, or assumption of additional DEBT. While poison put provisions are intended to protect DEBT INVESTORS, they can also be used by the issuing company as an ANTITAKEOVER DEFENSE, as any hostile approach leading to redemption will lead to a reduction in cash, making the company appear less attractive.

POLICY CAP The maximum amount payable by an INSURER to an INSURED, or a REINSURER to a CEDING INSURER, under an INSURANCE or REINSURANCE CONTRACT. Also known as AGGREGATE LIMIT, CAP, EXHAUSTION POINT.

POLITICAL RISK INSURANCE A form of INSURANCE that provides the INSURED with coverage against losses arising from various SOVEREIGN RISKS, including political disruption, EXPROPRIATION, NATIONALIZATION, CONTRACT repudiation, CAPITAL controls, and, in some instances, acts of terrorism. See also WRAPAROUND INSURANCE.

POLL TAX In the United Kingdom and continental Europe, a uniform TAX that can be levied on each citizen of a particular city, state, or other jurisdiction, according to local needs and rules.

PONZI SCHEME A FRAUD perpetrated on unwitting INVESTORS, named after Charles Ponzi who operated a large scheme in the early twentieth century. Ponzi schemes can take various forms, but often involve some form of pyramiding structure, where new client funds are used to repay funds placed by original clients; the scheme can only work as long as new funds continue to flow in.

POOL (1) A SYNDICATE of INSURERS or REINSURERS organized to underwrite a LINE of RISK. Each pool member shares in PREMIUMS, losses, and LOSS ADJUSTMENT EXPENSES. (2) A group of ASSETS combined into a PORTFOLIO for SECURITIZATION or COLLATERAL management purposes. (1) See also REINSURANCE POOL.

POOLED PORTFOLIO COLLATERAL A COLLATERAL management technique where ASSETS securing a PORTFOLIO of DERIVATIVES or other CREDIT-sensitive transactions are held in a general POOL that can be applied to incremental transactions as they arise; pooled collateral can generally be managed on a dynamic basis through the right of substitution. See also CROSS COLLATERAL AGREEMENT, TRANSACTION-SPECIFIC COLLATERAL.

POOLING (1) The process of combining DEBIT and CREDIT balances in a corporate customer's disparate BANK ACCOUNTS to derive a net balance; interest is credited on a positive balance, and debited on a negative balance. (2) See RISK POOLING. (1) Also known as BALANCE CONCENTRATION, NOTIONAL POOLING.

POOLING OF INTERESTS ACCOUNTING See MERGER ACCOUNTING.

POOP AND SCOOP [COL] An illegal practice where a group of INVESTORS circulates false negative news about a company in order to drive down the price of its COMMON STOCK; once the price has been pushed down, the investors purchase shares and wait for a rebound. This type of scheme is typically targeted at small, thinly traded stocks. See also PUMP AND DUMP.

PORCUPINE PROVISION [COL] See ANTITAKEOVER DEFENSE.

PORTABLE ALPHA (1) An INVESTMENT MANAGEMENT technique that involves separating ALPHA (specific performance) from BETA (market performance) and neutralizing the latter, so that pure MARKET RISK no longer factors into the investment performance of the FUND manager. When alpha can be decomposed from beta, it is said to be portable, as it is no longer dependent on market performance and can be created in any investment setting. (2) A set of SECURITIES representing a collection of ACTIVE BETS, with EXPECTED RETURNS that are theoretically uncorrelated with market returns.

PORTABLE PENSION In the United Kingdom, an employee PENSION account that can be moved between employers as the employee changes jobs.

PORTFOLIO A group of ASSETS that is managed jointly, often to provide proper DIVERSIFICATION, RISK MANAGEMENT, or INVESTMENT opportunities that cannot be obtained by holding individual assets. See also PORTFOLIO DIVERSIFICATION, PORTFOLIO RISK, PORTFOLIO THEORY.

PORTFOLIO CONSTRUCTION The general process used by HEDGE FUND, MUTUAL FUND, and INVESTMENT managers to create a PORTFOLIO of investments with particular RISK and RETURN characteristics. The construction process, which may be led by a fund's CHIEF INVESTMENT OFFICER or investment committee, takes account of the fund's specific mandate, its ability to take risk, and its return targets.

PORTFOLIO DIVERSIFICATION The practice of combining SECURITIES that are not correlated with one another in order to diffuse RISK. See also DIVERSIFICATION, DIVERSIFIABLE RISK, NONDIVERSIFIABLE RISK, PORTFOLIO THEORY.

PORTFOLIO INSURANCE A technique that allows participants to benefit from a rising market by increasing exposure to COMMON STOCKS and protecting against a declining market by decreasing exposure. The primary downside RISK MANAGEMENT application is centered on the sale of INDEX FUTURES to protect an INVESTMENT PORTFOLIO against a fall in prices.

PORTFOLIO MANAGER A financial professional that invests the CAPITAL of investors in a range of SECURITIES. The manager may choose an active or passive strategy, and may specialize in particular ASSET classes, such as EQUITIES, FIXED INCOME, EMERGING MARKETS, and so forth. Also known as ASSET MANAGER, INVESTMENT MANAGER.

PORTFOLIO PUMPING [COL] A quarter-end or year-end practice where INVESTMENT MANAGERS purchase additional amounts of COMMON STOCK to supplement existing holdings in order to push up prices and improve end-of-period performance statistics. See also WINDOW DRESSING.

PORTFOLIO REINSURANCE A REINSURANCE CONTRACT granted over a CEDING INSURER's total PORTFOLIO of RISKS; the contract effectively provides the insurer with macro protection against all LINES of INSURANCE business written.

PORTFOLIO RETURN　The income generated by a group of ASSETS over a defined horizon. Income may be derived from DIVIDENDS, YIELD, and/or CAPITAL GAINS, depending on the characteristics of the SECURITIES. The total RETURN of the portfolio is equal to the sum of the returns on each individual asset, and is given by:

$$R_p = \sum_{x=1}^{z} w_x R_x$$

where R_p is the return of the portfolio, R_x is the return of asset x in the portfolio, w_x is the weight of asset x in the portfolio, Z is the number of assets in the portfolio. See also EXPECTED PORTFOLIO RETURN.

PORTFOLIO RISK　The RISK of loss arising from adverse movements in a PORTFOLIO of ASSETS or businesses. Portfolio risks can often be managed or mitigated through DIVERSIFICATION techniques, including those that make use of uncorrelated exposures, and through certain MACROHEDGES. Portfolio risk between assets in a portfolio can be measured through the use of a VARIANCE/COVARIANCE MATRIX. The risk of a two asset portfolio is given by:

$$\sigma^2(R_p) = \sigma^2(R_1) + \sigma^2(R_2) + 2w_1 w_2 cov(R_1, R_2)$$

where R_p is the return of the portfolio, R_1 is the return of asset 1, R_2 is the return of asset 2, $\sigma^2(R_1)$ is the variance of the return of asset 1, $\sigma^2(R_2)$ is the variance of the return of asset 2, w_1 is the weight of asset 1 in the portfolio, w_2 is the weight of asset 2 in the portfolio, $cov(R_1, R_2)$ is the covariance between assets 1 and 2.

The generalized formula for a portfolio containing Z assets is given by:

$$\sigma^2(R_p) = \sum_{g=1}^{z} \sum_{h=1}^{z} w_g w_h cov(R_g, R_h)$$

Note that the terms for which h = g results in the variance of the Z assets, while the terms for which h ≠ g yields all covariances among the Z assets. See also CORRELATION, CORRELATION RISK.

PORTFOLIO THEORY　The practice of analyzing and managing INVESTMENTS on a PORTFOLIO, rather than SECURITY-specific, basis. The process is based on measuring portfolio ASSET RISKS and RETURNS (including those that are characterized as DIVERSIFIABLE and NONDIVERSIFIABLE RISKS), creating investment allocation strategies, and optimizing portfolio components. The ultimate goal is to create a diversified portfolio of investments that maximizes return for a given level of risk.

POSITION TRADING   A speculative TRADING strategy based on holding a LONG POSITION or SHORT POSITION for several weeks or months. Position trading, though relatively short-term in nature, has a longer horizon than MOMENTUM TRADING.

POSITIVE BASIS   A market state where the price of the cash or SPOT MARKET SECURITY is greater than the price of the underlying FUTURES contract. See also BASIS RISK, NEGATIVE BASIS.

POSITIVE CARRY   Any transaction or trade where the RETURNS generated by an ASSET are greater than the financing and storage charges required to support the asset. See also CARRY, CARRY TRADE, NEGATIVE CARRY.

POSITIVE CONVEXITY   A characteristic of certain financial ASSETS where gains are greater, and losses are smaller, than those of LINEAR INSTRUMENTS or those with NEGATIVE CONVEXITY. LONG OPTIONS, and BONDS with no OPTIONALITY feature positive convexity. See also NEGATIVE CONVEXITY, NONLINEAR INSTRUMENT, POSITIVE GAMMA.

POSITIVE GAMMA   MARKET RISK exposure to large price moves in the UNDERLYING generated through the purchase of PUT OPTIONS or CALL OPTIONS. In common with other POSITIVE CONVEXITY instruments, positive gamma positions feature gains that are greater and losses that are smaller than instruments with NEGATIVE CONVEXITY. See also GAMMA, NEGATIVE GAMMA.

POSITIVE GAP   A general measure of a company's exposure to INTEREST RATE REPRICING RISK. A positive gap arises when RATE SENSITIVE ASSETS reprice faster than LIABILITIES (e.g., have shorter DURATION), meaning a company will experience a loss if rates fall and a gain if rates rise. Also known as ASSET SENSITIVE. See also GAP, GAPPING, NEGATIVE GAP.

POSITIVE OBLIGATION   See AFFIRMATIVE OBLIGATION

POSITIVE WORKING CAPITAL   A financial state where a company's CURRENT ASSETS exceed its CURRENT LIABILITIES. Positive working capital indicates the availability of sufficient LIQUIDITY to cover OBLIGATIONS coming due. See also NEGATIVE WORKING CAPITAL.

POSITIVE YIELD CURVE   A TERM STRUCTURE where short-term INTEREST RATES are lower than long-term interest rates. The positive yield curve is the most common state of the term structure in financial systems operating under normal market conditions (i.e., low INFLATION, stable economic growth). Also known as UPWARD SLOPING YIELD CURVE. See also FLAT YIELD CURVE, KINKED YIELD CURVE, NEGATIVE YIELD CURVE, YIELD CURVE.

POST-FUNDED POLICY   See RETROSPECTIVE FINITE POLICY.

POST-LOSS FINANCING   Funding that is arranged in response to, rather than in anticipation of, a loss event, and which may come from cash or RESERVES, RETAINED EARNINGS, LOANS or DEBT, or EQUITY issuance. In some instances post-loss financing may prove more expensive and uncertain than PRE-LOSS FINANCING, as CAPITAL may not be available and/or the company may have entered a period of FINANCIAL DISTRESS. See also LOSS FINANCING.

POT   [COL] A portion of a NEW ISSUE that is retained by the LEAD MANAGER to facilitate large block sales to INSTITUTIONAL INVESTORS.

POTENTIAL EXPOSURE   A measure of the current and future CREDIT RISK exposure of a financial CONTRACT with uncertain or variable value, such as a DERIVATIVE, REPURCHASE AGREEMENT, or LOAN COMMITMENT. It is often calculated as the sum of ACTUAL EXPOSURE (MARK-TO-MARKET value) and FRACTIONAL EXPOSURE (an estimate of future value obtained through statistical or SIMULATION-based models). Also known as RISK EQUIVALENT EXPOSURE.

POTENTIAL MARKET RISK   See FRACTIONAL EXPOSURE.

POWER BARRIER OPTION   An OVER-THE-COUNTER COMPLEX OPTION with an exponential PAYOFF that is either created (i.e., knocks-in) or extinguished (i.e., knocks-out) when a particular BARRIER is breached. See also POWER OPTION, BARRIER OPTION.

POWER-OF-ATTORNEY   A legal authorization given by one party (the PRINCIPAL) to another party (the ATTORNEY-IN-FACT) to deal in specified, and binding, transactions on its behalf.

POWER OPTION   (1) An OPTION that grants the buyer an exponential PAYOFF if the CONTRACT moves/finishes IN-THE-MONEY. A power option raises the price of the UNDERLYING reference to a prespecified exponent (or power) and compares the result against a predefined STRIKE PRICE to determine any economic gain. (2) An option contract with an UNDERLYING that references electricity prices in a particular pool or grid. Power options can be traded OVER-THE-COUNTER and via certain EXCHANGES. (1) Also known as LEVERAGED OPTION, TURBO OPTION. (2) See also ELECTRICITY SWAP.

POWER SWAP   (1) An OVER-THE-COUNTER COMPLEX SWAP that generates a PAYOFF by multiplying the FIXED RATE or FLOATING RATE payments by a LEVERAGE factor; the use of leverage compounds the upward or downward movement of the market reference, magnifying potential RISK and RETURN. Leverage can be applied to any swap and can be defined in any fashion. (2) See ELECTRICITY SWAP. (1) Also known as LEVERAGED SWAP, RATIO SWAP.

PPI   See PRODUCER PRICE INDEX.

PREANNOUNCEMENT   A process used by a PUBLIC COMPANY where it releases financial or corporate information (particularly forecast earnings) to the marketplace ahead of a formally scheduled release date to allow the market to absorb the information and dampen the potential impact on its STOCK PRICE.

PRECIPITATION DERIVATIVE An OVER-THE-COUNTER WEATHER DERIVATIVE that provides protection against, or exposure to, snowfall or rainfall based on the amount of solid or liquid precipitation falling in a given location over a set period of time. Precipitation derivatives can be used to HEDGE inputs or outputs that are sensitive to, or impacted by, rainfall or snowfall. See also TEMPERATURE DERIVATIVE.

PREDATORY LENDING Unethical, and sometimes illegal, LENDING practices followed by certain FINANCIAL INSTITUTIONS that seek to take advantage of RETAIL CLIENTS through excessive fees and charges or through unfavorable and prejudicial terms.

PREEMPTION RIGHT See PREEMPTIVE RIGHT.

PREEMPTIVE RIGHT The RIGHT of existing SHAREHOLDERS to invest in a NEW ISSUE of COMMON STOCK before it is offered to the market at large; only when shareholders have waived or transferred this right can new shares be offered to new shareholders. Where preemptive rights do not specifically exist, shareholders may still be protected through SUBSCRIPTION WARRANTS. Also known as ANTIDILUTION PROVISION, PREEMPTION RIGHT, SUBSCRIPTION PRIVILEGE. See also RIGHTS ISSUE.

PREFERENCE The transfer of valuable property within 90 days of a company's BANKRUPTCY filing; preference payments made by the company to third parties that prejudice or impair the position of CREDITORS, or which favor one creditor over others, may be subject to CLAWBACK by the TRUSTEE or RECEIVER. Also known as VOIDABLE PREFERENCE. See also PREFERENCE PERIOD.

PREFERENCE OPTION See CHOOSER OPTION.

PREFERENCE PERIOD A 90-day period preceding a company's BANKRUPTCY filing. See also PREFERENCE.

PREFERENCE SHARE In the United Kingdom, PREFERRED STOCK.

PREFERENTIAL CREDITOR In the United Kingdom, a PREFERRED CREDITOR.

PREFERENTIAL DEBT In the United Kingdom, DEBT that receives preferred repayment status in the event of BANKRUPTCY, accorded to PREFERENTIAL CREDITORS.

PREFERRED CREDITOR A CREDITOR that is repaid after holders of SECURED DEBT, but before unsecured creditors, typically defined to include PENSION TRUSTEES and employees owed salary or other compensation. Also known as PREFERENTIAL CREDITOR.

PREFERRED RISK An INSURED with a lower PROBABILITY of generating a loss and CLAIM than a standard applicant; INSURERS attempt to identify such RISKS for inclusion in their PORTFOLIOS in order to maximize UNDERWRITING income and minimize SETTLEMENTS.

PREFERRED STOCK   A CAPITAL SECURITY issued by a company that pays INVESTORS periodic DIVIDENDS, but does not convey VOTING RIGHTS (although consent from two-thirds of preferred investors is often required on any matter that will affect the seniority of their CLAIM). Preferred stock investors rank senior to COMMON STOCK investors in the event of BANKRUPTCY, but junior to BOND investors and LOAN holders. Preferreds can be issued in various forms (with most differences related to the setting, timing, and accumulation of dividend payments), including CUMULATIVE PREFERRED STOCK, NONCUMULATIVE PREFERRED STOCK, and ADJUSTABLE RATE PREFERRED STOCK. See also PREFERENCE SHARE.

PRE-LOSS FINANCING   Funding that is arranged in advance of a loss situation, typically through mechanisms such as INSURANCE, DERIVATIVES, and CONTINGENT CAPITAL. Pre-loss financing may be less expensive than POST-LOSS FINANCING, as it can be arranged before any instance of FINANCIAL DISTRESS and can be developed on a committed basis so that funds are available when required. See also LOSS FINANCING.

PREMARKET   The period before the official opening of TRADING on a specific EXCHANGE or marketplace. Trading activity may occur in the premarket period through ELECTRONIC COMMUNICATIONS NETWORKS or other ALTERNATIVE TRADING SYSTEMS.

PREMIUM   (1) The payment made by the purchaser to the seller of an EXCHANGE-traded or OVER-THE-COUNTER OPTION. By accepting the premium, the seller is obligated to perform under the terms of the contract when the buyer exercises its rights. Premium comprises of TIME VALUE and INTRINSIC VALUE, and the premium an option seller charges depends on the price and VOLATILITY of the UNDERLYING reference, the RISK-FREE RATE, and time to EXPIRY. (2) The payment made by an INSURED to an INSURER (or REINSURER) for a future compensatory payment under the terms of an INSURANCE POLICY. Insurance premiums are determined through ACTUARIAL PRICING based on EXPECTED LOSS ratios and LOADS. (3) The upfront or periodic payment made by an INVESTOR to an INSURER for an ANNUITY that will provide a future cash inflow. (4) The MARKET VALUE in excess of PAR VALUE on a FIXED INCOME SECURITY. (5) The excess of a TENDER OFFER over a target company's STOCK price in a corporate MERGER or ACQUISITION. (6) For CONVERTIBLE BONDS, see PREMIUM OVER BOND VALUE. (1) Also known as OPTION MONEY. (2) Also known as RISK PREMIUM.

PREMIUM BOND   A BOND that trades at a PREMIUM to its PAR VALUE. See also DISCOUNT BOND, PAR BOND.

PREMIUM CAPACITY   The ability for an INSURER or REINSURER to write a large volume of POLICIES on the same LINE or RISK.

PREMIUM CURRENCY   A CURRENCY that trades at a higher value than another currency in the FORWARD market. See also DISCOUNT CURRENCY.

PREMIUM LOADING   The MARGIN an INSURER requires in order to cover overhead expenses (EXPENSE LOADING) and generate an appropriate PROFIT; premium loading is one of two components, along with PURE PREMIUM, used to determine FAIR PREMIUM.

PREMIUM OVER BOND VALUE   The value ascribed to the EQUITY characteristics of a CONVERTIBLE BOND, or the difference between the MARKET VALUE of a convertible and an equivalent STRAIGHT BOND without the EMBEDDED OPTION. In general, the higher the CONVERSION PRICE, the greater the premium over bond value. Also known as PREMIUM.

PREMIUM RAID   An attempt by a RAIDER or acquiring company to quickly purchase a block of a TARGET's COMMON STOCK by offering SHAREHOLDERS a significant PREMIUM to the prevailing stock price. See also DAWN RAID, SATURDAY NIGHT SPECIAL.

PREMIUM SWAP   An OVER-THE-COUNTER NONPAR SWAP where the receiver of FIXED RATES grants an upfront payment to the FLOATING RATE payer in exchange for a higher ongoing fixed rate inflow. See also DISCOUNT SWAP.

PREMIUM TAX   A TAX payable by an INSURER to a state or jurisdiction based on the amount of PREMIUMS earned from INSURANCE activities. Premium taxes are generally included in EXPENSE LOADING.

PREMIUMS IN FORCE   A measure of an INSURER's UNDERWRITING business, measured as PREMIUM earned on all INSURANCE policies that have not lapsed or have not been cancelled.

PREPACK   [COL] See PREPACKAGED BANKRUPTCY.

PREPACKAGED BANKRUPTCY   In the United States, a filing under CHAPTER 11 of the US BANKRUPTCY Code where CREDITORS agree in advance to REORGANIZATION terms in order to accelerate the process and minimize the time the company spends under bankruptcy protection. A prepackaged bankruptcy is arranged when the company and its business franchise are deemed to have significant value, and bankruptcy negotiations can be arranged with a minimum of conflict among STAKEHOLDERS. Also known as PREPACK. See also CHAPTER 7, CHAPTER 9, CHAPTER 13.

PREPAYMENT   (1) The early repayment of a MORTGAGE by a BORROWER as a result of the sale of the underlying home/property or a REFINANCING to take advantage of a lower INTEREST RATE environment. (2) The payment of any sum of money for goods or services that have not yet been received. A prepayment is reflected as an ASSET on the BALANCE SHEET. (1) See also PREPAYMENT MODEL, PREPAYMENT SPEED.

PREPAYMENT MODEL   An analytic process used to estimate the PREPAYMENT SPEED of MORTGAGES comprising a POOL or PASS-THROUGH SECURITY, which can then be used to value the ASSET. Common models include the constant prepayment rate model, which assumes mortgage

PRINCIPAL prepayments occur at a constant annual rate that can be estimated from historical mortgage data, and the Public Securities Association standard prepayment model, which assumes mortgage PREPAYMENTS occur at variable speeds (e.g., 0.2%/month for 30 months, then 6% annually).

PREPAYMENT SPEED The rate at which underlying commercial or residential MORTGAGES in a POOL or PASS-THROUGH SECURITY are expected to repay (i.e., as rates decline, PREPAYMENTS accelerate as REFINANCINGS increase; as rates rise, prepayments decelerate as refinancings slow). Prepayment speed is an essential component of pricing and HEDGING MORTGAGE-BACKED SECURITIES and can be estimated through a PREPAYMENT MODEL or SIMULATION process.

PREPETITION PHASE A stage of FINANCIAL DISTRESS, such as the VICINITY OF INSOLVENCY, when a company is preparing to file a BANKRUPTCY petition. During this period the rights of CREDITORS often supersede those of SHAREHOLDERS, as DIRECTORS and executives attempt to preserve as much ENTERPRISE VALUE as possible in advance of a REORGANIZATION or LIQUIDATION.

PRE-REFUNDING A new BOND issue floated by a company in order to repay an existing bond issue at the FIRST CALL DATE; proceeds of the pre-refunding are generally invested in low-RISK SECURITIES until the original bond can be called and redeemed. Pre-refunding typically occurs in an environment where INTEREST RATES have declined enough to make the REFINANCING an economically beneficial process.

PRESENT EXPECTED VALUE An ACTUARIAL PRICING method of calculating PREMIUM for INSURANCE coverage, generally via:

$$PEV = Prob_{occ} \, (Face_{pol}) \, (PV_{factor})$$

where $Prob_{occ}$ is the PROBABILITY of loss occurrence, $Face_{pol}$ is the FACE VALUE of the POLICY, and PV_{factor} is a PRESENT VALUE factor.

PRESENT VALUE A financial computation where future CASH FLOWS are discounted back to current terms through use of an appropriate DISCOUNT RATE or COST OF CAPITAL. The general form of the equation is given as:

$$PV = \frac{CF}{(1+r)^t}$$

where CF is the future cash flow, r is the discount rate, t is the future period.

The present value of a cash flow that is subject to CONTINUOUS DISCOUNTING is given as:

$$PV = CFe^{-rN}$$

where e is the exponential constant, N is the number of years over which the compounding occurs.

The computation for multiple periods is given as:

$$PV = \sum_{t=1}^{n} \frac{CF_t}{(1+r)^t}$$

where CF_t is the expected cash flow at time t, n is the number of periods, and other terms are as defined above.

The present value of a recurring cash flow, as in an ANNUITY, is given as:

$$PV_{ann} = CF\left[\frac{1}{r} - \frac{1}{r(1+r)^t}\right]$$

See also DISCOUNTED CASH FLOW, FUTURE VALUE, NET PRESENT VALUE.

PRESENT VALUE FACTOR   See DISCOUNT FACTOR.

PRESENTING BANK   A BANK that seeks payment on a BILL OF EXCHANGE, DRAFT, or CHECK from the bank on which the order has been drawn.

PRESETTLEMENT RISK   See FRACTIONAL EXPOSURE.

PRESIDING DIRECTOR   See LEAD INDEPENDENT DIRECTOR.

PRICE-BOOK RATIO   A measure that compares market and ACCOUNTING values to determine potential undervaluation or overvaluation of a company. Price-book is generally computed via:

$$P/B = \frac{S}{BVPS}$$

where S is the current STOCK price and BVPS is BOOK VALUE per share.

A high ratio, or an increasing ratio over time, may indicate a growth stock, while a low ratio may suggest an opportunity to purchase the stock of a company that has not realized its valuation potential.

PRICE COMPRESSION   A phenomenon where the price of a CALLABLE BOND remains close to its call redemption price in a declining INTEREST RATE environment since the likelihood of a call, redemption, and REFINANCING increases.

PRICE CONTROL   Caps or ceilings placed by a government authority on specific goods or services, generally as an attempt to control INFLATION. Price controls run contrary to free market economic principles and are more characteristic of certain COMMAND ECONOMIES.

PRICE DISCOVERY   The process of establishing a fair market price for an ASSET through the interaction of buyers and sellers via AUCTION or quotation, typically through an organized marketplace such as a physical or electronic EXCHANGE.

PRICE/EARNINGS (P/E) RATIO A measure of a company's value and EARNINGS RISK, computed from the latest reported earnings in the general form of:

$$P/E = \frac{S}{EPS}$$

where S is the STOCK price and EPS is EARNINGS PER SHARE.

A company's P/E can be compared against past performance, the market, or a specific industry norm to determine relative value and performance. Alternatively, a target stock price can be imputed by using EPS and an industry or company estimate of the P/E ratio. The higher the P/E, the more INVESTORS are paying for the stock, and the greater the expectation of earnings growth. Lower P/E stocks tend to carry less RISK, as earnings expectations are lower; mature companies generally feature lower P/Es than aggressive or start-up firms. Also known as MULTIPLE. See also FORWARD PRICE/EARNINGS RATIO, TRAILING PRICE/EARNINGS RATIO.

PRICE ELASTICITY The ratio of a proportional change in quantity supplied or demanded for a proportional change in price; the greater the price elasticity, the more sensitive SUPPLY or DEMAND to changes in price. See also ELASTICITY.

PRICE KEEPING OPERATIONS A technique used by the Japanese monetary authorities to "encourage" its FINANCIAL INSTITUTIONS to actively buy SECURITIES in order to provide price supports at key levels.

PRICE LEVEL ACCOUNTING See INFLATION ACCOUNTING.

PRICE LIMIT A boundary placed on certain EXCHANGE-traded ASSETS (e.g., FUTURES, OPTIONS, COMMON STOCKS) that limits the amount of upward or downward price movement that can occur during a TRADING session. A price limit is a form of CIRCUIT BREAKER that is intended to control excessive VOLATILITY and/or market overreaction.

PRICE-SENSITIVE INFORMATION See INSIDE INFORMATION.

PRICE SPREAD See BEAR SPREAD, BULL SPREAD.

PRICE SUPPORT A floor placed by a government authority on the price of a particular good, often an agricultural COMMODITY, typically implemented through the purchase of a particular amount of the good or the payment of any price differential between the agreed floor and the open market price.

PRICE TAKER A small INVESTOR that has no ability to impact or influence SECURITIES prices, and must simply accept the BID or OFFER in the marketplace.

PRICE TALK   [COL] An estimate of the potential pricing on a NEW ISSUE of SECURITIES or a LOAN based on presoundings in the market by the LEAD MANAGER or ARRANGER.

PRIMA FACIE   [LAT] Appearance of truth that is taken as fact, until there is evidence to the contrary.

PRIMACY   In INSURANCE, a rule that indicates which specific insurance coverage takes precedence when multiple coverage exists, in order to avoid dispute or conflict. See also APPORTIONMENT, DIVIDED COVER, OVERLAPPING INSURANCE, PRO-RATA.

PRIMARY DEALER   A FINANCIAL INSTITUTION, officially approved by government authorities, which is permitted to deal in the PRIMARY MARKET for GOVERNMENT BONDS. In order to create an efficient, transparent, and well-controlled process, CENTRAL BANKS and monetary authorities issuing government securities often deal through a primary dealer network. An institution must generally meet certain minimum standards of financial strength and adhere to certain quoting and pricing rules to qualify as a primary dealer. In exchange for participating in government securities auctions and acting as a MARKET MAKER, the dealer is generally given full access to ORDER flows.

PRIMARY INSURER   See INSURER.

PRIMARY LAYER   The main layer of INSURANCE coverage in PROPERTY AND CASUALTY INSURANCE, which exists between the DEDUCTIBLE and the POLICY CAP. The primary layer bears the initial losses once the deductible has been met. Also known as BURNING LAYER.

PRIMARY MARKET   The general marketplace for the FLOTATION of NEW ISSUE SECURITIES, including NOTES, BONDS, COMMON STOCK, PREFERRED STOCK, and CONVERTIBLE BONDS, on behalf of corporate or sovereign ISSUERS. Once securities are placed and the UNDERWRITING SYNDICATE "breaks" the primary market phase is concluded. Any subsequent TRADING activity forms part of the SECONDARY MARKET.

PRIMARY OFFERING   The sale of a corporate or sovereign ISSUER's SECURITIES in the PRIMARY MARKET, including INITIAL PUBLIC OFFERINGS and DEBT NEW ISSUES. Subsequent new issues launched in the primary market are considered SECONDARY OFFERINGS.

PRIME BROKER   A BANK, INVESTMENT BANK, or SECURITIES DEALER that provides HEDGE FUNDS and other institutional INVESTORS with a full range of PRIME BROKERAGE services.

PRIME BROKERAGE   A suite of services provided by a PRIME BROKER to institutional clients (including HEDGE FUNDS and other large INVESTORS) that includes trade EXECUTION, SECURITIES lending and financing, trade SETTLEMENT, CUSTODY, PORTFOLIO analysis, and valuation and reporting. See also SYNTHETIC PRIME BROKERAGE.

PRIME RATE   In the United States, a semifloating INTEREST RATE reflecting the unsecured lending rate that BANKS charge their best corporate customers.

PRIME RATE FUND   A MUTUAL FUND or CLOSED-END FUND that invests primarily in corporate LOANS tied to the PRIME RATE. Prime rate funds feature limited LIQUIDITY as a result of the ILLIQUID nature of the SECONDARY MARKET for corporate loans.

PRINCIPAL   (1) The primary, or authorizing, party in a transaction or business relationship. (2) The FACE VALUE of a financial transaction, such as a LOAN, BOND, or SWAP. (1) See also AGENT. (2) See also NOTIONAL.

PRINCIPAL INVESTMENT   See PRIVATE EQUITY.

PRINCIPAL-ONLY (PO) STRIP   A component of a stripped MORTGAGE-BACKED SECURITY or COLLATERALIZED MORTGAGE OBLIGATION that is entitled only to PRINCIPAL payments from the underlying SECURITIES; INTEREST COUPONS are redirected to the INTEREST-ONLY (IO) STRIP. The price of a PO strip declines as INTEREST RATES rise since higher rates slow REFINANCING and result in slower principal repayments. Since PO strips lack the additional CASH FLOW buffer generated by the coupons, they feature more price VOLATILITY than other FIXED INCOME securities.

PRINCIPAL PROTECTED BOND   See GUARANTEED PRINCIPAL BOND.

PRIOR LIEN BOND   A BOND, often issued in a corporate REORGANIZATION, that gives INVESTORS a first CLAIM on the issuer's ASSETS, even if the SECURITY is equally senior to other outstanding securities.

PRIOR-PERIOD ADJUSTMENTS   Significant changes to a company's financial accounts based on changes in ACCOUNTING policies or the correction of errors, which must be reflected in the RETAINED EARNINGS account.

PRIOR PREFERRED STOCK   PREFERRED STOCK that ranks senior to a company's other preferred stock issues. Within the preferred stock class, prior preferreds are entitled to a first CLAIM on DIVIDENDS, and in a BANKRUPTCY and LIQUIDATION scenario, a first claim on the company's ASSETS. See also SECONDARY PREFERRED STOCK.

PRIVATE BANK   (1) A BANK that specializes in wealth management services for high NET WORTH clients, including INVESTMENT MANAGEMENT, TRUST and CUSTODY services, FOREIGN EXCHANGE, and so forth. It may be established as a separate unit or division of a large international bank, or as a dedicated, stand-alone entity. (2) A bank that is not publicly owned.

PRIVATE BANKER   A professional working at a BANK that is primarily responsible for managing the INVESTMENT PORTFOLIOS of high net worth individuals on a discretionary or nondiscretionary basis, and providing associated TRUST and CREDIT services. See also BANKER, FINANCIER, INVESTMENT BANKER.

PRIVATE COMPANY   A company whose SHARES are held by the DIRECTORS and SHAREHOLDERS, but which do not trade publicly. A private company is not typically subject to the same public disclosure rules as PUBLIC COMPANIES. See also CLOSE COMPANY, CLOSELY HELD COMPANY.

PRIVATE EQUITY   A proprietary INVESTMENT by a VENTURE CAPITAL FUND, INVESTMENT BANK, or MERCHANT BANK in the CAPITAL of a PRIVATE COMPANY or PUBLIC COMPANY. Private equity stakes are generally held for several years, and exit is generally arranged through an INITIAL PUBLIC OFFERING or the sale of the company to a third party. Private equity activities can involve direct investment in the pre-IPO EQUITY of a company, or it may relate to investment in LEVERAGED BUYOUTS, BRIDGE EQUITY, VENTURE CAPITAL, DISTRESSED ASSETS, or RESTRUCTURINGS. Also known as PRINCIPAL INVESTMENT. See also J-CURVE, PRIVATE INVESTMENT IN PUBLIC EQUITY.

PRIVATE INVESTMENT IN PUBLIC EQUITY (PIPE)   An INVESTMENT by INVESTORS in the public EQUITY SECURITIES of company (e.g., COMMON STOCK, PREFERRED STOCK, CONVERTIBLE BONDS), often at a below-market price. The PIPE may be registered with REGULATORS or it may be arranged as a PRIVATE PLACEMENT.

PRIVATE LIMITED COMPANY   A corporate entity that offers LIMITED LIABILITY to its SHAREHOLDERS but which restricts the ability of shareholders to sell their SHARES in the open market or without first offering them to existing shareholders. Private limited companies generally do not have to adhere to the same financial disclosure requirements as PUBLIC COMPANIES.

PRIVATE PLACEMENT   A DEBT SECURITY that is not registered with a REGULATOR and can therefore only be sold on a CAVEAT EMPTOR basis to a very limited number of sophisticated INVESTORS. Private placements are highly ILLIQUID and are generally only transferable to the original SYNDICATE or other QUALIFIED INSTITUTIONAL BUYERS when REGULATIONS permit. In the United States, a SAFE HARBOR RULE is provided by SECURITIES AND EXCHANGE COMMISSION RULE 144A, which allows limited resale of securities that have not been registered. See also PRIVATE PLACING, REGISTRATION STATEMENT.

PRIVATE PLACING   In the United Kingdom, a PRIVATE PLACEMENT.

PRIVATIZATION   The act of converting a government or state-run company into a publicly owned company. The privatization typically generates a windfall gain for the government, and allows the company to operate as a private enterprise (though the government may retain a GOLDEN SHARE for a specified period of time).

PRIVILEGED SUBSCRIPTION ISSUE   See RIGHTS ISSUE.

PRO-FORMA   [LAT] Literally "as a formality;" in the financial sector it relates to the presentation of hypothetical or projected corporate BALANCE SHEET,

INCOME STATEMENT, and/or STATEMENT OF CASH FLOWS to reflect the potential impact of expected EARNINGS, a NEW ISSUE, or a CORPORATE FINANCE transaction. Pro-forma statements are used by INVESTORS considering an INVESTMENT, BANKS arranging a financing, or companies considering an ACQUISITION as a gauge of the possible future financial position of a company. See also PRO-FORMA EARNINGS REPORT.

PRO-FORMA BALANCE SHEET A projected BALANCE SHEET for a future period prepared by a company for internal management purposes; such pro-forma balance sheet statements are not released publicly. Balance sheet items can be projected using the ANALYSIS OF ACCOUNTS METHOD or the PERCENTAGE OF SALES METHOD. See also PRO-FORMA EARNINGS REPORT, PRO-FORMA INCOME STATEMENT.

PRO-FORMA EARNINGS REPORT A FINANCIAL STATEMENT that expresses PROFITS by excluding exceptional costs or including exceptional gains; although pro-forma reports are widely used by companies and analysts, they do not typically conform to GENERALLY ACCEPTED ACCOUNTING PRINCIPLES or INTERNATIONAL ACCOUNTING STANDARDS and must be interpreted with care.

PRO-FORMA INCOME STATEMENT A projected INCOME STATEMENT for a future period prepared by a company for internal management purposes; such pro-forma income statements are not released publicly. Income statement can be projected using the ANALYSIS OF ACCOUNTS method or the PERCENTAGE OF SALES METHOD. See also PRO-FORMA BALANCE SHEET, PRO-FORMA EARNINGS REPORT.

PRO-RATA [LAT] Literally "proportional allocation;" in the financial sector it reflects an allocation of NEW ISSUE SECURITIES to INVESTORS in proportion to the ORDERS submitted. In INSURANCE, it relates to a clause in a CONTRACT indicating that any SETTLEMENT to the INSURED will be in proportion to the total amount of insurance in force on the same PERIL. See also APPORTIONMENT, DIVIDED COVER, OVERLAPPING INSURANCE, PRIMACY.

PROBABILITY A statistical measure that indicates the likelihood or chance that an event will occur. Probability is widely used to measure uncertain or risky events, including those impacting the financial markets.

PROBABILITY OF DEFAULT See DEFAULT RATE.

PROBABILITY OF RUIN The likelihood that the distribution of average losses exceeds a BENCHMARK SOLVENCY value (i.e., a minimum amount of CAPITAL surplus or tangible NET WORTH), leading to a company's BANKRUPTCY. Probability of ruin is incorporated in certain DEFAULT models.

PROCESS RISK See OPERATIONAL RISK.

PRODUCER PRICE INDEX An INFLATION measure at the wholesale level based on production components by COMMODITY, industry, and processing stage. The producer price INDEX may measure the prices of underlying goods and commodities, but not associated services (in the United States the complete index includes volatile food and energy components, while the core index excludes both). See also CONSUMER PRICE INDEX, HARMONIZED INDEX OF CONSUMER PRICES, RETAIL PRICE INDEX.

PRODUCT GUARANTEE INSURANCE   A form of INSURANCE cover that provides the INSURED with restitution in the event a product it introduces to the marketplace is found to be defective, and which requires a recall and refund or repair. See also PRODUCT LIABILITY INSURANCE.

PRODUCT LIABILITY INSURANCE   A form of INSURANCE cover that provides the INSURED with restitution in the event a product it introduces into the marketplace is found to be defective, and creates a legal LIABILITY. See also PRODUCT GUARANTEE INSURANCE.

PROFIT   Any excess or surplus remaining after all costs have been subtracted from the REVENUE or selling price of a good or service or any surplus arising from the disposal of an asset at a price that is favorable compared to its original contract price. See also LOSS.

PROFIT AND LOSS ACCOUNT   In the United Kingdom, the INCOME STATEMENT.

PROFIT AND LOSS EXPLAIN   A financial process commonly used by BANKS, INVESTMENT BANKS, and SECURITIES FIRMS following MARK-TO-MARKET ACCOUNTING rules where the sources of daily PROFITS and LOSSES are examined in detail. The process involves decomposing profits and losses and relating them to specific activities, including TRADING, market-making, COMMISSIONS, and fee-generating business; this allows an institution to understand how it earns and loses money and assists in the RISK MANAGEMENT control process. Profit and loss explain is also a central component of the BACKTESTING of VALUE-AT-RISK models.

PROFIT FORECAST   An estimate provided by a company or developed by an INVESTMENT ANALYST related to expected PROFITS for a forthcoming period.

PROFIT MARGIN   See NET PROFIT MARGIN.

PROFIT TAKING   The process of selling or covering an ASSET, INVESTMENT or other financial transaction in order to crystallize UNREALIZED PROFITS, converting them into REALIZED GAINS.

PROFIT WARNING   A preemptive statement issued by a company to the marketplace in advance of a formally scheduled earnings announcement that indicates an impending shortfall in PROFITS expected to be reported during the official reporting period. See also PREANNOUNCEMENT.

PROFITABILITY INDEX   A method of determining the advisability of making a CAPITAL INVESTMENT based on the NET PRESENT VALUE framework. The profitability index can be computed as:

$$PI = \frac{PV_{in}}{PV_{out}}$$

where PV$_{in}$ is the PRESENT VALUE of cash inflows, PV$_{out}$ is the present value of cash outflows.

In general, if PI > 1.0 the investment is expected to create value for SHAREHOLDERS and should be accepted; if PI < 1.0 the investment should be rejected, and if PI = 1.0, then the company should be indifferent. See also INTERNAL RATE OF RETURN.

PROFITEER An individual or company that charges exorbitant prices for goods and services that are in short SUPPLY during a time of crisis (natural disaster, war).

PROGRAM TRADING   (1) The general process of executing TRADES in financial ASSETS through computerized platforms and customized ALGORITHMS. (2) See INDEX ARBITRAGE.

PROGRESSIVE TAX A TAX scheme which directly or indirectly places a greater burden on higher income households by increasing the tax rate on the amount subject to taxation. INCOME taxes and luxury goods taxes are considered progressive taxes. See also PROPORTIONAL TAX, REGRESSIVE TAX.

PROHIBITED RISK   See UNINSURABLE RISK.

PROJECT FINANCE   LOAN funding that is provided by a BANK to an entity that is developing an infrastructure project, and where the project is typically designed to generate CASH FLOWS that can be used in the repayment of the loan. Project finance transactions may be partially or totally arranged on a NONRECOURSE basis, though they may also feature CREDIT ENHANCEMENT provided by the sponsor (e.g., third party GUARANTEES). Banks supplying funding analyze in considerable detail the nature and risks of individual projects (including MARKET RISK, operating risk, construction risk, SOVEREIGN RISK, and so forth), given the importance of the project in generating cash flows for repayment. Most transactions feature long-term MATURITIES (in accordance with the long-term nature of the projects), though more complex financing packages may comprise a series of short- and long-term loan tranches. Also known as PROJECT FINANCING.

PROJECT FINANCING   See PROJECT FINANCE.

PROMISED YIELD   See YIELD TO MATURITY.

PROMISSORY NOTE   A written promise by one party to pay another party a stated sum on a certain date or upon presentation; the promise represents the maker's LIABILITY. A promissory note may be transferred to another party as a NEGOTIABLE INSTRUMENT through an ENDORSEMENT; the act of endorsing the note allows the BENEFICIARY to convert it into cash. Also known as NOTE.

PROMPT DATE   The specific date on which payment is due from the buyer on a good purchased from a seller.

PROMPT MONTH   See NEARBY CONTRACT.

PROOF OF LOSS Documentary evidence an INSURED must present an INSURER when submitting a CLAIM under an INSURANCE policy. Since an insurance CONTRACT requires the insured to have an INSURABLE INTEREST, proof of loss is an essential element in ensuring validity.

PROPERTY AND CASUALTY INSURANCE In the United States, INSURANCE coverage for damage or loss to property. The standard CONTRACT specifies PERILS, limits, and duration, and whether coverage includes CONSEQUENTIAL LOSSES or is restricted to DIRECT LOSSES. Certain perils, such as damage or destruction from war, terrorism, or neglect in preserving damaged property from further loss, are often excluded from coverage. Property and casualty insurance generally requires the INSURED to agree to SUBROGATION. Also known as PROPERTY INSURANCE. See also PROPERTY AND LIABILITY INSURANCE.

PROPERTY AND LIABILITY INSURANCE INSURANCE coverage for an INSURED whose property is damaged or destroyed by a PERIL, or whose negligence causes another property to be destroyed. See also PROPERTY AND CASUALTY INSURANCE.

PROPERTY INSURANCE See PROPERTY AND CASUALTY INSURANCE.

PROPERTY PER RISK EXCESS OF LOSS A REINSURANCE agreement providing the PRIMARY INSURER with cover for any loss in excess of the specified retention on each type of RISK.

PROPERTY TAX A TAX levied on various forms of real estate, including residential homes, commercial buildings, and undeveloped land. Schemes for levying property tax depend on national and local practice, but generally center on applying a percentage amount on an appraised value.

PROPORTIONAL AGREEMENT A QUOTA SHARE or SURPLUS SHARE REINSURANCE agreement requiring the INSURER and REINSURER to share PREMIUMS, RISKS, LOSSES, and LOSS ADJUSTMENT EXPENSES on the basis of a predefined formula, such as a fixed or variable percentage of policy limits, or a monetary value amount. Also known as PROPORTIONAL TREATY. See also EXCESS OF LOSS AGREEMENT.

PROPORTIONAL TAX A TAX scheme where the tax rate is fixed as the amount subject to taxation increases, implying an equal burden on high- and low-income households, though in practice may be regressive in certain areas, e.g., consumption. In practice proportional taxes are relatively uncommon. Also known as FLAT TAX. See also PROGRESSIVE TAX, REGRESSIVE TAX.

PROPORTIONAL TREATY See PROPORTIONAL AGREEMENT.

PROSPECTIVE FINITE POLICY An INSURANCE POLICY that seeks primarily to shift the timing risk of losses that are expected to occur in the future. In common with other FINITE RISK POLICIES, the prospective agreement is primarily a RISK FINANCING rather than RISK TRANSFER vehicle. See also RETROSPECTIVE FINITE POLICY.

PROSPECTUS A REGISTRATION or information statement filed by an ISSUER with a SECURITIES commissioner or registrar of CORPORATIONS, and distributed in final form to INVESTORS. The prospectus conveys particulars regarding a public PRIMARY OFFERING or SECONDARY OFFERING, relevant financial details regarding the issue and issuer, and the nature of potential RISKS arising from a purchase of securities. Core information generally includes form, denomination, and transfer of securities; status (seniority); form of NEGATIVE PLEDGE; INTEREST, DIVIDEND, and other payment details; REDEMPTION, issuer CALL and investor PUT features; TAX matters; EVENTS OF DEFAULT; issuer FINANCIAL STATEMENTS; and, form of SUBSCRIPTION AGREEMENT. Also known as OFFERING CIRCULAR, STATUTORY PROSPECTUS. See also RED HERRING.

PROTECTED BID A BID quotation on a STOCK that is displayed via an ELECTRONIC TRADING center, is disseminated via a national market system and is the best bid available in the market. See also PROTECTED OFFER.

PROTECTED CELL COMPANY A multiuser CAPTIVE with individual accounts ("cells") that clients hire for SELF-INSURANCE programs. Individual cells are separated by statute, which prevents commingling of ASSETS and RISKS, and ensures the assets of each client remain safe in the event other cell clients encounter FINANCIAL DISTRESS. Protected cell companies are widely used by firms that are interested in self-insurance but do not want to establish and manage a captive of their own. See also AGENCY CAPTIVE, GROUP CAPTIVE, PURE CAPTIVE, RENT-A-CAPTIVE, CAPTIVE, SENIOR CAPTIVE, SISTER CAPTIVE.

PROTECTED OFFER An OFFER quotation on a STOCK that is displayed via an ELECTRONIC TRADING center, is disseminated via a national market system and is the best offer available in the market. See also PROTECTED BID.

PROTECTION BUYER An institution that buys a CREDIT DERIVATIVE contract for a PREMIUM, creating a SHORT position in the CREDIT DEFAULT RISK of the REFERENCE ENTITY or REFERENCE OBLIGATION. See also PROTECTION SELLER.

PROTECTION PAYMENT The amount due to the PROTECTION BUYER from the PROTECTION SELLER in the event a REFERENCE ENTITY or REFERENCE OBLIGATION triggers a DEFAULT under a CREDIT DERIVATIVE contract.

PROTECTION SELLER An institution that sells a CREDIT DERIVATIVE contract for a PREMIUM, creating a LONG position in the CREDIT DEFAULT RISK of the REFERENCE ENTITY or REFERENCE OBLIGATION. See also PROTECTION BUYER.

PROTECTIVE STOP Any INVESTMENT strategy that employs a STOP ORDER to protect downside RISK.

PROTEST A certification sought by a holder of PROMISSORY NOTE or BILL OF EXCHANGE that has been dishonored or refused payment, typically required in order to commence legal proceedings.

PROVISION (1) A stipulation in a legal agreement or CONTRACT. (2) A non-cash account established from EARNINGS and reflected through the INCOME STATEMENT that is intended to cover a known or potential LIABILITY (such as a bad LOAN or anticipated TAXES) or an expected reduction in value (such as DEPRECIATION on an ASSET). See also BAD DEBT PROVISION, LOAN LOSS PROVISION.

PROXIMATE CAUSE See DIRECT LOSS.

PROXY (1) A document that conveys a COMMON STOCK SHAREHOLDER's right to vote. (2) A person or institution authorized to vote on behalf of a shareholder.

PROXY CONTEST A HOSTILE TAKEOVER technique where the acquiring company attempts to persuade SHAREHOLDERS of the TARGET to vote for their PROXIES against the incumbent DIRECTORS and in support of a new slate of DIRECTORS favorably disposed to the takeover. Proxy contests can be lengthy, and the existence of defenses such as STAGGERED BOARDS or DEAD HAND CLAUSES can delay or block the process. Also known as PROXY FIGHT.

PROXY FIGHT See PROXY CONTEST.

PRUDENCE CONCEPT A central ACCOUNTING CONCEPT that indicates a company should be prudent and generally conservative in recognizing its PROFIT (i.e., a profit should not be recognized until a sale is complete) and in recording costs and establishing PROVISIONS (i.e., a provision should be established as soon as there is a belief that such will be required in the future). See also CONSISTENCY CONCEPT, GOING CONCERN CONCEPT, MATCHING CONCEPT.

PRUDENTIAL RATIO See CAPITAL ADEQUACY RATIO.

PUBLIC COMPANY A company that has issued SHARES to INVESTORS through an INITIAL PUBLIC OFFERING, and which is listed and traded on a STOCK EXCHANGE. See also LISTED COMPANY, PRIVATE COMPANY

PUBLIC DEBT Any form of DEBT incurred by a government and its direct AGENTS.

PUBLIC FINANCE A field of study within FINANCE centered on government REVENUES (e.g., TAXES), EXPENSES, and DEBT, and how these impact an economy and its STAKEHOLDERS.

PUBLIC ISSUE See PUBLIC OFFERING.

PUBLIC LIMITED COMPANY (PLC) In the United Kingdom a corporate entity with LIMITED LIABILITY, registered under the Companies Act, which is publicly listed and traded.

PUBLIC OFFERING   A form of NEW ISSUE in which the ISSUER invites the public to INVEST in SHARES or other SECURITIES directly, without the use of an INTERMEDIARY. Also known as PUBLIC ISSUE.

PUBLIC SECTOR   The broad component of the economy that is related to the government, which typically centers on social services, health, defense, and any state-run CORPORATIONS.

PUBLISHED ACCOUNTS   In the United Kingdom, the minimum elements of FINANCIAL STATEMENTS of companies that are required to file such under law.

PUFFERY   [COL] A legal, if questionable, sales practice where BROKERS promote the positive aspects/upside of a potential INVESTMENT while deemphasizing RISKS/negative points in order to entice clients to invest.

PUKE POINT   [COL] A capitulation price, or the price at which a DEALER or TRADER decides to sell some, or all, of a money-losing position.

PULL TO PAR   A phenomenon where the price of a FIXED INCOME SECURITY will migrate toward its PAR VALUE as MATURITY approaches. This occurs because the INVESTOR receives REDEMPTION value (i.e., par value) once the security is redeemed by the ISSUER. Also known as PULL TO REDEMPTION.

PULL TO REDEMPTION   See PULL TO PAR.

PUMP AND DUMP   [COL] An illegal practice where a group of INVESTORS circulates positive, but false, news about a company in order to lure new buyers in and drive the STOCK price up ("pump"); once the price has reached a certain level the group sells its shares ("dump") at a profit, leaving duped investors with positions in a falling market. This type of scheme is typically targeted at small, thinly traded stocks. See also DAISY CHAIN, POOP AND SCOOP.

PUNT   [COL] (1) A risky or speculative position. (2) The act of SPECULATION.

PUNTER   [COL] A SPECULATOR.

PUP COMPANY   [COL] The subsidiary of an INSURER that writes SPECIAL RISK INSURANCE on behalf of the parent company or other group companies.

PURCHASE   ACQUISITION   ACCOUNTING See   ACQUISITION ACCOUNTING.

PURCHASE GROUP   See SYNDICATE.

PURCHASE GROUP AGREEMENT   A CONTRACT between the members of the SYNDICATE (or PURCHASE GROUP) involved in UNDERWRITING a NEW ISSUE of SECURITIES that authorizes formation of the syndicate, designates the LEAD MANAGER, establishes deal allocations, responsibilities, and LIABILITIES, and defines the duration of the syndicate. The ISSUER is not a party to the purchase group agreement (the relationship between issuer and syndicate is contained in the UNDERWRITING AGREEMENT).

PURCHASE TRANSACTION   An ACCOUNTING methodology used for an ACQUISITION which involves a cash payment to the firm being acquired. The process adds revalued ASSETS, LIABILITIES, and EQUITY to the acquirer's BALANCE SHEET, with any difference between the merger price and fair MARKET VALUE reflected in the GOODWILL account (which is DEPRECIATED over a defined number of years). See also MERGER ACCOUNTING.

PURCHASED GOODWILL   Any form of GOODWILL that a company obtains through the ACQUISITION of another company or business.

PURCHASING POWER PARITY   An economic theory indicating that purchasing power across countries should be equal when goods, services, labor, and CAPITAL can be transported without restriction. Since barriers and frictions exist, cross-border purchasing power is not equal, suggesting that FOREIGN EXCHANGE RATES need to adjust over the long term to reflect the amount of goods and services that can be purchased with each CURRENCY.

PURCHASING POWER RISK   See INFLATION RISK.

PURE ARBITRAGE   (1) Any ARBITRAGE strategy that makes use of external, or borrowed, funds rather than internal funds. (2) Any arbitrage strategy that is executed in a truly riskless manner, by simultaneously buying and selling the same ASSET in different MARKETS to take advantage of a price discrepancy. (1,2) See also QUASI ARBITRAGE.

PURE BOND VALUE   See INVESTMENT VALUE.

PURE CAPTIVE   A licensed INSURER or REINSURER that is wholly owned by a single sponsor and writes INSURANCE cover solely or primarily for the sponsoring firm. Although the pure captive structure allows for greater management control, TAX treatment of PREMIUMS may not be favorable as the amount of true RISK TRANSFER outside the group structure is generally negligible. Also known as a SINGLE PARENT CAPTIVE. See also AGENCY CAPTIVE, CAPTIVE, GROUP CAPTIVE, PROTECTED CELL COMPANY, RENT-A-CAPTIVE, SENIOR CAPTIVE, SISTER CAPTIVE.

PURE CATASTROPHE SWAP   An OVER-THE-COUNTER SWAP transaction that allows INSURERS or REINSURERS to exchange uncorrelated CATASTROPHIC HAZARDS in their PORTFOLIOS in order to improve DIVERSIFICATION. See also CATASTROPHE REINSURANCE SWAP.

PURE PLAY   [COL] A company that is very focused in its business operations and has little or no DIVERSIFICATION in other areas. This often makes it simpler for INVESTORS to discern the RISKS and RETURNS that can be obtained from investing in such a company's STOCK.

PURE PREMIUM   The amount an INSURER needs to charge to cover EXPECTED LOSSES and LOSS ADJUSTMENT EXPENSES; pure premium is one of two components, along with PREMIUM LOADING, used to determine FAIR PREMIUM. See also EXPENSE LOADING.

PURE PREMIUM RATING METHOD A method of determining the PREMIUM on PROPERTY AND CASUALTY INSURANCE that excludes PREMIUM LOADING factors, generally computed as:

$$PP = \frac{Loss + LAE}{U}$$

where Loss is the amount of losses per year, LAE is the LOSS ADJUSTMENT EXPENSE per year, and U is the number of exposure units (e.g., policies).

PURE RISK A RISK exposure that can result only in a loss or no loss, but no possibility of a gain. Also known as STANDARD RISK. See also SPECULATIVE RISK.

PURPOSE LOAN A LOAN, collateralized by SECURITIES and subject to MARGIN rules, where the proceeds are used to purchase other securities. Also known as MARGIN LOAN. See also NONPURPOSE LOAN.

PUT See PUT OPTION.

PUT-CALL PARITY Relationships in OPTION pricing that must hold true in order for no-ARBITRAGE conditions to exist. The primary parity relationship indicates that the sum of the price of a CALL OPTION and the PRESENT VALUE of the STRIKE PRICE must equal the sum of the price of the PUT OPTION and the UNDERLYING ASSET. If parity does not hold, ARBITRAGE opportunities will arise and persist until ARBITRAGEURS force the discrepancy to disappear. Put-call parity is summarized as:

$$c + Xe^{-r_f t} = p + S$$

where c is the price of the call option, X is the strike price, p is the price of the put option, S is the underlying STOCK (or asset) price, r_f is the RISK-FREE RATE, t is the time to maturity, and e is the exponential constant.

PUT-CALL RATIO The ratio of OPEN INTEREST in EXCHANGE-TRADED PUT OPTIONS to CALL OPTIONS, and an indicator of market sentiment; a put-call ratio that favors puts may be indicative of BEARISH sentiment, while one that favors calls may indicate a BULLISH sentiment.

PUT ON A CALL A COMPOUND OPTION that grants the buyer the right to sell an underlying CALL OPTION to the seller of the compound. See also CALL ON A CALL, CALL ON A PUT, PUT ON A PUT.

PUT ON A PUT A COMPOUND OPTION that grants the buyer the right to sell an underlying PUT OPTION to the seller of the compound. See also CALL ON A CALL, CALL ON A PUT, PUT ON A CALL.

PUT ON THE BEST OF N-ASSETS An OVER-THE-COUNTER COMPLEX OPTION that grants the buyer a PAYOFF based on the difference between a predefined STRIKE PRICE and the best performing ASSET in a PORTFOLIO. See also CALL ON THE BEST OF N-ASSETS, CALL ON THE WORST OF N-ASSETS, MULTI-INDEX OPTION, OPTION ON THE BEST/WORST OF N-ASSETS, PUT ON THE WORST OF N-ASSETS.

PUT ON THE MINIMUM An OVER-THE-COUNTER COMPLEX OPTION that grants the buyer a PAYOFF based on the difference between a predefined STRIKE PRICE and the lowest price achieved by the UNDERLYING reference ASSET over the life of the transaction. See also OPTION ON THE MAXIMUM/MINIMUM, CALL ON THE MAXIMUM, LOOKBACK OPTION.

PUT ON THE WORST OF N-ASSETS An OVER-THE-COUNTER COMPLEX OPTION that grants the buyer a PAYOFF based on the difference between a pre-defined STRIKE PRICE and the worst performing ASSET in a PORTFOLIO. See also CALL ON THE BEST OF N-ASSETS, CALL ON THE WORST OF N-ASSETS, MULTI-INDEX OPTION, OPTION ON THE BEST/WORST OF N-ASSETS, PUT ON THE BEST OF N-ASSETS.

PUT OPTION A DERIVATIVE CONTRACT that gives the buyer the RIGHT, but not the obligation, to sell an UNDERLYING ASSET to the seller at a set STRIKE PRICE at, or before, EXPIRY; in exchange, the buyer pays the seller a PREMIUM. The PAYOFF to the put buyer is given as:

max(0, strike price – asset price)

Puts, which can be written on a broad range of financial and COMMODITY references, are available as EXCHANGE-traded and OVER-THE-COUNTER contracts, and can be structured as AMERICAN OPTIONS, BERMUDAN OPTIONS, or EUROPEAN OPTIONS.

Long put payoff profile

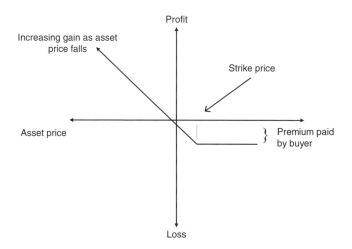

Short put payoff profile

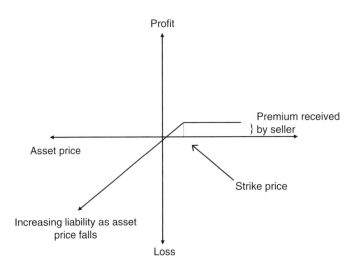

See also CALL OPTION.

PUT PRICE   The price INVESTORS can expect to receive for a PUTABLE BOND if the OPTION to put the securities back to the ISSUER is exercised. Also known as REDEMPTION PRICE.

PUT PROTECTED EQUITY   A CONTINGENT EQUITY facility where a company buys a PUT OPTION on its own COMMON STOCK from an INTERMEDIARY, generating an economic gain which increases RETAINED EARNINGS if the value of its stock declines (such as in the aftermath of a large loss resulting from a CATASTROPHIC HAZARD). See also LOSS EQUITY PUT.

PUT PROVISION   A clause contained in the INDENTURE of a BOND that specifies the terms under which the INVESTOR may PUT the outstanding SECURITIES to the ISSUER. The provision indicates the PUT PRICE and any relevant LOCKOUT PERIOD. See also CALL PROVISION.

PUT SPREAD   An OPTION position created by buying and selling PUT OPTIONS with the same EXPIRY but different STRIKE PRICES (i.e., the purchaser of a put spread buys a closer-to-the-money put option and sells a farther out-of-the-money put option (a BEARISH strategy), the seller of a put spread does the reverse (a BULLISH strategy). The spread limits the gain/LIABILITY to an area defined by the two strikes. See also BULL SPREAD, BEAR SPREAD, CALL SPREAD.

PUT SWAPTION   See PAYER SWAPTION.

PUTABLE ASSET SWAP   A structured DERIVATIVE comprised of a PUTABLE SWAP and an underlying BOND. The INVESTOR in the structure retains a PUT OPTION on the bond, allowing it to sell the package back to the seller at a given STRIKE CREDIT SPREAD. If the spread widens during the life of the transaction (e.g., the price of the asset falls as a result of specific or general market/credit conditions), the investor puts the package to the seller, receiving PRINCIPAL and INTEREST defined by the strike spread. See also CALLABLE ASSET SWAP.

PUTABLE BOND A BOND with embedded PUT OPTIONS which gives INVESTORS the RIGHT to sell the SECURITY back to the ISSUER at a predetermined PUT PRICE, generally a PREMIUM to PAR VALUE; in exchange for granting investors the put, the ISSUER obtains a lower COUPON. An investor may choose to put the bond when the PRESENT VALUE of the future CASH FLOWS from the bond is lower than the put price. From the issuer's perspective, a putable bond can be considered the equivalent of a nonputable bond and a SHORT POSITION in a put option with a STRIKE PRICE equal to the bond's put price. See also CALLABLE BOND, HYBRID BOND.

PUTABLE COMMON STOCK   A form of COMMON STOCK where the issuing company floats SHARES that feature a PUT OPTION agreement, giving INVESTORS the right to sell the stock back to the company at a future time and STRIKE price. Such issues are not particularly common, as a falling stock price moves the investor's option IN-THE-MONEY, precisely when the company may be experiencing FINANCIAL DISTRESS. See also CALLABLE COMMON STOCK.

PUTABLE CONVERTIBLE BOND   A CONVERTIBLE BOND that contains a PUT OPTION which gives INVESTORS the RIGHT to sell the SECURITIES back to the ISSUER at a PREMIUM to PAR VALUE on a specific date(s); in exchange for granting investors the put, the issuer obtains a lower COUPON. The putable structure is offered in one of two forms: a single premium put, allowing for a one-time EXERCISE (commonly used in the EUROMARKETS) and a rolling premium put, allowing for multiple exercise opportunities on predefined dates. See also CONDITIONAL PUT CONVERTIBLE BOND.

PUTABLE SWAP   An OVER-THE-COUNTER SWAP structure that gives the institution receiving FIXED RATES the OPTION to cancel the transaction at a future date. See also CALLABLE SWAP, CANCELLABLE SWAP.

PYRAMID   A corporate structure that relies on the use of HOLDING COMPANIES and SUBSIDIARIES to generate multiple layers of FINANCING. A pyramid structure is legal but adds complexity to the analysis process, and may be difficult for LENDERS to monitor.

Q

QFII   See QUALIFIED FOREIGN INSTITUTIONAL INVESTORS.

QIB   See QUALIFIED INSTITUTIONAL BUYER.

QT (QUESTIONED TRADE)   See DK.

QUAD WITCH   [COL] See QUADRUPLE WITCHING DAY.

QUADRUPLE WITCHING DAY   A single business day when INDEX FUTURES, index OPTIONS, individual EQUITY options and SINGLE STOCK FUTURES all settle simultaneously, which occurs once each quarter (i.e., the third Friday in March, June, September, and December). There is evidence to indicate that volume and VOLATILITY increase during these days as market participants rebalance their positions. See also TRIPLE WITCHING DAY.

QUALIFIED FOREIGN INSTITUTIONAL INVESTORS (QFII)   An INVESTOR that is authorized to purchase A-SHARES (Yuan-denominated) on the SHANGHAI STOCK EXCHANGE or the Shenzhen Stock Exchange. The program was authorized by the Chinese monetary authorities in 2003 and places QUOTAS on the amount of shares each QFII is permitted to acquire.

QUALIFIED INSTITUTIONAL BUYER (QIB)   An INSTITUTIONAL INVESTOR that is authorized to purchase and sell to other QIBs and DEALERS PRIVATE PLACEMENTS and other SECURITIES that have not been floated in the public markets. The QIB resale mechanism injects additional LIQUIDITY into otherwise UNMARKETABLE SECURITIES. In the United States, a SECURITIES AND EXCHANGE COMMISSION SAFE HARBOR, RULE 144A, allows QIB resales provided that the number of QIBs and the minimum size of their participation are specified in the selling documents or private placement agreement.

QUALIFIED OPINION   An AUDIT OPINION by an EXTERNAL AUDITOR indicating that the accuracy of a company's FINANCIAL STATEMENTS cannot be verified because of omissions or lack of information, e.g., the auditor is unable to ascertain TAX or legal LIABILITIES associated with certain transactions or is unable to confirm details regarding the company's INVENTORY or ACCOUNTS RECEIVABLE. See also ADVERSE OPINION, UNQUALIFIED OPINION.

QUANGO [COL]   See QUASI AUTONOMOUS NONGOVERNMENTAL ORGANIZATION.

QUANTITATIVE EASING   A form of MONETARY POLICY where government authorities purchase GOVERNMENT SECURITIES from the open market, thereby increasing MONEY SUPPLY. This policy tends to be enacted when further easing is required but INTEREST RATES are already near 0% and cannot be reduced further.

QUANTITY ADJUSTED OPTION   See QUANTO.

QUANTITY THEORY OF MONEY   An economic theory put forth by philosopher David Hume in the eighteenth century (and popularized by others since) which relates the level of prices with the amount of MONEY in the system. In particular, the following relationship is proposed:

$$MV = PQ$$

where M is the amount of money in circulation, V is the VELOCITY OF MONEY, P is the level of prices, Q is the real output of an economy.

QUANTO   An OPTION that converts gains from an underlying DERIVATIVE into a target CURRENCY at a predetermined FOREIGN EXCHANGE RATE. The quanto allows an INVESTOR to participate in a foreign market/ASSET while protecting it from exchange rate RISK. Also known as GUARANTEED EXCHANGE RATE OPTION, QUANTITY ADJUSTED OPTION.

QUANTO SWAP   See DIFFERENTIAL SWAP.

QUARTERLY REPORT   See 10-Q

QUASI ARBITRAGE   Any ARBITRAGE strategy that makes use of internal, rather than external or borrowed, funds. See also PURE ARBITRAGE.

QUASI AUTONOMOUS NONGOVERNMENTAL ORGANIZATION (QUANGO)   A semigovernmental organization that is financed by, and features specific authorities that have been devolved from, a national or state government. See also GOVERNMENT-SPONSORED ENTERPRISE, QUASI AUTONOMOUS NONGOVERNMENTAL ORGANIZATION.

QUESTIONED TRADE   See DK.

QUICK ASSETS   A measure of a firm's most LIQUID ASSETS, generally taken to include cash, MARKETABLE SECURITIES (e.g., FIXED INCOME SECURITIES, COMMON STOCK, PREFERRED STOCK) and ACCOUNTS RECEIVABLE. The quick asset measure is precisely equal to CURRENT ASSETS less INVENTORY. See also QUICK RATIO.

Q

QUICK RATIO   A measure of a company's ability to meet OBLIGATIONS that are coming due with its most LIQUID ASSETS, typically computed as:

$$OR = QA/CL$$

where QA is QUICK ASSETS and CL is CURRENT LIABILITIES.

A quick ratio above 1.0 indicates that the company has sufficient CASH FLOW from maturing or saleable assets to meet its short-term OBLIGATIONS; a ratio below 1.0 suggests the possibility of LIQUIDITY RISK pressures. Since the quick ratio only includes truly liquid assets as a potential source of cash, it is a more conservative measure than the CURRENT RATIO. Also known as LIQUID RATIO.

QUIET PERIOD   [COL] The period of time during which a company in the process of registering a NEW ISSUE of SECURITIES is prohibited from releasing any public relations material or other sensitive information.

QUOTA   An allotment or maximum amount; in the context of TRADE it relates to the specific amount of a good or COMMODITY that can be IMPORTED or EXPORTED.

QUOTA SHARE   In REINSURANCE, a PROPORTIONAL AGREEMENT where an INSURER and REINSURER agree to split PREMIUMS, RISKS, losses, and LOSS ADJUSTMENT EXPENSES as a fixed percentage of the policy limit rather than a specific monetary amount. See also SURPLUS SHARE.

QUOTATION   (1) An estimate of the cost of a particular service or coverage, as in INSURANCE. (2) An indication of the price of a SECURITY or other ASSET. Also known as QUOTE. (2) See also FIRM QUOTE, INDICATIVE QUOTE.

QUOTE   See QUOTATION.

QUOTE-DRIVEN MARKET   A marketplace where DEALERS or MARKET MAKERS give prices to BROKERS or TRADERS, who can then buy or sell. Prices are typically adjusted to reflect ORDER flow and SUPPLY and DEMAND forces. Institutional OVER-THE-COUNTER markets are often quote driven. See also DEALER MARKET, ORDER-DRIVEN MARKET.

QUOTED SPREAD   The difference between the BID and the OFFER before a transaction occurs; the quoted spread may be a FIRM QUOTE or an INDICATIVE QUOTE.

R

R-SQUARED   See COEFFICIENT OF DETERMINATION.

RAIDER   [COL] A hostile acquirer that attempts to purchase another company, often to engage in ASSET STRIPPING or to receive GREENMAIL payments. Although raiders were especially active during the HOSTILE TAKEOVER phase of the 1980s, they still exist.

RAINBOW OPTION   See MULTI-INDEX OPTION.

RAINMAKER   [COL] A financial services professional that is capable of generating a significant amount of new business for an employing BANK or INVESTMENT BANK. The rainmaker generally refers to bankers that are capable of winning MANDATES to arrange NEW ISSUES or CORPORATE FINANCE transactions, but can also apply to institutional salespeople, BROKERS, or traders that are extremely successful in their respective areas.

RALLY   A rise in the price of a SECURITY or market, which is seen as a BULLISH signal. A rally may be of short or long duration, depending on fundamental and technical factors. See also RELIEF RALLY.

RAMPING   [COL] The process of trying to push up the value of a STOCK or other SECURITY through a combination of short-term buying and spreading of positive news, with the aim of trying to secure a short-term price rise so that an existing LONG POSITION can be sold at a profit.

RANDOM VARIABLE   An event or observation with an uncertain outcome; a random variable may be discrete (appearing at specified time intervals) or continuous (appearing at any time), and it may be limited to a defined value or carry any value. Samplings of random variables are often used in SIMULATION processes that generate ASSET prices or distributions.

RANDOM WALK   A financial theory indicating that ASSET prices move in a random and unpredictable (though not irrational) fashion, suggesting that future prices cannot be predicted by past or current prices; the longer the time period associated with the asset observations, the greater the possible dispersion of prices. More formally, the random walk is a STOCHASTIC PROCESS where asset prices are RANDOM VARIABLES, with each price increment independent and identically distributed. See also EFFICIENT MARKET HYPOTHESIS.

Additional references: Cootner (1964); Samuelson (1965).

RANGE FLOATER   See RANGE FLOATING RATE NOTE.

RANGE FLOATING RATE NOTE (FRN)   A STRUCTURED NOTE that provides the INVESTOR with an enhanced COUPON if the FLOATING RATE reference trades within a predefined range; for every day the reference falls outside the band the investor loses one day's interest. The security is effectively a standard FRN with a strip of embedded BINARY OPTIONS. Also known as ACCRUAL

NOTE, DAY COUNT NOTE, RANGE FLOATER. See also CAPPED FLOATING RATE NOTE, INVERSE FLOATING RATE NOTE, PERPETUAL FLOATING RATE NOTE, RANGE KNOCK-OUT FLOATING RATE NOTE.

RANGE FORWARD   See ZERO COST COLLAR.

RANGE KNOCK-OUT FLOATER   See RANGE KNOCK-OUT FLOATING RATE NOTE.

RANGE KNOCK-OUT FLOATING RATE NOTE (FRN)   A STRUCTURED NOTE that provides the INVESTOR with larger COUPONS than a RANGE FLOATING RATE NOTE but ceases paying INTEREST for an entire period (typically one quarter) if the reference trades outside the range for a single day. The security is effectively a standard FRN with a strip of embedded KNOCK-OUT OPTIONS. Also known as RANGE KNOCK-OUT FLOATER. See also CAPPED FLOATING RATE NOTE, INVERSE FLOATING RATE NOTE, PERPETUAL FLOATING RATE NOTE.

RAROC   See RISK-ADJUSTED RETURN ON CAPITAL.

RATCHET OPTION   See CLIQUET OPTION.

RATE   See INTEREST RATE.

RATE LOCK   A mechanism that guarantees a BORROWER an underlying INTEREST RATE on a LOAN for a period ranging from 30 to 90 days. The rate lock ensures the borrower faces a known financing cost, as long as the loan is concluded during the effective period. Also known as LOCK-IN PROVISION. See also DROP LOCK, SPREAD LOCK.

RATE MAKING   In INSURANCE, the process of establishing PREMIUM rates so that they adequately cover EXPECTED LOSSES and are reasonable and non-discriminatory. When supplemented by relevant LOAD factors, the INSURER obtains the FAIR PREMIUM that it charges INSUREDS. See also EXPENSE LOADING, PREMIUM LOADING, PURE PREMIUM.

RATE OF EXCHANGE   See FOREIGN EXCHANGE RATE.

RATE OF INTEREST   See INTEREST RATE.

RATE OF RETURN   See RETURN.

RATE ON LINE   A measure of an INSURER's or REINSURER's gross profitability, generally calculated as:

$$ROL = \frac{Pr}{Line}$$

where Pr is PREMIUM and Line is the amount of the LINE provided by the insurer or reinsurer.

The higher the rate on line, the more gross profit the insurer earns.

RATE-SENSITIVE ASSETS   ASSETS of a FINANCIAL INSTITUTION that are exposed to changes in INTEREST RATES (e.g., FIXED INCOME INVESTMENTS,

REVERSE REPURCHASE AGREEMENTS, LOANS). Measurement of rate-sensitive assets is an essential component of GAP MANAGEMENT; by determining sensitivity to changes in interest rates, a financial institution can manage its exposure to DIRECTIONAL RISK, CURVE RISK, and REPRICING RISK. See also ASSET MANAGEMENT, RATE-SENSITIVE LIABILITIES.

RATE-SENSITIVE LIABILITIES   LIABILITIES of a FINANCIAL INSTITUTION that are exposed to changes in INTEREST RATES (e.g., DEPOSITS, REPURCHASE AGREEMENTS, BONDS). Measurement of rate-sensitive liabilities is an essential component of GAP MANAGEMENT; by determining sensitivity to changes in interest rates, a financial institution can manage its exposure to DIRECTIONAL RISK, CURVE RISK, and REPRICING RISK. See also ASSET MANAGEMENT, RATE-SENSITIVE ASSETS.

RATING MIGRATION   The evolution of a company's CREDIT RATING over time, providing potential CREDITORS and INVESTORS with a historical view on how the company's financial strength has fared over time, and how it might evolve in the future. The rating migration is typically shown as a percentage PROBABILITY that a rating will remain unchanged, be downgraded, or be upgraded over particular time horizons that range from one to several years. Also known as MIGRATION, TRANSITION.

RATIO ANALYSIS   A financial analysis technique used by INVESTMENT ANALYSIS and CREDIT ANALYSTS that uses ACCOUNTING information from a company's FINANCIAL STATEMENTS to compute relative and absolute strength/weakness in key areas such as profitability, activity, liquidity, LEVERAGE, and SOLVENCY.

RATIO HORIZONTAL SPREAD   See TIME SPREAD.

RATIO SWAP   See POWER SWAP.

RATIO VERTICAL SPREAD   An OPTION SPREAD that is designed to generate profits from VOLATILITY. Ratio vertical spreads are created through the purchase of a smaller quantity of closer-to-the-money PUT OPTIONS or CALL OPTIONS and the sale of a larger quantity of farther-from-the-money puts or calls. See also BACKSPREAD.

RATIO WRITING   An OPTION position where an option writer sells a combination of COVERED OPTIONS and NAKED OPTIONS, in specific quantities or ratios. The RISKS associated with the strategy are lower than they are with a pure naked option strategy, but higher than on a covered option approach.

RATIONALIZATION   A process undertaken by a company to reduce its operations in order to improve efficiencies and lower costs. Rationalization may involve the disposal of certain business lines or operating SUBSIDIARIES, the closure of production facilities and/or the dismissal of some amount of employees. See also DOWNSIZING, RIGHTSIZING.

RAW MATERIAL INVENTORY   A class of INVENTORY held by a company that includes all materials and resources used in the production of goods intended for sale. See also FINISHED GOODS INVENTORY, WORK-IN-PROCESS INVENTORY.

RBA   See RESERVE BANK OF AUSTRALIA.

REACQUIRED STOCK   See TREASURY STOCK.

REAL ESTATE INVESTMENT TRUST (REIT)   An INVESTMENT COMPANY or INVESTMENT TRUST that raises CAPITAL from INVESTORS and invests proceeds on a TAX-advantaged basis in INCOME-producing real estate; in the United States, if 95% of income generated by the REIT is distributed to investors, EARNINGS are exempt from federal taxation. A REIT may be created as an EQUITY TRUST, which owns and operates real estate, or a MORTGAGE trust, which lends to developers on a secured basis.

REAL ESTATE MORTGAGE INVESTMENT CONDUIT (REMIC)   An INVESTMENT vehicle that raises funds from INVESTORS and uses the proceeds to acquire commercial and residential MORTGAGE-related ASSETS. REMICs, which can be structured as CORPORATIONS, INVESTMENT TRUSTS, or LIMITED PARTNERSHIPS, purchase WHOLE LOANS, COLLATERALIZED MORTGAGE OBLIGATIONS, and/or MORTGAGE-BACKED SECURITIES through the issuance of DEBT in TRANCHES with unique MATURITIES, RISK classes, and levels of SUBORDINATION. Each tranche gives investors an undivided interest in the underlying assets.

REAL EXCHANGE RATE   A FOREIGN EXCHANGE RATE that has been calibrated to take account of INFLATION.

REAL INTEREST RATE   The core level of INTEREST RATES, excluding the effects of INFLATION, typically computed as:

$$1 + r_{real} = \frac{1 + r_{nom}}{1 + r_{inf}}$$

where r_{real} is the real rate, r_{nom} is the nominal rate, and r_{inf} is the inflation rate. See also NOMINAL INTEREST RATE, REAL YIELD.

REAL MONEY ACCOUNT   See REAL MONEY INVESTOR.

REAL MONEY INVESTOR   An INSTITUTIONAL INVESTOR, such as a PENSION FUND or INSURANCE FUND, that tends to have a stable, medium/long-term INVESTMENT outlook, is unlikely to use significant LEVERAGE and is unlikely to quickly enter and exit specific ASSETS or markets. HEDGE FUNDS, though classed as institutional investors, are not considered to be real money investors. Also known as REAL MONEY ACCOUNT.

REAL OPTION   The right, but not the obligation, a company has to enter into a new CAPITAL INVESTMENT or to exit an existing capital investment. The general concept is based on the framework developed for financial OPTIONS, though real option decisions tend to be much more complex and opaque. The associated REAL OPTION VALUATION process is used as an alternative or supplement to more traditional CAPITAL BUDGETING and DISCOUNTED CASH FLOW exercises. In general, real options cannot be traded between parties, though some real options can be sold to other parties.

REAL OPTION ANALYSIS See REAL OPTION VALUATION.

REAL OPTION VALUATION A framework used to evaluate REAL OPTIONS that attempts to factor in the multiplicity of decisions that exist in a typical INVESTMENT project (e.g., initial investment, expansion, abandonment, deferral of funding, and so forth). In order to take account of these multiple decisions, their associated uncertainties and an array of EXERCISE possibilities, the real option valuation framework employs RISK-adjusted probabilities and LATTICE MODELS to generate a quantitative result. Also known as REAL OPTION ANALYSIS.

REAL RETURN BOND In Canada, an INFLATION-LINKED SECURITY.

REAL YIELD The YIELD on a SECURITY that has been calibrated to take account of INFLATION. Real yield is lower than the computed or nominal yield in an inflationary environment.

REALIZED GAIN Gains on an ASSET (resulting from a positive change in valuation) that have been crystallized for ACCOUNTING purposes on the INCOME STATEMENT. A gain is realized through disposal of the asset. See also REALIZED LOSS, UNREALIZED PROFIT.

REALIZED LOSS Losses on an ASSET (resulting from a negative change in valuation) that have been crystallized for ACCOUNTING purposes on the INCOME STATEMENT. A loss is realized through disposal of the asset. See also REALIZED GAIN, UNREALIZED LOSS.

REALIZED SPREAD The difference between the weighted average of the BIDS and OFFERS of executed SECURITIES transactions over a specific period of time. See also EFFECTIVE SPREAD, QUOTED SPREAD.

REALIZED VOLATILITY SWAP An OVER-THE-COUNTER COMPLEX SWAP involving the exchange of realized, or actual, VOLATILITY and IMPLIED VOLATILITY on a given market reference. Realized volatility is the floating volatility of the underlying reference INDEX evident over the life of the transaction, while implied volatility is the fixed volatility rate contracted between buyer and seller at the start of the transaction. Realized volatility swaps are used in the EQUITY and FOREIGN EXCHANGE markets. See also VARIANCE SWAP.

REBALANCING (1) The process of adjusting an INVESTMENT PORTFOLIO by adding or removing certain SECURITIES or ASSETS to reflect a change in the market. (2)The process of adjusting an existing HEDGE after a market move in order to preserve its efficacy in neutralizing RISK.

REBATE (1) A refund, provided by a company to its customers, related to the purchase of specified goods or services (2) A refund provided by an INTERMEDIARY to a client executing a TRADE.

RECAPITALIZATION (1) The general process of RESTRUCTURING the financial CAPITAL of a company, generally by increasing EQUITY and reducing DEBT. Recapitalization can apply to companies that are solvent as well as those that are in the process of REORGANIZATION following filing of BANKRUPTCY protection. (2) The act of converting the nature and voting characteristics of a company's COMMON STOCK by assigning more or less VOTING RIGHTS to individual shares. (1) Also known as DELEVERAGING. (2) See also DUAL CLASS RECAPITALIZATION.

RECEIVABLE See ACCOUNTS RECEIVABLE.

RECEIVABLES SECURITIZATION A SECURITIZATION structure where the underlying COLLATERAL POOL comprises of eligible short-term ACCOUNTS RECEIVABLE. In a standard structure a SPECIAL PURPOSE ENTITY is created by the seller to hold the receivables, which serve as collateral for NOTES issued to INVESTORS. Funding can also be obtained via CONDUITS, which issue receivables-backed COMMERCIAL PAPER to INVESTORS. Stand-alone term receivables securitizations are also arranged on occasion. In all structures the pool of receivables must conform to specific eligibility criteria related to CREDIT quality, MATURITY, and concentration; standard RESERVES are typically established to provide additional protection.

RECEIVER A party named by a BANKRUPTCY court to act as AGENT for a bankrupt DEBTOR while maintaining ASSETS for the benefit of CREDITORS. A receiver may be given different levels of operating discretion by the courts, from managing the business of the company in bankruptcy to simply dealing with the disposal of property. Also known as ADMINISTRATOR. See also RECEIVERSHIP.

RECEIVER EXTENDIBLE SWAP An EXTENDIBLE SWAP that is formed from a combination of a fixed receiver SWAP and a RECEIVER SWAPTION.

RECEIVER SWAPTION A SWAPTION granting the buyer the right to enter into an OVER-THE-COUNTER INTEREST RATE SWAP to receive FIXED RATES and pay FLOATING RATES. The buyer will to EXERCISE the receiver swaption as floating rates fall below a particular STRIKE PRICE. Also known as CALL SWAPTION. See also PAYER SWAPTION.

RECEIVERSHIP A state where a company has filed for BANKRUPTCY and is being overseen by a RECEIVER until courts decide on LIQUIDATION or REORGANIZATION.

RECESSION A period of economic contraction within a national ECONOMY as part of the ongoing BUSINESS CYCLE. A recession, which may be defined as two or more consecutive quarters of falling output (as measured through GROSS DOMESTIC PRODUCT), may feature falling INVESTMENT and rising UNEMPLOYMENT. See also DEPRESSION.

RECIPROCAL EXCHANGE An unincorporated association where INSUREDS amalgamate their RISKS in order to insure one another; existing members actively attempt to recruit new members to spread risks even more widely. The affairs of the reciprocal exchange, including collection of PREMIUMS, adjustment of losses, and payment of CLAIMS, are often administered by an ATTORNEY-IN-FACT. Also known as RECIPROCAL INSURANCE EXCHANGE.

RECIPROCAL INSURANCE EXCHANGE   See RECIPROCAL EXCHANGE.

RECIPROCAL RATE   The inverse of the commonly quoted FOREIGN EXCHANGE RATE for a given CURRENCY pair. While the foreign exchange markets typically quote in terms of currency per US dollar or US dollar per currency, the reciprocal rate denominates the same quote in inverse terms. See also AMERICAN TERMS, EUROPEAN TERMS.

RECIPROCITY   In general, the exchange between two parties of certain actions or services for receipt of substantial similar actions or services. In BANKING reciprocity is commonly encountered in CAPITAL-raising, DEPOSIT, and UNDERWRITING activities.

RECOMBINING TREE   See LATTICE MODEL.

RECONCILIATION   In ACCOUNTING the process of comparing DEBITS and CREDITS on transactions flowing through a company's ledgers to ensure proper treatment and balance. Reconciliation may be carried out on a formal basis every week, month, or quarter.

RECONSTITUTION   The process of reassembling the CORPUS (or PRINCIPAL) and INTEREST COUPONS of a SECURITY that has previously been decomposed into STRIPS, often to take advantage of ARBITRAGE opportunities. This occurs, for instance, in the US TREASURY BOND market and the UK GILT market, where long-term securities are routinely split into ZERO COUPON BONDS and coupon streams. See also STRIPPING.

RECOUPONING   The process of MARKING-TO-MARKET and settling a PORTFOLIO of DERIVATIVES in order to reduce ACTUAL EXPOSURE between COUNTERPARTIES. A net cash SETTLEMENT is paid to the party holding the contracts with current value and the derivatives are then rewritten, or recouponed, at current market levels. The process is then repeated at a future settlement period.

RECOURSE   The ability for a LENDER to seek repayment from a BORROWER rather than the ASSET or project that is being financed, or the right to a CLAIM on a contracting party. The greater the degree of recourse, the greater the repayment options to the lender. A CONTRACT agreed on a full recourse basis means the original seller of a product, maker of a NEGOTIABLE INSTRUMENT, or borrower under a CREDIT facility is liable for repayment. See also FULL RECOURSE LOAN, NONRECOURSE, NONRECOURSE LOAN, PARTIAL RECOURSE LOAN.

RECOVERY   The amount received by CREDITORS after BANKRUPTCY proceedings have concluded, typically related to the SENIORITY of the CLAIM and/or the amount of COLLATERAL held. Secured creditors typically recover the greater percentage of their outstanding claims (e.g., 40%–100% RECOVERY RATE), followed by senior, unsecured creditors (20%–50%) and junior, unsecured creditors (10%–40%); subordinated debt holders, PREFERRED STOCK INVESTORS, and COMMON STOCK investors receive the smallest recoveries. The actual amount of recovery is dependent on the value of a company in LIQUIDATION or REORGANIZATION, as well as the total amount of outstanding claims. See also LOSS-GIVEN DEFAULT.

RECOVERY RATE   The percentage of an OBLIGATION or CLAIM recovered by a CREDITOR following a defaulted DEBTOR's BANKRUPTCY proceedings. See also LOSS-GIVEN DEFAULT, RECOVERY.

RED HERRING   [COL] In the United States, a preliminary REGISTRATION STATEMENT, filed by a company with the SECURITIES AND EXCHANGE COMMISSION, related to a forthcoming NEW ISSUE of SECURITIES. The red herring contains no price or issue size details, and is updated regularly until it becomes the final PROSPECTUS. The document derives its name from the red ink that is used to warn that the circular is not an attempt to sell securities in advance of registration statement approval. Also known as PATHFINDER PROSPECTUS.

RED-LINING   [COL] Refusal by a BANK to provide funds, or an INSURER to supply INSURANCE cover, in particular areas or sectors as a result of previous negative experiences and/or losses. Red-lining that is discriminatory or prejudicial is illegal in many jurisdictions.

REDEEMABLE BOND   See CALLABLE BOND.

REDEMPTION   The process of paying off and extinguishing an issue of SECURITIES as per the terms stated in the OFFERING DOCUMENT or PROSPECTUS, or otherwise reflected on the SCRIP.

REDEMPTION DATE   The date on which an issue of SECURITIES can be paid off by the ISSUER, or the specific MATURITY DATE of the issue.

REDEMPTION PRICE   See CALL PRICE, PUT PRICE.

REDEMPTION VALUE   The value or price at which a SECURITY will be redeemed at MATURITY.

REDISCOUNTING   The process of discounting a NEGOTIABLE INSTRUMENT a second time, e.g., a BANK first DISCOUNTS a BILL OF EXCHANGE, and a CENTRAL BANK then rediscounts the bank's discounted bill when presented. Each act of rediscounting implicitly reflects a charge taken for the obligor's CREDIT RISK.

REFERENCE CREDIT   See REFERENCE ENTITY.

REFERENCE ENTITY   The ISSUER to whose DEFAULT a CREDIT DERIVATIVE CONTRACT refers. Default on any of the issuer's DEBT obligations will trigger a payout under the credit derivative contract. Also known as REFERENCE CREDIT. See also REFERENCE OBLIGATION.

REFERENCE INDEX An INDEX that is used as the pricing indicator in a DERIVATIVE transaction, such as those related to EQUITIES or COMMODITIES.

REFERENCE OBLIGATION The specific DEBT obligation of an ISSUER to whose DEFAULT a CREDIT DERIVATIVE CONTRACT refers. In order to trigger a payout under the credit derivative contract the specific obligation must be in default. See also REFERENCE ENTITY.

REFERENCE RATE An INTEREST RATE that is used as the pricing indicator in a financing or DERIVATIVE transaction. In most cases the reference rate is a well-established and transparent BENCHMARK, such as LIBOR, EURIBOR, EONIA, PRIME RATE, and so forth.

REFINANCING The process of renewing an existing financing facility, such as a LOAN. Refinancing is common amongst BORROWERS when INTEREST RATES decline and the cost savings of repaying and renewing an existing facility are greater than the fees payable for a new financing. Refinancing may also occur at the original MATURITY of an existing facility as a form of extension or ROLLOVER.

REFINANCING RISK See REPRICING RISK.

REFLATION An act of stimulating an ECONOMY, generally through an increase in MONEY SUPPLY and/or a reduction in TAXES. See also DEFLATION, INFLATION.

REFUNDING A process where the ISSUER of a BOND repays INVESTORS at a predefined REDEMPTION price. Refunding can only occur when a bond issue is CALLABLE, and is generally arranged in a declining INTEREST RATE environment, when a NEW ISSUE of cheaper bonds can be floated to replace the refunded bonds. See also REFUNDING PROTECTION.

REFUNDING PROTECTION A clause in an INDENTURE that prohibits an ISSUER from redeeming a BOND for a stated period of time from proceeds of an issue floated at a lower cost and ranking equal, or senior, to the original bond. See also REFUNDING.

REGIONAL BANK In certain countries, a BANK that operates primarily outside of the main money centers, focusing its activities on one or more states in a single region or on a specific locality. Regional banks are common in countries such as the United States and Japan. See also MONEY CENTER BANK.

REGIONAL EXCHANGE In certain countries, an EXCHANGE that serves as an additional exchange in the local marketplace fulfilling a specific function for listing and trading but not holding dominant market shares. Regional exchanges exist for both STOCKS and COMMODITIES.

REGISTERED CAPITAL See AUTHORIZED CAPITAL.

REGISTERED COMPANY   In the United States, a company that has filed a REGISTRATION STATEMENT with the SECURITIES AND EXCHANGE COMMISSION in preparation for an INITIAL PUBLIC OFFERING of COMMON STOCK, or an ADD-ON. In the United Kingdom, a PUBLIC LIMITED COMPANY or a PRIVATE COMPANY that is registered under the Companies Act and has completed the COMPANY FORMATION process.

REGISTERED OFFICE   The official address of a REGISTERED COMPANY.

REGISTERED SECURITY   Any NEW ISSUE of SECURITIES that must adhere to requirements set forth by a national REGULATOR prior to FLOTATION, listing, and TRADING. Registered securities must generally be supported by a detailed REGISTRATION STATEMENT that provides information on the proposed issue of securities and the ISSUER. See also BEARER SECURITY, PRIVATE PLACEMENT.

REGISTRAR   A party that is appointed to maintain the registry of SHAREHOLDERS of a given company. BANKS and TRUST companies often fulfill the role of registrar.

REGISTRATION STATEMENT   A detailed statement accompanying a NEW ISSUE of public SECURITIES that contains details on both the ISSUER and the issue. In the United States, the SECURITIES AND EXCHANGE COMMISSION requires that all public offerings of securities include information on the proposed issue of securities and associated RISK factors, and the nature and condition of, and prospects for, the issuer. Small offerings (under $500,000) as well as PRIVATE PLACEMENTS, TREASURY BONDS/NOTES, and AGENCY SECURITIES, are exempt from the registration statement requirement. See also EXEMPT SECURITY, PROSPECTUS, RED HERRING.

REGRESSION   See REGRESSION ANALYSIS.

REGRESSION ANALYSIS   A statistical process that seeks to determine the relationship between a dependent variable (regressand) and one or more independent variables (regressors). Regression may be computed on a linear or nonlinear basis. The general form of the simple linear equation is given as:

$$y_i = \beta_o + \beta_1 x_i + \epsilon_i \text{ , for i = 1 to N data points}$$

where y is the dependent variable, x is the independent variable, β is the regression parameter, ε is the residual or error term. Also known as REGRESSION.

REGRESSIVE TAX   A TAX scheme which directly or indirectly places a greater burden on lower income households (relative to resources) by reducing the tax rate as the amount subject to taxation increases. Sales taxes and sin taxes (e.g., extra levies on tobacco and alcohol) are considered regressive taxes. See also PROGRESSIVE TAX, PROPORTIONAL TAX.

REGULAR CHOOSER OPTION   See CHOOSER OPTION.

REGULATED ELECTRONIC COMMUNICATIONS NETWORK (ECN) An ELECTRONIC COMMUNICATIONS NETWORK that is authorized by REGULATORS to operate as an EXCHANGE. Regulated ECNs must adhere to financial and reporting requirements imposed by authorities, and may be required to arrange for CLEARING of transactions through an independent CLEARINGHOUSE. See also DEALER MARKET ELECTRONIC COMMUNICATIONS NETWORK, HYBRID ELECTRONIC COMMUNICATIONS NETWORK.

REGULATION A series of rules, restriction, controls, and oversight imposed on markets, industry sectors, and/or individual institutions by a government authority in an effort to ensure proper protections within the marketplace and fair treatment of individuals and competitors. See also DEREGULATION, REGULATOR.

REGULATION FAIR DISCLOSURE In the United States, a SECURITIES AND EXCHANGE COMMISSION rule that requires a company to issue sensitive information to the public broadly rather than selectively. The rule eliminates the information access privileges often granted to research analysts of BANKS, INVESTMENT BANKS, and SECURITIES FIRMS.

REGULATION NMS In the United States, Regulation National Market System (NMS) put forth by the SECURITIES AND EXCHANGE COMMISSION, which seeks to consolidate and strengthen the framework for TRADING and EXECUTION on a variety of EXCHANGES and electronic platforms. The key elements of the regulation focus on ORDER protection (via TRADE-THROUGH and PROTECTED BIDS and OFFERS), order access, pricing increments, and market data/information display.

REGULATION T In the United States, a FEDERAL RESERVE BOARD REGULATION related to extensions of CREDIT by BROKER/DEALERS and SECURITIES FIRMS to their clients. Regulation T LOANS must be secured by MARGIN comprised of ELIGIBLE SECURITIES and capped at certain LOAN-TO-VALUE levels; minimum margin levels must be maintained and supplemented as necessary through the MAINTENANCE MARGIN process. See also NONPURPOSE LOAN, PURPOSE LOAN.

REGULATOR A government body that is responsible for overseeing the activities of particular companies or markets, and for establishing minimum standards of conduct. Certain industries, such as BANKING, may feature multiple regulators, one of which may emerge as the primary regulator. Regulated companies operating in multiple countries may also be subject to regulation by each national authority.

REGULATORY ARBITRAGE The process of taking advantage of internal or external differences in the regulatory treatment of business activities in order to decrease regulatory costs or expand into products or markets normally off limits. See also REGULATORY CONSOLIDATION, REGULATORY HARMONIZATION.

REGULATORY CAPITAL   CAPITAL resources that financial institutions must allocate to their FINANCIAL RISKS in order to comply with applicable national regulatory requirements. REGULATORS often establish minimum thresholds to ensure SOLVENCY under a range of stress loss scenarios. See also ECONOMIC CAPITAL, RISK-ADJUSTED CAPITAL, TIER 1 CAPITAL, TIER 2 CAPITAL.

REGULATORY COMPLIANCE RISK   The RISK of loss arising from failure to comply with regulatory rules related to business, TRADING, LENDING, authorized dealing personnel, reporting, disclosure, or capitalization. A subcategory of OPERATIONAL RISK.

REGULATORY CONSOLIDATION   The process of combining separate REGULATORS with a specific focus under a single "umbrella" in order to unify treatment of markets, products, and forums and eliminate inefficiencies and instances of REGULATORY ARBITRAGE. A fully consolidated regulator might be responsible for BANKING, SECURITIES, INSURANCE, INVESTMENT MANAGEMENT, and listed markets. See also REGULATORY HARMONIZATION.

REGULATORY FORBEARANCE   A decision by a national REGULATOR or authority not to enforce a specific regulation, generally to avoid destabilizing or aggravating an unstable market or situation.

REGULATORY HARMONIZATION   The process of ensuring that rules for business and financial activities are generally similar across countries in order to reduce instances of cross-border REGULATORY ARBITRAGE. See also REGULATORY CONSOLIDATION.

REHYPOTHECATION   The act of pledging COLLATERAL taken in a lending or SECURITIES FINANCING transaction to secure additional collateralized financing.

REINSTATEMENT   The reactivation of an INSURANCE CONTRACT that has lapsed due to nonpayment of PREMIUM by the INSURED. In reinstating a contract an INSURER reserves the right to charge a higher PREMIUM or modify coverage terms.

REINSURANCE   A RISK TRANSFER from an INSURER to a REINSURER that provides an insurer with cover for specified INSURANCE exposures. The agreement may be arranged as FACULTATIVE REINSURANCE (i.e., customized, one-off) or TREATY REINSURANCE (i.e., standardized, multiple exposure).

REINSURANCE BROKER   A BROKER representing the CEDING INSURER in placing business with a REINSURER.

REINSURANCE CAPACITY   (1) The amount of REINSURANCE available to INSURERS from the reinsurance market at large or from an individual REINSURER. (2) The amount of PREMIUM that an individual reinsurer is able to write for specific types of RISKS.

REINSURANCE CREDIT   A CREDIT balance on a CEDING INSURER's BALANCE SHEET that reflects PREMIUMS CEDED to, and losses recoverable from, REINSURERS. The credit balance, which is a reflection of RISK TRANSFER, permits an insurer to write additional primary INSURANCE coverage for INSUREDS.

REINSURANCE FACILITY   See REINSURANCE POOL.

REINSURANCE POOL   A group of REINSURERS that agrees to UNDERWRITE RISKS on a joint basis; under a typical POOL each member agrees to pay a fixed percentage of any loss, or a percentage of any loss above a defined RETENTION level. Also known as REINSURANCE FACILITY.

REINSURANCE SIDECAR   A form of REINSURANCE developed in response to the need for additional UNDERWRITING CAPACITY in the face of specific catastrophes. The sidecar functions in a manner similar to traditional QUOTA SHARE, except that its CAPITAL is raised privately, it supports a single CEDANT, and has a finite life (generally less than 2 years).

REINSURED   An INSURER that CEDES a particular RISK to a REINSURER through a REINSURANCE agreement.

REINSURER   An INSURER that provides REINSURANCE coverage to other insurers through FACULTATIVE REINSURANCE or TREATY REINSURANCE agreements.

REINVESTMENT RATE   The INTEREST RATE at which CAPITAL can be reinvested as it is earned and once existing INVESTMENTS mature. See also REPRICING RISK.

REINVESTMENT RISK   See REPRICING RISK.

REIT   See REAL ESTATE INVESTMENT TRUST.

RELATED PARTY   Any party (individual or corporate) that is in some way associated with a second party. In a corporate context this relates to the relationship between HOLDING COMPANIES, PARENT companies, SUBSIDIARIES, AFFILIATES, and/or JOINT VENTURES.

RELATED-PARTY TRANSACTION   A financial transaction conducted between a company and a related entity, such as a PARENT, HOLDING COMPANY, SUBSIDIARY, AFFILIATE, JOINT VENTURE, or SPECIAL PURPOSE ENTITY. Common related-party transactions include paying or receiving DIVIDENDS, accepting or granting LOANS, HEDGING RISKS, and transferring CAPITAL.

RELATIONSHIP BANKING   A model of BANKING where a FINANCIAL INSTITUTION attempts to provide its clients with a full range of products and services and to engage in a continuous and detailed dialog about business requirements in order to create a long-term business relationship. A client choosing a relationship bank may expect rapid response, competitive pricing, and assistance as required. See also TRANSACTIONAL BANKING.

RELATIONSHIP MODEL   A general corporate system that is characterized by concentrated ownership stakes and cross-SHAREHOLDINGS, LIQUID

CAPITAL MARKETS, and a relatively inactive CORPORATE CONTROL MARKET; formal legal dealings are often supplemented by informal negotiation arising from long-term business relationships. Germany and Japan are representative examples of the relationship model. See also HYBRID MODEL, MARKET MODEL.

RELATIVE VALUATION   A quantitative VALUATION method used to estimate the STOCK price of a company based on the use of multiples rather than DISCOUNTED CASH FLOWS. The framework is based on identifying peer ratios that reflect the price of the stock and some underlying CASH FLOW measure (the "base," such as net earnings, EARNINGS BEFORE INTEREST AND TAXES, sales, and so forth), computing the average of those peer multiples, and then applying the multiples to the base of the ratio of the target company that is being valued; the end result is the estimated price of the target company's stock. Also known as COMPARABLES TRANSACTION ANALYSIS.

RELATIVE VALUE ARBITRAGE   A general ARBITRAGE strategy where an INVESTOR or HEDGE FUND manager can establish arbitrage positions in any one of several different, and often unrelated, ASSET classes. As with other arbitrage strategies, the fundamental goal is to identify price discrepancies which can be converted into profits and to monetize them through a combination of unleveraged or LEVERAGED LONG and SHORT positions.

RELIEF RALLY   A RALLY in the broader market that comes after a significant sell-off or BEARISH phase. The rally may be short-lived if fundamental and technical factors have not actually changed.

REMARKETABLE ASSET SWAP   See CALLABLE ASSET SWAP.

REMIC   See REAL ESTATE MORTGAGE INVESTMENT CONDUIT.

REMITTING BANK   See COLLECTING BANK.

RENEGOTIATED LOAN   A LOAN where the original terms of CONTRACT (i.e., MATURITY, amount, INTEREST RATE, repayment frequency) are altered to avoid forcing the lending BANK to commence FORECLOSURE proceedings. A renegotiated loan may involve an extension of the maturity, a lowering of the interest rate, or a change in the PRINCIPAL AMORTIZATION schedule. Although the loan may perform under the new terms, the bank may still be required to establish LOAN LOSS RESERVES. See also RESCHEDULING, RESTRUCTURING, SOFT LOAN.

RENT   A periodic payment made by a renting party to a property owner for the use of residential or commercial property.

RENT-A-CAPTIVE   A licensed INSURER or REINSURER that makes an account available to a firm that wishes to SELF-INSURE but does not want to administer its own CAPTIVE program. A rent-a-captive prevents account commingling by segregating ASSETS, LIABILITIES, and RISK exposures into individual accounts that are separated through a SHAREHOLDER'S agreement. See also AGENCY

CAPTIVE, CAPTIVE, GROUP CAPTIVE, PROTECTED CELL COMPANY, PURE CAPTIVE, SENIOR CAPTIVE, SISTER CAPTIVE.

RENT RIGHT The financial benefit granted to an INVESTOR through a SHARE of COMMON STOCK, comprised of a PRO-RATA share of the discounted future CASH FLOWS of the company (which manifests itself via share price appreciation) and any periodic DIVIDENDS that might be paid. See also CONTROL RIGHT.

RENTES [FR] In France, a PERPETUAL BOND issued by the government which pays a FIXED RATE of INTEREST.

REOPENING A SECONDARY OFFERING of a new TRANCHE of SECURITIES under an existing issue with a defined COUPON and MATURITY. Frequent ISSUERS often use reopenings in order to concentrate LIQUIDITY in a smaller number of issues and establish more robust BENCHMARKS.

REORGANIZATION A state of corporate BANKRUPTCY that results in an agreement among CREDITORS and the bankruptcy court to restructure, rather than liquidate, an insolvent company. In order for a company to emerge from reorganization, creditors must be willing to accept concessions related to the value of their CLAIMS. A TRUSTEE, RECEIVER, or administrator is typically appointed to manage the affairs of the company while in reorganization and prepare a reorganization plan for court approval. If no trustee is appointed, the company itself becomes a DEBTOR-IN-POSSESSION (DIP) and must assume the responsibilities. If agreement is not reached on the reorganization plan the bankruptcy judge may order implementation via a CRAMDOWN or may opt for LIQUIDATION.

REORGANIZATION BOND See INCOME BOND.

REPACKAGING The process of converting an existing SECURITY into an alternate form through the use of DERIVATIVES or other financial instruments. The intent is to create a new ASSET or LIABILITY with a different PAYOFF or funding profile.

REPATRIATION The return of an individual or CAPITAL from an overseas locale back to a home country.

REPLACEMENT COST (1) In ACCOUNTING, the amount required to replace an ASSET based on its BOOK VALUE, accumulated DEPRECIATION, and obsolescence. In some cases replacement cost requires subjective input and judgment, particularly if the asset has become obsolete. (2) See ACTUAL EXPOSURE.

REPLICATION The process of duplicating an INDEX, HEDGE, or INVESTMENT strategy through physical ASSETS or DERIVATIVE CONTRACTS.

REPO [COL] See REPURCHASE AGREEMENT.

REPO RATE The INTEREST RATE a BORROWER pays a LENDER in a REPURCHASE AGREEMENT transaction. The repo rate, which is set according to the specific terms of the transaction (including MATURITY and underlying COLLATERAL), is generally lower than equivalent unsecured CREDIT from a BANK since the exposure is secured by collateral.

REPRESENTATION (1) A statement of fact that an INSURED provides to the INSURER when applying for INSURANCE coverage. An insurer routinely relies on representations as part of its UNDERWRITING process. (2) A statement of fact that an ISSUER of SECURITIES or a BORROWER under a CREDIT facility supplies to the BANK arranging the FINANCING. See also MISREPRESENTATION, WARRANTY.

REPRICING RISK The RISK that a maturing ASSET or LIABILITY will be reinvested or refinanced at a less favorable rate. Assets that reprice in a lower-rate environment and liabilities that reprice in a higher-rate environment create an opportunity cost or loss. Also known as REFINANCING RISK, REINVESTMENT RISK. See also NEGATIVE GAP, POSITIVE GAP, RATE-SENSITIVE ASSETS, RATE-SENSITIVE LIABILITIES.

REPUDIATION The act of abrogating, or refusing to perform legal requirements under, a CONTRACT.

REPURCHASE AGREEMENT A financial transaction involving the sale, and future repurchase, of securities for cash. Through the exchange, the repurchase agreement party effectively borrows money from the REVERSE REPURCHASE AGREEMENT party on a collateralized basis, paying a financing charge (REPO RATE) for doing so. Repurchase agreements carry MATURITIES ranging from overnight to several months, and are generally secured by high-quality COLLATERAL such as US TREASURY NOTES, TREASURY BONDS, JAPANESE GOVERNMENT BONDS, GILTS, or BUNDS. Repurchase agreements are generally MARKED-TO-MARKET daily via the reverse party, and MARGIN is called or returned as needed. Also known as REPO. See also DOLLAR ROLL, GENERAL COLLATERAL, GENSAKI, OPEN REPURCHASE AGREEMENT, OVERNIGHT REPURCHASE AGREEMENT, SPECIAL, TERM REPURCHASE AGREEMENT.

REPUTATIONAL RISK The RISK a company faces in negative publicity or damage to its public image, resulting in a negative impact on its ability to conduct business. Reputational risk is often classified as a form of OPERATIONAL RISK.

REQUEST FOR PROPOSAL (RFP) An invitation given by a company to suppliers of goods/services to submit a bid for the provision of such goods/services based on specific parameters specified by the company.

RESALE See REVERSE REPURCHASE AGREEMENT.

RESCHEDULING Negotiation between a CREDITOR and a DEBTOR on an existing LOAN with new terms and conditions, including those that may be more favorable to the debtor, in order to avoid any instance of nonaccrual or FORECLOSURE. Also known as DEBT RESTRUCTURING. See also DEBT FORGIVENESS, RENEGOTIATED LOAN, RESTRUCTURING.

RESCISSION   The cancellation of a CONTRACT by mutual agreement or court order, which returns the parties to their positions prior to the commencement of the contract.

RESERVE ASSETS   (1) Any ASSETS that are available to a country for financing BALANCE OF PAYMENTS imbalances and for intervening in the FOREIGN EXCHANGE markets. (2) Funds held by a BANK with a CENTRAL BANK.

RESERVE BANK OF AUSTRALIA (RBA)   The CENTRAL BANK of Australia, established in 1911 as the Commonwealth Bank of Australia, with all powers and duties transferred to the successor RBA in 1959. The RBA is primarily responsible for conducting MONETARY POLICY via the Reserve Bank Board. It is also responsible for issuing CURRENCY, managing the domestic payments system, regulating FINANCIAL INSTITUTIONS and markets within the country, and managing the country's RESERVES.

RESERVE CURRENCY   A CURRENCY featuring full CURRENCY CONVERTIBILITY on the CURRENT ACCOUNT and CAPITAL ACCOUNT, and which is widely used in international TRADE, finance, and FOREIGN EXCHANGE transactions. Reserve currencies are typically associated with national economies that have strong industrial bases and low INFLATION rates. Dollars, EURO, sterling, and yen are examples of reserve currencies. Also known as HARD CURRENCY. See also CONVERTIBLE CURRENCY, EXOTIC CURRENCY.

RESERVE ORDER   An ORDER on an EXCHANGE that is only partially visible in the exchange's order book – the balance remains hidden, and is only fed into the order book as executions take place. Reserve orders are a form of DARK LIQUIDITY. Also known as ICEBERG. See also HIDDEN ORDER.

RESERVE REQUIREMENTS   A minimum percentage of total ASSETS that FINANCIAL INSTITUTIONS must hold in highly LIQUID form to ensure sufficient ability to meet DEPOSITS or other demand LIABILITIES as they mature or are presented for repayment. In addition to reinforcing LIQUIDITY, CENTRAL BANKS and monetary authorities often use reserve requirements as a tool of MONETARY POLICY.

RESERVES   Funds segregated by a company to cover future LIABILITIES, CLAIMS, obligations, or uncertainties. Reserves, which are often established as CONTRA-ACCOUNTS on the ASSET side of the BALANCE SHEET, may be designated in different forms. In BANKING these may include legal or regulatory reserves (noninterest bearing DEPOSITS held with a CENTRAL BANK) and LOAN LOSS RESERVES (funds set aside for NONPERFORMING LOANS). In INSURANCE they may include UNEARNED PREMIUM RESERVES (funds set aside to reflect the timing differences between upfront receipt of PREMIUM and the TAIL of written policies) and EXPECTED LOSS reserves (funds set aside to cover expected claims). In some cases reserves may be hidden or implicit, such as unrealized CAPITAL gains within a SECURITIES PORTFOLIO. In many systems ACCOUNTING rules control the establishment and release of reserves so that firms cannot use them to manipulate their EARNINGS.

RESET BOND   A BOND with a provision that allows the INTEREST RATE to be adjusted so that the SECURITY always trades at its original value. A reset bond can be beneficial for ISSUERS in a declining rate environment, but can be problematic if rates rise or CREDIT SPREADS widen; the act of keeping the bond trading at PAR VALUE through an upward adjustment in the rate can lead to financial pressures for certain issuers. See also RESET PAYMENT IN KIND BOND.

RESET OPTION   See PARTIAL LOOKBACK OPTION.

RESET PAYMENT IN KIND (PIK) BOND   A PAYMENT IN KIND SECURITY with a requirement that the ISSUER float additional BONDS to INVESTORS in order to keep the original securities trading at PAR VALUE. Reset PIKs are generally issued by weaker companies that are unable to secure better financing terms, and can prove risky: if the issuer's credit deteriorates and the price of the original bonds declines, it will have to issue more bonds, which will increase LEVERAGE, lower CREDIT quality, and result in further price declines and more issuance, in a self-fulfilling cycle. See also RESET BOND.

RESIDENTIAL MORTGAGE   A MORTGAGE that is granted to support the financing of a single family residential property. A residential mortgage can be structured as a FIXED RATE mortgage, ADJUSTABLE RATE MORTGAGE, or HYBRID ADJUSTABLE RATE MORTGAGE, with a MATURITY that can range from 10 to 30 years; INTEREST only options are also available. LOAN-TO-VALUE is typically set at 80%, though this can be lowered for lower credit quality borrowers (SUBPRIME MORTGAGE borrowers) or those choosing to disclose less financial information (ALT-A borrowers). See also GRADUATED PAYMENT MORTGAGE.

RESIDENTIAL MORTGAGE-BACKED SECURITY (RMBS)   A form of MORTGAGE-BACKED SECURITY where the COLLATERAL POOL underlying the security comprises of RESIDENTIAL MORTGAGES, which may be prime (high quality), subprime (lowest quality) and conforming (adhering to government programs and thereby benefiting from a government guarantee), or nonconforming (not adhering to government programs). Since residential mortgages typically allow borrowers to prepay the outstanding loan prior to maturity, PREPAYMENT RISK in an RMBS is relatively high and factors into the pricing of the securities. A standard RMBS is structured as a PASS-THROUGH SECURITY, giving investors partial ownership in a pool of residential mortgages and the attendant PRINCIPAL and INTEREST payments that occur over the life of the transaction. RMBS without specific GUARANTEES makes use of the SUBORDINATION mechanism to create TRANCHES with different CREDIT RATINGS.

RESIDUAL   See RESIDUAL SECURITY.

RESIDUAL INCOME   (1) INCOME earned from intellectual property, such as royalties. (2) Income earned over and above some RISK-FREE RATE or minimum HURDLE RATE.

RESIDUAL RIGHT   Discretionary powers and authorities delegated by DIRECTORS to EXECUTIVE MANAGEMENT, allowing executives to act as AGENTS and make decisions related to the daily management of the firm, including financing plans, ACQUISITIONS, INVESTMENTS, production and marketing, and employee matters.

RESIDUAL RISK   See BASIS RISK.

RESIDUAL SECURITY   (1) A financial instrument that can increase a company's DILUTION if EXERCISED into COMMON STOCK, including CONVERTIBLE BONDS, WARRANTS, RIGHTS, and OPTIONS. (2) The most junior TRANCHE in a SECURITIZATION, bearing the first losses from any DEFAULTS in the ASSET POOL; in exchange for this increased RISK, the security generally carries the prospect of greater RETURNS. The residual is the last element of the structure to receive cash, payable only after all other tranches have been serviced. The value of the residual is often quite uncertain as CASH FLOWS may be impacted by a number of dynamic market variables that can cause a cash flow deficit or surplus. (2) Also known as EQUITY TRANCHE, FIRST LOSS PIECE.

RESIDUAL VALUE   The anticipated value of an ASSET at the conclusion of a LEASE; value may be determined by prior agreement or through an independent appraisal at the conclusion of a LEASE or at the end of the asset's useful life. Also known as DISPOSAL VALUE. See also NET RESIDUAL VALUE, RESIDUAL VALUE GUARANTEE, RESIDUAL VALUE SECURITIZATION, SALVAGE VALUE.

RESIDUAL VALUE GUARANTEE   A contingent FINANCIAL GUARANTEE that provides a company with a CAPITAL infusion if it experiences a shortfall in the RESIDUAL VALUE of ASSETS that have been LEASED. See also RESIDUAL VALUE SECURITIZATION.

RESIDUAL VALUE SECURITIZATION   An INSURANCE-LINKED SECURITY that protects an issuing firm from the RESIDUAL VALUE RISKS embedded in a variety of fixed ASSET LEASES by shifting exposure to CAPITAL MARKETS INVESTORS. If the ISSUER experiences a shortfall in residual value, it reduces or suspends PRINCIPAL and/or COUPONS payable on the SECURITIES, thus protecting itself against the economic shortfall. See also CATASTROPHE BOND, LIFE ACQUISITION COST SECURITIZATION, MORTGAGE DEFAULT SECURITIZATION, WEATHER BOND.

RESIDUAL VARIANCE   ASSET RETURNS that deviate from the SECURITY MARKET LINE or a SECURITY/PORTFOLIO relationship. Residual variance can be computed via:

$$\varepsilon_{j,t} = r_{j,t} - (A + \beta_j \, (r_{m,t}))$$

where $r_{j,t}$ is the return on security j at time t, $r_{m,t}$ is the return on the market portfolio at time t, β_j is the BETA of security j, and A is the intercept of the security market line or security/portfolio relationship. See also ARBITRAGE PRICING THEORY, CAPITAL ASSET PRICING MODEL, CAPITAL MARKET LINE.

RESISTANCE LEVEL A TECHNICAL ANALYSIS charting figure of a SECURITY or INDEX price level that withstands repeated bouts of buying pressure. If the price manages to breach the resistance level after several repeated attempts, further upward moves may follow (as in a BREAKOUT).

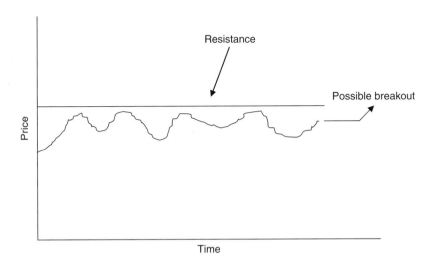

See also SUPPORT LEVEL.

RESOLUTION   A motion that is adopted by a specific body, such as a group of SHAREHOLDERS during the ANNUAL GENERAL MEETING of a company, typically through a majority vote in the affirmative. Once approved, it becomes part of the governing operations of a company.

RESTITUTION   (1) Compensation that is paid to a party that has sustained loss or injury by one who is responsible for causing the loss or injury, excluding noneconomic damages. (2) A refund of MONEY or property that belongs rightfully to another.

RESTORATION PREMIUM The PREMIUM paid by an INSURED to an INSURER to restore an INSURANCE POLICY to its previous limits after a loss has occurred and a SETTLEMENT has been received.

RESTRICTED RETAINED EARNINGS   See RESTRICTED SURPLUS.

RESTRICTED STOCK   SHARES of a company's COMMON STOCK granted to executives and employees as a form of compensation, and which generally vest over a multiyear period; awards may also be granted in the form of CALL

OPTIONS. Restricted stock grants result in the creation of new shares and are thus dilutive.

RESTRICTED SURPLUS In the United States, that portion of RETAINED EARNINGS that cannot be distributed via DIVIDENDS to COMMON STOCK investors. The restriction may occur, for example, as a result of arrears on CUMULATIVE PREFERRED STOCK dividends, which must be paid first. Also known as RESTRICTED RETAINED EARNINGS. See also UNDISTRIBUTABLE RESERVES.

RESTRICTIVE ENDORSEMENT An ENDORSEMENT on a BILL OF EXCHANGE that limits the ability of the bill to be further negotiated or transferred.

RESTRUCTURING The process of adjusting the LIABILITIES of a company in order to reduce the possibility of further FINANCIAL DISTRESS and/or to avoid BANKRUPTCY. A restructuring, which may involve a WAIVER, deferral, RESCHEDULING, STANDSTILL AGREEMENT, or exchange of liabilities, generally leaves CREDITORS with less value and/or more CREDIT RISK, and the company with a more manageable DEBT burden. Also known as DEBT RESTRUCTURING. See also DEBT FORGIVENESS.

RETAIL BANKING An element of BANKING focused on providing services to individual customers, primarily through CHECKING ACCOUNTS, DEPOSITS, SAVINGS ACCOUNTS, consumer LOANS, CREDIT CARDS, and MORTGAGES.

RETAIL INVESTOR An individual INVESTOR that generally transacts in relatively small amounts, and in simple (though not riskless) financial products. See also INSTITUTIONAL INVESTOR.

RETAIL PRICE INDEX (RPI) In the United Kingdom, an INFLATION measure based on the retail prices of goods and services (and also including rents, utilities, and MORTGAGE payments); all computations are inclusive of VALUE-ADDED TAX. A separate INDEX (RPIX), which excludes mortgage payments, is also tabulated. See also CONSUMER PRICE INDEX, HARMONIZED INDEX OF CONSUMER PRICES, PRODUCER PRICE INDEX.

RETAINED EARNINGS The portion of a company's EQUITY CAPITAL account comprised of net EARNINGS generated and kept within the business, after all DIVIDENDS have been paid to COMMON STOCK and PREFERRED STOCK INVESTORS. See also RETAINED PROFITS. Also known as EARNED SURPLUS, EARNINGS RETAINED, UNDISTRIBUTED EARNINGS. See also PAID-IN CAPITAL.

RETAINED PROFITS In the United Kingdom, RETAINED EARNINGS.

RETENTION (1) Any RISK preserved, knowingly or unknowingly, by an individual or an institution. Unknowing retention might arise from misunderstanding the nature of an exposure, while knowing retention is generally the result of a conscious decision to keep a particular amount of exposure for financial or strategic reasons. (2) In INSURANCE, RISK retained by an INSURED through a DEDUCTIBLE, EXCLUSIONS, and/or POLICY CAP. Policies with large deductibles, small policy caps, and minimal exclusions result in less RISK TRANSFER and more retention. (3) In a NEW ISSUE of SECURITIES, the amount allocated to SYNDICATE members less the amount held in the POT. (1), (2) Also known as ASSUMPTION OF RISK. (1) See also PASSIVE RETENTION, RISK RETENTION.

RETROCEDANT   A REINSURER that CEDES RISK to another REINSURER through a RETROCESSION CONTRACT.

RETROCEDE   The process of transferring RISK from one REINSURER to another reinsurer through a RETROCESSION CONTRACT.. See also CEDE, RETROCEDANT, RETROCESSIONAIRE.

RETROCESSION   A form of REINSURANCE CONTRACT that allows a REINSURER to transfer designated RISKS to another reinsurer in order to manage and diversify its PORTFOLIO of REINSURANCE exposures. See also RETROCEDANT, RETROCESSIONAIRE.

RETROCESSIONAIRE   A REINSURER accepting RISK from another REINSURER through a RETROCESSION CONTRACT. See also RETROCEDANT.

RETROSPECTIVE AGGREGATE LOSS COVER   A FINITE INSURANCE CONTRACT that allows the INSURED to finance existing losses and losses INCURRED BUT NOT REPORTED by paying the INSURER a PREMIUM and ceding its LIABILITIES. The insured must still pay for losses above a specified amount when they are incurred, and thus retains some timing risk. See also LOSS PORTFOLIO TRANSFER, RETROSPECTIVE FINITE POLICY.

RETROSPECTIVE FINITE POLICY   A FINITE INSURANCE CONTRACT that allows the INSURED to manage the timing RISKS of LIABILITIES that already exist and losses that have already occurred. Common structures include the ADVERSE DEVELOPMENT COVER, LOSS PORTFOLIO TRANSFER, and RETROSPECTIVE AGGREGATE LOSS COVER. Also known as a POST-FUNDED POLICY. See also PROSPECTIVE FINITE POLICY.

RETROSPECTIVE RATING   In INSURANCE, the process of adjusting PREMIUM rates to reflect actual current year losses. The retrospective approach is based on an initial premium plus an adjustment as loss experience is crystallized.

RETROSPECTIVE SCRUTINY   A legal review by REGULATORS and other external parties of a bankrupt company's history of financial deterioration, with a focus on the actions of the BOARD OF DIRECTORS during the period leading up to FINANCIAL DISTRESS.

RETROSPECTIVELY RATED POLICY   A LOSS-SENSITIVE INSURANCE CONTRACT requiring the INSURED to pay an initial PREMIUM to an INSURER and, at some future time, make an additional premium payment (i.e., a retrospective premium) or receive a refund (i.e., a retrospective refund), depending on the size of any losses that occur.

RETURN   The economic value generated by an INVESTMENT, generally expressed as a percentage of the amount of the original investment. Return may be generated through DIVIDENDS, COUPONS, and/or CAPITAL GAINS. Also known as RATE OF RETURN. See also DIVIDEND YIELD, EXPECTED RETURN, RETURN ON ASSETS, RETURN ON EQUITY, YIELD.

RETURN ON ASSETS (ROA)   A measure of the RETURN a firm generates from the average ASSETS it holds during a reporting period. ROA can be computed via:

$$ROA = \frac{NI_n}{ATA_n}$$

where NI_n is net income in period n, and ATA_n is average total assets during period n.

  The higher the ratio, the greater the profitability of the assets.

RETURN ON EQUITY (ROE)   A measure of the RETURN a firm generates for SHAREHOLDERS that have supplied CAPITAL. ROE, which is not adjusted for the effects of FINANCIAL RISK or OPERATING RISK, can be computed in different forms, including:

$$ROE = \frac{NI_n}{EQ_n}$$

$$ROE = \frac{EPS_n}{BVEqPS_n}$$

where NI_n is NET INCOME in period n, Eq_n is EQUITY in period n, EPS_n is EARNINGS PER SHARE in period n, and $BVEqPS_n$ is BOOK VALUE equity per share in period n.

  The higher the ratio, the greater the profitability on invested equity. See also RISK-ADJUSTED RETURN ON CAPITAL.

RETURN ON INVESTMENT (ROI)   A measure of the operating RETURN a firm generates from a core base of CAPITAL resources, computed as:

$$ROI = \frac{EBIT}{TC}$$

where EBIT is EARNINGS BEFORE INTEREST AND TAXES, and TC is total capital, or the sum of COMMON STOCK, PREFERRED STOCK, and LONG-TERM DEBT.

The higher the ratio, the greater the operating profitability on capital resources.

RETURN PERIOD   In INSURANCE, the average time within which an event of a particular magnitude is reached/exceeded. The return period, which is inversely proportional to frequency of occurrence, is commonly used in analyzing CATASTROPHIC HAZARDS; the lower the frequency of occurrence, the longer the return period.

RETURNED CHECK   A CHECK that is returned by a PAYEE to the BANK on which its drawn as a result of insufficient funds in the DRAWER's CHECKING ACCOUNT. A returned check is generally subject to a BANK CHARGE.

REVALORIZATION   Replacement of a CURRENCY with a new one, typically as an attempt to signal a new start for a national ECONOMY and financial system that has been impacted by high INFLATION and a weak currency.

REVALUATION   The process of reassessing the value of an ASSET or LIABILITY to reflect a current value. Adjustments are carried through a revaluation RESERVE account.

REVENUE   The amount of MONEY received by a company for selling its goods or services, taking account of any merchandise returned or other monies refunded. The simplified revenue computation multiplies units sold by the price per unit. Also known as GROSS REVENUE. See also COST OF GOODS SOLD.

REVENUE AND CUSTOMS, HM   In the United Kingdom, the consolidated government authority formed in 2005 from the previously separate Inland Revenue and HM Customs and Excise authorities, now responsible for direct TAX collection, VALUE-ADDED TAX collection, and customs and excise DUTIES collection.

REVENUE BOND   In the United States, a municipal SECURITY that pays INVESTORS PRINCIPAL and INTEREST from specific REVENUE streams generated by the project funded through the bond. A revenue bond is generally a NONRECOURSE obligation, and is thus backed only by the project and not the credit resources of the municipal ISSUER. Revenue bonds can be issued as utility, housing, education, transportation, and health-care securities. See also GENERAL OBLIGATION BOND.

REVERSAL   A TECHNICAL ANALYSIS charting pattern that depicts a prolonged change in the upward or downward direction of a SECURITY or INDEX.

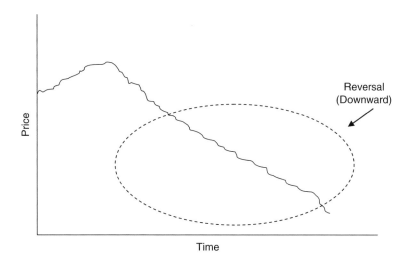

REVERSE   [COL] See REVERSE REPURCHASE AGREEMENT.

REVERSE BARRIER OPTION   A COMPLEX DERIVATIVE CONTRACT that creates or extinguishes an underlying IN-THE-MONEY EUROPEAN OPTION as the price of the market reference moves through a specified BARRIER. Four versions of the barrier option are commonly used, including the DOWN AND IN OPTION, DOWN AND OUT OPTION, UP AND IN OPTION, and UP AND OUT OPTION. See also REVERSE KNOCK-IN OPTION, REVERSE KNOCK-OUT OPTION.

REVERSE CASH-AND-CARRY ARBITRAGE   An ARBITRAGE strategy where a profit can be secured by buying a FORWARD or FUTURE, selling the UNDERLYING ASSET, and lending the proceeds until MATURITY. The arbitrage only works when the forward price is less than the SPOT PRICE plus the COST OF CARRY. See also CASH-AND-CARRY ARBITRAGE.

REVERSE CONVERTIBLE BOND   A BOND that can be exchanged into COMMON STOCK at the OPTION of the ISSUER rather than the INVESTOR. The issuing company might choose to convert if it is attempting to decrease its LEVERAGE and improve its overall CREDITWORTHINESS. See also CONVERTIBLE BOND, MANDATORY CONVERTIBLE BOND.

REVERSE DUTCH AUCTION   An AUCTION which features one buyer and many sellers, and where the price rises from a low BID until a party agrees to sell at the stated price.

REVERSE FLOATER SWAP   See INVERSE FLOATER SWAP.

REVERSE FLOATING RATE NOTE   See INVERSE FLOATING RATE NOTE.

REVERSE HEAD AND SHOULDERS   [COL] A TECHNICAL ANALYSIS charting formation of a SECURITY or INDEX that features a supporting price plateau, followed by a dip, and a reversal to a second supporting price plateau; the formation of a reverse head and shoulders might then lead to a BREAKOUT on the upside or downside.

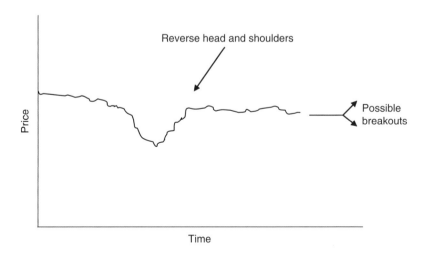

See also HEAD AND SHOULDERS.

REVERSE INDEX PRINCIPAL SWAP   An OVER-THE-COUNTER COMPLEX SWAP with a NOTIONAL PRINCIPAL that increases as a FLOATING RATE reference declines through prespecified BARRIER levels. As the notional increases, fixed and floating rate payments associated with the swap become larger. A reverse index principal swap can be used to HEDGE CASH FLOWS associated with an accreting ASSET. See also ACCRETING SWAP, AMORTIZING SWAP, INDEX PRINCIPAL SWAP, VARIABLE PRINCIPAL SWAP.

REVERSE KNOCK-IN OPTION   A BARRIER OPTION that creates an underlying IN-THE-MONEY option once the BARRIER is breached, i.e., the barrier is above the STRIKE PRICE in the case of a reverse knock-in CALL, and below the strike in the case of the reverse knock-in PUT. Also known as KICK-IN OPTION. See also REVERSE KNOCK-OUT OPTION.

REVERSE KNOCK-OUT OPTION   A BARRIER OPTION that extinguishes an underlying IN-THE-MONEY option once the BARRIER is breached, i.e., the barrier is above the STRIKE PRICE in the case of a reverse knock-out CALL, and below the strike in the case of the reverse knock-out PUT. Also known as KICK-OUT OPTION. See also REVERSE KNOCK-IN OPTION.

REVERSE LEVERAGED BUYOUT (LBO)   A transaction where a company that has been taken private through a LEVERAGED BUYOUT (LBO) is floated publicly through an INITIAL PUBLIC OFFERING. A reverse LBO generally occurs after the company has been streamlined and operating efficiencies have been created by the LBO management group.

REVERSE MERGER   See REVERSE TAKEOVER.

REVERSE MORTGAGE   A MORTGAGE where the BORROWER receives payments (monthly, lump sum, or as a CREDIT LINE) from the LENDER based on accumulated EQUITY in the property. The reverse mortgage comes due if the property is sold, required payments are not made, or the property deteriorates as a result of lack of care. In general, the transaction terminates when the last surviving borrower dies or sells the home.

REVERSE REPO   [COL] See REVERSE REPURCHASE AGREEMENT.

REVERSE REPURCHASE AGREEMENT   A financial transaction involving the purchase, and future resale, of SECURITIES for cash. Through the exchange, the reverse repurchase agreement party effectively lends funds to the REPURCHASE AGREEMENT party on a collateralized basis, charging a financing rate (REPO RATE) for doing so. Reverse repurchase agreements have MATURITIES ranging from overnight to several months, and are generally secured by high-quality COLLATERAL such as TREASURY NOTES, TREASURY BONDS, JAPANESE GOVERNMENT BONDS, BUNDS, or GILTS. Reverse repurchase agreements are generally MARKED-TO-MARKET daily via the lending party, and MARGIN is called or returned as needed. Also known as RESALE, REVERSE, REVERSE REPO. See also DOLLAR ROLL, GENERAL COLLATERAL, GENSAKI, OPEN REPURCHASE AGREEMENT, OVERNIGHT REPURCHASE AGREEMENT, REVERSE TO MATURITY, SPECIAL, TERM REPURCHASE AGREEMENT.

REVERSE STOCK SPLIT   A corporate action that increases the PAR VALUE of a company's COMMON STOCK while reducing the number of SHARES outstanding. A reverse stock split may be undertaken to improve the optics of the stock price level or reduce the administrative burden of tracking a larger amount of shares and SHAREHOLDERS; although there is no change in the MARKET VALUE of the company, a reverse split is occasionally viewed as a sign of financial weakness. See also STOCK SPLIT.

REVERSE TAKEOVER   The ACQUISITION by a smaller company of a larger company, or the acquisition of PUBLIC COMPANY (generally a SHELL COMPANY) by a PRIVATE COMPANY in order to gain a STOCK EXCHANGE listing. Also known as REVERSE MERGER.

REVERSE TO MATURITY   A REVERSE REPURCHASE AGREEMENT with a MATURITY equal to the maturity of the underlying ASSET being lent; a reverse to maturity often involves collateralization of high COUPON SECURITIES that the holder does not want to sell.

REVERSE TYING   [COL] A practice where a BANK or INVESTMENT BANK agrees to purchase goods or services from a company in exchange for the company's agreement to award it with lucrative fee-based NEW ISSUE or CORPORATE FINANCE MANDATES. In some jurisdictions the practice is illegal, as it constitutes a violation of fair trading practices. See also TYING.

REVERSE W FORMATION   See DOUBLE TOP.

REVOLVER   [COL] See REVOLVING CREDIT FACILITY.

REVOLVING BANK FACILITY   See REVOLVING CREDIT FACILITY.

REVOLVING CREDIT FACILITY   A secured or unsecured CREDIT line with a MATURITY ranging from 6 months to 5+ years that a BORROWER can draw down and repay multiple times. A typical facility requires the borrower to pay the BANK an annual COMMITMENT FEE on the entire line in order to keep it available for future use; those without a fee may be withdrawn by the bank at will. In some instances banks require borrowers to repay the facility in full before allowing further draw-downs or renewals (a process known as a CLEANUP CALL). Also known as LINE OF CREDIT, REVOLVER, REVOLVING BANK FACILITY. See also BANK LINE, COMMITTED FUNDING, EVERGREEN, LOAN COMMITMENT.

REVOLVING UNDERWRITING FACILITY (RUF)   A medium-term EURONOTE facility that guarantees the BORROWER funds through the issuance of NOTES or a draw-down under a CREDIT line. If the TENDER PANEL arranging the RUF on behalf of the ISSUER is unable to place the notes it supplies funds through a REVOLVING CREDIT FACILITY. See also NOTE ISSUANCE FACILITY.

RFP   See REQUEST FOR PROPOSAL.

RHO   A measure of the change in the value of an OPTION for a change in the RISK-FREE RATE, with all other variables held constant. The rhos of the CALL OPTION and PUT OPTION under the BLACK-SCHOLES MODEL are given by:

$$\rho_c = tXe^{-r_f t} N(d_2)$$

$$\rho_p = tXe^{-r_f t} N(-d_2)$$

where

$$d_2 = \frac{\ln\left(\frac{S}{X}\right) + \left(r_f - \frac{\sigma^2}{2}\right)t}{\sigma\sqrt{t}}$$

S is the stock price, X is the STRIKE PRICE, t is the time to MATURITY, r_f is the risk-free rate, σ_2 is the VARIANCE, and where the N value of $N(d_2)$ can be obtained from a standard table of PROBABILITY functions.

The rhos of LONG and SHORT puts and calls are shown as:

	Long call	Long put	Short call	Short put
Rho	+	−	+	−

See also DELTA, GAMMA, GREEKS, VEGA, THETA.

RIBA   [ARB] INTEREST payable or receivable on a CONTRACT, which is prohibited under the rules of ISLAMIC FINANCE. See also GHARAR.

RICH   [COL] An ASSET that is perceived by market participants to be expensive compared with alternatives (i.e., the SPREAD is too narrow in the case of a risky BOND or the price too high in the case of a COMMON STOCK, CURRENCY, or COMMODITY). Those believing the asset is rich will seek to profit by selling it, either directly or through an ARBITRAGE transaction. See also CHEAP.

RIDER   An ENDORSEMENT to an INSURANCE POLICY that modifies the provisions of coverage. The terms contained in the rider supersede those contained in the original policy.

RIDING THE CURVE   [COL] See ROLLING DOWN THE CURVE.

RIGHT OF SUBSTITUTION   The legal ability for a BORROWER and/or LENDER to replace COLLATERAL securing a financial transaction with other ASSETS that feature at least the same minimum value and marketability.

RIGHTS ISSUE   An offer of new COMMON STOCK to existing SHAREHOLDERS at a DISCOUNT to the company's current STOCK price, in an amount proportional to existing holdings; rights that are not EXERCISED or sold to other INVESTORS may be taken up by an UNDERWRITING group through a STANDBY COMMITMENT. A rights issue must be arranged if new EQUITY is sought, unless a company has already arranged for a WAIVER OF PREEMPTIVE RIGHTS. Also known as PRIVILEGED SUBSCRIPTION ISSUE, RIGHTS OFFERING, SUBSCRIPTION RIGHTS. See also SUBSCRIPTION WARRANT.

RIGHTS OFFERING   See RIGHTS ISSUE.

RIGHTSIZING   [COL] The process of restructuring corporate operations, typically through employee redundancies, ASSET sales, and/or discontinuation of certain products, services, or business divisions.

RING-FENCING   The process of legally or structurally isolating a portion of a company's ASSETS or business operations into a separate SUBSIDIARY or management unit in order to allow it to file for BANKRUPTCY or to be sold or wound down.

RING TRADING   A TRADING mechanism used on EXCHANGES that still feature physical, rather than electronic, trading, where BROKERS, DEALERS, and/or MARKET MAKERS assemble at appointed times in a "ring" to make a market in a particular ASSET. Also known as CALLOVER. See also OPEN OUTCRY.

RIO TRADE   [COL] A large TRADE executed in an attempt to reverse losses on existing positions; thus named because if the strategy fails the trader may be tempted to flee, e.g. take the next plane to Rio.

RISING BOTTOM   A TECHNICAL ANALYSIS charting figure of a SECURITY or INDEX depicting rising prices and an increasing support level; a rising bottom is generally considered to be a BULLISH signal.

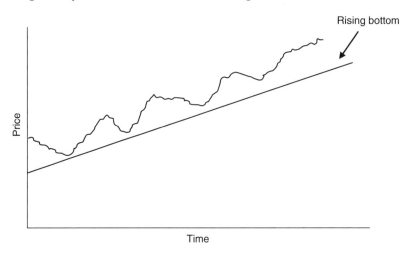

See also ASCENDING TOP, DESCENDING BOTTOM, FALLING TOP.

RISK   Uncertainty or unpredictability associated with a future outcome or event. From a corporate and financial perspective, risk can be broadly divided into SPECULATIVE RISK and PURE RISK, and may also be classed as FINANCIAL RISK and OPERATING RISK.

RISK-ADJUSTED ASSETS   See RISK-WEIGHTED ASSETS.

RISK-ADJUSTED CAPITAL   ECONOMIC CAPITAL, calibrated for specific dimensions of FINANCIAL RISK and/or OPERATING RISK, which a company allocates internally to support unexpected losses. Riskier activities attract a greater amount of capital since they have the potential of generating larger financial losses; SPECULATIVE RISKS that a company assumes or preserves for profit reasons must therefore generate a greater RETURN than those that are less risky. Risk-adjusted capital is often estimated by applying a risk weighting to a class of exposure and then ensuring a minimum level of capital is kept against the risk-weighted exposure at all times. See also REGULATORY CAPITAL, RISK-ADJUSTED RETURN ON CAPITAL.

RISK-ADJUSTED RETURN ON CAPITAL (RAROC)   The RETURN earned on CAPITAL after adjustments for the effects of FINANCIAL RISK and/or OPERATING RISK. By risk-adjusting returns on CAPITAL, the true costs/earnings of risk can be properly compared. RAROC can be computed via:

$$RAROC = \frac{NI_n}{RAEq_n}$$

where NI_n is NET INCOME in period n and $RAEq_n$ is the RISK-ADJUSTED CAPITAL allocated in support of the INCOME-producing business in period n. An alternative computation adjusts the returns for riskiness and leaves capital unadjusted.

RISK ARBITRAGE   A common ARBITRAGE technique related to MERGERS and ACQUISITIONS, where an ARBITRAGEUR purchases SHARES in a TARGET company, while simultaneously arranging a SHORT SALE in the shares of the ACQUIRER. The investor is effectively betting on the PROBABILITY the transaction will be completed at the stated price terms: if the deal is consummated, the spread between the two share prices will converge to zero at closing date, otherwise the spread will widen. The characteristics of this strategy feature more SPECULATIVE RISK than PURE ARBITRAGE. Also known as MERGER ARBITRAGE.

RISK AVERSION   A characteristic of an individual or institution that prefers less, rather than more, RISK, and is willing to pay a price or accept a lower RETURN for protection/mitigation (through, for example, INSURANCE, DERIVATIVES, or other methods of RISK TRANSFER or HEDGING). See also RISK NEUTRALITY, RISK SEEKING.

RISK BUDGETING   A process of allocating RISK CAPITAL within an INVESTMENT PORTFOLIO, typically based on principles related to MODERN PORTFOLIO THEORY. Risk budgeting, through use of marginal and cumulative risk and RETURN measures, as well as tools such as MEAN VARIANCE OPTIMIZATION, seeks to balance the potential for losses with the possibility of generating returns within the PORTFOLIO CONSTRUCTION framework.

RISK CAPACITY   The ability for an institution to accept the transfer of RISK from another party. Risk capacity is generally based on an institution's financial resources, expertise, and operating mandate.

RISK CAPITAL   (1) The amount of ECONOMIC CAPITAL financial institutions require in order to support RISK-related activities, such as TRADING, LENDING, and UNDERWRITING. Risk capital may be allocated through internal processes and/or regulatory measures. For BANKS, risk capital is generally set as a percentage of the exposures arising from MARKET RISK and CREDIT RISK. For SECURITIES FIRMS net capital is allocated primarily against open market risks. For INSURERS risk capital is held in support of net INSURANCE written. (2) INVESTMENT capital pledged by a VENTURE CAPITAL or PRIVATE EQUITY FUND in a speculative venture. (1) See also REGULATORY CAPITAL, RISK-ADJUSTED RETURN ON CAPITAL.

RISK EQUIVALENT EXPOSURE   See POTENTIAL EXPOSURE.

RISK FACTOR   (1) A source of RISK, including one of a financial or operating nature. (2) A named risk included in FOOTNOTES to the FINANCIAL STATEMENTS of a company, an OFFERING MEMORANDUM, PROSPECTUS,

REGISTRATION STATEMENT, or other INVESTMENT offering intended to warn potential INVESTORS or STAKEHOLDERS on the possibility of loss. Risk factors may include MARKET RISKS, CREDIT RISKS, litigation, and so forth.

RISK FINANCING   The general class of RISK MANAGEMENT products and mechanisms that seeks primarily to shift the timing of RISK-related losses rather than their permanent transfer to a third party; an institution engaged in risk financing simply delays funding of losses until a future period. See also FINITE INSURANCE, FINITE REINSURANCE.

RISK-FREE RATE   The DEFAULT-free BENCHMARK INTEREST RATE accorded to sovereign nations with the strongest CREDIT RATINGS. The risk-free rate is often used as the base reference rate for the pricing of credit-risky LOANS, BONDS, and DERIVATIVES. See also DISCOUNT RATE, RISK PREMIUM.

RISK IDENTIFICATION   The first stage of the RISK MANAGEMENT PROCESS, where a firm defines its actual, perceived, or anticipated FINANCIAL RISKS and OPERATING RISKS. See also RISK MANAGEMENT, RISK MONITORING, RISK QUANTIFICATION.

RISK MANAGEMENT   The third stage of the RISK MANAGEMENT PROCESS, where a firm decides whether to control, retain, eliminate, or expand its FINANCIAL RISKS and OPERATING RISKS. This process may be guided by cost-benefit analysis, available financial resources, and corporate operating directives. See also RISK IDENTIFICATION, RISK MONITORING, RISK QUANTIFICATION.

RISK MANAGEMENT PROCESS   A four-stage process centered on identifying, quantifying, managing, and monitoring FINANCIAL RISK and OPERATING RISK. See also RISK IDENTIFICATION, RISK MANAGEMENT, RISK MONITORING, RISK QUANTIFICATION.

RISK MANAGEMENT TECHNIQUES   A broad group of methods, including LOSS CONTROL, LOSS FINANCING, and RISK REDUCTION, which companies and sovereign entities often use to manage FINANCIAL RISKS and OPERATING RISKS.

RISK MARGIN   See RISK PREMIUM.

RISK MONITORING   The fourth stage of the RISK MANAGEMENT PROCESS, where a firm tracks and reports its RISK exposures and communicates them to internal and external STAKEHOLDERS. See also RISK IDENTIFICATION, RISK MANAGEMENT, RISK QUANTIFICATION.

RISK NEUTRAL VALUATION   A framework, developed by Cox, Ross, and Rubenstein and used in certain OPTION pricing models, which indicates that as long as the expected RETURN and DISCOUNT RATE used as inputs reflect the same degree of RISK AVERSION, they have no impact on the price of an option.

RISK NEUTRALITY   A characteristic of an individual or institution that accepts the average RETURN or EXPECTED VALUE available on a given

INVESTMENT opportunity, is indifferent to different choices that provide the same return, or requires no excess return for assuming a risk. See also RISK AVERSION, RISK SEEKING.

RISK PHILOSOPHY   A formal expression of a firm's view on RISK, including its corporate goals related to risk, the focus of its risk activities, and STAKEHOLDER expectations regarding risk activities. See also RISK TOLERANCE.

RISK POOLING   A practical implementation of DIVERSIFICATION, and a fundamental mechanism of the RISK MANAGEMENT markets and the INSURANCE mechanism, based on the concept that independent (i.e., uncorrelated) risks can be combined to reduce the overall level of risk. Also known as POOLING.

RISK PREMIUM   (1) A payment made by a RISK-averse firm to a third party to secure *ex-ante* protection against financial loss from a specific risk exposure. (2) The MARGIN added to the RISK-FREE RATE to compensate for the risk of DEFAULT; the sum of the two yields the DISCOUNT RATE, or the total rate used to discount the value of future risky cash flows. (1) See also PREMIUM. (2) Also known as RISK MARGIN.

RISK QUANTIFICATION   The second stage of the RISK MANAGEMENT PROCESS, where a firm uses mathematical, statistical, or actuarial techniques to estimate the economic impact of FINANCIAL RISKS and OPERATING RISKS on its operations. See also RISK IDENTIFICATION, RISK MANAGEMENT, RISK MONITORING.

RISK REDUCTION   A RISK MANAGEMENT TECHNIQUE based on either withdrawal from a business with particular RISK characteristics or DIVERSIFICATION of exposures through RISK POOLING. The intent in either case is to reduce the overall level of FINANCIAL RISK and/or OPERATING RISK to a level consistent with a firm's RISK TOLERANCE. See also LOSS CONTROL, LOSS FINANCING.

RISK RETENTION   A LOSS FINANCING technique where a company chooses to preserve, rather than transfer or HEDGE, a portion of its FINANCIAL RISK and/or OPERATING RISK. See also HEDGING, RETENTION, RISK RETENTION GROUP, RISK TRANSFER, SELF-INSURANCE.

RISK RETENTION GROUP   A RETENTION vehicle, conceptually similar to a GROUP CAPTIVE, where several companies with similar RISKS combine and then spread their exposures via RISK POOLING.

RISK REVERSAL   (1) In the FOREIGN EXCHANGE market, the difference in VOLATILITY between OUT-OF-THE-MONEY CALL and PUT options with the same STRIKE and EXPIRY DATE, providing an indication of VOLATILITY SKEW and VOLATILITY SMILE. (2) See COLLAR.

RISK SEEKING   A characteristic of an individual or institution that seeks RISK, reflecting a preference for an INVESTMENT with a higher expected RETURN and higher average risk. See also RISK AVERSION, RISK NEUTRALITY.

RISK TOLERANCE   A quantitative expression of a firm's view on RISK, generally based on the amount it is willing to lose through exposure to FINANCIAL RISK and/or OPERATING RISK, the amount it can earn in assuming or preserving risk or must pay to transfer it, and the financial resources it has at its disposal to support risky activities. See also RISK PHILOSOPHY.

RISK TRANSFER   A LOSS FINANCING technique where one party shifts an exposure to another party, paying a small, certain cost (such as a PREMIUM or fee) in exchange for coverage of uncertain losses. A standard INSURANCE POLICY is a common risk transfer mechanism. See also RISK RETENTION, HEDGING.

RISK-WEIGHTED ASSETS (RWA)   ASSETS of a BANK that have been adjusted, or weighted, by specific RISK WEIGHTS that are designed to reflect their relative degree of RISK. The weights are governed by BASLE II for participating banks, and range from 0% for cash and high-quality GOVERNMENT SECURITIES to 100% for LOANS to less creditworthy borrowers. OFF-BALANCE SHEET contracts are included in the risk adjustment process. Also known as RISK-ADJUSTED ASSETS.

RISK WEIGHTS   The assignment of weights to specific classes of RISKS, used in the computation of RISK-WEIGHTED ASSETS for CAPITAL ADEQUACY purposes under the STANDARDIZED APPROACH of BASLE II.

Obligations of sovereigns:

Credit rating	AAA to AA–	A+ to A–	BBB+ to BBB–	B+ to B–	Below B–	Unrated
Risk weight (%)	0	20	50	100	150	100

Note that claims on supranationals carry a risk weight of 0%

Obligations of banks and securities companies:

Credit rating	AAA to AA–	A+ to A–	BBB+ to BBB–	B+ to B–	Below B–	Unrated
Risk weight (%)	20	50	100	100	150	100

Obligations of corporates:

Credit rating	AAA to AA–	A+ to A–	BBB+ to BBB–	Below B–	Unrated
Risk weight (%)	20	50	100	150	100

Retail products (credit cards, auto loans, personal finance, and small business) risk weight: 75%

Residential property risk weight: 35%

Commercial real estate risk weight: 100%

Other assets risk weight: 100%

Cash risk weight: 0%

RMBS   See RESIDENTIAL MORTGAGE-BACKED SECURITY.

ROA   See RETURN ON ASSETS.

ROADSHOW   [COL] A series of sales and marketing presentations held for INSTITUTIONAL INVESTORS by a company or sovereign entity preparing to launch a NEW ISSUE of SECURITIES; the focus of such meetings is on the ISSUER'S financial standing and prospects, and on a general review of the planned new issue. Roadshows are typically arranged and managed by the LEAD MANAGER and/or other institutions forming part of the SYNDICATE. Also known as DOG AND PONY SHOW. See also NONDEAL ROADSHOW.

ROE   See RETURN ON EQUITY.

ROI   See RETURN ON INVESTMENT.

ROLL DOWN   The process of exchanging one OPTION position for a new one with a lower STRIKE PRICE by closing out the original position. See also ROLL FORWARD, ROLL UP.

ROLL FORWARD   The process of exchanging one OPTION position for a new one with a longer MATURITY date by closing out the original position. See also ROLL DOWN, ROLL UP.

ROLL UP   The process of exchanging one OPTION position for a new one with a higher STRIKE PRICE by closing out the original position. See also ROLL DOWN, ROLL FORWARD.

ROLLER COASTER   [COL] See VARIABLE PRINCIPAL SWAP.

ROLLING DOWN THE CURVE   [COL] An INVESTMENT strategy involving the purchase of long-term BONDS in anticipation of CAPITAL GAINS as YIELDS decline. Also known as RIDING THE CURVE.

ROLLING HEDGE   A HEDGING strategy, generally applied to long-term RISK exposures, that requires the HEDGER to purchase or sell the NEARBY or NEXT NEARBY DERIVATIVE CONTRACT, close it out prior to MATURITY, reestablish it with the next contract, and so forth, until the final exposure being protected enters the LIQUID part of the market. Through this process the hedger effectively stacks, and then "rolls," the hedge from one contract to the next. Though the strategy reduces or eliminates DIRECTIONAL RISK, it creates CURVE RISK: if the near term FUTURES price is below the expiring contract price (e.g., the market is in BACKWARDATION), stacking and rolling is profitable, otherwise it is unprofitable. Also known as a STACK AND ROLL. See also STRIP HEDGE.

ROLLOVER   (1) The process of renewing or reissuing a REPURCHASE AGREEMENT, REVOLVING CREDIT FACILITY, EVERGREEN, DEPOSIT, COMMERCIAL PAPER, ACCOUNT PAYABLE, or NOTE coming due. The rollover provides the DEBTOR with continued funding and the INVESTOR/CREDITOR with continued RETURNS. (2) The simultaneous sale and purchase of FOREIGN EXCHANGE for one-day settlement, as in a SPOT NEXT or TOM NEXT transaction.

ROUND LOT A SECURITIES ORDER executed in the standard TRADING size associated with the security marketplace. Round lots typically carry lower COMMISSIONS or fees than small size ODD LOTS.

ROUND TRIP [COL] The purchase and sale of a SECURITY or EXCHANGE-TRADED DERIVATIVE, generally over a short period of time.

ROUTER LOGIC The mathematical instructions embedded in an ALGORITHM that indicate where to route each individual CHILD ORDER and/or a PARENT ORDER in order to take advantage of available trading LIQUIDITY. See also ORDER GENERATION LOGIC, ORDER PLACEMENT LOGIC.

RPI See RETAIL PRICE INDEX.

RUF See REVOLVING UNDERWRITING FACILITY.

RULE 144A In the United States, a SECURITIES AND EXCHANGE COMMISSION SAFE HARBOR allowing limited resale of SECURITIES that have not been registered (e.g., PRIVATE PLACEMENTS) among QUALIFIED INSTITUTIONAL BUYERS (QIB) and DEALERS, provided the maximum number of QIBs and the minimum size of their participation are specified in the selling documents or private placement agreement. Rule 144A is designed to create LIQUIDITY in securities that otherwise have limited marketability.

RULE 415 REGISTRATION See SHELF REGISTRATION.

RULES-BASED TRADING See ALGORITHMIC TRADING.

RUN See BANK RUN.

RUN TO SETTLEMENT Any EXCHANGE-TRADED DERIVATIVE CONTRACT that has been allowed to mature without being offset by an equal and opposite position or otherwise closed out, indicating that a physical or cash settlement will result.

RUNOFF Future CLAIMS that an INSURER expects to pay and which are already covered by RESERVES.

RUNNING BROKER An INTERMEDIARY BILL BROKER interposed between DISCOUNT HOUSES and bill holders, who brings the parties together but does not DISCOUNT bills.

RUNNING THE BOOKS [COL] The act of serving as a LEAD MANAGER in an UNDERWRITING.

RUNNING YIELD See FLAT YIELD.

RWA See RISK-WEIGHTED ASSETS.

S

S&L   See SAVINGS AND LOAN ASSOCIATION.

S&P 500   See STANDARD AND POOR'S 500.

SA   See SOCIETE ANONYME, SOCIEDAD ANONIMA.

SAFE CUSTODY   The process of keeping in trust with a BANK any ASSETS with physical value.

SAFE HARBOR RULE   [COL] A provision in law or REGULATION that permits a company to avoid LIABILITY if it is attempting to comply with rules in good faith. Examples include: the repurchase of TREASURY STOCK is permissible under rules that normally prohibit a company from repurchasing its own SECURITIES; the disposal of COLLATERAL upon DEFAULT by a COUNTERPARTY to a DERIVATIVE CONTRACT (or REPURCHASE AGREEMENT) is allowed under AUTOMATIC STAY rules that normally forbid disposal; the limited resale of securities that have not been registered is permissible under rules that otherwise ban such sales.

SALAM   [ARB] A prepaid FORWARD CONTRACT used in ISLAMIC FINANCE in order to adhere to rules which prohibit the exchange of RIBA (interest). See also IJARA, MURABAHA, SUKUK.

SALE AND LEASEBACK   A transaction involving the sale of a real ASSET by one party and an agreement to LEASE the same asset back from the acquirer on a long-term basis. The sale and leaseback allows the seller/LESSEE to inject LIQUIDITY into its BALANCE SHEET and the acquirer/LESSOR to obtain the TAX and financial benefits generated by the lease.

SALVAGE VALUE   The value of a CAPITAL INVESTMENT at the time of its disposal or discontinuation. See also RESIDUAL VALUE.

SAME DAY FUNDS   Funds that can be transferred or withdrawn on the same business day they are presented or collected, such as FEDERAL FUNDS transmitted via the FED WIRE or electronic transfers arranged via the CLEARINGHOUSE INTERBANK PAYMENT SYSTEM or CLEARINGHOUSE AUTOMATED PAYMENT SYSTEM.

SAMURAI   [JPN, COL] A BOND, NOTE, or CERTIFICATE OF DEPOSIT issued in Japanese yen in the Japanese markets by a foreign company. See also DAIMYO, GEISHA, SHIBOSAI, SHOGUN.

SANDWICH LEASE   A LEASE transaction where a party leases equipment from one party and then subleases the same equipment to a second party, becoming a LESSOR and LESSEE in the process both earning and paying lease payments during the life of the transaction.

SANDWICH SPREAD   Any OPTION SPREAD strategy that gains from low VOLATILITY, such as a LONG POSITION in a BUTTERFLY or CONDOR SPREAD.

SARBANES-OXLEY ACT 2002   In the United States, legislation enacted to improve CORPORATE GOVERNANCE, the quality of FINANCIAL STATEMENTS, and the accountability of a company's financial officers and executives.

SATURDAY NIGHT SPECIAL   [COL] A sudden TAKEOVER attempt by one company of another through a rapid and unexpected TENDER OFFER. See also DAWN RAID, PREMIUM RAID.

SAVINGS   The process of setting aside a certain amount of INCOME after EXPENSES have been paid and placing the funds in a SAVINGS ACCOUNT or some other INVESTMENT vehicle for future use.

SAVINGS ACCOUNT   A BANK ACCOUNT where a depositor earns INTEREST on the balance. Funds can generally be removed at will by the depositor, though some BANKS place term or notice restrictions.

SAVINGS AND LOAN (S&L) ASSOCIATION   In the United States, a state or federally chartered DEPOSITORY institution that is primarily involved in accepting retail DEPOSITS and granting residential MORTGAGES. Although S&Ls can also engage in certain commercial LOAN transactions, most retain their traditional retail focus. Also known as THRIFT. See also BUILDING SOCIETY, SAVINGS BANK.

SAVINGS BANK   A SAVINGS AND LOAN (United States) or BUILDING SOCIETY (United Kingdom), focused on retail DEPOSITS and residential MORTGAGES.

SAVINGS RATE   The degree to which households in a country allocate INCOME to SAVINGS. A low savings rate is indicative of higher consumption, and vice-versa.

SCALE EFFECT   See ECONOMIES OF SCALE.

SCALPER   [COL] (1) A MARKET MAKER or DEALER that charges an excessive SPREAD on a transaction, in contravention of established rules. (2) An INVESTMENT ADVISOR or BROKER that takes a position in an INVESTMENT before advising clients to do so, and then exits at a profit; such pre-positioning is illegal in certain national systems.

SCENARIO ANALYSIS   Hypothetical "what if" computations that reveal the PROFIT or LOSS impact from any RISK exposures that are subject to a particular market shock, such as a movement in EQUITY prices or FOREIGN EXCHANGE RATES, a shift in a YIELD CURVE, or a change in VOLATILITY or CREDIT SPREADS. Scenarios are widely used by FINANCIAL INSTITUTIONS to understand how PORTFOLIOS of MARKET RISKS or CREDIT RISKS react under various low-PROBABILITY/high-severity stress situations. The most extreme scenarios ignore any benefits obtained from DIVERSIFICATION and can be computed through techniques such as MAXIMUM LOSS. Also known as STRESS TESTING.

SCHATZ   [GER, COL] Abbreviated form of Bundesschatz, a subcategory of German GOVERNMENT BONDS (BUNDS), issued in the 2-year sector with fixed COUPONS. Two-year Federal savings NOTES (Bundesschatzbriefe) are also available for purchase by the retail sector.

SCHATZWECHSEL   [GER] A TREASURY BILL issued by the German government, generally carrying a MATURITY of 3 months.

SCHEDULE RATING   A pricing method for INSURANCE that involves modification of a general PREMIUM-rate class based on the specific characteristics of the coverage; the adjustment is typically based on charges or credits to a base premium. See also EXPERIENCE RATING.

SCHULDSCHEIN   [GER] Abbreviated form of Schuldscheindarlehen, or German certificates of indebtedness. Schuldschein represent transferable interests in LOANS between BORROWERS and BANKS; the certificates allow loan interests to be transferred to other INVESTORS, creating a certain amount of SECONDARY TRADING and LIQUIDITY in the CONTRACTS.

SCORCHED EARTH DEFENSES   [COL] ANTITAKEOVER DEFENSES designed to create a significant amount of "corporate destruction" if enacted. A company using scorched earth techniques may convey their existence to would-be acquirers in order to dissuade any potential action. See also CROWN JEWEL DEFENSE, DEAD HAND CLAUSE, LOBSTER TRAP, MACARONI DEFENSE, PAC MAN DEFENSE, POISON PILL.

SCRIP   (1) Physical CAPITAL certificates with value, such as a COMMON STOCK certificate or BEARER BOND certificate. (2) Temporary certificates issued for a STOCK SPLIT or a SPIN-OFF that can be used to purchase underlying SHARES of common stock.

SCRIP ISSUE   In the United Kingdom, a STOCK SPLIT.

SDR   See SPECIAL DRAWING RIGHT.

SEAQ   See STOCK EXCHANGE AUTOMATED QUOTATIONS SYSTEM.

SEASONED SECURITY   A SECURITY that has been outstanding in the SECONDARY MARKET for a period of at least several months and has a history of prices and volume. The established track record often makes seasoned securities more marketable than newly issued securities that have just completed the PRIMARY MARKET process.

SEAT   [COL] A transferable membership on the NEW YORK STOCK EXCHANGE, generally held by an individual (acting for his/her own account or as an officer, partner, or representative of a BANK, INVESTMENT BANK, SECURITIES FIRM, or BROKER/DEALER), which permits direct dealing on the floor of the EXCHANGE.

SEATS   See STOCK EXCHANGE ALTERNATIVE TRADING SERVICE.

SEC   See SECURITIES AND EXCHANGE COMMISSION.

SECOND BANKING DIRECTIVE   In the EUROPEAN UNION, a directive governing the ability and process for licensing of BANKS within the Union.

SECOND LIEN LOAN   A form of SYNDICATED LOAN where COLLATERAL CLAIMS securing the borrowing rank behind those of the first loan to be secured by the collateral (which may be considered the first lien loan). Second lien loans generally have less restrictions on any maintenance COVENANTS. See also COVENANT LITE LOAN

SECOND MORTGAGE   An additional MORTGAGE taken by a homeowner on the same property, which a BANK will only grant if the combination of the two mortgages is below a specified percentage of the appraised value of the property, and the borrower's income can support the DEBT SERVICE.

SECONDARY BANK   In the United Kingdom, a non-BANK FINANCIAL INSTITUTION that performs many of the functions of a BANK but does not typically offer CHECKING ACCOUNTS or SAVINGS ACCOUNTS.

SECONDARY DISTRIBUTION   A resale of existing SECURITIES on behalf of an existing INVESTOR, generally arranged by a BANK or SECURITIES FIRM; the seller, rather than the buyer, is obliged to pay COMMISSION for the redistribution. If the transaction involves COMMON STOCK, no new EQUITY is created and no DILUTION occurs; if it involves DEBT, no new LEVERAGE is added to the ISSUER's BALANCE SHEET.

SECONDARY MARKET   The general marketplace for buying and selling a SECURITY or ASSET that has already been issued or created. The secondary market for any particular asset varies by level of participation, VOLATILITY, REGULATION, and market need; some markets are extremely active and LIQUID, while others are ILLIQUID, trading only infrequently. Also known as AFTERMARKET. See also GRAY MARKET, PRIMARY MARKET, SEASONED SECURITY.

SECONDARY OFFERING   Any NEW ISSUE of SECURITIES that occurs after an ISSUER's inaugural PRIMARY OFFERING. See also ADD-ON.

SECONDARY PREFERRED STOCK   PREFERRED STOCK that is subordinate to an ISSUER's other preferred stock, including PRIOR PREFERRED STOCK. Such issues, which rank just above COMMON STOCK in seniority, are relatively rare.

SECONDARY RESERVES   RESERVES in excess of those that FINANCIAL INSTITUTIONS are required to hold for regulatory reasons. Secondary reserves are often used as an emergency buffer to meet unexpected obligations; accordingly, they are generally held in the form of very LIQUID, low-RISK SECURITIES that can be converted into cash very quickly.

SECONDARY TRADING   Any TRADING in SECURITIES or LOANS that occurs after PRIMARY MARKET issuance is completed. Secondary trading may take place through an EXCHANGE or OVER-THE-COUNTER. In certain cases MARKET MAKERS make TWO-WAY PRICES in order to ensure a minimum level of activity.

SECTOR OPTION   An OVER-THE-COUNTER or EXCHANGE-traded OPTION that references the price or VOLATILITY of an entire industrial or regional sector (e.g., BANKS, automobile manufacturers, technology companies, emerging markets). Although the sector contract provides DIVERSIFICATION among individual COMMON STOCKS, it still creates a concentration in a broad group.

SECURED   A FINANCING or LIABILITY that is backed by some form of support, such as COLLATERAL or GUARANTEE. See also UNSECURED.

SECURED CREDITOR   A CREDITOR that has lent MONEY to an individual or company on the basis of COLLATERAL. See also SECURED DEBT, UNSECURED CREDITOR.

SECURED DEBT   A BOND or LOAN that is collateralized by a CLAIM on the ASSETS of the BORROWER/ISSUER. Secured debt holders rank above all other claimholders in the event the borrower/issuer DEFAULTS. See also SENIOR DEBT, SUBORDINATED DEBT.

SECURED INTEREST   A legal CLAIM of the LENDER over ASSETS pledged by a BORROWER to secure an OBLIGATION. The security interest grants priority over unsecured creditors and provides the right of FORECLOSURE in the event of DEFAULT. Also known as LIEN. See also FLOATING CHARGE.

SECURED LENDING   Any form of FINANCING where the BORROWER pledges COLLATERAL to the LENDER to support repayment in the event of DEFAULT.

SECURITIES AND EXCHANGE COMMISSION (SEC)   A US Federal agency created in 1934 that is responsible for regulatory matters related to the public SECURITIES markets, including REGISTRATION, issuance, and TRADING of BONDS and EQUITY, oversight of INTERMEDIARIES participating in the markets, and protection of INVESTORS.

SECURITIES EXCHANGE ACT 1934   In the United States, the legislation that led to the creation of the SECURITIES AND EXCHANGE COMMISSION and the enforcement of regulations regarding the financial marketplace that were created in the Securities Act of 1933.

SECURITIES FINANCING   The general segment of transactions based on LENDING/BORROWING cash versus SECURITIES-based COLLATERAL. This includes general securities lending, REPURCHASE and REVERSE REPURCHASE AGREEMENTS, and BUY/SELLBACKS.

SECURITIES FIRM   A FINANCIAL INSTITUTION that is primarily involved in originating and issuing new DEBT and EQUITY issues, TRADING SECURITIES and other financial instruments, and executing TRADES on behalf of clients. Securities firms that also deal in the broadest range of CORPORATE FINANCE transactions are more appropriately considered INVESTMENT BANKS.

SECURITIES INDUSTRY AND FINANCIAL MARKETS ASSOCIATION (SIFMA)   In the United States, a trade group that represents the interests of

SECURITIES FIRMS, BANKS, and INVESTMENT MANAGERS, created in 2006 through the MERGER of two previously existing trade groups, the Bond Market Association and the Securities Industry Association.

SECURITIES INVESTOR PROTECTION CORPORATION (SIPC) In the United States, a government mandated nonprofit organization designed to provide INVESTORS with protection of funds in ACCOUNTS held by SECURITIES FIRMS. Each account is covered to a maximum amount through a fund that is financed by PREMIUMS levied on participating securities firms.

SECURITIZATION The process of repackaging ASSETS, LIABILITIES, or CASH FLOWS into tradable SECURITIES for RISK transfer or CAPITAL ARBITRAGE reasons. Securitizations are often based on MORTGAGES (MORTGAGE-BACKED SECURITIES), mortgage-backed securities (COLLATERALIZED MORTGAGE OBLIGATIONS), corporate BONDS (COLLATERALIZED BOND OBLIGATIONS), corporate LOANS (COLLATERALIZED LOAN OBLIGATIONS), RECEIVABLES, and INSURANCE risks (INSURANCE-LINKED SECURITIES). In a typical securitization, a TRUST or SPECIAL-PURPOSE ENTITY is established to issue NOTES (effectively ASSET-BACKED SECURITIES (ABS) to INVESTORS, using the proceeds to purchase the pool of assets which generate CASH FLOWS that provide PRINCIPAL and INTEREST to INVESTORS; a certain level of OVERCOLLATERALIZATION is likely to exist in the asset pool. Services may be provided by a TRUSTEE, CUSTODIAN, or AGENT. The ABS may feature internal credit enhancement through the issuance of multiple TRANCHES with varying degrees of SENIORITY/SUBORDINATION (as in diagram), e.g., in accordance with an established WATERFALL or TIME TRANCHING, the senior tranches receive PRINCIPAL before the SUBORDINATED tranches. Alternatively, the ABS may be secured through external credit enhancement, such as a LETTER OF CREDIT issued by a BANK or a guarantee from a MONOLINE INSURER. A BANK may also supply a LIQUIDITY FACILITY to bridge cash flow gaps.

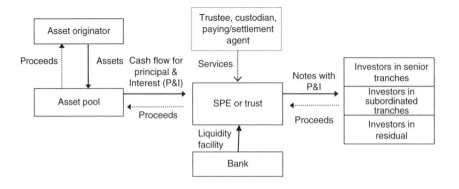

See also SYNTHETIC SECURITIZATION, TRUE SALE SECURITIZATION.

SECURITIZED ASSET   Any ASSET that has been structured through a SECURITIZATION process or program.

SECURITY   (1) A standardized, marketable, and tradable CAPITAL instrument, such as a BOND, COMMON STOCK, or PREFERRED STOCK, that provides INVESTORS with a particular RETURN for a given set of RISKS. Its standardization creates fungibility and thus a degree of LIQUIDITY. (2) A mechanism that provides an additional method of repayment on a financial transaction; common forms of security include GUARANTEES, COLLATERAL, and LETTERS OF CREDIT. (1) See also BEARER SECURITY, DATED SECURITY, REGISTERED SECURITY, SECURITIZATION, UNDATED SECURITY.

SECURITY MARKET LINE   A financial relationship linking the RETURN and the NONDIVERSIFIABLE RISK of a LEVERAGED SECURITY. The security market line depicts PORTFOLIOS that maximize RETURN for a given level of BORROWING and RISK (reflected through BETA). The expected return is given as:

$$E\left(r_j\right) = r_f + \beta_j \left[E\left(r_m\right) - r_f\right]$$

where $E(r_j)$ is the expected return for security j, $E(r_m)$ is the expected return for the market portfolio, r_f is the RISK-FREE RATE, and β_j is the beta of security j. See also ARBITRAGE PRICING THEORY, CAPITAL ASSET PRICING MODEL.
    Additional references: Jensen (1972); Merton (1973); Roll (1977); Ross (1976).

SEDOL   See STOCK EXCHANGE DAILY OFFICIAL LIST.

SEED CAPITAL   A sum of CAPITAL that is provided to a start-up firm to prepare business plans, prototypes, and basic hiring. Seed capital may be raised formally or informally, and typically precedes more robust capital allocations gained through VENTURE CAPITAL.

SEIGNIORAGE   The REVENUE a country derives from the issuance of CURRENCY. Excessive seigniorage can lead to instances of currency DEVALUATION and INFLATION.

SELF-ASSESSMENT   A process carried out by a TAX payer, where an estimate of tax due is computed based on actual and anticipated EARNINGS and is then sent to the relevant tax authority.

SELF-FINANCING   A state where a company is able to raise the financing it requires through its own operations, indicating that is does not need to rely on BANKS or the CAPITAL MARKETS for funding. In practice, companies often rely on a combination of self-financing and external funding to run their operations.

SELF-FUNDING   See SELF-INSURANCE.

SELF-INSURANCE   A method of RISK RETENTION where an institution preserves particular types and amounts of RISK and finances EXPECTED LOSSES by creating an internal fund or establishing a CAPTIVE. Self-insurance is generally applied to exposures that are highly predictable and noncatastrophic, or which cannot be covered by traditional INSURANCE contracts as a result of excessive cost. Also known as SELF-FUNDING.

SELF-INSURANCE RETENTION   See DEDUCTIBLE.

SELF-LIQUIDATING LOAN   A secured or unsecured WORKING CAPITAL LOAN that is repaid through the sale of the INVENTORY being financed; self-liquidating loans are generally used to finance inventories used to meet seasonal DEMAND for products. Also known as ASSET CONVERSION LOAN.

SELF-REGULATORY ORGANIZATION (SRO)   An organization that is granted oversight powers by REGULATORS in order to manage daily business affairs. An SRO establishes its own oversight guidelines based on overarching external REGULATIONS, approves the admittance of new participants, and supervises the activities of those already active in the marketplace. Certain STOCK and FUTURES EXCHANGES operate as SROs; they are typically divided into separate units, including one to deal with commercial business and the other to ensure that the business unit complies with all relevant rules.

SELF-TENDER   A STOCK BUYBACK arranged by a company based on regular open market purchases that increases the TREASURY STOCK CONTRA-ACCOUNT and reduces the EQUITY account. A self-tender might be used when a company believes it periodically has excess capital that is not generating an adequate RETURN for SHAREHOLDERS.

SELL DOWN   The process of reducing exposure on a new LOAN or BOND, through SYNDICATIONS, participations, and sub-UNDERWRITINGS; the sell-down process generally applies to financial intermediaries that are not part of the original SYNDICATE or UNDERWRITING GROUP.

SELL PLUS ORDER   An ORDER to execute a SECURITIES sale only if the price is higher than the preceding TRADE.

SELL-SIDE   [COL] FINANCIAL INSTITUTIONS, such as BANKS, INVESTMENT BANKS, MERCHANT BANKS, or UNIVERSAL BANKS, that provide services, including investment advice, NEW ISSUES, and other product offerings, and trading EXECUTION, to client firms in exchange for fees and commissions (i.e., "selling"). See also BUY-SIDE.

SELL THE BOOK ORDER   An ORDER to sell as much of a current position as possible at the prevailing market price.

SELLERS' MARKET   A market condition where DEMAND exceeds SUPPLY, causing prices to rise and giving potential sellers a greater opportunity to achieve a favorable OFFER price. See also BUYERS' MARKET.

SELLER'S OPTION   A transaction where the seller of SECURITIES has the OPTION to deliver a security at a future time, generally 6 to 60 days after TRADE date.

SELLING AWAY   [COL] An illegal practice where a BROKER at a SECURITIES FIRM or BROKER/DEALER sells clients' financial products originated by another securities firm. In the event of problems or losses, clients may not have RECOURSE to the broker's employing firm.

SELLING CONCESSION   The DISCOUNT at which a NEW ISSUE is allocated to SYNDICATE members. The selling concession comprises approximately half the UNDERWRITING SPREAD, or the difference between the price paid to the ISSUER and the public offering price.

SELLING GROUP   See SYNDICATE.

SELLING OUT   The process followed by a SECURITIES FIRM, BROKER/ DEALER, or BANK of disposing of SECURITIES or other ASSETS that a client has failed to purchase under the terms of an ORDER. The client is typically invoiced for any difference between the selling price and the order price.

SELLING THE WINGS   [COL] A practice of selling deep OUT-OF-THE-MONEY OPTIONS, allowing the seller to generate PREMIUM in the process. Though the options are struck far out-of-the-money and thus have a high PROBABILITY of expiring worthless, a sharp market move can force the SHORT option positions IN-THE-MONEY, increasing the payout to the buyer. Such short options are characterized by NEGATIVE GAMMA and negative VEGA.

SELLOUT   The process of liquidating a MARGIN LOAN or EXCHANGE-TRADED DERIVATIVE when payment is not received for SECURITIES or a VARIATION MARGIN call is not met. Sellout leads to *de facto* cancellation of the underlying loan or derivative.

SEMIVARIANCE   A statistical measure that focuses on all outcomes that occur below the MEAN. Such a measure is useful in an examination of loss distributions.

SENIOR CAPTIVE   A CAPTIVE that functions as an expanded form of the PURE CAPTIVE, writing a sufficiently large amount of third party business that it is generally entitled to greater TAX benefits than the pure captive. See also AGENCY CAPTIVE, GROUP CAPTIVE, PROTECTED CELL COMPANY, RENT-A-CAPTIVE, SISTER CAPTIVE.

SENIOR DEBT   (1) A BOND or LOAN that ranks higher in CLAIM priority than SUBORDINATED DEBT (JUNIOR DEBT). (2) See SENIOR UNSECURED DEBT.

SENIOR SECURED DEBT   A form of SENIOR DEBT with COLLATERAL or SECURITY pledged in support of repayment in the event of a BORROWER'S DEFAULT.

SENIOR SUBORDINATED DEBT   The lowest ranking form of SENIOR DEBT. Senior subordinated CLAIMS receive payment after senior INVESTORS or CREDITORS, but before JUNIOR investors or creditors and EQUITY investors.

SENIOR UNSECURED DEBT A form of SENIOR DEBT without any COLLATERAL or SECURITY pledged in support of repayment in the event of DEFAULT. Also known as SENIOR DEBT.

SENIORITY The ranking of a company's LIABILITIES within its overall CAPITAL STRUCTURE. In the event of BANKRUPTCY, the most senior liabilities receive recompense before less senior liabilities.

SEQUENTIAL PAY BOND A standard COLLATERALIZED MORTGAGE OBLIGATION that pays INVESTORS CASH FLOWS from the underlying MORTGAGE-BACKED SECURITIES in strict sequence. Subordinated TRANCHES only receive payments once senior tranches have been paid. See also PLANNED AMORTIZATION CLASS BOND, TARGETED AMORTIZATION CLASS BOND.

SERIAL BOND One of a group of BONDS issued by a single company or municipality that matures over a period of successive years. See also SERIES BOND.

SERIES BOND One of a group of BONDS issued by a single company or municipality under the same INDENTURE. Each bond in the series may have a unique COUPON and MATURITY. See also SERIAL BOND.

SERVICING (1) The process of collecting PRINCIPAL and INTEREST on LOANS generally, and MORTGAGES specifically. The function is generally performed by a FINANCIAL INSTITUTION acting as a TRUSTEE or servicing AGENT. In the mortgage sector the originator of the loan may retain the servicing rights, charging a fee for performing the function, or it may sell the rights to a third party. (2) Within the SECURITIZATION market, services to ensure timely and accurate payment processing, TAX and compliance reporting, ASSET tracking, delinquency monitoring, INVESTOR reporting, and similar functions, all of which are used to ensure the operational integrity of the securitization structure. The servicing functions may be carried out by primary servicers, master servicers, specialized servicers, or backup servicers, each with its own set of functions. (1) Also known as LOAN SERVICING.

SET-OFF A NETTING arrangement where an institution and a COUNTERPARTY in DEFAULT agree to terminate all transactions and net payments due or owed under all existing CONTRACTS. See also NOVATION, PAYMENT NETTING.

SETS See STOCK EXCHANGE TRADING SYSTEM.

SETTLEMENT (1) A process where two contracting parties complete an exchange of cash for an ASSET (PHYSICAL SETTLEMENT) or for its equivalent value in cash (CASH SETTLEMENT). When settlement is complete, a process that may take several hours to several days for standard financial CONTRACTS, the transaction is considered to be concluded. (2) In INSURANCE, the disposition of a CLAIM made by an INSURED under a policy, generally based on the degree of loss and the nature of the coverage. (1) See also SETTLEMENT RISK, VALUE DATE.

SETTLEMENT DATE   See VALUE DATE.

SETTLEMENT PRICE   (1) The last price at which an EXCHANGE-TRADED DERIVATIVE closes, typically computed on the last day of the delivery month. (2) The closing price on a COMMODITY or other traded ASSET.

SETTLEMENT RISK   The RISK of loss arising from failure by one party to a CONTRACT to receive cash or ASSETS after it has already delivered assets or cash to a second party. Settlement risk is common in the FOREIGN EXCHANGE and international SECURITIES markets, where time zone differences and local SETTLEMENT practices can lead to payment and receipt gaps of hours, days, or weeks. A subcategory of CREDIT RISK. Also known as CLEAN RISK, DELIVERY RISK, HERSTATT RISK. See also CONTINGENT CREDIT RISK, CORRELATED CREDIT RISK, DAYLIGHT RISK, DIRECT CREDIT RISK, SOVEREIGN RISK, TRADING CREDIT RISK.

SEVERABILITY CLAUSE   A COVENANT in a DIRECTOR and officers' LIABILITY INSURANCE POLICY that permits the INSURER to avoid making a SETTLEMENT payment if a director is found to have committed FRAUD; however, it must still pay legal fees and any judgments against all remaining directors.

SEVERAL BUT NOT JOINT   A legal condition where each party to a transaction is liable only for its part of the process and not all others; several but not joint LIABILITY is commonly used in the UNDERWRITING of BONDS, where each SYNDICATE member is only responsible for distributing the portion of bonds it has been allocated. See also JOINT AND SEVERAL.

SEVERITY RATE   A measure of the expected or potential size of a loss, used by INSURERS to compute appropriate PREMIUM rates.

SHADOW CALENDAR   [COL] A list of NEW ISSUES of SECURITIES that are currently in REGISTRATION with a securities commissioner or REGULATOR but which have no firm offering date. See also PIPELINE.

SHADOW STOCK   [COL] See PHANTOM STOCK.

SHANGHAI STOCK EXCHANGE (SSE)   The main STOCK EXCHANGE of China, formally established in 1990 (though its roots date back to the 1890s), and responsible for trading STOCKS, BONDS and FUNDS on an electronic basis. The SSE trades A-SHARES (denominated in Yuan) and B-SHARES (denominated in dollars), with the SSE Composite serving as the main BENCHMARK INDEX of the country. The SSE is one of three stock exchanges in China, operating alongside the HONG KONG STOCK EXCHANGE and the smaller Shenzhen Stock Exchange.

SHARE   A unit of STOCK representing partial ownership in the company that has issued the stock. The share represents certain RENT RIGHTS and legal rights, and in most instances is freely transferable.

SHARE ACCOUNT   In the United States, an ACCOUNT granted to a member of a CREDIT UNION, into which DIVIDENDS are paid.

SHARE CAPITAL   CAPITAL raised by a company through the issuance of SHARES to INVESTORS. See also AUTHORIZED CAPITAL, PAID-IN CAPITAL.

SHARE CERTIFICATE   In the United Kingdom, a STOCK CERTIFICATE.

SHARE DIVIDEND   In the United Kingdom, a STOCK DIVIDEND.

SHARE INDEX   In the United Kingdom, a STOCK INDEX.

SHARE OPTION   In the United Kingdom, a STOCK OPTION.

SHARE PREMIUM   In the United Kingdom, an ACCOUNT that reflects the difference between the PAR VALUE of SHARES and the issue price of the shares. It is treated as a form of UNDISTRIBUTABLE RESERVES. See also CAPITAL SURPLUS.

SHARE SPLIT   In the United Kingdom, a STOCK SPLIT.

SHAREHOLDER   An INVESTOR holding one or more SHARES of COMMON STOCK in a CORPORATION. In many jurisdictions each shareholder, as a fractional owner of the corporation, holds a legal right (e.g., the right to vote on specific issues) and a RENT RIGHT (e.g., the right to receive appropriate distribution of profits, which may include CAPITAL GAINS and/or DIVIDENDS).

SHAREHOLDER ACTIVISM   A process by which SHAREHOLDERS of a company use the legal rights inherent in their shareholdings to require the BOARD OF DIRECTORS to consider, and the shareholder body at large to vote on, specific issues. In addition to the formal process of shareholder voting, activism can extend to public or private dialog with directors or EXECUTIVE MANAGEMENT in an attempt to consider and resolve certain issues.

SHAREHOLDER VALUE   The total value of a PUBLIC COMPANY accruing to the SHAREHOLDERS. Maximization of shareholder value is a goal of many companies and is typically reflected through strong business operations which allow for payment of DIVIDENDS and an increase in the STOCK price.

SHAREHOLDERS EQUITY   The sum of a company's RETAINED EARNINGS and SHARE CAPITAL, reflective of any decrease through TREASURY STOCK purchases.

SHARES OUTSTANDING   See OUTSTANDING SHARES.

SHARK   [COL] An individual or institution that is able to detect any single strategy being used within the DARK POOL sector and use that knowledge to FRONT RUN or position itself to profit. This is typically done through ALGORITHMS that are specifically designed to identify revealing trading patterns. See also GAMING, PINGING.

SHARK REPELLENT   [COL] See ANTITAKEOVER DEFENSE.

SHARPE INDEX   A measure of RISK-adjusted PORTFOLIO performance that compares the RISK PREMIUM (or RETURN) of the portfolio with its risk (as measured through STANDARD DEVIATION). The Sharpe index, which uses the CAPITAL MARKET LINE as a BENCHMARK, can be computed via:

$$SI = \frac{E\left(r_p\right) - r_f}{\sigma\left(r_p\right)}$$

where $E(r_p)$ is the expected return of the portfolio, r_f is the risk-free rate, and $\sigma(r_p)$ is the standard deviation of the portfolio. In general, the higher the ratio, the better the investment strategy on a risk-return basis. Also known as SHARPE RATIO. See also TREYNOR INDEX, JENSEN INDEX.

Additional reference: Sharpe (1966).

SHARPE RATIO   See SHARPE INDEX.

SHELF REGISTRATION In the United States, a SECURITIES AND EXCHANGE COMMISSION rule that requires ISSUERS to file SECURITIES registrations only once every two years; this allows registration in advance for future issues of BONDS, COMMON STOCK, or PREFERRED STOCK. Once the shelf registration is filed, subsequent issuance need only be accompanied by a small amount of updated INVESTOR disclosure, allowing launch to occur at very short notice. Also known as RULE 415 REGISTRATION.

SHELL [COL] A form of corporate organization that holds no significant operations of its own, apart from certain ownership stakes in ASSETS or other INVESTMENTS, and which is often created for TAX-purposes in tax-friendly jurisdictions.

SHELL COMPANY A company that is registered, and in some cases listed on a STOCK EXCHANGE, but which has no specific operations. A shell company may be used in a REVERSE TAKEOVER by a PRIVATE COMPANY.

SHIBOSAI [JPN] A PRIVATE PLACEMENT denominated in Japanese yen, issued by a foreign company in Japan. See also DAIMYO, GEISHA, SAMURAI, SHOGUN.

SHIKKO YAKUIN [JPN] The corporate executive officer under the Japanese SINGLE BOARD SYSTEM, responsible for separating the supervisory and executive duties embedded in the BOARD OF DIRECTORS.

SHOCK LOSS A catastrophic loss that is so severe that an INSURER providing INSURANCE coverage related to the loss may suffer FINANCIAL DISTRESS. In practice insurers protect against shock loss by using REINSURANCE mechanisms and DIVERSIFICATION techniques, and establishing internal limits related to maximum UNDERWRITING exposures. See also CLASH LOSS.

SHOE [COL] See GREENSHOE.

SHOGUN [JPN, COL] A BOND, NOTE, or CERTIFICATE OF DEPOSIT issued in a foreign CURRENCY in the Japanese markets by a foreign company. See also DAIMYO, GEISHA, SAMURAI, SHIBOSAI.

SHOKEN [JPN] A Japanese SECURITIES FIRM.

SHORT   See SHORT POSITION.

SHORT AGAINST THE BOX   [COL] A practice of BORROWING SECURITIES from a SECURITIES FIRM or BROKER/DEALER and selling them SHORT in order to protect gains embedded in an offsetting LONG POSITION. From a TAX perspective, shorting against the box is generally considered a "constructive sale" that generates a CAPITAL GAINS LIABILITY.

SHORT ARBITRAGE   An ARBITRAGE strategy employed in the FUTURES market when the FORWARD RATE is higher than the futures rate, indicating that the cash market is underpriced to the futures market; the strategy calls for buying the UNDERLYING ASSET and selling futures. See also LONG ARBITRAGE.

SHORT BILL   A BILL OF EXCHANGE that is payable on demand or on very short notice.

SHORT CARRY   The CARRY generated by a SHORT position, defined for FIXED INCOME positions as daily financing income less daily COUPON cost. See also LONG CARRY.

SHORT COUPON   A COUPON falling between a normal current coupon period, often associated with the first INTEREST payment on a BOND or NOTE; subsequent coupons generally revert to a normal monthly, semiannual, or annual cycle.

SHORT COVERING   The process where BEAR INVESTORS or SPECULATORS with SHORT positions repurchase the STOCK or ASSET in order to reduce or flatten their shorts. Short covering occurs when a BEAR SQUEEZE is anticipated or underway.

SHORT END   [COL] The short MATURITIES of the YIELD CURVE, generally considered to include those less than 3 years. See also BELLY OF THE CURVE, LONG END.

SHORT HEDGE   A SHORT POSITION in a DERIVATIVE or financial instrument that is used to protect a natural LONG POSITION. As falling prices create a loss on the natural long position, the short hedge produces an offsetting gain; the reverse occurs with rising prices. See also LONG HEDGE.

SHORT INTEREST   The amount of SECURITIES or ASSETS sold SHORT that have not been repurchased or closed out. In general, the greater the level of short interest, the greater the likelihood that INVESTORS are expecting a decline in a security or market; however, a large short interest balance lasting for an extended period of time may also lead to buying pressure as short investors and SPECULATORS seek to cover their positions.

SHORT INTEREST RATIO   The ratio of shares of STOCK sold SHORT versus average daily TRADING volume, often used as a technical indicator to determine whether the market is OVERBOUGHT or OVERSOLD. See also SHORT INTEREST.

SHORT POSITION   A borrowed and sold position that benefits from price depreciation. In order to neutralize a short, the position has to be repurchased in the market; if the repurchase price is lower than the initial selling price, a profit results. The economics of the short position must take account of the financing costs associated with BORROWING the shorted ASSET. Also known as SHORT. See also LONG POSITION, NAKED SHORTING, SHORT SALE, SHORT SELLER.

SHORT RATE MODEL   A form of mathematical model used in the pricing of INTEREST RATE DERIVATIVES which relies on the use of a short (e.g., one period) rate as the center of modeling process, generally a RISK-FREE RATE. Short rate models may be constructed as SINGLE FACTOR MODELS or MULTIFACTOR MODELS. See also FORWARD RATE MODEL.

SHORT SALE   The sale of a borrowed position that establishes a SHORT POSITION. The party selling short expects that the market price of the ASSET, SECURITY, or INDEX sold short will decline. See also NAKED SHORTING.

SHORT SELLER   An INVESTOR, HEDGER, or SPECULATOR that engages in SHORT SALES in order to capitalize on expectations that the price of an ASSET, SECURITY, or INDEX will decline.

SHORT SELLING   The act of creating a SHORT SALE.

SHORT SQUEEZE   [COL] An attempt by one or more institutions to accumulate a sufficient amount of an ASSET so that higher prices can be demanded from those forced to cover (i.e., repurchase) their SHORT POSITIONS. Short covering exacerbates the situation, as more covering drives up the price of the target SECURITY, forcing more covering, and so forth, in a continuous cycle. A sustained short squeeze generally works only with assets that have unique characteristics and/or low TRADING volume. See also BEAR TRAP.

SHORT TENDER   The process of using borrowed COMMON STOCK to fulfill the terms of a TENDER OFFER.

SHORT-TERM DEBT   Any form of DEBT with a MATURITY of less than 1 year. See also CURRENT LIABILITIES, LONG-TERM DEBT, MEDIUM-TERM DEBT.

SHORT-TERM MONETARY SUPPORT   Funds made available by the EUROPEAN CENTRAL BANK to member nations that have not yet adopted the EURO for assistance in managing BUDGET DEFICITS. The funds are typically due and repayable within 3 months.

SHORT THE BASIS   An ARBITRAGE or TRADING strategy where a SHORT POSITION in a cash instrument is HEDGED by a LONG POSITION in FUTURES or FORWARDS.

SHOUT OPTION   An OVER-THE-COUNTER COMPLEX OPTION that allows the buyer to lock in any gains when a "shout" is declared (i.e., the buyer formally declares its intention to lock in); gains are not lost if the market subsequently retraces. See also CLIQUET OPTION, FIXED STRIKE SHOUT OPTION, FLOATING STRIKE SHOUT OPTION, LADDER OPTION.

SIFMA See SECURITIES INDUSTRY AND FINANCIAL MARKETS ASSOCIATION.

SIGHT DEPOSIT   Any form of DEPOSIT placed by a DEPOSITOR with a BANK that can be withdrawn on demand.

SIGHT DRAFT A BILL OF EXCHANGE, DRAFT, or NEGOTIABLE INSTRUMENT that is payable to the holder upon presentation.

SILENT PARTNERSHIP   A form of PARTNERSHIP where one of the PARTNERS provides CAPITAL but does not participate in the management of the operation. Also known as SLEEPING PARTNERSHIP. See also ACTIVE PARTNERSHIP, GENERAL PARTNERSHIP, LIMITED PARTNERSHIP.

SIMPLE BREAKEVEN A measure of the number of years it takes for the YIELD ADVANTAGE of a CONVERTIBLE BOND to cover the initial CONVERSION PREMIUM paid by the INVESTOR in acquiring the bond, typically computed as:

$$SBE = \frac{Conv_{prem}}{YA}$$

where $Conv_{prem}$ is the conversion premium and YA is the yield advantage. See also ADJUSTED BREAKEVEN, EQUIVALENT BREAKEVEN.

SIMPLE COMPOUNDING   See COMPOUNDING.

SIMPLE YIELD   A method of computing the annual YIELD on a BOND, commonly used in the JAPANESE GOVERNMENT BOND market. The standard form of the calculation is:

$$SY = \frac{C + \left[\frac{Par - P}{t} \right]}{P}$$

where C is the annual COUPON, Par is the PAR VALUE of the bond, P is the price of the bond, and t is the number of years until MATURITY. See also BOND EQUIVALENT YIELD, CURRENT YIELD, DISCOUNT YIELD, TAXABLE EQUIVALENT YIELD, YIELD TO CALL, YIELD TO MATURITY.

SIMULATION   A statistical process used to estimate the possible price paths of ASSETS over future periods by assuming that prices move randomly over time, but that possible values can be defined in terms of a particular distribution with known MEAN and VARIANCE and associated CONFIDENCE LEVELS. Possible future moves can then be used to value CONTRACTS and PORTFOLIOS with dynamic characteristics. Simulation is widely used in SCENARIO ANALYSIS and computation of DERIVATIVE prices and RISKS.

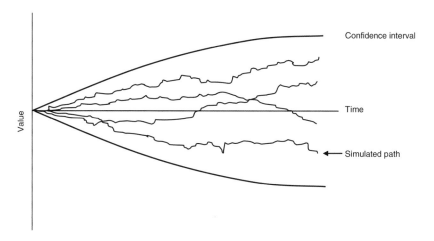

See also SIMULATION METHOD.

SIMULATION METHOD A process of estimating the FRACTIONAL EXPOSURE of an INTEREST RATE SWAP through the SIMULATION of future INTEREST RATES. Given a predefined statistical distribution, CONFIDENCE LEVELS, starting interest rate, time intervals, and mathematical relationship of future rate movements, a random generation of an artificial future path can be created, with swap REPLACEMENT COSTS calculated at each interval. Thousands of realizations yield a set of discounted swap replacement costs, and the average can be used as a representation of the discounted replacement cost at each time interval during the life of the swap. The sum of average discounted replacement costs generates a percentage RISK FACTOR that can be applied to the NOTIONAL PRINCIPAL to obtain the fractional exposure. See also HISTORICAL METHOD, OPTION METHOD.

SIMULTANEOUS PAY BOND See PLANNED AMORTIZATION CLASS (PAC) BOND.

SIN STOCK [COL] The STOCKS of companies involved in "sin" industries, generally taken to mean tobacco, spirits, and gaming.

SINGLE BOARD SYSTEM A corporate system where one BOARD OF DIRECTORS oversees and guides the activities of EXECUTIVE MANAGEMENT. DIRECTORS are generally nominated through an internal committee and/or management recommendations, and are formally elected by SHAREHOLDERS via PROXY at the ANNUAL GENERAL MEETING. The board is guided by the chairman (who may or may not also be the chief executive) and ranges in size from 10 to 20 directors, though it can grow to more than 30 in some systems. See also DUAL BOARD SYSTEM.

SINGLE FACTOR MODEL A form of mathematical model used in the pricing of INTEREST RATE DERIVATIVES in which all of the uncertainty related to the future movement of interest rates is captured in a single factor, generally a short-term rate. The entire TERM STRUCTURE is evolved from the single rate. Also known as ONE FACTOR MODEL. See also FORWARD RATE MODEL, MULTIFACTOR MODEL, SHORT RATE MODEL.

SINGLE LIFE ANNUITY   An ANNUITY that is paid only to the BENEFICIARY during his/her lifetime, with no subsequent transfer to a survivor.

SINGLE MARKET   The framework established in 1986 under the Single European Act requiring EUROPEAN COMMUNITY nations to create the framework for removal of barriers to TRADE, capital movement, and personal movement by 1992. Also known as EUROPE 1992.

SINGLE PARENT CAPTIVE   See PURE CAPTIVE.

SINGLE PEG   A MANAGED FOREIGN EXCHANGE RATE technique management where a country's CENTRAL BANK or monetary authority pegs the value of its currency to another CURRENCY. See also COMPOSITE PEG.

SINGLE PREMIUM INSURANCE   A form of life INSURANCE where the INSURED pays in one sum of money to secure the policy, rather than a series of regular PREMIUMS.

SINGLE STOCK FUTURE   A FUTURES CONTRACT where the UNDERLYING reference ASSET is a STOCK, generally a LIQUID, large capitalization issue. Single stock futures are traded on selective EXCHANGES.

SINGLE TEXT METHOD   A process where existing, and disparate, INSURANCE CONTRACTS are redrafted into a new master policy so that all covered PERILS are included under a single agreement. See also ATTACHMENT METHOD.

SINGLE TRANCHE COLLATERALIZED DEBT OBLIGATION   A form of SYNTHETIC COLLATERALIZED DEBT OBLIGATION (CDO) where the transaction is created with reference to only one specific TRANCHE of the CDO rather than the full CAPITAL structure. The single tranche, which can reference any portion of the structure (from the RESIDUAL tranche to the SUPER SENIOR tranche), is created by pooling individual CREDIT DEFAULT SWAPS, which serve as the reference pool. In some cases the transaction allows for dynamic substitution of reference credits in the pool.

SINKER   [COL] A BOND that contains a SINKING FUND provision in the INDENTURE.

SINKING FUND   (1) Funds that are accumulated in a segregated account in order to retire DEBT on a specific schedule. The sinking fund can be satisfied by direct contributions to the account or by redeeming or repurchasing the debt. (2) A SELF-INSURANCE fund that a company establishes to cover RISKS that it chooses to retain. (1) See also DOUBLING OPTION, SINKER.

SIPC   See SECURITIES INVESTOR PROTECTION CORPORATION.

SISTER CAPTIVE   A CAPTIVE formed as a licensed INSURER or REINSURER that acts as an extension of the PURE CAPTIVE, writing INSURANCE cover primarily for other companies forming part of the same "economic family," i.e., SUBSIDIARIES or AFFILIATES of the PARENT or HOLDING COMPANY sponsor. A sister captive may or may not receive the benefit of favorable TAX treatment, depending on the nature of the economic relationships between group companies and the amount of true third party business that is conducted. See also AGENCY CAPTIVE, GROUP CAPTIVE, PROTECTED CELL COMPANY, RENT-A-CAPTIVE, SENIOR CAPTIVE.

SIV   See STRUCTURED INVESTMENT VEHICLE.

SIV LITE   [COL] A form of a STRUCTURED INVESTMENT VEHICLE that features a finite life and generally a higher degree of LEVERAGE.

SIZE   [COL] A large offering of, or position in, SECURITIES or other financial ASSETS.

SKEWNESS   A measure of the symmetry of a statistical distribution. A distribution with positive skewness has a right-hand tail that is longer than the left-hand tail, while one with negative skewness has a longer left-hand tail. In a positively skewed distribution the PROBABILITY that the outcome is higher is larger than the probability that it is lower, and vice-versa in the case of a negatively skewed distribution. Skewness is often referred to as the third MOMENT about the MEAN. Skewness is given by:

$$\frac{1}{N\sigma^2}\sum_{i=1}^{N}\left(x_i - \mu\right)^3$$

where N is the number of observations, x_i is an observation, μ is the mean, σ is the STANDARD DEVIATION.

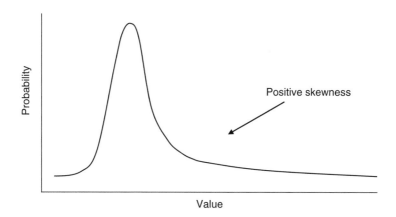

See also KURTOSIS, NORMAL DISTRIBUTION.

SKIP DAY SETTLEMENT   A market practice where the SETTLEMENT of SECURITIES takes place one day after the normal settlement day.

SLEEPING BEAUTY   [COL] A company that is a possible TAKEOVER candidate as a result of large cash holdings, undervalued ASSETS, and/or underperforming operations.

SLEEPING PARTNERSHIP   See SILENT PARTNERSHIP.

SLIP   A document prepared by a BROKER for an UNDERWRITER at LLOYD'S OF LONDON which contains all relevant information on the RISK being underwritten and the specific terms and conditions. The underwriter agreeing to accept the risk signs the slip, which is then circulated by the broker to other underwriters, until the coverage is completed.

SLOW LOAN   A LOAN where the BORROWER has become delinquent on INTEREST and/or PRINCIPAL payments; a slow loan must generally be reclassified as a NONACCRUAL LOAN and LOAN LOSS RESERVES must be allocated in anticipation of a possible write-off.

SMALL AND MEDIUM ENTERPRISE (SME) LOAN   A LOAN arranged and extended by a BANK or FINANCIAL INSTITUTION to a small or medium-sized company. The loan may have a fixed or floating INTEREST RATE and PRINCIPAL repayment that amortizes according to a set schedule or is repayable in the form of a BALLOON LOAN or BULLET LOAN. Since SMEs may not have the resources and CREDIT RATINGS of large, MULTINATIONAL COMPANIES, they may be required to secure the loan through a PLEDGE on specific ASSETS.

SMALL CAP STOCK   The COMMON STOCK of a company with a small MARKET CAPITALIZATION, typically under $1 billion. See also ANKLE BITER, LARGE CAP STOCK, MICROSTOCK, MID-CAP STOCK.

SMALL COMPANY   In the United Kingdom, a PRIVATE COMPANY with NET WORTH, REVENUES, and staffing that do not exceed specified levels, and which are therefore permitted to prepare FINANCIAL STATEMENTS according to a different set of rules than those applied to PUBLIC COMPANIES.

SMALL GROUP   In the United Kingdom, a group with NET WORTH, REVENUES, and staffing that do not exceed specified levels, and which are therefore permitted to prepare FINANCIAL STATEMENTS according to a different set of rules than those applied to PUBLIC COMPANIES.

SMALL ORDER EXECUTION SYSTEM (SOES)   An electronic EXECUTION system that bypasses BROKERS for AGENCY ORDERS of less than 1,000 SHARES on any NASDAQ-listed SECURITY.

SMALL PRINT   See FINE PRINT.

SMART CARD   A plastic card with an embedded microchip that contains details of the holder's financial and other records, and which can be used for a variety of purposes, including withdrawal or transfer of MONEY.

SMART MONEY   [COL] Sophisticated and successful INSTITUTIONAL INVESTORS that have a strong record of performance in INVESTMENT and which are often the first to identify and exploit market opportunities.

SMART ORDER ROUTER (SOR)   A coding mechanism in an ELECTRONIC TRADING platform that divides an ORDER according to the rules defined in an ALGORITHM and then selects the proper destination(s) so that EXECUTION can be fulfilled. An SOR maintains compliance with order protection and best execution requirements and generally permits prioritization of venues based on TRANSACTION COSTS.

SME LOAN   See SMALL AND MEDIUM ENTERPRISE LOAN.

SMOOTHING   [COL] The process of manipulating FINANCIAL STATEMENTS in order to create a more appealing, less volatile, picture of earnings. Though such smoothing is contrary to ACCOUNTING principles that mandate a true and fair evaluation of the financial position, it can be difficult to detect and prevent in all cases.

SMURFING   [COL] A process in MONEY LAUNDERING where a large sum of MONEY is divided into many small transactions in order to integrate it into the financial system without detection by the authorities.

SNAKE   [COL] A FOREIGN EXCHANGE regime developed in 1972 to keep certain European CURRENCIES TRADING within a BAND. The snake was ultimately replaced by the more robust and formalized EUROPEAN MONETARY SYSTEM.

SNIF   See STANDBY NOTE ISSUANCE FACILITY.

SNIFFER   [COL] An ALGORITHM that is used for PINGING and, ultimately, GAMING of a DARK POOL. Also known as SWEEPER.

SNOWBALLING   [COL] A market phase where the activation of STOP ORDERS leads to additional upward or downward market movements, which trigger more stop orders, and so forth, until a significant sequence of stops and market moves have occurred. See also GATHER IN THE STOPS.

SOCIAL SECURITY   In the United States, United Kingdom, and certain other countries, a government-run entitlement program providing retirees with retirement INCOME, unemployment income, and/or disability/health benefits.

SOCIALLY RESPONSIBLE INVESTMENT   A form of INVESTMENT strategy that considers social or environmental issues (in addition to RISK and RETURN parameters) during the PORTFOLIO CONSTRUCTION process. Socially responsible investment may be effected by specifically excluding certain types of corporate investments from a portfolio or by constructively engaging with corporate management, via SHAREHOLDER ACTIVISM and management dialog, in the promotion of certain behaviors or actions perceived to be socially beneficial. Fiduciary duties may preclude the involvement of certain INSTITUTIONAL INVESTORS in this sector, since this form of investment may not lead to a maximization of returns. In certain jurisdictions, legal restrictions may also place limits on the amount of socially responsible investment that can be undertaken. Also known as ETHICAL INVESTMENT.

SOCIEDAD ANONIMA (SA) [SPN] In Mexico, Portugal, and certain other countries a CORPORATION that is publicly traded. In all countries minimum CAPITAL requirements must be met in order to qualify.

SOCIETA A RESPONSABILITA LIMITATA (SrL) [ITA] In Italy, a LIMITED LIABILITY COMPANY.

SOCIETA PER AZIONI (SpA) [ITA] In Italy, a limited share company.

SOCIETE ANONYME (SA) [FR] In France, Belgium, Luxembourg, and certain other countries, a CORPORATION that is publicly traded. In all countries minimum CAPITAL requirements must be met in order to qualify.

SOES See SMALL ORDER EXECUTION SYSTEM.

SOFT CALL PROTECTION A CALL PROTECTION provision in an INDENTURE that prevents the ISSUER from calling and redeeming an outstanding SECURITY unless a certain price has been reached (for a standard BOND) or the STOCK price exceeds the CONVERSION PRICE by a defined percentage (for a CONVERTIBLE BOND). See also HARD CALL PROTECTION, NONCALLABLE BOND.

SOFT DOLLARS Indirect reciprocal payments made by clients to FINANCIAL INSTITUTIONS for services rendered. In commercial banking a client may be required to keep non-INTEREST-bearing COMPENSATING BALANCES with a BANK in exchange for a LOAN; in SECURITIES dealing a client may pay higher BROKER COMMISSIONS in exchange for research and other FIDUCIARY services. See also HARD DOLLARS.

SOFT LANDING A stabilization program enacted by a CENTRAL BANK or monetary authority that attempts to avoid economic RECESSION following a period of excess DEMAND and rising INFLATION. A soft landing may be difficult to achieve; if FISCAL POLICY or MONETARY POLICY is too accommodative INFLATION will continue, and if they are too restrictive a sharp slowdown will occur before stability can be regained. See also HARD LANDING.

SOFT LOAN A LOAN with favorable terms for the BORROWER, including below-market INTEREST RATES, long repayment periods, and a continual deferral or ROLLOVER of PRINCIPAL. A BANK may grant a soft loan in order to win future business, build a client relationship, or achieve some other relationship-driven goal.

SOFT MARKET An INSURANCE market cycle where excess SUPPLY of RISK CAPACITY from the insurance sector leads to lower pricing of PREMIUMS. A soft market arises when loss experience of INSURERS has been favorable for a period of time and insurers are willing to write new cover and expand business; the excess CAPITAL used to cover risks leads to an extremely competitive environment. See also HARD MARKET.

SOFTS [COL] A range of perishable COMMODITIES and related DERIVATIVES, originally applied to tropical commodities such as coffee, sugar, and cocoa, but now generally taken to also include GRAINS, cotton, and orange juice.

SOLE PROPRIETORSHIP   A form of business organization that features a single owner, who bears unlimited personal LIABILITY with regard to incurred DEBTS and the actions of employee. A sole proprietorship does not exist as a separate TAX-paying entity, meaning all INCOME generated by the operation is incorporated in the owner's personal tax returns. See also GENERAL PARTNERSHIP, LIMITED PARTNERSHIP, LIMITED LIABILITY PARTNERSHIP.

SOLVENCY   A normal state of financial operations for a company functioning as a going concern, where the value of ASSETS exceeds the value of LIABILITIES (i.e., positive EQUITY) and all DEBTS and OBLIGATIONS falling due in the normal course of business are paid on a timely basis. See also INSOLVENCY.

SONIA   See STERLING OVERNIGHT INDEX AVERAGE.

SOR   See SMART ORDER ROUTER.

SORT CODE   A numeric code contained on a CHECK that is used to identify the drawing BANK and the DRAWER'S ACCOUNT.

SOURCE AND APPLICATION OF FUNDS   In the United Kingdom, a CASH FLOW statement reflecting the nature and magnitude of financing and how the financing has been used, along with any resulting changes in WORKING CAPITAL. It has been replaced by the STATEMENT OF CASH FLOWS.

SOURCE OF CASH   A transaction that results in a cash inflow to a company; any source of cash is reflected in the CASH FLOW STATEMENT. Typical sources include NET INCOME, DEPRECIATION, medium- and long-term DEBT issuance, COMMON STOCK and PREFERRED STOCK issuance, decreases in ASSET balances (e.g., ACCOUNTS RECEIVABLE, INVESTMENTS), increases in LIABILITIES (e.g., ACCOUNTS PAYABLE, deferrals). See also USE OF CASH.

SOVEREIGN LOAN   A LOAN made by a BANK, MULTILATERAL DEVELOPMENT BANK, or government authority to another government.

SOVEREIGN RISK   The RISK of loss arising from an action by a sovereign nation, including DEFAULT, MORATORIUM, EXCHANGE CONTROLS, or currency DEVALUATION. A subcategory of CREDIT RISK. See also CONTINGENT CREDIT RISK, CORRELATED CREDIT RISK, COUNTRY RISK, DIRECT CREDIT RISK, SETTLEMENT RISK, TRADING CREDIT RISK.

SOVEREIGN WEALTH FUND   A government-owned INVESTMENT FUND, operated through the CENTRAL BANK or monetary authority, that invests in a range of real and financial ASSETS in a variety of other countries and marketplaces. Sovereign wealth funds typically apply a medium- to long-term horizon to their investment strategies.

SpA   See SOCIETA PER AZIONI.

SPARK SPREAD   [COL] A SPREAD in the energy market reflecting the price differential between natural gas and electricity; the spread can be traded through a single FUTURE or OPTION contract on certain EXCHANGES. A HEDGER or SPECULATOR can buy the spark spread (e.g., purchase gas and sell electricity) to take advantage of positive MARGINS in generation, and sell the spread (e.g., sell gas and purchase electricity) to profit from negative margins. See also CRACK SPREAD.

SPE   See SPECIAL-PURPOSE ENTITY.

SPECIAL   [COL] COLLATERAL in the REPURCHASE AGREEMENT market that is in tight SUPPLY, and which therefore allows a repurchase agreement BORROWER to obtain a lower BORROWING rate. See also GENERAL COLLATERAL.

SPECIAL CROSSING   In the United Kingdom, a restriction placed on a CHECK that permits the check to be deposited only in the named BANK.

SPECIAL DIVIDEND   A mechanism that enables a company to return CAPITAL to its SHAREHOLDERS; by granting a one-time DIVIDEND to current INVESTORS, it reduces the RETAINED EARNINGS account by the necessary amount. A company may declare a special dividend when it is consistently unable to identify INVESTMENT or expansion opportunities that can generate an adequate RETURN for investors. See also CUTTING THE MELON, STOCK BUYBACK.

SPECIAL DRAWING RIGHT (SDR)   A CURRENCY introduced in 1970 by the INTERNATIONAL MONETARY FUND to supplement national RESERVES and maintain FOREIGN EXCHANGE stability. The SDR is a neutral unit of account allocated in proportion to the GROSS DOMESTIC PRODUCT of each country, and is backed by the CREDIT of participating countries. The SDR is convertible into GOLD and HARD CURRENCIES.

SPECIAL-PURPOSE ENTITY (SPE)   An off BALANCE SHEET company, often incorporated as a BANKRUPTCY-remote entity in a favorable TAX jurisdiction, which is used to arrange SECURITIZATION, financing, DERIVATIVE, and/or tax-related transactions on behalf of the corporate sponsor. In order to avoid CONSOLIDATION into the corporate operation, an SPE may be established as a charitable TRUST that is nominally owned by a third party. To gain the benefits of particular transactions, the corporate sponsor must generally hold a nominal amount of the EQUITY. Also known as SPECIAL-PURPOSE VEHICLE, VARIABLE INTEREST ENTITY.

SPECIAL-PURPOSE VEHICLE (SPV)   See SPECIAL-PURPOSE ENTITY.

SPECIAL RISK INSURANCE   Customized INSURANCE coverage that is unique and situation-specific, and which cannot be priced through standard actuarial techniques or managed via RISK POOLING. The INSURER UNDERWRITING the special risk policy generally attempts to price the exposure as conservatively as possible and limit the amount underwritten. Also known as SPECIFIC INSURANCE. See also PUP COMPANY.

SPECIALIST   An individual or firm on an EXCHANGE that acts as a MARKET MAKER in a particular COMMON STOCK. The specialist manages an auction book of BIDS and OFFERS and attempts to maintain a balanced and orderly market at all times. Under certain exchange rules a specialist can deal for its own account as a proprietary DEALER but must adhere to AFFIRMATIVE OBLIGATION (i.e., taking one side of a TRADE if no offsetting ORDER is available in the market) and NEGATIVE OBLIGATION (i.e., not participating in a trade if an order can be matched).

SPECIE   Coinage issued by a country.

SPECIFIC EXCESS REINSURANCE An EXCESS OF LOSS (XOL) REINSURANCE CONTRACT written on a FACULTATIVE basis that provides cover for a PRIMARY INSURER's policy.

SPECIFIC INSURANCE   See SPECIAL RISK INSURANCE.

SPECIFIC RISK   See DIVERSIFIABLE RISK.

SPECIFIC STOP LOSS INSURANCE   An INSURANCE POLICY that becomes effective when a CLAIM breaches an INSURED's predefined SELF-INSURANCE threshold.

SPECULATION   A strategy that involves taking a position in an ASSET or market through financial instruments (e.g., STOCK, BONDS) or DERIVATIVES in an attempt to generate PROFITS; resulting gains and losses are not offset by underlying exposures/positions, as in a HEDGE transaction. See also ARBITRAGE, SPECULATOR.

SPECULATIVE RISK   A RISK exposure that yields the possibility of either a PROFIT or a LOSS. See also PURE RISK.

SPECULATOR   An individual or firm engaged in SPECULATION in an attempt to generate PROFITS. Speculators are an essential driver of market LIQUIDITY, helping balance or support flows arising from parties that are engaged in HEDGING or ARBITRAGE.

SPIDER   [COL] See STANDARD AND POOR'S DEPOSITORY RECEIPT.

SPIN-OFF   See DEMERGER.

SPINNING   [COL] An illegal practice where BANKS, INVESTMENT BANKS, or SECURITIES FIRMS UNDERWRITING a NEW ISSUE grant executives of favored corporate clients allocations in an attempt to win future CORPORATE FINANCE business.

SPLIT-COUPON BOND   A BOND that functions as a ZERO COUPON BOND for a prespecified period of time and then converts into a standard COUPON-bearing instrument, paying INTEREST on a regular basis.

SPLIT-OFF   See DEMERGER.

SPONSOR   A BANK that advises a company on an INITIAL PUBLIC OFFERING and arranges all dimensions of the process, including the creation of PROSPECTUS and the nomination of an UNDERWRITING SYNDICATE.

SPOO   [COL] The FUTURES CONTRACT on the STANDARD AND POOR'S 500 INDEX, traded via the CHICAGO MERCANTILE EXCHANGE, named after the ticker SPU allocated to one of the quarterly contracts.

SPOT   A transaction in the current, or cash, market. See also SPOT MARKET, SPOT PRICE, SPOT RATE.

SPOT MARKET   The current, or cash, market for an ASSET, which generally involves SETTLEMENT within 13 days (depending on the underlying asset). Also known as CASH MARKET. See also FORWARD MARKET.

SPOT NEXT   The purchase of FOREIGN EXCHANGE for delivery the day after SPOT delivery (which is generally two business days after TRADE date); the delivery price in a spot next deal is adjusted for the extra day. See also TOM NEXT.

SPOT PRICE   The price of an ASSET in the current, or cash, market. Also known as CASH PRICE. See also FORWARD PRICE.

SPOT RATE   (1) A FOREIGN EXCHANGE RATE in the current, or cash, market. (2) The theoretical rate on a ZERO COUPON BOND, derived from STRIPPING THE YIELD CURVE. (2) Also known as CASH RATE. (2) See also FORWARD RATE.

SPREAD   (1) In general, two or more financial instruments that are combined to produce an exposure to, or protection against, price or VOLATILITY references. The spread strategy can be applied to COMMON STOCKS, OPTIONS, FIXED INCOME SECURITIES, CREDIT references, or cross-market/ASSET classes. (2) In TRADING and market making, the difference between the BID and OFFER. (3) In a NEW ISSUE transaction, see UNDERWRITING SPREAD. (1) See also BULL SPREAD, BEAR SPREAD. (2) See also EFFECTIVE SPREAD, QUOTED SPREAD, REALIZED SPREAD.

SPREAD LOCK   A financial CONTRACT that GUARANTEES a BOND ISSUER or an INTEREST RATE SWAP party a fixed SPREAD over a reference BENCHMARK for a specific period of time prior to issuance or TRADE EXECUTION. The spread lock ensures that the issuance or execution price will be a function solely of the reference benchmark rather than of the CREDIT SPREAD. See also DROP LOCK, RATE LOCK.

SPREAD LOSS   A form of FINITE REINSURANCE where the CEDING INSURER pays a PREMIUM into an EXPERIENCE ACCOUNT every year of a multiyear CONTRACT period; the experience account generates an agreed rate and is used to pay losses as they occur. If a deficit arises in the account at the end of any year, the ceding insurer covers the shortfall through an additional contribution; if a surplus results, the reinsurer returns the excess. If the spread loss account is in surplus at the end of the contract, the ceding insurer and reinsurer share profits on a preagreed basis.

SPREAD OPTION   A COMPLEX OPTION that grants the buyer a PAYOFF based on the difference between two reference ASSETS versus a predefined STRIKE PRICE; the assets may be drawn from similar or different classes/markets. Also known as DIFFERENCE OPTION, OUTPERFORMANCE OPTION, UNDERPERFORMANCE OPTION. See also MULTI-INDEX OPTION, YIELD CURVE OPTION.

SPREAD RISK   The RISK of loss due to adverse changes between two reference ASSETS with a common link, such as a risk-free asset and a CREDIT-risky asset pegged to the risk-free asset. A subcategory of MARKET RISK.

SPRING LOADING   [COL] A form of financial manipulation where the pre-ACQUISITION EARNINGS of a company to be purchased are understated in order to give the acquiring company an earnings boost and the appearance of financial strength following the acquisition.

SPV   See SPECIAL-PURPOSE VEHICLE.

SQUARE   [COL] (1) A RISK position that has been neutralized, i.e., an offset between a LONG POSITION and a SHORT POSITION, or an UNDERLYING ASSET or exposure and its associated HEDGE. (2) The process of neutralizing the risk of a position.

SQUARE ROOT RULE   A statistical property used in financial mathematics indicating that the STANDARD DEVIATION of the changes in a market variable, such as a STOCK or BOND price, is proportional to the square root of time.

SQUEEZE   [COL] A lack of sufficient acceptable ASSETS deliverable into an EXCHANGE-TRADED DERIVATIVE or as cover for a SHORT POSITION, which can lead to price distortions. See also SHORT SQUEEZE.

SREP   See SUPERVISORY REVIEW AND EVALUATION PROCESS.

SrL   SOCIETA A RESPONSABILITA LIMITATA.

SRO   See SELF-REGULATORY ORGANIZATION.

SSE   See SHANGHAI STOCK EXCHANGE.

STACK AND ROLL   [COL] See ROLLING HEDGE.

STAG   [COL] See FLIPPER.

STAGFLATION   A phenomenon where INFLATION is increasing while economic output is stagnant or declining; UNEMPLOYMENT may also be rising at the same time.

STAGGERED BOARD   An ANTITAKEOVER DEFENSE tactic where an external TENDER OFFER for a company automatically triggers a change in the company's DIRECTOR reelection policy, from annual to staggered (e.g., only a third of directors reelected every year, so that the entire board can only be replaced over a 3-year period). This means a suitor will be unable to engage in a PROXY CONTEST to remove the board and undo POISON PILLS or other defenses within a 1-year time frame.

STAGS   Acronym for Sterling Transfer Accruing Government Security, a STRIP SECURITY in the UK GILT sector.

STAKEHOLDERS   From a GOVERNANCE perspective, the group of parties that have a legal, financial, and/or social interest in a company and its success, and are impacted directly or indirectly by the actions a company takes. See also DIRECT STAKEHOLDERS, INDIRECT STAKEHOLDERS.

STALKING HORSE   [COL] An INVESTOR that makes an initial BID for a bankrupt company's ASSETS. Once the stalking horse bid is submitted, other investors can join in the bidding process, but cannot bid below the initial bid.

STAMP DUTY   A TAX levied by authorities on specific types of financial transactions. The duty may be applied to an ISSUER of SECURITIES in the PRIMARY MARKET, a buyer and/or seller of securities in the SECONDARY MARKET, or a BORROWER of funds through a LOAN or other CREDIT mechanism.

STANDARD AND POOR'S 500 (S&P 500)   A BENCHMARK INDEX of the US stock market comprised of 500 LARGE CAP STOCKS representing the industrial, transportation, financial, and utility sectors; the index is rebalanced periodically as industries and corporate leadership change. The S&P 500 can be traded directly through EXCHANGE-TRADED FUNDS and DERIVATIVES.

STANDARD AND POOR'S DEPOSITORY RECEIPT (SPDR)   A tradable SHARE of a UNIT TRUST that holds a STANDARD AND POOR'S 500 portfolio (and that automatically adjusts for INDEX-REBALANCING). As in other EXCHANGE-traded FUNDS, the SPDR creates and redeems shares on a continuous basis, depending on supply and demand. Also known as SPIDER.

STANDARD DEVIATION   A measure of RISK, variability, or dispersion that indicates the magnitude by which an outcome will differ from the EXPECTED VALUE, or the degree to which an observation deviates from the MEAN of a distribution. It is generally computed via:

$$\sigma = \sqrt{\frac{\sum_{i=1}^{n}(x_i - \mu)^2}{N}}$$

where x_i is an observation, μ is the mean, and N is the number of observations. See also VARIANCE.

STANDARD RATE   The flat rate of VALUE-ADDED TAX (VAT) that is applied to any good or service in a VAT system unless it is specifically exempt, which varies by country.

STANDARD RISK   See PURE RISK.

STANDARDIZED APPROACH   A method of computing CREDIT RISK exposures under PILLAR I of BASLE II, which follows the framework established under the original BASLE ACCORD, where various classes of RISKS are assigned RISK WEIGHTS to determine capital requirements.

STANDBY AGREEMENT   (1) An agreement where the UNDERWRITERS of a RIGHTS ISSUE agree to purchase any unsold SHARES after SHAREHOLDERS exercise their PREEMPTIVE RIGHTS, thereby ensuring the company gains the full amount of anticipated proceeds. (2) Agreements between the INTERNATIONAL MONETARY FUND and its member countries that allow the members to immediately access supplemental funds for emergency purposes. (1) Also known as STANDBY UNDERWRITING.

STANDBY CREDIT   See STANDBY LETTER OF CREDIT.

STANDBY LETTER OF CREDIT   A contingent LETTER OF CREDIT obligation of the issuing BANK that becomes effective only if the drawing customer fails to perform on a specific transaction. If performance does not occur as planned, the bank automatically pays the BENEFICIARY of the letter of credit and then attempts to recover CASH FLOWS from the customer. Also known as STANDBY CREDIT. See also CONFIRMED LETTER OF CREDIT, DIRECT PAY LETTER OF CREDIT, TRANSFERABLE LETTER OF CREDIT, IRREVOCABLE LETTER OF CREDIT.

STANDBY NOTE ISSUANCE FACILITY (SNIF)   A banking facility that guarantees INVESTORS payment if the ISSUER of SECURITIES floated under a NOTE ISSUANCE FACILITY DEFAULTS on its OBLIGATION. The guaranteeing BANK charges the issuer a fee in exchange for assuming the contingent LIABILITY.

STANDBY UNDERWRITING   See STANDBY AGREEMENT.

STANDING ORDER   Authorization granted by an ACCOUNT holder to a BANK to allow for recurring direct DEBITS to be made in payment of a good or service.

STANDSTILL AGREEMENT   (1) A formal agreement between a RAIDER or acquiring company and a TARGET company, where the acquirer agrees not to purchase any additional SHARES in the target until further negotiations regarding a possible deal can be conducted. (2) An agreement by one or more CREDITORS not to force the collection of payment on a LOAN or FINANCING agreement in order to avoid an EVENT OF DEFAULT or CREDIT EVENT. Once a standstill has been agreed, the parties may seek a RESTRUCTURING of the terms and conditions of the financing. (2) An agreement between two or more BANKS providing CREDIT to a DEBTOR in FINANCIAL DISTRESS that they shall act in concert rather than independently in order not to force the debtor into BANKRUPTCY.

STAPLED STOCK   [COL] See PAIRED SHARES.

STATEMENT OF AUDITING STANDARDS   Official statements released by ACCOUNTING bodies indicating the specific principles and procedures that AUDITORS must follow when auditing a company.

STATEMENT OF CASH FLOWS   A key FINANCIAL STATEMENT produced by a company that reflects its CASH FLOW position. This statement draws together items from the INCOME STATEMENT and BALANCE SHEET to reveal the nature of the firm's cash sources and uses, and its net cash position at the end of a reporting period. The basic cash flow statement is generally divided into three segments: OPERATING CASH FLOW, INVESTING CASH FLOW, and FINANCING CASH FLOW, though this can vary somewhat by country, accounting regime, and/or industry sector. The summarized cash flow statement takes the following general form:

Statement of Cash Flows

Operating cash flow
Net income
+ Depreciation
−Increase in working capital
+ Decrease in working capital
= Net operating cash flow

Investing cash flow
Sale of securities
+ Sale of PP&E
−Purchase of securities
−Purchase of PP&E
= Net investing cash flow

Financing cash flow
Issuance of debt, stock
−Repayment of debt
−Repurchase of stock
−Payment of dividends
= Net financing cash flow

= Net cash surplus/deficit

Also known as CASH FLOW STATEMENT.

STATEMENT OF CHANGES IN FINANCIAL POSITION   In the United States, a statement reflecting changes in a company's CASH FLOW and WORKING CAPITAL balances, now generally reported by the STATEMENT OF CASH FLOWS. See also SOURCE AND APPLICATION OF FUNDS.

STATEMENT OF STANDARD ACCOUNT PRACTICE   In the United Kingdom, a series of ACCOUNTING STANDARDS developed by the Accounting Standards Committee, many of which have been superseded by the FINANCIAL REPORTING STANDARDS.

STATIC COLLATERALIZED DEBT OBLIGATION   A COLLATERALIZED DEBT OBLIGATION (CDO) that does not permit the manager to substitute reference CREDITS in the POOL. This form of CDO provides the INVESTORS with complete transparency on the composition of the PORTFOLIO and carries lower fees than MANAGED CDOs, but does not allow the substitution of deteriorating credits. See also SINGLE TRANCHE COLLATERALIZED DEBT OBLIGATION, SYNTHETIC COLLATERALIZED DEBT OBLIGATION.

STATISTICAL ARBITRAGE   A quantitative ARBITRAGE strategy where an INVESTOR or HEDGE FUND manager makes use of mathematical and statistical techniques to analyze certain indicators of individual STOCKS (e.g., DIVIDEND YIELDS, price/book value, and so on) and how these impact market performance in order to create a statistical model that can consistently outperform a BENCHMARK or market INDEX. Once a statistical arbitrage model has been developed and tested, it can be programmed to handle selections and buying/selling executions automatically. A successful implementation of this strategy yields small and consistent, rather than large and infrequent, profits.

STATISTICAL FACTOR MODEL A MULTIFACTOR RISK MODEL based on historical STOCK PRICE data that seeks to explain observable returns through identification of linear combinations of RISK FACTORS. The sensitivity of a stock price to each linear factor can be estimated through such a model, allowing the projection of EXPECTED RETURNS. See also FUNDAMENTAL FACTOR MODEL, MACROECONOMIC FACTOR MODEL.

STATUTORY ACCOUNTS ACCOUNTS or FINANCIAL STATEMENTS that must be prepared and submitted as indicated under relevant law statutes.

STATUTORY AUDIT An AUDIT that must be performed on a company or other organization as indicated under relevant law statutes.

STATUTORY BOND A SURETY BOND that a government authority or REGULATOR may require contractors, businesses, or FIDUCIARIES to post for work performance affecting the public interest. The intent of the statutory bond is to ensure adequate third party financial protection in the event the contract party fails to perform as intended.

STATUTORY DAMAGES DAMAGES awarded to a plaintiff that are limited by some relevant statute. See also LIQUIDATED DAMAGES, UNLIQUIDATED DAMAGES.

STATUTORY PROFIT In INSURANCE, a measure of an INSURER's profitability, typically defined as earned PREMIUMS less total EXPENSES and losses paid.

STATUTORY PROSPECTUS See PROSPECTUS.

STATUTORY RESERVE A RESERVE that INSURERS are required to maintain to ensure they can withstand potential losses from RISKS they have underwritten and can remain solvent. Methods of computing the minimum amount of the statutory reserve vary, although most are based on loss frequency calculations.

STATUTORY TAX RATE The legal mandated TAX rate applied to INCOME or sales. In many jurisdictions multiple statutory tax rates are applied to different levels of income, while a single statutory tax rate is applied to sales (e.g., a flat sales tax). See also AVERAGE TAX RATE, EFFECTIVE TAX RATE, MARGINAL TAX RATE.

STATUTORY VOTING The conventional corporate method of assigning one SHAREHOLDER vote to each share of COMMON STOCK and requiring that each vote be apportioned equally to DIRECTOR nominees. See also CUMULATIVE VOTING.

STEP-DOWN BOND A BOND (or NOTE) that pays a decreasing COUPON during the life of the SECURITY. The security may be putable by the INVESTOR at predefined dates. See also STEP-UP BOND.

STEP-UP BOND A BOND (or NOTE) that pays an increasing COUPON if the SECURITY is not called by the ISSUER. The step-up may occur on one or several predefined dates. See also STEP-DOWN BOND.

STERILIZATION Action by a CENTRAL BANK or monetary authority to increase or decrease a nation's MONEY SUPPLY to offset any changes caused by active intervention in the FOREIGN EXCHANGE markets. If a country has a greater amount of foreign exchange RESERVES as a result of its intervention activities, its money supply will increase and cause the central bank to sell GOVERNMENT BONDS as an offset; if reserves decline and the money supply contracts, the central bank will purchase government bonds. See also DIRTY FLOAT.

STERLING OVERNIGHT INDEX AVERAGE (SONIA) The Sterling overnight INDEX average of INTEREST RATES on unsecured DEPOSITS between BANKS in the London market.

STICKINESS [COL] (1) The tendency for a financial indicator, such as INFLATION and UNEMPLOYMENT, to remain at a particular level, despite a changing market environment. (2) The degree to which DEMAND DEPOSITS placed by retail customers with a BANK remain *in situ* in the face of a changing environment (e.g., more alternatives, higher fees, lower deposit rates).

STICKY DEAL [COL] See HUNG DEAL.

STOCHASTIC PROCESS A mathematical process used to describe the continuous and dynamic movement of ASSET prices. Certain OPTION pricing models use a stochastic process to generate values. See also MARKOV PROCESS.

STOCK (1) See COMMON STOCK, PREFERRED STOCK. (2) In the United Kingdom, a FIXED INTEREST SECURITY. (3) See INVENTORY. (3) See also FIRST IN FIRST OUT, LAST IN FIRST OUT.

STOCK BUYBACK A mechanism for returning CAPITAL to SHAREHOLDERS by repurchasing and retiring a specified amount of outstanding COMMON STOCK. From an ACCOUNTING perspective the buyback has the effect of increasing the TREASURY STOCK CONTRA-ACCOUNT, thus reducing the overall EQUITY account. The buyback may be conducted via direct open market purchases, a general TENDER OFFER to shareholders, or direct negotiation with a major INVESTOR; a buyback arranged on a regular basis through a formulaic process is known as a SELF-TENDER. Also known as STOCK REPURCHASE. See also SPECIAL DIVIDEND.

STOCK CERTIFICATE A nonnegotiable physical certificate that denotes SHARE ownership in a PUBLIC COMPANY. See also SHARE CERTIFICATE.

STOCK DIVIDEND A regular corporate DIVIDEND that is payable to COMMON STOCK SHAREHOLDERS of record in the form of additional

SHARES of stock rather than cash. Also known as ACCUMULATING SHARE, BONUS ISSUE, BONUS SHARE. See also CASH DIVIDEND.

STOCK EXCHANGE   An EXCHANGE that specializes in TRADING of STOCKS and other EQUITY-related instruments (such as INDEXES, stock-based EXCHANGE-TRADED FUNDS, and OPTIONS). The exchange may operate through physical or electronic mechanisms and is typically regulated by the country's financial REGULATORS. See also STOCK MARKET.

STOCK EXCHANGE ALTERNATIVE TRADING SERVICE (SEATS)   A screen-based service used on the LONDON STOCK EXCHANGE's ALTERNATIVE INVESTMENT MARKET.

STOCK EXCHANGE AUTOMATED QUOTATIONS SYSTEM (SEAQ)   A computerized service used on the LONDON STOCK EXCHANGE to record and reflect TRADES that have been executed.

STOCK EXCHANGE DAILY OFFICIAL LIST (SEDOL)   The SECURITY identification code used by the LONDON STOCK EXCHANGE. See also COMMITTEE ON UNIFORM SECURITIES IDENTIFICATION PROCEDURES, CUSIP INTERNATIONAL NUMBER, INTERNATIONAL SECURITIES IDENTIFICATION NUMBER.

STOCK EXCHANGE TRADING SYSTEM (SETS)   An electronic ORDER-driven TRADING system of the LONDON STOCK EXCHANGE that matches BIDS and OFFERS of the FTSE 100 companies and certain other LARGE CAP STOCKS.

STOCK INDEX   An INDEX that includes a large number of quoted STOCKS, and which serves as a reference BENCHMARK for a country's stock market. In many cases stock indexes are directly traded through DERIVATIVES and EXCHANGE-TRADED FUNDS, and can serve as a convenient INVESTMENT and RISK MANAGEMENT tool. Also known as SHARE INDEX.

STOCK LOAN   A form of SECURED LENDING within the class of EQUITY FINANCE where the BORROWER posts SHARES to the LENDER in exchange for cash. A HAIRCUT is typically applied in order to protect against market movements in the price of the shares which might render some portion of the loan unsecured.

STOCK MARKET   The general marketplace for issuing, buying, and selling of STOCKS, including COMMON STOCK and PREFERRED STOCK. The stock market is a central element of the global CAPITAL MARKET, ensuring ISSUERS have the ability to raise EQUITY capital and INVESTORS have access to trading LIQUIDITY. Each national stock market has its own characteristics, procedures, and conventions, though most trading occurs on an EXCHANGE (electronic or physical) and many valuation and PRICE DISCOVERY techniques are similar. See also COMMODITY MARKET, FOREIGN EXCHANGE MARKET, STOCK MARKET.

STOCK OPTION   A CALL OPTION or a PUT OPTION with a company's STOCK as the UNDERLYING reference. Also known as SHARE OPTION.

STOCK PICKING   [COL] An INVESTMENT strategy where a PORTFOLIO MANAGER selects individual STOCKS based on FUNDAMENTAL ANALYSIS or TECHNICAL ANALYSIS in an attempt to outperform a broad INDEX or BENCHMARK.

STOCK PRICE   The quoted value of the STOCK of an issuing company.

STOCK REPURCHASE   See STOCK BUYBACK.

STOCK SPLIT   A corporate action that reduces the PAR VALUE of a company's COMMON STOCK while increasing the number of SHARES outstanding. A split is often undertaken in order to broaden the INVESTOR base by lowering the minimum purchase price of a share; although there is no change in the MARKET VALUE of the company, a stock split is generally viewed as a sign of strength. Also known as SHARE SPLIT. See also REVERSE STOCK SPLIT, SCRIP ISSUE.

STOCK SWAP   (1) A MERGER or ACQUISITION involving the exchange of COMMON STOCK between two companies; the transaction is generally accounted for as a POOLING OF INTERESTS. (2) A TAX-motivated transaction where an INVESTOR with UNREALIZED LOSSES in a stock PORTFOLIO sells the positions, realizes the losses, and uses the losses to offset CAPITAL GAINS on other SECURITIES; excess losses from the stock swap can be carried forward to future periods, subject to certain limitations. (2) See also TAX CARRYBACK, TAX CARRYFORWARD.

STOCK SYMBOL   An alphanumeric code comprised of several characters which uniquely identifies a PUBLIC COMPANY for TRADING purposes on an EXCHANGE.

STOP LIMIT ORDER   An ORDER to buy or sell SECURITIES at a limit price once the stop level is reached, rather than the market price characteristic of a traditional STOP ORDER.

STOP LOSS ORDER   A STOP ORDER to sell a SECURITY at the market once a particular price level is reached. The stop loss does not guarantee a specific EXECUTION price; it simply invokes an order to sell at the stop level.

STOP LOSS REINSURANCE   A REINSURANCE CONTRACT that protects the CEDING INSURER against an aggregate amount of CLAIMS in excess of a specified percentage of earned PREMIUMS; stop loss reinsurance effectively protects the insurer against the possibility that the sum of individual losses from the INSURANCE it has UNDERWRITTEN will be greater than expected. In most instances the REINSURER is only liable up to a defined percentage of the losses or a maximum value amount.

STOP ORDER   An ORDER to purchase or sell SECURITIES once a particular price level is reached on the upside or downside. The stop order does not GUARANTEE specific price EXECUTION, simply that the order will become an effective purchase or sale and will then be filled at the best available price. The most common stop order is the STOP LOSS ORDER. See also LIMIT ORDER, MARKET ORDER, TIME ORDER.

STOP OUT PRICE   The lowest price at which GOVERNMENT BILLS are sold in an AUCTION MARKET process.

STOPPED OUT   [COL] A situation when the market price of a given SECURITY or ASSET moves below a particular level and triggers a STOP LOSS ORDER.

STORY PAPER   [COL] A SECURITY with unusual characteristics that requires detailed explanations or disclosure in order to attract INVESTORS. Story paper must occasionally be sold at a higher YIELD (or a larger price DISCOUNT) than comparable "conventional" securities as a result of its unique or complex qualities.

STRADDLE   An OPTION SPREAD designed to take advantage of VOLATILITY rather than market direction. A straddle is created through the purchase or sale of options with identical STRIKE PRICES and EXPIRIES; a LONG straddle consists of a long PUT OPTION and a long CALL OPTION, while a SHORT straddle consists of a short put and call. The purchaser of the straddle gains on the put or call if there is significant market movement; the seller gains if markets remain calm and both options expire OUT-OF-THE-MONEY.

Payoff profile of long straddle position

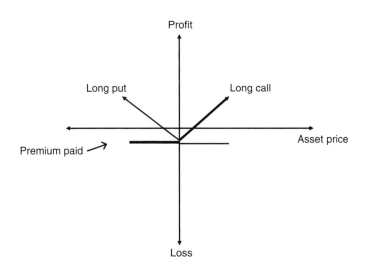

Payoff profile of short straddle

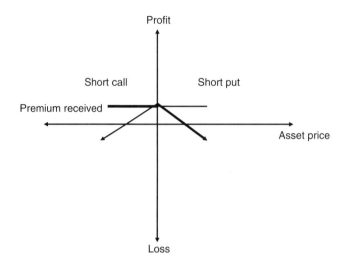

See also STRANGLE.

STRAIGHT BOND   (1) A NONCALLABLE BOND. (2) In the EUROMARKETS, a bond with a FIXED RATE COUPON. (3) A GILT with a BULLET repayment.

STRAIGHT-LINE DEPRECIATION A DEPRECIATION mechanism that applies equal reductions in value to a depreciable ASSET based on the expected life of the asset. Straight-line methods are commonly applied to FIXED ASSETS that are not expected to become obsolete before the end of their economically useful lives. See also ACCELERATED DEPRECIATION.

STRAIGHT-LINE INTERPOLATION   See LINEAR INTERPOLATION.

STRANGLE   An OPTION SPREAD designed to take advantage of VOLATILITY rather than market direction. A strangle is created through the purchase or sale of options with different STRIKE PRICES but the same EXPIRIES: a LONG strangle consists of a long PUT OPTION and a long CALL OPTION, each with a different STRIKE PRICE, while a SHORT strangle consists of a short put and call with unique strikes. The purchaser of the strangle gains on the put or call if there is significant market movement; the seller gains if markets remain calm and both options expire OUT-OF-THE-MONEY.

Payoff profile of long strangle

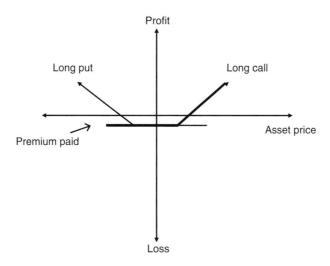

Payoff profile of short strangle

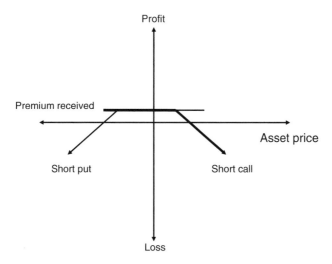

STRAP   An OPTION SPREAD designed to take advantage of VOLATILITY. A LONG strap, which is created through a long PUT OPTION and two long CALL

OPTIONS with the same STRIKE PRICE, is characterized by unlimited profit potential and limited downside RISK; the short strap, simply a short put and two short calls with identical strikes, has limited profit potential and unlimited downside risk. See also STRIP.

STRATEGIC ASSET ALLOCATION   One of two phases in the ASSET ALLOCATION process, where an INVESTOR or INVESTMENT MANAGER develops a weighting of asset classes for the PORTFOLIO that is intended to be preserved over a long-term horizon. By doing so, the manager is effectively defining a BENCHMARK. See also TACTICAL ASSET ALLOCATION.

STREET   [COL] See WALL STREET.

STREET NAME   [COL] Client-owned SECURITIES that are registered to a BANK, BROKER/DEALER, or third party NOMINEE rather than the client. Securities held in street name eliminate the need to physically deliver securities to the client.

STRESS TESTING   See SCENARIO ANALYSIS.

STRICT LIABILITY   A LIABILITY motion requiring that the plaintiff need only prove harm in a specific manner in order to collect damages and need not demonstrate the methods, motivations, or intent leading to the damage.

STRIKE   See STRIKE PRICE.

STRIKE PRICE   The agreed price, rate, or level at which an OPTION begins creating value for the buyer and a LIABILITY for the seller. When the market price exceeds the strike price for a CALL OPTION, or falls below the strike for a PUT OPTION, INTRINSIC VALUE is created. Also known as EXERCISE PRICE, STRIKE, STRIKING PRICE.

STRIKING PRICE   See STRIKE PRICE.

STRIP   (1) An OPTION SPREAD designed to take advantage of VOLATILITY. A LONG strip, which is created through a long CALL OPTION and two long PUT OPTIONS with the same STRIKE PRICE, is characterized by unlimited PROFIT potential and limited downside RISK; the short strip, which is simply a short call and two short puts with the same strikes, has limited profit potential and unlimited downside risk. (2) A SECURITY that has been split into CORPUS and COUPONS, enabling each component to be priced and traded separately. In the United States the Treasury Department conducts a stripping program of GOVERNMENT NOTES and GOVERNMENT BONDS to create STRIPS (Separate Trading of Registered Interest and Principal Securities). In the United Kingdom the BANK OF ENGLAND operates a GILT stripping program known as the STAGS (Sterling Transfer Accruing Government Securities); similar programs exist in other countries. Individual FINANCIAL INSTITUTIONS also create their own private-label strips of government bonds and MORTGAGE-BACKED SECURITIES. (1) See also STRAP. (2) See also COUPON STRIPPING, INTEREST-ONLY STRIP, PRINCIPAL-ONLY STRIP, RECONSTITUTION, STRIPPING.

STRIP HEDGE A HEDGE based on the use of sequential OVER-THE-COUNTER or EXCHANGE-traded CONTRACTS that match or approximate future CASH FLOWS associated with the underlying RISK being hedged. A successful strip hedge can eliminate DIRECTIONAL RISK and CURVE RISK. See also ROLLING HEDGE.

STRIPPING The process of separating a BOND's CORPUS and INTEREST COUPONS so that they can be traded separately. Stripping is done by government agencies and FINANCIAL INSTITUTIONS, often by creating separate TRUST vehicles that hold the original SECURITIES and issue new, decomposed securities. See also RECONSTITUTION.

STRIPPING THE YIELD CURVE [COL] The process of deconstructing the PAR YIELD CURVE (i.e., the yield curve observable from COUPON instruments trading in the market) to obtain a ZERO COUPON YIELD CURVE. Stripping the yield curve commences with identifying several coupon instruments traded in the market, converting the first one into a zero coupon rate, using the second coupon instrument and the first derived zero coupon rate to determine the second zero coupon rate, and so forth, until an entire zero coupon curve has been created. The zero coupon curve is then converted into an IMPLIED FORWARD CURVE in order to value transactions requiring an estimate of FORWARD RATES. Also known as BOOTSTRAPPING.

STRIPS Acronym for Separate Trading of Registered Interest and Principal Securities, a STRIP SECURITY in the US marketplace

STRONG HANDS [COL] A holder of an EXCHANGE-TRADED DERIVATIVE that expects to receive the UNDERLYING ASSET at EXPIRY or EXERCISE. See also WEAK HANDS

STRUCTURAL MODEL A form of CREDIT DEFAULT MODEL that defines the PROBABILITY of COUNTERPARTY DEFAULT in terms of a firm's ASSETS, LIABILITIES, and CAPITAL structure. Default occurs when a boundary value, such as a liability or negative NET WORTH threshold, is reached. See also INTENSITY MODEL.

STRUCTURAL SUBORDINATION The relative degree of SUBORDINATION between CREDITORS of a HOLDING COMPANY and creditors of an associated operating company. A holding company that has extensive LEVERAGE and is heavily reliant on the operating company for UPSTREAMING of DIVIDENDS to cover its DEBT SERVICE places its creditors in a structurally subordinate position to the creditors of the operating company, which has its own cash generating capabilities.

STRUCTURED FINANCE The general category of financing and RISK MANAGEMENT solutions offered by BANKS to institutional clients seeking to achieve specific results that cannot be readily met with standard financial products. Structured finance can involve combinations of LOANS, BONDS, and DERIVATIVES, as well as SECURITIZATION techniques and off-balance sheet vehicles, to achieve goals of RISK TRANSFER, liquidity management, and/or funding. See also ASSET-BACKED SECURITY, COLLATERALIZED DEBT OBLIGATION, FINANCIAL ENGINEERING.

STRUCTURED INVESTMENT VEHICLE (SIV) An off-BALANCE SHEET, SPECIAL-PURPOSE ENTITY that is used primarily for ARBITRAGE purposes, raising funds via ASSET-BACKED COMMERCIAL PAPER, MEDIUM-TERM NOTES, and SUBORDINATED DEBT and using the proceeds to INVEST in a range of ASSETS. The SIV has an open-end life and must adhere to certain investment criteria in order to maintain its CREDIT RATINGS. If it fails to do so, it must deleverage the vehicle through sales of assets. See also SIV LITE.

STRUCTURED NOTE A NOTE or BOND containing EMBEDDED OPTIONS that creates a customized payout for INVESTORS. The options, which carry varying degrees of potential RISK, allow RETURNS to be linked to a variety of different ASSETS on a leveraged or unleveraged basis. Structured notes may be issued as PRIVATE PLACEMENTS and often feature very limited LIQUIDITY as a result of their unique structural characteristics. Common structured notes include the INVERSE FLOATING RATE NOTE, LEVERAGED NOTE, multiple INDEX note, RANGE FLOATING RATE NOTE, and RANGE KNOCK-OUT FLOATING RATE NOTE. See also COMPLEX STRUCTURED PRODUCT.

STUB [COL] (1) The NEARBY FUTURES CONTRACT on EURODOLLARS. (2) A SHORT COUPON on a NOTE or a BOND.

STUCK DEAL [COL] See HUNG DEAL

STYLE DRIFT A phenomenon when a HEDGE FUND or INVESTMENT COMPANY deviates from its original INVESTMENT focus and expertise in an attempt to find new opportunities to deploy CAPITAL. Style drift can introduce additional RISK into a fund, as managers may lack the requisite base of knowledge needed to effectively manage the ASSETS.

SUBINVESTMENT GRADE A CREDIT RATING designation applied to any ISSUER of SECURITIES that is rated below BBB- by Standard and Poor's or Baa3 by Moody's Investors Services. Subinvestment-grade credits have weaker financial profiles than INVESTMENT GRADE credits, and thus a greater likelihood of encountering FINANCIAL DISTRESS leading to DEFAULT.

SUBORDINATED DEBT A LIABILITY that ranks below SECURED DEBT and SENIOR DEBT in CLAIMS priority in the event of a DEFAULT by the DEBTOR. Subordinated debt can be issued with varying levels of SUBORDINATION, making a given obligation senior to one liability and subordinate to another one. Subordinated debt holders do not receive any restitution in BANKRUPTCY until all senior debt holders have been compensated; in exchange for accepting the subordinated position, they demand a higher RISK PREMIUM on CAPITAL invested. Also known as JUNIOR DEBT, MEZZANINE FINANCING. See also SUBORDINATED PERPETUAL DEBT.

SUBORDINATED PERPETUAL DEBT A COUPON-bearing BOND that has no PRINCIPAL REDEMPTION feature and ranks junior to all other DEBT CLAIMS.

The bond functions as permanent FINANCING or quasi-EQUITY (although it ranks senior to COMMON STOCK). See also SUBORDINATED DEBT.

SUBORDINATION The ranking of CLAIMS priority of a NOTE, BOND, or LOAN in the event of DEFAULT by the ISSUER or BORROWER; the greater the subordination, the lower the claims priority, and the lower the CREDITOR RECOVERY RATE following BANKRUPTCY proceedings. The degree of creditor subordination may also be influenced by an ISSUER's or BORROWER's corporate structure, with HOLDING COMPANY creditors generally subordinate to operating company creditors as a result of STRUCTURAL SUBORDINATION. Subordination is also commonly used in the structuring of a range of ASSET-BACKED SECURITIES, where distinct TRANCHES are created by establishing a specific level of subordination within the capital structure. Tranches with the most subordination bear the first losses in DEFAULT and thus carry the lowest CREDIT RATINGS and highest returns; those with the least subordination bear the last losses and feature the highest credit ratings and lowest returns. See also ABSOLUTE PRIORITY RULE.

SUBPRIME LOAN A LOAN granted to a weak individual or corporate BORROWER, including one that may have had a history of prior loan delinquency or DEFAULT. Subprime loans, which are generally secured against a specific ASSET (e.g., a residence, commercial property), typically have much lower LOAN-TO-VALUE ratios than conventional loans in order to protect the lender in the event of default. Also known as B & C LOAN, NONPRIME LOAN.

SUBPRIME MORTGAGE A residential MORTGAGE that is granted to a BORROWER that has a relatively weak CREDIT standing, including borrowers that may have previously DEFAULTED on other DEBT obligations. Subprime mortgages may be characterized by higher rates to compensate for poorer credit quality.

SUBROGATION (1) The transfer of rights of loss recovery from the INSURED to the INSURER, allowing the insurer to seek its own restitution. The insured, whose rights are transferred, is known as the subrosor; the insurer accepting the subrogated rights is known as the subrosee. (2) The right to substitute one CREDIT for another in settling a CLAIM or transferring ownership.

SUBSCRIBER A party to an initial SUBSCRIPTION of SHARES.

SUBSCRIPTION An offer to purchase SECURITIES, exercisable for a specific period of time.

SUBSCRIPTION AGREEMENT An agreement between the LEAD MANAGER, SYNDICATE members, and an ISSUER to offer SECURITIES at the issue price less an agreed SELLING CONCESSION. The agreement delineates instances where the transaction can be cancelled (through FORCE MAJEURE) and contains details related to TAXES, expenses, listing fees, COMMISSIONS, and STAMP DUTIES. A form of the subscription agreement is often included in the final PROSPECTUS. See also SYNDICATE AGREEMENT.

SUBSCRIPTION PRIVILEGE See PREEMPTIVE RIGHT.

SUBSCRIPTION RIGHTS　See RIGHTS ISSUE.

SUBSCRIPTION WARRANT A WARRANT granted to existing SHAREHOLDERS of a company's COMMON STOCK, giving them the RIGHT to purchase SHARES of an ADD-ON issue, generally in an amount proportional to their current shareholdings, at a price that is below the current market. Subscription warrants may be issued when PREEMPTIVE RIGHTS do not exist. See also RIGHTS ISSUE.

SUBSIDIARY A subholding of a PARENT company or HOLDING COMPANY, which may be engaged in a specific line of business operations and operate partly or totally apart from the rest of the organization. A subsidiary may have significant operations and resources in its own right, or may have to rely on the standing of its parent or holding company to secure its LIABILITIES.

SUBSIDY A form of financial assistance provided by a government authority in support of a specific venture or to cover a deficit resulting from the sale of goods or services at less than cost.

SUCKER'S RALLY　[COL] See DEAD CAT BOUNCE.

SUITABILITY RISK The RISK of loss arising from clients claiming financial injury on transactions with characteristics that might be regarded as "unsuitable" (i.e., too speculative, risky, or leveraged, insufficient disclosure, ineffective HEDGE). See also ULTRA VIRES.

SUKUK [ARB] A rent certificate or BOND alternative used in ISLAMIC FINANCE which adheres to restrictions related to RIBA and GHARAR. See also IJARA, MURABAHA, SALAM.

SUNK COST An EXPENSE of a company that can never be recovered once incurred. It can be considered as an avoidable FIXED COST that must be analyzed in the context of OPPORTUNITY COST.

SUNSHINE TRADE　[COL] A large ORDER in a SECURITY that is made public before EXECUTION, in order to increase transparency and reduce any potential for confusion.

SUPER SENIOR　[COL] The top-rated TRANCHE of a SECURITIZATION, so named as it does not suffer any losses until all other tranches in a structure have absorbed pool losses, including those of the AAA-rated tranche. In this regard it is often known as a SUPER AAA.

SUPERANNUATION In the United Kingdom, a retirement PENSION FUND that is financed through employee deductions.

SUPERCYCLE　See KONDRATIEFF WAVE.

SUPERMAJORITY VOTE An ANTITAKEOVER DEFENSE requiring a supermajority, rather than just simple majority, vote by SHAREHOLDERS on a proposed CORPORATE FINANCE or corporate control action.

SUPERSINKER　[COL] A TRANCHE of a MORTGAGE-BACKED SECURITY or COLLATERALIZED MORTGAGE OBLIGATION with an average life that is shorter than other tranches in the series. The tranche is retired at an acceler-ated rate through early PREPAYMENTS.

SUPERVISORY BOARD The first BOARD OF DIRECTORS in the DUAL BOARD SYSTEM, responsible for appointing, supervising, and advising mem-bers of the MANAGEMENT BOARD, and developing fundamental corporate strategy. Supervisory board directors are generally nominated through an internal committee and/or EXECUTIVE MANAGEMENT recommendations, and are formally elected by SHAREHOLDERS via PROXY at the ANNUAL GENERAL MEETING; in countries following LABOR CODETERMINATION, one or more labor representatives is appointed to the board. Board size can vary from 10 to 30 DIRECTORS, depending on the national system.

SUPERVISORY REVIEW AND EVALUATION PROCESS (SREP) An element of PILLAR II of the BASLE II framework, in which a national REGULATOR reviews the INTERNAL CAPITAL ADEQUACY ASSESSMENT PROCESS of a par-ticipating BANK.

SUPPLY The amount of a good or service that an individual or institution will be willing to provide at a given price. In general, supply increases with price. See also DEMAND, ELASTICITY.

SUPPORT BOND See COMPANION BOND.

SUPPORT LEVEL A TECHNICAL ANALYSIS chart reflecting a SECURITY or INDEX price level that withstands repeated bouts of selling pressure. If the price breaches the support level after several repeated attempts, further down-ward moves may follow (as in a BREAKOUT). See also RESISTANCE LEVEL.

SURETY (1) A GUARANTEE of CONTRACT fulfillment. (2) The party respon-sible for performing under a SURETY BOND should the original contract party DEFAULT on its obligations.

SURETY BOND A financial agreement where an INSURER assumes the role of the contracting party in completing a transaction or project in the event the contracting party DEFAULTS on its performance obligations. A conventional surety bond features three parties: the PRINCIPAL, who is responsible for per-forming on the underlying contract, task, or transaction; the SURETY, who performs upon the DEFAULT of the principal; and, the obligee, who is owed the right of performance. Surety bonds are commonly used in project financ-ings and municipal/government developments. See also COMPLETION BOND, PERFORMANCE BOND.

SURPLUS LINES INSURANCE INSURANCE cover that cannot be obtained from an ADMITTED INSURER and which must therefore be provided by a NONADMITTED INSURER. Also known as EXCESS SURPLUS LINES INSURANCE.

SURPLUS NOTES SUBORDINATED DEBT that functions in a manner simi-lar to CONTINGENT SURPLUS NOTES, except that SECURITIES are issued directly by the company rather than through a TRUST. Surplus notes have

MATURITIES ranging from 10 to 30 years, and must generally be approved by INSURANCE REGULATORS.

SURPLUS SHARE   In REINSURANCE, a PROPORTIONAL AGREEMENT where the REINSURER agrees to accept RISK on a variable percentage basis above the INSURER's DEDUCTIBLE, up to a defined maximum; the amount the CEDING INSURER retains is referred to as a LINE and is expressed in monetary terms. See also QUOTA SHARE.

SURRENDER VALUE   The amount of SAVINGS accumulated in a whole life INSURANCE POLICY, UNIT-LINKED POLICY, or similar vehicle, generated through the payment and INVESTMENT of periodic PREMIUMS, and payable to the INSURED upon termination of the policy. The amount of the surrender value depends on the performance of the specific INVESTMENTS underlying the policy. Also known as CASH SURRENDER VALUE.

SUSPENSE ACCOUNT   An ACCOUNT that is used to record balances related to unresolved errors or incomplete transactions that are awaiting finalization.

SWAP   (1) A customized OVER-THE-COUNTER DERIVATIVE involving the periodic exchange of payments between two parties in order to achieve a specific goal related to HEDGING, ARBITRAGING, or SPECULATING. Swaps are defined in terms of a NOTIONAL PRINCIPAL, MATURITY, and payment/ receipt terms; transactions generally have maturities ranging from 1 to 10 years, although longer deals are possible. Swaps are available on various references from the FIXED INCOME, EQUITY, FOREIGN EXCHANGE, COMMODITY, and CREDIT markets; common transactions include INTEREST RATE SWAPS, COMMODITY SWAPS, CREDIT DEFAULT SWAPS, CURRENCY SWAPS, EQUITY SWAPS, and TOTAL RETURN SWAPS. (2) In the FOREIGN EXCHANGE market, a pair of SPOT and FORWARD transactions, where the spot offsets or unwinds the forward. (1) See also BASIS SWAP, CATASTROPHE REINSURANCE SWAP, COMPLEX SWAP, DISCOUNT SWAP, NONPAR SWAP, PREMIUM SWAP, PURE CATASTROPHE SWAP.

SWAP SPREAD   The differential between an INTEREST RATE SWAP or CURRENCY SWAP rate (representing the CREDIT RISK of BANK counter-parties), and a BENCHMARK GOVERNMENT BOND rate (representing a sovereign RISK-FREE RATE). The swap spread serves as a proxy for the credit quality of large banks that actively quote and TRADE swaps, with a widening of spreads reflecting credit deterioration in the sector, and a narrowing reflecting improvement. See also ASSET SWAP SPREAD, BOND SWAP SPREAD.

SWAPTION   An OVER-THE-COUNTER OPTION on a SWAP, available in the form of a RECEIVER SWAPTION and a PAYER SWAPTION. The purchaser of a swaption has the RIGHT, but not the obligation, to enter into an underlying swap transaction at a predetermined rate at a future time.

SWAPTION ARBITRAGE A common ARBITRAGE technique that seeks to exploit differences between the IMPLIED VOLATILITY of SWAPTIONS and CAPS/FLOORS.

SWEEP A service provided by certain BANKS to their customers, which takes excess cash balances out of deposit accounts and reinvests them in overnight funds, thereby generating a YIELD.

Also know as END OF DAY SWEEP.

SWEEP-TO-FILL ORDER A MARKET ORDER which is divided into several individual orders to capture the best available price at that point in time, in order to ensure fast EXECUTION. The order gives greater weight to speed of execution than price. See also INTERMARKET SWEEP ORDER.

SWEEPER [COL] See SNIFFER.

SWEETENER [COL] See KICKER.

SWF See SOVEREIGN WEALTH FUND.

SWING LOAN See BRIDGE LOAN.

SWING TRADING A TRADING strategy based on buying and selling SECURITIES for short periods of time (often intra-day) in order to take advantage of perceived overreactions. Swing trading is essentially a form of very short-term MOMENTUM TRADING. See also POSITION TRADING.

SWINGLINE A short-term backup LINE OF CREDIT that can be drawn by the BORROWER when needed. Swinglines are often used by COMMERCIAL PAPER ISSUERS as a backup in the event INVESTORS are unwilling to ROLL OVER maturing paper. The swingline may be structured as a REVOLVING CREDIT FACILITY, REVOLVING UNDERWRITING FACILITY, or LETTER OF CREDIT facility. Also known as BACKUP LINE.

SWISSIE [COL] The Swiss Franc.

SWITCH TRADE (1) A transaction that involves replacing one INVESTMENT with a different investment. (2) A process where an importer that is unable to make payment on goods purchased is permitted by the exporter to transfer the OBLIGATION to a second importer.

SYMMETRIC PAYOFF A PAYOFF PROFILE on a DERIVATIVE where the gain or loss is the same for given market price changes; the gain or loss may be linear or nonlinear. A FUTURE and a FORWARD are characterized by symmetric profiles, gaining or losing equally for a range of market prices. See also ASYMMETRIC PAYOFF, LINEAR PAYOFF, NONLINEAR PAYOFF.

SYNDICATE (1) A group of FINANCIAL INSTITUTIONS that UNDERWRITES a NEW ISSUE of SECURITIES, typically by purchasing them at a DISCOUNT from the ISSUER and reselling them to INVESTORS at a fixed price in the PRIMARY MARKET. In some cases the syndicate will act as AGENT, placing securities through a BEST EFFORTS UNDERWRITING. (2) The process of selling or distributing securities or LOANS. (3) A group of INSURERS or REINSURERS that agree to jointly underwrite a RISK exposure. (1) Also known as PURCHASE GROUP, SELLING GROUP, UNDERWRITING GROUP. (2) See also SYNDICATION. (3) See also POOL.

SYNDICATE AGREEMENT   An agreement related to an UNDERWRITING of SECURITIES that assigns RIGHTS and responsibilities to each participating SYNDICATE member. The agreement designates the LEAD MANAGER, the securities allotment by member, the duration of the syndicate, offering mechanism, and fees; the syndicate agreement generally expires one to two months after the securities placement. Also known as UNDERWRITING AGREEMENT. See also SUBSCRIPTION AGREEMENT.

SYNDICATE MANAGER   See LEAD MANAGER.

SYNDICATED LOAN   A LOAN granted by a banking group to a corporate BORROWER and then sold to smaller banks and hold-to-MATURITY INSTITUTIONAL INVESTORS. A syndicated loan is distinct from a PARTICIPATION LOAN, as the funding banks are known to the borrower. A syndicated loan can be structured as a REVOLVING CREDIT FACILITY, TERM LOAN, LETTER OF CREDIT facility, or ACQUISITION LINE. The syndicated loan is structured and managed by the ARRANGER.

SYNDICATION   A process where a SYNDICATE UNDERWRITING a NEW ISSUE or a BANK arranging a LOAN sells portions of the OBLIGATION to other financial intermediaries. Syndication is a common means of distributing PRIMARY or SECONDARY OFFERINGS, and is used to supplement direct sales to INVESTORS.

SYNERGY   The potential value that can be created by combining two firms, as in a MERGER or ACQUISITION. Synergies may be financial (e.g., increased DEBT capacity, TAX benefits, higher payback on CAPITAL INVESTMENTS) and/or operating (e.g., ECONOMIES OF SCALE, pricing power, market or geographic expansion) in nature.

SYNTHETIC ASSET-BACKED SECURITY   An ASSET-BACKED SECURITY (ABS) structure that is created through the use of CREDIT DERIVATIVES, such as CREDIT DEFAULT SWAPS, rather than conventional underlying ASSET pools. Synthetic ABS may be created when there is a short supply of physical bonds, when one party wishes to establish a short position where it might not otherwise be possible, or when the economic benefits of creating a synthetic package are more favorable for one or both parties. The mechanics and documentation used in synthetic ABS are identical to those used in standard CDS transactions.

SYNTHETIC CATASTROPHE BOND   An OPTION on a CATASTROPHE BOND that permits, but does not obligate, the ISSUER to launch a bond transaction if needed in order to HEDGE or transfer RISK exposures.

SYNTHETIC COLLATERALIZED DEBT OBLIGATION (CDO) A COLLATERALIZED DEBT OBLIGATION (CDO) that is created on an unfunded basis through the use of CREDIT DERIVATIVES, including TOTAL RETURN SWAPS, BASKET OPTIONS, and/or BASKET SWAPS. Under a synthetic structure, the economic RISK of the reference ASSET pool is transferred, but the legal ownership remains on the BALANCE SHEET of the sponsoring BANK. A synthetic CDO may be structured as a BALANCE SHEET CDO or an ARBITRAGE CDO, and may be managed statically or dynamically. See also CASH COLLATERALIZED DEBT OBLIGATION.

SYNTHETIC CONVERTIBLE BOND A SECURITY package issued by a company or FINANCIAL INSTITUTION that comprises of discounted SUBORDINATED DEBT and EQUITY WARRANTS, resulting in the same RISK and RETURN characteristics of a conventional CONVERTIBLE BOND. The individual components of the package can be decomposed and traded separately.

SYNTHETIC CREDIT FACILITY See SYNTHETIC LENDING FACILITY.

SYNTHETIC GUARANTEED INVESTMENT CONTRACT A GUARANTEED INVESTMENT CONTRACT (GIC) where the ASSET PORTFOLIO that underlies the contract is owned by the contract holder and held in a TRUST ACCOUNT. The actual assets are managed by a third party INVESTMENT MANAGER. This stands in contrast to a standard GIC, where the asset portfolio is owned and managed by the INSURER. See also PARTICIPATING GUARANTEED INVESTMENT CONTRACT, NONPARTICIPATING GUARANTEED INVESTMENT CONTRACT.

SYNTHETIC LENDING FACILITY A FORWARD commitment to purchase REVOLVING CREDIT AGREEMENTS or undrawn LOANS. The facility allows an INVESTOR to participate in an unfunded revolver or loan, receiving a COMMITMENT FEE while the facility remains undrawn, and requiring it to provide funding in the event the BORROWER elects to draw down. This is equivalent to the investor selling a PUT OPTION to the INTERMEDIARY on a REVOLVING CREDIT LINE or NOTE underwriting program arranged for a third party borrower. Also known as ASSET SWAPTION, SYNTHETIC CREDIT FACILITY.

SYNTHETIC LONG POSITION A combination of a LONG CALL OPTION and a SHORT PUT OPTION with identical STRIKE PRICES that replicates the economics of a LONG POSITION. See also SYNTHETIC SHORT POSITION.

SYNTHETIC OPTION An OPTION position created through the combination of a LONG or SHORT option on an UNDERLYING SECURITY or ASSET and a long or short position in the same underlying security/asset.

Synthetic option =	Underlying +	Option
Long call =	Long underlying +	Long put
Long put =	Short underlying +	Long call
Short put =	Long underlying +	Short call
Short call =	Short underlying +	Short put

SYNTHETIC PRIME BROKERAGE A service offered by certain PRIME BROKERS to institutional clients that makes use of TOTAL RETURN SWAPS to synthetically reproduce a desired PORTFOLIO.

SYNTHETIC SECURITIZATION A form of SECURITIZATION where a SPECIAL-PURPOSE ENTITY (SPE) or TRUST issues NOTES to INVESTORS with an economic RETURN that is linked to the performance of a POOL of reference ASSETS. The SPE uses the proceeds of the notes to purchase unrelated high-quality qualifying ASSETS, and simultaneously provides the originator with RISK protection in exchange for a PREMIUM. The COUPONS from the qualifying assets and the premium are used to service the notes, while the qualifying assets are used to secure the investors' interests. Under the synthetic structure the originator retains the actual assets on its balance sheet. See also TRUE SALE SECURITIZATION.

SYNTHETIC SHORT POSITION A combination of a LONG PUT OPTION and a SHORT CALL OPTION with identical STRIKE PRICES that replicates the economics of a SHORT POSITION. See also SYNTHETIC LONG POSITION.

SYNTHETIC UNDERLYING An ASSET position created through the combination of two LONG or SHORT OPTIONS on the same UNDERLYING SECURITY or ASSET.

Synthetic underlying =	Option +	Option
Long underlying =	Long call +	Short put
Short underlying =	Short call +	Long put

See also SYNTHETIC LONG POSITION, SYNTHETIC SHORT POSITION.

SYSTEMATIC RISK   See NONDIVERSIFIABLE RISK.

SYSTEMATIC TACTICAL ASSET ALLOCATION   A form of TACTICAL ASSET ALLOCATION where short-term adjustments to the PORTFOLIO are based primarily on output provided by a forecasting model, making the process relatively objective. See also DISCRETIONARY TACTICAL ASSET ALLOCATION.

SYSTEMIC RISK   RISKS that are imposed on an entire financial system and which have the possibility of creating significant financial damage.

T

TAC BOND   See TARGETED AMORTIZATION CLASS BOND.

TACTICAL ASSET ALLOCATION One of two phases in the ASSET ALLOCATION process, where an INVESTOR or INVESTMENT MANAGER adjusts, on a tactical basis, the weighting of asset classes in the PORTFOLIO to take account of short-term (e.g., quarterly) market opportunities. Deviating from portfolio weightings involves forecasting market RETURNS, and identifying suitable INVESTMENTS via the PORTFOLIO CONSTRUCTION process. See also DISCRETIONARY TACTICAL ASSET ALLOCATION, STRATEGIC ASSET ALLOCATION, SYSTEMATIC TACTICAL ASSET ALLOCATION.

TAG ALONG RIGHTS [COL] Legal RIGHTS designed to protect MINORITY INTERESTS in the event of a TAKEOVER bid. If a bid occurs and majority SHAREHOLDERS tender their SHARES, then MINORITY INTEREST holders have the right to join on the same terms. Tag along rights must be specifically negotiated in a CORPORATE FINANCE transaction. See also DRAG ALONG RIGHTS.

TAIL [COL] (1) The extreme portion of a statistical distribution (e.g., NORMAL DISTRIBUTION, LOGNORMAL DISTRIBUTION) used to estimate EXPECTED LOSSES and unexpected losses. Tails, which can be difficult to estimate with accuracy, are important to BANKS and INSURERS attempting to establish extreme loss values. (2) In an AUCTION of SECURITIES, the differential between the average COMPETITIVE BID submitted and the highest YIELD (lowest price) accepted (i.e., the STOP OUT PRICE); a long tail indicates a weak auction, a short tail a strong auction. (3) In INSURANCE, the time between the receipt of PREMIUM and the payment of a CLAIM. (4) Price figures quoted after a decimal point. (1) See also EXTREME VALUE THEORY, KURTOSIS. (2) See also BID-TO-COVER. (4) See also PIP, POINT.

TAIL COVERAGE INSURANCE coverage that extends beyond the end of the standard policy. Tail coverage is useful in the case of a CLAIMS MADE BASIS policy, which only provides restitution for claims received during the policy period.

TAILGATING [COL] A practice where a BROKER replicates a client's TRADE in a proprietary account. Although tailgating is not strictly illegal (as is FRONT RUNNING), it can be regarded as unethical. See also COAT-TAILING.

TAILING A HEDGE A process where an EXCHANGE-TRADED DERIVATIVE HEDGE is DISCOUNTED using a PRESENT VALUE FACTOR in order to take account of the fact that exchange-traded positions are MARKED-TO-MARKET and settled every day.

TAKE-OUT The replacement of one form of FINANCING with another one, often associated with the replacement of a temporary BRIDGE LOAN with a long-term BOND or LOAN.

TAKE THE OFFER   [COL] A buyer's willingness to accept the seller's price on a transaction. Also known as LIFT THE OFFER. See also HIT THE BID.

TAKEDOWN   (1) An advance or drawing of funds by a BORROWER under a REVOLVING CREDIT FACILITY. (2) The amount of a NEW ISSUE of SECURITIES a SYNDICATE member agrees to purchase and resell to clients.

TAKEOVER   A CORPORATE FINANCE transaction where one company offers to acquire another company in order to expand its client, product, or market scope, or achieve some other strategic goal. The transaction may be structured as a FRIENDLY TAKEOVER or HOSTILE TAKEOVER, and may be based on an all-cash offer, or a mix of cash and the acquiring company's SHARES. Hostile takeover attempts may be delayed or thwarted through ANTITAKEOVER DEFENSES and ANTITAKEOVER LAWS. See also TAKEOVER BID.

TAKEOVER BID   The price an acquiring company is willing to pay for a TARGET company. The bid value is generally represented as a particular PREMIUM to the target's share price. See also ANY-AND-ALL BID, TAKEOVER, TWO-TIER BID.

TAKEOVER VALUE   See BREAKUP VALUE.

TAKING DELIVERY   The process where the buyer of an EXCHANGE-TRADED DERIVATIVE submits a notice to accept delivery of any physical ASSET underlying the CONTRACT.

TAP ISSUE   In the United Kingdom, an issue of GOVERNMENT BILLS sold directly to governmental entities without using GILT-EDGED MARKET MAKERS.

TAPE   [COL] The listing of STOCK prices on an EXCHANGE, reflecting updates as new BIDS and OFFERS are executed.

TARGET   [COL] A company that is the subject of an ACQUISITION offer from an ACQUIRER. See also ACQUISITION, BLACK KNIGHT, GRAY KNIGHT, HOSTILE TAKEOVER, WHITE KNIGHT.

TARGETED AMORTIZATION CLASS (TAC) BOND   A TRANCHE of a COLLATERALIZED MORTGAGE OBLIGATION (CMO) that exhibits reasonable price and RETURN stability by deflecting some amount of PREPAYMENT RISK to a COMPANION BOND. The companion bond shields the TAC from accelerating PREPAYMENTS, providing INVESTORS with a constant YIELD for a select PREPAYMENT SPEED (rather than a band of speeds, as is characteristic of the PLANNED AMORTIZATION CLASS BOND). See also SEQUENTIAL PAY BOND.

TARIFF   A TAX that is levied on goods that are imported into a country.

TAX   An amount of MONEY that is levied by a government as a means of generating public REVENUES. Taxes may be applied to INCOME (including wages, earnings, DIVIDENDS, INTEREST, CAPITAL GAINS), real estate and property, estates/inheritance, and goods and services (excise, AD VALOREM). See also PROGRESSIVE TAX, PROPORTIONAL TAX, REGRESSIVE TAX.

TAX AVOIDANCE   The process of seeking to minimize TAX paid to a government authority through legal and legitimate use of the tax code and any LOOPHOLES. See also TAX EVASION, TAX SHELTER

TAX BURDEN   The amount of TAX that an individual or organization pays after taking advantage of all relevant deductibility, CREDIT, and avoidance measures. See also TAX INCIDENCE.

TAX CARRYBACK   A TAX benefit generated by applying eligible losses to a current tax LIABILITY. In the United States, capital or operating losses can be offset against profits for the 3 prior years. Also known as CARRYBACK LOSS. See also TAX CARRYFORWARD, TAX UMBRELLA.

TAX CARRYFORWARD   A TAX benefit generated by applying eligible losses to a future tax LIABILITY. In the United States, losses can be carried forward to offset future profits for 5 years (capital losses) and 15 years (operating losses). Also known as CARRYFORWARD LOSS. See also TAX CARRYBACK, TAX UMBRELLA.

TAX CREDIT   (1) A CREDIT, or benefit, granted to a person or organization paying TAXES which results in an effective reduction in the tax LIABILITY. A tax credit can be created by taking advantage of certain government incentives. (2) A credit toward interim tax payments made on amounts due in the future.

TAX DEDUCTIBILITY   A transaction or event that permits a person or organization paying TAXES to reduce taxes payable by reducing INCOME before applying the relevant tax rate.

TAX EVASION   The process of seeking to minimize TAX paid to a government authority through illegal means, such as underreporting of INCOME or failing to disclose offshore ASSETS. See also TAX AVOIDANCE.

TAX HAVEN   A jurisdiction that features a lower TAX rate, or even tax-free, environment as a way of fostering business and CAPITAL formation. In order to qualify for the tax benefits of such a haven, a person or organization must typically fulfill minimum residence or business requirements. Popular tax havens include the Cayman Islands, Bahamas, Liechtenstein, Monaco, and the Netherlands Antilles.

TAX INCIDENCE   The party that ultimately bears the impact of TAXES, which may or may not be the person or organization nominally paying taxes. If the TAX BURDEN can be shifted to third parties through price increases on taxable goods and services, the tax incidence is indirectly spread out.

TAX LOSS   A loss made in one period that can be used to offset previous or future INCOME via TAX CARRYBACK or TAX CARRYFORWARD provisions.

TAX SHELTER   A legal business or INVESTMENT scheme or transaction that is intended to reduce a person's or organization's TAX LIABILITY. See also TAX AVOIDANCE.

TAX SHIELD   A TAX benefit generated through INTEREST deductibility on LOANS, BONDS, and other DEBT funding instruments (i.e., interest EXPENSE is deducted from OPERATING INCOME before a tax rate is applied). In general, the higher the marginal corporate tax rate, the greater the benefits derived from the shield. The PRESENT VALUE of a tax shield is given as:

$$PV_{TS} = TR \left[\frac{D(r_{davg})}{r_{davg}} \right]$$

where TR is the effective tax rate, D is total debt, and r_{davg} is the average cost of the debt. See also TAX UMBRELLA.

TAX UMBRELLA   Any TAX transaction that is intended to decrease a company's effective tax rate, generally considered to include TAX CARRYBACKS, TAX CARRYFORWARDS, and TAX SHIELDS.

TAX YEAR   See FISCAL YEAR.

TAXABLE EQUIVALENT YIELD   The YIELD on a TAX-free FIXED INCOME SECURITY grossed up to allow comparison with taxable INVESTMENT alternatives. The taxable equivalent yield is generally computed via:

$$TEY = \frac{y_{TF}}{(1 - TR)}$$

where y_{TF} is the tax-free yield and TR is the effective tax rate. See also BOND EQUIVALENT YIELD, DISCOUNT YIELD, SIMPLE YIELD, YIELD TO CALL, YIELD TO MATURITY.

TAXABLE PERSON   Any individual, organization, or corporate entity that is subject to TAX on INCOME earned or, in a VALUE-ADDED TAX regime, tax on the TAXABLE SUPPLY.

TAXABLE SUPPLY   In systems using a VALUE-ADDED TAX, the goods or services which are subject to TAX.

TBA   See TO BE ANNOUNCED.

TEAR-UP PRICE   The price at which a BANK or DEALER will close out, or buy out, a client's DERIVATIVE transaction. The tear-up price is generally a function of the transaction's current MARK-TO-MARKET value and a PROFIT SPREAD. Also known as UNWIND PRICE.

TEASER   [COL] A below-market INTEREST RATE on a LOAN used to entice an individual or company to borrow funds, or an above-market rate on a DEPOSIT used to entice clients into placing funds. The favorable teaser rate generally lasts for up to several quarters and then reverts to normal market levels.

TECHNICAL ANALYSIS   SECURITY and market analysis techniques that are based on the concept that past price formations repeat in particular patterns and can thus be used to forecast future movements. Technical analysts believe that historical price patterns have a bearing on both present and future price movements, suggesting that their views stand in contrast to theories such as the EFFICIENT MARKET HYPOTHESIS and RANDOM WALK. The technical analysis process involves charting techniques such as HEAD AND SHOULDERS, REVERSE HEAD AND SHOULDERS, ASCENDING TOPS, FALLING TOPS, DESCENDING BOTTOMS, RISING BOTTOMS, DOUBLE TOPS, REVERSE DOUBLE TOPS, FLAGS, PENNANTS, TRIANGLES, SUPPORT LEVELS, and RESISTANCE LEVELS, among others. Technical analysis also relies on other statistical tools, such as MOVING AVERAGES and MOMENTUM OSCILLATORS. See also FUNDAMENTAL ANALYSIS.

Additional reference: Edwards and Magee (2001).

TED SPREAD   See TREASURY-EURODOLLAR SPREAD.

TEENY   [COL] The smallest trading unit in US TREASURY BONDS and AGENCY SECURITIES, i.e., 1/64th of $1.

TEMPERATURE DERIVATIVE   An OVER-THE-COUNTER or EXCHANGE-traded WEATHER DERIVATIVE that references the movement of a temperature INDEX, such as cumulative average temperatures, heating degree days, or cooling degree days. A temperature derivative involves the exchange of payments based on the actual movement of the temperature index against a predefined level. Most CONTRACTS are traded on a seasonal basis (e.g., the summer cooling season and the winter heating season) and are based on a particular reference city. Since temperature is not a tradable commodity, all contracts feature FINANCIAL SETTLEMENT. See also TEMPERATURE-LINKED BOND.

TEMPERATURE-LINKED BOND   An INSURANCE-LINKED SECURITY with COUPON INTEREST and/or PRINCIPAL REDEMPTION contingent on the level of cumulative temperatures in a particular city, group of cities, or region. The BOND provides INVESTORS with an alternative INVESTMENT opportunity and the ISSUER with a HEDGE or RISK TRANSFER mechanism. See also TEMPERATURE DERIVATIVE.

TENDER   (1) The act of delivering SHARES of a company that is being acquired by another company in order to receive in exchange shares of the acquiring company, or the delivery of shares into a STOCK BUYBACK. (2) The act of offering an ASSET or SECURITY for sale. (1) See also TENDER OFFER. (2) See also FIXED-PRICE TENDER.

TENDER OFFER   A publicly announced offer by a company or RAIDER to purchase the COMMON STOCK of a TARGET company at a stated price. The offer price, known as a TAKEOVER BID, is generally made at a PREMIUM to the market in order to induce SHAREHOLDERS to sell (or "tender") their SHARES. Tender offers do not require specific shareholder approval or the specific support of the incumbent BOARD OF DIRECTORS or EXECUTIVE MANAGEMENT. See also FRIENDLY TAKEOVER, HOSTILE TAKEOVER, TAKEOVER, TWO-TIER BID.

TENDER PANEL   A SYNDICATE of BANKS backing an ISSUER's REVOLVING UNDERWRITING FACILITY, NOTE ISSUANCE FACILITY, or MULTIPLE OPTION FACILITY. The panel sells NOTES on behalf of the ISSUER on a best efforts basis and purchases any SECURITIES that remain unsold, thus providing the issuer with funds.

TENOR   The time period between issuance and MATURITY of a SECURITY.

TERM ASSURANCE   In the United Kingdom, TERM INSURANCE.

TERM BILL   A BILL OF EXCHANGE that is due and payable on a specific date. Also known as PERIOD BILL.

TERM INSURANCE   A form of life INSURANCE with a finite expiration date. Term life is the simplest form of life insurance, offering no specific SAVINGS or INVESTMENT features, simply a lump sum payout in the event of mortality of the named INSURED. Also known as TERM ASSURANCE.

TERM LOAN   A LOAN with a MATURITY ranging from 1 to 15+ years, generally used to fund medium- and long-term ASSETS such as INVENTORY and plant and equipment. A term loan may be secured or unsecured, carry a FIXED RATE or FLOATING RATE, and contain general or specific performance COVENANTS.

TERM REPURCHASE AGREEMENT   A REPURCHASE AGREEMENT with a final MATURITY ranging from 7 to 30 days; the opposite side of the transaction is referred to as a term REVERSE REPURCHASE AGREEMENT. See also OPEN REPURCHASE AGREEMENT, OVERNIGHT REPURCHASE AGREEMENT.

TERM STRUCTURE   The level of INTEREST RATES across time/MATURITY, generated through the construction of a YIELD CURVE. The same concept can also be applied to other RISK FACTORS with a maturity sequence, such as VOLATILITY and CREDIT SPREADS. See also EXPECTATIONS THEORY, LIQUIDITY PREFERENCE THEORY, MARKET SEGMENTATION THEORY. Additional references: Cox, Ingersoll, and Ross (1981); Hicks (1946); Meiselman (1962).

TERMINAL EXPECTED RISK EXPOSURE   POTENTIAL EXPOSURE of an OVER-THE-COUNTER DERIVATIVE that is based on the final MATURITY of the transaction and the expected movement of the UNDERLYING market reference. See also AVERAGE EXPECTED RISK EXPOSURE, AVERAGE WORST-CASE RISK EXPOSURE, TERMINAL WORST-CASE RISK EXPOSURE.

TERMINAL EXPOSURE   POTENTIAL EXPOSURE of an OVER-THE-COUNTER DERIVATIVE that is based on the final MATURITY of the transaction. See also AVERAGE EXPOSURE.

TERMINAL MARKET A TRADING center for a particular good or COMMODITY, rather than its original production center.

TERMINAL VALUE A method of estimating the value of a company over a long-term horizon, designed to overcome the challenges inherent in reliably forecasting earnings, DIVIDENDS, or CASH FLOWS beyond the medium term. Terminal value, which is used in various VALUATION models, can be estimated via a liquidation value (e.g., an estimate of the proceeds generated through the disposal of a company's ASSETS), multiple approach value (e.g., an estimate based on applying a multiple to earnings or REVENUES based on market comparables) or stable growth value (e.g., an estimate that assumes cash flows to the firm will grow at a stable rate beyond a specific time horizon, and then discounting the cash flows by the difference between COST OF CAPITAL and the growth constant).

TERMINAL WORST-CASE RISK EXPOSURE POTENTIAL EXPOSURE of an OVER-THE-COUNTER DERIVATIVE that is based on the final MATURITY of the transaction and the worst-case movement of the UNDERLYING market reference. See also AVERAGE EXPECTED RISK EXPOSURE, AVERAGE WORST-CASE RISK EXPOSURE, TERMINAL EXPECTED RISK EXPOSURE.

TERMINATION FEE A fee paid by an acquiring company to a BANK providing financing for an ACQUISITION, payable only if the financing is not utilized. See also BREAKUP FEE.

TERMINATION OPTION An OPTION embedded in an OVER-THE-COUNTER SWAP that permits one or both parties to terminate the transaction based on the passage of time or the occurrence of a triggering CREDIT event (often a CREDIT RATING downgrade). A firm might employ a termination option to help mitigate the effects of counterparty CREDIT RISK on very long-term transactions.

TERP See THEORETICAL EX-RIGHTS PRICE.

TEXAS HEDGE [COL] A financial transaction that increases RISK or produces losses under all market scenarios, i.e., it does the opposite of what a properly functioning HEDGE is meant to do.

THEORETICAL EX-RIGHTS PRICE (TERP) The theoretical price a company's STOCK will have upon the completion of a RIGHTS ISSUE, reflecting the degree of DILUTION and the amount of rights taken up by existing SHAREHOLDERS.

THEORETICAL FUTURES PRICE The ARBITRAGE-free price of a FUTURES contract, equal to the SPOT PRICE plus the COST OF CARRY.

THETA A change in the value of an OPTION for a change in the passage of time, with all other variables held constant. The thetas of the CALL OPTION and PUT OPTION under the BLACK-SCHOLES MODEL are given by:

$$\theta_c = -\frac{\delta C}{\delta t} = -\frac{S\sigma}{2\sqrt{t}}N'(d_1) - r_f X e^{-r_f t} N(d_2)$$

$$\theta_p = -\frac{\delta P}{\delta t} = -\frac{S\sigma}{2\sqrt{t}}N'(d_1) + r_f X e^{-r_f t} N(-d_2)$$

where

$$d_1 = \frac{ln\left(\frac{S}{X}\right) + \left(r_f + \frac{\sigma^2}{2}\right)t}{\sigma\sqrt{t}}$$

$$d_2 = \frac{ln\left(\frac{S}{X}\right) + \left(r_f - \frac{\sigma^2}{2}\right)t}{\sigma\sqrt{t}}$$

and S is the STOCK price, X is the STRIKE PRICE, t is the time to MATURITY, r_f is the RISK-FREE RATE, σ^2 is the VARIANCE, and where the N values of N(d1) and N(d2) can be obtained from standard tables of PROBABILITY functions.

The thetas of long and short puts and calls are shown as:

	Long call	Long put	Short call	Short put
Theta	+	+	−	−

Also known as OMEGA. See also DELTA, GAMMA, GREEKS, RHO, TIME DECAY, TIME VALUE, VEGA.

THETA NEUTRAL   A PORTFOLIO of OPTIONS that is neutral with respect to its THETA, meaning that it is HEDGED with regard to daily TIME DECAY. See also DELTA NEUTRAL, GAMMA NEUTRAL, VEGA NEUTRAL.

THIN MARKET   [COL] An ILLIQUID market that features low volume, wide BID-OFFER SPREADS, and high price VOLATILITY; a thin market may also feature periods of strictly one-way activity and periodic ORDER IMBALANCES. See also DEEP MARKET, TIGHT MARKET.

THIRD MARKET   [COL] (1) The general marketplace for TRADING of OVER-THE-COUNTER instruments. (2) EXCHANGE trading between nonmember firms, or between a member and nonmember firm.

THIRD PARTY ENHANCEMENT   Any form of support obtained from a third party CREDIT support provider, such as a GUARANTEE, SURETY BOND, or LETTER OF CREDIT. Such enhancements are used to increase the CREDITWORTHINESS of a transaction, often in lieu of posting physical or financial ASSETS as COLLATERAL.

THRIFT   See SAVINGS AND LOAN ASSOCIATION.

THROUGHPUT CONTRACT   A form of take-or-pay CONTRACT often used in PROJECT FINANCE deals in the energy industry that obliges producers to pass a certain minimum amount of product through a processing facility or pipeline for a fixed period of time. The existence of such a contract serves as a form of GUARANTEE in support of a project financing. See also TOLLING CONTRACT.

TIBOR   See TOKYO INTERBANK OFFERED RATE.

TICK VALUE   The value of a single price increment of an EXCHANGE-TRADED DERIVATIVE CONTRACT.

TIDE PROVISION   A "3-year independent director evaluation" provision included in certain POISON PILL defenses to make them more acceptable to SHAREHOLDERS. The provisions require DIRECTORS to evaluate the nature and status of poison pill defenses every three years to ensure that they remain equitable and appropriate, and do not harm or prejudice shareholder interests.

TIED LOAN   A LOAN granted by one country to another country, with the express condition that the proceeds be used to buy goods and services from the lending country.

TIER 1 CAPITAL   Core REGULATORY CAPITAL for BANKS, defined by the BANK FOR INTERNATIONAL SETTLEMENTS as COMMON STOCK, RETAINED EARNINGS, PERPETUAL PREFERRED STOCK, and disclosed RESERVES. See also ECONOMIC CAPITAL, TIER 2 CAPITAL.

TIER 2 CAPITAL   Supplementary REGULATORY CAPITAL for BANKS, defined by the BANK FOR INTERNATIONAL SETTLEMENTS as hybrid DEBT/EQUITY SECURITIES (including MANDATORY CONVERTIBLE BONDS), SUBORDINATED DEBT with MATURITIES in excess of 5 years, PERPETUAL DEBT, PREFERRED STOCK with a stated MATURITY, LOAN LOSS RESERVES, UNREALIZED PROFITS on INVESTMENTS, and HIDDEN RESERVES. See also ECONOMIC CAPITAL, TIER 1 CAPITAL.

TIGHT MARKET   [COL] A LIQUID market that features large volume and strong two-way flows, and narrow BID-OFFER SPREADS. ORDER IMBALANCES and one-way quotations are rare in a tight market. See also DEEP MARKET, THIN MARKET.

TIGR   See TREASURY INVESTORS GROWTH RECEIPT.

TIME AND DISTANCE REINSURANCE   A FINITE REINSURANCE CONTRACT, generally structured as EXCESS OF LOSS (XOL) REINSURANCE, where the REINSURER agrees to pay the CEDING INSURER an agreed schedule of loss payments in the future, without assuming any LIABILITY for losses in excess of those contained in the schedule. In exchange, the insurer pays the reinsurer a PREMIUM that is equal to the PRESENT VALUE of the loss payments.

TIME DECAY   Daily gain or loss impacting the TIME VALUE component of OPTION PREMIUM due to the passage of time; time decay is often used as a practical expression of THETA.

TIME DEPOSIT   A nonnegotiable DEPOSIT issued by a BANK that pays periodic FIXED RATE or FLOATING RATE COUPONS for a period ranging from several months to several years. The deposit can only be redeemed by the DEPOSITOR on the stated MATURITY and cannot be transferred on a secondary basis. See also CERTIFICATE OF DEPOSIT, INTERBANK DEPOSIT, LOCKUP CERTIFICATE OF DEPOSIT, NEGOTIABLE CERTIFICATE OF DEPOSIT.

TIME DRAFT   See BANKER'S ACCEPTANCE.

TIME ORDER   An ORDER to purchase or sell SECURITIES with a specific time constraint, such as at the close or open of a market, or at some future date. See also LIMIT ORDER, MARKET ORDER, STOP ORDER.

TIME SPREAD   An OPTION SPREAD designed to take advantage of perceived price or VOLATILITY discrepancies in the FORWARD MARKET. Time spreads are created through the purchase or sale of OPTIONS with identical STRIKE PRICES but different EXPIRIES. A LONG time spread consists of a SHORT POSITION in a near MATURITY PUT OPTION or CALL OPTION and a LONG POSITION in a far maturity put or call; a SHORT time spread consists of a long position in a near maturity put or call, and a short position in a far maturity put or call. Time spreads can also be established through FUTURES and FORWARDS. Also known as CALENDAR SPREAD, RATIO HORIZONTAL SPREAD.

TIME-TO-DECAY RISK   See FRACTIONAL EXPOSURE.

TIME TRANCHING   An internal CREDIT enhancement mechanism used in a SECURITIZATION transaction that directs the repayment of PRINCIPAL to the most SENIOR TRANCHES first; once the senior tranche has been repaid, CASH FLOWS are redirected to increasingly SUBORDINATED tranches. See also WATERFALL.

TIME VALUE   One of two components, which along with INTRINSIC VALUE, comprises the value of an OPTION. Time value measures the remaining economic worth of the CONTRACT that is specifically attributable to time, i.e., the time remaining for the UNDERLYING reference to move IN-THE-MONEY (or further in-the-money). Since time is a wasting ASSET, time value declines on a daily basis for the option buyer until it reaches zero at expiry. Longer term options have greater time value than shorter time options, while in-the-money and OUT-OF-THE-MONEY options have less time value than AT-THE-MONEY options. See also THETA, TIME DECAY.

TIME VALUE OF MONEY   A central financial concept indicating that the FUTURE VALUE of a sum of money invested today, in an INTEREST-bearing ASSET, is worth more than its current value. By extension, the future value of a sum can be DISCOUNTED at a DISCOUNT RATE to obtain today's PRESENT VALUE.

TIME WEIGHTED AVERAGE PRICE (TWAP)   An ORDER rule often implemented via ALGORITHMS which divides a PARENT ORDER against linear

VOLUME during a defined TRADING period in order to achieve a better average fill price. See also VOLUME WEIGHTED AVERAGE PRICE.

TIMES INTEREST EARNED A measure of a firm's ability to cover its DEBT, generally measured as:

$$TIE = \frac{EBIT}{Int}$$

where EBIT is EARNINGS BEFORE INTEREST AND TAXES and Int is interest EXPENSE.

The greater the ratio, the stronger the firm's INTEREST COVERAGE.

TIMING OPTION See DEFERRAL OPTION.

TIPS See TREASURY INFLATION-PROTECTED SECURITY.

TO BE ANNOUNCED (TBA) The common name given to a MORTGAGE-BACKED SECURITY (issued by the GOVERNMENT NATIONAL MORTGAGE ASSOCIATION, FEDERAL NATIONAL MORTGAGE ASSOCIATION, or FEDERAL HOME LOAN MORTGAGE CORPORATION) that TRADES as a WHEN ISSUED (WI) SECURITY, i.e., announced but not yet priced or settled. While in the "WI" period informal, but legally binding, GRAY MARKET TRADING occurs between DEALERS. Once the TBA has settled, it trades in the same manner as any other SEASONED SECURITY.

TOBIN'S Q RATIO A corporate valuation measure developed by economist Tobin, computed as:

$$Q = \frac{MV}{BV}$$

where MV is the MARKET VALUE of the firm and BV is the BOOK VALUE of the firm (measured on a REPLACEMENT COST basis).

A Q ratio below 1.0 means the firm is earning less than its required rate of RETURN; each marginal dollar invested in ASSETS fails to produce future CASH FLOWS whose PRESENT VALUE is equal to the marginal dollar invested. A ratio above 1.0 means the firm is exceeding the required rate of RETURN.

TOKKIN [JPN] An INVESTMENT FUND held by a corporate client and managed by a BANK, the ASSETS of which are generally invested in STOCKS.

TOKYO INTERBANK OFFERED RATE (TIBOR) The OFFER side of the yen-based Tokyo INTERBANK DEPOSIT market, or the rate at which prime BANKS are willing to lend funds. TIBOR, which is set every business day, is quoted for deposits in a range of MATURITIES and serves as an important base reference for other financial instruments (e.g., DERIVATIVES, FLOATING RATE NOTES) with a FLOATING RATE component.

TOKYO STOCK EXCHANGE (TSE)   The primary STOCK EXCHANGE of Japan, originally established in 1878, consolidated in 1943, and reformed in 1949. The exchange features three sections (LARGE CAP STOCKS, MID-CAP STOCKS, and start-up company stocks) and has operated on an electronic basis since the closure of its FLOOR in 1999. See also OSAKA STOCK EXCHANGE.

TOKYO STOCK PRICE INDEX (TOPIX)   A BENCHMARK INDEX of the Japanese STOCK market comprised of all COMMON STOCKS listed on the first section of the TOKYO STOCK EXCHANGE, with further subdivisions by size and industry. The TOPIX can be traded directly through EXCHANGE-TRADED FUNDS and DERIVATIVES.

TOLLING CONTRACT   A form of take-or-pay CONTRACT often used for processing and transportation/distribution in the energy industry that does not require the processor or transporter to purchase input/feedstock or sell the output. See also THROUGHPUT CONTRACT.

TOM NEXT   [COL] Abbreviated form of "tomorrow-next," referring to FOREIGN EXCHANGE and MONEY MARKET transactions that are executed tomorrow (t + 1) for delivery the day after that (t + 2). Also known as DEALING OVER TOMORROW, ROLLOVER.

TOMBSTONE   [COL] An advertisement announcing the completion of a NEW ISSUE of DEBT or EQUITY SECURITIES. The tombstone provides details of the transaction, along with the UNDERWRITING GROUP responsible for distributing the issue, and constitutes an informational advertisement rather than a solicitation to sell securities (any explicit advertisement in support of a new issue, apart from the PROSPECTUS, is illegal).

TON   [COL] Common reference for one hundred million. See also BUCK, YARD.

TOO BIG TO FAIL   [COL] A FINANCIAL INSTITUTION that is so large and integral to the effective functioning of a local, regional, or global system that its failure would have systemic repercussions that could create instability for a much larger population of institutions. Institutions that are considered too big to fail generally enjoy implicit (though rarely explicit) support from a CENTRAL BANK or monetary authority, and might expect to receive a bailout in the event of FINANCIAL DISTRESS.

TOP TICK   [COL] The EXECUTION of a TRADE at, or near, the peak of the market.

TOPIX   See TOKYO STOCK PRICE INDEX.

TOPPY   [COL] See FROTHY.

TORPEDO STOCK   [COL] A COMMON STOCK that has fallen dramatically and is expected to continue declining, generally as a result of poor financial performance and uncertain prospects.

TORT   An intentional or unintentional act of negligence by an individual or company, excluding breach of CONTRACT. A party damaged by a tort may seek remedy in court through a damage lawsuit.

TOTAL CONTROL   A process or structure where effective corporate control is gained through complete ownership. This exists primarily in the case of family-owned or PRIVATE COMPANIES, where accumulation or retention of a total block of SHARES is feasible. See also LEGAL MECHANISM CONTROL, MAJORITY CONTROL, MANAGEMENT CONTROL, MINORITY CONTROL, VOTING TRUST CONTROL.

TOTAL COST   The sum of a company's VARIABLE COSTS and FIXED COSTS.

TOTAL RATE OF RETURN SWAP   See TOTAL RETURN SWAP.

TOTAL RETURN SWAP   An OVER-THE-COUNTER SWAP that synthetically replicates the economic flows of a reference ASSET or INDEX, such as a CREDIT-risky BOND or EQUITY index, over a stated MATURITY (generally ranging from 6 months to 5 years). A generic total return swap involves the exchange of a periodic COUPON or upfront CASH FLOW plus any appreciation in the price of the reference for any depreciation in the reference. The contract permits BALANCE SHEET exposures or INVESTMENTS to be reproduced off balance sheet, on a LEVERAGED basis. Also known as CONTRACT FOR DIFFERENCES, TOTAL RATE OF RETURN SWAP.

TOXIC ASSET   [COL] A financial instrument that is considered to be very risky, generally one with high VOLATILITY and significant CREDIT RISK, MARKET RISK, and/or LIQUIDITY RISK. A Toxic asset may be developed by design (e.g., a STRUCTURED NOTE with a risky profile),or it may be the by-product of a SYNTHETIC ASSET (e.g. a RESIDUAL, COMPANION BOND, or exotic TRANCHE of a COLLATERALIZED DEBT OBLIGATION or COLLATERALIZED MORTGAGE OBLIGATION) that proves difficult to sell to INVESTORS or which has fallen out of favor.

TOXIC POOL   [COL] A DARK POOL that plays host to aggressive traders or those with rapid execution strategies who may be able to take advantage of INVESTORS with a more passive approach.

TRACKER FUND   See INDEX FUND.

TRACKING ERROR   A measure of the divergence between the performance of an INVESTMENT PORTFOLIO and a target or BENCHMARK INDEX, which generally arises as a result of transaction costs, portfolio composition (including a smaller number of SECURITIES used in the portfolio), and ASSET pricing differentials. Minimizing tracking error is a central element of successful INDEXING. (2) The realized VOLATILITY of a PORTFOLIO's ACTIVE RISK, measured on an ex-post basis as the realized annualized STANDARD DEVIATION of the difference between the portfolio's RETURN and the BENCHMARK's RETURN. (2) See also TRACKING RISK.

TRACKING RISK   A mechanism for estimating the ACTIVE RISK contained in a PORTFOLIO with ACTIVE BETS. It can be computed as the forecast of the annualized STANDARD DEVIATION of the difference between the PORTFOLIO's RETURN and the BENCHMARK's RETURN; since the forecast is model-driven, it must only be regarded as an estimate. See also TRACKING ERROR.

TRACKING STOCK   A COMMON STOCK based on a portion of a company's operations (i.e., a separate SUBSIDIARY or business unit). Tracking stocks are priced and traded independently of the company's primary stock and are permitted to pay a DIVIDEND; however, they carry no VOTING RIGHTS and have no legal CLAIM on the main company's ASSETS.

TRADE   (1) A transaction involving the purchase or sale of SECURITIES, COMMODITIES, FOREIGN EXCHANGE or DERIVATIVES, on an EXCHANGE or OVER-THE-COUNTER. (2) The purchase or sale of goods or services across borders.

TRADE BARRIER   Any restrictions created by a country in order to impede or limit free TRADE with other countries. Barriers may come in different guises, including QUOTAS, TARIFFS, DUTIES, and restrictive REGULATIONS.

TRADE BILL   A BILL OF EXCHANGE that is used to purchase goods.

TRADE CREDIT   (1) A form of financing extended by a company to its customers, created when customers are permitted to pay for goods or services at some future date. Trade credit is not referenced through specific documentation, as in a standard LOAN, but is generated informally at the time of sale. The implicit cost of credit can be determined by computing the difference between the DISCOUNT received for immediate cash payment, and the full invoice price for payment at any point after the discount period. (2) Funds lent to an exporter which are repaid when the importer receives and pays for the goods. (1) Also known as DEALER CREDIT, MERCHANDISE CREDIT. (1) See also ACCEPTANCE CREDIT.

TRADE CREDITORS   See ACCOUNTS PAYABLE.

TRADE DEBTORS   See ACCOUNTS RECEIVABLE.

TRADE GAP   The difference between a country's IMPORTS and EXPORTS, which may be either positive (trade surplus) or negative (trade deficit).

TRADED AWAY   [COL] A prospective financial transaction or deal with a client that one BANK loses to another bank.

TRADE-THROUGH   The purchase or sale of a STOCK during regular TRADING hours, either as PRINCIPAL or AGENT, at a price that is lower than a PROTECTED BID or higher than a PROTECTED OFFER.

TRADING   The process of buying and selling ASSETS in order to generate PROFITS from market movements and BID and OFFER SPREADS. Trading is a common line of business for BANKS, INVESTMENT BANKS, SECURITIES FIRMS, BROKER/DEALERS, HEDGE FUNDS, and certain MUTUAL FUNDS.

TRADING BOOK An ACCOUNT used by a DEALER, MARKET MAKER or proprietary TRADER that contains all OPEN POSITIONS, including SECURITIES, DERIVATIVES, and other CONTRACTS, along with any relevant HEDGES.

TRADING BOOK ACCOUNTING An ACCOUNTING process used by a BANK where certain ASSETS, such as SECURITIES and DERIVATIVES that are held for TRADING purposes, follow a MARK-TO-MARKET approach to profit and loss recognition, with changes in fair value booked to the OPERATING INCOME account within the INCOME STATEMENT. See also AVAILABLE FOR SALE ACCOUNTING, BANKING BOOK ACCOUNTING.

TRADING CREDIT RISK The RISK of loss associated with DEFAULT by a COUNTERPARTY on a financial transaction that dynamically changes in value, such as a DERIVATIVE or REVERSE REPURCHASE AGREEMENT. A loss on default is not always certain; when the transaction generates bilateral CREDIT RISK (as in a FORWARD or SWAP), the contract may have value to the counterparty rather than the INTERMEDIARY at the time of default, indicating that the credit provider sustains no loss. A subcategory of CREDIT RISK. See also CONTINGENT CREDIT RISK, CORRELATED CREDIT RISK, DIRECT CREDIT RISK, SETTLEMENT RISK, SOVEREIGN RISK.

TRADING CURB See CIRCUIT BREAKER.

TRADING HALT The temporary stop of all TRADING activities on an EXCHANGE, which may be the result of breaching a CIRCUIT BREAKER or the onset of an operational or technical difficulty, or a stop in the activities of one SECURITY as a result of breaking news which is expected to have a market impact.

TRADING INDEX (TRIN) A measure of STOCK market strength that compares the number of companies advancing and declining to volume. The general TRIN formula is given as:

$$TRIN = \left[\frac{\left(\dfrac{Adv_{num}}{Dec_{num}} \right)}{\left(\dfrac{Adv_{vol}}{Dec_{vol}} \right)} \right]$$

where Adv_{num} is the number of advancing issues, Dec_{num} is the number of declining issues, Adv_{vol} is the volume of advancing issues, and Dec_{vol} is the volume of declining issues.

A TRIN below 1.0 is considered a BULLISH signal, while a result above 1.0 is a BEARISH signal. Also known as ARMS INDEX.

TRADING PIT A section of an EXCHANGE that is used for TRADING of a specific ASSET. Trading pits still exist on certain exchanges, but are gradually disappearing as OPEN OUTCRY trading shifts to electronic trading. Also known as PIT.

TRADING PROFIT   In the United Kingdom, OPERATING INCOME.

TRADING SPECIAL   [COL] A condition where a SECURITY used as COLLATERAL in the REPURCHASE AGREEMENT market has become SPECIAL.

TRADING UPFRONT   [COL] A market situation where the REFERENCE CREDIT in a CREDIT DEFAULT SWAP (CDS) is perceived to be of such weak credit quality that the seller of the swap demands, in addition to the periodic premium payments that accompany a standard CDS, an upfront PREMIUM payment to compensate for the increased likelihood of DEFAULT.

TRAILING PRICE/EARNINGS RATIO   A PRICE/EARNINGS RATIO that is computed on a rolling basis based on the most recent 12 months' financial results, with the latest quarterly or semiannual results replacing the oldest data points. See also FORWARD PRICE/EARNINGS RATIO.

TRANCHE   [FR] A slice or portion of a SECURITIES issue or financing that is characterized by unique features related to CURRENCY, COUPON, MATURITY, CREDIT RATING, and seniority. Tranching is commonly used in SECURITIZATION, multicurrency LOANS, and CERTIFICATES OF DEPOSIT in order to create a range of INVESTMENT selections.

TRANCHETTE   A small issue of GILTS issued by the BANK OF ENGLAND, intended primarily for RETAIL INVESTORS.

TRANSACTION BALANCE   See IDLE BALANCE.

TRANSACTION COST   The costs associated with entering into a financial or INVESTMENT transaction, including COMMISSIONS, fees, STAMP DUTIES and/or TAXES, as well as certain indirect costs that support research and operational support. The greater the friction costs, the higher the breakeven point on the initial investment. Also known as FRICTION COST.

TRANSACTION RISK   The RISK of loss arising from adverse CURRENCY movements on corporate operations; PROFITS or LOSSES from such risks are typically reflected directly through the corporate INCOME STATEMENT. Dealings that give rise to transaction risk may be hedged through CURRENCY DERIVATIVES in order to decrease the possibility of loss. Also known as CURRENCY TRANSACTION RISK. See also TRANSLATION RISK.

TRANSACTION-SPECIFIC COLLATERAL   A COLLATERAL management technique where collateral is taken on an incremental basis in support of each discrete CREDIT-sensitive transaction. Individual pieces of collateral security are thus associated with specific transactions; as transactions mature or are unwound, the specific collateral is released. See also CROSS COLLATERAL AGREEMENT, POOLED PORTFOLIO COLLATERAL.

TRANSACTIONAL BANKING   A model of BANKING where a FINANCIAL INSTITUTION focuses primarily on providing clients with specific transactional services and support, often attempting to be the low-cost provider on a volume basis of CHECKING, DEPOSITS, TRADE EXECUTION, and LENDING. See also RELATIONSHIP BANKING.

TRANSFER The act of moving an ASSET from one person, ACCOUNT, or company to another. The asset involved may include MONEY, SECURITIES, COMMODITIES, or other property, and it may be accomplished physically or electronically.

TRANSFER PAYMENT Noncompensatory MONIES given by a government to the public, such as SOCIAL SECURITY benefits or other PENSION or welfare benefits.

TRANSFER PRICING Prices charged internally for goods or services within a company, which are ultimately factored into the cost of production.

TRANSFERABLE LETTER OF CREDIT A LETTER OF CREDIT that gives the BENEFICIARY the option of shifting some, or all, of the facility to a third party, such as a SUBSIDIARY or JOINT VENTURE partner. The transfer must first be approved by the issuing BANK. See also CONFIRMED LETTER OF CREDIT, DIRECT PAY LETTER OF CREDIT, IRREVOCABLE LETTER OF CREDIT, STANDBY LETTER OF CREDIT.

TRANSFERABLE REVOLVING UNDERWRITING FACILITY (TRUF) A REVOLVING UNDERWRITING FACILITY giving the original UNDERWRITER the RIGHT to transfer its commitment to another BANK.

TRANSFEREE A person or company to whom the TRANSFER of an ASSET is made. See also TRANSFEROR.

TRANSFEROR A person or company that TRANSFERS an ASSET. See also TRANSFEREE.

TRANSITION See RATING MIGRATION.

TRANSITION PROBABILITY The likelihood that a company's CREDIT RATING will migrate from one rating class to another; such PROBABILITIES are essential components of CREDIT MARK-TO-MARKET MODELS. See also RATING MIGRATION

TRANSLATION RISK The RISK arising from converting ASSETS and LIABILITIES from one CURRENCY to another, with any gains or losses reflected directly in the EQUITY account on the corporate BALANCE SHEET. Translation risk may arise when a company operates SUBSIDIARIES in different countries, and can be protected through a balance sheet HEDGE. See also TRANSACTION RISK.

TRAVELER'S CHECK A prepaid CHECK issued by a BANK that can be exchanged for local CURRENCY or used to pay for goods and services in foreign countries. The check must be signed and countersigned and accompanied by proof of identity in order to be valid.

TREASURER A professional within a company that is responsible for managing all items related to financing, HEDGING, and INVESTMENT, forming part of the TREASURY function.

TREASURY A function within a company that deals with financing, HEDGING, and INVESTMENT.

TREASURY BILL In the United States and certain other countries, a MONEY MARKET instrument issued by a government as a funding mechanism and a tool for conducting MONETARY POLICY. Treasury bills are typically issued on a DISCOUNT, rather than COUPON-bearing, basis through weekly and monthly auctions, and have maturities extending from 3 to 12 months. See also TREASURY BOND, TREASURY INFLATION-PROTECTED SECURITY, TREASURY NOTE.

TREASURY BILL RATE The INTEREST RATE applicable to an issue of TREASURY BILLS. Since Treasury bills are generally issued as DISCOUNT instruments, the interest rate is implicit rather than explicit.

TREASURY BOND In the United States and certain other countries, a DEBT instrument issued by the government as a funding mechanism. Treasury bonds are often issued on an AUCTION basis through PRIMARY DEALERS as FIXED RATE, COUPON-bearing, instruments with MATURITIES extending from 10 to 20 years. See also TREASURY BILL, TREASURY INFLATION-PROTECTED SECURITY, TREASURY NOTE.

TREASURY-EURODOLLAR (TED) SPREAD The YIELD differential between EURODOLLAR DEPOSITS and TREASURY BILLS of the same MATURITY. The TED SPREAD provides an indication of the relative CREDIT performance of the banking sector, with a widening of the spread reflecting weakness or deterioration, and a tightening signaling an improvement.

TREASURY INFLATION-PROTECTED SECURITY (TIPS) A US TREASURY NOTE or TREASURY BOND with a RETURN that is linked to the level of INFLATION (as measured by the CONSUMER PRICE INDEX). TIPS are available in a range of medium- to long-term MATURITIES and are sold in small minimum denominations so that they may be purchased by RETAIL INVESTORS. TIPS pay fixed COUPONS on a regular cycle and the PRINCIPAL repayment is adjusted at maturity to reflect inflation performance.

TREASURY INVESTORS GROWTH RECEIPT (TIGR) A ZERO COUPON BOND issued by the US Treasury.

TREASURY MANAGEMENT The financial management of a company's short-term ASSET and LIABILITY positions and short-term CASH FLOWS, with the aim of ensuring appropriate amounts of daily funding and LIQUIDITY, and proper management of MARKET RISKS (e.g., INTEREST RATE RISK and FOREIGN EXCHANGE RISK). The focus of treasury management is on the OPERATING CYCLE and the CASH FLOW CYCLE of the business.

TREASURY NOTE In the United States and certain other countries, a DEBT instrument issued by the government as a funding mechanism. Treasury notes are often issued on an AUCTION basis through PRIMARY DEALERS as FIXED RATE, COUPON-bearing, instruments with MATURITIES extending from 1 to 10 years. See also TREASURY BILL, TREASURY BOND, TREASURY INFLATION-PROTECTED SECURITY.

TREASURY STOCK   Outstanding COMMON STOCK that is repurchased by a company, at which point it is classified as STOCK that is authorized and issued but is no longer outstanding. The repurchase, which is shown as a net reduction in total EQUITY through a CONTRA ACCOUNT, can be arranged through a single STOCK BUYBACK or via a regular, formulaic, repurchase known as a SELF-TENDER. In the United States, a SECURITIES AND EXCHANGE COMMISSION SAFE HARBOR (Rule 10b-18) allows a company to repurchase its own stock without being charged with SECURITIES manipulation. Also known as REACQUIRED STOCK.

TREATY FACILITY   A mechanism allowing a CAPTIVE to access the REINSURANCE markets for large exposures. The facility generally reinsures a small percentage of the captive's exposures and then RETROCEDES the balance through TREATY REINSURANCE.

TREATY OF ROME   A treaty executed in 1957 that led to the formation of the EUROPEAN ECONOMIC COMMUNITY (as predecessor of the EUROPEAN UNION).

TREATY REINSURANCE   A REINSURANCE agreement where the primary INSURER agrees to CEDE to a REINSURER a portion of all RISKS conforming to preagreed guidelines. Since conforming risks must be assumed by the reinsurer, the insurer is assured of necessary coverage; it also means, however, that the insurer cannot retain in its own PORTFOLIO a full share of conforming risks that may be especially profitable. See also FACULTATIVE REINSURANCE, QUOTA SHARE, SURPLUS SHARE, TREATY FACILITY.

TRENDLINE   A TECHNICAL ANALYSIS charting technique created by connecting the highest or lowest prices of a SECURITY or market over time; the resulting line is indicative of an overall directional trend.

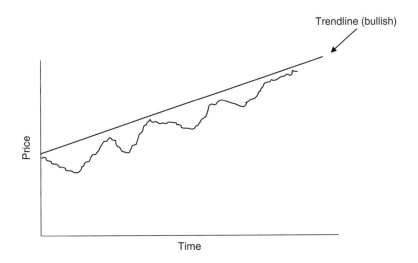

TREYNOR INDEX   A measure of RISK-adjusted PORTFOLIO performance that compares the RISK PREMIUM (or RETURN) earned by the PORTFOLIO with the risk of the portfolio (as reflected through the portfolio BETA). The Treynor index, which uses the SECURITY MARKET LINE as a BENCHMARK, can be computed via:

$$TI = \frac{E(r_p) - r_f}{\beta_p}$$

where $E(r_p)$ is the expected return of the portfolio, r_f is the RISK-FREE RATE, and β_p is the beta of the portfolio. See also JENSEN INDEX, SHARPE INDEX. Additional reference: Treynor (1965).

TRIAL BALANCE   A tool used in the DOUBLE ENTRY ACCOUNTING system that adds all ledger account DEBIT columns and CREDIT columns in order to ensure they are in balance. If the two are not in balance, an error has occurred (e.g., error in posting JOURNAL ENTRIES, omission of an account, and so forth).

TRIAL FINANCIAL STATEMENTS The preliminary, un-AUDITED FINANCIAL STATEMENTS of a company. Trial financial statements are intended for internal use rather than public disclosure.

TRIANGLE   A TECHNICAL ANALYSIS charting technique that depicts the price of a SECURITY or market in a formation with two base points and a top that gives the appearance of a triangle; a triangle features multiple rallies and retreats, with each subsequent peak occurring at a lower level than the previous one. A BREAKOUT from a triangle may portend a much larger move to the upside or downside.

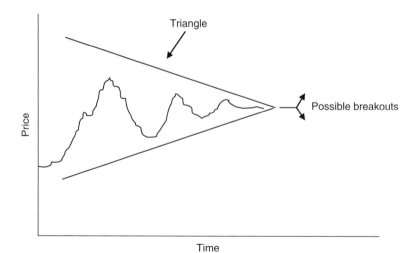

TRIGGER (1) A value or event threshold embedded in an INSURANCE POLICY that determines whether an INSURED (or BENEFICIARY) will receive a compensatory payment in the event of loss. A generic insurance contract has a single trigger, i.e., whether a named PERIL has created a loss. More complex structures, including DUAL TRIGGERS and TRIPLE TRIGGERS, require the onset of additional events (or breach of particular values) before providing loss payments. Similar triggers are found in INSURANCE-LINKED SECURITIES, and indicate whether an ISSUER's PRINCIPAL and/or INTEREST payments will be suspended. (2) A form of COVENANT in BANK credit agreements and BOND INDENTURES. (3) The value that must be surpassed in a COVERAGE TEST on a COLLATERALIZED DEBT OBLIGATION to continue payments to increasingly subordinated TRANCHES under the CASH FLOW WATERFALL.

TRIN See TRADING INDEX.

TRIPLE TRIGGER An INSURANCE mechanism that provides the INSURED with a payout only if three separate TRIGGER events occur; one trigger is often related to a traditional insurance RISK (e.g., destruction in plant and equipment leading to business interruption), while the second and third may relate to insurance or FINANCIAL RISKS (e.g., a decline in operating revenues of a certain amount and a fall in the STOCK price to a particular level). Since all three events must occur in order for a SETTLEMENT to take place, the PREMIUM is generally lower than it is on a standard insurance CONTRACT. See also DUAL TRIGGER, MULTIPLE TRIGGER PRODUCT.

TRIPLE WITCHING DAY [COL] A single business day when INDEX FUTURES, index OPTIONS, and individual EQUITY options all settle, which occurs once each quarter (i.e., the third Friday in March, June, September, and December). There is evidence to indicate that volume and VOLATILITY increase during triple witching days as INVESTORS, HEDGERS, and SPECULATORS rebalance their positions. See also QUADRUPLE WITCHING DAY.

TRUE AND FAIR VIEW In the United Kingdom, FAIR PRESENTATION.

TRUE SALE SECURITIZATION A form of SECURITIZATION that involves the transfer or assignment of a POOL of reference ASSETS from the originator to a SPECIAL PURPOSE ENTITY (SPE) or TRUST, which then issues NOTES to INVESTORS; the originator, however, retains legal TITLE to the assets. The TRUSTEE, through a power of attorney from the originator, has the ability to transfer legal title to the SPE, if necessary. See also SYNTHETIC SECURITIZATION.

TRUST (1) A legal vehicle that permits ownership of property by one party for the express benefit of another party. The TRUSTEE receives TITLE to, but cannot benefit from, the property, and is legally obliged to manage the property in a prudent manner on behalf of the ultimate BENEFICIARY. (2) A monopolistic business entity formed through consolidation or amalgamation of various existing CORPORATIONS, prevalent primarily during the early twentieth century.

TRUST DEED   See INDENTURE.

TRUST FUND   An INVESTMENT FUND that holds the ASSETS of a TRUST, and which is directed by the TRUSTEE.

TRUST PREFERRED STOCK   A type of HYBRID CAPITAL SECURITY where a TRUST purchases the junior ranking SUBORDINATED DEBT of the issuing company (generally a BANK), and passes through the periodic COUPONS to INVESTORS in the form of cumulative DIVIDENDS. Trust preferreds generally feature a minimum maturity of 30 years with OPTIONAL REDEMPTION, and qualify as REGULATORY CAPITAL. The securities have a ranking in DEFAULT that is senior to COMMON STOCK and PREFERRED STOCK and PARI PASSU with other junior subordinated debt. See also JUNIOR SUBORDINATED DEBENTURE, PERPETUAL PREFERRED STOCK.

TRUSTEE   (1) In general, a party that administers a TRUST. A trustee is typically designated as the legal owner of property being administered on behalf of a BENEFICIARY; all actions taken by the trustee must be done in the best interests of the beneficiary. (2) In a BOND issue, an institution responsible for enforcing terms of the INDENTURE, managing the SINKING FUND, collecting PRINCIPAL and INTEREST from the ISSUER for disbursement to INVESTORS, investing and disbursing cash balances, and holding COLLATERAL for the ultimate benefit of bond investors.

TRUSTEE IN BANKRUPTCY   A FIDUCIARY appointed by a court or CREDITOR to manage the affairs of a company that has filed for BANKRUPTCY. In the United States a trustee in bankruptcy is appointed under CHAPTER 7 to oversee LIQUIDATION and dispersal of ASSETS. A trustee may or may not be appointed under CHAPTER 11; if no trustee is appointed a DEBTOR-IN-POSSESSION assumes the role and responsibilities of the trustee, including the development of a REORGANIZATION plan. See also PREFERENTIAL DEBT.

TSE   See TOKYO STOCK EXCHANGE.

TUNNEL   [COL] See ZERO COST COLLAR.

TURBO OPTION   See POWER OPTION.

TURKEY   [COL] A bad INVESTMENT, or a promising deal that has soured.

TURN   [COL] The difference between the BID and OFFER on a SECURITY, or the amount that a DEALER or MARKET MAKER can earn by buying at the bid and selling at the offer.

TURNOVER   (1) In the United Kingdom, GROSS REVENUE. (2) The amount of TRADING volume on an EXCHANGE, in total or in a specific SECURITY. (3) The activity in a specific ASSET account, such as INVENTORY. (2) Also known as VOLUME.

TWAP   See TIME WEIGHTED AVERAGE PRICE.

TWIN-IN BARRIER OPTION   An OVER-THE-COUNTER COMPLEX OPTION that is created when an upper or lower BARRIER is breached. The inclusion of two barriers, which increase the probability of triggering, generally makes the structure more expensive than a standard KNOCK-IN OPTION. See also BARRIER OPTION, TWIN-OUT BARRIER OPTION.

TWIN-OUT BARRIER OPTION   An OVER-THE-COUNTER COMPLEX OPTION that is extinguished when an upper or lower barrier is breached. The inclusion of two barriers, which increases the probability of triggering, generally makes the structure cheaper than a standard KNOCK-OUT OPTION. See also BARRIER OPTION, TWIN-IN BARRIER OPTION.

TWIST   The process of moving the YIELD CURVE up or down by a different number of BASIS POINTS in the short and long MATURITIES of the curve and recalculating the value of a FIXED INCOME transaction or PORTFOLIO. The curve twist reveals the sensitivity of the fixed income position(s) to unequal changes in the curve and can be used to compute hypothetical PROFITS and LOSSES or the effectiveness of a possible HEDGE strategy. Twists can be created by holding constant short-term rates while raising/lowering long-term rates, holding constant long-term rates while raising/lowering short-term rates, raising short-term rates and lowering long-term rates, or raising long-term rates and lowering short-term rates. See also PARALLEL SHIFT.

TWISTING   [COL] See CHURNING.

TWO-FACTOR INTEREST RATE MODEL   An OPTION pricing model that values BOND options by generating an entire YIELD CURVE through two variables, such as a short-term rate and a drift or reversion factor. Although such models are more complex to calibrate and implement than ONE-FACTOR INTEREST RATE MODELS, they can generate more precise results.

TWO-TIER BID   A TAKEOVER BID that features a more attractive price for INVESTORS willing to tender their SHARES by the first cutoff date; those choosing not to tender by a certain date are offered a less favorable deal. See also ANY-AND-ALL BID, FAIR PRICE PROVISION.

TWO-WAY MARKET   See TWO-WAY PRICES.

TWO-WAY PRICES   A BID and an OFFER on an individual SECURITY as quoted by a MARKET MAKER or other DEALER. In certain cases institutions that choose to act as market makers must be prepared to quote two-way prices in all market conditions. Also known as MAKING A MARKET, TWO-WAY MARKET.

TYING   [COL] A practice where a BANK, INVESTMENT BANK, or SECURITIES FIRM grants a client a LOAN with a low MARGIN only if the client agrees to award it more lucrative financial business, such as an UNDERWRITING or CORPORATE FINANCE transaction. In some jurisdictions the practice constitutes a violation of fair trading practices and is illegal. See also REVERSE TYING.

U

UBERRIMAE FIDEI [LAT] Literally "in utmost good faith;" a characteristic commonly applied to INSURANCE POLICIES, where the INSURED and INSURER disclose all relevant information and express intention to carry out their respective obligations in good faith.

ULTIMATE NET LOSS A computation performed by an INSURER that reflects the net economic loss sustained in INSURANCE activities, generally calculated via:

$$UNL = - (Cl + LAE) + (Reins + Sal + Sub)$$

where Cl is CLAIMS loss, LAE is LOSS ADJUSTMENT EXPENSE, Reins is recovery from REINSURANCE CONTRACTS in force, Sal is recovery from salvage value, and Sub is recovery from SUBROGATION rights.

ULTRA VIRES [LAT] Literally "outside one's jurisdiction;" any action or financial dealing undertaken by a company or municipal authority that is beyond the scope of authority dictated by CORPORATE CHARTER, municipal bylaws, or state/federal/national laws. Ultra vires actions are not generally defensible and leave open the possibility of third party legal proceedings against those committing the actions. Use of DERIVATIVES, STRUCTURED NOTES with embedded LEVERAGE, and other risky instruments have been cited by the courts, in certain instances, to be ultra vires.

UMBRELLA POLICY An INSURANCE POLICY that provides the INSURED with additional coverage for specific LIABILITY and/or various named PERILS. The umbrella policy works in tandem with an insured's existing policies to provide EXCESS LAYER coverage or ensure that any potential gaps that exist are appropriately filled.

UMBRELLA REINSURANCE A REINSURANCE CONTRACT that covers MULTIPLE PERIL POLICIES. All treaties written under the umbrella comprise a single block of business, so REINSURERS participating in the agreement cannot select which treaty to reinsure.

UNAUTHORIZED INSURANCE See NONADMITTED INSURANCE.

UNAUTHORIZED INSURER See NONADMITTED INSURER.

UNBUNDLING [COL] The process of decomposing and segregating individual financial services offered by BANKS so that customers can more precisely take advantage of, and pay for, those services they actually require.

UNCOMMITTED FACILITY A CREDIT line granted by a BANK to a company that can be withdrawn by the bank at will if it has not been drawn. Since the facility can easily be taken away, it is not considered a reliable source of financing. See also COMMITTED FUNDING.

UNCOVERED OPTION See NAKED OPTION.

UNDATED SECURITY Any SECURITY that lacks a defined MATURITY, such as PERPETUAL DEBT, COMMON STOCK, and most forms of PREFERRED STOCK.

UNDERBANKED A future NEW ISSUE of SECURITIES with few INDICATIONS OF INTEREST, suggesting that the deal may be difficult for the SYNDICATE to place with INVESTORS unless pricing or other deal terms are altered.

UNDERCAPITALIZATION Any situation where a company lacks enough CAPITAL to support its operations on a continuing basis. Undercapitalization may result from large losses that deplete capital resources, or from growth in ASSETS that outpaces any capital-raising efforts.

UNDERFUNDED PENSION PLAN A form of FUNDED PENSION PLAN in which invested proceeds are insufficient to meet the requirements of future pensioners, primarily as a result of underperformance of the INVESTMENT PORTFOLIO underlying the pension.

UNDERINSURANCE (1) Insufficient INSURANCE to cover an INSURABLE RISK, leaving the INSURED exposed to financial loss. (2) Failure by the insured to meet COINSURANCE requirements specified by the INSURER. (1) See also OVERINSURANCE.

UNDERINVESTMENT PROBLEM A situation where a company in FINANCIAL DISTRESS is urged by CREDITORS to invest in projects with low RISKS and low RETURNS. Such INVESTMENTS are intended to protect the ASSET position of the firm for the benefit of creditors rather than maximize ENTERPRISE VALUE for the benefit of SHAREHOLDERS.

UNDERLYING The ASSET or market reference defining or underpinning a DERIVATIVE contract.

UNDERPERFORMANCE OPTION An OVER-THE-COUNTER COMPLEX OPTION that grants the buyer a PAYOFF based on the underperformance of a market reference or SPREAD against a predefined STRIKE PRICE. See also OUTPERFORMANCE OPTION, SPREAD OPTION.

UNDERSTANDABILITY A principle of ACCOUNTING indicating that financial terms and information must be presented in a way that can be understood by an individual with some degree of business knowledge, that it should include essential information and should not include irrelevant or overly detailed information.

UNDERSUBSCRIPTION A situation where the number of ORDERS for a NEW ISSUE of SECURITIES is lower than the available SUPPLY, suggesting the price of the security could decline at launch. Depending on the nature of the CAPITAL commitment, the UNDERWRITERS may take up a shortfall in orders. See also OVERSUBSCRIPTION.

UNDERWATER [COL] (1) A market situation where an OPTION is so far OUT-OF-THE-MONEY that it is virtually worthless. (2) An INVESTMENT position with a MARKET VALUE that is below BOOK VALUE or carrying value, and which will crystallize a loss if sold.

UNDERWRITER   (1) A FINANCIAL INSTITUTION involved in UNDERWRITING a NEW ISSUE of SECURITIES. (2) An INSURER or REINSURER that analyzes, prices, and accepts or rejects INSURABLE RISKS. (1) See also SYNDICATE.

UNDERWRITER'S LIABILITY   The LIABILITY an UNDERWRITER faces in arranging and issuing SECURITIES for a company. If DUE DILIGENCE has not been performed (or has been performed with errors), or if financial disclosure contained in the PROSPECTUS is incorrect, INVESTORS holding securities that ultimately DEFAULT may be able to recover their losses from the underwriter.

UNDERWRITING   (1) In the SECURITIES industry, the process of issuing NOTES, BONDS, CONVERTIBLE BONDS, COMMON STOCK, or PREFERRED STOCK in the PRIMARY MARKET on behalf of an ISSUER. (2) In the banking and INSURANCE industries, the process of thoroughly evaluating a RISK exposure and determining whether anticipated profitability is commensurate with EXPECTED LOSS. In banking this is often done through CREDIT analysis; in insurance it is accomplished through ACTUARIAL PRICING and analysis. (1) See also ALL-OR-NONE UNDERWRITING, BEST EFFORTS UNDERWRITING, BOUGHT DEAL.

UNDERWRITING AGREEMENT   See SYNDICATE AGREEMENT.

UNDERWRITING GROUP   See SYNDICATE.

UNDERWRITING INCOME   In INSURANCE, the net amount earned from core insurance UNDERWRITING activities, typically computed as:

$$UI = Pr - (IL + LAE + UE + Div)$$

where Pr is PREMIUM, IL is INCURRED LOSSES, LAE is LOSS ADJUSTMENT EXPENSES, UE is underwriting EXPENSE, and Div is policyholder DIVIDENDS.

UNDERWRITING RISK   (1) The RISK that a SYNDICATE of BANKS or SECURITIES FIRMS UNDERWRITING a NEW ISSUE on a BOUGHT DEAL basis will be unable to place securities with INVESTORS, indicating that they will be required to fund any shortfall from their own resources. (2) The risk that the PREMIUM an INSURER charges INSUREDS will prove insufficient to cover future losses, and that losses and LOSS ADJUSTMENT EXPENSES will not be properly covered by RESERVES.

UNDERWRITING SPREAD   In a NEW ISSUE, the difference between the amount paid by the SYNDICATE to the ISSUER and the price at which SECURITIES are offered to INVESTORS. The spread varies by issuer, class of issue, market conditions, and marketplace, and can range from 4% to 7% for COMMON STOCK to less than 1% for NOTES and BONDS. Also known as GROSS SPREAD, SPREAD. See also SELLING CONCESSION.

UNDISCLOSED FACTORING   A form of FACTORING where the underlying does not want the presence of a factor to be revealed. Apart from this confidentiality, the roles of seller and factor remain the same as in a conventional factoring arrangement.

UNDISTRIBUTABLE RESERVES In the United Kingdom, that portion of CAPITAL that cannot be distributed, including SHARE CAPITAL, the SHARE PREMIUM, and certain other RESERVES and unrealized profit accounts. See also RESTRICTED SURPLUS.

UNDISTRIBUTED PROFITS See RETAINED EARNINGS.

UNDUE INFLUENCE Any form of influence that can be interpreted as coercion in the preparation and execution of a CONTRACT, and which may render the contract null and void by a court.

UNEARNED PREMIUM RESERVE A RESERVE that contains a portion of the advance PREMIUM paid by an INSURED to an INSURER (or a CEDING INSURER to REINSURER) to cover the amount of INSURANCE (or REINSURANCE) that is still in force. Since premiums are normally charged at the inception of a policy but potential LIABILITY exists until the policy terminates, the reserve reflects the amount needed to cover EXPECTED LOSS prior to expiry. The amount of the reserve associated with a specific policy declines as contract expiry draws closer.

UNEMPLOYMENT Lack of employment for able workers, and a key measure of the state of an ECONOMY in the BUSINESS CYCLE. During recovery and growth phases unemployment is low as demand for productive labor increases; during slowdown and RECESSION phases unemployment rises as demand for labor declines in line with reduced economic output.

UNEXPECTED CREDIT LOSS The difference between EXPECTED CREDIT LOSS and WORST-CASE CREDIT LOSS; alternatively, the difference between the MEAN of the credit loss distribution function and a point represented by multiple STANDARD DEVIATIONS from the mean.

UNFAIR PREFERENCE The transfer of ASSETS or the payment of sums to a CREDITOR by a party that is about to declare BANKRUPTCY. Such a transfer may be declared void by the courts and be subject to CLAWBACK.

UNFUNDED PENSION PLAN A PENSION SYSTEM in which current employees pay for the benefits of existing pensioners (e.g., pay as you go). See also FUNDED PENSION PLAN, UNDERFUNDED PENSION PLAN.

UNIFORM PRICE AUCTION A type of AUCTION MARKET in which buyers submit BIDS reflecting the price they will pay for a given quantity of an item. The orders are then allocated from highest to lowest, until the total SUPPLY of items is exhausted. Thereafter, bidders pay a per unit price that is equal to the lowest winning bid, rather than the original bid submitted.

UNILATERAL COLLATERAL A COLLATERAL agreement where only one party to a transaction is required to post SECURITY; this generally occurs when one of the two COUNTERPARTIES to a transaction has a materially lower CREDIT RATING than the second party. See also BILATERAL COLLATERAL.

UNINCORPORATED BUSINESS   Any form of business organization where the owner bears UNLIMITED LIABILITY for any DEBTS incurred.

UNINSURABLE RISK   A RISK that cannot be covered by INSURANCE as it fails to meet the standard requirements set forth for an INSURABLE RISK, i.e., the risk can produce a loss that is not definable or fortuitous, or the risk is catastrophic and cannot be transferred through payment of an economically reasonable PREMIUM. Also known as PROHIBITED RISK.

UNISSUED STOCK   COMMON STOCK that is authorized for issuance through a firm's CORPORATE CHARTER, but has not yet been floated; unissued stock stands in contrast to TREASURY STOCK, which is issued but no longer outstanding.

UNIT INVESTMENT TRUST   See CLOSED-END FUND.

UNIT LINKED POLICY   In the United Kingdom, a form of life INSURANCE where the amount paid to a BENEFICIARY in the event of mortality of the INSURED depends on the value of the INVESTMENT PORTFOLIO underlying the policy, which comprises of SHARES in a UNIT TRUST. Since the policy has a SAVINGS component, it has a SURRENDER VALUE that can be realized upon termination of the policy.

UNIT TRUST   (1) In the United Kingdom, a FUND where INVESTORS contribute CAPITAL that is used to acquire a PORTFOLIO of earning ASSETS; investors receive a proportional share of any RETURNS generated. A unit trust is legally constructed as a TRUST, with a TRUSTEE appointed as a guardian to hold assets on behalf of the BENEFICIAL OWNERS under the terms of a trust DEED. A separate INVESTMENT MANAGEMENT company is responsible for managing the portfolios and making investment decisions. Investors purchase individual units in the fund, which can be open-ended; subsequent sales and purchases of units are arranged through the investment manager. (2) See MUTUAL FUND. (3) See CLOSED-END FUND.

UNIVERSAL BANK   A BANK that engages in traditional commercial banking activities (i.e., LENDING, DEPOSIT-taking) and SECURITIES activities (i.e., TRADING securities, UNDERWRITING NEW ISSUES, arranging CORPORATE FINANCE transactions, granting INVESTMENT advice). Europe has featured a system of universal banking for many years; the same has not existed in the United States as a result of regulatory restrictions (these were dismantled in the millennium via the GRAMM-LEACH-BLILEY ACT). See also BANCASSURANCE, COMMERCIAL BANK, INVESTMENT BANK.

UNLIMITED COMPANY   A form of corporate organization in which SHAREHOLDERS do not benefit from the tenet of LIMITED LIABILITY.

UNLIMITED LIABILITY   A concept and structure where the personal ASSETS of INVESTORS, GENERAL PARTNERS, or sole proprietors are at RISK in the event of a business loss; the extent of financial LIABILITY is not bounded as it is in a LIMITED LIABILITY company. See also PIERCING THE CORPORATE VEIL.

UNLIQUIDATED DAMAGES   DAMAGES awarded to a plaintiff that can only be estimated ex-post by the courts. See also LIQUIDATED DAMAGES, STATUTORY DAMAGES.

UNLISTED SECURITY   Any SECURITY that is not formally listed on an EXCHANGE, and which need not comply with exchange rules related to disclosure. Unlisted securities are typically issued by small companies and are very ILLIQUID.

UNMATCHED BOOK   A PORTFOLIO of ASSETS and LIABILITIES (such as the LOANS and DEPOSITS of a BANK, or the REPURCHASE AGREEMENTS and REVERSE REPURCHASE AGREEMENTS of a SECURITIES FIRM), with unequal MATURITIES or DURATIONS. An unmatched book increases an institution's exposure to MARKET RISK and/or LIQUIDITY RISK, but provides for the possibility of a greater RETURN on CAPITAL. See also GAP, GAPPING, MATCHED BOOK, MISMATCH, OPEN BOOK.

UNQUALIFIED OPINION   An AUDIT OPINION by an EXTERNAL AUDITOR indicating that a company's FINANCIAL STATEMENTS present a fair and accurate view of its financial position and conform to accepted ACCOUNTING PRINCIPLES. Also known as CLEAN OPINION. See also ADVERSE OPINION, QUALIFIED OPINION.

UNREALIZED GAIN   Gains on an ASSET (resulting from a positive change in valuation) that have not yet been realized or "locked in" for ACCOUNTING purposes. An unrealized profit can only be realized through disposal or establishment of a HEDGE. Also known as PAPER PROFIT. See also REALIZED GAIN, UNREALIZED LOSS.

UNREALIZED LOSS   Losses on an ASSET (resulting from a negative change in valuation) that have not yet been realized or "locked in" for ACCOUNTING purposes. An unrealized loss can only be realized through disposal. Also known as PAPER LOSS. See also REALIZED LOSS, UNREALIZED GAIN.

UNREGISTERED STOCK   STOCK that is not registered with the relevant SECURITIES REGULATOR and which cannot therefore be TRADED on a public basis.

UNSECURED   A financing or LIABILITY that is not backed by any type of support, e.g., no COLLATERAL or GUARANTEE. See also SECURED.

UNSECURED CREDITOR   A CREDITOR that has lent MONEY to an individual or company without taking any COLLATERAL as SECURITY. See also SECURED CREDITOR, UNSECURED DEBT.

UNSECURED DEBT   A BOND or LOAN without any COLLATERAL backing; the sole source of repayment for INVESTORS or LENDERS comes from the DEBTOR'S financial resources. Unsecured debt is most common among BORROWERS/ISSUERS with strong CREDIT RATINGS. See also SECURED DEBT.

UNWIND   The process of settling two or more DERIVATIVE transactions between two COUNTERPARTIES in order to reduce CREDIT RISK exposures and crystallize any MARK-TO-MARKET gain or loss. The unwinding process terminates all affected CONTRACTS and is thus a more efficient method than entering into BACK-TO-BACK SWAPS.

UNWIND PRICE   See TEAR-UP PRICE.

UP AND IN OPTION   A COMPLEX OPTION that creates a standard EUROPEAN OPTION if the price of the UNDERLYING market reference rises above a predefined BARRIER. See also BARRIER OPTION, DOWN AND IN OPTION, DOWN AND OUT OPTION, KNOCK-IN OPTION, REVERSE KNOCK-IN OPTION, UP AND OUT OPTION.

UP AND OUT OPTION   A COMPLEX OPTION that extinguishes a standard EUROPEAN OPTION if the price of the UNDERLYING market reference rises above a predefined BARRIER. If the barrier is not breached the European option remains in effect. See also BARRIER OPTION, DOWN AND IN OPTION, DOWN AND OUT OPTION, KNOCK-OUT OPTION, REVERSE KNOCK-OUT OPTION, UP AND IN OPTION.

UPFRONT COLLATERAL   A process where an institution takes initial COLLATERAL from its COUNTERPARTY in an amount sufficient to cover expected POTENTIAL EXPOSURE for the entire life of the transaction. Under this arrangement no periodic evaluations or collateral calls are required. See also PERIODIC COLLATERAL.

UPSTAIRS MARKET   [COL] TRADES executed through a BROKER/DEALER, or between two broker/dealers, that do not flow through an EXCHANGE. Upstairs market transactions cannot occur at prices that are prejudicial to customers. See also CROSSED TRADE.

UPSTREAM   (1) The process of channeling funds from a SUBSIDIARY to a PARENT or HOLDING COMPANY. This may occur when the parent or holding company is restricted in some way from raising funds directly. (2) The segment of the energy industry that is focused on exploration, extraction, and production. See also DOWNSTREAM.

UPTICK   See PLUS TICK.

UPTICK RULE   A rule imposed by the SECURITIES AND EXCHANGE COMMISSION that only permits a SHORT SALE in a SECURITY or INDEX ARBITRAGE program to be initiated on a PLUS TICK or ZERO PLUS TICK. The rule is intended to halt a self-fulfilling downward spiral, where each downtick leads to further short selling.

UPWARD SLOPING YIELD CURVE   See POSITIVE YIELD CURVE.

USANCE   The time period during which a BILL OF EXCHANGE must be paid.

USE OF CASH A transaction that leads to a cash outflow from a company; any use of cash is reflected in the CASH FLOW STATEMENT. Typical uses of cash include net losses, CAPITAL EXPENDITURES, purchases of INVESTMENTS, repayment of medium- and long-term DEBT, repurchase of COMMON STOCK, payment of DIVIDENDS, increases in ASSET balances (e.g., ACCOUNTS RECEIVABLE, INVENTORIES), and decreases in LIABILITIES (e.g., ACCOUNTS PAYABLE, deferrals). See also SOURCE OF CASH.

USURY The practice of charging an excessive INTEREST RATE on any class of DEBT or LIABILITY; in many national systems usury is prohibited by law through the establishment of maximum interest rate ceilings.

UTILIZATION RATE The portion of a REVOLVING CREDIT FACILITY that is drawn down by the BORROWER, and which must be repaid according to scheduled terms.

V

VALORIZATION A process used by a government authority to artificially support or increase the price of an ASSET or COMMODITY, often by constraining SUPPLY.

VALUATION See CORPORATE VALUATION.

VALUE-ADDED TAX (VAT) An indirect TAX applied in certain national systems that is payable by producers and consumers of goods and services. A tax is levied on each incremental stage of the production process that adds value to the good or service being produced. See also AD VALOREM.

VALUE-AT-RISK (VAR) A statistical measure that estimates how much a PORTFOLIO of ASSETS and LIABILITIES might lose in a given time period as a result of MARKET RISK. VAR, which can be implemented through the VARIANCE/COVARIANCE, historical, or SIMULATION methods, is based on assumptions related to LIQUIDATION period, shape of the statistical distribution, desired CONFIDENCE LEVEL, and VOLATILITIES and CORRELATIONS between portfolio CONTRACTS. Though widely used, the measure has shortcomings related to statistical assumptions and uncertainty regarding the magnitude of potential losses in the TAIL of the distribution. The general computation for VAR is given as:

$$VAR_{1-\alpha}(r_p) = -\min\{z \mid (P(r_p \leq z) > \alpha)\}$$

where r_p is the return on a portfolio of assets, P is the probability, $1 - \alpha$ is the confidence level (e.g., α set to 1% or 5%), z is the relevant Z-SCORE. See also BACKTESTING, EXTREME VALUE THEORY, MAXIMUM LOSS, PROFIT AND LOSS EXPLAIN.

VALUE CHAIN A sequence of linked activities supporting the production of a good, where each activity adds a particular value to the end product. Common value chain activities include logistics, production, marketing, and distribution, along with supporting functions such as research and development, human resources, and technology.

VALUE DATE The date on which funds become GOOD MONEY, or a SECURITIES or FOREIGN EXCHANGE transaction is settled. Also known as SETTLEMENT DATE.

VALUED CONTRACT An INSURANCE POLICY that provides the INSURED with a stated payout amount, agreed on an ex-ante basis, in the event of a loss. Valued contracts are generally associated with life insurance policies, which specify a certain sum payable to the BENEFICIARY upon the death of the insured. See also INDEMNITY CONTRACT.

VANILLA [COL] A standard or conventional financial transaction, rather than one with esoteric or complex parameters, RISKS, or PAYOFF profiles.

Since vanilla transactions are common, they tend to feature the greatest LIQUIDITY and the narrowest BID-OFFER SPREADS. Also known as PLAIN VANILLA.

VAR   See VALUE-AT-RISK.

VARIABLE ANNUITY   An ANNUITY where PREMIUMS received from the INVESTOR are used to purchase accumulation units with variable value determined by the worth of the SECURITIES in the INSURER's INVESTMENT PORTFOLIO. When the benefits are ultimately paid to the ANNUITANT, units are converted into a fixed number, crystallizing the payout.

VARIABLE COST   An expense that changes in proportion to a company's output, increasing as output increases and decreasing as output decreases (e.g., raw materials used in production). Variable cost is one of two elements, along with FIXED COST, which comprise TOTAL COSTS. It can also be computed as the sum of the MARGINAL COSTS.

VARIABLE INTEREST ENTITY (VIE)   See SPECIAL-PURPOSE ENTITY.

VARIABLE LIFE ASSURANCE   In the United Kingdom, form of life ASSURANCE in which PREMIUMS are invested in UNIT TRUSTS and where the amount of coverage can be altered by the INSURED. See also VARIABLE LIFE INSURANCE.

VARIABLE LIFE INSURANCE   In the United States, a form of whole life INSURANCE in which PREMIUMS are invested in a range of SECURITIES on a TAX-deferred basis. Since the policy features standard INVESTMENT RISKS it is treated as a form of security and sold with a PROSPECTUS. See also VARIABLE LIFE ASSURANCE.

VARIABLE LIMIT   A provision in a PROPERTY AND CASUALTY INSURANCE POLICY that automatically increases the size of the INSURED's limit at each anniversary date, to coincide with increased value attributable to the underlying property being insured. The insured retains the sole right not to increase the limit on each specified date.

VARIABLE PRINCIPAL SWAP   The general class of OVER-THE-COUNTER SWAPS with NOTIONAL PRINCIPAL amounts that increase or decrease according to time or the movement of a reference INDEX, generally INTEREST RATES. Payments made or received vary according to the movement of both the market reference and the notional size of the transaction. Also known as ROLLER COASTER. See also ACCRETING SWAP, AMORTIZING SWAP, INDEX PRINCIPAL SWAP, MORTGAGE SWAP, REVERSE INDEX PRINCIPAL SWAP.

V

VARIABLE RATE CERTIFICATE OF DEPOSIT (VRCD)   See FLOATING RATE CERTIFICATE OF DEPOSIT.

VARIABLE RATE DEMAND NOTE   A NOTE issued by a BANK that pays a FLOATING RATE based on PRIME RATE or LIBOR, and which is redeemable on demand by the INVESTOR.

VARIABLE RATE MORTGAGE In the United Kingdom, an ADJUSTABLE RATE MORTGAGE.

VARIABLE RATE NOTE (VRN) A form of FLOATING RATE NOTE where both the reference INTEREST RATE (e.g., LIBOR, EURIBOR) and the MARGIN over the reference are adjusted at periodic intervals, generally every quarter. The resetting of the margin is a function of SUPPLY and DEMAND conditions, as well as the market perception of the ISSUER's CREDITWORTHINESS.

VARIABLE RATE PREFERRED STOCK See ADJUSTABLE RATE PREFERRED STOCK.

VARIABLE RATE SECURITY See FLOATING RATE SECURITY.

VARIABLE STRIKE OPTION See DEFERRED STRIKE OPTION.

VARIANCE A measure of RISK, variability, or dispersion, reflecting the magnitude by which an outcome differs from the EXPECTED VALUE, or the degree to which an observation deviates from the MEAN of a distribution. Variance, which is the second MOMENT about the mean and equal to the STANDARD DEVIATION squared, can be computed as:

$$\sigma^2 = \left[\frac{\sum_{i=1}^{n}(x_i - \mu)^2}{N} \right]$$

where x_i is an observation, μ is the mean, and N is the number of observations.

VARIANCE/COVARIANCE MATRIX A matrix of COVARIANCES between the variables in a vector, reflecting VARIANCES on the diagonal and covariances on the off-diagonal. The matrix is commonly used in PORTFOLIO analysis and VALUE-AT-RISK computations. The general form of a two-variable matrix is given as:

$$v = \begin{bmatrix} \sigma_x^2 & cov_{xy} \\ cov_{yx} & \sigma_y^2 \end{bmatrix}$$

where x, y are variables, cov is the covariance between the variables and σ^2 is the variance of each variable.

VARIANCE SWAP An OVER-THE-COUNTER COMPLEX SWAP involving the exchange of the difference between the square of realized VOLATILITY and the square of IMPLIED VOLATILITY related to a defined market reference. Realized volatility is the floating volatility of the underlying reference INDEX evident over the life of the transaction, while implied volatility is the fixed volatility rate contracted between buyer and seller at the start of the transaction. Since the contract is a NONLINEAR INSTRUMENT it provides the purchaser with POSITIVE CONVEXITY (i.e., gains are larger when realized volatility is greater than implied volatility, and losses are smaller when the reverse occurs). Variance swaps are often used in the EQUITY and FOREIGN EXCHANGE markets. See also REALIZED VOLATILITY SWAP.

VARIATION MARGIN (1) Incremental SECURITY (generally cash, a LETTER OF CREDIT, or high-quality BONDS) posted by the buyer or seller of an EXCHANGE-TRADED DERIVATIVE CONTRACT once the MAINTENANCE MARGIN level has been breached. If variation margin is not posted with the CLEARINGHOUSE as required, the underlying contract is closed out. (2) Incremental security (generally cash) posted by a BORROWER under a MARGIN LOAN agreement once the TRIGGER level has been breached.

(1) See also INITIAL MARGIN, CLEARING MARGIN.

VAT See VALUE-ADDED TAX.

VEGA The change in the value of an OPTION for a change in VOLATILITY, with all other variables held constant. The vegas of the CALL OPTION and PUT OPTION computed under the BLACK-SCHOLES MODEL (which are equivalent) are given by:

$$V_c = \frac{\delta c}{\delta \sigma} = S\sqrt{t}N'(d_1)$$

$$V_p = \frac{\delta P}{\delta \sigma} = S\sqrt{t}N'(d_1)$$

$$N'(d_1) = \frac{1}{\sqrt{2\pi}}e^{\frac{-d_1^2}{2}}$$

and S is the STOCK price, t is the time to MATURITY, σ is the STANDARD DEVIATION, and where the value of N'(d1) can be obtained from a standard table of PROBABILITY functions.

The vegas of long and short puts and calls are shown as:

	Long call	Long put	Short call	Short put
Vega	+	+	−	−

Also known as KAPPA, LAMBDA. See also DELTA, GREEKS, THETA, RHO, GAMMA.

VEGA NEUTRAL A PORTFOLIO of OPTIONS that is neutral with respect to its VEGA, meaning that it is HEDGED against moves in VOLATILITY. See also DELTA NEUTRAL, GAMMA NEUTRAL, THETA NEUTRAL.

VELOCITY OF CIRCULATION   See VELOCITY OF MONEY.

VELOCITY OF MONEY   The average number of times a given unit or amount of MONEY in a system changes hands (or is spent) over a defined time period. Velocity is used in various economic theories, such as the QUANTITY THEORY OF MONEY. Also known as VELOCITY OF CIRCULATION.

VENTURE CAPITAL   CAPITAL invested in a new, often high-RISK, venture, generally in exchange for a pre-INITIAL PUBLIC OFFERING EQUITY stake. Venture capital specialists raise FUNDS from INVESTORS and play an active role in the strategic direction of the ventures being sponsored (through an advisory or board level position). The venture capital cycle is multiyear in nature, beginning with fund raising, moving to DUE DILIGENCE on potential ventures, investing committed fund capital (generally in stages over time), managing the performance of individual portfolio ventures and then crystallizing profits through a predefined exit strategy. See also DOWN ROUND, HARVEST, J-CURVE, MEZZANINE FINANCING.

VERTICAL LAYERING   A practice where different REINSURERS assume the RISK of different loss layers under an EXCESS OF LOSS (XOL) REINSURANCE agreement. Each reinsurer becomes liable for its own layer of coverage between a specific ATTACHMENT level and individual POLICY CAP. Under this approach not every reinsurer is susceptible to losses and CLAIMS once the underlying DEDUCTIBLE is exceeded; the higher vertical layers may not be exposed unless the losses are large. See also EXCESS LAYER, HORIZONTAL LAYERING.

VERTICAL MERGER   A MERGER between companies that represent different components or stages of the service or industrial process. A vertical merger may be arranged if a company wishes to control or influence the majority of the processes that are used in the production of goods and services, including raw material extraction, processing, production, warehousing, transporting, shipping, and retailing. See also CONGLOMERATE MERGER, HORIZONTAL MERGER.

VERTICAL SPREAD   See BEAR SPREAD, BULL SPREAD.

VESTED BENEFIT   A benefit, such as a PENSION or STOCK ownership interest, that is owed by a company to an employee, and which the employee is entitled to if he/she departs.

VESTED INTEREST   A right of ownership in, and use of, an ASSET on an immediate basis, and which is not dependent on the outcome of a future event.

VICINITY OF INSOLVENCY   A legal concept where the FIDUCIARY DUTIES of DIRECTORS shift from SHAREHOLDERS to CREDITORS prior to the actual INSOLVENCY of a company. This occurs when a company is almost certain to become insolvent (though has not yet met the technical definition) and is designed to protect the interests of creditors by ensuring actions are taken to protect as much ASSET value as possible.

VIE   See VARIABLE INTEREST ENTITY.

VIS MAJOR   [LAT] Literally, "overpowering force;" an unavoidable calamity or catastrophic event that can impact the financial profile of a firm, causing it to seek RISK TRANSFER solutions through INSURANCE, REINSURANCE, or DERIVATIVES. See also FORCE MAJEURE.

VISIBLE   Any good that is exported from, or imported into, a country. Visibles form a key element of a country's BALANCE OF TRADE and BALANCE OF PAYMENTS accounts. See also INVISIBLE ASSET.

VISIBLE LIQUIDITY   See DISPLAYED LIQUIDITY.

VISIBLE MARKET   Any SECURITIES market that provides a significant or total degree of transparency with regard to ORDER BOOKS and EXECUTION. EXCHANGES and ELECTRONIC COMMUNICATIONS NETWORKS are the main examples of such markets. See also DARK POOL.

VISIBLE SUPPLY   See PIPELINE.

VIX   See VOLATILITY INDEX

VOIDABLE CONTRACT   A valid CONTRACT that can be cancelled for cause on the basis of FRAUD or MISREPRESENTATION.

VOIDABLE PREFERENCE   See PREFERENCE.

VOLATILITY   A measure of the price movement of a reference ASSET or market; in general, a reference with high volatility is deemed to be riskier than one with low volatility. Measures of volatility may be backward-looking (HISTORICAL VOLATILITY) or forward-looking (IMPLIED VOLATILITY) and are used in a broad range of financial applications, including pricing of OPTIONS and other DERIVATIVES, computation of CREDIT RISK exposure, and determination of VALUE-AT-RISK. See also STANDARD DEVIATION, VARIANCE, VEGA, VOLATILITY SKEW, VOLATILITY SMILE, VOLATILITY STRATEGY.

VOLATILITY ARBITRAGE   An ARBITRAGE strategy where an INVESTOR or HEDGE FUND manager seeks to profit from discrepancies between IMPLIED VOLATILITY on individual STOCKS, BASKETS, or INDEXES, typically by applying a MEAN REVERSION model (which compares implied volatility with HISTORICAL VOLATILITY, under the assumption that implied volatility will revert to a historical MEAN) or a AUTOREGRESSIVE CONDITIONAL HETER-OSKEDASTICITY model (which uses prior volatility data points to forecast the future path of volatility). In order to monetize a particular view, a manager can source LONG or SHORT volatility positions from OPTIONS, CONVERTIBLE BONDS, WARRANTS or VARIANCE/VOLATILITY SWAPS.

VOLATILITY INDEX (VIX)   An INDEX that is used in the OPTION market that reflects the price movement of an EQUITY index. The VIX, which is managed by the Chicago Board Options EXCHANGE, is often used as a proxy of RISK AVERSION, with a high VIX level representing market fear and risk aversion, and a low VIX level representing market confidence and expanded risk appetite. The value of the VIX is obtained through a weighted average of IMPLIED VOLATILITIES, and results in an estimate of future volatility.

VOLATILITY SKEW   The difference in VOLATILITY between OUT-OF-THE-MONEY PUT OPTIONS and CALL OPTIONS. In certain markets puts trade at a higher IMPLIED VOLATILITY than calls, reflecting the fact that buyers and sellers value RISK protection more highly on the downside than on the upside. See also VOLATILITY SMILE.

VOLATILITY SMILE   A comparison of the IMPLIED VOLATILITY of an OPTION with its STRIKE PRICE. A "conventional" smile attributes greater implied volatility to IN-THE-MONEY OPTIONS and OUT-OF-THE-MONEY OPTIONS, although in some markets out-of-the-money options trade at the highest volatility under the assumption that INVESTORS wish to protect against the disaster scenario (which occurs more frequently than financial theory normally suggests, i.e., the FAT TAIL phenomenon) by purchasing less expensive out-of-the-money contracts.

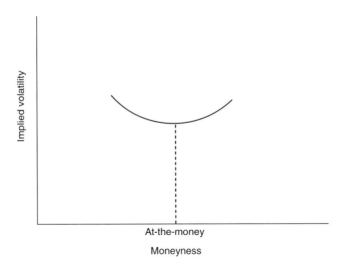

See also VOLATILITY SKEW.

VOLATILITY STRATEGY   An OPTION strategy that seeks to take advantage of changes in IMPLIED VOLATILITY or historical volatility, rather than market direction. Common volatility strategies include STRADDLES, STRANGLES, BUTTERFLY SPREADS, CONDOR SPREADS, CALENDAR SPREADS, BACKSPREADS, and RATIO VERTICAL SPREADS. Similar strategies can be created through VOLATILITY SWAPS. See also DIRECTIONAL STRATEGY.

VOLATILITY SWAP   A general class of OVER-THE-COUNTER SWAPS involving the exchange of realized (actual) VOLATILITY of an UNDERLYING reference for fixed volatility. Volatility swaps provide a mechanism for directly participating in, or protecting against, ASSET or market movement, obviating the need for indirect participation using OPTIONS. Volatility swaps generally have MATURITIES ranging from 6 months to 5 years, and can be structured in the form of REALIZED VOLATILITY SWAPS and VARIANCE SWAPS.

VOLUME   See TURNOVER.

VOLUME WEIGHTED AVERAGE PRICE (VWAP)   An ORDER rule often implemented via ALGORITHMS which divides a PARENT ORDER in proportion to the historical VOLUME achieved during a defined TRADING period in order to achieve a better average fill price. The general form of the VWAP is given as:

$$VWAP = \frac{\sum (\# \, of \, shares \, purchased * share \, price)}{Total \, shares \, purchased}$$

See also TIME WEIGHTED AVERAGE PRICE.

VOLUMETRIC RISK   The RISK of loss from volume imbalances, which can be impacted by changes in both price and quantity. Certain RISK MANAGEMENT structures, such as MULTIPLE TRIGGER PRODUCTS, allow simultaneous management of both dimensions of RISK.

VOLUNTARY BANKRUPTCY   A process where a DEBTOR files a petition for BANKRUPTCY protection, invoking an AUTOMATIC STAY. Once filed, the debtor's operations may be placed under the management of a TRUSTEE (or administrator) or they may remain with the debtor itself (who becomes a DEBTOR-IN-POSSESSION). See also INVOLUNTARY BANKRUPTCY.

VOLUNTARY LIQUIDATION   LIQUIDATION of a company that has become insolvent, following approval by SHAREHOLDERS, and in some systems CREDITORS. Any proceeds from the liquidation are apportioned to creditors and INVESTORS in order of seniority.

VORSTAND   [GER] The MANAGEMENT BOARD of a German CORPORATION. See also AUFSICHTSRAT.

VOSTRO   [LAT] Literally "your account"; a local account held on behalf of a foreign BANK to accommodate local CURRENCY business, e.g., a Japanese bank maintains a US bank's yen vostro account so that the US bank can manage its yen inflows and outflows. See also NOSTRO.

VOTING CAP   Corporate or regulatory provisions allowing companies to restrict votes to a particular percentage of a company's STOCK, regardless of the ownership stake held. Voting caps can be used as an ANTITAKEOVER DEFENSE or as a method of diffusing the power of control blocks.

VOTING RIGHTS   Legal rights accorded to SHAREHOLDERS, allowing them to vote for specific topics at a company's ANNUAL GENERAL MEETING or during a special meeting. In most instances, each SHARE is granted one vote.

VOTING TRUST CONTROL   A process or structure where effective corporate control is gained through TRUSTEES who have total, or near total, discretion over how to vote SHARES. This mechanism represents a true separation of ownership and control, as the trustees do not technically own the stock but exercise the CONTROL RIGHTS embedded in the shares. See also LEGAL MECHANISM CONTROL, MAJORITY CONTROL, MANAGEMENT CONTROL, MINORITY CONTROL, TOTAL CONTROL.

VRCD   See VARIABLE RATE CERTIFICATE OF DEPOSIT.

VRN   See VARIABLE RATE NOTE.

VULTURE BID   [COL] A deep-discount BID by an INVESTOR or INVESTMENT group for DISTRESSED ASSETS or SECURITIES of uncertain worth, or those that must be liquidated by an eager seller. See also FIRE SALE, VULTURE FUND.

VULTURE FUND   [COL] A LIMITED PARTNERSHIP or private fund that invests in DISTRESSED ASSETS, including SECURITIES and real property. Also known as a DISTRESSED FUND.

VWAP   See VOLUME WEIGHTED AVERAGE PRICE.

W

W FORMATION   See DOUBLE BOTTOM.

WAC   See WEIGHTED AVERAGE COUPON.

WACC   See WEIGHTED AVERAGE COST OF CAPITAL

WAGE EARNER'S PLAN   See CHAPTER 13.

WAGERING CONTRACT   See GAMING CONTRACT.

WAIVER   The act by one or more CREDITORS of temporarily or permanently permitting the breach of a previously established COVENANT under a LOAN or financing agreement in order to avoid an EVENT OF DEFAULT or CREDIT EVENT.

WAIVER OF PREEMPTIVE RIGHTS   An INVESTOR's agreement to relinquish the affirmative right to obtain new SHARES of COMMON STOCK when they are issued. Once a waiver is granted, the investor has no further legal ability to take up shares before they are offered in the marketplace at large. See also PREEMPTIVE RIGHT, RIGHTS ISSUE.

WALL STREET   [COL] The collective group of FINANCIAL INSTITUTIONS and EXCHANGES in New York, a small number of which are physically located on Wall Street. Also known as THE STREET.

WALLPAPER   [COL] Any SECURITY that has become worthless.

WAM   See WEIGHTED AVERAGE MATURITY.

WAR CHEST   [COL] (1) Cash and NEAR CASH held by a company or RAIDER for the express purpose of acquiring another company, often via a HOSTILE TAKEOVER. (2) Funds that can be used by a TARGET company to defend against a possible hostile takeover attempt, i.e., repurchasing shares in the market, declaring a SPECIAL DIVIDEND for existing SHAREHOLDERS.

WAREHOUSE BOND   A SURETY BOND guaranteeing that goods or INVENTORY stored in a public warehouse will be delivered upon presentation of authorizing documents.

WAREHOUSE RECEIPT   Documentary evidence of INVENTORY placed in storage in a public warehouse. A warehouse provides no GUARANTEE as to the quality or condition of the inventory and does not provide INSURANCE against damage; it simply evidences existence of the inventory. Inventory blocked by a warehouse receipt can only be sold or transferred by the bearer of the receipt, meaning the receipt functions as a mechanism for collateralizing a LOAN.

W

WAREHOUSING   (1) The process of holding ASSETS, such as MORTGAGES, ACCOUNTS RECEIVABLE, or corporate BONDS and LOANS, in a CONDUIT until they are repackaged for SECURITIZATION. The institution warehousing the securities faces full MARKET RISK and CREDIT RISK on the underlying assets. (2) The process of assuming a RISK position (e.g., a block of SECURITIES) in advance of a HEDGE or sale to another party.

WARRANT   A form of long-term OPTION (i.e., 3- to 5-year MATURITY), generally issued as a private instrument and often attached to a BOND issue to lower funding costs (and typically detached and traded separately). Warrants are often issued on a company's COMMON STOCK (e.g., an EQUITY WARRANT), but are also available on FIXED INCOME, FOREIGN EXCHANGE, equity INDEX, and COMMODITY references. See also BOND WITH WARRANT, COVERED WARRANT, EQUITY WARRANT, EX-WARRANT.

WARRANTY   A PLEDGE by a company, INSURED, or SECURITIES ISSUER indicating that specific conditions related to the commencement or fulfillment of a CONTRACT exist. Warranties may be relied upon by another party to the transaction as an element of the contract, and any breach may lead to cancellation. See also REPRESENTATION.

WASH SALE   The purchase and sale of a SECURITY over a short time frame, which, for nonfinancial institutions operating in certain national systems, may qualify for TAX loss benefits. Wash sales that are done in a coordinated fashion with other parties with the intent of manipulating or PEGGING the price of a security are illegal. See also BED AND BREAKFASTING.

WASTING ASSET   Any ASSET with a value that decays over time, such as a LEASE or plant and equipment.

WATERED STOCK   COMMON STOCK of a company with ASSETS that are overvalued and do not accurately convey the financial position of the firm. Watered stock may also arise from companies that feature significant operating losses, excessive DIVIDEND payments, or overcapitalized operations.

WATERFALL   [COL] The order of CASH FLOW distributions related to a SECURITIZATION. As the underlying POOL in a securitization generates cash, it is paid to INVESTORS in a strict order of priority which relates to the level of TRANCHE SUBORDINATION. The payment to each successive level in the waterfall depends on successful passing of relevant COVERAGE TESTS. In a typical structure the distribution of INTEREST proceeds may be allocated as follows: HEDGE EXPENSES and fees, and then the senior tranche, after which a coverage test is performed. If successful, the waterfall passes cash to the junior tranche; if not successful, cash is redirected to the payment of the PRINCIPAL on the senior tranche. If cash is redirected, the junior tranche receives an incremental future PRINCIPAL payment making it a *de-facto* PAYMENT-IN-KIND SECURITY. Assuming again the first test is successful and junior interest is paid, a second coverage test is performed, with success leading to interest paid to the junior subordinated tranche and ultimately the RESIDUAL SECURITY. Failure of the second test leads to a redirection of the waterfall in favor of further reduction in principal of the senior, and then junior, tranches. A similar waterfall can be created for the principal repayment proceeds of the pool, though coverage tests are not necessary as cash flow is distributed in order of seniority until proceeds are exhausted. Also known as CASH FLOW WATERFALL.

WEAK HANDS   [COL] A holder of an EXCHANGE-TRADED DERIVATIVE that is not expecting to receive or take delivery of the underlying ASSET, intending instead to close out the position prior to EXPIRY or EXERCISE. RETAIL INVESTORS and SPECULATORS typically have "weak hands." See also STRONG HANDS.

WEALTH   The total of all ASSETS that can produce INCOME, typically measured net of any LIABILITIES required for supporting such assets.

WEALTH EFFECT   The change in AGGREGATE DEMAND for a given change in the value of ASSETS. In general, an increase in the value of assets can lead to growth in consumption and a decline in SAVINGS, while a reduction in the value of assets can lead to the reverse.

WEATHER BOND   A SECURITIZATION of a noncatastrophic weather RISK, including temperature and precipitation. Repayment of PRINCIPAL and/or COUPONS is contingent on the occurrence of a defined loss-making weather event; if a specified loss occurs, the ISSUER of the BOND may delay or cease making payments to INVESTORS, meaning that it has HEDGED its exposure. See also CATASTROPHE BOND, LIFE ACQUISITION COST SECURITIZATION, MORTGAGE DEFAULT SECURITIZATION, RESIDUAL VALUE SECURITIZATION.

WEATHER DERIVATIVE   An EXCHANGE-TRADED DERIVATIVE or OVER-THE-COUNTER DERIVATIVE with an UNDERLYING reference based on the performance of noncatastrophic weather references such as temperature, precipitation, wind, and streamflow. TEMPERATURE DERIVATIVES and PRECIPITATION DERIVATIVES are the two most common forms of weather derivatives.

WEIGHTED AVERAGE   A method of computing the MEAN of a set of variables by assigning a weight to each observation which is related to its overall contribution to the entire set of variables.

WEIGHTED AVERAGE COST OF CAPITAL (WACC) See COST OF CAPITAL.

WEIGHTED AVERAGE COUPON (WAC) The average COUPON on MORTGAGES, LOANS, or other ASSETS forming part of a SECURITIZATION, weighted by value. See also WEIGHTED AVERAGE MATURITY.

WEIGHTED AVERAGE MATURITY (WAM) The average MATURITY of MORTGAGES, LOANS, or other ASSETS forming party of a SECURITIZATION, weighted by value. See also WEIGHTED AVERAGE COUPON.

WEINER PROCESS   A STOCHASTIC PROCESS that is normally distributed with EXPECTED VALUE of 0 and VARIANCE of 1 at each time interval t. Under a Weiner process, values at time t and t + 1 are independent (i.e., they have a CORRELATION COEFFICIENT of 0), meaning that a Weiner process is also a MARKOV PROCESS. The Weiner process is used in certain OPTION pricing models.

WET BARRELS [COL] Physically delivered, rather than financially settled, crude oil. TRADERS dealing in wet barrels generally have need of the physical commodity for production, refining, or supply purposes.

WET LEASE   A LEASE agreement used in the airline industry, where one airline (acting as LESSOR) provides an aircraft to a second airline (the LESSEE), along with associated crew, maintenance, and insurance. The lessee supplies fuel and pays for airport fees and duties.

WHEN-IN-THE-MONEY OPTION   See CONTINGENT PREMIUM OPTION.

WHEN-ISSUED (WI) SECURITY   Any SECURITY that has been announced but not yet priced or settled. While in the "WI" period informal, but legally binding, GRAY MARKET TRADING occurs between DEALERS. Once the WI security has settled, it trades in the same manner as all other SEASONED SECURITIES. See also TO BE ANNOUNCED, WHEN-ISSUED TREASURY.

WHEN-ISSUED TREASURY (WIT)   A US TREASURY NOTE or TREASURY BOND that has been announced but not yet priced or settled. While in the "WI" period informal, but legally binding, GRAY MARKET TRADING occurs between DEALERS. Once the WIT has settled, it trades in the same manner as all other seasoned Treasury issues. See also TO BE ANNOUNCED, WHEN-ISSUED SECURITY.

WHIPSAW   [COL] A fall in the price of a SECURITY, triggering a STOP LOSS ORDER and sale, followed by a price rebound. Alternatively, a rise in the price, triggering a buy order and purchase, followed by a price decline.

WHISPER NUMBERS [COL] The release of projected corporate earnings guidance by a company's management in advance of a full public announcement. In the United States this has been limited through SECURITIES AND EXCHANGE COMMISSION REGULATION FAIR DISCLOSURE, which prohibits selective disclosure to specific parties such as BANK research analysts.

WHISPER STOCK [COL] The COMMON STOCK of a company that is rumored to be the target of a potential TAKEOVER transaction. A whisper stock may exhibit unusual price and volume patterns as a result of the rumors.

WHISTLEBLOWER   [COL] An employee who reports internal infractions to senior levels of management in order to reveal or contain a problem. A whistleblower often comes in contact with information that might not be apparent or available to other control functions and is thus an additional element of the GOVERNANCE process.

WHITE KNIGHT   [COL] A company that assumes the role of a friendly partner by acquiring a controlling stake in a company that is the subject of a HOSTILE TAKEOVER. See also BLACK KNIGHT, GRAY KNIGHT, WHITE SQUIRE.

WHITE SQUIRE   [COL] A company that assumes the role of a friendly partner by acquiring a substantial, though not controlling, stake in a company that is the subject of a HOSTILE TAKEOVER. See also BLACK KNIGHT, GRAY KNIGHT, WHITE KNIGHT.

WHOLE LIFE ASSURANCE In the United Kingdom, WHOLE LIFE INSURANCE.

WHOLE LIFE INSURANCE   A form of life INSURANCE in which the INSURER pays the INSURED's BENEFICIARY a defined sum on the death of the insured, and which is characterized by fixed PREMIUM payments and a SURRENDER VALUE that builds over time through INVESTMENT of premiums. See also WHOLE LIFE ASSURANCE.

WHOLE LOAN   A commercial or residential MORTGAGE sold to an INVESTOR complete with servicing rights (e.g., collection of PRINCIPAL and INTEREST). Whole loans are periodically sold to CONDUITS for subsequent private label SECURITIZATION.

WHOLESALE BANKING   A business model followed by certain BANKS where the focus of activities is on corporate and institutional, rather than retail, customers. Dedicated wholesale banks do not operate large branch networks.

WHOLESALE MARKETS BROKERS ASSOCIATION (WMBA)   In the United Kingdom, a trade association for BROKERS operating in the MONEY MARKETS, also responsible for tabulating the EURONIA and SONIA FLOATING RATE references.

WHOLLY OWNED SUBSIDIARY   A SUBSIDIARY that is 100% owned by a PARENT or HOLDING COMPANY.

WI   See WHEN-ISSUED SECURITY.

WIDOWS AND ORPHANS   [COL] An individual or institution that is considered to be an unsophisticated INVESTOR. Certain SECURITIES laws exist to protect widows and orphans from being financially damaged through bad financial advice or FRAUD. See also AUNT MILLIE.

WILLINGNESS TO PERFORM   A COUNTERPARTY's intent to perform on its financial OBLIGATIONS, unrelated to its financial capability of doing so. In some instances a company may choose not to perform on its contracts if it believes it has been misguided by a financial INTERMEDIARY or its AGENT, or if legal or regulatory circumstances forbid it from completing its OBLIGATIONS. See also ABILITY TO PERFORM.

WINDING-UP   [COL] See LIQUIDATION.

WINDOW DRESSING   [COL] The practice of altering the appearance of corporate FINANCIAL STATEMENTS through various short-term transactions, with the primary goal of presenting an improved financial position during reporting periods. Although such alterations may be legal from a strict ACCOUNTING and regulatory standpoint, they may be ethically questionable.

WIRE TRANSFER   An electronic ORDER for the payment of funds from one party to another. Various wire mechanisms exist to accommodate such transfers, including the Fed Wire, CLEARINGHOUSE AUTOMATED PAYMENT SYSTEM, and the CLEARINGHOUSE INTERBANK PAYMENT SYSTEM.

WIT   See WHEN-ISSUED TREASURY.

WITH RECOURSE   An implicit legal right giving the holder of a BILL OF EXCHANGE legal recourse to the seller of the bill in the event the DRAWER fails to pay. This right exists unless the bill is specifically endorsed to read WITHOUT RECOURSE.

WITHHOLDING TAX   Any TAX that is withheld at the source of the INCOME. Withholding taxes are commonly applied to wages and certain DIVIDENDS.

WITHOUT   [COL] An indication that only a one-way quote is available on a particular SECURITY; rather than quoting a standard BID and OFFER, a MARKET MAKER or DEALER may quote a "bid without" or an "offer without."

WITHOUT PREJUDICE   A declaration made by a party so that any information covered by the declaration is privileged and protected, and cannot therefore be used in a legal proceeding or as legal evidence.

WITHOUT RECOURSE   An amendment to a BILL OF EXCHANGE indicating that the holder of the bill has no legal recourse to the seller of the bill in the event the DRAWER fails to pay. See also WITH RECOURSE.

WMBA   See WHOLESALE MARKETS BROKERS ASSOCIATION.

WORK-IN-PROCESS INVENTORY   A class of INVENTORY held by a company that includes goods that are in various stages of production but not yet ready for sale. See also FINISHED GOODS INVENTORY, RAW MATERIAL INVENTORY.

WORKING CAPITAL   A measure of a company's short-term operating resources, i.e., CURRENT ASSETS and CURRENT LIABILITIES. Also known as CURRENT CAPITAL, NET CURRENT ASSETS. See also GROSS WORKING CAPITAL, NET WORKING CAPITAL, WORKING CAPITAL LOAN.

WORKING CAPITAL LOAN   A short-term business LOAN used to purchase short-term ASSETS, often INVENTORY used for production and resale. The CREDIT may be unsecured or secured on the assets being financed, and is generally payable within 60 to 90 days. See also WORKING CAPITAL.

WORKOUT AGREEMENT   An agreement between a BORROWER and LENDER to restructure existing LOAN terms, including repayment schedule, MATURITY, and/or rate, in order to avoid any act of DEFAULT and FORECLOSURE. A loan subject to a workout agreement is likely to be fully covered by a lender's LOAN LOSS RESERVES. See also NONPERFORMING LOAN, SLOW LOAN.

WORLD BANK   See INTERNATIONAL BANK FOR RECONSTRUCTION AND DEVELOPMENT (IBRD).

WORLD TRADE ORGANIZATION (WTO)   A supranational organization, created in 1994 as a successor body to the GENERAL AGREEMENT ON TARIFFS AND TRADE (GATT), that manages functions and negotiations related to multi-lateral TRADE in goods and services.

WORST-CASE CREDIT LOSS   A potential extreme CREDIT loss represented by a point multiple STANDARD DEVIATIONS from the MEAN value of the credit LOSS DISTRIBUTION function. Financial institutions allocate CAPITAL in support of worst-case credit losses. See also EXPECTED CREDIT LOSS, UNEXPECTED CREDIT LOSS.

WRAP   [COL] Any form of GUARANTEE or support applied to a SECURITY to enhance its CREDITWORTHINESS.

WRAPAROUND INSURANCE   An INSURANCE POLICY covering various aspects of SOVEREIGN RISK, including embargo, sanction, loss, abandonment, control, and EXPROPRIATION. See also POLITICAL RISK INSURANCE.

WRITE   (1) The process of selling an OPTION. (2) The process of UNDERWRITING an INSURANCE policy for an INSURED.

WRITEOFF   (1) The process of reducing the value of a FIXED ASSET according to a DEPRECIATION schedule. (2) The process of classifying a CREDIT as uncollectible, and charging it against a BAD DEBT RESERVE or a LOAN LOSS RESERVE.

WRONGFUL TRADING   In the United Kingdom, a state where a company continues to operate even though it has reason to believe that it has reached a state of INSOLVENCY. Personal LIABILITIES may accrue to DIRECTORS in certain instances.

WTO   See WORLD TRADE ORGANIZATION.

X

XD See EX-DIVIDEND.

XOL AGREEMENT See EXCESS OF LOSS AGREEMENT.

XR See EX-RIGHTS.

XW See EX-WARRANT.

Y

YANKEE [COL] A BOND, NOTE, or CERTIFICATE OF DEPOSIT issued in US dollars in the US markets by a foreign company.

YARD [COL] Common reference for billion. See also BUCK, TON.

YIELD The percentage RETURN derived from an INVESTMENT, typically determined by dividing the EARNINGS from the investment by the initial amount invested. Yield is a relevant return measure for FIXED INCOME instruments, as well as DIVIDEND-paying COMMON STOCK and PREFERRED STOCK. See also BOND EQUIVALENT YIELD, CURRENT YIELD, DISCOUNT YIELD, DIVIDEND YIELD, SIMPLE YIELD, TAXABLE EQUIVALENT YIELD, YIELD TO CALL, YIELD TO MATURITY.

YIELD ADVANTAGE The additional SPREAD an INVESTOR gains from holding a CONVERTIBLE BOND instead of the equivalent COMMON STOCK, typically computed as:

$$YA = FY - DY$$

where FY is the FLAT YIELD and DY is the DIVIDEND YIELD. See also SIMPLE BREAKEVEN.

YIELD BURNING [COL] An illegal practice in MUNICIPAL BOND refinancings where UNDERWRITERS charge excessive prices for TREASURY BONDS purchased and held in escrow before retirement of existing bonds. The high Treasury prices result in a "burning down" of the YIELD.

YIELD CURVE A plot of INTEREST RATES against MATURITIES that results in the creation of a TERM STRUCTURE. In a "normal" interest rate environment the yield curve is upward sloping (i.e., POSITIVE YIELD CURVE), meaning it costs more to borrow long-term funds than short-term funds, or the investment yield on long-term securities is higher than it is on short-term securities. Other market scenarios include the NEGATIVE YIELD CURVE, which features short-term rates that are higher than long-term rates, and the KINKED YIELD CURVE, which features medium-term rates that are higher than both short- and long-term rates. The shape of the yield curve is influenced by economic, LIQUIDITY, and monetary factors, as well as general market expectations. Yield curves are widely used in financial RISK MANAGEMENT to price and HEDGE securities and DERIVATIVES. See also EXPECTATIONS THEORY, IMPLIED FORWARD CURVE, LIQUIDITY PREFERENCE THEORY, MARKET SEGMENTATION THEORY, PAR YIELD CURVE, TERM STRUCTURE, ZERO COUPON YIELD CURVE.

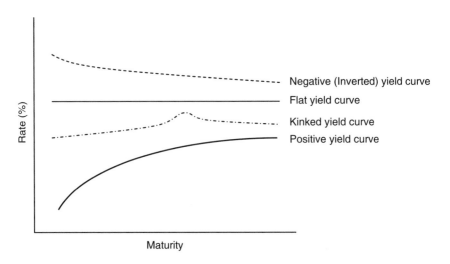

Maturity

YIELD CURVE INTERPOLATION   See INTERPOLATION.

YIELD CURVE OPTION   A SPREAD OPTION that grants the buyer a payoff based on the difference between two points on a YIELD CURVE against a pre-defined STRIKE PRICE. By embedding the two references in a single option CONTRACT, the purchaser gains cost and efficiency advantages.

YIELD ENHANCEMENT   A financial strategy designed to increase an INVESTOR's core RETURNS; most YIELD-enhancing techniques, such as SPREAD trades and COVERED CALL and COVERED PUT strategies, are intended to be low RISK, i.e., limited downside with moderate upside. See also ARBITRAGE, SPECULATION, HEDGING.

YIELD TO CALL   A method of measuring the YIELD of a CALLABLE BOND, computed as the percentage annualized RETURN on a BOND to the FIRST CALL date. The general formula is given as:

$$YTC = \sum_{t=1}^{n^*} \frac{c}{(1+y)^t} + \frac{M^*}{(1+y)^n}$$

where C is COUPON INTEREST, y is the yield, n^* is the number of periods until the first call date, and M^* is the callable bond price. See also YIELD TO MATURITY.

YIELD TO MATURITY   A common method of measuring the YIELD on a COUPON-bearing SECURITY, computed as the percentage annualized return on a BOND until its final MATURITY. The general formula is given as:

$$YTM = \sum_{t=1}^{n} \frac{c}{(1+y)^t} + \frac{M}{(1+y)^n}$$

where C is the COUPON INTEREST, y is the yield, n is the number of periods, and M is the redemption value of the bond at maturity (generally PAR VALUE). Also known as EFFECTIVE YIELD, GROSS REDEMPTION YIELD, PROMISED YIELD. See also YIELD TO CALL.

Z

Z-BOND See ACCRUAL BOND.

Z-SCORE (1) A measure used to predict the likelihood of BANKRUPTCY. The model is based on a weighted average of five key financial ratios:

1.2 * WORKING CAPITAL/Total ASSETS +
1.4 * RETAINED EARNINGS/Total Assets +
3.3 * EARNINGS BEFORE INTEREST AND TAXES/Total Assets +
0.6 * MARKET VALUE of EQUITY/BOOK VALUE of DEBT +
1.0 * Sales/Total Assets

A z-score less than 2.675 is indicative of impending bankruptcy. The original z-score measure has been updated (though not supplanted) by a modified Zeta^{TM} model with proprietary parameters. (2) A statistical measure that indicates how many STANDARD DEVIATIONS above or below the MEAN a particular random variable lies; the standard deviation is therefore a unit measure of the z-score, and is given by:

$$z = \frac{x - \mu}{\sigma}$$

where x is the random variable to be standardized, μ is the population MEAN, σ is the population STANDARD DEVIATION.

(1) Additional reference: Altman (1968).

ZAIBATSU [JPN] A Japanese corporate conglomerate with a central company controlling the ownership and activities of other companies. The zaibatsu structure was banned in the mid-1940s and replaced by the KEIRETSU.

ZAITECH [JPN] Financial SPECULATION undertaken by many Japanese companies in order to boost nonoperating income. The practice was very widespread during the late 1980s and early 1990s, although it continues to feature to some degree. Transactions involving STRUCTURED NOTES and DERIVATIVES, often with LEVERAGED EQUITY and FOREIGN EXCHANGE RISKS, are popular vehicles for zaitech activities.

ZERO COST COLLAR An OPTION SPREAD consisting of a LONG POSITION in a CAP or CALL OPTION and a SHORT POSITION in a FLOOR or PUT OPTION, or vice versa. The sale of one option offsets the PREMIUM payable on the second option, resulting in "zero cost." Also known as CYLINDER, RANGE FORWARD, TUNNEL. See also COLLAR.

ZERO COUPON BOND A deep-DISCOUNT BOND that is sold and traded at a DISCOUNT to PAR VALUE and pays no periodic COUPON interest during the life of the issue. The difference between the discounted value and the par

REDEMPTION VALUE generates an implicit RETURN to the INVESTOR. The price of a coupon bond is typically computed as:

$$P = \frac{M}{(1+r)^n}$$

where r is the DISCOUNT RATE, n is the number of periods, and M is the redemption value of the bond at MATURITY (generally par value).

ZERO COUPON CONVERTIBLE BOND A discounted CONVERTIBLE BOND exchangeable into the ISSUER's COMMON STOCK, often issued with a CONVERSION PREMIUM of 15% to 25% and used primarily in the US markets. Since the SECURITY is structured as a ZERO COUPON BOND it pays no current COUPON while it remains a bond, but accrues INTEREST. The zero coupon convertible is often PUTABLE by the INVESTOR back to the ISSUER at the current redemption price (i.e., accreted value).

ZERO COUPON INFLATION SWAP An OVER-THE-COUNTER SWAP involving the exchange of floating and fixed INFLATION at MATURITY, with no intervening payments during the life of the transaction. Zero coupon inflation swaps, which generally reference an inflation INDEX of consumer prices, are often structured as long-term transactions, with maturities exceeding 10 years. See also ANNUAL INFLATION SWAP, INFLATION SWAP.

ZERO COUPON SWAP An OVER-THE-COUNTER SWAP involving the exchange of periodic INTEREST payments by one party in return for receipt of a single BULLET payment at maturity. A zero coupon swap acts as a de-facto LOAN for the party contracting to pay at maturity.

ZERO COUPON YIELD CURVE A YIELD CURVE representing DISCOUNT RATES across maturities, starting from the present. The zero coupon curve is generally constructed from an observable PAR YIELD CURVE through a process known as STRIPPING THE YIELD CURVE (or BOOTSTRAPPING). The zero coupon curve is then used to construct the IMPLIED FORWARD CURVE, which is used to price instruments requiring a forward estimate of rates.

ZERO MINUS TICK Sale of a SECURITY at the same price as the last transaction, but lower than the transaction prior to that one. A SHORT SALE cannot be initiated on a zero minus tick. See also MINUS TICK, PLUS TICK, ZERO PLUS TICK.

ZERO PLUS TICK Sale of a SECURITY at the same price as the last transaction, but higher than the transaction prior to that one. A SHORT SALE can be initiated on a zero plus tick. See also MINUS TICK, PLUS TICK, ZERO MINUS TICK.

ZOMBIE [COL] A company that is in technical INSOLVENCY but continues to operate, pending the finalization of a RESTRUCTURING, REORGANIZATION, or bailout.

Z

Appendix: Summary of Accounting Standards

Financial Accounting Standards

FAS 1 Disclosure of Foreign Currency Translation Information, superseded by FAS 8 and FAS 52

FAS 2 Accounting for Research and Development Costs

FAS 3 Reporting Accounting Changes in Interim Financial Statements, replaced by FAS 154

FAS 4 Reporting Gains and Losses from Extinguishment of Debt, rescinded by FAS 145

FAS 5 Accounting for Contingencies, amended by FAS 11, 112, and 114

FAS 6 Classification of Short-Term Obligations Expected to Be Refinanced

FAS 7 Accounting and Reporting by Development Stage Enterprises

FAS 8 Accounting for the Translation of Foreign Currency Transactions and Foreign Currency Financial, superseded by FAS 52

FAS 9 Accounting for Income Taxes: Oil and Gas Producing Companies, superseded by FAS 19

FAS 10 Extension of "Grandfather" Provisions for Business Combinations, superseded by FAS 141

FAS 11 Accounting for Contingencies: Transition Method – an amendment of FAS 5

FAS 12 Accounting for Certain Marketable Securities, superseded by FAS 115

FAS 13 Accounting for Leases, amended by FAS 17, 22, 23, 26, 27, 28, 29, 91, 98, and 145

FAS 14 Financial Reporting for Segments of a Business Enterprise, superseded by FAS 131

FAS 15 Accounting by Debtors and Creditors for Troubled Debt Restructurings, amended by FAS 114

FAS 16 Prior Period Adjustments

FAS 17 Accounting for Leases: Initial Direct Costs, amendment of FAS 13, rescinded by FAS 91

FAS 18 Financial Reporting for Segments of a Business Enterprise: Interim Financial Statements, amendment of FAS 14, superseded by FAS 131

FAS 19 Financial Accounting and Reporting by Oil and Gas Producing Companies, amended by FAS 25 and FAS 69

FAS 20 Accounting for Forward Exchange Contracts, amendment of FAS 8, superseded by FAS 52

FAS 21 Suspension of the Reporting of Earnings per Share and Segment Information by Nonpublic Enterprises, amended by Opinion 15 and FAS 14, superseded by FAS 131

FAS 22 Changes in the Provisions of Lease Agreements Resulting from Refundings of Tax-Exempt Debt, amendment of FAS 13

FAS 23 Inception of the Lease, amendment of FAS 13

FAS 24 Reporting Segment Information in Financial Statements That Are Presented in Another Enterprise's Financial Report, amendment of FAS 14, superseded by FAS 131

FAS 25 Suspension of Certain Accounting Requirements for Oil and Gas Producing Companies, amendment of FAS 19, amended by FAS 69

FAS 26   Profit Recognition on Sales-Type Leases of Real Estate, amendment of FAS 13, rescinded by FAS 98

FAS 27   Classification of Renewals or Extensions of Existing Sales-Type or Direct Financing Leases, amendment of FAS 13

FAS 28   Accounting for Sales with Leasebacks, amendment of FAS 13

FAS 29   Determining Contingent Rentals, amendment of FAS 13

FAS 30   Disclosure of Information about Major Customers, amendment of FAS 14, superseded by FAS 131

FAS 31   Accounting for Tax Benefits Related to U.K. Tax Legislation Concerning Stock Relief, superseded by FAS 96

FAS 32   Specialized Accounting and Reporting Principles and Practices in AICPA Statements of Position and Guides on Accounting and Auditing Matters, amendment of Opinion 20, rescinded by FAS 111

FAS 33   Financial Reporting and Changing Prices September, superseded by FAS 89

FAS 34   Capitalization of Interest Cost October, amended by FAS 42, 58, and 62

FAS 35   Accounting and Reporting by Defined Benefit Pension Plans, amended by FAS 59, 75, and 110

FAS 36   Disclosure of Pension Information, amendment of Opinion 8, superseded by FAS 87

FAS 37   Balance Sheet Classification of Deferred Income Taxes, amendment of Opinion 11

FAS 38   Accounting for Preacquisition Contingencies of Purchased Enterprises, amendment of Opinion 16, superseded by FAS 141

FAS 39   Financial Reporting and Changing Prices: Specialized Assets – Mining and Oil and Gas, supplement to FAS 33, superseded by FAS 89

FAS 40   Financial Reporting and Changing Prices: Specialized Assets – Timberlands and Growing Timber, supplement to FAS 33, superseded by FAS 89

FAS 41   Financial Reporting and Changing Prices: Specialized Assets – Income-Producing Real Estate, supplement to FAS 33, superseded by FAS 89

FAS 42   Determining Materiality for Capitalization of Interest Cost, amendment of FAS 34

FAS 43   Accounting for Compensated Absences

FAS 44   Accounting for Intangible Assets of Motor Carriers, rescinded by FAS 145

FAS 45   Accounting for Franchise Fee Revenue, amended by FAS 112

FAS 46   Financial Reporting and Changing Prices: Motion Picture Films, superseded by FAS 89

FAS 47   Disclosure of Long-Term Obligations

FAS 48   Revenue Recognition When Right of Return Exists

FAS 49   Accounting for Product Financing Arrangements

FAS 50   Financial Reporting in the Record and Music Industry

FAS 51   Financial Reporting by Cable Television Companies

FAS 52   Foreign Currency Translation

FAS 53   Financial Reporting by Producers and Distributors of Motion Picture Films, rescinded by FAS 139

FAS 54   Financial Reporting and Changing Prices: Investment Companies, amendment of FAS 33, superseded by FAS 89

FAS 55   Determining whether a Convertible Security is a Common Stock Equivalent, amendment of Opinion 15, superseded by FAS 111

FAS 56   Designation of AICPA Guide and Statement of Position (SOP) 81–1 on Contractor Accounting and SOP 81–2 concerning Hospital-Related Organizations as Preferable for Purposes of Applying APB Opinion 20, amendment of FAS 32, superseded by FAS 111

FAS 57   Related Party Disclosures

FAS 58   Capitalization of Interest Cost in Financial Statements That Include Investments Accounted for by the Equity Method – an amendment of FAS 34

FAS 59   Deferral of the Effective Date of Certain Accounting Requirements for Pension Plans of State and Local Governmental Units, amendment of FAS 35, superseded by FAS 75

FAS 60   Accounting and Reporting by Insurance Enterprises, amended by FAS 91 and 120

FAS 61   Accounting for Title Plant

FAS 62   Capitalization of Interest Cost in Situations Involving Certain Tax-Exempt Borrowings and Certain Gifts and Grants, amendment of FAS 34

FAS 63   Financial Reporting by Broadcasters, amended FAS 139

FAS 64   Extinguishments of Debt Made to Satisfy Sinking-Fund Requirements, amendment of FAS 4, rescinded by FAS 145

FAS 65   Accounting for Certain Mortgage Banking Activities, amended by FAS 91, 122, and 134

FAS 66   Accounting for Sales of Real Estate, amended by FAS 98 and 152

FAS 67   Accounting for Costs and Initial Rental Operations of Real Estate Projects, amended by FAS 152

FAS 68   Research and Development Arrangements

FAS 69   Disclosures about Oil and Gas Producing Activities, amendment of FAS 19, 25, 33, and 39

FAS 70   Financial Reporting and Changing Prices: Foreign Currency Translation, amendment of FAS 33, superseded by FAS 89

FAS 71   Accounting for the Effects of Certain Types of Regulation, amended by FAS 90 and 92

FAS 72   Accounting for Certain Acquisitions of Banking or Thrift Institutions, amendment of Opinion 17, an interpretation of Opinions 16 and 17, and an amendment of FAS 9, rescinded by FAS 147

FAS 73   Reporting a Change in Accounting for Railroad Track Structures, amendment of Opinion 20, superseded by FAS 154

FAS 74   ccounting for Special Termination Benefits Paid to Employees, superseded by FAS 88

FAS 75   Deferral of the Effective Date of Certain Accounting Requirements for Pension Plans of State and Local Governmental Units, amendment of FAS 35, rescinded by FAS 135

FAS 76   Extinguishment of Debt, amendment of Opinion 26, superseded by FAS 125

FAS 77   Reporting by Transferors for Transfers of Receivables with Recourse, superseded by FAS 125

FAS 78   Classification of Obligations That Are Callable by the Creditor, an amendment of ARB 43

FAS 79   Elimination of Certain Disclosures for Business Combinations by Nonpublic Enterprises, amendment of Opinion 16, superseded by FAS 141

FAS 80   Accounting for Futures Contracts, superseded by FAS 133

FAS 81   Disclosure of Postretirement Health Care and Life Insurance Benefits, superseded by FAS 106

FAS 82   Financial Reporting and Changing Prices: Elimination of Certain Disclosures, amendment of FAS 33, superseded by FAS 89

FAS 83   Designation of AICPA Guides and Statement of Position on Accounting by Brokers and Dealers in Securities, by Employee Benefit Plans, and by Banks as Preferable for Purposes of Applying APB Opinion 20, amendment FAS 32 and Opinion 30 and a rescission of FAS Interpretation 10, superseded by FAS 111

FAS 84   Induced Conversions of Convertible Debt, amendment Opinion 26

FAS 85   Yield Test for Determining whether a Convertible Security is a Common Stock Equivalent, amendment of Opinion 15, superseded by FAS 128

FAS 86   Accounting for the Costs of Computer Software to Be Sold, Leased, or Otherwise Marketed

FAS 87   Employers' Accounting for Pensions, amended by FAS 132R and 158

FAS 88   Employers' Accounting for Settlements and Curtailments of Defined Benefit Pension Plans and for Termination Benefits, amended by FAS 132R and 158

FAS 89   Financial Reporting and Changing Prices, amended by FAS 139

FAS 90   Regulated Enterprises – Accounting for Abandonments and Disallowances of Plant Costs, amendment of FAS 71

FAS 91   Accounting for Nonrefundable Fees and Costs Associated with Originating or Acquiring Loans and Initial Direct Costs of Leases, amendment of FAS 13, 60, and 65 and a rescission of FAS 17, amended by FAS 98

FAS 92   Regulated Enterprises – Accounting for Phase-in Plans, an amendment of FAS 71

FAS 93   Recognition of Depreciation by Not-for-Profit Organizations, amended by FAS 99

FAS 94   Consolidation of All Majority-owned Subsidiaries, amendment of ARB 51, with related amendments of Opinion 18 and ARB 43

FAS 95   Statement of Cash Flows, amended by FAS 102 and 104

FAS 96   Accounting for Income Taxes, superseded by FAS 109

FAS 97   Accounting and Reporting by Insurance Enterprises for Certain Long-Duration Contracts and for Realized Gains and Losses from the Sale of Investments, amended by FAS 120

FAS 98   Accounting for Leases: Sale-Leaseback Transactions Involving Real Estate, Sales-Type Leases of Real Estate, Definition of the Lease Term, and Initial Direct Costs of Direct Financing Leases, amendment of FAS 13, 66, and 91 and a rescission of FAS 26

FAS 99   Deferral of the Effective Date of Recognition of Depreciation by Not-for-Profit Organizations, amendment of FAS 93

FAS 100   Accounting for Income Taxes-Deferral of the Effective Date of FAS 96, amendment of FAS 96, superseded by FAS 103

FAS 101   Regulated Enterprises – Accounting for the Discontinuation of Application of FAS 71

FAS 102   Statement of Cash Flows – Exemption of Certain Enterprises and Classification of Cash Flows from Certain Securities Acquired for Resale, amendment of FAS 95

FAS 103   Accounting for Income Taxes – Deferral of the Effective Date of FAS 96, amendment of FAS 96, superseded by FAS 108

FAS 104   Statement of Cash Flows – Net Reporting of Certain Cash Receipts and Cash Payments and Classification of Cash Flows from Hedging Transactions, amendment of FAS 95

FAS 105   Disclosure of Information about Financial Instruments with Off-Balance-Sheet Risk and Financial Instruments with Concentrations of Credit Risk, March 1990, superseded by FAS 133

FAS 106   Employers' Accounting for Postretirement Benefits Other Than Pensions, amended by FAS 132R and 158

FAS 107   Disclosures about Fair Value of Financial Instruments, amended FAS 126

FAS 108   Accounting for Income Taxes – Deferral of the Effective Date of FAS 96, amendment of FAS 96, superseded by FAS 109

FAS 109   Accounting for Income Taxes

FAS 110   Reporting by Defined Benefit Pension Plans of Investment Contracts, amendment of FAS 35

FAS 111   Rescission of FAS 32 and Technical Corrections

FAS 112   Employers' Accounting for Postemployment Benefits, amendment of FAS 5 and 43

FAS 113   Accounting and Reporting for Reinsurance of Short-Duration and Long-Duration Contracts, amended by FAS 120

FAS 114   Accounting by Creditors for Impairment of a Loan, amendment of FAS 5 and 15, amended by FAS 118

FAS 115   Accounting for Certain Investments in Debt and Equity Securities, amended by FAS 159

FAS 116   Accounting for Contributions Received and Contributions Made

FAS 117   Financial Statements of Not-for-Profit Organizations June 1993

FAS 118   Accounting by Creditors for Impairment of a Loan-Income Recognition and Disclosures, amendment of FAS 114

FAS 119   Disclosure about Derivative Financial Instruments and Fair Value of Financial Instruments, superseded by FAS 133

FAS 120   Accounting and Reporting by Mutual Life Insurance Enterprises and by Insurance Enterprises for Certain Long-Duration Participating Contracts, amendment of FAS 60, 97, and 113

FAS 121   Accounting for the Impairment of Long-Lived Assets and for Long-Lived Assets to Be Disposed, superseded by FAS 144

FAS 122   Accounting for Mortgage Servicing Rights, amendment of FAS 65, superseded by FAS 125

FAS 123   Accounting for Stock-Based Compensation

FAS 123R Share-Based Payment

FAS 124   Accounting for Certain Investments Held by Not-for-Profit Organizations

FAS 125   Accounting for Transfers and Servicing of Financial Assets and Extinguishments of Liabilities, replaced by FAS 140

FAS 126   Exemption from Certain Required Disclosures about Financial Instruments for Certain Nonpublic Entities, amendment to FAS 107

FAS 127   Deferral of the Effective Date of Certain Provisions of FAS 125, superseded by FAS 140

FAS 128   Earnings per Share, amended by FAS 150 and 160

FAS 129   Disclosure of Information about Capital Structure

FAS 130   Reporting Comprehensive Income

FAS 131   Disclosures about Segments of an Enterprise and Related Information

FAS 132   Employers' Disclosures about Pensions and Other Postretirement Benefits, amendment of FAS 87, 88, and 106

FAS 132R Employers' Disclosures about Pensions and Other Postretirement Benefits, amendment of FAS 87, 88, and 106, amended by FAS 158

FAS 133   Accounting for Derivative Instruments and Hedging Activities, amended by FAS 137, 138, 155, 161, and FAS 133–1 and FIN 45–4

FAS 134   Accounting for Mortgage-Backed Securities Retained after the Securitization of Mortgage Loans Held for Sale by a Mortgage Banking Enterprise, amendment of FAS 65

FAS 135   Rescission of FAS 75 and Technical Corrections

FAS 136   Transfers of Assets to a Not-for-Profit Organization or Charitable Trust That Raises or Holds Contributions for Others

FAS 137   Accounting for Derivative Instruments and Hedging Activities – Deferral of the Effective Date of FAS 133, an amendment of FAS 133

FAS 138   Accounting for Certain Derivative Instruments and Certain Hedging Activities, amendment of FAS 133

FAS 139   Rescission of FAS 53 and amendments to FAS 63, 89, and 121

FAS 140   Accounting for Transfers and Servicing of Financial Assets and Extinguishments of Liabilities, replacement of FAS 125, amended by FAS 155 and 156

FAS 141   Business Combinations

FAS 142   Goodwill and Other Intangible Assets

FAS 143   Accounting for Asset Retirement Obligations

FAS 144   Accounting for the Impairment or Disposal of Long-Lived Assets

FAS 145   Rescission of FAS 4, 44, and 64, Amendment of 13 and Technical Corrections

FAS 146   Accounting for Costs Associated with Exit or Disposal Activities

FAS 147   Acquisitions of Certain Financial Institutions, amendment of FAS 72 and 144

FAS 148   Accounting for Stock-Based Compensation – Transition and Disclosure, amendment of FAS 123, superseded by FAS 123R

FAS 149   Amendment of Statement 133 on Derivative Instruments and Hedging Activities

FAS 150   Accounting for Certain Financial Instruments with Characteristics of both Liabilities and Equity

FAS 151   Inventory Costs, amendment of ARB 43

FAS 152   Accounting for Real Estate Time-Sharing Transactions, amendment of FAS 66 and 67

FAS 153   Exchanges of Non-monetary Assets, amendment of APB Opinion 29

FAS 154   Accounting Changes and Error Corrections, replacement of APB 20 and FAS 3

FAS 155   Accounting for Certain Hybrid Financial Instruments, amendment of FAS 133 and 140

FAS 156   Accounting for Servicing of Financial Assets, amendment of FAS 140

FAS 157   Fair Value Measurements

FAS 158   Employers' Accounting for Defined Benefit Pension and Other Postretirement Plans, amendment of FAS 87, 88, 106, and 132R

FAS 159   The Fair Value Option for Financial Assets and Financial Liabilities, including amendment of FAS 115

FAS 160   Noncontrolling Interests in Consolidated Financial Statements, amendment of ARB 51

FAS 161   Disclosures about Derivative Instruments and Hedging Activities, amendment of FAS 133

FAS 162   The Hierarchy of Generally Accepted Accounting Principles

FAS 163   Accounting for Financial Guarantee Insurance Contracts

FAS 164   Not-for-Profit Entities: Mergers and Acquisitions, including amendment of FAS 142

Financial Reporting Standards

FRS 1   Cash Flow Statements

FRS 2   Accounting for Subsidiary Undertakings

FRS 3   Reporting Financial Performance

FRS 4   Capital Instruments

FRS 5   Reporting the Substance of Transactions

FRS 6   Acquisitions and Mergers

FRS 7   Fair Values in Acquisition Accounting

FRS 8   Related Party Disclosures

FRS 9   Associates and Joint Ventures

FRS 10   Goodwill and Intangible Assets

FRS 11   Impairment of Fixed Assets and Goodwill

FRS 12   Provisions, Contingent Liabilities, and Contingent Assets

FRS 13   Derivatives and other Financial Instruments: Disclosures

FRS 14   Earnings per Share

FRS 15   Tangible Fixed Assets

FRS 16   Current Tax
FRS 17   Retirement Benefits
FRS 18   Accounting Policies
FRS 19   Deferred Tax
FRS 20   (IFRS 2) Share-based Payment
FRS 21   (IAS 10) Events after the Balance Sheet Date
FRS 22   (IAS 33) Earnings per share
FRS 23   (IAS 21) The Effects of Changes in Foreign Exchange Rates
FRS 24   (IAS 29) Financial Reporting in Hyperinflationary Economies
FRS 25   (IAS 32) Financial Instruments: Disclosure and Presentation
FRS 26   (IAS 39) Financial Instruments: Recognition and Measurement
FRS 27   Life Assurance
FRS 28   Corresponding Amounts
FRS 29   (IFRS 7) Financial Instruments: Disclosures FRSSE Financial Reporting Standard
    for Smaller Entities

International Financial Reporting Standards

IFRS 1   First-time Adoption of International Financial Reporting Standards
IFRS 2   Share-Based Payment
IFRS 3   Business Combinations
IFRS 4   Insurance Contracts
IFRS 5   Noncurrent Assets Held for Sale and Discontinued Operations
IFRS 6   Exploration for and Evaluation of Mineral Assets
IFRS 7   Financial Instruments: Disclosures
IFRS 8   Operating Segments
FPPFS   Framework for the Preparation and Presentation of Financial Statements

International Accounting Standards

IAS 1   Presentation of Financial Statements
IAS 2   Inventories
IAS 3   Consolidated Financial Statements, superseded by IAS 27 and 28.
IAS 4   Depreciation Accounting, replaced by IAS 16, 22, and 38.
IAS 5   Information to Be Disclosed in Financial Statements, superseded by IAS 1.
IAS 6   Accounting Responses to Changing Prices, superseded by IAS 15, which was
    ultimately withdrawn.
IAS 7   Statement of Cash Flows
IAS 8   Accounting Policies, Changes in Accounting Estimates and Errors
IAS 9   Accounting for Research and Development Activities, superseded by IAS 38
IAS 10   Events after the Reporting Period
IAS 11   Construction Contracts
IAS 12   Income Taxes
IAS 13   Presentation of Current Assets and Current Liabilities, superseded by IAS 1
IAS 14   Segment Reporting
IAS 15   Information Reflecting the Effects of Changing Prices, ultimately withdrawn.
IAS 16   Property, Plant, and Equipment
IAS 17   Leases
IAS 18   Revenue
IAS 19   Employee Benefits
IAS 20   Accounting for Government Grants and Disclosure of Government Assistance

IAS 21   The Effects of Changes in Foreign Exchange Rates
IAS 22   Business Combinations, superseded by IFRS 3.
IAS 23   Borrowing Costs
IAS 24   Related Party Disclosures
IAS 25   Accounting for Investments, superseded by IAS 39 and 40.
IAS 26   Accounting and Reporting by Retirement Benefit Plans
IAS 27   Consolidated and Separate Financial Statements
IAS 28   Investments in Associates
IAS 29   Financial Reporting in Hyperinflationary Economies
IAS 30   Disclosures in the Financial Statements of Banks and Similar Financial Institutions, superseded by IFRS 7.
IAS 31   Interests in Joint Ventures
IAS 32   Financial Instruments: Presentation – Disclosure provisions, superseded by IFRS 7
IAS 33   Earnings per Share
IAS 34   Interim Financial Reporting
IAS 35   Discontinuing Operations, superseded by IFRS 5
IAS 36   Impairment of Assets
IAS 37   Provisions, Contingent Liabilities, and Contingent Assets
IAS 38   Intangible Assets
IAS 39   Financial Instruments: Recognition and Measurement
IAS 40   Investment Property
IAS 41   Agriculture

Selected References

Altman, E. (1968) "Financial ratios, discriminatory analysis, and the prediction of corporate bankruptcy," *Journal of Finance*, September, Vol. 23, No. 4, pp. 589–609.

Berle, A. and Means, G. (1991) *The Modern Corporation and Private Property* (rev. edn of 1932 original), New Brunswick, NJ: Transaction.

Black, F. and Scholes, M. (1973) "The pricing of options and corporate liabilities," *Journal of Political Economy*, May–June, pp. 637–59.

Cootner, P. (1964) *The Random Character of Stock Market Prices*, Boston: MIT Press.

Cox, J., Ingersoll, J., and Ross, S. (1981) "A re-examination of traditional hypotheses about the term structure of interest rates," *Journal of Finance*, September, Vol. 36, pp. 769–99.

Cox, J., Ross, S., and Rubinstein, M. (1979) "Option pricing: a simplified approach," *Journal of Financial Economics*, Vol. 7, pp. 229–63.

Cox, J. and Rubinstein, M. (1985) *Options Markets*, Englewood Cliffs, NJ: Prentice Hall.

Edwards, R. and Magee, J. (2001) *Technical Analysis of Stock Trends*, 8th edn, Florida: St Lucie Press.

Fama, E. (1970) "Efficient capital markets: a review of theory and empirical work," *Journal of Finance*, Vol. 25, pp. 383–417.

Friedman, M. and Schwartz, A.J. (1963). "Money and Business Cycles," *Review of Economics and Statistics*, Vol. 45, No. 1, Part 2, Supplement, pp. 32–64.

Graham, B. and Dodd, D. (1962) *Security Analysis*, 4th edn, New York: McGraw-Hill.

Hicks, J. (1946) *Value and Capital*, 2nd edn, Oxford: Oxford University Press.

Jensen, M. (1969) "Risk, the pricing of capital assets, and the evaluation of investment portfolios," *Journal of Business*, Vol. 42, No. 2, pp. 167–247.

Jensen, M. (1972) *Studies in the Theory of Capital Markets*, New York: Praeger.

Keynes, John Maynard (1936), *The General Theory of Employment, Interest and Money*, London: Macmillan.

Lintner, J. (1956) "Distribution of incomes of corporations among dividends, retained earnings, and taxes," *American Economic Review*, Vol. 46, pp. 97–113.

Lutz, F. and Lutz, V. (1951) *The Theory of Investment in the Firm*, Princeton: Princeton University Press.

Markowitz, H. (1952) "Portfolio selection," *Journal of Finance*, March, Vol. 7, pp.77–91.

Meiselman, D. (1962) *The Term Structure of Interest Rates*, Englewood Cliffs, NJ: Prentice-Hall.

Merton, R. (1973) "An intertemporal capital asset pricing model," *Econometrica*, Vol. 41, No. 5, pp. 867–87.

Miller, M. and Modigliani, F. (1958) "The cost of capital, corporation finance, and the theory of investment," *American Economic Review*, June, Vol. 48, pp. 261–97.

Miller, M. and Modigliani, F. (1961) "Dividend policy and growth: the valuation of shares," *Journal of Business*, October, Vol. 34, pp. 411–33.

Rendleman, R. and Bartter, B. (1979) "Two state option pricing," *Journal of Finance*, Vol. 34, No. 5, pp. 182–92.

Roll, R. (1977) "A critique of the asset pricing theory's tests," *Journal of Financial Economics*, March, Vol. 4, No. 2, pp. 129–76.

Roll. R. and Ross, S. (1980) "An empirical investigation of arbitrage pricing theory," *Journal of Finance*, December, Vol. 35, pp. 1073–103.

Ross, S. (1976) "The arbitrage theory of capital asset pricing," *Journal of Economic Theory*, Vol. 13, pp. 341–60.

Samuelson, P. (1965) "Proof that properly anticipated prices fluctuate randomly," *Industrial Management Review*, Vol. 6, No. 2, pp. 41–9.

Sharpe, W. (1964) "Capital asset prices: A theory of market equilibrium," *Journal of Finance*, September, Vol. 19, No. 3, pp. 425–42.

Sharpe, W. (1966) "Mutual fund performance," *Journal of Business*, January, Vol. 39, No. 1, pp. 119–38.

Sharpe, W. (1971) *Portfolio Theory*: Capital Markets, New York: McGraw-Hill.

Treynor, J. (1965) "How to rate management investment funds," *Harvard Business Review*, January–February, pp. 312–25.